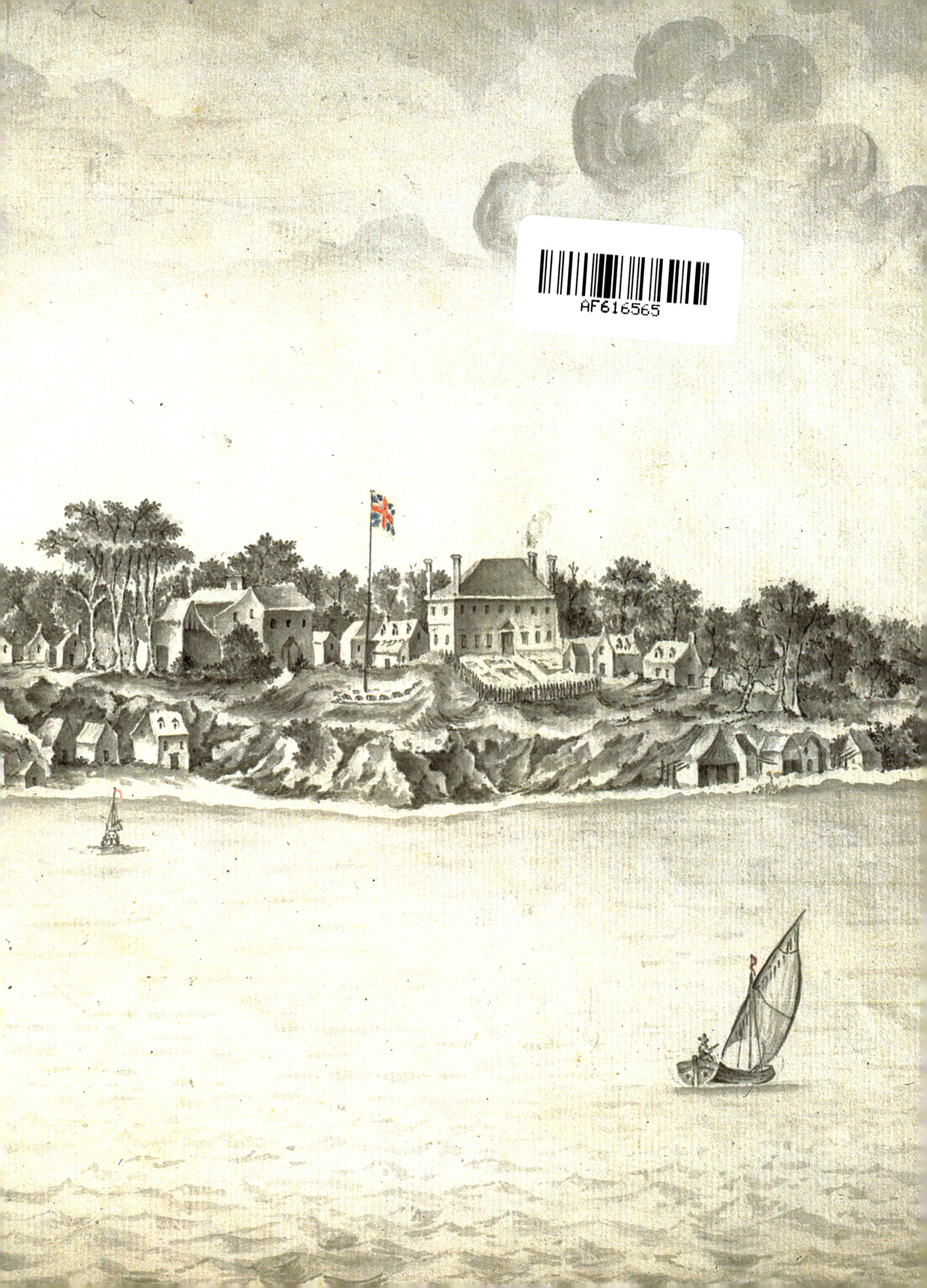

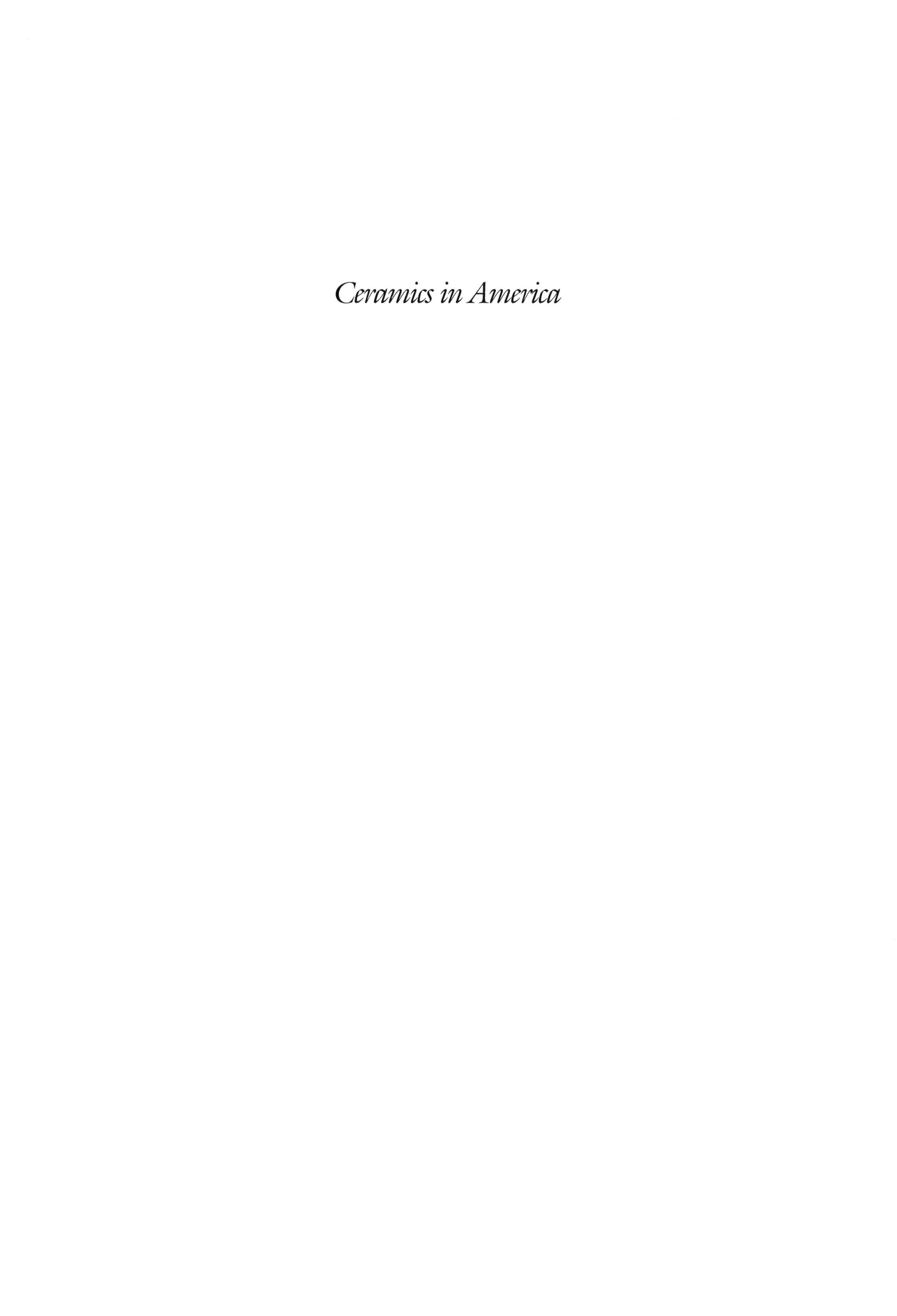

Ceramics in America

CERAMICS

IN AMERICA

2004

Edited by Robert Hunter

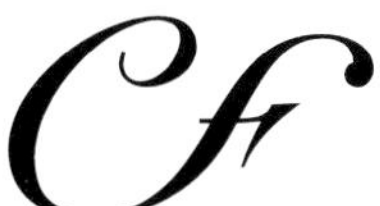

Published by the CHIPSTONE FOUNDATION

Distributed by University Press of New England

Hanover and London

Cover Illustration: Detail of English pearlware punch bowl, ca. 1780. (Chipstone Foundation; photo, Gavin Ashworth.)

Design: Wynne Patterson, VT
Copyediting: Mary Gladue, CT
Proofreading: Fronia W. Simpson, VT
Printing: Balding + Mansell, Norwich, UK
Typesetting: Aardvark Type, CT

Published by the Chipstone Foundation
7820 North Club Circle, Milwaukee, WI 53217

Printed in England 5 4 3 2 1

ISSN 1533–7154
ISBN 0–9724353–3–6

Contents

Editorial Statement

Ceramics in America is an interdisciplinary journal intended for collectors, historical archaeologists, curators, decorative arts students, social historians, and contemporary studio potters. Authors are encouraged to submit articles on the broad role of historical ceramics in the American context including essays on ceramic history, archaeological research, ceramic technology, social history, studio pottery, and ceramic collecting. Short illustrated notes on new ceramic discoveries are particularly wanted. References to be compiled in an annual bibliography, including electronic sources, may also be submitted. Manuscripts must be typed, double-spaced, illustrated with high-quality color transparencies, and prepared in accordance with the *Chicago Manual of Style*. Computer disk copy is requested but not required. The Chipstone Foundation will offer significant honoraria for manuscripts accepted for publication and reimburse authors for all photography approved in writing by the editor.

Low resolution digital images or photographs of poor quality will not be accepted for publication.

A style guide is available for prospective authors by request and can be sent via email.

Robert Hunter

Robert Hunter

Introduction

▼ WITH EACH ISSUE of *Ceramics in America* it becomes increasingly apparent that there is no simple story line for our ceramic history. The complexity of that history is underscored by the fact that no single volume offers a comprehensive assessment of America's regionally diverse ceramics. Surveys of Chinese or English ceramics are relatively easy to find, but despite a number of publications on specific American types or individual potteries, huge gaps remain.

How will these gaps be filled? For every professional ceramic historian there are dozens if not hundreds of enthusiastic collectors on the front line of ceramic research. Each region has its own cadre of specialists competing at flea markets and auctions for that prized specimen of locally made pottery. Unfortunately, in the past the specimen typically was stored away for safekeeping, rarely seen except in the occasional family photograph album, as many collectors are secretive and highly competitive. The truth is, it makes good economic sense not to share too much about one's personal collecting interests or habits, information that could increase competition and raise prices.

This secretiveness is changing as more and more scholars and collectors are connecting to the Internet, where images and details about items in even the most remote country auction can be viewed with just a few keystrokes. Some collectors now have websites for their collections, and the clandestine contents of museum storerooms, previously viewable only through the graces of an accommodating curator, are increasingly available through the electronic medium. With this growing accessibility, collectors must share with professional historians the responsibility to publish. Although their scholarship might not be academically wrought, or is sometimes clumsy or even outright speculative, these enthusiasts are America's ceramics chroniclers.

This issue of *Ceramics in America* is filled with such an admixture of academic and collector research, and it is the sincere enthusiasm of both types of authors that best connects their stories.

English-made clay tobacco pipe fragments have long provided archaeologists with a useful chronology for dating colonial-period archaeological assemblages. The colonists themselves made tobacco pipes as well, and the ethnicity of the makers—African American, Native American, and white—has preoccupied archaeological discussions for more than a decade. Al Luckenbach reports on the discovery of a circa 1660 American pipe manufactory in Anne Arundel County, Maryland. Using pipe fragments, kiln remains, kiln furniture, and even raw clay, Luckenbach is able to firmly identify American pipe maker Emanuel Drue. Building on archaeologist Dan Mouer's assertion that locally made pipes are manifestations of early American folk art, Luckenbach demonstrates the importance of the manufactory's discovery for students of tobacco pipe technology and Chesapeake material culture.

Another archaeology story recounts the discovery of America's first stoneware manufactory—that of the "Poor Potter" of Yorktown, Virginia. Norman Barka's painstaking excavation of William Rogers's circa 1720 pottery site uncovered a large workshop complex that included the well-preserved remains of two kilns and thousands of earthenware and stoneware waster fragments. The historical significance of this site—its contribution to the story of America's domestically made ceramics, as well as its revolutionary role in initiating an independence from imported products—cannot be overstated. Even with Barka's persistence in the labor-intensive analysis of the site and its artifacts, research on this vast body of material will continue into the foreseeable future.

William Rogers was the eighteenth-century Yorktown entrepreneur who owned and operated the pottery, but virtually nothing is known about the actual potters. Martha McCartney and Edward Ayres's historical essay explains the pottery's role in light of Rogers's activities as a brewer and merchant. Of greater significance is their suggestion that his workforce was composed of indentured convict labor from England and augmented with African-American slaves. Barka's ceramic analysis indicates that Rogers's master potters were trained in state-of-the-art London stoneware technology and that some of them were well versed in Germanic-style earthenwares. Future research may help to identify these master craftsmen and explain their presence in the colonial America context.

Yorktown potters with European training had to adapt to the locally available clays and fuels. In an unusual twist, Australian contributors Ross Ramsay, Judith Hansen, and Gael Ramsay show how clay from the western part of North Carolina may have served as the key ingredient needed for a circa 1744 London-made porcelain body. Employing a combination of historical research, connoisseurship, and rigorous chemical analysis, the authors present a convincing argument that the so-called A-marked porcelain group depended on this "Cherokee" clay for its success. Their article challenges the long-held notion that the manufacture of English porcelain was strictly a homegrown enterprise.

In addition to the flow and exchange of materials and expertise, innovative technology is essential to ceramic invention. Jonathan Rickard and Don Carpentier examine the adaptation of the engine-turning lathe for decorating late-eighteenth-century forms. While Josiah Wedgwood may deserve the credit for adapting this metalworking device to the pottery industry, Rickard and Carpentier can be recognized as the first ceramic historians to fully discuss and illustrate the inner workings of the machine. Ceramic students are the beneficiaries of Carpentier's quest to design and build from scratch his own engine-turning lathe, and one of the great eighteenth-century technological mysteries is now better understood.

Identifying decorative as well as technological characteristics is essential to building regional ceramic typologies and chronologies. Based on years of personal collecting, Don Horvath and Richard Duez present their thoughtful research on the earthenware potters of Morgantown, West Virginia. The Morgantown story benefits from the preservation of a number of pots and related hand tools acquired from the Thompson family pottery in the late nineteenth century by Walter Hough, a curator of ethnology at the U.S. National Museum. Horvath and Duez show with their article the evolving exercise of identifying local potters and their products in the absence of firmly dated examples. A future article by these authors will survey the exceptional Morgantown stonewares produced by the Thompson family.

The British potter Bernard Leach likely would have relished the opportunity to examine the pots and tools of Morgantown's nineteenth-century potters. Well known to students of contemporary ceramics but probably unfamiliar to collectors of historical wares, Leach's *The Potter's Book* is considered the bible of the British studio pottery movement, espousing both the philosophy and the aesthetics of Asian and British ceramic history. Emmanuel Cooper, editor of the international journal *Ceramic Review* and author of the recent comprehensive biography of Leach, offers a lively essay chronicling the potter's several visits to America in the 1950s and 1960s. He captures both Leach's quick dismissal of America as "a new amalgam of races" lacking the pottery traditions of Chinese or English cultures, and his almost proselytizing fervor for encouraging American potters to find a "taproot" with which to ground their efforts.

Two articles on nineteenth-century American stoneware, with their emphasis on the sturdy, functional, and aesthetic nature of these utilitarian pots, offer ample evidence of an established taproot for American stoneware traditions, however. Luke Zipp leads off with new information about Henry Remmey Sr. and Henry Remmey Jr. in Baltimore circa 1807–1829 that rewrites the canon about these members of America's best-known potting family. The author provides firm evidence of the Remmeys' employment history in Baltimore and discusses the artistry of their work in the context of the area's utilitarian stoneware production.

Another regional stoneware potter long recognized by local collectors is George N. Fulton, who worked in rural Virginia during the second half of the nineteenth century. Pulling together an extensive survey of extant pots, archaeology, and historical information, archaeologist and collector Kurt Russ documents this traditional potter's career, which spanned forty years and flourished in the face of increasing mechanization of the stoneware industry. Unlike many anonymous potters, Fulton decorated and signed many of his pots with a flourish indicative of a master potter confident in his abilities, a trait highly sought by collectors today.

Collecting without an underlying research interest is usually a somewhat soulless pursuit that can result in an accumulation with little meaning. At the other end of that spectrum are the enlightened endeavors of Ivor Noël Hume, for whom research drives the collecting. Long interested in the story of British brown stonewares, Noël Hume recently has given chase to the subject of the ubiquitous sprig-molded English brown hunting mug. Unhappy with the few standard references on the subject, he has pursued the age-old problems of establishing chronologies and tracing design sources and factory attributions by using detective work, old-fashioned connoisseurship, and a huge dose of his famous serendipity. The result is as important for methodology as for its conclusions, the most lasting of which is that research—and, by extension, collecting—is rarely finished. More undocumented brown stoneware jugs were surfacing even as this journal was going to press.

Further evidence that ceramic research is never finished is reflected in the wide range of short articles assembled by Merry Outlaw for the journal's New Discoveries section. In addition, Amy Earls's solicitation of many insightful and occasionally provocative book reviews continues to guide readers—as does her bibliographic checklist—to the more interesting publications pertaining to our field.

Upcoming issues of *Ceramics in America* will include more regional studies of American stoneware and earthenware potteries. Tentatively scheduled for 2006, for example, is an issue devoted to a review of the current scholarship related to southern ceramic traditions. Suggestions and comments regarding this and other future topics can be submitted via email at <CeramicJournal@aol.com>. Selected articles from previous volumes can be accessed by visiting the Chipstone Foundation's website at <http//:www.chipstone.org.>.

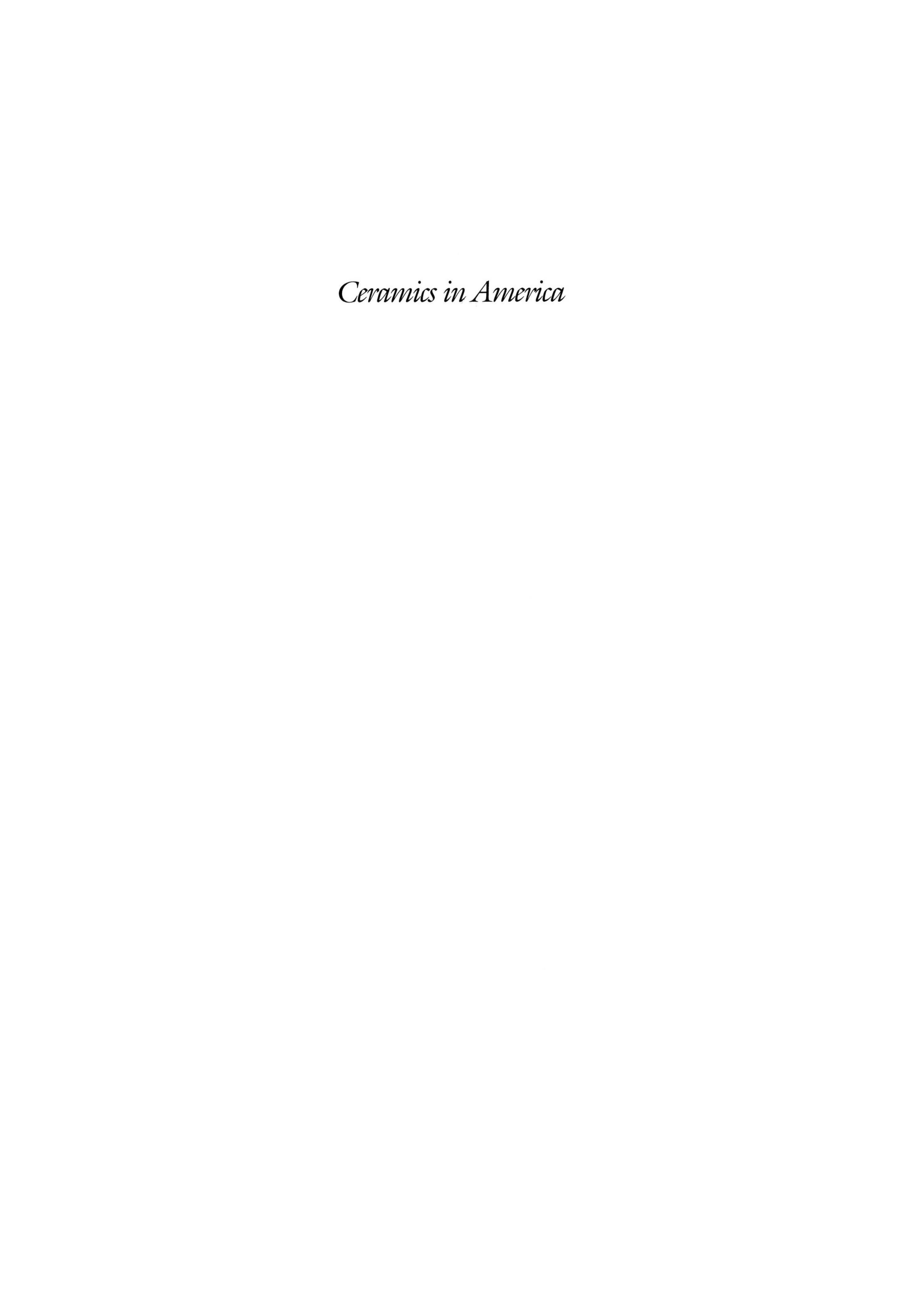

Ceramics in America

Al Luckenbach

The Swan Cove Kiln: Chesapeake Tobacco Pipe Production, Circa 1650–1669

▼ CHESAPEAKE PIPES *are notable because they are craft items, meticulously made, and beautifully decorated. They are the most intriguing surviving examples of folk art of the early Chesapeake. The care and effort which attended the creation of these artifacts attest to their symbolic importance for those who used them. The designs on these pipes have things to tell us about life in a distant past. If we can "read" these pipes, perhaps we can hope to fathom something of the essence of American culture as it was created from the interactions of diverse people on the early Chesapeake frontier.*[1]

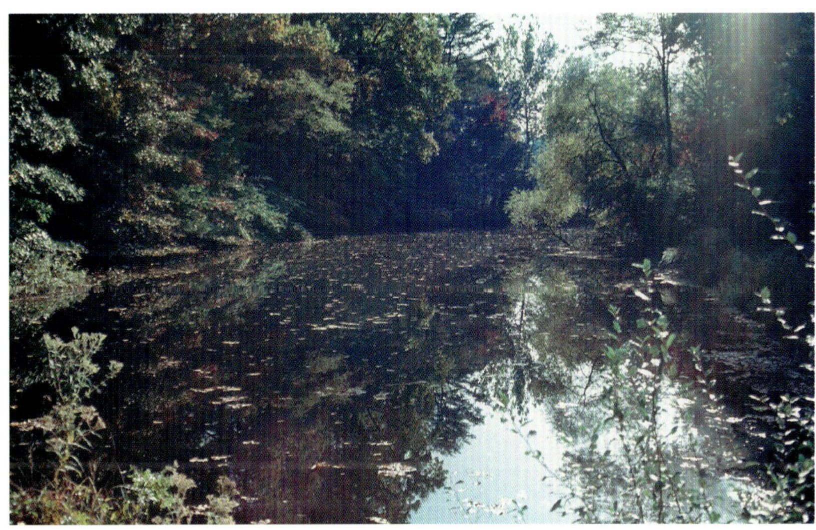

Figure 1 Today Swan Cove is a small, abayed pond. Three hundred and fifty years ago it was probably navigable for small boats—the main form of transportation for the Puritan settlement of Providence. (Photo, Al Luckenbach.)

The Swan Cove Site

Between the protective arms of Greenbury and Hackett's Points, Whitehall Bay opens out on the broader Chesapeake Bay near the mouth of the Severn River. In the mid-seventeenth century, off a tributary called Ferry Creek (or Mill Creek as it is known today), a small but navigable cove was named for its current inhabitants, native swans (fig. 1).

Englishman Emanuel Drue lived out his life on Swan Cove in the 1650s and 1660s, when the region was on the frontier of European settlement. Only a decade or so earlier, however, what is now Anne Arundel County, Maryland, had been the sole domain of the Susquehannoch Indians (fig. 2), who harvested the region's natural resources—oysters, fish, terrapin, migratory fowl—flourishing in almost unimaginable abundance.

Drue apparently pursued a lifestyle like those of his neighbors. He lived in a scattered, hamlet-style settlement called Providence, a Puritan town

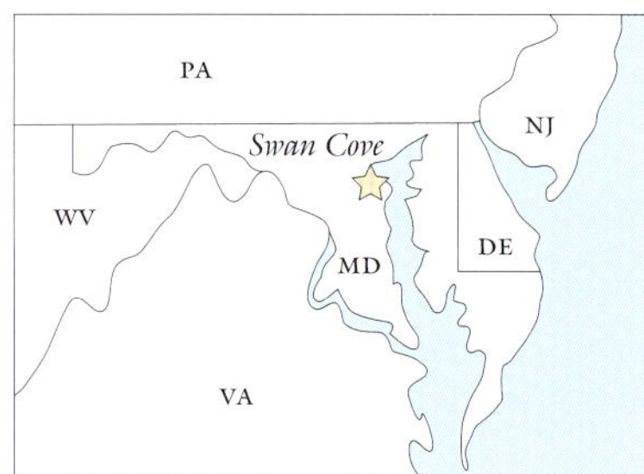

Figure 2 The Swan Cove kiln site was discovered in Anne Arundel County, Maryland, on the western shore of the Chesapeake Bay.

established in 1649 at the mouth of the Severn.[2] Documentation from Providence, the county's earliest settlement, records Drue's presence and calls him a "planter," a term applied to landed individuals who grew tobacco, the principal crop of the Chesapeake Bay.[3] Domestic debris recovered by archaeologists at the site of Drue's home indicates a diet and material standard of living similar to findings discovered elsewhere in the community and surrounding region.

In addition to the mix of domestic debris, extensive remains of Drue's cottage industry—the manufacture of clay tobacco pipes (fig. 3)—were recovered. Apparently, Emanuel Drue was not only a planter but also a potter, a scientist, and, as archaeologist Dan Mouer suggests, an artist in clay. The surviving historical record contains scarcely any clues to support these extraordinary facts. Indeed, only a single line in the two-page probate inventory taken at Drue's death in 1669 hints at his diversity, listing "One payre of pype Moulds brass and materials belong to them" (fig. 4).[4]

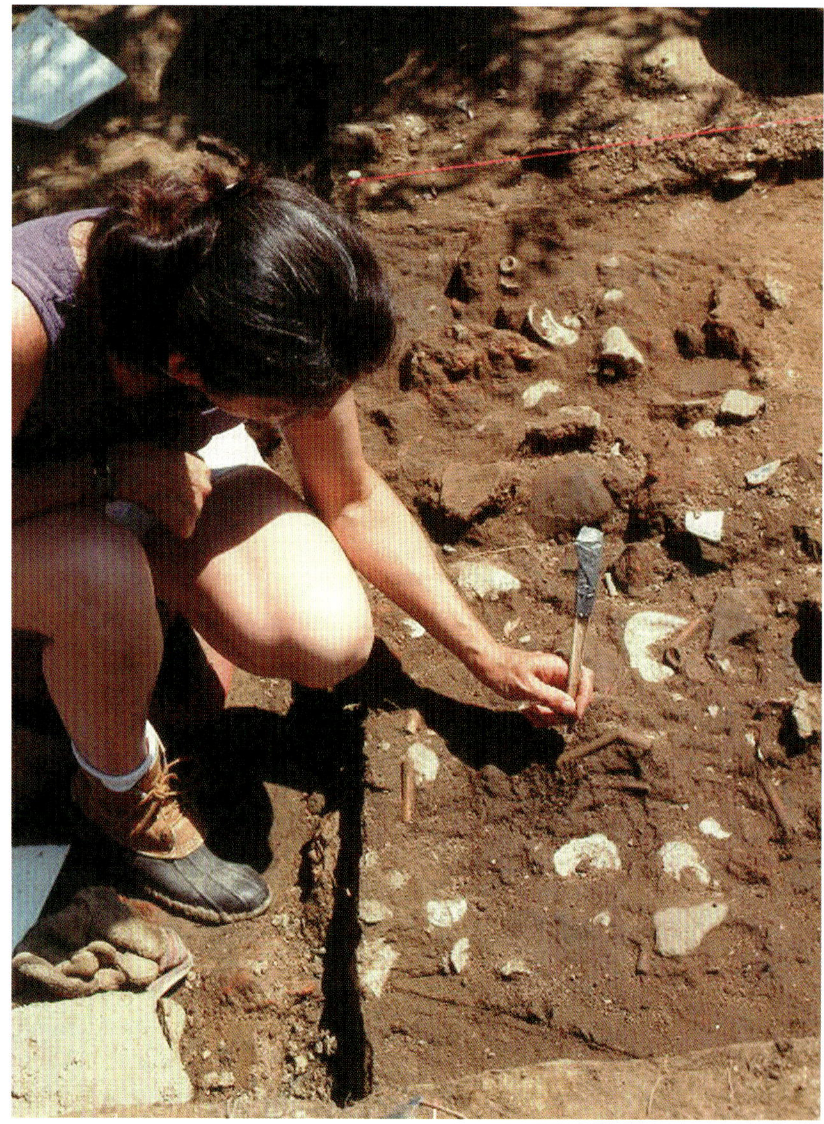

Figure 3 Anne Arundel County's Historic Sites Planner, Donna Ware, excavates Feature 19 at Swan Cove. This feature was one of several undisturbed trash pits filled with pipe kiln debris and wasters. (Photo, Al Luckenbach.)

Figure 4 Emanuel Drue's 1669 estate inventory listing. (Courtesy, Maryland State Archives.)

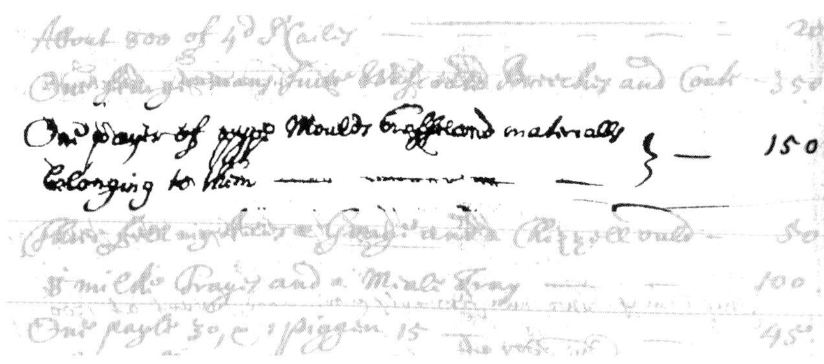
One payre of pype Moulds [illegible] materialls
Belonging to them — 150

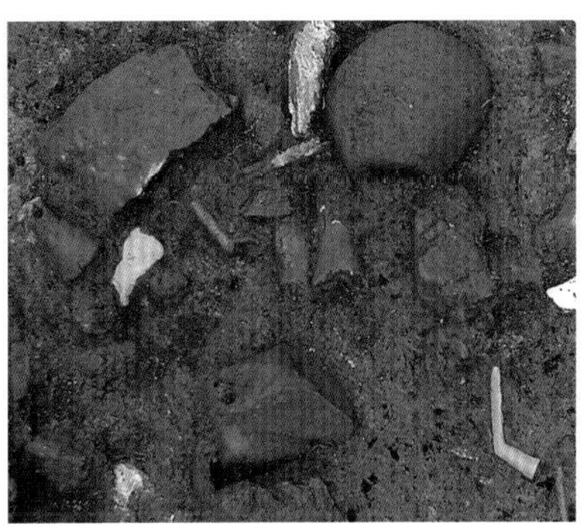

Figure 5 A detail from Feature 7 at Swan Cove shows muffle fragments, loaves, a prop, glazed cobbles, and pipe wasters, along with domestic debris such as oysters and delftware sherds. Feature 7 contained over 160 pounds of kiln debris along with nearly 1,200 pipe fragments. (Photo, Al Luckenbach.)

While excavating the Swan Cove site, however, archaeologists from Anne Arundel County's Lost Towns Project discovered clear evidence that a state-of-the-art industrial kiln once existed there, constructed in the style of pipe kilns of the same period in England.[5] Discovery of the kiln site has been a remarkable payoff for two generations of archaeologists investigating the manufacture of Chesapeake tobacco pipes.

Emanuel Drue's Pipe Kiln

Although the search continues, the centuries-old foundation of the kiln remains elusive. It is possible that it did not survive the ravages of time, as plowing, erosion, grading, and ditch digging have all occurred on the site. Nonetheless, the vast quantity of kiln debris found inside several intact trash features appears to represent periodic rebuilding of the structure and contains invaluable clues to the nature of its construction (figs. 5–8).

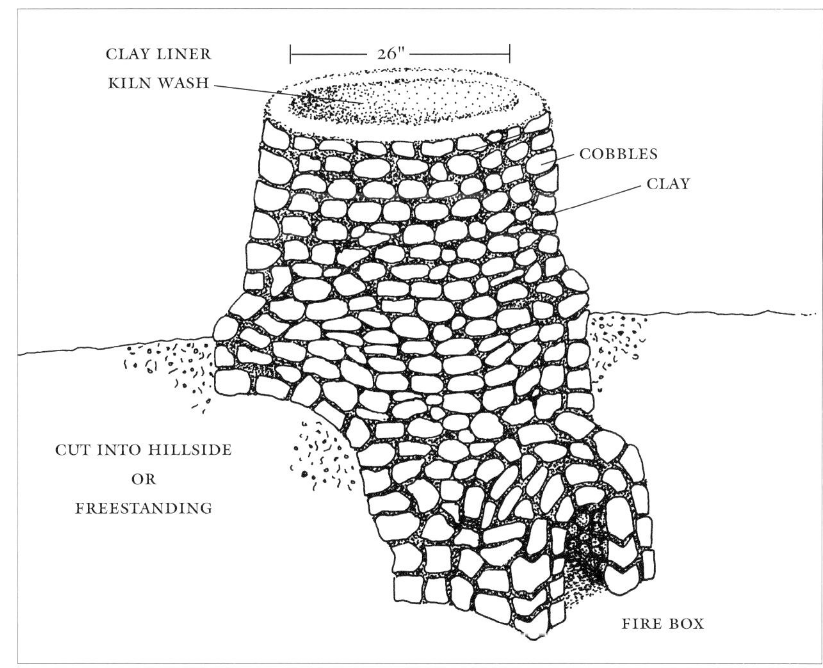

Figure 6 Conjectural drawing of the Emanuel Drue pipe kiln. (Drawing, Lost Towns Project, Anne Arundel County, Maryland.)

Handmade clay objects called *loaves,* shaped vaguely like fresh-baked bread, represent part of the kiln's interior structure. Loaves exhibit clear evidence of high firing on one face (top or side) and a soft, "salmon brick"

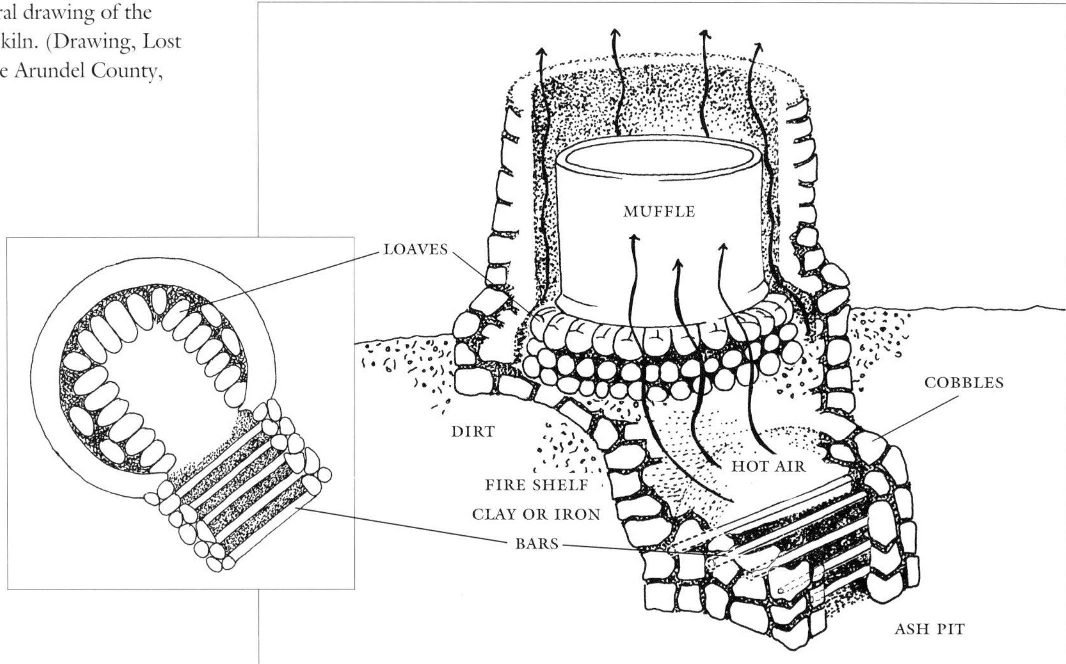

Figure 7 Conjectural drawing of the Emanuel Drue pipe kiln. (Drawing, Lost Towns Project, Anne Arundel County, Maryland.)

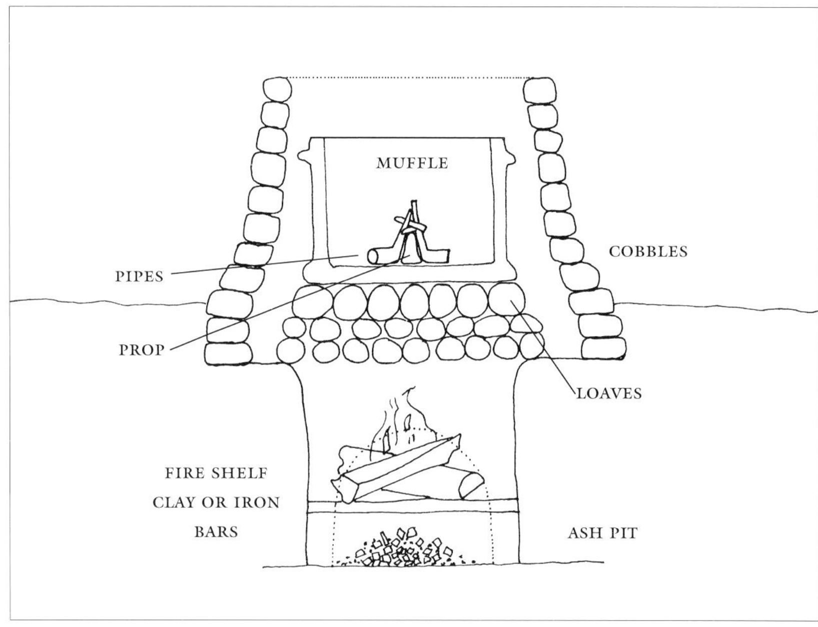

Figure 8 Conjectural drawing of the Emanuel Drue pipe kiln showing the placement of the muffle and the interior arrangement of the pipes and props. (Drawing, Lost Towns Project, Anne Arundel County, Maryland.)

consistency on the other. Drue's fingerprints confirm the handmade nature of these ovoid shapes (fig. 9), which were either an integral part of the kiln floor or objects that had been set in place. Interestingly, no traditional, rectangular-shaped bricks have been found, although they would have been easy for Drue to make. Even the imported, yellow Dutch bricks commonly encountered on other Providence sites are not in evidence at Swan Cove. Numerous river cobbles have been recovered, however, that appear to have been used in the kiln construction, as some recovered examples display one surface with a vitrified glaze resulting from exposure to extremely high temperatures (fig. 10).

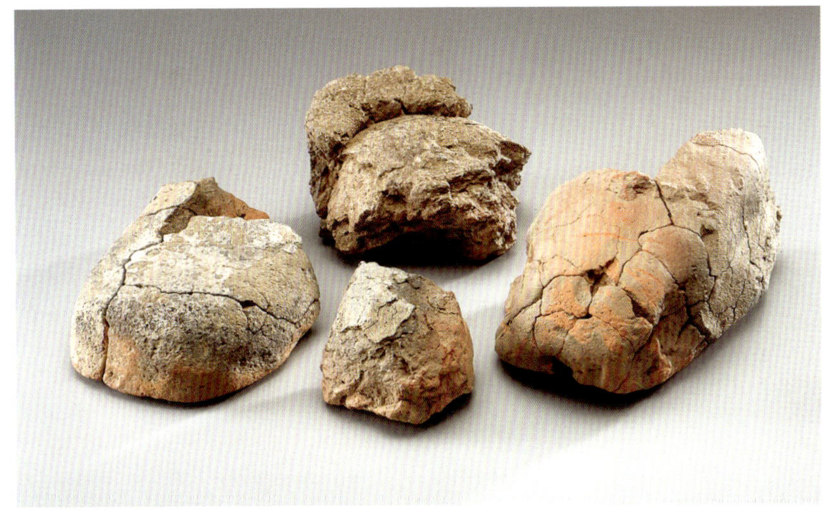

Figure 9 Crude, handmade, redware objects roughly the size and shape of bread were given the term *loaves*. These apparently took the place of more traditional bricks in the kiln's flooring and perhaps its sides. (Photo, Gavin Ashworth.)

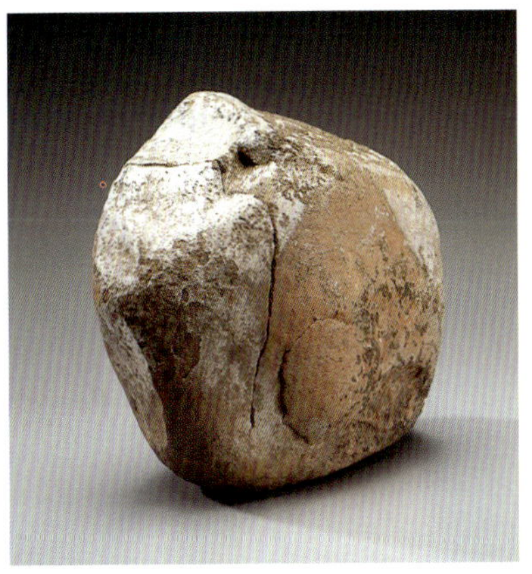

Figure 10 Numerous non-native quartzite cobbles, many of which display heat alterations, litter the Swan Cove site. The vitrified surface of this extreme example clearly indicates their use as part of the kiln's construction. (Photo, Gavin Ashworth.)

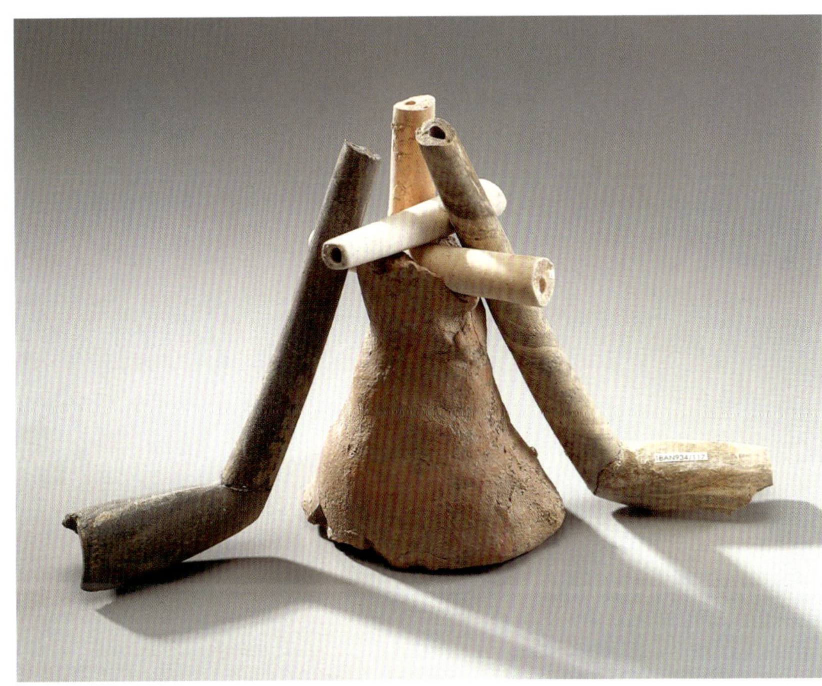

Figure 11 A redware cross-pipe prop was built incorporating broken pipe stem fragments and used to brace tobacco pipes during the firing of Emanuel Drue's kiln. Two examples were recovered. (Photo, Gavin Ashworth.)

Fragments of Dutch roof pantiles were also found with the kiln debris. At other Providence sites these reddish tiles were used for roofing material, as originally intended. At Swan Cove, their dark burned color indicates they had been subjected to the kiln's high temperatures after breaking, and must have served in some fashion as spacers or props during firings. British archaeologist and tobacco kiln expert Allan Peacey submits they may also have been used to seal the tops of the kiln muffles (receptacles protecting the pipes) before firing.[6] Recovered heat-altered redware sherds may have served a similar function.[7]

Other, more traditional kiln furniture has survived, including the unique form of a "cross-pipe" prop (fig. 11) that heretofore has been known only from an example found in Chelmsford, England.[8] Flattened pipe bowl wasters (fig. 12) further attest to the use of such props.

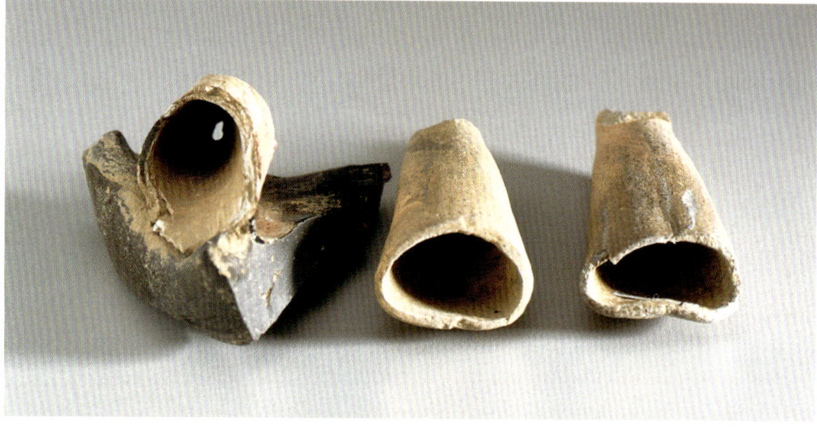

Figure 12 Pipe bowl wasters demonstrating distortion caused during firing while leaning against cross-pipe props. (Photo, Gavin Ashworth.)

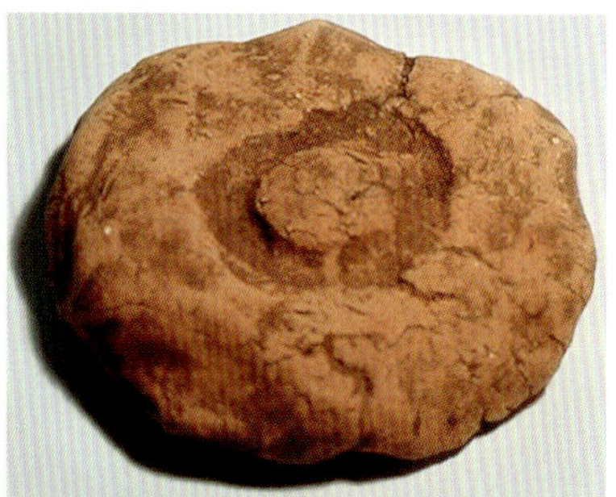

Figure 13 A redware object called a "bun," which may have been used to stack props. (Photo, Al Luckenbach.)

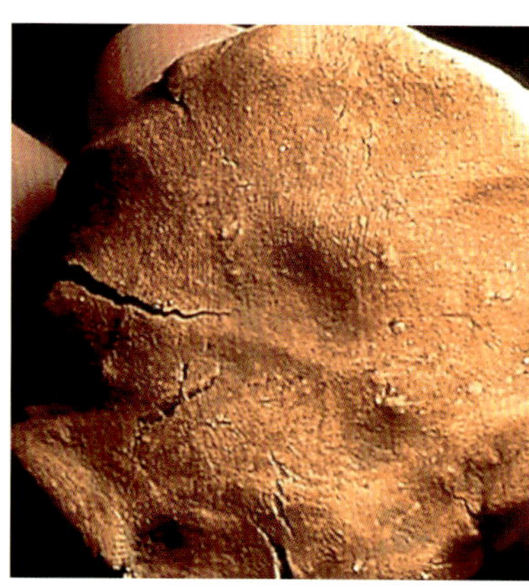

Figure 14 The reverse side of the bun bears the clear impressions of finger and palm prints. Presumably these belong to Emanuel Drue, imprinted over 350 years ago. (Photo, Al Luckenbach.)

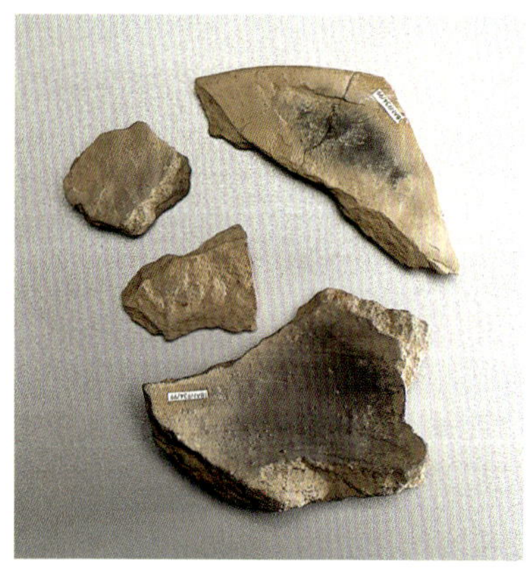

Figure 15 A crude, highly fired redware dish, which Emanuel Drue presumably made for some expedient purpose involving pipe making. (Photo, Gavin Ashworth.)

Another, fairly enigmatic find is, perhaps, a "bun" (fig. 13), at least based on the definitions contained in a study of English kilns by Allan Peacey.[9] The bun's reverse side is notable for having captured what is presumably Drue's palm print (fig. 14). Fragments of a possible kiln "dish" were also found (fig. 15), and its crude, handmade form argues strongly for a limited or specific use.

By far the most numerous kiln-related artifacts are fragments of muffles or saggers—large, rough, ceramic vessels that held the pipes during firing. Whether they are actually muffles or saggers is an interesting definitional dilemma. Functionally, if they can be moved in and out of the kiln, they should be termed saggers, and those from Swan Cove show no clear

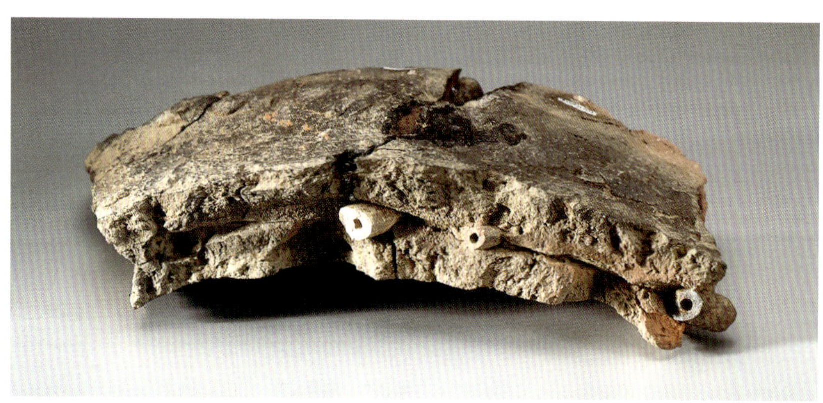

Figure 16 A fragment of the muffle showing the utilization of broken pipe stems as a bond between coils during construction. (Photo, Gavin Ashworth.)

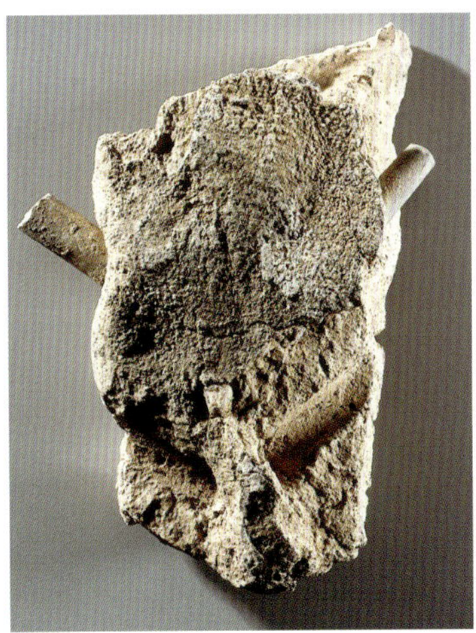

Figure 17 Muffle sherd from the side showing herringbone pattern produced with pipe stems on alternating coils. (Photo, Gavin Ashworth.)

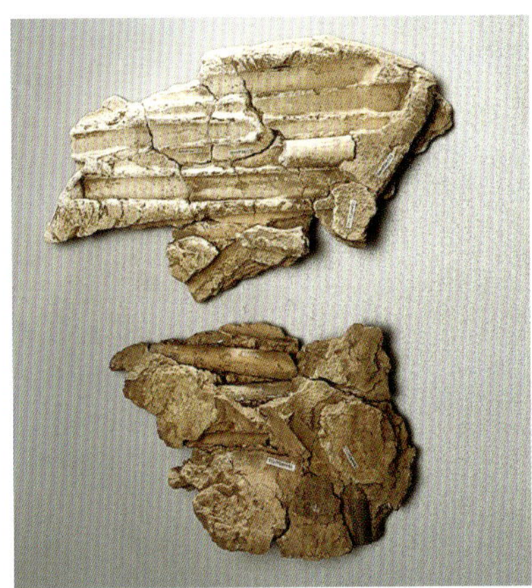

Figure 18 The interior base of each muffle contained layers of broken pipe stems. (Photo, Gavin Ashworth.)

evidence of having been permanently fixed. On the other hand, they fit the definition of muffles compositionally, since they are vessels tempered with pipe fragments, a trait unknown in saggers.[10]

The muffle's intriguing physical attributes reveal important clues to Drue's manufacturing activities (figs. 16–18). Essentially, muffles are large clay vats with buttresses that separate them in the kiln. Their clay is tempered by the unusual addition of similarly sized pipe-stem wasters. Arranged in alternating, angled rows, the pipe fragments form a herringbone pattern, a style that Peacey attributes to the general London area, the possible origin of Drue's training.[11]

To keep the muffle's interior smooth, an interior wash or slip of fine clay, or "lute," was periodically applied, resulting in a laminar or layering effect (fig. 19). Unfortunately the number of layers—up to eight have been noted—does not necessarily indicate an equal number of firings, since the wash was not replaced each time. The interior wash was also one of the first clues indicating Drue's access to a clay that fired to pure white. Other examples of alternating white and terracotta clays have also been observed.

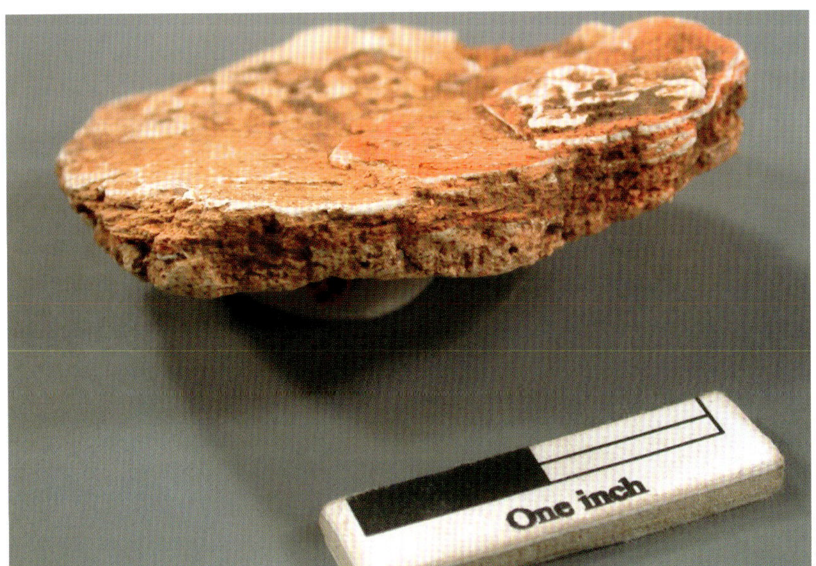

Figure 19 Repeated application of a clay wash on the muffle interior produced a laminar structure called "lute." (Photo, David Gadsby.)

Drue's Tobacco Pipes

The pipes produced by Emanuel Drue would appear overwhelmingly to be products of the two molds mentioned in his 1669 inventory. They include an angular elbow type, a classic "Chesapeake pipe" form, Drue Type A

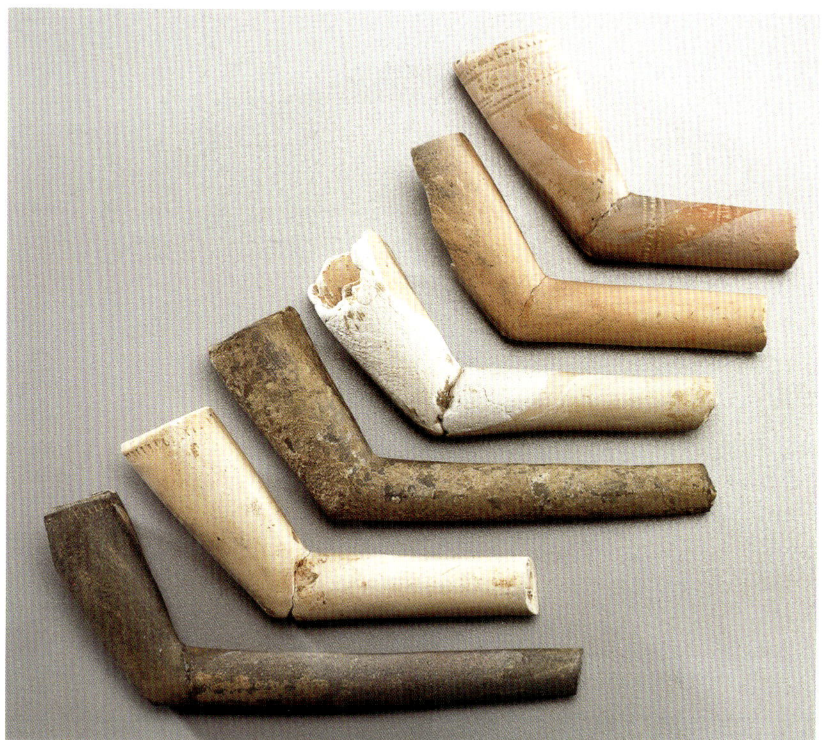

Figure 20 The Drue tobacco pipe Type A is a typical Chesapeake-style angular-elbow pipe. (Photo, Gavin Ashworth.)

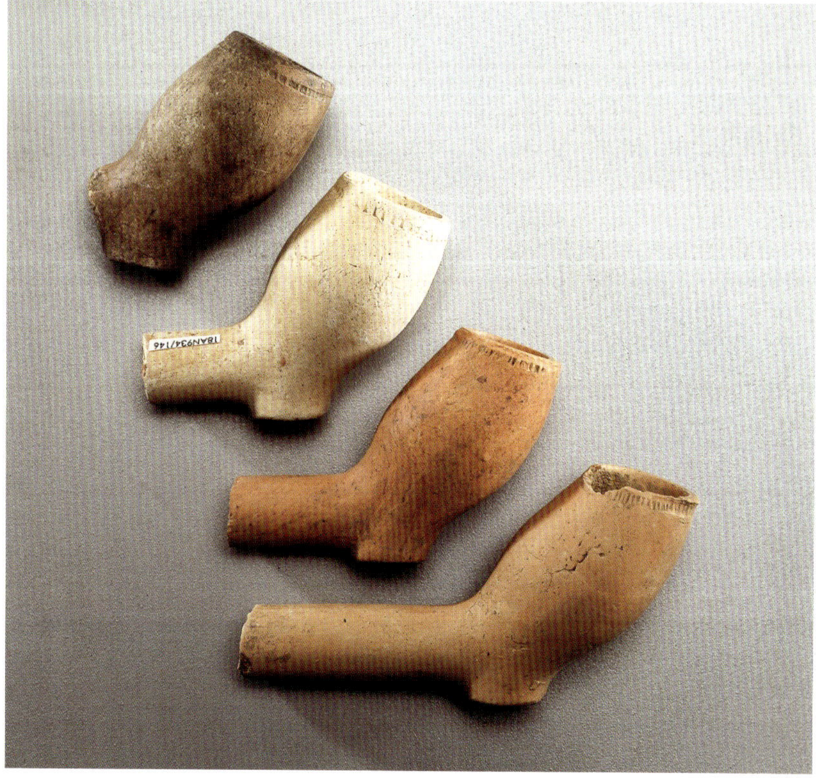

Figure 21 Drue's Type B tobacco pipe is in the form of a classic English "belly bowl," typical of the mid-seventeenth century. (Photo, Gavin Ashworth.)

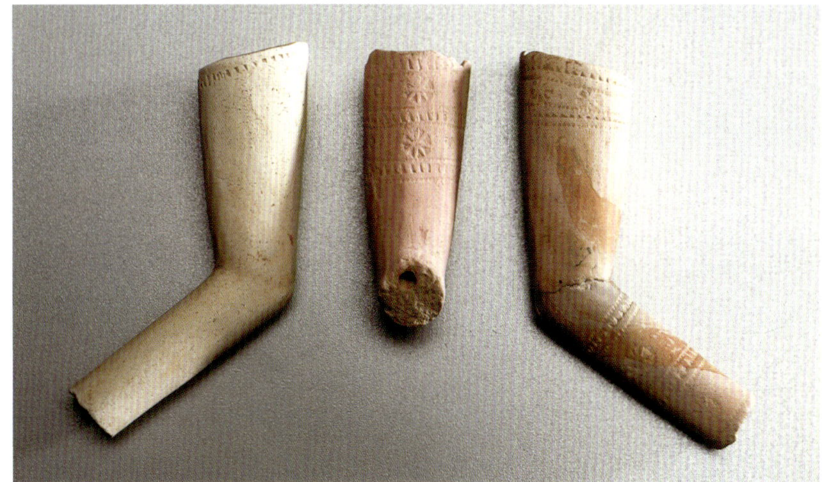

Figure 22 Variations of Chesapeake-style decoration appearing on Drue Type A pipe examples. (Photo, Gavin Ashworth.)

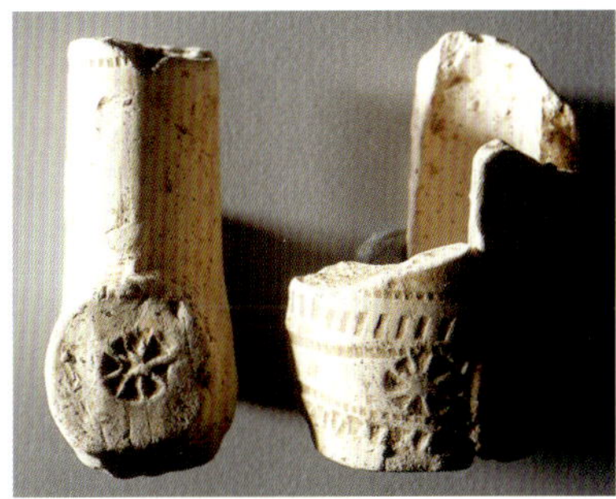

Figure 23 Unique examples of exuberant Chesapeake-style decoration on Drue Type B, perhaps representing a single specimen. (Photo, Gavin Ashworth.)

(fig. 20), and a traditional mid-century, English belly-bowl form, Drue Type B (fig. 21). Appearing in approximately equal numbers, the distinction between the two is further reinforced by separate, decorative vocabularies.

Type A bowls seem to follow a decorative grammar derived from the Chesapeake, and not England. They occur in a wide range of colors, including the use of colorfully agatized clays. Besides the application of an exterior slip, they also show a propensity for elaborate decoration (fig. 22).

Drue Type B bowls are decorated in the English style. Although appearing in a wide range of color variations (decidedly not an English characteristic), decoration is limited to simple rouletting around the rim. There are only two exceptions: one—a small fragment of a white belly bowl—appears to have a wheel stamp on its side, and another bears a wheel stamp applied to the base of its heel, much like a traditional English maker's mark (fig. 23). Minimalism and conformity to Old World vocabularies appear to be the predominant decorative traits of Type B.

The imprints of at least eight different pipe-decorating tools have been noted, including three decorative stamps, a smaller circular punch, and four distinct rouletting tools (fig. 24). One of the rarest artifacts recovered

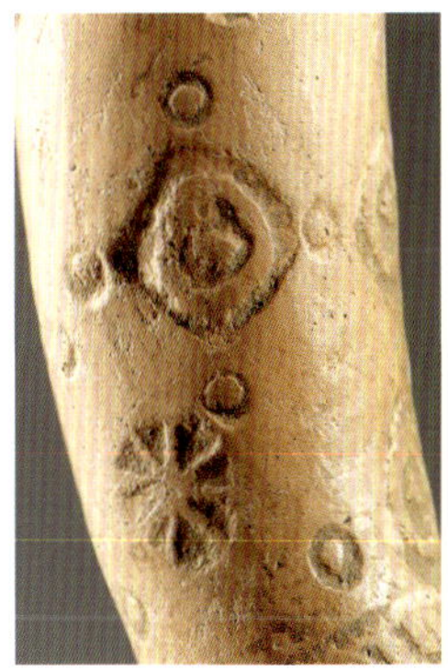

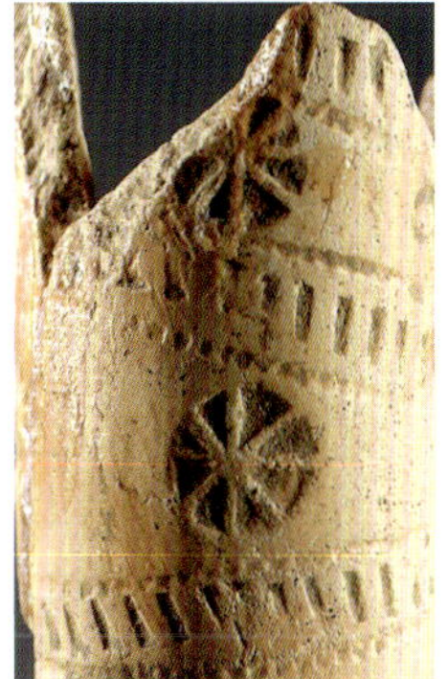

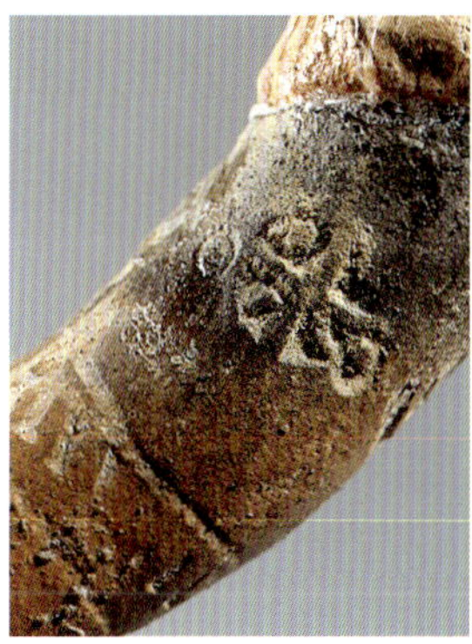

Figure 24 Three different stamps were utilized by Emanuel Drue in the production and decoration of his pipes. These have been termed Stamp Types 1, 2, and 3. (Photo, Gavin Ashworth.)

from the Swan Cove site is a decorative stamp used by Drue (fig. 25). Even in England, only two have been found during the investigation of over 140 kiln sites; comparable examples from the New World are unknown.[12]

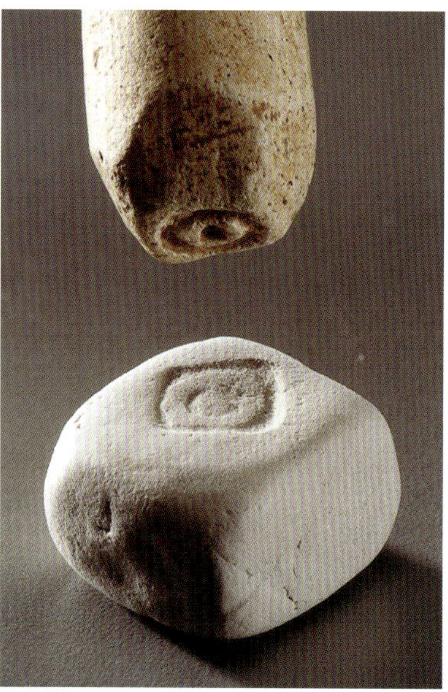

Figure 25 Stamp tool found at Swan Cove that was used to produce Type 1. This frequently utilized tool was found broken in half and appears to be constructed from an unbored pipe stem. (Photo, Gavin Ashworth.)

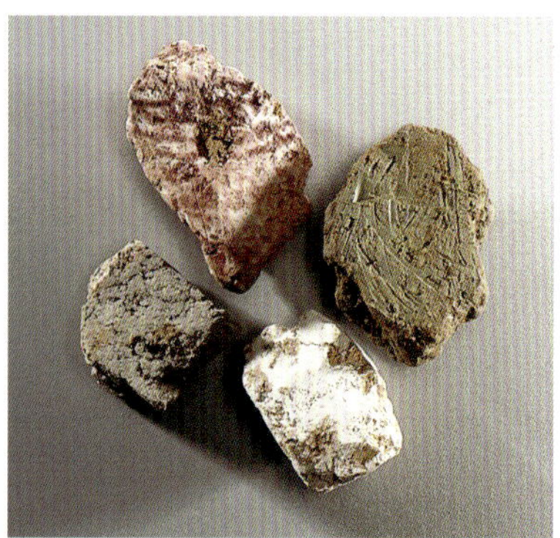

Figure 26 Raw, unfired clay from intact feature deposits at Swan Cove. These "gourmet clays" were utilized by Drue to produce products that were amazingly variable in color. (Photo, Gavin Ashworth.)

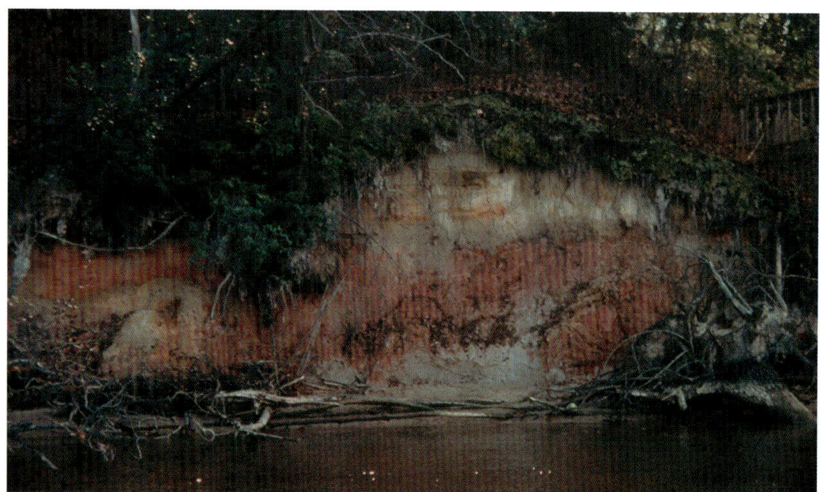

Figure 27 Source of white, pink, and green clays exposed on the banks of the Severn River that were exploited by Drue. This bank is located over thirteen miles away from Swan Cove. (Photo, C. Jane Cox.)

All of Drue's products display an astonishing rainbow of colors. It was first assumed that this variety was indicative of a lack of temperature and oxygen controls in Drue's kiln, since variables of heat can make identical clays fire to different shades and hues. However, as intact trash deposits were excavated and numerous lumps of discarded, unfired clay were recovered, it became apparent that Drue was deliberately experimenting with the production of pipes from different colored clays. Slate gray, green, white, yellow, pink, and variegated pink-white varieties were encountered by excavators. Soon the expression "gourmet clay" was added to the vocabulary (fig. 26). Eventually the clay's sources were located a little more than thirteen miles upstream from the site, on the banks of the Severn River (fig. 27).[13]

Importantly, Drue did more than simply experiment with different color clays; he also mixed them to create agate bodies, created different colored washes, and used clay slips for trailed decoration (fig. 28). His productions reflect both the mind of a scientist and the sensibilities of an artist.

The recovery of two (or three) unique handmade pipes confirms that Drue occasionally felt the need for artistic expression beyond the production of his two standard pipes. This expression is reflected by an example (Drue Type C) recovered from the home of Drue's neighbor, Robert Burle (fig. 29).[14]

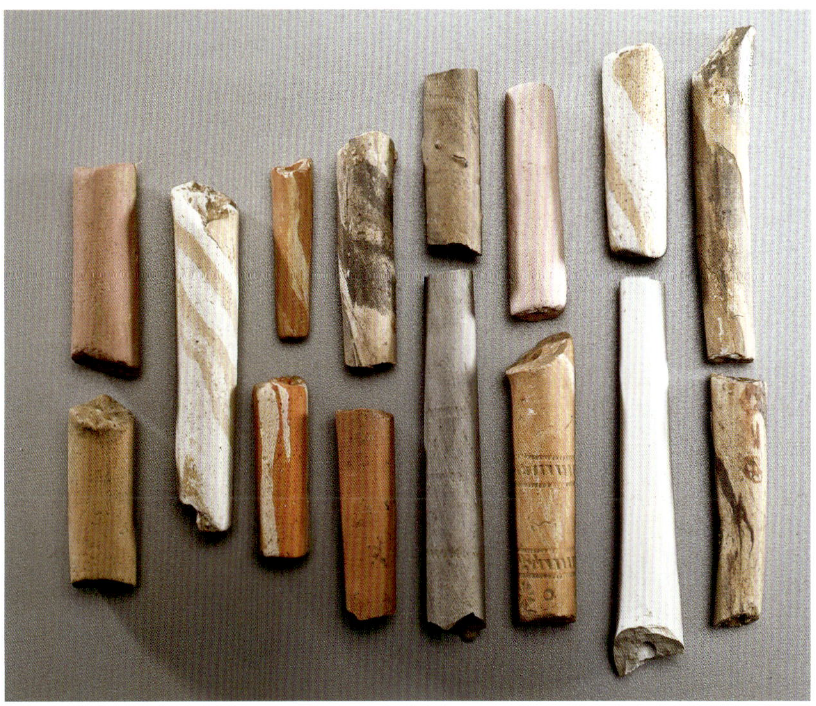

Figure 28 Tobacco pipe stems, Emanuel Drue, Maryland. Examples of the myriad color variations achieved by Drue through the mixing of different color clays as well as slipping their exteriors. (Photo, Gavin Ashworth.)

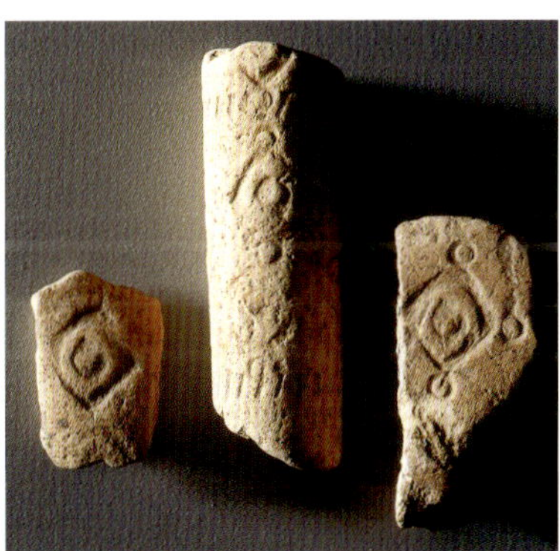

Figure 29 Three pieces of a pipe with a distinctive, very large heel termed Drue Type C. These sherds were excavated at the Burle Site at Providence nearly a decade before the stamp itself was recovered at Swan Cove. (Photo, Gavin Ashworth.)

Another remarkable pipe, most likely a presentation piece, is Drue's Type D (fig. 30). This extremely unusual pipe seems to have a single parallel—an example recovered in Holland that resides in Don Duco's pipe museum in Amsterdam.[15] The Dutch example is called a "crumm horn pipe" and has been assigned a date of circa 1650.[16]

Until more is learned about Drue's life before he settled in Providence, the hows and whys of his crumm horn pipe could be the source of endless speculation. Most important, perhaps, is the decorative extreme this pipe represents. The Drue crumm horn shows the results of ninety-four individual hand actions involving six different tools—not an economic method

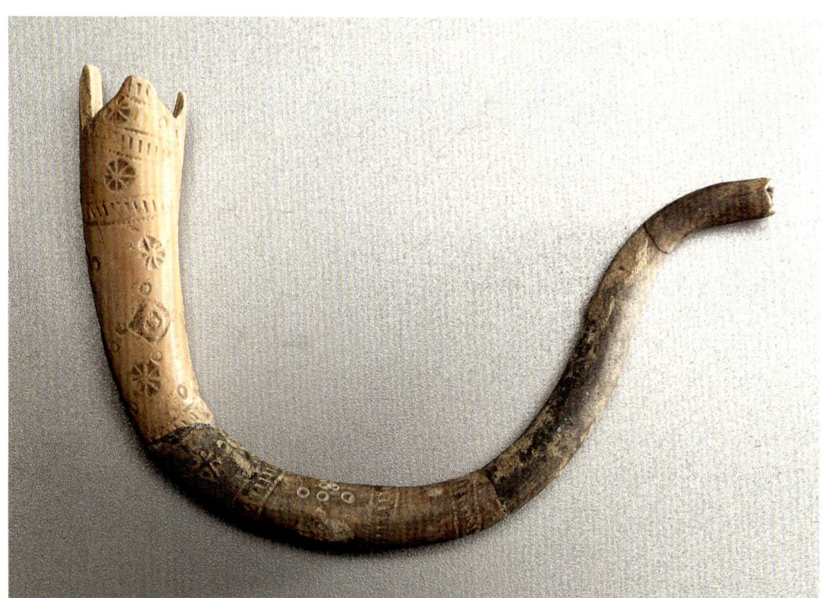

Figure 30 Drue Type D. (Photo, Gavin Ashworth.) Called a "crumm horn" (or crooked horn) pipe in Holland, this example is assumed to be one of Drue's presentation pieces. It is a unique form, with ninety-four separate decorative elements.

for the manufacture of what some perceive to be a fragile and disposable item. This industrious process is particularly noteworthy since the value of labor in the Chesapeake was so high that its expense was considered a driving force in the economy, influencing aspects as diverse as housing construction and the advancement of the slave trade.[17]

Shifting the Paradigm

The terracotta "Chesapeake pipe" and its cultural implications have been a hot topic in seventeenth-century historical archaeology virtually since the inception of the field. From decade to decade, paradigms concerning both the nature of the manufacturing of these pipes and the social implications of their use have changed. For example, the thinking about the pipe's makers has shifted from Native Americans to African Americans to a Creole population that included a European component.[18] Similar theoretical shifts have occurred in perceiving pipe manufacture and use as signs of trade with native populations; as a response to economic vagaries, such as declining tobacco prices; as expressions of African cultural continuity; and as evidence of master-servant relationships.[19] The findings at Swan Cove will further impact these studies—and, thereby, the study of lifeways in seventeenth-century Virginia and Maryland—because convention has been challenged on three theoretical fronts.[20]

The first and most basic shift concerns the archaeologist's ability to accurately identify Chesapeake pipes. The pure white products of Drue's Type B belly-bowl mold defy any previous attribution as Chesapeake pipes. No small matter, in view of the theoretical importance assigned to these artifacts. Archaeologists must now inspect such pipes for evidence of Drue's rouletting tools and hope (probably in vain) that no other manufacturers were making similarly problematic products.

A second shift involves the assumed locus of production. The scraps, trimmings, and "blobs" that have constituted the previous evidence of pipe manufacturing in the Chesapeake appear to have been handmade pipes fired in home fireplaces.[21] The Swan Cove site establishes that Drue possessed a kiln rivaling anything in Europe at the time. His was not expedient experimentation or the effort of a landless individual "who could not afford the most inexpensive imported commodities," but rather the intentional construction of a landed, middle-class planter.[22] Notably, Drue's classic terracotta products received the most elaborate decoration. At a time when labor costs were high, this calls into question theories based on the reasoning that the pipe's "cheap" nature implies greater use in times of economic depression, or greater employment by the Chesapeake's lower economic class.[23]

Finally, the manufacturer of Chesapeake pipes, at least in this case, was neither a Native American nor an African nor a Creole, but a white, Anglo-Saxon Protestant. Whether Drue had learned his trade in England, Holland, or even Virginia, it is clear that he was adapting "modern" manufacturing techniques with New World influences as an outlet for a distinct expression of folk art.[24] If the Chesapeake pipe can be considered among the known expressions of seventeenth-century folk art, as maintained by Dan Mouer, then Emanuel Drue's crumm horn pipe must stand near the pinnacle of this body of work.[25]

1. Daniel L. Mouer, "Chesapeake Creoles: The Creation of Folk Culture in Colonial Virginia," in *The Archaeology of Seventeenth Century Virginia,* edited by Theodore J. Renhart and Dennis J. Pogue (Richmond: The Archaeological Society of Virginia, 1993), p. 129.

2. Al Luckenbach, *Providence 1649: The History and Archaeology of Anne Arundel County, Maryland's First European Settlement* (Annapolis: Maryland State Archives; Crownsville: Maryland Historical Trust, 1995).

3. Al Luckenbach and C. Jane Cox, "Tobacco-Pipe Manufacturing in Early Maryland: The Swan Cove Site (ca. 1660–1669)," in *The Clay Tobacco-Pipe in Anne Arundel County, Maryland (1650–1730),* edited by Al Luckenbach, C. Jane Cox, and John Kille (Annapolis: Anne Arundel County Trust for Preservation, 2002) pp. 46–63.

4. Emanuel Drue Probate Inventory, 1670, p. 67, Maryland State Archives, Annapolis.

5. The author wishes to thank amateur archaeologist Bob Ogle for first reporting this site, and the Storck family for their kind permission to excavate and for their donation of artifacts.

6. Allan Peacey, personal communication, 2001.

7. David Gadsby, "Industrial Re-use of Domestic Ceramics at Swan Cove (18AN934)," *Maryland Archaeology* (Archeological Society of Maryland) 38, no. 1 (2002): 19–26.

8. Allan Peacey, "IV. The Development of the Clay Tobacco Pipe Kiln in the British Isles," in *The Archaeology of the Clay Tobacco Pipe,* vol. 16, edited by Peter Davey, BAR British Series, 246 (Oxford: B.A.R., 1996), pp. 40, 269.

9. Ibid., pp. 37–39.

10. Ibid., p. 15.

11. Peacey, personal communication, October 2001.

12. Peacey, "Development of the Clay Tobacco Pipe Kiln," pp. 86–87.

13. A waterborne expedition including C. Jane Cox from the Lost Towns Project and Steven Bilicki from the Maryland Historical Trust made this discovery.

14. Shawn Sharpe, Al Luckenbach, and John Kille, "Burle's Town Land (ca. 1649–1676): A Marked Abundance of Pipes," in *Clay Tobacco-Pipe in Anne Arundel County,* pp. 28–39.

15. Don Duco, personal communication, October 2001.

16. Ibid.

17. Cary Carson, Norman F. Barka, William M. Kelso, Garry W. Stone, and Dell Upton, "Impermanent Architecture in the Southern American Colonies," *Winterthur Portfolio* 16 (summer/autumn 1981): 135–96. See also Paul A. Shackel, "Town Plans and Everyday Material Culture: An Archaeology of Social Relations in Colonial Maryland's Capital Cities," in

Historical Archaeology of the Chesapeake, edited by Paul A. Shackel and Barbara J. Little (Washington, D.C.: Smithsonian Institution Press, 1994), pp. 91–94.

18. Matthew C. Emerson, "Decorated Clay Pipes from the Chesapeake" (Ph.D. diss., University of Michigan, Ann Arbor, 1988); Matthew C. Emerson, "Decorated Clay Pipes from the Chesapeake: An African Connection," in *Historical Archaeology of the Chesapeake Bay*, edited by Paul A. Shackel and Barbara J. Little (Washington, D.C.: Smithsonian Institution Press, 1994), pp. 45–46.

19. For examples, see Susan L. Henry, "Terra-cotta Pipes in 17th Century Maryland and Virginia: A Preliminary Study," *Historical Archaeology* 13 (1979): 14–38; Henry M. Miller, *A Search for the "Citty of Saint Maries": Report on the 1981 Excavations in St. Mary's City, Maryland* (St. Mary's City: St. Mary's City Commission, 1983), p. 84; Luckenbach, *Providence 1649*, p. 18; and Fraser Neiman and Julia King, "Who Smoked Chesapeake Pipes?" (paper presented at Society for Historical Archaeology Conference, Salt Lake City, 1999).

20. R. Westwood Winfree, "A Comment upon Indian Brown Clay Pipes," *Quarterly Bulletin of the Archaeological Society of Virginia* 24 (1969): 79; Henry, "Terra-cotta Pipes," pp. 16–17; Miller, *Search for the "Citty of Saint Maries,"* p. 84; Emerson, "Decorated Clay Pipes from the Chesapeake" (1988); Mouer, "Chesapeake Creoles," pp. 152–53; Emerson, "Decorated Clay Pipes from the Chesapeake" (1994), pp. 45–46; Neiman and King, "Who Smoked Chesapeake Pipes?"

21. Ann Markel and Tom Davidson, personal communications, December 2000; for reference to firing in home fireplaces, see Emerson, "Decorated Clay Pipes from Chesapeake" (1988), p. 36.

22. Emerson, "Decorated Clay Pipes from Chesapeake" (1994), pp. 44–45.

23. Henry, "Terra-cotta Pipes"; Neiman and King, "Who Smokes Chesapeake Pipes?"

24. Research being conducted by Taft Kiser and the author indicates that a pipemaker (called the "Bookbinder") from the Chesapeake Beach area of Virginia is the only other maker known to incorporate marbleized clays in the fashion Drue did. This similarity suggests Drue may have migrated from this region ca. 1650, when large numbers of Puritans moved from this part of Virginia to Providence, Maryland.

25. Mouer, "Chesapeake Creoles."

Norman F. Barka

Archaeology of a Colonial Pottery Factory: The Kilns and Ceramics of the "Poor Potter" of Yorktown

▼ THE DISCOVERY IN 1966 of the "Poor Potter" manufacturing site in Yorktown, Virginia, is one of the most significant industrial finds in historical archaeology. Excavation of the site has revealed the rare preservation of two kilns and abundant evidence of the production of a large variety of pottery, including the earliest stoneware made in America (fig. 1). The site also stands out historically because of its size and technological advancement in kiln and factory design. The establishment and operation of this well-developed pottery complex was a remarkable industrial achievement. As well, its development clearly flaunted British mercantile policy, especially as Yorktown was located only a short distance from Williamsburg, the seat of British colonial government in Virginia.[1]

Documentary and archaeological evidence of pottery kiln sites—or, indeed, any manufacturing site—is not always easy to find. Such mundane and ordinary structures and activities were rarely recorded by potters or by contemporary citizens, and relatively few kiln sites are known. The relative completeness of the Poor Potter site makes it a valuable tool for the study of kiln technology, pottery production, trade, and early-eighteenth-century consumer demands.

The Identity of the "Poor Potter"

The term "poor potter" is first mentioned in the documentary record by the royal governor of the Virginia colony, William Gooch, in 1732; in subsequent years, until 1741, Governor Gooch sent required reports dealing with trade and manufacture in Virginia to England's Board of Trade. The content of these reports and other documents was meager at best, and in essence asserted that the government need not worry about damage to English trade because the potter's work was of little consequence. The last known reference by Gooch was in his 1741 dispatch, in which he mentioned the potter's death. By the 1950s, archaeological research was providing further evidence of local manufacture of ceramic wares, suggesting that Governor Gooch had made a conscious attempt to disguise Yorktown's burgeoning industry.[2]

It appears that only one person, William Rogers, can definitively be associated with the Yorktown pottery operation: he was a well-established businessman and entrepreneur in Yorktown during the early eighteenth century; he owned the two lots on which the pottery factory was built; and the inventory of his estate taken at the time of his death in December 1739 lists many items that would have been associated with a pottery operation.[3]

Figure 1 Earthenware and stoneware "wasters" recovered from the William Rogers site in Yorktown, Virginia, ca. 1720–1745. (Courtesy, National Park Service, Colonial National Historical Park, Yorktown Collection; all artifact photos by Gavin Ashworth.)

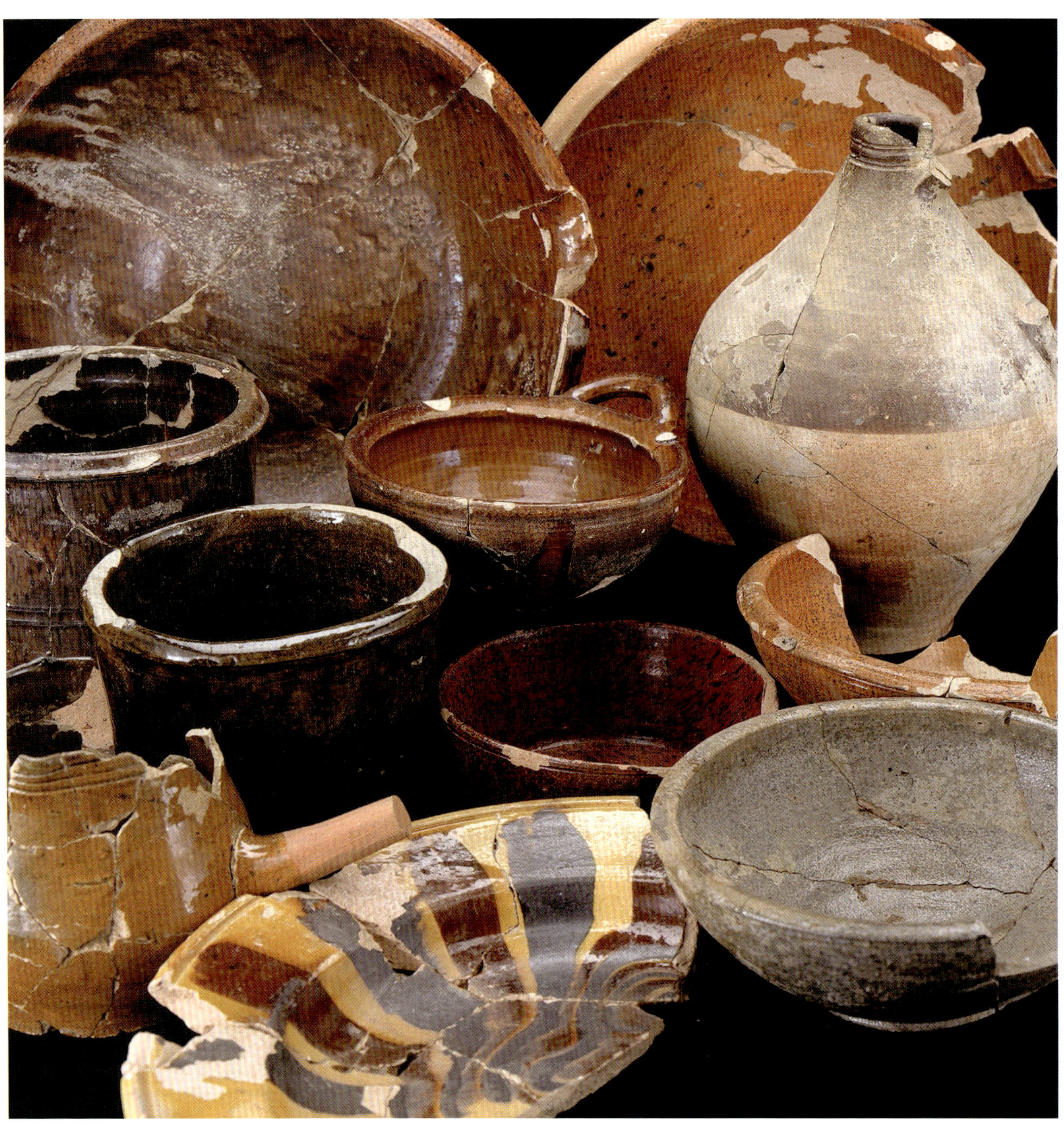

There is little question today that William Rogers was the "poor potter," but he probably was not a potter and he certainly was not poor. In addition to being a successful brewer and respected businessman (see McCartney and Ayres, "Yorktown's 'Poor Potter': A Man Wise Beyond Discretion," pp. 49–59 in this issue), there is sufficient evidence to establish that he was the owner of one of the largest, most significant, and most successful pottery factories in colonial America.

William Rogers was born sometime between 1680 and 1688 across the Thames from London in Southwark or Lambeth, major pottery-producing areas in the seventeenth and eighteenth centuries. Although very little information about him survives, there are many families named Rogers who lived in Southwark and Lambeth.

Rogers probably arrived in Yorktown in 1710. Established as a port town in 1691, Yorktown had soon become a thriving community of fifty or more buildings, including homes, storehouses, a church, and a courthouse. Lawyers, merchants, tailors, craftsmen, and blacksmiths were just some of the citizenry making up the town's permanent residents.

In 1711 William Rogers acquired two half-acre lots, Lots 51 and 55, on the northwest edge of town, where he probably lived until his death in 1739. Since these lots became the eventual site of the pottery factory, Rogers's proprietorship indicates that he was seriously involved with the pottery operation.

Archaeological excavations of the property turned up the remains of numerous buildings, two kilns, waster pits, and a number of features. Written documentation also speaks. Various court records dating to the 1720s indicate that Rogers sold quantities of earthenwares to various plantations in Virginia and Maryland, among them Marlborough, Menokin, and Wicocomico. And a subsequent owner of the lots, George Chaplin, a butcher, received a deed in 1770 describing them as those "commonly known by the name of the Pothouse lots."

In 1759, twenty years after Rogers's death, his daughter, Sarah, listed other structures that were probably situated on the lots, namely a dwelling, a garden, a stable, and a pothouse. Rogers also owned additional property in and around Yorktown, including several ships and a waterfront warehouse, and it is likely that Rogers's family continued his success and operated his business until at least 1745.

Rogers and British Mercantilism

The British mercantile system of the eighteenth century had as its goal the supply of British manufactured goods to the colonies and the discouragement of any colonial manufacture that would compete with and thereby lessen the need for British exports. The British Board of Trade regulated colonial commerce through the appointed governors of the colonies. Some governors enforced Board of Trade policy, others neglected it. There is no evidence to suggest that the Board of Trade or British pottery manufacturers ever complained about Rogers's pottery factory or even knew of the prodigious quantities of quality ware that it produced.

Rogers opened the Yorktown pottery works in or around 1720 during the administration of Colonel Alexander Spotswood, who ran the colony from nearby Williamsburg. Governor Spotswood must have known about the enterprise in Yorktown, so his silence on its operation indicates at least tacit approval. Governor Hugh Drysdale succeeded Spotswood in 1722, but he, too, maintained silent approval of the pottery factory.

In 1727 William Gooch, who was sympathetic to home manufacture, became governor of the colony. In contrast to Spotswood and Drysdale, Gooch reported on the activities of a "poor potter" but never mentioned William Rogers by name. The responses by Gooch to queries put forth by the Board of Trade from 1732 to 1742 are both protective and favorable in tone. It is likely that Governor Gooch used the term "poor potter" to mislead the Board of Trade and mask the true nature of the Yorktown pottery industry. "Poor potter" would have implied either an impoverished potter or a potter who produced inferior quality pots. Rogers was neither. He sold not only large quantities of earthenwares but also excellent salt-glazed stoneware vessels, and the mugs he produced are virtually indistinguishable in quality from those produced in England. Gooch had to mention the Yorktown enterprise because of its ever-increasing size and production, but clearly he tried to minimize the operation so as not to alarm the Board of Trade. His reports to the Board of Trade provide an exercise in reading between the lines.

In order to operate an enterprise the size of the Yorktown pottery, Rogers would have needed a large number of skilled and unskilled laborers, and he might have used skilled potters from England and Europe. Evidence shows he used the labor of indentured servants and slaves, some of whom also could have been skilled potters. (See McCartney and Ayres, pp. 51–52.)

Archaeological Research

The William Rogers site was discovered when the author excavated a large waster pit on Lot 51 (fig. 2). From 1966 to 1970, with the help of students from the College of William and Mary and other interested individuals, a testing program was carried out on limited portions of the site. In the fall of 1970, the first of two kilns—designated the "Large Kiln"—was discovered and subsequently excavated (figs. 3, 4). Associated with the Large Kiln were two artifacts purposefully buried as part of a dedication ritual (figs. 5–7). The author recalls the day these incredibly significant objects were uncovered:

> The discovery of two well-preserved eighteenth century pottery kilns at the Poor Potter's site in Yorktown was a rare experience for any historical archaeologist. In addition, the finding of these two extraordinary pots at the same site was downright unbelievable. After thirty years, I still find it difficult to believe, but the story of this adventure is true. On a beautiful, and what was to be a very eventful day in 1970, I drove to Yorktown as I had planned to spend some time defining the back side of the recently discovered large kiln. Troweling the soil in this area revealed a darker pit-like feature measuring about one foot in diameter. After recording it, I began to excavate the feature and my trowel scraped what appeared to be

a pottery sherd. Digging farther into the feature, a pottery vessel began to emerge and within a short time a complete pot had been uncovered—a bowl-like porringer, with a triangular handle and raised annular base, completely lead glazed and orange in color, and buried upside down. I could not believe my eyes, but the next discovery was equally thrilling. Brushing the dirt off the exterior surface of the pot below the handle revealed the initials "AG" and the date "1720"; both letters and numbers had been incised into the pot prior to glazing. Lifting the porringer out of the soil matrix revealed another astonishing "treasure," a small white tin-glazed cup with a handle, exquisitely potted, with blue floral decoration on the exterior and the lip of the rim painted red. After overcoming a sense of exhilaration over these unique discoveries, I thought about the meaning of the extraordinary finds. What a special day it was for both the "poor potter," who made and buried the pot in 1720, and for me, who found it 250 years later.[+]

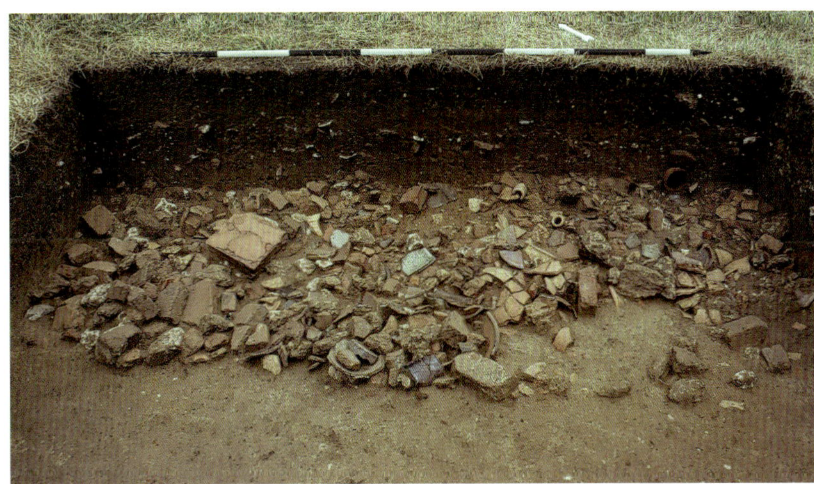

Figure 2 Photograph showing the initial stages of the excavation of one of several waster pits discovered on the site. (Photo, Norman F. Barka.)

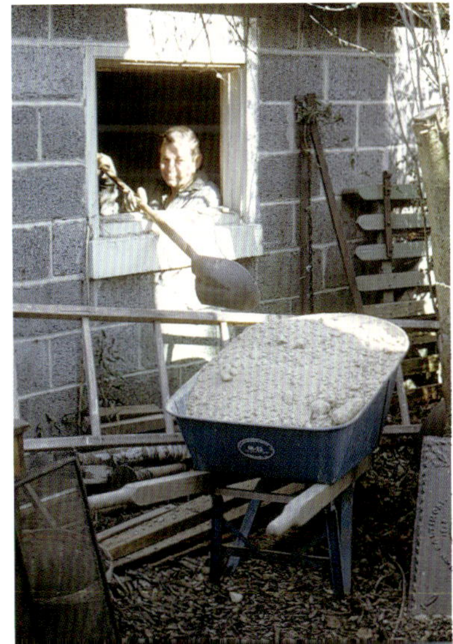

Figure 3 Excavator removing soil from within the car garage over the buried William Rogers's kiln complex. (Photo, Norman F. Barka.)

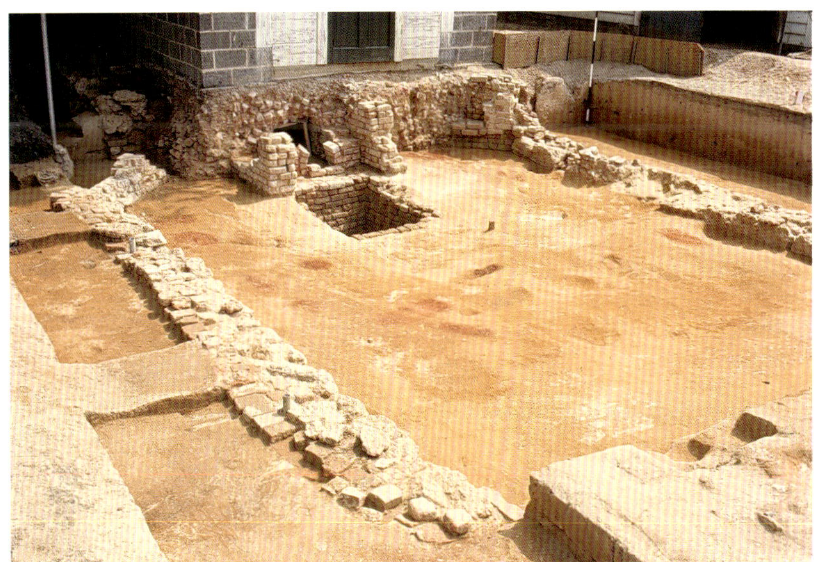

Figure 4 View of archaeological excavation of the William Rogers's pottery complex with portions of the kiln exposed beneath a cinder block garage. (Photo, Norman F. Barka.)

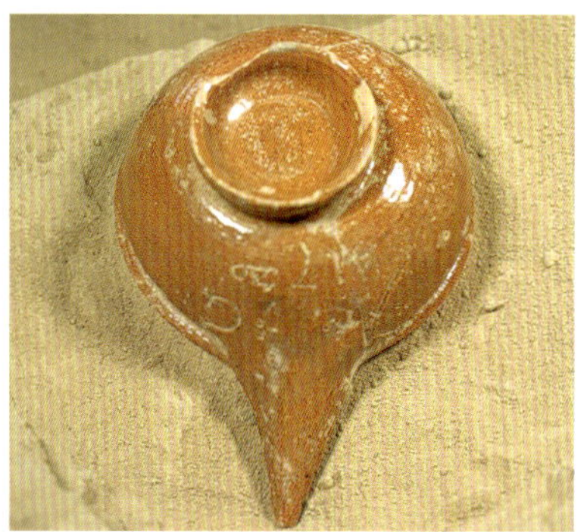
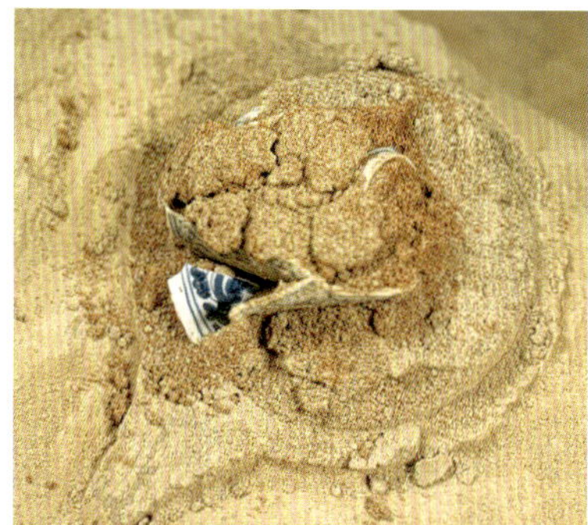
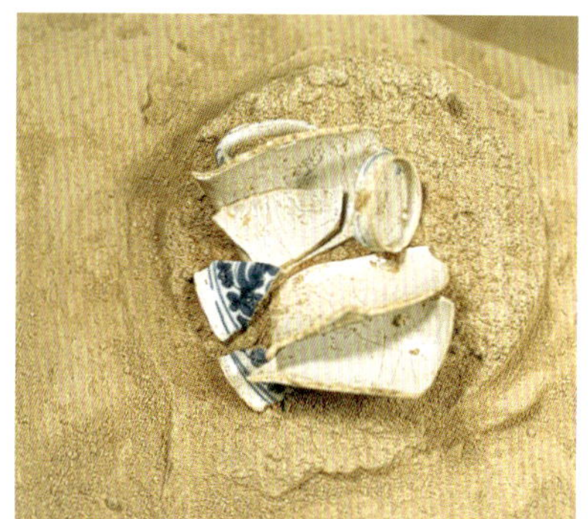

Figure 5 The discovery and excavation of William Rogers's porringer and London delft capuchinne. (Photos, Norman F. Barka.)

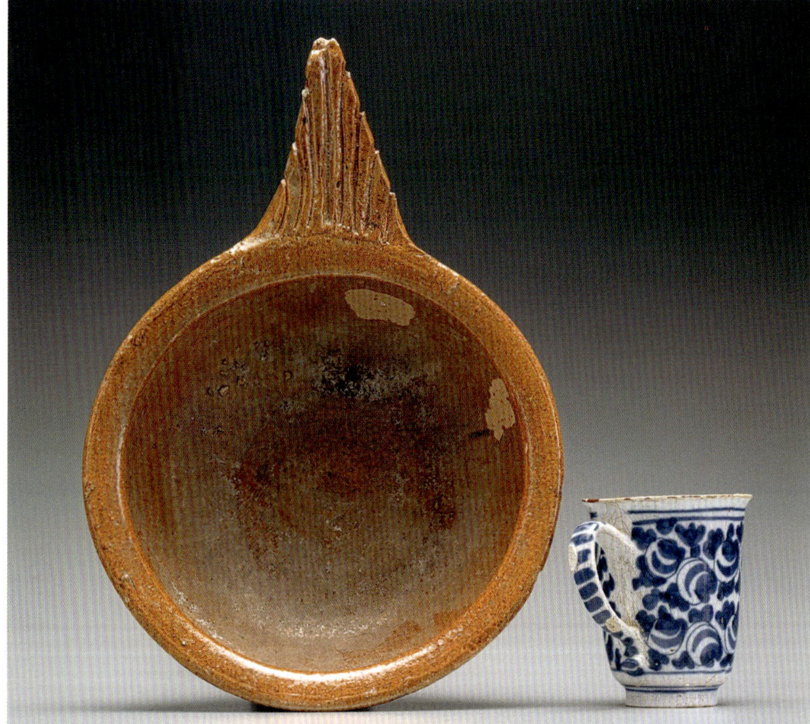
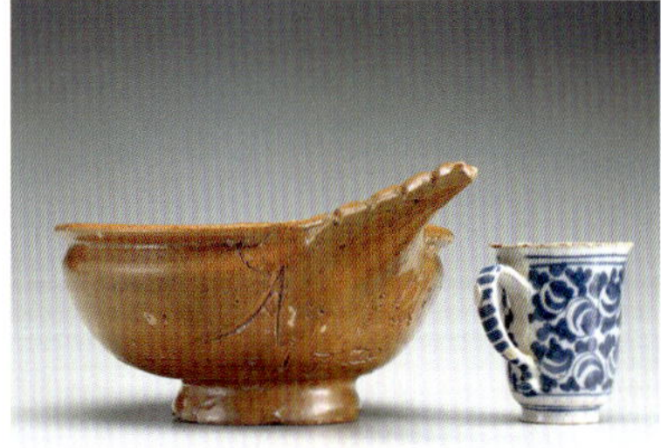

Figure 6 Porringer and coffee cup. *Porringer:* William Rogers, Yorktown, Virginia, 1720. Lead-glazed earthenware. D. 6½". *Coffee cup:* London, ca. 1700. Tin-glazed earthenware. H. 2⅝". (Courtesy, National Park Service, Colonial National Historical Park, Yorktown Collection.) COLO Y 7096, COLO Y 7097. These special objects may represent the material evidence of a dedication rite or ceremony marking the first successful firing of the large kiln. The initials "AG" on the porringer might refer to the initials of the potter, who remains unidentified, and "1720" to the first year of production at the site. The tin-glazed cup, made in London, England, in the period 1700–1720, would have been especially valued by the potter because of its fine quality; it may also have reaffirmed connections the potter had with the tin-glazing industry in Lambeth or Southwark. In any case, the burial of these pots was likely a special event to ensure good luck in the pottery business. The porringer may be the earliest dated American-made piece ever found in a kiln context.

Expanded excavations during the summer of 1972, the first to be sponsored on this site by the National Park Service, uncovered the remains of the probable workshop room and buildings interconnected with the Large Kiln (fig. 8).

In the fall of 1975, William and Mary personnel began the excavation of a second kiln, designated the "Small Kiln" (figs. 9, 10). Approximately fifty percent of Lots 51 and 55 have been tested or excavated as of this writing,

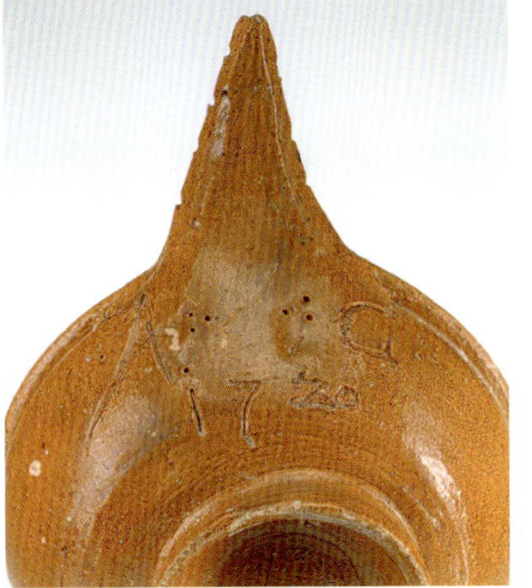

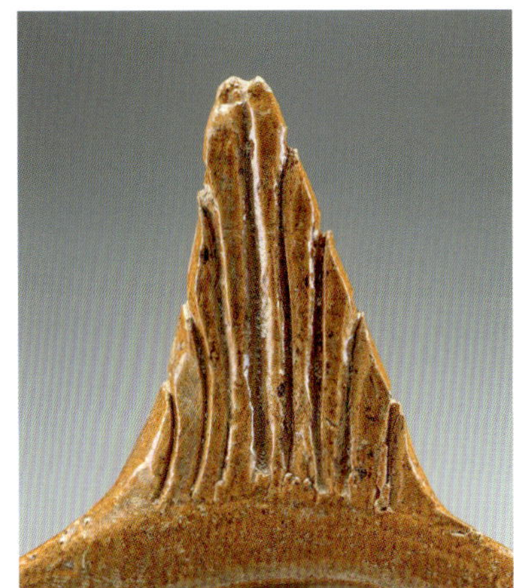

Figure 7 Detail of the back and front of the dedication porringer illustrated in fig. 6. Its solid handle is triangular-shaped with incised parallel line decoration on the upper, flat portion. At least one bisque handle fragment has been found at the site, signifying that the porringer was made at the site.

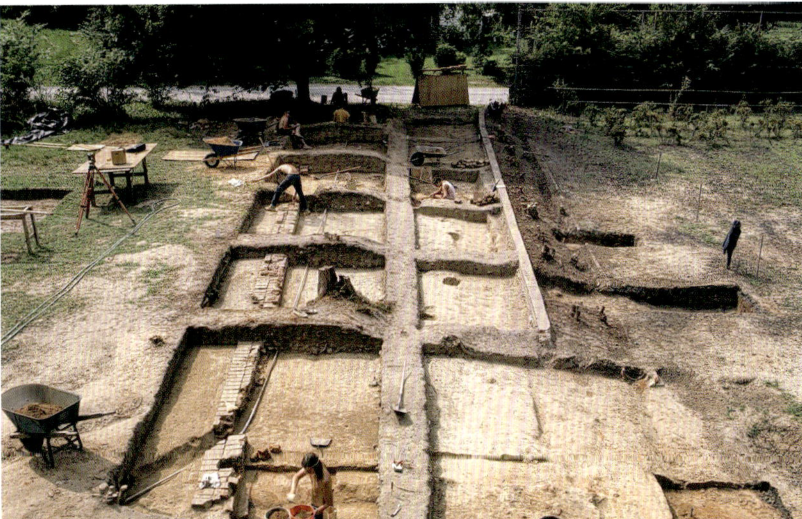

Figure 8 View of the archaeological excavation, facing north. (Photo, Norman F. Barka.) Note the brick foundation of the workshop complex at left.

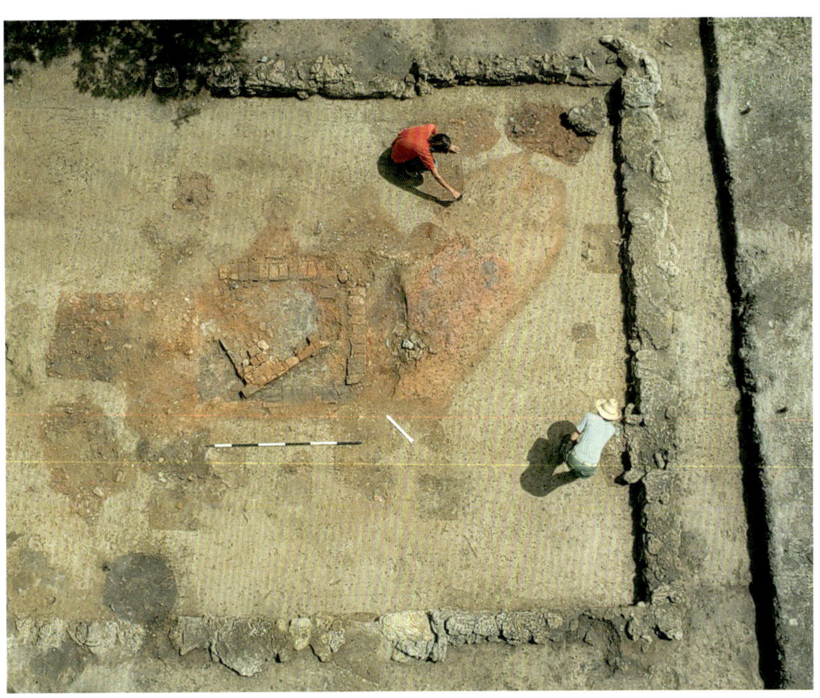

Figure 9 Overhead view of the Small Kiln prior to excavation. (Photo, Norman F. Barka.)

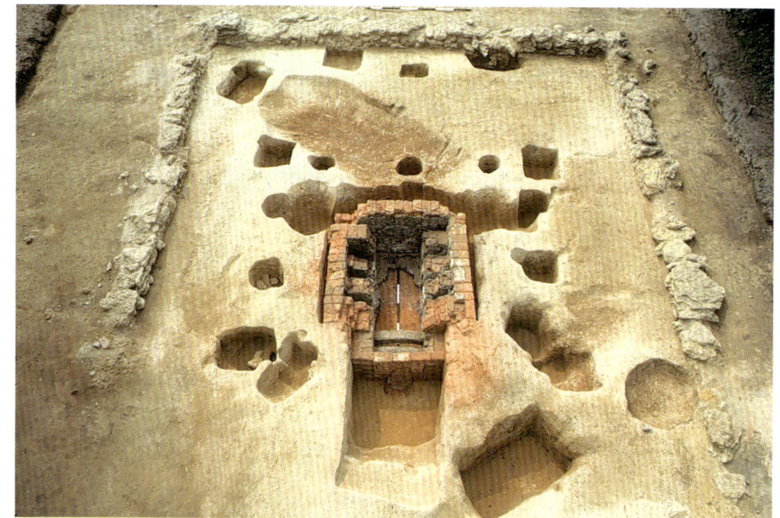

Figure 10 Overhead view of the completed excavation of the Small Kiln. (Photo, Norman F. Barka.) The traces of a marl foundation and a series of postholes represent the remains of the contemporary structures associated with the kiln.

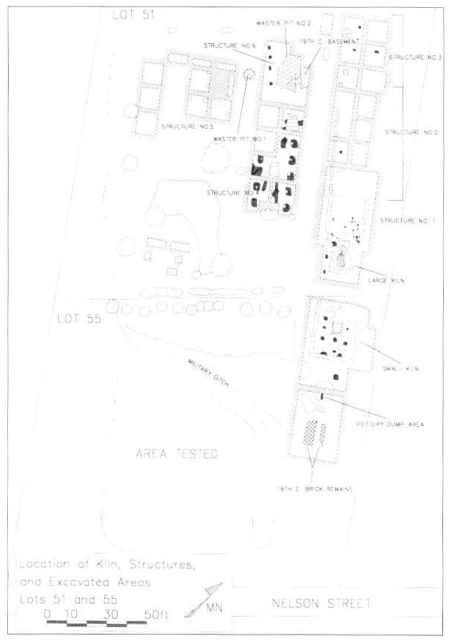

Figure 11 A plan drawing of the excavations detailing the locations of the kilns and related structures and features.

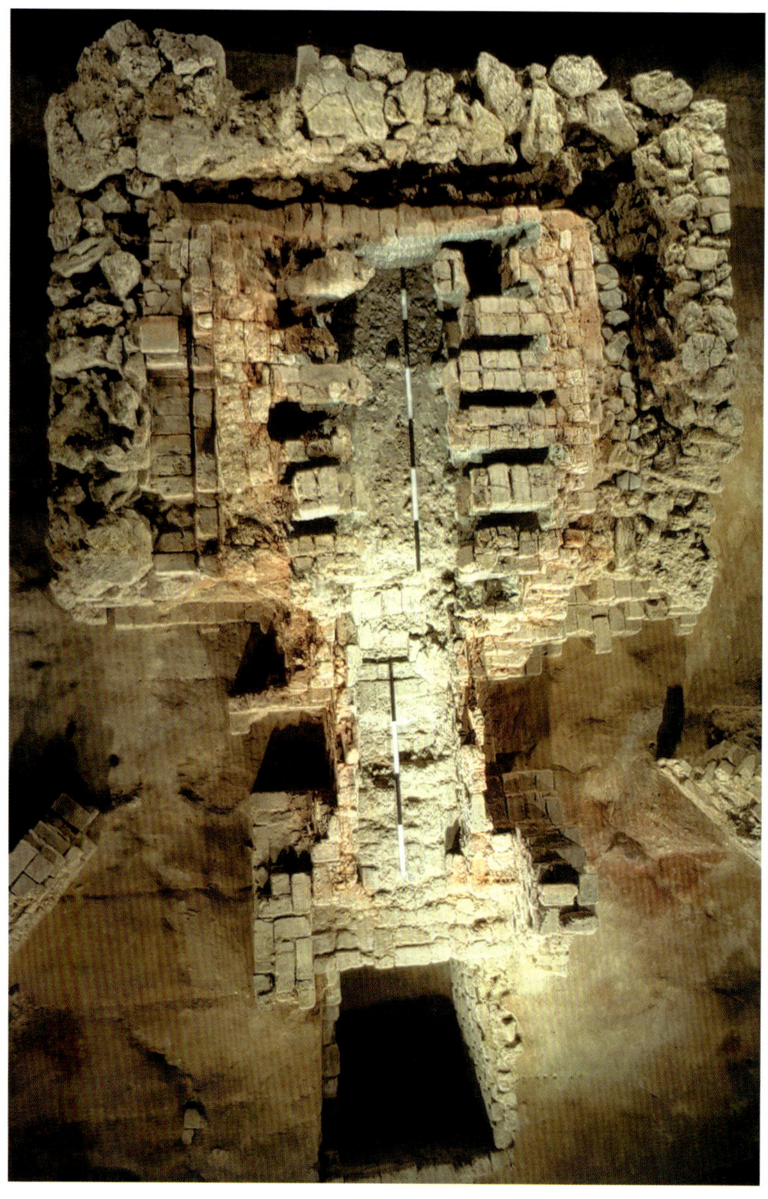

Figure 12 An overhead view of the Large Kiln. (Photo, Norman F. Barka.)

uncovering two kilns, a workshop building complex, several post-in-the-ground structures, and two waster pits (fig. 11). It is believed that the major components of the pottery factory were uncovered in the archaeological research carried out from 1966 to around 1981.

The Yorktown pottery factory was a large operation, consisting of a symmetrical complex of buildings and features. The main pottery complex probably consisted of a row of interconnected buildings, rooms, and kilns located on the east side of Lots 51 and 55. The complex measures about 170 feet in length (north-south) and 20–22 feet in width, extending from the edge of Read Street to within one hundred feet of Nelson Street. Both the Large and Small Kilns were situated toward the south end. The archaeological and architectural evidence suggests that pots were thrown, dried, and glazed in a large workshop room or rooms and fired in one of the two kilns.

Large Kiln

The Large Kiln was built of brick and marl (figs. 12, 13). Rectangular in shape, it was of the updraft type, with a lower heat chamber and an upper pot chamber (fig. 14). The foundation for the kiln and an adjoining room immediately north of the kiln had been constructed in a large rectangular hole measuring 37 feet by 22 feet to a depth of 4.4 feet below ground surface. The lower one-third or so of the kiln, or the majority of the heat chamber, was situated below ground level, with the pot chamber floor approximately at ground level (fig. 15).

Figure 13 An oblique view of the Large Kiln. (Photo, Norman F. Barka.)

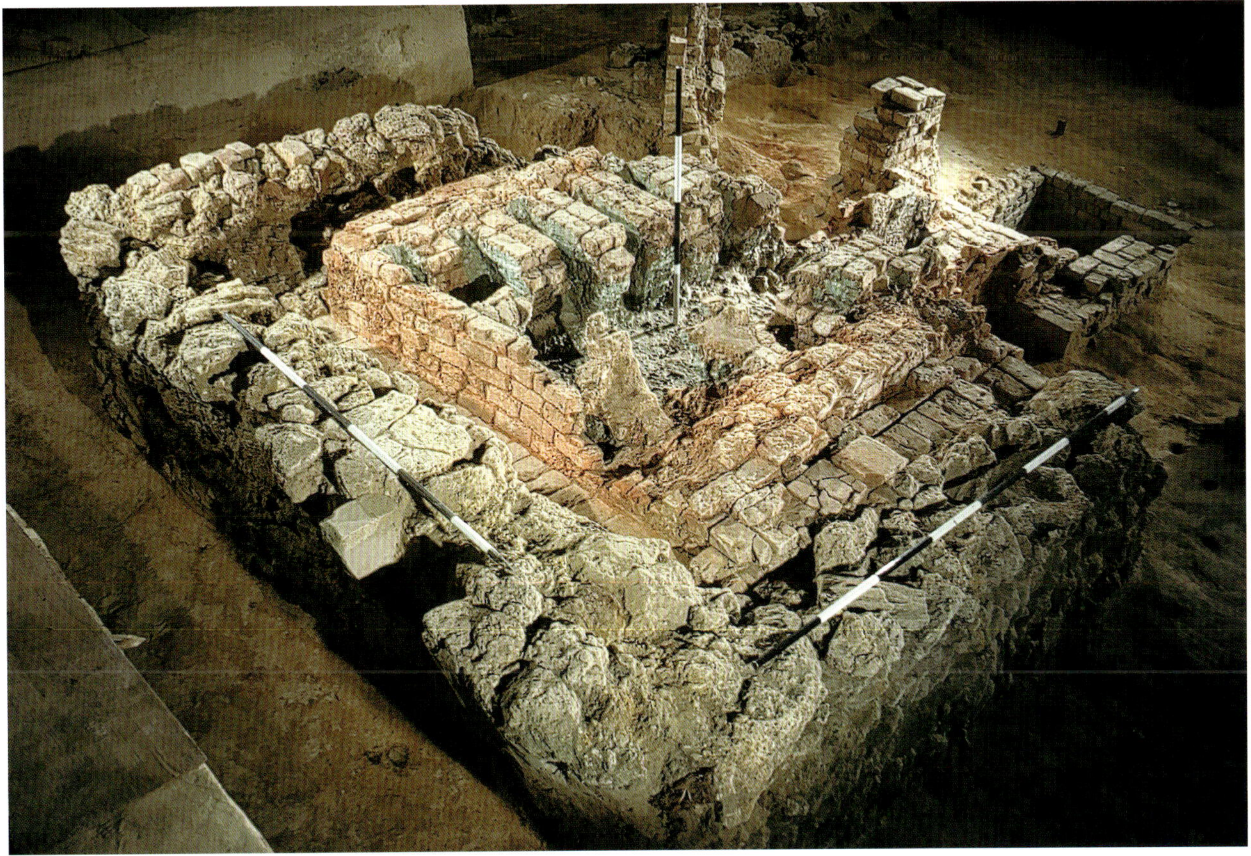

Figure 14 A drawing of the remains of the Large Kiln. (Unless otherwise noted, all drawings courtesy of the Department of Anthropology, College of William and Mary, Williamsburg, Va.)

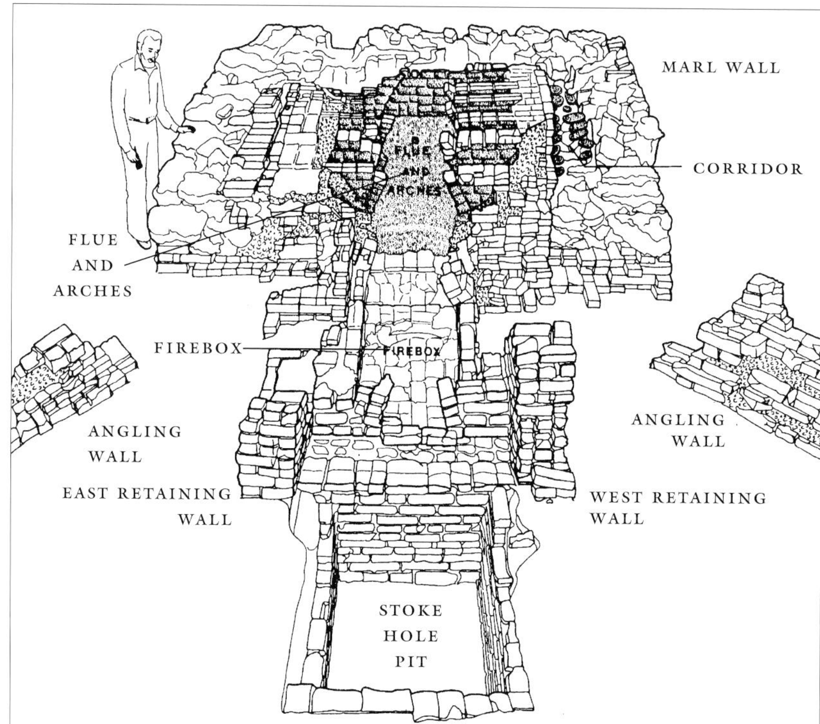

Figure 15 A cross section of the Large Kiln.

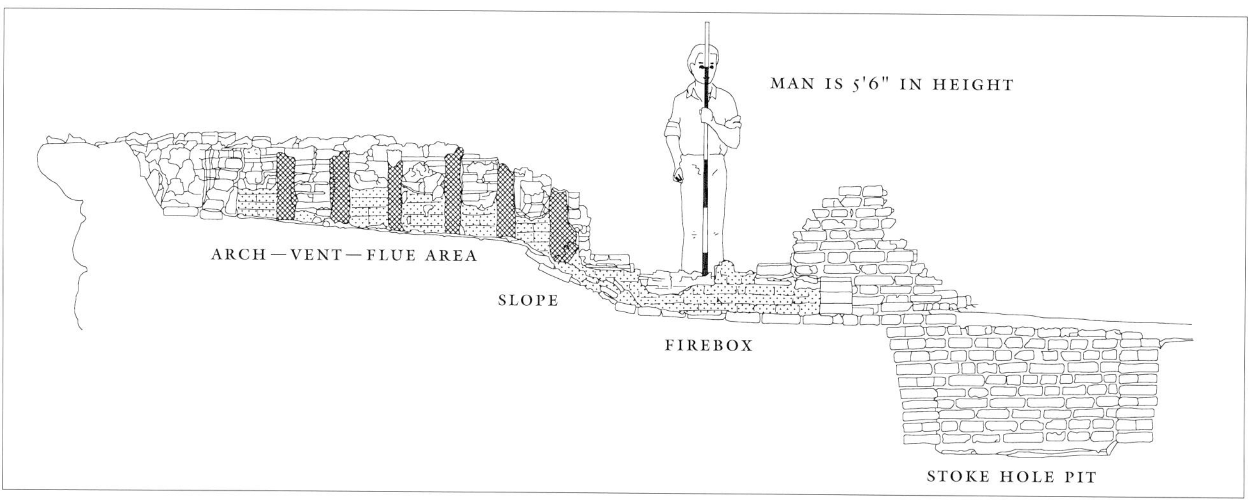

The building (designated Structure 1) directly associated with the kiln is bounded on the south by the kiln, on the east and west by marl walls, and on the north by steps cut into subsoil that lead into a large structure, the presumed main workshop building (designated Structure 2). The Large Kiln is a well-built, well-planned structure, symmetrical in plan. A firebox and stoke hole project from the north side into the center of Structure 1.

The kiln itself measures 21.6 feet by 13.3 feet and, for discussion purposes, can be divided into three parts: flue-arch-vent area; firebox with adjacent stoke-hole pit; and adjacent brick and marl walls and corridor.

The central brick portion of the lower heat chamber consisted of a main flue spanned by arches separated by vents or open areas that circulated hot air. This area also served as a foundation for the pot chamber located directly above. The entire flue-arch-vent area was constructed of red nonfire brick. Vertical brick walls extended upward from the outer portions of this area to contain the heat generated in the firebox, which is connected to the flue on the kiln's north side. The heat chamber floor was formed by the top of the arch system. The flue-arch-vent area measures 8.5 feet square, exclusive of the firebox and stoke-hole pit, and survives to a height of thirteen courses of brick, or 3.32 feet above sterile soil.

The flue measures 2.2 feet in width by 6 feet in length, its floor sloping gently from south to north, where it connects with a shorter and steeper slope. The total flue-firebox length is 11.7 feet. The flue was formed by a series of six parallel arches, each separated by vents. The arches were catenary in shape, the midpoint of each reaching an estimated height of 3 feet from the flue floor. The arches survive to various elevations, the highest at 1.84 feet above the flue floor. The angle of the arch is currently about 19° inward from the vertical, and both arch and arch supports are one brick wide.

The arches were separated from one another by four-inch vents, which paralleled the six arches across the width of the heat chamber. The vents as well as the arches were positioned at right angles to the flue. Originally extending about one foot into the pot chamber and terminating at the same height as the arches' upper surface, the vents enabled the flue's hot air to travel upward into the heat chamber. The maximum surviving horizontal length of the vents is 1.8 feet (east-west). The interior surfaces of the arches and vents are thoroughly coated by a fairly thick layer of bluish green salt glaze, making it impossible to discern interior brick characteristics.

When found, the flue-arch-vent area was filled with a 1.7 foot deep deposit of soil, artifacts, rubble, and kiln debris, with the majority of finds consisting of kiln furniture. The lower layer probably was contemporary with the kiln's operation, as a great deal of kiln furniture was present at this level. Finds included numerous props, separators, and pads.

The firebox is the area of the kiln where heat was generated through the combustion of wood logs. Heat traveled into the kiln flue and up through the vents and into the pot chambers. The firebox extended from the kiln's north side to a stoke-hole pit. Both structures were constructed entirely of brick. The firebox, which connects to the flue, measures the same width, 2.2 feet. It has a flat brick floor and extends for a length of 4 feet, from an arched firemouth on the north to a point where the floor rises at a 37 degree angle to meet the sloping flue floor.

The two parallel walls of the firebox survive to a height of 1.8 feet. Both walls are continuously glazed on the inner (toward the fire) surface. The glaze is coarser than the salt glaze found on the flue-arch-vent surfaces because the intense heat melted the brick. The firebox floor bricks are heavily fire-affected but not glazed. Its walls show evidence of rebuilding, as occasional bricks with glazed surfaces are noticeable on the exterior. The upper brick course of the firebox walls curves slightly inward, suggesting that an arched roof had been in place. When first excavated, a low arched firemouth was present on its north side. The firemouth's opening measured 1.5 feet in height and 1.2 feet in width. This feature was subsequently destroyed by vandals, although a photographic record survives.

The firebox is flanked on both sides by brick retaining or support walls. Each wall is laid in Flemish bond and is 1½ bricks wide, surviving to a maximum of 2.6 feet high, or twelve courses of brick. The walls are each 4 feet in length and do not extend the full span of the firebox. Each wall's north end extends about 1.8 feet beyond the firemouth, forming boundaries for a short brick platform, which continues between the firemouth and stoke-hole pit. Unlike the firebox bricks, the platform bricks are not glazed by heat. Measuring 4 feet long and 1.4 feet wide, the platform served as a small loading and utility area between the stoke-hole pit and firemouth.

To the immediate north of the firebox, and separated by the platform, there is a stoke-hole pit, a brick-walled box with a dirt (subsoil) floor. The pit's floor as found is nearly 2½ feet below the level of the firebox floor. By standing in the hole, the potter could more easily load logs into the firebox and stoke the fire. It also may have served as a temporary repository for the hot coals and ash raked out from the firebox through the firemouth. When found, the stoke-hole pit contained numerous strata of ash. The pit may have served one other function: if the kiln's temperature became too high, the fire could be drawn or raked out through the stoke hole into the stoke-hole pit, thereby reducing the temperature.

The stoke-hole pit is slightly trapezoidal in plan, the end nearest the firebox slightly narrower than the opposite (north) end. The pit measures 4 feet in length and 2.65 feet in height. All four walls were built of thirteen courses of red brick, but survive to heights varying between nine and eleven courses. The firebox fill, platform area, and stoke-hole pit consisted of strata of rubble, ash, and numerous examples of kiln furniture.

The flue-arch-vent area, made entirely of brick, is flanked on three sides by a continuous wall of irregular marl blocks, probably quarried from the cliffs of the nearby York River. Extending to 3.47 feet in height, 1.5–2.5 feet in width, and 10.4–13.3 feet in length, it may have functioned as an insulating barrier between the heat chamber and the ground.

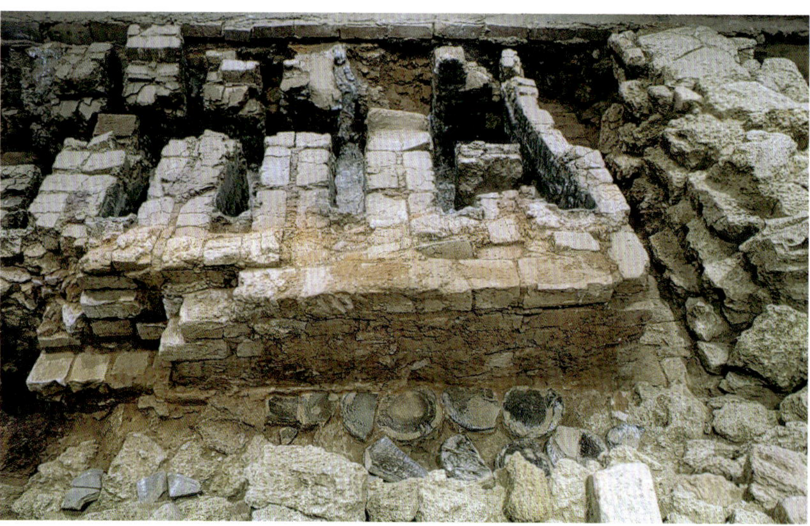

Figure 16 View of the corridor on the west side of the Large Kiln. (Photo, Norman F. Barka.) This area was paved with flat saggar lids, saggar bases, and body fragments. Measuring 1.2 feet wide and 8 feet long, the corridor may have allowed the potter to peer through spy holes in the kiln wall to judge the pot chamber's temperature.

On the south and east sides, the marl walls directly articulate with the outer walls of the flue-arch-vent area. On the west side there is a corridor paved with flat saggar lids, saggar bases, and body fragments (fig. 16). Measuring 1.2 feet wide and 8 feet long, the corridor may have allowed the potter to peer through spy holes in the kiln wall to judge the pot chamber's temperature.

Small Kiln

A smaller kiln was found about 23 feet south of the Large Kiln. It, too, is well preserved due to the presence of a below-ground heat chamber (fig. 17). However, the upper pot chamber, originally situated above ground level, has been destroyed. The Small Kiln has a Bourry-like firebox, differing slightly from the Large Kiln, which has an extended firebox.[5] Nonetheless, both are similar in basic design—updraft kilns with an upper pot chamber resting on a lower heat chamber. The Small Kiln measures 12.7 feet by 5.75 feet and consists of a lower heat chamber made entirely of brick, a stokehole pit with earthen steps leading into it, and filled builders' trenches (fig. 18). It, like the Large Kiln, had been built into a hole dug three feet into the subsoil. The present archaeological remains are well preserved to a maximum height of 2.9 feet, or twelve to thirteen courses of brick.

The heat chamber has maximum dimensions of 7.1 feet (north-south) by 5.5 feet. The chamber consisted of outer brick walls, interior arch supports, and arches designed to promote heat circulation through flues and an interior firebox area (fig. 19). The north wall contains a stoke hole. Brickwork, for the most part, was laid in random bonding patterns. The south wall exhibits numerous salt-glazed headers. Four arches supported the pot chamber floor above, and a fifth arch within the south wall probably served to strengthen the kiln's rear wall. The stoke hole in the north wall was found plugged with a clay slab on its exterior side; the interior portion of the stoke hole had been plugged with eight brickbats.

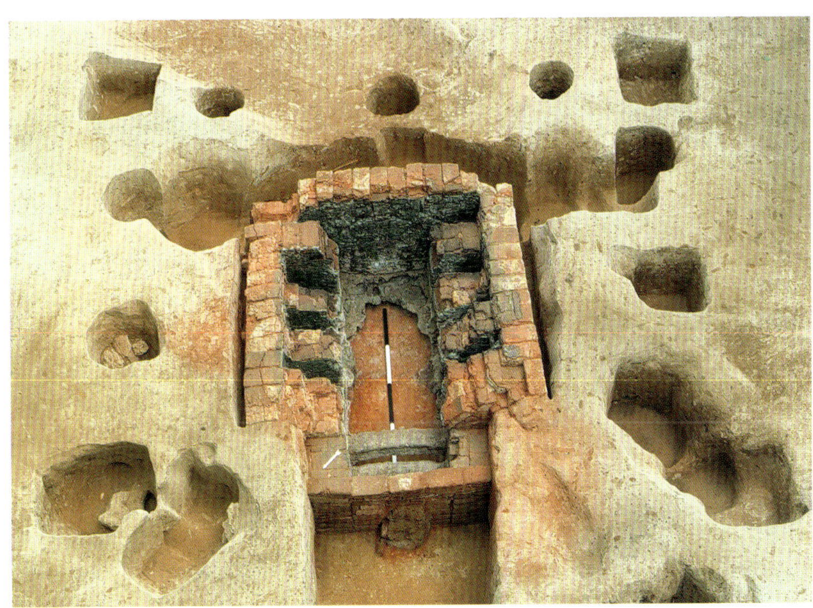

Figure 17 A view of the excavated Small Kiln, facing south. (Photo, Norman F. Barka.)

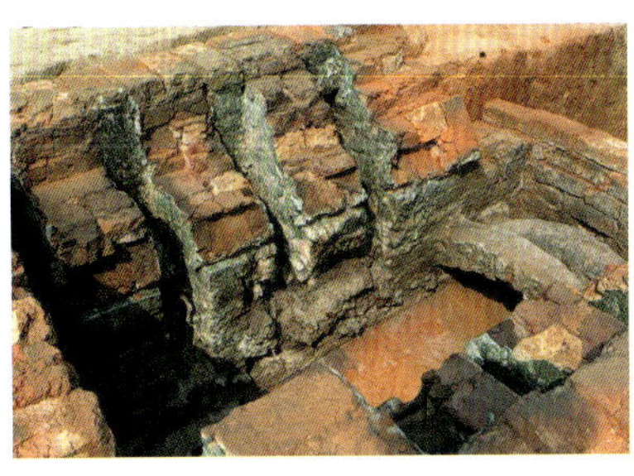

Figure 18 An oblique view of the Small Kiln. (Photo, Norman F. Barka.)

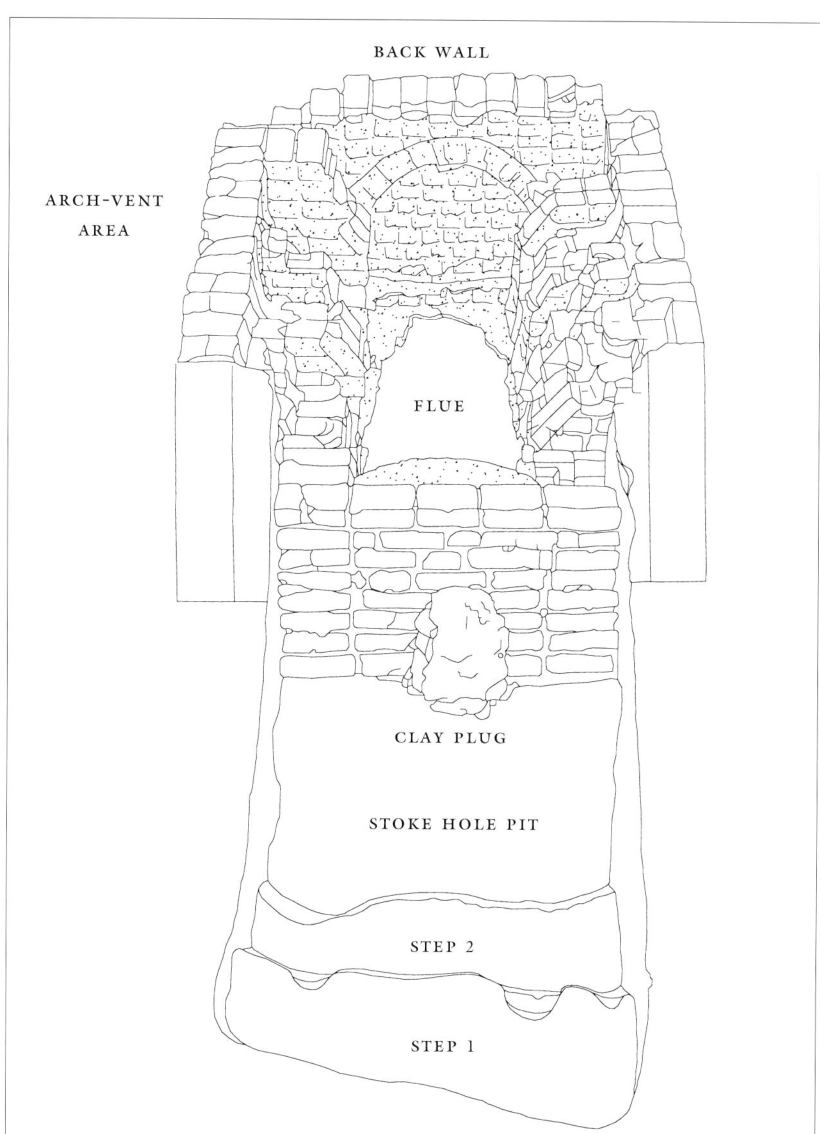

Figure 19 A drawing of the remains of the Small Kiln.

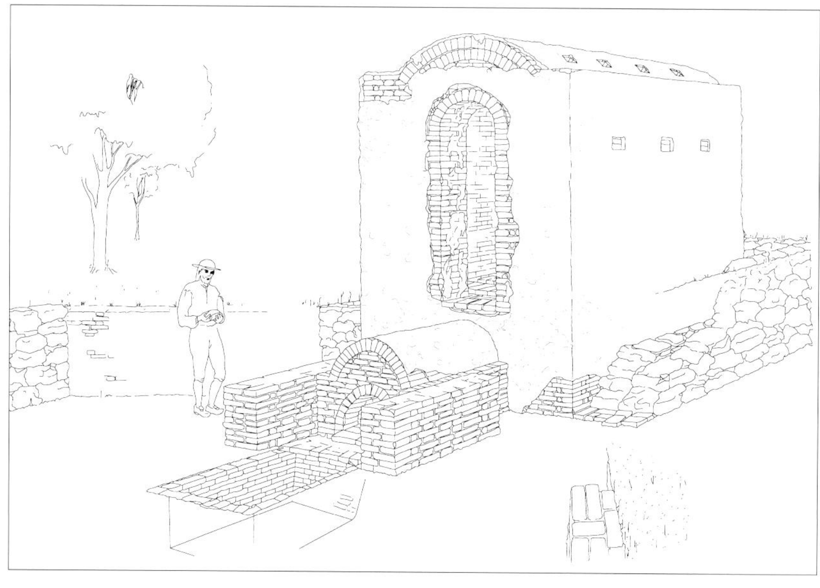

Figure 20 An artist's reconstruction of the Large Kiln.

The chamber's interior contained four arch supports and flue arches, four minor flues, a main flue, and two lower arches that formed the firebox area, all of which were heavily salt-glazed. The main flue is 2 feet wide and extends from the north wall to the south wall, a distance of 5.8 feet. At right angles to the main flue and on each side are four smaller flues, each 0.4 feet wide. These eight flues, essentially spaces between brick arches, were passages through which hot air circulated in the main flue-firebox area and entered the upper pot chamber.

In addition to the flues, four brick arches once spanned the main flue, each arch supported by seven to eight courses of brick. Arches were separated from one another by the minor flues, a distance of 0.4 feet. The vertical dimension of the main flue was about 2.1 feet, and the pot chamber's floor was about 2.5 feet above the kiln's lowest part. The kiln's firebox is defined by two completely preserved brick arches, situated between arch 1 and the kiln's north wall, and two ledges above the arches on the side walls of the kiln.

The kiln was approached using two earthen steps formed in an excavated hole on the north side. At the bottom the potter had a small area from which to load wood onto the firebox ledges and to rake ashes out of the kiln. When found, the kiln and stoke-hole pit were filled with brick rubble and soil. A lower ash level, contemporary with the operation of the kiln, contained fragments of bisque and glazed stoneware and earthenware, indicating that both might have been fired together. Stoneware mugs made up the majority of the small sample.

A marl wall is present on three sides of the Small Kiln, but is missing on the fourth side that faces the Large Kiln, suggesting that the area in between was accessible to both kilns. This wall and thirty-five postholes/postmolds represent the remains of the structures that once served the Small Kiln. Those situated immediately around the kiln itself suggest that the Small Kiln was braced by wooden logs. A system of vertical, horizontal, and, perhaps, angling logs may have supported the kiln from movement caused by the heating and cooling brick. The kiln and bracing posts were flanked on three sides by a 24-foot-square structure represented by low marl walls and postholes/postmolds. This structure undoubtedly supported a cover to protect the Small Kiln from rain. The Large Kiln also must have been protected from the elements, but postholes were not discerned and may have been destroyed during the construction of the modern garage.

Both Yorktown kilns were similar in design and construction. Each had below-ground heat chambers incorporating a series of arches and vents that regulated heat flow while simultaneously supporting the pot chamber floor above. The Large Kiln was the major production unit at the factory. Based on the heat chamber's size and shape, the Large Kiln's stacking area is estimated at 310 cubic feet, a good-sized kiln (fig. 20). The kiln was fired by shoving logs through the small arched firemouth or stoke hole located on the north side of the firebox. The pot chamber entrance was also located on the north side, since that faces both the workshop room and building. It is probable that a movable wooden stairway was built over the firebox area, providing access to the pot chamber doorway, which was bricked up before each firing. The Large Kiln roof was arched and contained slots or holes for heat and smoke escape (fig. 21). The roof must have looked like the kiln drawn by Piccolpasso in 1548.[6]

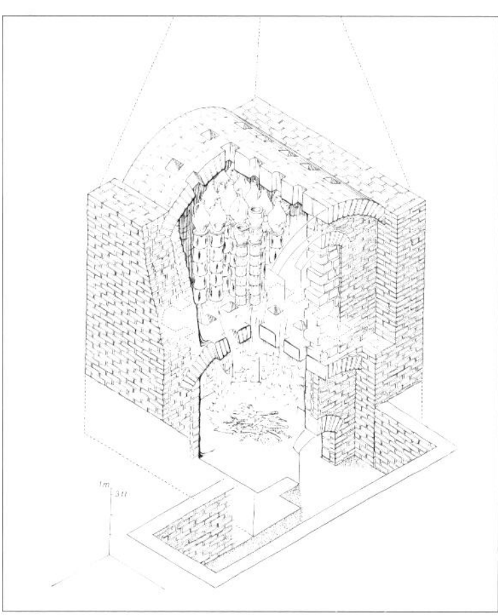

Figure 21 An artist's reconstruction of an English stoneware kiln similar to the type employed at the William Rogers pottery. (Chris Green, *John Dwight's Fulham Pottery: Excavations 1971–79* [London: English Heritage, 1999], fig. 22; drawing © Chris Green.)

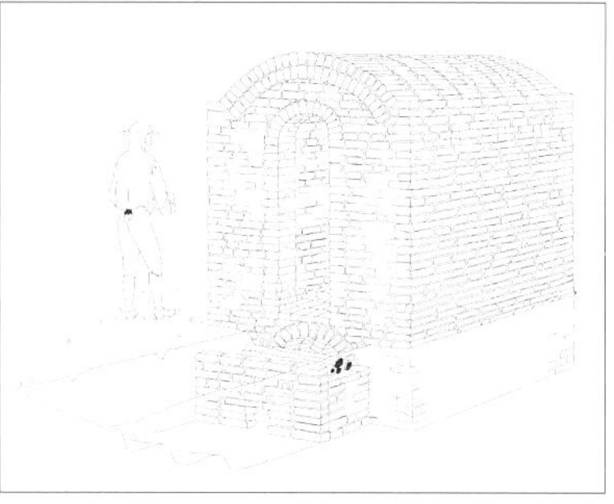

Figure 22 An artist's reconstruction of the Small Kiln.

The Small Kiln had a capacity roughly one-quarter the size of the Large Kiln, and was estimated at 80 cubic feet (fig. 22). A Bourry-like firebox was formed by a shorter and narrower projection of the kiln's north side. Two brick shelves or hobs, each one brick wide, flanked either side of the main flue. Located slightly below these shelves were two arches, beneath which is a stoke hole. The brick shelves supported the ends of the logs, which served as fuel. Air could pass easily beneath the burning logs and combustion could take place in the firebox. The primary air would enter at or near the top of the firebox and flames would travel downward and enter the firebox arch. Embers fell into the area below, but an intact secondary grate formed by two smaller arches below the hob on the kiln's north side would catch and suspend any partially burnt wood for more complete combustion. This firebox was quite sophisticated for its time.

Other Buildings and Features

As previously mentioned, there are several possible workshop buildings connected with the Large Kiln. A workshop room (Structure 1) was delineated by marl foundation walls 2 feet wide and 19 feet long. The subsoil floor situated some 4 feet below ground surface survives to a height of only 0.8 feet. Originally, these walls probably reached upward at least to ground level. The room measures 23 feet (north-south) by 17.5 feet. Its southern boundary is determined by two yellow brick walls, each angling inward about 45 degrees toward the Large Kiln to which they once articulated.

Structure 1 may have served as an area in which a variety of tasks were performed—stacking wood for burning, storing pots before firing, and, perhaps, carrying out the final glazing or dipping operations, as evidenced by eighteen maroon-colored soil stains in the subsoil floor surface. A volume of about 1,584 cubic feet of brick rubble and pottery was excavated in this room. All fill represents post-fill debris, materials deposited there once the pottery factory had ceased operation.

Structure 2 was a building with interior dimensions of 54 feet by 17 feet that connected with the north end of Structure 1. Only the west wall is extant because of recent disturbances to the area. The west brick wall of Structure 2 is 54 feet long and, given the symmetry of the factory complex, the east wall would have had the same dimensions. The higher floor level of Structure 2 gradually merges with the lower Structure 1 floor through a stepped slope carved into the subsoil. It is likely there were wooden steps or a ramplike structure for easy access between the two rooms. No evidence of a fireplace was found in Structure 2, giving further credence to the belief that Structures 1–3 were actually interconnected units of one long building. In summary, Structure 2 was a long building of the same width as Structure 1; because it had been disturbed, however, its function is difficult to interpret.

Evidence regarding Structure 3 is similarly incomplete because portions of the building have been destroyed. At this layer, light gray clay covers an area that measures 17 feet by 8 feet. One of the more interesting characteristics was a layer of white ash, immediately below which were four ash-filled postmolds (each 0.3 feet square) connected to one another by narrow, shallow ash-filled trenches. Measuring 3 feet square, it may represent the former location of a wooden clay working or throwing table or bench, or perhaps a potter's wheel.

Archaeological excavations revealed Structure 4 approximately 17 feet east of Structures 1 and 2. This post-in-the-ground building measured 32 feet (north-south) by 16 feet. The wooden building could have been another workshop/storage building or even a dwelling. There were many additional eighteenth- and nineteenth-century finds, as the entire extent of Lots 51 and 55 was covered with below-ground archaeological remains: several waster pits filled with large quantities of mostly broken pottery; the remains of at least one additional post-in-the-ground structure; a brick-lined basement with a bulkhead entrance; evidence of plow scars; and various trash pits.

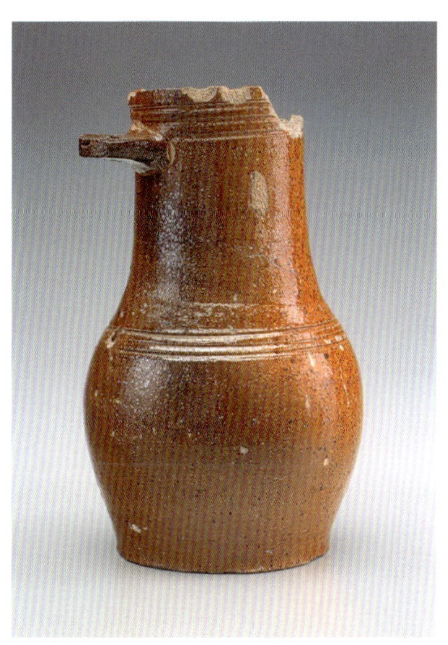

Figure 23 Bird bottle, William Rogers, Yorktown, Virginia, 1720–1745. Lead-glazed earthenware. H. 8½". (Courtesy, Department of Archaeological Research, Colonial Williamsburg.) William Rogers's inventory lists "4 doz bird bottles."

Ceramics

The "Poor Potter" factory produced large quantities of utilitarian pottery over a period of approximately twenty-five years. Both lead-glazed earthenwares and salt-glazed stonewares were made in a variety of shapes. About 140,000 sherds were studied from the Yorktown site. Earthenware was more prevalent than stoneware. The number of bisque and glazed sherds found was nearly equal, giving credence to the importance of two separate firings of wares. Bisque stoneware, however, occurred more frequently than glazed earthenware by three to one, possibly signifying more breakage during bisque firing. Although the presence of bisque stoneware on the site is significant, its frequency in relation to glazed stoneware is low. Most sherds found were body fragments, but the shape of nearly 68 percent of the sherds

Figure 24 Front and back views of the bird bottle illustrated in fig. 23. Note the perforated tab in the front to seat a dowel, which would serve as a perch. The back of the bottle was cut while the pot was wet (before firing) to provide a notch for hanging under the eaves of a building.

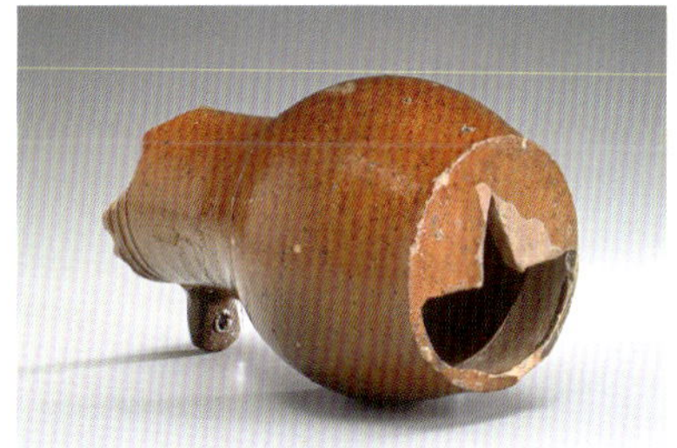

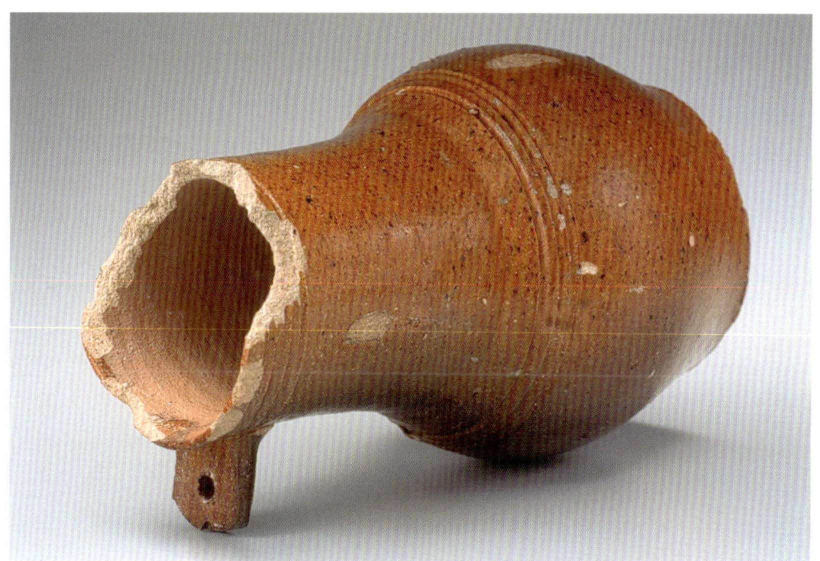

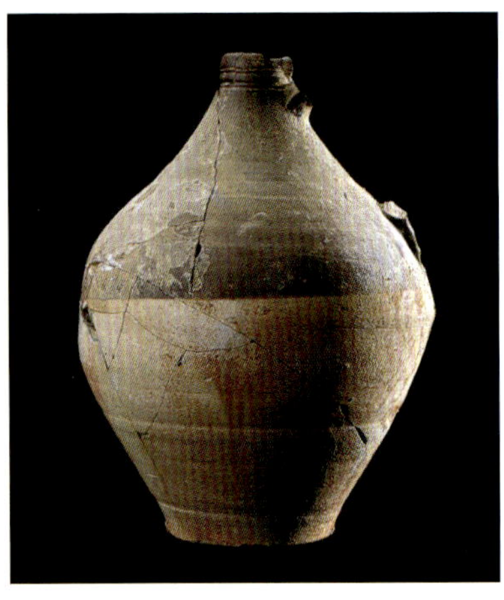

Figure 25 Bottle, William Rogers, Yorktown, Virginia, 1720–1745. Salt-glazed stoneware. H. 10¾". (Courtesy, National Park Service, Colonial National Historical Park, Yorktown Collection.) COLO Y 71262. In addition to large bottles, a number of fragments from small bottles and flasks (or pocket bottles) were found of the type mentioned in the 1739 inventory. Bottles displayed variation in cordon patterns near the rim, as well as different handle types. A "WR" crown stamp mark is displayed on the shoulder of this example. Capacity seems to vary from one to three gallons, possibly larger.

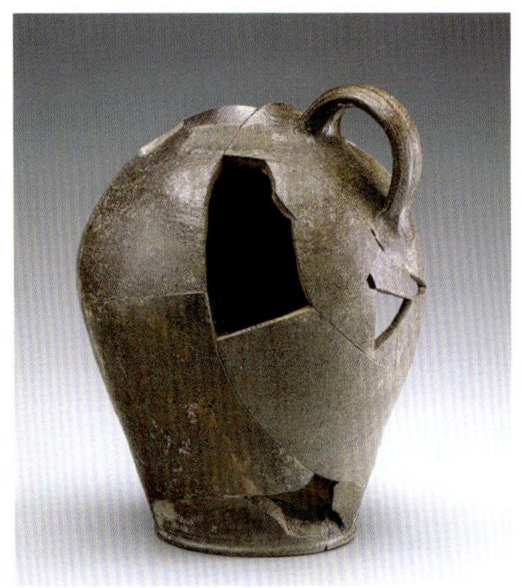

Figure 26 Bottle, William Rogers, Yorktown, Virginia, 1720–1745. Salt-glazed stoneware (lip missing). (Department of Archaeological Research, Colonial Williamsburg.) This example was excavated from an eighteenth-century context in Williamsburg.

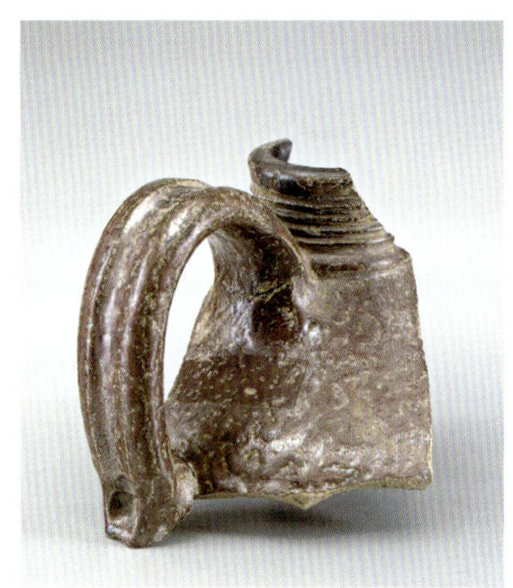

Figure 27 Bottle neck fragment, William Rogers, Yorktown, Virginia, 1720–1745. Salt-glazed stoneware. (Courtesy, National Park Service, Colonial National Historical Park, Yorktown Collection.) COLO Y 15191. This neck fragment is from a large bottle, of three-gallon capacity or possibly more.

found could not be identified, leaving the main study sample of 32 percent (45,374 sherds). Of this amount, 42 percent (18,932) was kiln furniture.

Analysis of the identifiable sherds disclosed a minimum of twenty-three forms (figs. 23–27). Of these, twenty-one were produced in earthenware, fifteen in stoneware. Ten forms were produced in either earthenware or stoneware and thirteen forms were made in both wares. Nearly all the shapes were found in both bisque and glazed varieties. Milk pans constituted nearly 40 percent of the identified sherds. Mugs were the second most frequent form, followed by bottles, bowls, storage jars, platters, pipkins, and cream pots.

The shapes produced range from coarse utilitarian, lead-glazed milk pans with knife-trimmed bases to delicate, finely thrown, salt-glazed teapots with expertly turned lids. The potters were well experienced in the craft, as is evident from the quality of the kilns and ceramic products. However, the lack of relative dating evidence eliminates the possibility of knowing what forms were produced contemporaneously.

The products of the Yorktown pottery can be grouped into the following functional categories:

Food processing. Pipkins or cooking pots; saucepans (possibly used for cooking puddings, pastries, etc.); bowls (for preparing foods); milk pans (used in cream collection); colanders (for washing vegetables, making cheese); churns (for making butter).

Food and drink storage. Storage jars and bottles (for storage of solid foods [jars] or liquids); cream pots may have been used to store butter and other foods.

Beverage consumption. Mugs were made in several different sizes.

TABLE 1. *Ceramic Shapes Produced at the William Rogers Site*		
FORM	EARTHENWARE	STONEWARE
Betty lamp	√	
Bird bottle	√	
Bottle	√	√
Bowl	√	√
Chafing dish	√	
Chamber pot	√	√
Churn	√	√
Colander	√	√
Cream pot	√	
Floor tile	√	
Funnel	√	
Jar	√	√
Jug	√	√
Milk pan	√	
Mug	√	√
Pipkin	√	√
Plate	√	√
Charger	√	
Porringer	√	
Saggar		√
Saucepan	√	√
Storage jar	√	√
Stove tile	√	√
Teapot	√	√
TOTAL	23	15

Beverage serving. Handled jugs and teapots.

Food consumption–serving. A variety of porringers, plates, and chargers were probably utilized as food receptacles.

Health/hygiene. Chamber pots were the only known vessels to be used in this category.

Other vessels. Bird bottles, betty lamps, funnels, and chafing dishes.

Many technological and artistic innovations can be found in the products of the Rogers pottery; indeed, there is much evidence of experimentation, as a number of actual test pots were found. A variety of small bisque

Figure 28 Bottle neck fragment, William Rogers, Yorktown, Virginia, 1720–1745. Lead-glazed earthenware. (Courtesy, National Park Service, Colonial National Historical Park, Yorktown Collection.) COLO Y 15616. This large earthenware bottle fragment is covered in a slip and colored with manganese.

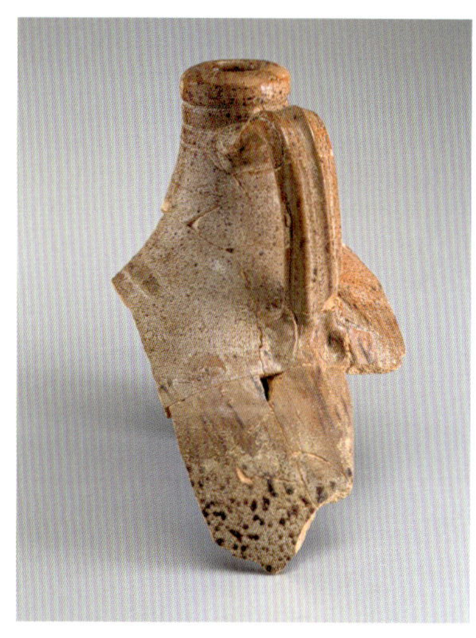

Figure 29 Bowls, William Rogers, Yorktown, Virginia, 1720–1745. Biscuit earthenware. H. 5". (Courtesy, National Park Service, Colonial National Historical Park, Yorktown Collection.) COLO Y 71193, COLO Y 71188. Bowls had up to ten variations in rim style and five basal types. Earthenware forms were fired twice, first to biscuit and then glazed and fired again.

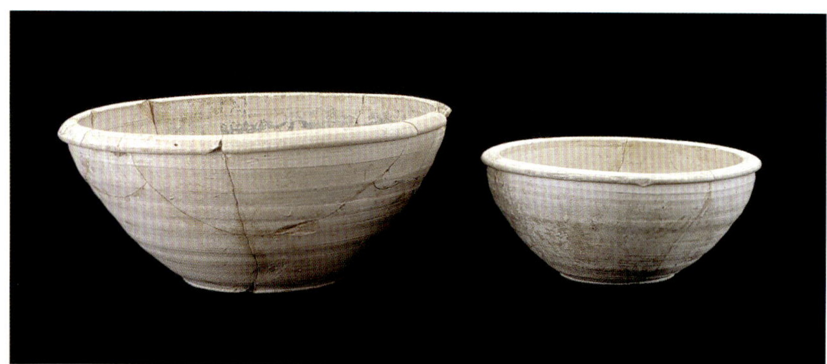

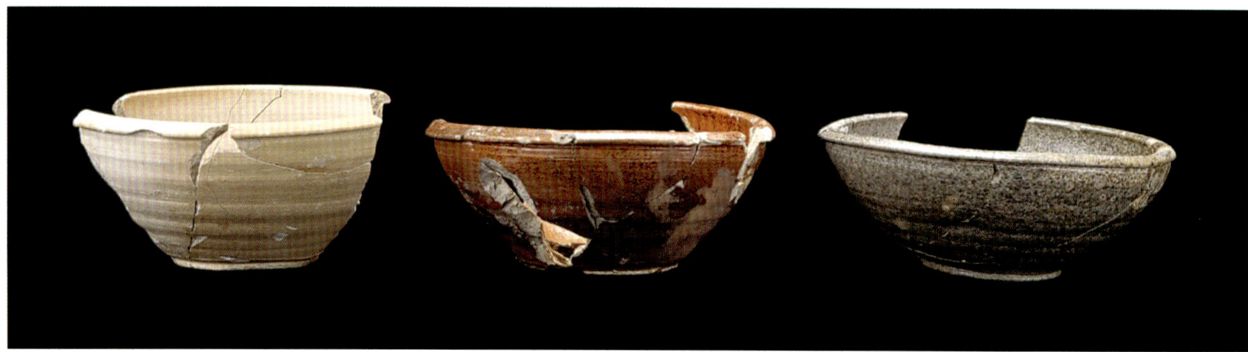

Figure 30 Bowls, William Rogers, Yorktown, Virginia, 1720–1745. Biscuit and lead-glazed earthenware. D. 8½". (Courtesy, National Park Service, Colonial National Historical Park, Yorktown Collection.) COLO Y 71183, COLO Y 71189, COLO Y 71185. Many bowls had a rim diameter of approximately 8", equating to one-quart capacity, although a larger example, with a rim diameter of 20", was excavated.

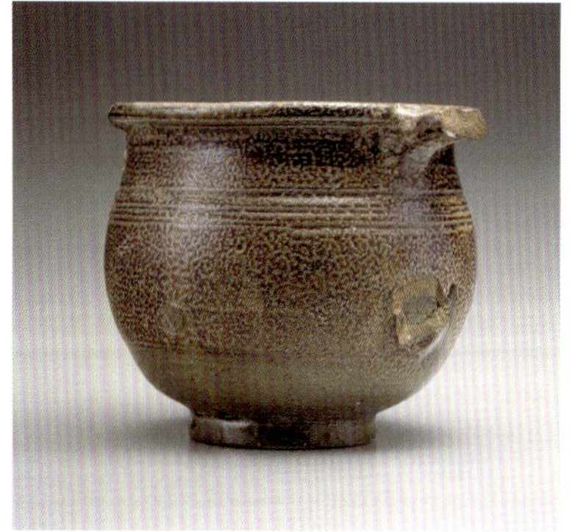

Figure 31 Chamber pot, William Rogers, Yorktown, Virginia, 1720–1745. Salt-glazed stoneware. H. 5¾". (Courtesy, National Park Service, Colonial National Historical Park, Yorktown Collection.) COLO Y 14270. Many size variations of both stoneware and earthenware chamber pots were found on the site. A lead-glazed earthenware vessel without handles was recovered that would have served as the receptacle in a closestool.

Figure 32 Chamber pot, William Rogers, Yorktown, Virginia, 1720–1745. H. 5½". Lead-glazed earthenware. (Department of Archaeological Research, Colonial Williamsburg.) This warped and overfired example was recovered from a well in Williamsburg, indicating that Rogers's seconds had a market.

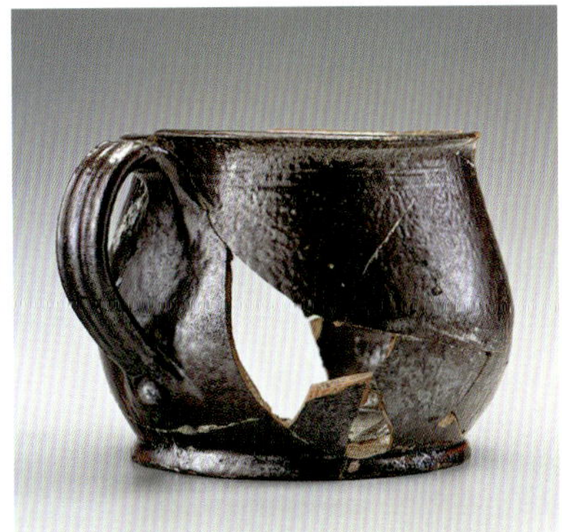

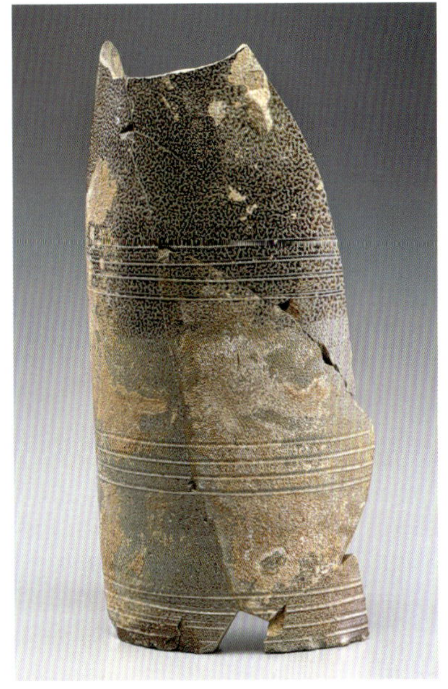

Figure 33 Churn, William Rogers, Yorktown, Virginia, 1720–1745. Salt-glazed stoneware. H. (approx) 17½". (Courtesy, National Park Service, Colonial National Historical Park, Yorktown Collection.) COLO Y 14427a. This tall cylindrical form tapers in circumference from base to mouth. It is one of the few forms to have been decorated with incised leaf and flower motifs. One fragment with a hole in its center may be a churn lid. The Yorktown churns may be the earliest clay butter churns made in America.

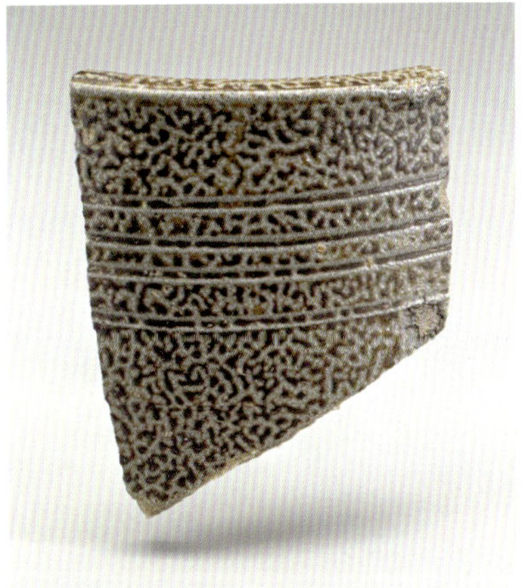

Figure 34 Detail of rim fragment associated with the churn illustrated in fig. 33. (Courtesy, National Park Service, Colonial National Historical Park, Yorktown Collection.) COLO Y 14427b. Note the heavy iron oxide wash evident on this example.

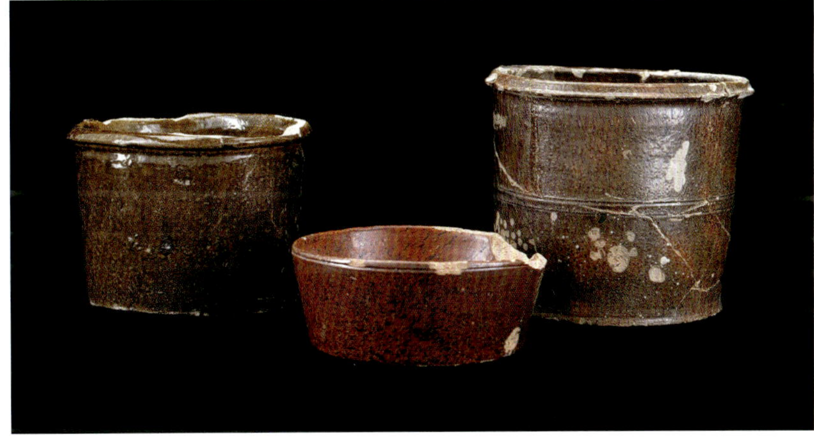

Figure 35 Cream jars and saucepan, William Rogers, Yorktown, Virginia, 1720–1745. Lead-glazed earthenware. H. 4 13/16", 2⅜", and 7⅜". (Courtesy, National Park Service, Colonial National Historical Park, Yorktown Collection.) COLO Y 71195, COLO Y 71184, COLO Y 71196.

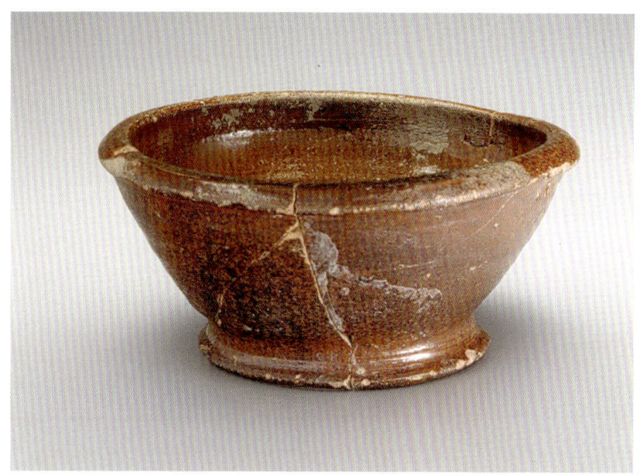

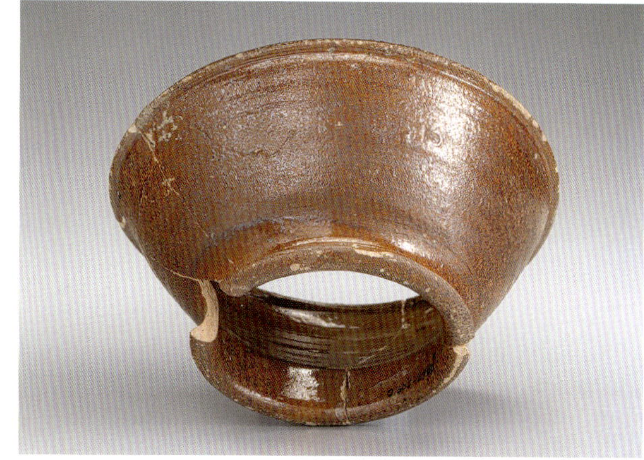

Figure 36 Funnel, William Rogers, Yorktown, Virginia, 1720–1745. Lead-glazed earthenware. H. 4½". (Department of Archaeological Research, Colonial Williamsburg.) This lead-glazed, bowl-like form has two open ends, one smaller than the other for channeling ingredients from one container to the other.

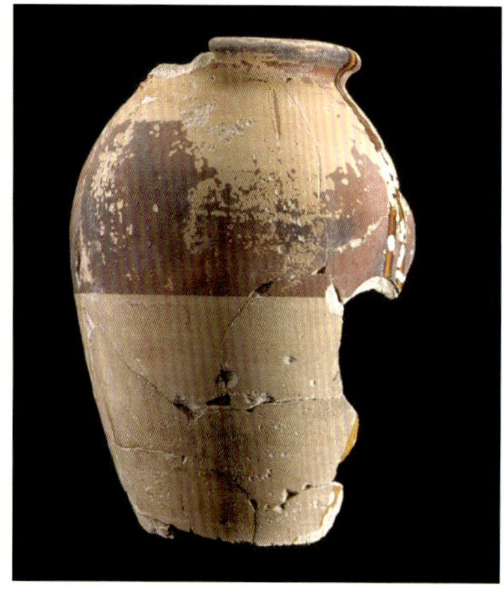

Figure 37 Jar, William Rogers, Yorktown, Virginia, 1720–1745. Lead-glazed earthenware. H. 13½". (Courtesy, National Park Service, Colonial National Historical Park, Yorktown Collection.) COLO Y 71198. Both lead-glazed earthenware and salt-glazed stoneware storage jars were apparently made in large quantities. The heights of the measurable examples range from 7½" to 17". These heights may conform to a standard range of sizes from one-half gallon up to as large as five gallons.

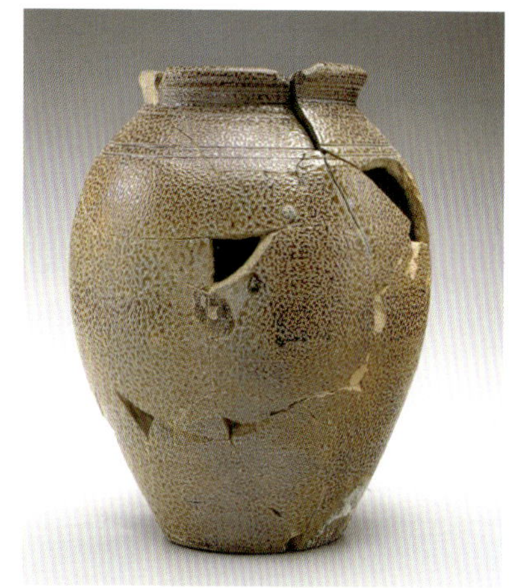

Figure 38 Jar, William Rogers, Yorktown, Virginia, 1720–1745. Salt-glazed stoneware. H. 10". (Courtesy, National Park Service, Colonial National Historical Park, Yorktown Collection.) COLO Y 15072. The upper portion of this typical stoneware jar has been dipped in iron oxide. Handles are present only on the largest examples.

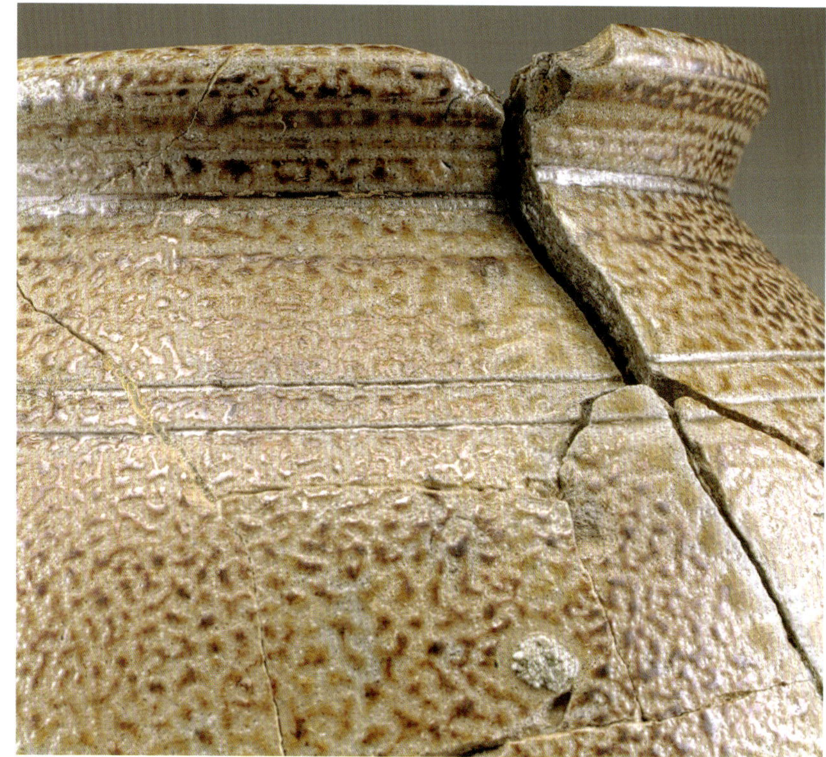

Figure 39 Detail of the jar illustrated in fig. 38. Note the major distortion along the firing crack that helps identify this jar as a waster.

Figure 40 Milk pans, William Rogers, Yorktown, Virginia, 1720–1745. Biscuit and lead-glazed earthenware. D. 13½–14½". (Courtesy, National Park Service, Colonial National Historical Park, Yorktown Collection.) COLO Y 71251, COLO Y 71253. These wide, flat-based vessels have curved, out-sloping walls and one spout in the rim. While most examples were bisque and lead-glazed earthenwares, a few stoneware milk pans were found. Pans were partially glazed, mostly on the interior, and showed sixteen rim variants. Heights vary from 2–4", with the majority measuring 3¼". Rim diameters also vary from 10–19", with the majority measuring 16". Base diameters measure from 6–9".

The major earthenware production in Yorktown was the milk pan, which was used to separate cream from milk when making cheese and butter. Milk was poured into these shallow pans and left until the cream had risen to the surface. Skimmed off, the cream was placed into a cream pot until enough had accumulated for churning butter or making cheese. Milk pan spouts were formed by pressing down on the rim with two thumbs.

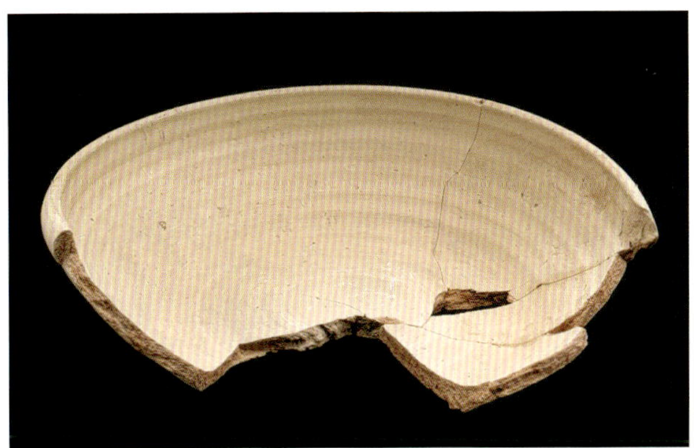

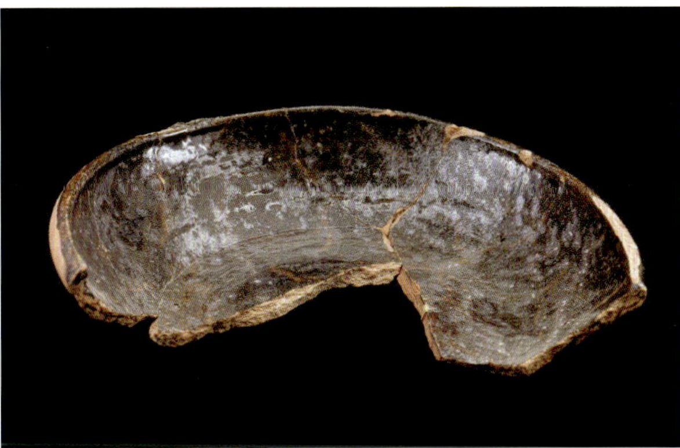

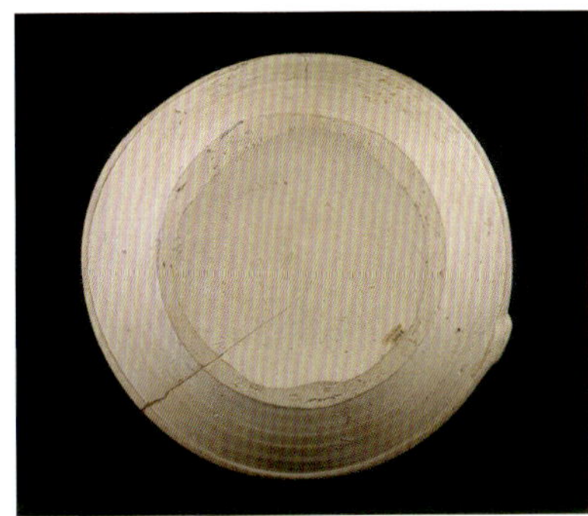

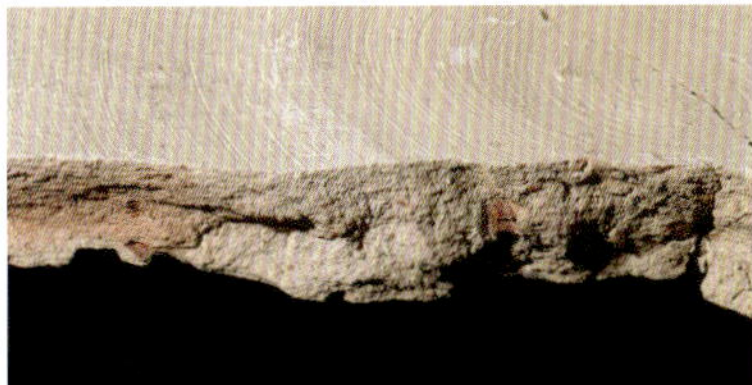

Figure 41 Detail of cross section of the bisque clay body of the milk pan illustrated at left in fig. 40. Note the brick red inclusions of hematite, a characteristic of the Rogers's pottery earthenware.

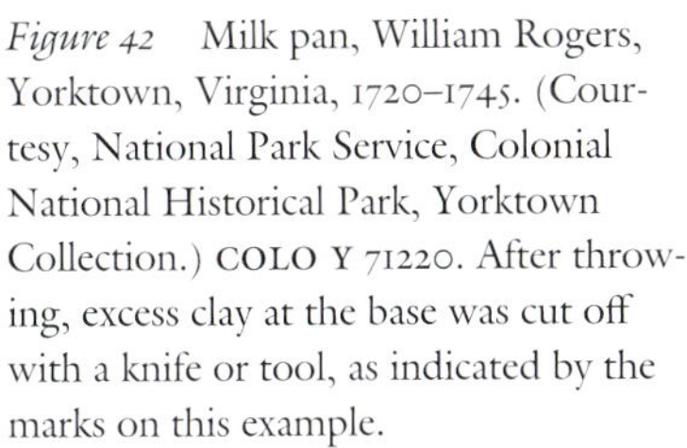

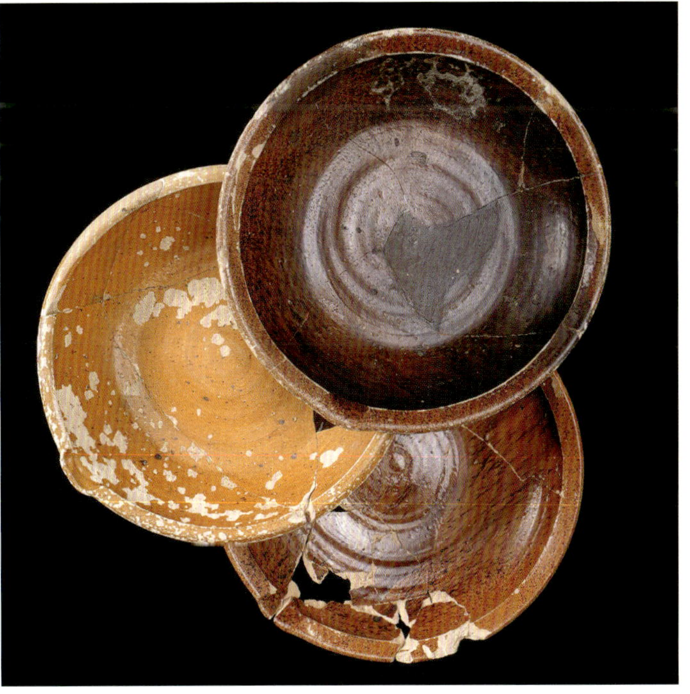

Figure 42 Milk pan, William Rogers, Yorktown, Virginia, 1720–1745. (Courtesy, National Park Service, Colonial National Historical Park, Yorktown Collection.) COLO Y 71220. After throwing, excess clay at the base was cut off with a knife or tool, as indicated by the marks on this example.

Figure 43 Milk pans, William Rogers, Yorktown, Virginia, 1720–1745. (Courtesy, National Park Service, Colonial National Historical Park, Yorktown Collection.) COLO Y 71191, COLO Y 71252, COLO Y 71199. Note the wide range of color due to variation in the firing environment within the kiln.

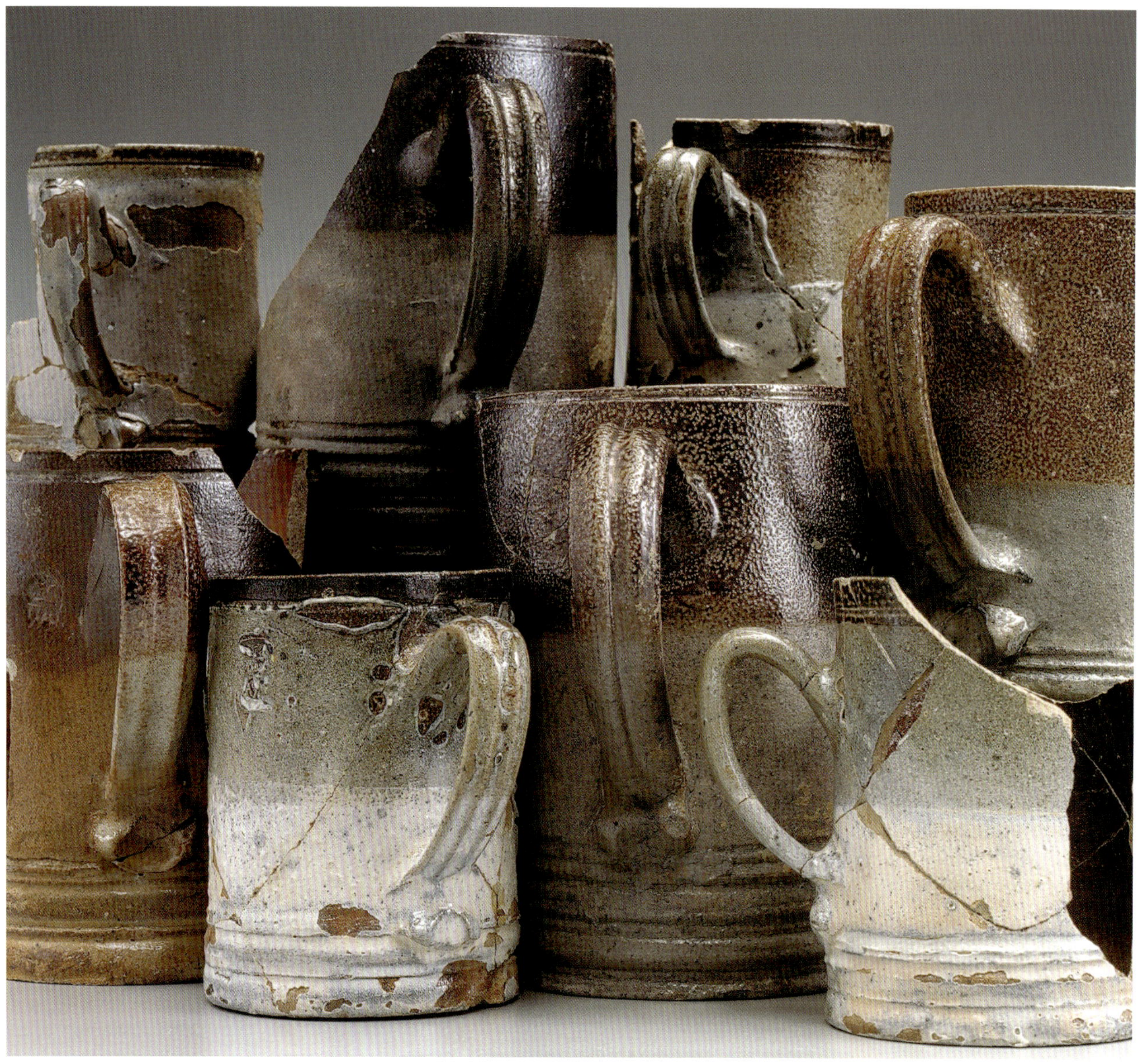

Figure 44 Mugs, William Rogers, Yorktown, Virginia, 1720–1745. Salt-glazed stoneware. (Courtesy, National Park Service, Colonial National Historical Park, Yorktown Collection.) One of the most common forms produced by William Rogers was the tavern mug. Bisque and glazed earthenware and stoneware were recovered. Earthenware mugs, yellow in color, were dipped in white slip or finished with a green glaze of dark brown or red-brown. Yorktown stoneware mugs were manufactured in the following sizes: ¼ pint, ½ pint, 1 pint, and 1½ pint; a few mug bases, large in diameter, were probably one quart in capacity. The stoneware mug (together with the teapot) was the highest quality pot made by the "poor potter." Its appearance and excellent potting rivaled those made in England; in fact, more time and care were spent making the Yorktown mugs, as they were the only form fired in saggars. Thirteen small stoneware mugs, each 3½" high and 2⅝" in diameter, appear to have been test pieces; all were found in association with the Small Kiln. Several show one or more slashlike incisions and some show evidence of a white slip, which in some cases had clearly peeled off the mugs but in others had produced a smooth white "glaze" under the salt glaze.

Figure 45 Mugs, William Rogers, Yorktown, Virginia, 1720–1745. Salt-glazed stoneware. H. $5\frac{7}{8}$" and $3\frac{9}{16}$". (Courtesy, National Park Service, Colonial National Historical Park, Yorktown Collection.) COLO Y 71102, COLO Y 10,884. The upper half of a stoneware mug was usually dipped in iron oxide and the lower part was sometimes dipped in white slip. Each mug has one strap handle, with the lower terminal folded back on itself and impressed.

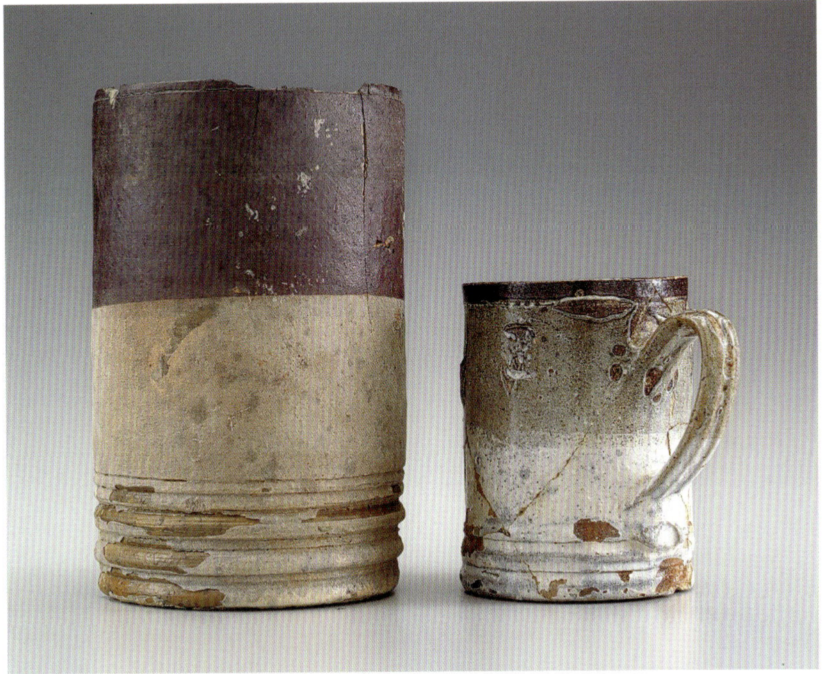

Figure 46 Mug, William Rogers, Yorktown, Virginia, 1720–1745. Salt-glazed stoneware. H. $3\frac{1}{2}$". (Courtesy, National Park Service, Colonial National Historical Park, Yorktown Collection.) COLO Y 47098. Many stoneware mugs are stamped with the initials "WR" beneath a crown, both of which are in relief within a depressed rectangle. The majority of these stamps are located to the left of the handle.

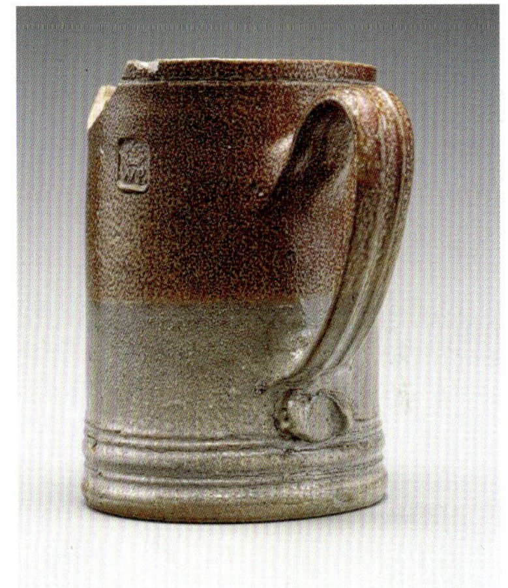

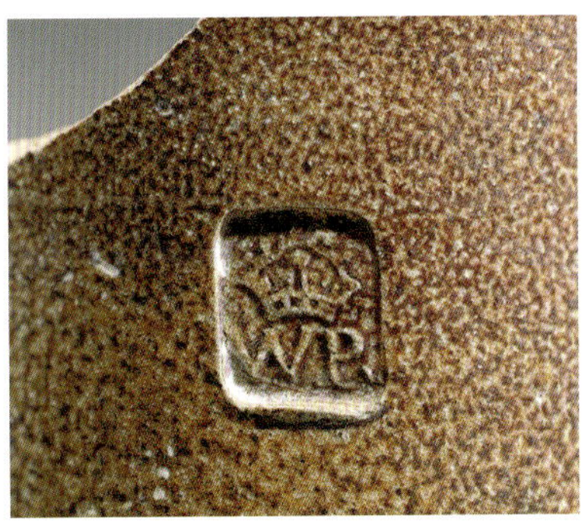

Figure 47 Detail of the "WR" excised mark on the mug illustrated in fig. 46. In 1700, during the reign of William III, regulation of the capacity sizes of tavern mugs was enacted that required vessels to be measured during manufacture and stamped with "WR" below a crown. It is interesting to observe that Rogers continued marking his products even though he was beyond the government's accountability for his wares. Perhaps these marks helped reassure his tavern keeper clients as to the veracity of the measures.

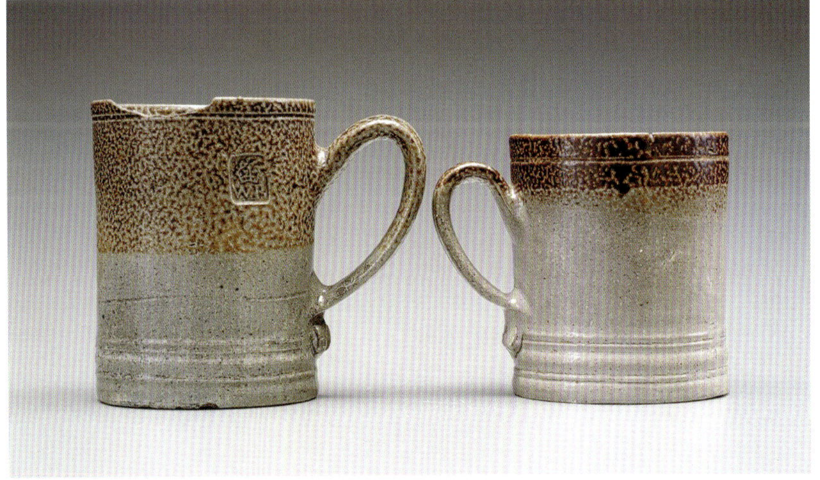

Figure 48 Mugs, William Rogers, Yorktown, Virginia, 1720–1745. Salt-glazed stoneware. H. $3\frac{1}{2}$" and $3\frac{1}{8}$". (Courtesy, National Park Service, Colonial National Historical Park, Yorktown Collection.) COLO Y 7098, COLO Y 7099.

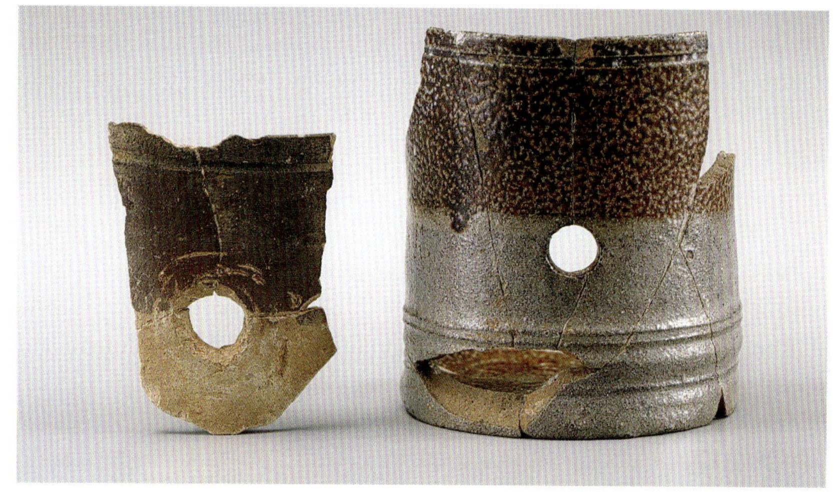

Figure 49 Mug fragments, William Rogers, Yorktown, Virginia, 1720–1745. Salt-glazed stoneware. H. (right) 2½". (Courtesy, National Park Service, Colonial National Historical Park, Yorktown Collection.) COLO Y 10,896, COLO Y 10,942. The function of the holes in these mugs has never been satisfactorily explained, but one suggestion is that they served as trial pieces which could have been extracted from the kiln during firing to check on the quality of glazing.

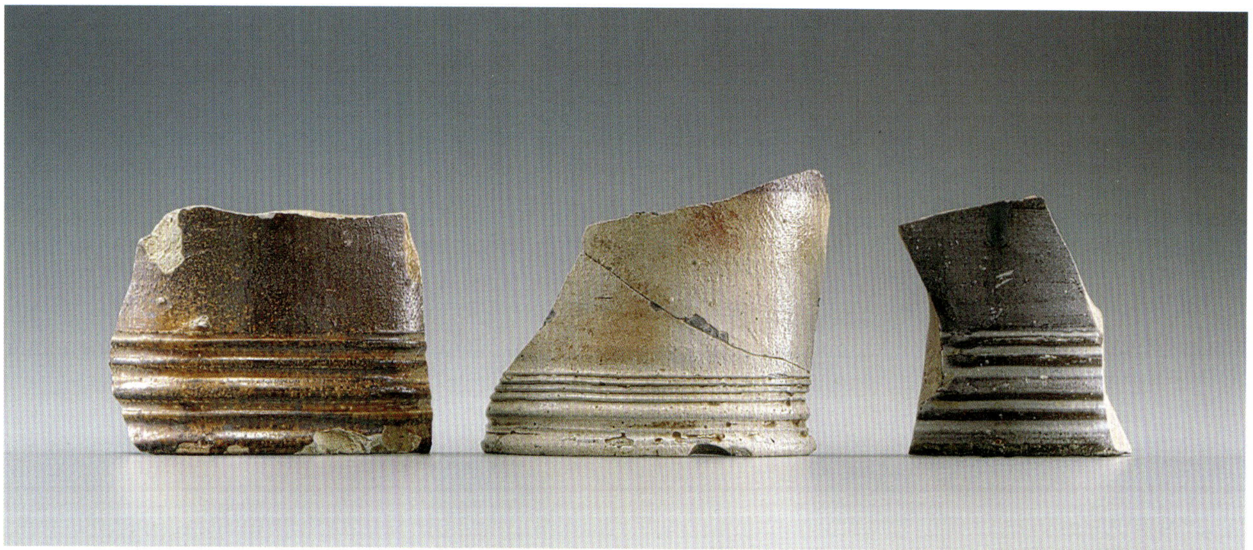

Figure 50 Mug base fragments, William Rogers, Yorktown, Virginia, 1720–1745. Salt-glazed stoneware. (Courtesy, National Park Service, Colonial National Historical Park, Yorktown Collection.) COLO Y 10,927, COLO Y 10,928, COLO Y 10,929. These examples show some of the variation in the cordoning treatment on the base of Rogers's mugs. At least eleven cordon variations occur on the mugs.

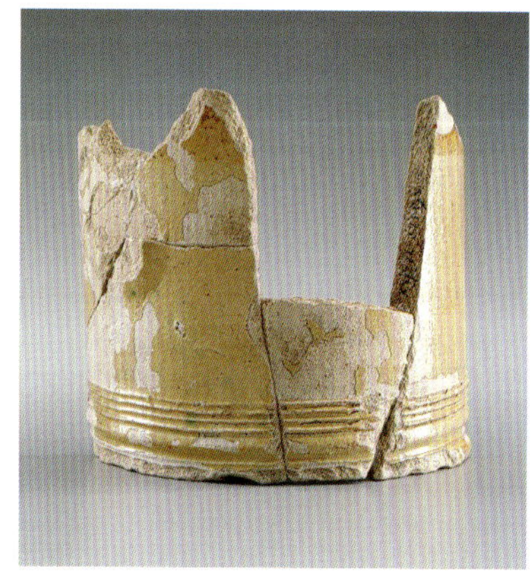

Figure 51 Mug base fragment, William Rogers, Yorktown, Virginia, 1720–1745. Lead-glazed earthenware. Diam. (approx.) 4". (Courtesy, National Park Service, Colonial National Historical Park, Yorktown Collection.) COLO Y 10,919. Some of the earthenware mugs were covered in a white slip before glazing; none yet identified bears the impressed "WR" stamp.

Figure 52 Pipkin, William Rogers, Yorktown, Virginia, 1720–1745. Lead-glazed earthenware. H. 4⅛". (Courtesy, National Park Service, Colonial National Historical Park, Yorktown Collection.) COLO Y 71194. Earthenware pipkins are cooking pots with a flat base or three legs, bulbous walls with a rim spout, and a solid or open handle applied at an angle. The handles are tapered and pulled, with cut or pinched-off ends. Some pipkins had large, hollow-thrown handles into which a wooden dowel could be inserted. Stonewares are thrown, solid cylinders, measuring 4½" in rim diameter, 3½" at base, and 4½" high. This nearly complete lead-glazed example shows how they were stacked directly on top of each other in the kiln. One footed pipkin, mostly lead-glazed with a wide cylindrical handle, was found in Gloucester Town, an eighteenth-century settlement facing Yorktown across the York River.

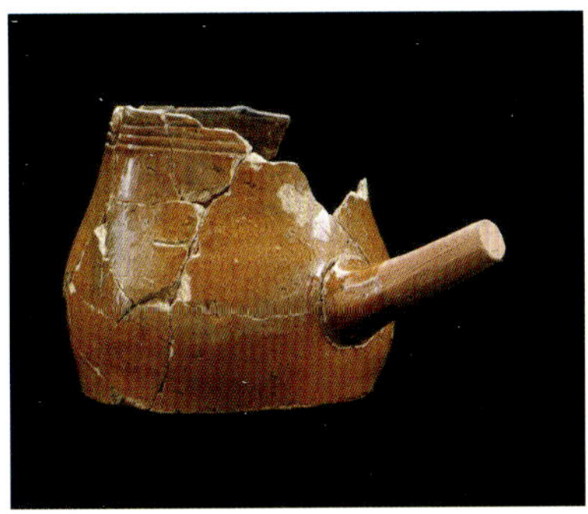

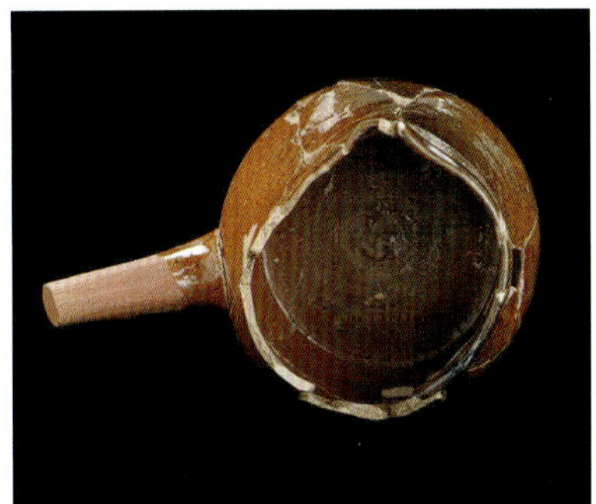

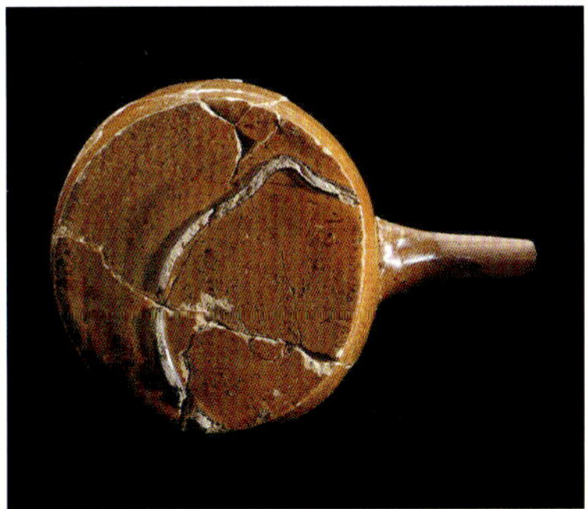

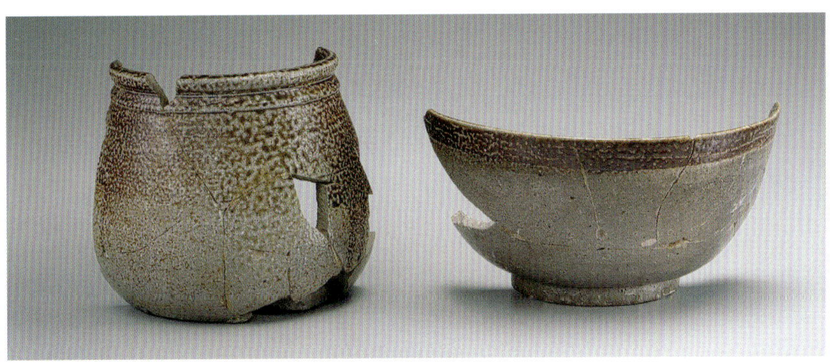

Figure 53 Pipkin and bowl, William Rogers, Yorktown, Virginia, 1720–1745. Salt-glazed stoneware. H. of pipkin: 4½". (Department of Archaeological Research, Colonial Williamsburg.) These are examples of Rogers's domestic stoneware vessels excavated in Williamsburg.

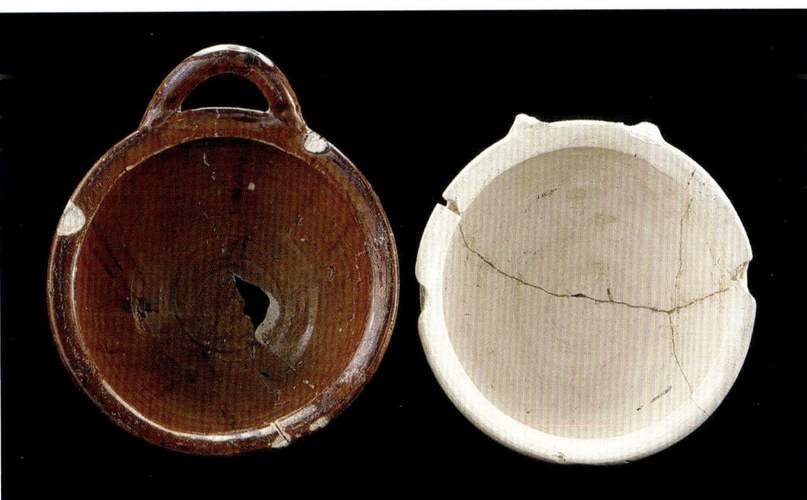

Figure 54 Porringers, William Rogers, Yorktown, Virginia, 1720–1745. Lead-glazed earthenware. Diam. 7". (Courtesy, National Park Service, Colonial National Historical Park, Yorktown Collection.) COLO Y 71190, COLO Y 71182. These bowl-like vessels have a flat base, curved out-sloping walls, flattened and usually down-sloping (toward the interior) rims, and a C-shaped, circular-sectioned handle attached to the rim. As with most of Rogers's earthenwares, the porringer has a reduced gray-green to red-orange color related to the kiln temperature and the atmosphere in the kiln.

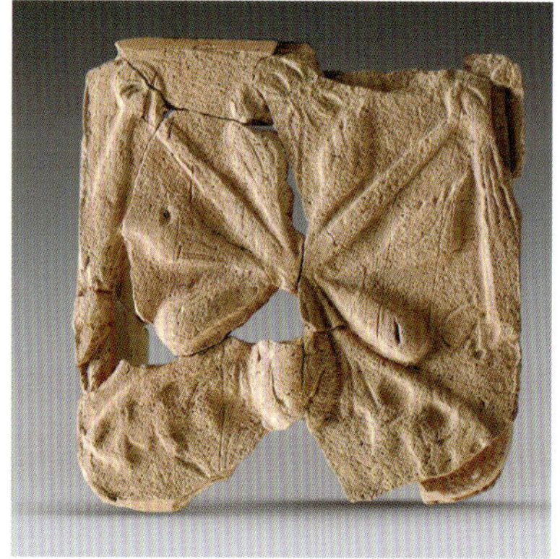

Figure 55 Stove tile, William Rogers, Yorktown, Virginia, 1720–1745. Earthenware. 7" square. (Courtesy, National Park Service, Colonial National Historical Park, Yorktown Collection.) COLO Y 8722a. This square tile has a raised design on one surface and an encircling wall or flange applied at right angles to the back of the flat tile. One-half of a complete specimen and 435 other fragments were found, all bisque; only three glazed fragments were found. The surface of the molded tile is decorated with a swag, six leaves, a pomegranate, and a flower. The total estimated sample found is 44 separate tiles. Stove-tile manufacture in Yorktown suggests the presence of a Dutch or German potter, as tile stoves were popular in Europe during the eighteenth century but not in England. Stove tiles of this type were also made in Moravian areas of North Carolina.

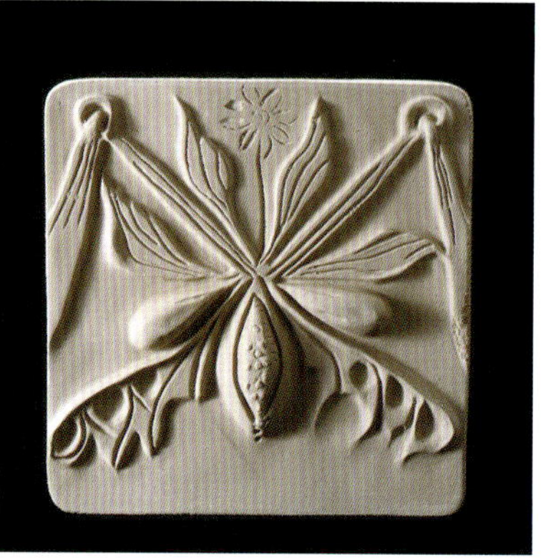

Figure 56 An artist's clay reconstruction of a William Rogers stove tile. (Courtesy, Patricia Kandle.)

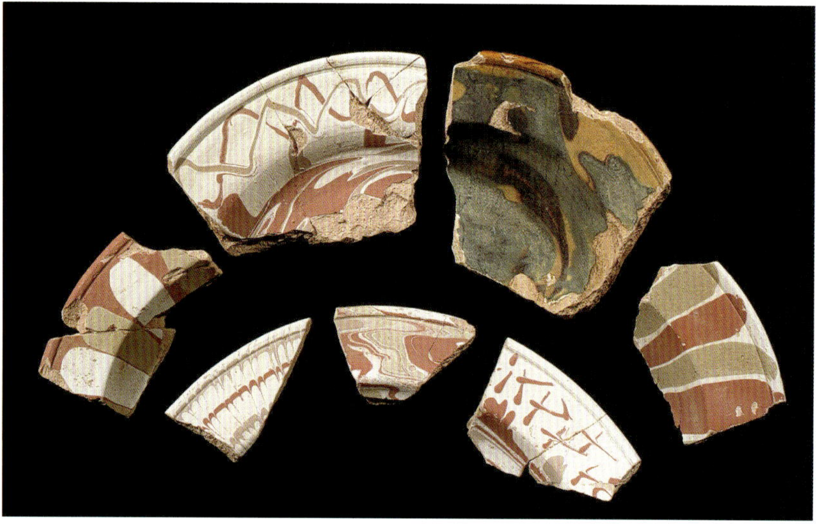

Figure 57 Dish fragments, William Rogers, Yorktown, Virginia, 1720–1745. Slipware. (Courtesy, National Park Service, Colonial National Historical Park, Yorktown Collection.) COLO Y 11490, COLO Y 11450, COLO Y 11854, COLO Y 11566, COLO Y 11853. A number of fragments from large, wide-rimmed low dishes with flat bases were recovered from the site. This form is usually slip-decorated but sometimes plain. The method of slip decoration includes trailing, combing, and marbleizing. These dishes range in diameter from 10–15" (with the majority being 14") and are about 2" high. They have a red to pinkish body, with glazed pieces usually yellow in color. The interior is lead-glazed. No examples of this important ceramic type have ever been found outside of the immediate pottery site.

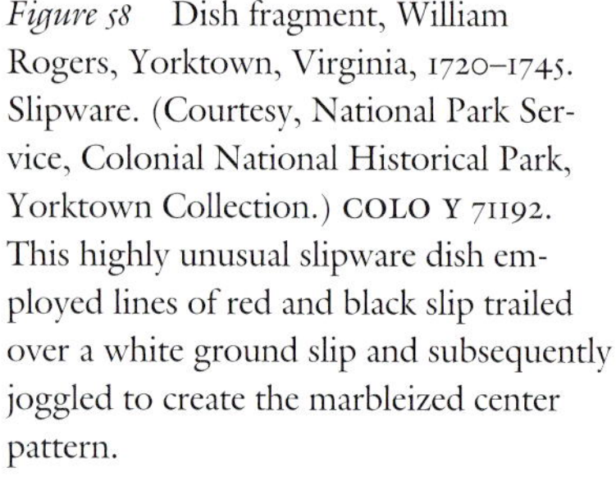

Figure 58 Dish fragment, William Rogers, Yorktown, Virginia, 1720–1745. Slipware. (Courtesy, National Park Service, Colonial National Historical Park, Yorktown Collection.) COLO Y 71192. This highly unusual slipware dish employed lines of red and black slip trailed over a white ground slip and subsequently joggled to create the marbleized center pattern.

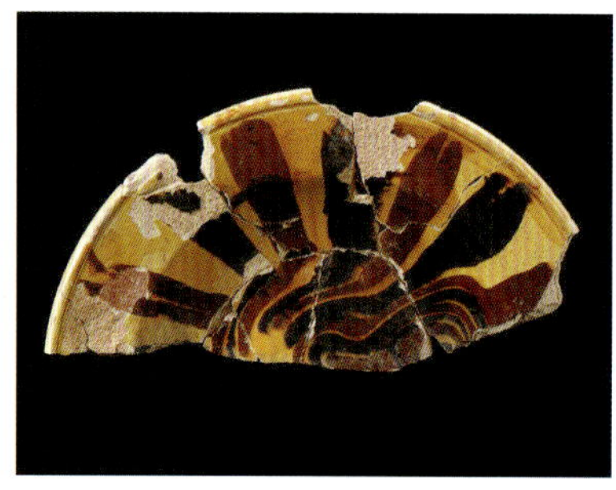

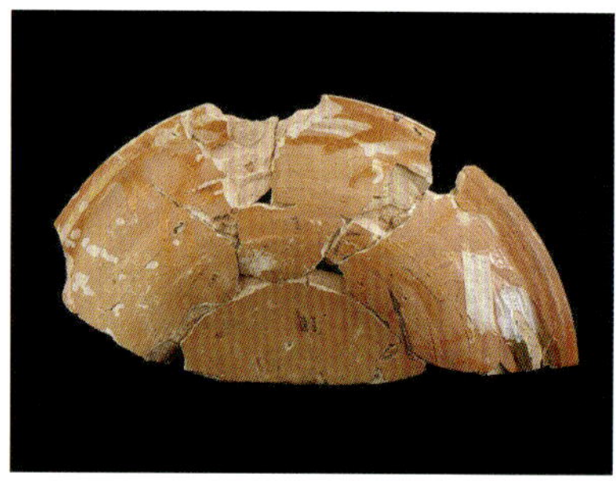

Figure 59 Reverse of the slipware dish fragment illustrated in fig. 58.

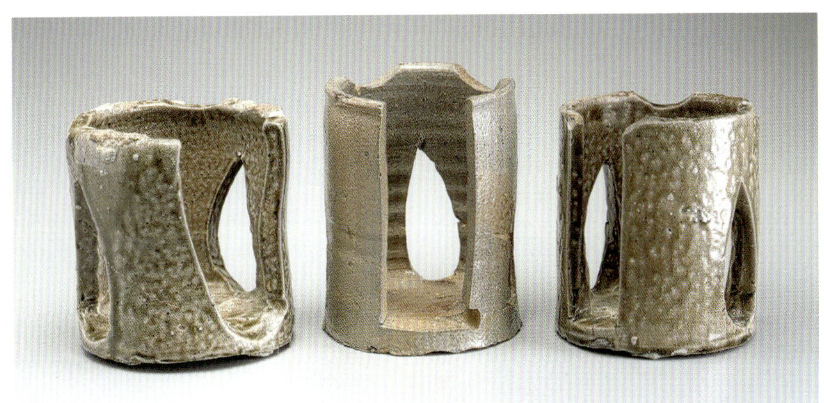

Figure 60 Saggars, William Rogers, Yorktown, Virginia, 1720–1745. H. 5½", 5¾", and 5". (Courtesy, National Park Service, Colonial National Historical Park, Yorktown Collection.) COLO Y 15928, COLO Y 38766, COLO Y 15934. A variety of saggars were employed at the Rogers's pottery to protect the stoneware mugs during firing. Made of refractory clay, the Yorktown saggars have four openings cut into the walls, permitting the entrance of heated air and volatilized salt. Three of the openings are teardrop-shaped; the fourth is a wide rectangular slit cut through the rim to facilitate air movement and subsequent removal of the glazed mug. Most saggars are heavily coated with salt glaze because of repeated use. Saggars range in diameter and height from 4–10", although there seem to have been three main sizes (corresponding to the different size stoneware mugs). The largest saggars are 9–10" in height and weigh about 8–10 pounds each. Saggars were stacked in columns in the kiln's pot chamber. The kiln's topmost saggar was topped by a lid. Individual saggars and stoneware pots were separated from one another—to prevent sticking during salt glazing—by props, pads, and wads of refractory clay generally referred to as kiln furniture. Thousands of saggar fragments and pieces of kiln furniture were found throughout the site.

Figure 61 Teapot fragments, William Rogers, Yorktown, Virginia, 1720–1745. Salt-glazed stoneware. (Courtesy, National Park Service, Colonial National Historical Park, Yorktown Collection.) COLO Y 37515, COLO Y 9813, COLO Y 9815, COLO Y 9816, COLO Y 9817. In addition to the large variety of coarse utilitarian ware, a number of finely thrown teaware pots were produced. Both lead-glazed and salt-glazed stoneware were found. These pots generally measured 4" high with a rim and basal diameter of 4". No examples of Rogers's teawares have been identified outside of the pottery site.

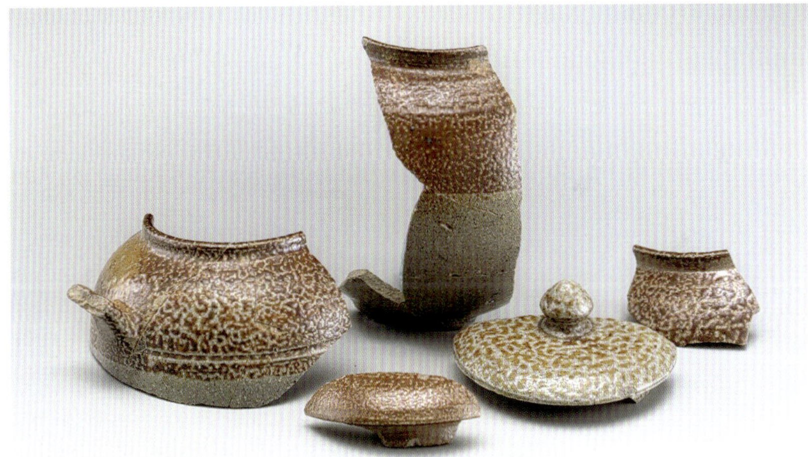

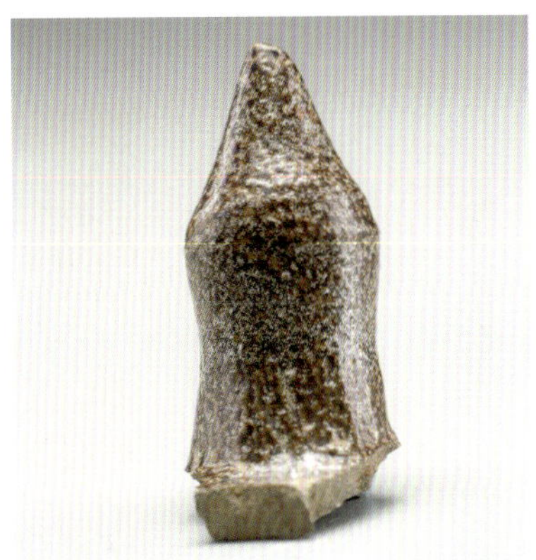

Figure 62 Coffee pot lid knop. William Rogers, Yorktown, Virginia, 1720–1745. Salt-glazed stoneware. (Courtesy, National Park Service, Colonial National Historical Park, Yorktown Collection.) COLO Y 9822. The shape and size of this fragment, based on parallels with English examples of the period, suggest that William Rogers may also have been making coffee pots.

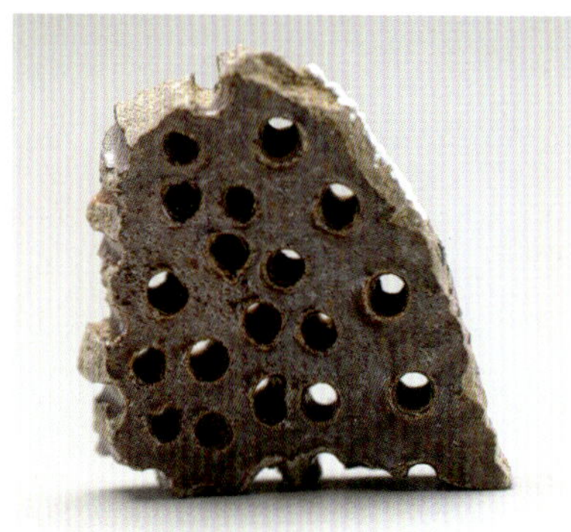

Figure 63 Fragment of a strainer from the interior of a salt-glazed stoneware teapot. (Courtesy, National Park Service, Colonial National Historical Park, Yorktown Collection.) COLO Y 9824.

earthenware pots, approximately eighty in number, were found in a dump area near waster pit 2. The pots vary between 3 and 5 inches in rim diameter and between 1 and 2 inches in height. The majority have numerals or initials crudely incised into the upper surface of each pot. Surface treatments and colorations are highly sophisticated, paralleling the best use of materials by London and Staffordshire potters. The potters used calcined flint in either the body slip or the glaze, dipping their mugs in a white slip to cover the dark body. Copper green glazes were used on at least twelve forms. Of particular importance are the large slip-decorated dishes employing a variety of techniques, including combing, trailing, and marbleizing.

The Yorktown churns were perhaps the first to be made in America. Unusual forms such as bird bottles, chafing dishes, colanders, and funnels show sound design for specific purposes. Robust forms, such as large, footed pipkins, have a peasant quality. Other forms—thin, cordoned mugs and delicate teapots with tight-fitting lids—show technical excellence.

Of tantamount importance is the evidence that William Rogers conducted America's first successful salt-glazed stoneware firings. At the Rogers site it seems that earthenwares and stonewares were fired in the same kiln. One significant discovery is the low firing temperature of hard-bodied stonewares. Apparently stonewares were fired in a range between C/06 (1,005° centigrade) and C/1 (1,125° centigrade), which is a temperature well within the firing range for coarse earthenware. The potters may have been using a refined earthenware body that became dense and mature and, therefore, well-salted at this low temperature. Earthenware clays are common in most areas of Yorktown, and undoubtedly this was one reason for establishing the pottery factory in or near the town. The source of stoneware clay, however, remains unknown.

With the exception of stove and floor tiles, which were mold-made, all Yorktown wares were formed or thrown on a potter's wheel. Most earthenware forms were glazed on both the interior and exterior. Eleven earthenware vessel forms were finished with a green lead glaze. It has been estimated that the Large Kiln would have required about 155 pounds of salt per firing and the Small Kiln about 40 pounds.

Close observation of pots and sherds found at the site reveals clues to kiln stacking methods. Since kiln shelving has not been found, wares had to be stacked. For example, milk pans were stacked on edge, in a series, one leaning against the other. At most, they were glazed only on the interior to just over the rim, so the glazed rim of the pan behind would rest on the unglazed back of the pan in front. The rims of some bisque milk pans have glaze adhering to their underside, indicating alternate bisque and glazed stacking. Bowls, porringers, and pipkins were stacked upside down on top of and overlapping one another, as shown by stacking scars. Bottles and storage jars were traditionally stacked base to base and rim to rim in columns.

In salt glaze firings, it was necessary to use a method that would keep pots from fusing together, since volatilized salt covers everything in the kiln. Kiln furniture—saggars, flat pads and wads, and cylinders or props—

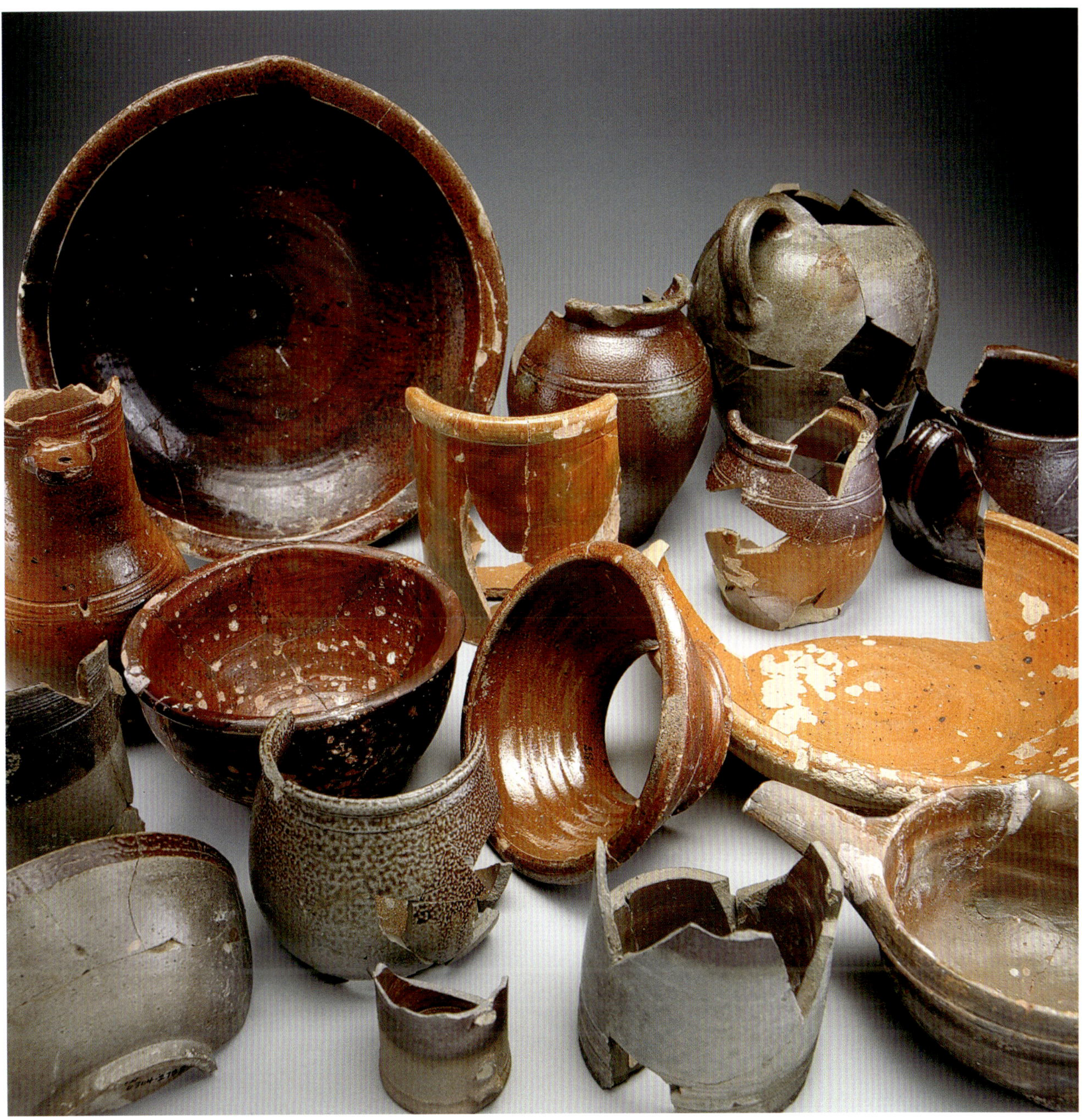

Figure 64 Probable examples of William Rogers earthenwares and stonewares, 1720–1745, excavated in Williamsburg. (Department of Archaeological Research, Colonial Williamsburg.) The success of William Rogers's pottery can be measured by the widespread distribution of his finished wares. Examples of his utilitarian forms are found at archaeological sites throughout the tidewater region of Virginia, with specimens also being reported from Maryland and North Carolina. Historical evidence suggests his wares may even have reached Caribbean ports.

was made and used for this purpose. It is probable that the only forms fired in saggars were mugs and possibly teapots.

As for the horizontal distribution of the site's pottery finds, the main factory complex—Small Kiln, Large Kiln, and Structures 1, 2, and 3—produced the overwhelming majority of pottery (116,000 sherds, or ninety percent of those sherds classified by provenance).

Conclusions

It is unfortunate that we know so little about the people who participated in this industrial enterprise. However, it seems probable that there was a strong Yorktown–London connection in kiln design in what has been called the tin-glaze pattern kiln.[7] Excavations of kilns at Norfolk House, Montague Close, Vauxhall, and Fulham provide evidence of rectangular kilns in which tin-glazed earthenware and stonewares had been fired.[8] The use of rectangular kilns for tin glazing goes back at least to Piccolpasso in 1548.[9] His rectangular kiln also resembles the Yorktown kilns in basic design: a lower heat chamber with a system of flues and arches beneath a pot chamber, which was bricked up during firing.

John Dwight of Fulham used a rectangular kiln for stoneware manufacture in the late seventeenth century. In the eighteenth century, rectangular kilns were gradually supplanted by circular bottle kilns, as the Vauxhall evidence indicates. Based on the English archaeological evidence, there is no doubt that the prototype for the Yorktown rectangular kilns was English.

The Yorktown kilns may be linked to the same English tin-glazing-to-stoneware tradition. The Yorktown potter(s) may have come from the London area and probably had worked in the Lambeth-Fulham vicinity. Perhaps this link with tin-glazed pottery explains the burial of the blue-on-white tin-glazed cup beneath the "1720" porringer. The cup was undoubtedly an object of sentimental value that would, it was hoped, bring good luck to the pottery operation.

The Yorktown potter may have influenced the development of other rectangular kilns in America. There are documentary references to a stoneware pottery operating in Lamberton, New Jersey, in the 1770s. In 1778, William Richards, a Philadelphia merchant, advertised for a stoneware potter. The pottery ceased to exist in 1787, the year Richards died. His updraft kiln seems to resemble the Yorktown kilns, measuring 14.5 feet by 8.5 feet with a firebox protruding an additional 3 feet at each end. Most of the kiln's upper chamber floor (8.5 by 3 feet in plan) survived intact.[10]

It is now a certainty that William Rogers was the "poor potter" of Yorktown, but, contrary to his appellation, he was not poor. From 1720 to 1745, Rogers and his heirs financed and operated the largest colonial pottery factory in America. He was an entrepreneur who also might have been a knowledgeable potter. If not the potter, he hired experienced potters whose high level of expertise can be seen in the well-built kilns, factory design, and size of the site, as well as in the products themselves, including finely made stonewares. Whether Rogers was a potter, an entrepreneur, or both, the politics of running a successful business in eighteenth-century Virginia required considerable skill.

ACKNOWLEDGMENTS I am grateful to all of the people who worked on this project, and it is unfortunate they are too numerous to be listed here. I would like to extend special thanks to Dean Bailey, however, who first showed me the supposed site; Malcolm Watkins and Ivor Noël Hume, who took an early interest in the "poor potter"; and J. C. Harrington, who arranged the first funding for excavation of the site. J. Palin Thorley visited the site many times, much to my benefit. Edward Ayres, Pattie Kandle, Linda Merrill, Chris Sheridan, and Shearon Vaughn contributed greatly to the final report to the National Park Service, as did Toni Gregg with her superb kiln reconstructive drawings. My three sons—Eric, David, and Daniel—spent many weekends at the site, excavating huge quantities of pottery. Andy Edwards, Jimmy Smith, and others did excellent fieldwork at the site, as did numerous anthropology students. Both David Riggs and Bill Pittman were very helpful in obtaining the photographs by Gavin Ashworth for this article. I am also grateful to David Orr for his support through the years. Finally, I am thrilled to have this article published in this very fine journal, skillfully edited by former William and Mary student Rob Hunter.

1. The initial discovery of the "Poor Potter" site was a waster pit on Lot 51, which contained numerous whole and partial pots, usually defective in some manner. It was not until 1970 that a kiln was found nearby. See the following reports: Norman F. Barka, "The Kiln and Ceramics of the 'Poor Potter' of Yorktown: A Preliminary Report," in *Ceramics in America,* edited by Ian M. G. Quimby (Winterthur, Del.: Winterthur Museum, 1972), pp. 291–18; Norman F. Barka and Chris Sheridan, "The Yorktown Pottery Industry, Yorktown, Virginia," *Northeast Historical Archaeology* 6, nos. 1–2 (1972); Erwin N. Thompson, *The Poor Potter of Yorktown, Colonial National Historical Park, Virginia,* Historic Structure Report, NPS 836 (Denver: Denver Service Center, Historic Preservation Team, National Park Service, 1974); Norman F. Barka, Edward Ayres, and Christine Sheridan, *The "Poor Potter of Yorktown": A Study of a Colonial Pottery Factory, Colonial National Historical Park, Virginia,* 3 vols. (Denver: U.S. Department of the Interior, National Park Service, 1984).

2. C. Malcolm Watkins and Ivor Noël Hume, *The "Poor Potter" of Yorktown* (Washington, D.C.: Smithsonian Institution Press, 1967).

3. Items linking Rogers with the "poor potter," taken from the Inventory and Appraisal of William Rogers the Estate, December 17, 1739, include:

> 1 pr. large Scales & Weights £2.10 a pcel crakt redware £2 a parcel crakt Stone Do £5 11 pocket bottles 3/8½ barrel Gun powder £2.10 1 old Sain & ropes £1.10 1 horse Mill £8 2300 lb. old Iron £9.11.8 26 doz qt Mugs £5.4 60 doz pt Do 7.10 11 doz Milk pans £2.4 9 large Cream potts 4/6 9 Midle Sized Do 3/ 12 Small Do 2 2 doz red Saucepans 4/ 2 doz porringers 4/ 6 Chamber potts 2/ 4 doz bird bottles 12/ 3 doz Lamps 9/ 4 doz small stone bottles 6/ 4 doz small dishes 8/ 6 doz puding pans 2/ 26 Cedar pailes £2.12 40 Bushels Salt £4

A total of 1,511 pottery vessels are listed in the inventory.

4. Personal communication with Rob Hunter, 2004.

5. The term *Bourry box* is derived from Emile Bourry, *A Treatise on Ceramic Industries: A Complete Manual for Pottery, Tile and Brick Manufacturers* (London: Scott Greenwood and Son, 1911). Emile Bourry described a firebox arrangement where the fuel is placed in an upper opening to rest on brick hobs. As the wood burns, the embers fall into the ash pit, providing continuous upward heat. The air supply, from an upper opening, moves first through the burning wood and then the ash pit before it enters the ware chamber.

6. Cipriano Piccolpasso, *The Three Books of the Potter's Art,* facsimile of 1548 ed., translated and edited by Bernard Rackham and Albert Van de Put (London: Victoria and Albert Museum, 1934).

7. Chris Green, *John Dwight's Fulham Pottery: Excavations 1971–79,* Archaeological Report, no. 6 (London: English Heritage, 1999): 28.

8. Brian J. Bloice, "Norfolk House, Lambeth: Excavations at a Delftware Kiln Site, 1968," *Post-Medieval Archaeology* 5 (1972): 99–159; Graham J. Dawson, "Two Delftware Kilns at Montague Close," *London Archaeologist* 1, no. 10 (1971): 228–31; Roy Edwards, "The Vauxhall Pottery, History and Excavations, 1977–81," *London Archaeologist* 4 (1981–82): 130–36, 148–54; Green, *John Dwight's Fulham Pottery,* pp. 21–28.

9. Piccolpasso, *Three Books of the Potter's Art.*

10. Richard Hunter, "Eighteenth-Century Stoneware Kiln of William Richards Found on the Lamberton Waterfront, Trenton, New Jersey," in *Ceramics in America,* edited by Robert Hunter (Hanover, N.H.: University Press of New England for the Chipstone Foundation, 2001), pp. 239–43.

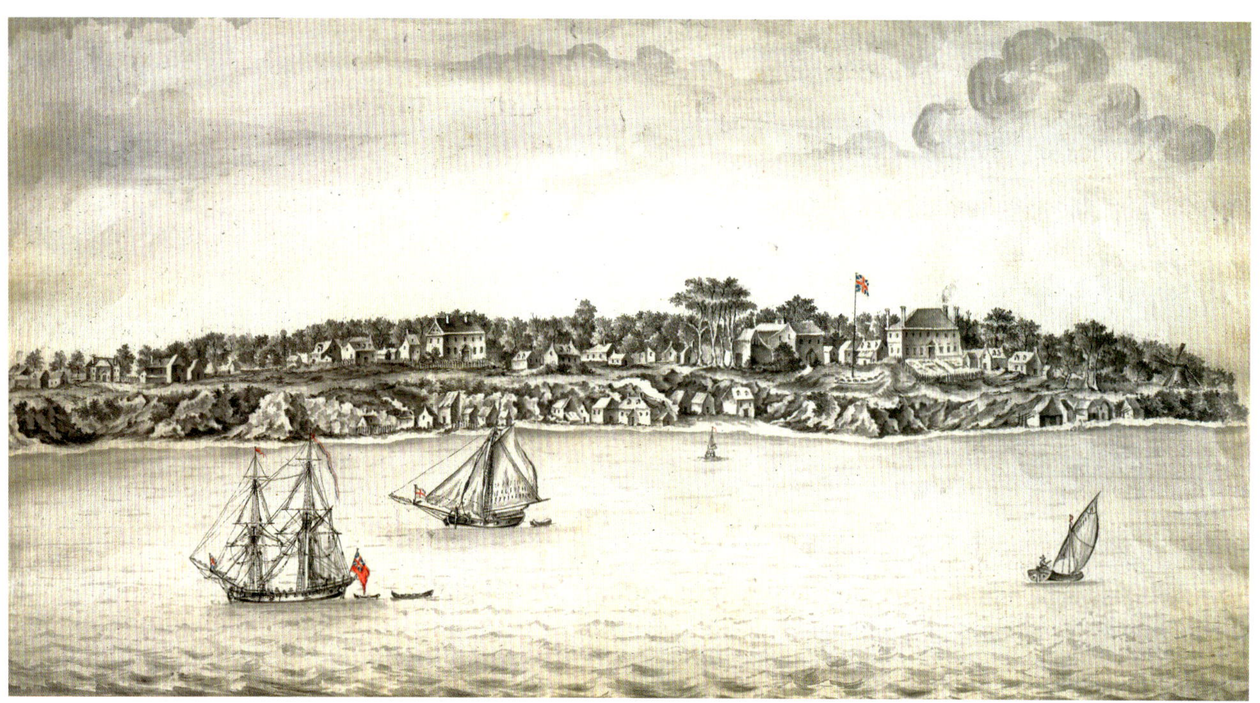

Figure 1 *View of the Town of York Virginia from the River*, 1754–1756. Colored drawing from Logbook #406 Voyage of HMS *Success* and HMS *Norwich* to Nova Scotia and Virginia. (Courtesy, The Mariner's Museum, Newport News, Va.) William Rogers supplied popular taverns in Williamsburg as well as Yorktown.

Martha W. McCartney and Edward Ayres

Yorktown's "Poor Potter": A Man Wise Beyond Discretion

▼ WILLIAM ROGERS, OWNER of the first Virginia pottery factory known to produce stoneware, resided in Yorktown. The extremely well-made salt-glazed stoneware and lead-glazed coarseware produced by his workers from 1720 until about 1745 were valued by consumers and enjoyed wide distribution. Shipping records suggest that these wares were exported to other North American colonies and perhaps to the West Indies.

The excavations that were undertaken between 1966 and 1982 by College of William and Mary archaeologist Dr. Norman Barka have culminated in the unearthing of William Rogers's pottery factory and kiln complex. A subsequent analysis of the wares produced at this site resulted in the development of a typology (see Barka, "Archaeology of a Colonial Pottery Factory," pp. 15–47 in this issue). Seminal research by historian Edward Ayres led to the identification of William Rogers as the owner of the Yorktown lot on which the pottery factory was located. Ayres also discovered that Virginia Governor William Gooch, when reporting to his superiors in England, purposefully downplayed the success of Rogers, whom he repeatedly referred to as the "poor potter." In truth, Rogers lacked neither skill nor financial resources.

Although very little is known about William Rogers of Yorktown prior to his arrival in Virginia, it is certain that his older brother, George, was a collar maker and resident of Braintree, in Essex, in southeastern England. A pair of monogrammed silver salts and a can, embellished with the initials FPM, and six silver spoons engraved with the letters WT^{F}R may provide clues to the identity of his forebears. Rogers came of age sometime prior to 1710 and married at least twice. When he made his will in 1739 he named as heirs his daughter Susanna, then a grown and married woman, and the three minor children he had with his wife Theodosia. William and Theodosia Rogers's son, William Jr., came of age between December 1739 and May 1741, so he probably was born about 1720.[1]

Edward Ayres has raised the possibility that William Rogers was a native of London and that he may have come from Southwark, an area known for its pottery factories, particularly its manufactories of stoneware. This hypothesis is based on correspondence between his grandson and a cousin named Samuel Rogers, who was a Southwark merchant. On the other hand, shipping records strongly suggest that Rogers had close ties to Bristol merchants; he maintained business relationships there for at least three decades.[2] In 1700 a William Rogers was among those who shipped goods from England to New England aboard the *Europe*. In 1707 he sent a shipment to Virginia and Boston aboard the *Virginia Merchant* of Plymouth, England. Many of the destinations to which British merchant William Rogers sent merchandise were the same ones to which the Captain William Rogers of Yorktown later dispatched ships. This pattern of commercial activity suggests that William Rogers of Yorktown made frequent trips to England during his first few years in the colony, perhaps as a factor or agent of a British mercantile firm. Or he might have been working closely with a kinsman, perhaps his father or an uncle, whose name he shared.[3]

Around 1709–1710 William Rogers began making plans to set up housekeeping in Yorktown, a community established in 1691 (fig. 1). In December 1710 he was credited with importing an African slave aboard the *Digges Frigate,* a sailing ship that belonged to the Digges family of the Bellfield plantation in York County. On May 19, 1711, he acquired Yorktown Lots 51 and 55, which were contiguous. Rogers, whose deed identified him as a brewer, was obliged to build "a good house" on each of his vacant lots within twelve months. If he failed to do so, his property automatically reverted to the town trustees, who had the right to sell them. This proviso was intended to quell real estate speculation and stimulate development. By January 21, 1712, William Rogers had paid for his lots and obtained an unencumbered title to them, and it was there that he established a family home, a pottery factory, and some ancillary structures.[4]

Court records suggest that before he developed his own property, Rogers rented one or more buildings in Yorktown and conducted business as a brewer and merchant. In January 1712 the executors of mariner John Martin successfully brought suit against Rogers, alleging that "for more than 12 months past" he had been in possession of "sundry houses" that belonged to the decedent's estate. On March 19, 1711, William Rogers was among the several York County men (most of whom were ordinary-keepers) who asked the county justices to set the rates that could be charged for various types of beverages. Rogers's beer, which could be sold for 6 pence a quart, apparently was considered far superior to "Virginia Midling Bear" and cider, the price of which was set at only 3¾ pence per quart. However, English beer was worth twice as much as Rogers's.[5] Rogers's brewing activities most likely took place in or near one of the "sundry houses" that he was renting from John Martin's estate, probably near the waterfront.

During the 1710s William Rogers frequently served as an agent of York County's court justices. This suggests that he was considered trustworthy and astute, and was a respected member of the community. Rogers often was called upon to appraise decedents' estates, serve as a juror, audit business accounts, and take witness testimony. Later, he served as captain of a troop of horse soldiers and even was responsible for seeing that a new county jail was built. Apparently he was not a deeply religious man, for he was fined on account of his chronic absences from church, a legal obligation in colonial Virginia, which had an officially sanctioned state church.[6]

Although it is unclear what impelled William Rogers to build a pottery factory, it is likely that as a savvy businessman he seized the opportunity to capitalize on local tavern-keepers' constant need for vessels. (Rogers's role as security for Williamsburg tavern-keeper Edward Ripping in 1714 would have reinforced his awareness of this potential market.) The relationship between the brewer's and potter's trades seems to have been a long-standing one. During the mid-seventeenth century there were at least three brew houses in Jamestown, the capital city, which had an abundance of taverns. Near at least one of these sites, archaeological evidence has been found that demonstrates that an apothecary, a brewer, and a potter were at work. One man known to have gone from one occupation to the other is Christian Whithelm, who was a brewer when he moved to London during the 1630s, but by the 1640s had become an apothecary and potter.[7] Apparently, those who needed substantial quantities of containers sometimes decided to make them.

In 1725 William Rogers sold a large quantity of earthenware to John Mercer, an Irishman and trader who settled on the Potomac River at Marlborough Town. Mercer began acquiring lots and continued until he had purchased much of the town. He built a mansion and constructed a mill, brewery, and glass factory. He also had a wharf, several warehouses, and a tavern.[8] This diversity in entrepreneurial activities, similar to the economic strategy employed by William Rogers, offered the assurance of good and reliable income.

In 1734 William Rogers became the official surveyor of Yorktown's landings, streets, and causeways, which he was obliged to keep in good repair. Archaeologists discovered in 1957 that Rogers sometimes used pot sherds to fill in low places in Yorktown's streets. Layers of Rogers stoneware sherds, several inches deep, were found beneath Main Street in front of Yorktown's Digges House. The technique of using potters' refuse to make a firmer base or roadbed is well documented in England.[9]

Historical documents reveal that white indentured servants and enslaved Africans and African Americans worked together in William Rogers's pottery factory at Yorktown. In December 1710 he paid for the transportation of a male African slave, named London, from London to Virginia. During the early to mid-1720s he purchased several young slaves, boys and girls between the ages of nine and fourteen. All of these children, to whom Rogers gave English names, came from Africa and arrived at Yorktown aboard sailing vessels that originated in Bristol or London.[10]

William Rogers also employed white indentured servants (or contract workers) in his pottery factory. Because he dealt regularly with merchants in Bristol and London, he would have been able to draw upon a labor pool that included workers with specialized expertise, and he may have deliberately sought someone who had the potter's skill. It is possible that one or more of the men and women whose contracts Rogers bought had a working knowledge of pot-making and would have been able to train others. William Rogers himself may have had some knowledge of the potter's craft.

The identities of seven of William Rogers's indentured servants are known because they ran afoul of the law and were brought before the justices of the county court. At least three had been sent to Virginia as convict servants.[11] Documents on file in the British Public Records Office reveal that during the early 1720s Rogers bought the contracts of male convicts from Middlesex (in the immediate vicinity of London), Yorkshire, and Devon. He may have purchased others, perhaps selectively. Advertisements that appeared in the *Virginia Gazette* during the eighteenth century attest to the wide variety of occupational skills to be found among Virginia's convict servants, and certainly those with specialized skills would have been in great demand despite their questionable pasts.

Throughout the years William Rogers's pottery factory was in business he had problems with his indentured servants. In August 1739 William Barbasore was jailed for breaking into two local storehouses, one of which belonged to his master. When confronted by his accusers, Barbasore admitted that he and another indentured servant (a blacksmith) had broken into Rogers's store and stolen two or three butter pots and a stoneware saucepan that they had carried off and sold. On another occasion the same two burglars robbed Rogers of fourteen pocket bottles. In both instances, the blacksmith had made keys for the purpose of unlocking the storehouses they intended to rob.[12]

A document dating to 1760 (two decades after William Rogers's death) mentions his daughter's not being entitled to a share of the profits from the wares produced at the pottery factory *because she did not inherit the slaves*.[13] This suggests that, at least by the end of his life, it was Rogers's slaves who produced the ceramic wares in his Yorktown pottery factory—indicating, perhaps, that Rogers decided indentured servants with questionable backgrounds were too problematic.

During the summer of 1711, shortly after purchasing two Yorktown lots, William Rogers appears to have been among those responsible for dispatching goods from Bristol, England, to what was then Carolina aboard

Figure 2 *View of the Town of Gloucester York River Virginia*, 1754–1756. Colored drawing from Logbook #406 Voyage of HMS *Success* and HMS *Norwich* to Nova Scotia and Virginia. Gloucestertown is located directly across from Yorktown on the north bank of the York River. (Courtesy, The Mariner's Museum, Newport News, Va.)

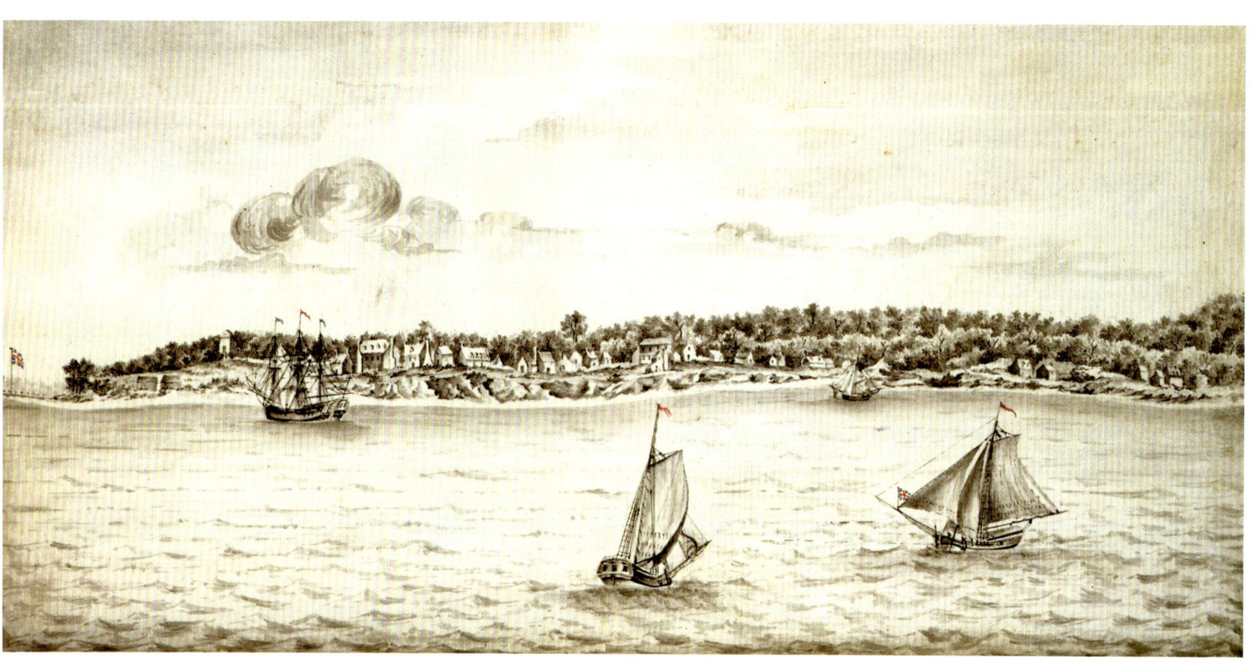

Figure 3 Miles Cary, *Plat of Gloucester Town*, 1707 (Robert Reade Thruston Papers; Filson Historical Society, Louisville, Ky.) Note Lots 7, 8, and 27.

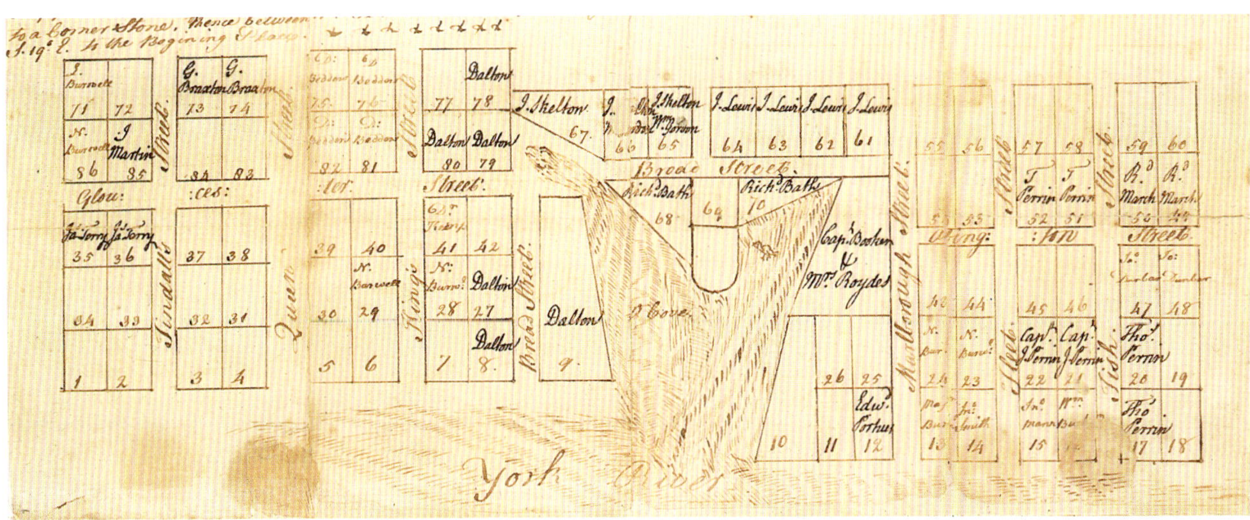

the galley *Carolina*. In mid-September 1715, Rogers, as the representative of William Hawksworth and Company of Bristol, had goods sent to Virginia aboard the *Bristol Merchant*. In 1716, trading as "William Rogers & Company," Rogers dispatched shipments from Bristol to Pennsylvania and Virginia. Part of Rogers's cargo was transported by the ship *Abingdon*, which belonged to a wealthy Virginia merchant and planter named William Dalton, who owned three waterfront lots in Gloucestertown, directly across the York River from Yorktown (figs. 2, 3).[14] Interestingly, archaeologists have discovered a large quantity of kiln furniture and pot sherds on one of Dalton's lots, artifacts associated with William Rogers's pottery factory (figs. 4–6).[15]

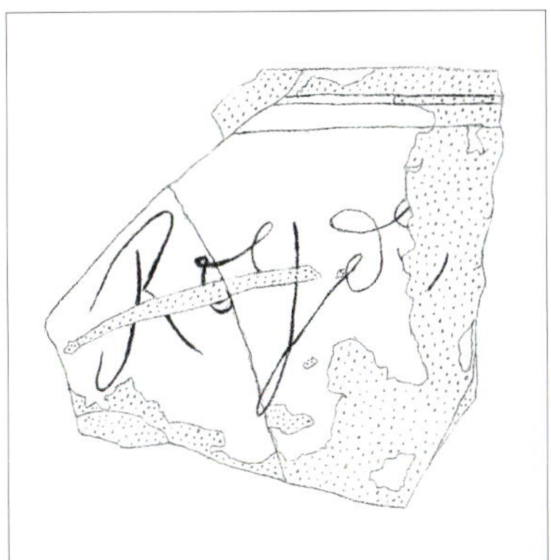

Figure 5 Drawing of the fragment illustrated in fig. 4 showing the "Rogers" inscription. (Drawing, Alain Outlaw.)

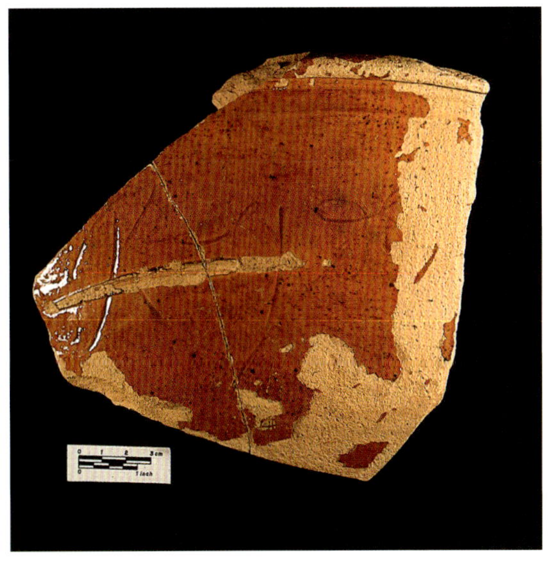

Figure 4 Fragment of a large bowl, William Rogers, Yorktown, Virginia, 1720–1745. Lead-glazed earthenware. This is the only known example of Rogers's pottery inscribed with his name. (Courtesy, Virginia Department of Historic Resources; photo, Alain Outlaw.)

Figure 6 Pipkin, William Rogers, Yorktown, Virginia, 1720–1745. Lead-glazed earthenware. H. 8¼". (Courtesy, Virginia Department of Historic Resouces; photo, David Hazzard.)

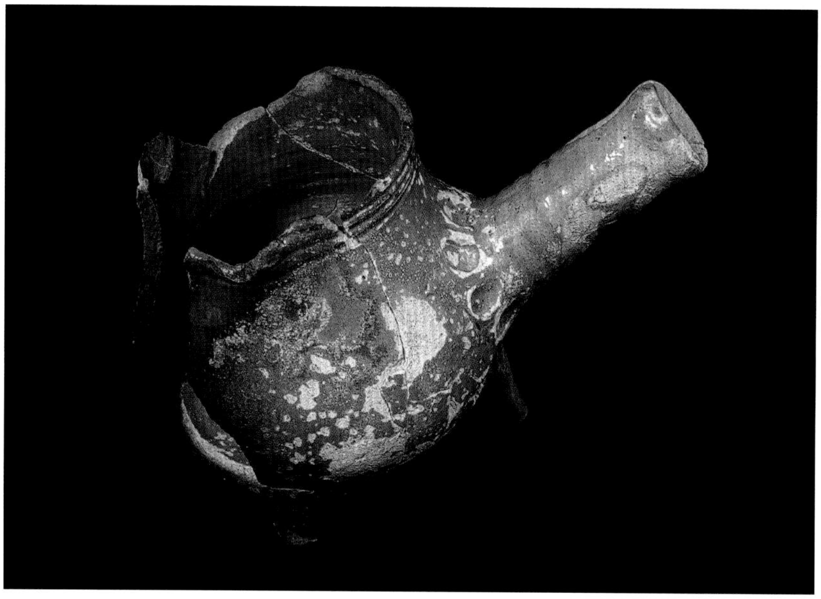

Figure 7 Peter Jefferson and Robert Brook, *A Map of the Northern Neck in Virginia,* 1713–1746. (Courtesy, The Library of Virginia.) Alexander Wordie transported Rogers's wares from Yorktown to Wiccocomoco and then to Monokin, Maryland.

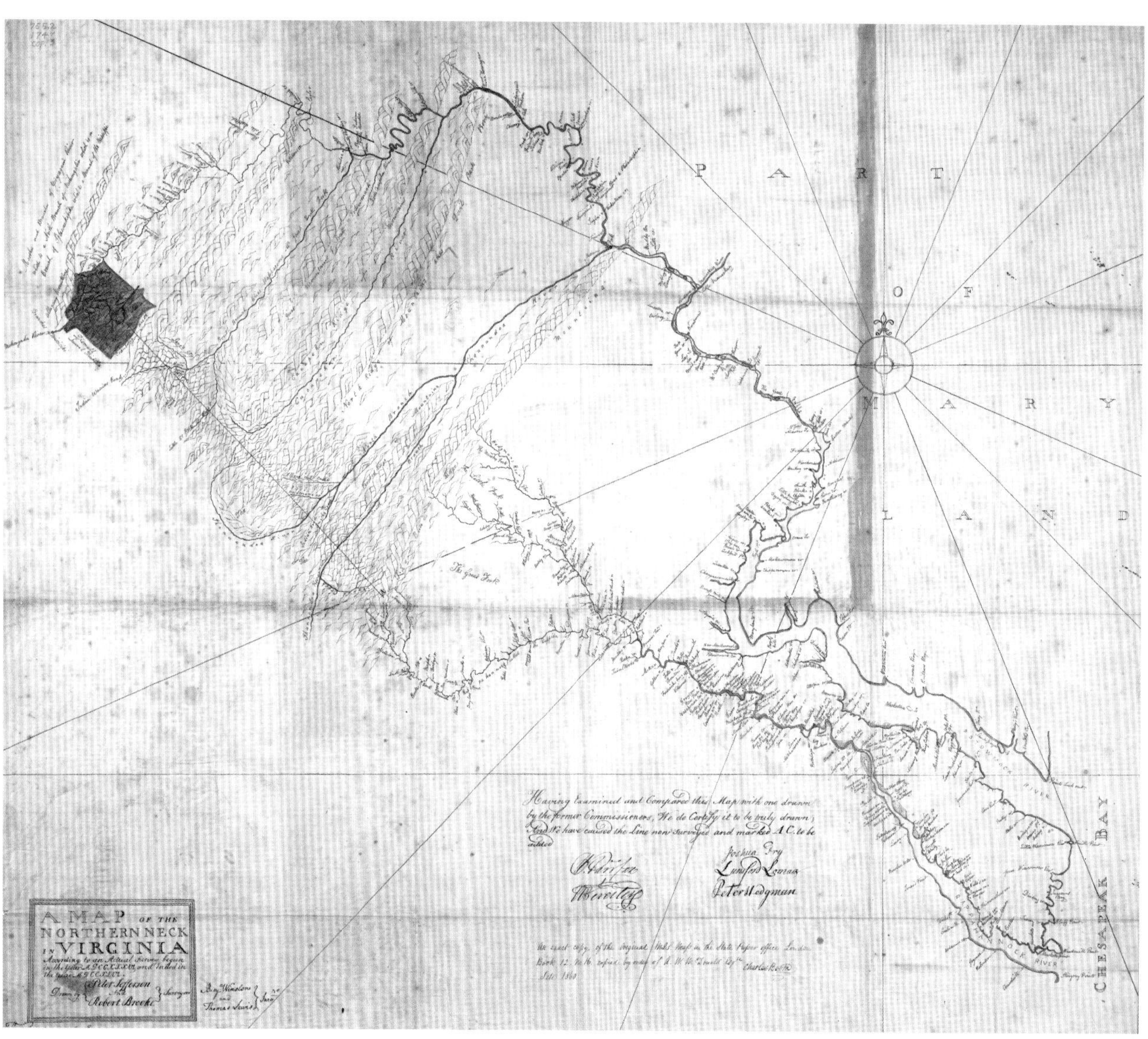

In late summer 1718 William Rogers dispatched goods from Bristol to Virginia aboard *The Little York,* a vessel that probably belonged to Yorktown, whose soubriquet was "Little York." Court documents reveal that by 1725 Rogers was mass-producing ceramics. He had filed suit against Alexander Wordie, who was to transport a large quantity of earthenware to Maryland and sell it on consignment.[16] By 1730 William Rogers had become the registered owner of a Virginia-built sloop, the *William and John,* with John Kelsale as master. In 1730–1731 the sloop plied coastal waters and transported "18 doz. pcs. earthenware" to Maryland (fig. 7). Shipping records reveal that George Page transported earthenware from Yorktown to Maryland in his shallop, perhaps obtaining the ceramics locally. Peter Frazier, who cleared customs in Yorktown in 1732, carried "a parcel of earthenware" to Maryland, as did *Virginia Gazette* publisher William Parks, who took shipments of goods to Maryland in 1734 and 1735.[17] William Rogers was listed as the owner of a 150-ton ship, the *Susanna,* in 1732 (a vessel of that name had transported convict servants to Virginia in 1727). In May 1739, shortly before his death, Rogers advertised that he had a small shallop for sale at Yorktown.[18]

Shipping returns published in the *Virginia Gazette* between 1739 and 1745, when the William Rogers pottery factory was in the hands of his heirs, indicate that vessels transported stoneware from Yorktown to North Carolina on a fairly regular basis. The late C. Malcolm Watkins noted that Rogers's stoneware may have been exported to New England, using as evidence Isaac Parker's September 1742 petition to Massachusetts authorities for permission to establish a stoneware manufactory in Charlestown. Parker proffered that, "There are large quantities of said ware imported into this Province every year from New York, Philadelphia, & Virginia." As William Rogers's pottery works seems to have been the only stoneware factory in Virginia, it is likely that Parker was speaking of wares made in Yorktown. More specific information comes from the shipping records associated with the ship *Friendship,* which entered the York River naval district in December 1733 and left in February 1734, carrying "a parcel of Virginia made Earthenware."[19]

However, Edward Ayres, who compared the quantities of ceramics being brought into Yorktown with the quantities being sent out, observed that more earthenware was being exported from Yorktown between 1725 and 1735 than between 1736 and 1740, when New England traders were more active. Pottery exports from Yorktown increased between 1741 and 1745, the years during which the late William Rogers's son-in-law was in possession of the lots on which the Rogers manufactory was located. Shipping records also reveal that the majority of the sailing vessels that left Yorktown with ceramics went to Maryland and North Carolina and that only a few went to New England and the West Indies.[20]

During the first quarter of the eighteenth century England had an aggressive protectionist policy regarding its manufactured goods. From the British perspective, the colonies existed for the Mother Country's benefit and they were expected to support England's mercantile system. To encourage dependency, the production of goods in the British colonies was discouraged. Included in the town acts passed by the Virginia Assembly between 1680 and 1705, intended to promote urban development, were economic incentives designed to attract those who engaged in crafts and trades. English officials opposed these acts, because they believed that encouraging manufacturing by the colonists would "take them off from the Planting of Tobacco, which would be of very ill consequence, not only in respect to the Exports of our Woolen and other Goods and Consequently *to the dependence that Colony ought to have on this Kingdom*." They proffered that the promotion of manufacturing would also be "a further Prejudice in relation to our shipping and navigation."[21] Thus, when William Rogers established his pottery factory in Yorktown, it was at a time when the colonists were discouraged from producing manufactured goods, especially those that might compete with commodities being exported by the Mother Country.

From 1700 on, Virginia's governors were asked to submit reports to the Commissioners for Trade and Plantations and to the Board of Trade, documenting the extent to which the colonists were producing marketable commodities. In 1713 Lieutenant Governor Alexander Spotswood, who had brought skilled German workers to the colony to establish an ironworks, reported that the decline in the colony's tobacco trade was due to the crop's low value. He added that "Unless a remedy is found the colony will be forced to turn to the manufacture of other goods." Spotswood noted that the "decay of the Tobacco trade" had led to "the collapse of the colony as a market for British manufactures."[22]

Lieutenant Governor William Gooch, who acted as the colony's chief executive from 1727 to 1749, was very sympathetic to the colonists' economic plight but also politically savvy. His carefully worded, deprecating responses to official queries about manufacturing in Virginia veiled the increased industrial development that was occurring, thanks to population growth and the need for a ready supply of locally produced goods. Gooch's offhand yet discreet references to Yorktown's "poor potter" (William Rogers) exemplify this obfuscatory approach.

In 1732 Gooch stated that Virginia's revenue laws were not prejudicial to British trade, and pointed out that there were fewer manufacturing enterprises in Virginia than in New England. He went on to say, "Nor indeed is there much ground to suspect that any kind of Manufactures will prevail in a Country where handycraft Labour is so dear." He added, however, that "There is one poor Potter's work of coarse earthen Ware, which is of so little Consequence, that I dare say there hath not been twenty Shillings worth less of that Commodity imported since it was sett up than there was before." When Gooch was queried by his superiors a year later, he reported that "Wee have at York Town upon York River one poor Potter's Work for Earthen Ware." He stated that the potter's production had not impinged upon British tax revenues, and that the only purchasers of the potter's wares were "the poorest Familys . . . who not being able to send to England for such Things would do without them if they could not get them here." Year after year Gooch downplayed the importance of the pottery works at Yorktown. In 1736 he said that "The same poor Potter's work is still continued at York Town without any great Improvement or Advantage to the Owner, or any Injury to the Trade of Great Britain." A year later Gooch commented that "The Potter continues his Business (at York Town in this Colony) of making Potts and Pans, with very little Advantage to himself, and without damage to Trade." In 1739 he noted that "The Poor Potter's operation" was unworthy of notice. Finally in 1741 he indicated that the "poor potter" was dead and that "the business of making potts & pans is of little advantage to his Family and as little Damage to the Trade of our Mother Country."[23]

As time went on William Rogers prospered. In 1731 he purchased a twenty-five-acre tract at Terrapin Point, near Yorktown, an outlying parcel that he used as a quarter or farm (a practice common to town dwellers both in the colonies and in Europe). It was there that his slaves, working under an overseer, kept his livestock and produced food crops. In September 1738 Rogers bought Lot 75 in Yorktown, as well as some neighboring acreage upon which he commenced building a brick house for his eldest daughter, Susanna. He and wife Theodosia made plans to build a house next door. In March 1739 Rogers purchased Lot K within what was known as the Gwyn Read subdivision, which bordered south and east on original Yorktown and which was only a block away from the Rogers's family home and pottery factory on Lots 51 and 55. A nineteenth-century reference to Lot K states that it was "a piece of land near an old clay hole on the back side of Yorktown."[24] This raises the possibility that the site was the source of the clay Rogers used in pottery manufacturing.

When William Rogers made his will in May 1739, he identified himself as a merchant. He bequeathed his Yorktown lots and buildings (which would have included the family home and pottery factory) to his nineteen- or twenty-year-old son, William Jr., to whom he also left a warehouse on the waterfront, "under the Hill." He also bequeathed to his son six enslaved males of African descent and an enslaved "India man," probably a West Indian. It is likely that some or all of these men were associated with the pottery factory. William Rogers instructed his executrix, wife Theodosia, to see "that no potters ware not burnt and fit for Sale shall be appraised."[25] This suggests that there was green ware on the premises at the time Rogers made his will and that he expected some to be present at the time of his demise.

The inventory of William Rogers's estate reveals that a large part of his wealth was invested in his slaves. However, his personal possessions show that he was a wealthy, erudite man of refined tastes. When he died, he was in possession of fine furnishings, silver serving vessels, gilt-framed pictures, and other objets d'art. He also owned—in all probability, a reflection of his brewing activities—a copper cistern, a cold still, a worm still, some casks, beer tubs, hops, and 240 quart bottles. It seems likely, then, that Rogers continued to generate income as a brewer while actively producing ceramics.[26]

William Rogers Jr., who came of age in 1740 or 1741, died young. As he died unmarried and intestate, the legal interest in the real and personal property he had inherited descended to his father's eldest brother, British collar maker George Rogers. He promptly conveyed his share of the Rogers estate to Thomas Reynolds, the husband of the elder William Rogers's daughter, Susanna. From 1742 to 1760 Susanna and her half sister Sarah retained legal possession of Yorktown Lots 51 and 55, which contained the Rogers pottery factory and family home. However, a Hanover County document reveals that Thomas Reynolds came into possession of—and retained—at least four of the Rogers slaves and therefore was entitled to virtually all of the income that the pottery factory produced. An advertisement that appeared in the June 20, 1745, edition of the *Virginia Gazette* announced that a variety of imported goods was to be sold in Williamsburg, as well as "All sorts of Rogers Earthen Ware, as cheap as [in] York." Shipments of Rogers pottery probably were being taken aboard vessels at Yorktown and transported to Maryland, for shipping returns dating to the summer of 1745 list "a parcel of earthenware." When Thomas Reynolds died in 1759 he was still in possession of the slaves apparently associated with pottery making. This raises the possibility that pottery was being fabricated at the Rogers manufactory for ten or more years after the demise of its founder.[27]

1. York County Wills and Inventories 18 (1732–1740): 537–40; York County Orders, Wills, and Inventories 19 (1740–1746): 8. York County's original colonial documents are on file in the York County Courthouse, Yorktown, Virginia; microfilms are available at the Rockefeller Library, Colonial Williamsburg Foundation, Williamsburg, Virginia.

2. York County Deeds, Administrations, and Bonds 5 (1741–1754): 64–66; York County Orders, Wills, and Inventories 19 (1740–1746): 193; Norman F. Barka, Edward Ayres, and Christine Sheridan, *The "Poor Potter" of Yorktown: A Study of a Colonial Pottery Factory; Colonial National Historical Park,* 3 vols. (Denver: U.S. Department of the Interior, National Park Service, 1984), 1: 18–19.

3. Peter Wilson Coldham, *The Complete Book of Emigrants in Bondage, 1700–1750* (Baltimore, Md.: Genealogical Publishing Company, 1992), pp. 11, 83, 127, 169, 180, 186–87, 218, 252, 487; British Public Records Office, London, Colonial Office Papers (hereafter C.O.) 5/1320, fol. 6.

4. Walter Minchinton, Celia M. King, and Peter B. Waite, eds., *Virginia Slave-Trade Statistics, 1698–1775* (Richmond: Virginia State Library, 1984), p. 41; York County Deeds and Bonds 20 (1701–1713): 365–66; York County Deeds, Orders, Wills 14 (1709–1716): pp. 82, 123.

5. York County Deeds, Orders, Wills 14 (1709–1716): 72–73, 119, 123.

6. Ibid., pp. 116, 119, 124, 136–37; 16, p. 575; 17, p. 74; York County Orders, Wills, and Inventories 15 (1716–1720): 14, 43, 86–89, 126, 357, 522.

7. Martha W. McCartney, *Documentary History of Jamestown Island,* 3 vols. (Williamsburg, Va.: National Park Service, 2000), 2: 106–22, 3: 396–37.

8. John Mercer, "Ledger Book, 1725–1732," fol. 27, Library of Virginia, Richmond, Va.; John W. Reps, *Tidewater Towns: City Planning in Colonial Virginia and Maryland* (Williamsburg, Va.: Colonial Williamsburg Foundation, 1972), p. 78.

9. C. Malcolm Watkins and Ivor Noël Hume, *The "Poor Potter" of Yorktown* (Washington, D.C.: Smithsonian Institution Press, 1967), p. 92; York County Orders, Wills, Inventories 18 (1732–1740): 157A.

10. C.O. 5/1320, fol. 6; York County Orders, Wills, and Inventories 16 (1720–1729): 25, 59, 248, 280; 18 (1732–1740): 223; Minchinton, King, and Waite, *Virginia Slave-Trade Statistics,* pp. 49–51. When William Rogers made his will in 1739, several of these individuals were still part of the household; York County Wills and Inventories 18 (1732–1740): 553–57.

11. Some of the men and women transported to the colonies were habitual criminals; the majority, however, was not.

12. York County Orders, Wills, and Inventories 18 (1732–1740): 513–14.

13. John Snelson, Letter Book, 1757–1775, entry for July 5, 1760, microfilm, Rockefeller Library, Colonial Williamsburg Foundation.

14. Dalton, who owned a plantation in Gloucester, sometimes sent shipments of pork, shingles, hams, pots of lard, beef, and beeswax to Barbados and Madeira. When William Dalton died, his widow, Sarah, married John Thruston, another Gloucestertown merchant, who owned Lot L in Yorktown's Gwyn Read subdivision, next door to William Rogers's Lot K (C.O. 5/1443, fol. 79; Polly C. Mason, comp., *Records of Colonial Gloucester County, Virginia: A Collection of Abstracts from Original Documents Concerning the Lands and People of Colonial Gloucester County,* 2 vols. (Newport News, Va.: Privately printed, 1946), 2: 58, 60.

15. Coldham, *Emigrants in Bondage,* pp. 11, 83, 17, 169, 180, 186–87, 218, 252, 487; Mason, *Records of Colonial Gloucester County,* 2: 58, 60; Miles Cary, Plan of Gloucestertown, 1707, Filson Club, Louisville, Ky.; David K. Hazzard, personal communication, April 2002.

16. York County Orders, Wills, and Inventories 16 (1720–1729): 380.

17. Parks established the *Maryland Gazette* in Annapolis in 1727 and then moved to Williamsburg, where he established a newspaper. Parks and his family owned property in both locations. He and Mrs. Sarah Packe of Williamsburg did business together and it is perhaps significant that Mrs. Packe and William Rogers sometimes transacted business; Martha W. McCartney, *A Documentary History of the Hanover Tavern Tract* (Williamsburg, Va.: Privately printed, 2002).

18. C.O. 5/1442, fol. 25; C.O. 5/1443, fols. 51, 68, 79–80, 102; C.O. 5/1444, fols. 1v, 12v; York County Orders, Wills, and Inventories 15 (1716–1720): 307, 317–18, 357–58, 388–89, 394, 439; Peter Wilson Coldham, *English Convicts In Colonial America. Middlesex: 1617 - 1775,* London: 1656 – 1775. 2 vols. (New Orleans, La.: Polyanthos, 1974 – 1976) 1: 304; William Parks, in *Virginia Gazette* (Williamsburg), May 4, 1739.

19. C.O. 5/1443, fols. 68, 79; Parks, in *Virginia Gazette,* June 24, September 21, November 2, 1739; January 24, 1741; July 4, 1745; Watkins and Noël Hume, *"Poor Potter" of Yorktown,* p. 84.

20. Barka, Ayres, and Sheridan, *"Poor Potter" of Yorktown,* 1: 174–77.

21. William W. Hening, ed., *The Statutes at Large; Being a Collection of All the Laws of Virginia, . . .* 13 vols. (Richmond: Samuel Pleasants, 1809–1813), 3: 404–5; William P. Palmer, ed., *Calendar of Virginia State Papers and Other Manuscripts . . . Preserved in the Capitol at Richmond,* 11 vols. (1875–1893; reprint, New York: Kraus Reprint, 1968), 1: 37–38 [emphasis added].

22. C.O. 5/1364, fols. 5–14; C.O. 5/1366, fols. 432–35.

23. C.O. 5/1323, fols. 62–66, 82, 93–94; C.O. 5/1324, fols. 3, 5–8, 20–21, 30–31, 59–60, 167–68.

24. York County Orders and Inventories 17 (1729–1732): 136; 18 (1732–1740): 478–80; York County Deeds, Administrations, Bonds 4 (1719–1726): 88–90; York County Deed Book 4 (1729–1740): 550–51; 21: 488–89; Robert Anderson, Papers, folder 319, Rockefeller Library, Colonial Williamsburg Foundation.

25. York County Wills and Inventories 18 (1732–1740): 537–40.

26. Ibid., pp. 544–45.

27. Parks, in *Virginia Gazette,* June 20, 1745; July 4, 1745; York County Orders, Wills and Inventories 21 (1760–1771): 99–102; John Snelson, Letter Book, 1757–1775, entry for July 5, 1760, microfilm, Rockefeller Library, Colonial Williamsburg Foundation.

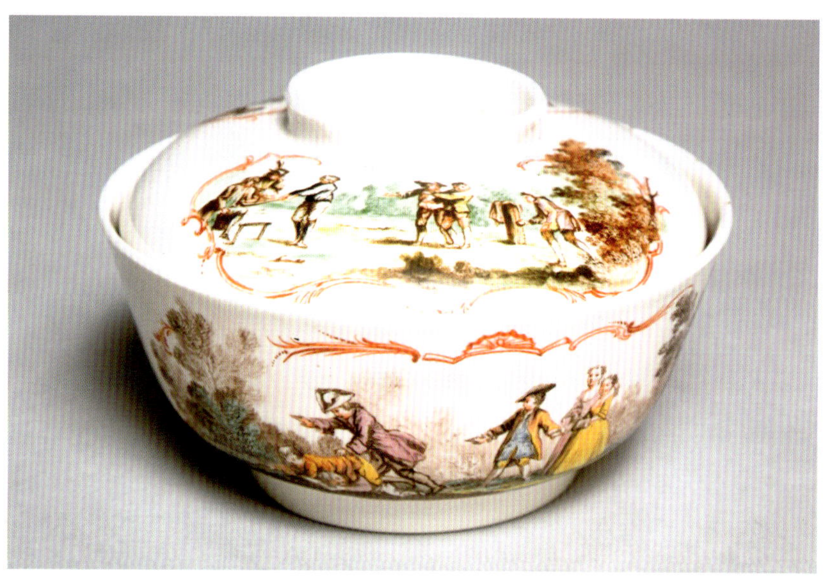

Figure 1 Covered bowl, East London, England, ca. 1744. Porcelain. H. 3⅛". (Collection of the Melbourne Cricket Club Museum, acc. no. M5369.1; photo, Erin O'Brien.) Decorated in enamels and marked on the base with an "A" in underglaze blue. This sugar bowl and cover, formerly in the Baer collection, are composed of a mixture of China clay and lime-soda frit in the proportion 60:40 (hydrous). This composition conforms to the 1744 patent of Heylyn and Frye, and it is proposed that whoever made this bowl was replicating the 1744 patent, which specified the use of Cherokee clay. This covered bowl is part of a partial tea set comprising a teapot and cover (see fig. 7), a cream jug, and three saucers.

W. Ross Ramsay, Judith A. Hansen, and E. Gael Ramsay

An "A-Marked" Porcelain Covered Bowl, Cherokee Clay, and Colonial America's Contribution to the English Porcelain Industry

▼ CRICKET, THE QUINTESSENTIAL English pastime, is in this account the link that brings together such seemingly disparate elements as a porcelain covered sugar bowl in the collection of the museum of the Melbourne Cricket Club (MCC), Cherokee clay obtained from North Carolina, the nascent English porcelain industry of 1743–1744, and colonial America's fledgling ceramic tradition.

The MCC covered bowl belongs to a small body of porcelains called the "A-marked" group (figs. 1–6), owing to the presence of either an incised "A" or a painted "A" in underglaze blue. Thirty-six objects of this type have been recognized to date (figs. 7, 9–12).[1] The attribution and origin of the group, which appears to have been given its name by Arthur Lane,[2] have been the subject of considerable debate. Lane, Robert J. Charleston, and John V. G. Mallet have all outlined the main features of the A-marked group, examples of which occur either as polychrome or, uncommonly, in the white.[3] Lane noted that the porcelain body, having a modified chonchoidal fracture, was harder than what was typical of English porcelains, and he suggested that the body was of a hybrid type containing some kaolin clay. Mallet has divided A-marked porcelains into two broad groupings: the *high style* and *stock pattern*.

The MCC sugar bowl under discussion belongs to the high-style group. Four vignettes of extraordinary quality and technique are painted on the bowl and cover, one of which illustrates cricket being played—quite different from the modern version of the game but possibly not unfamiliar to some Australian cricketers. The game appears to have started in England and subsequently has spread to her various territories and dominions. Yet, strangely, cricket has not been taken up to any degree in continental Europe, and because of this, the cricket scene depicted on the cover of the bowl proved to be a crucial factor in ascribing an English origin for the A-marked porcelains. Arthur Lane had been inclined to a Continental origin; however, the discovery in 1961 of a partial tea set with the associated covered sugar bowl resulted in a general acceptance that A-marked wares were of British origin.[4] Subsequently, its factory source has been widely debated. Hilary Young notes that, "with the exception of a few individual items or small groups, among the earlier porcelains only the rare 'A-marked' wares still await an attribution."[5] The quality of the potting, the porcelain body itself, and the startling enameling make this bowl the subject of considerable speculation.

With the discovery of high-fired porcelain by the Chinese in the T'ang period during the ninth century there developed a demand for such porcelaneous wares in Europe through trading and then for European production, initially in Florence under the patronage of Francesco de' Medici. Florentine porcelain was an artificial glassy or frit porcelain, known generally as soft paste porcelain. Subsequent examples now recognized include pieces related to Padua (ca. 1627–1638), Rouen (ca. 1690), St. Cloud (ca. 1693), Chantilly (1730), and Vincennes (1740).[6] The first English attempts at porcelain appear to have been by John Dwight, commencing around 1671–1672; in North America, experimental firings were conducted by Andrew Duché in Savannah, Georgia, by May 1738.[7]

In his paper dealing with the career of Andrew Duché, Graham Hood suggests that this potter, who was born in Philadelphia around 1710, could have been a pivotal figure in the most important period of the development of English and American ceramics. However, after discussing Duché's career, Hood concludes that while Duché undoubtedly remains an important figure in the development of ceramics in America, his failure to improve his rudimentary porcelain appears to have discouraged him. There is no evidence that Duché ever had a significant connection with subsequent English or American porcelain factories, nor is there evidence that the American clay deposits were discovered primarily by Duché, or that such clay was ever used for other than experimental purposes.[8] Brad Rauschenberg expressed a comparable view when he stated that although Andrew Duché likely knew about the ingredients for porcelain and probably did discover kaolin in the New Windsor area, and perhaps in the southern Appalachians, he never produced porcelain wares himself.[9] Such conclusions were correctly and understandably predicated on the absence of any porcelain wasters or wares that could be reliably accredited to Duché.

A new development to this story emerged in 2001 with the publication of an article by W. Ross H. Ramsay, Anton Gabszewicz, and E. Gael Ramsay dealing with the ceramic patent taken out in England in 1744 by Edward Heylyn and Thomas Frye.[10] Heylyn and Frye are of particular interest to Americans because they were two of the proprietors responsible for the establishment of the Bow porcelain manufactory (New Canton) in Essex around 1749–1750. This concern gained wide recognition in its day, with many of its wares being exported to the New World. It is generally regarded as a prototype, both with respect to the recipe utilized and for much of the decoration used in America's first porcelain manufactory, Bonnin and Morris in Philadelphia, which operated from 1770 to at least 1772.

The article on Heylyn and Frye's 1744 ceramic patent identifies the type of clay referred to in the patent, locates its probable source (in the Little Tennessee River catchment, Macon County, North Carolina), and identifies the group of English porcelain wares most likely made by Heylyn and Frye using this Cherokee clay.[11] The authors proposed that such wares probably belong to the A-marked group of porcelains, to which the covered sugar bowl belongs. Moreover, the authors argued that there is now very strong circumstantial evidence linking this Cherokee clay, the Bow manufactory of Heylyn and Frye, and A-marked porcelain wares with the first-generation American-born potter Andrew Duché. They conclude their article by noting that,

> If Andrew Duché did supply the raw clay as we suggest, then to what degree did he contribute to the Heylyn and Frye 1744 patent? It is unlikely that Duché supplied the clay without contributing in some way to the recipe from which the "A"-mark porcelain was manufactured. The intriguing unanswered question arises as to whether the results of Duché's experimental porcelain efforts are to be found, not in Georgia, USA, but rather amongst the earliest recorded clay-rich porcelains of England.[12]

This paper reassesses these conclusions in light of new information, unavailable at the time to both Graham Hood and Brad Rauschenberg, and with regard to the polychrome porcelain covered sugar bowl in the collections of the MCC. In addition, the generally held view that the initial attempts at porcelain making in America were the result of both technological and artistic endowment from Europe—principally England—is revisited. On the basis of the chemical results obtained from the bowl, there are now reasonable grounds for arguing that the English porcelain tradition owes a great deal more to colonial American entrepreneurial enterprise, raw materials, and technology than has been recognized to date.

The Melbourne Cricket Club Museum came into existence in the Australian summer of 1968–1969 to house an outstanding gift by a young English stockbroker named Anthony Baer. His gift comprised over twelve hundred items pertaining to the game of cricket, including artwork, prints, books, manuscripts, bronzes, silverware, textiles, and porcelain. This gift introduced to Australia one of the most extensive, intriguing, and valuable collections of cricketana known, with items dating from the early seventeenth to the mid-twentieth century.

Anthony Baer began collecting cricket-related items in London during his school years, and by the early 1960s his collection had outgrown his London apartment. The extent of this collection reflects not only Baer's interest but also his rapport with London's art and antique dealers, who notified him of any items of significance that appeared on the market. In the early 1960s Anthony Baer visited the MCC to watch an English-Australian Test cricket match. Such was his regard for the hospitality extended to visitors at the ground and for the prowess of the Australian cricketers that within two years of the Test match he offered his collection as an immediate gift to the MCC.

In 1961 at the Antique Dealers Fair in London a partial tea set from the P. and K. Embden collection was put up for sale.[13] The pieces included a teapot, cream jug, sugar bowl with cover, and three saucers. Anthony Baer acquired all but two of the saucers. The sugar bowl went to the MCC, and the remainder went to the Victoria and Albert Museum.

The cover and bowl (fig. 1) trace their form back to Chinese examples.[14] The cover and bowl are each decorated with two vignettes surrounded by a rococo frame in distinct *rouge de fer*. In a detailed discussion on the source of the decoration, Charleston and Mallet were able to show that all four

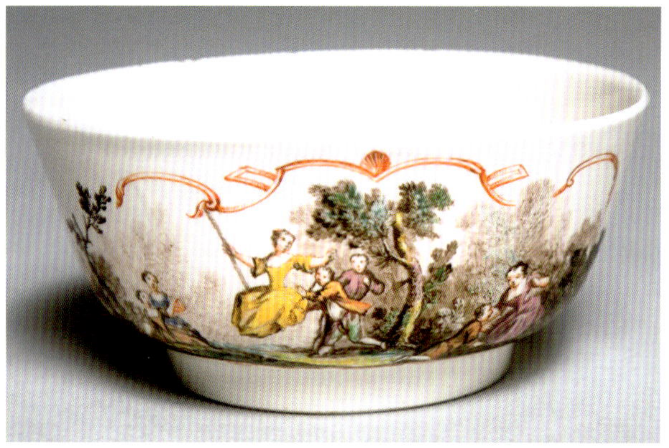

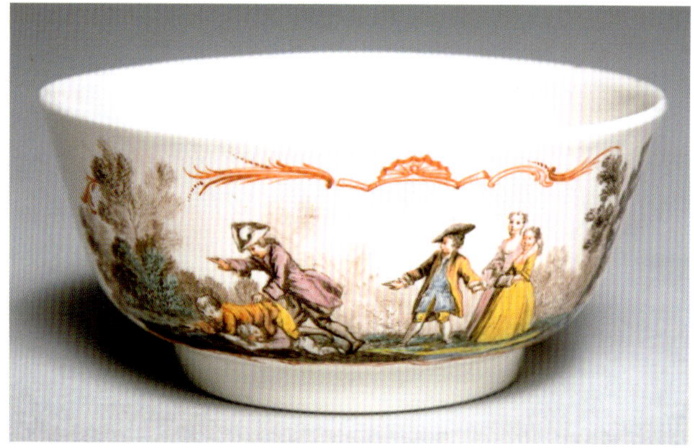

Figure 2 Side view of bowl illustrated in fig. 1. (Photo, Erin O'Brien.) The vignette *Swinging on the Rope,* located on one side of the covered bowl, is derived from a set of engravings by James Cole titled *The Second Part of Youthful Diversions,* 1739. The palette comprises an iron red, as seen in the scrolled cartouche. In addition there is blue-green, grass green, vibrant mid-blue, brown grading to dark brown, black, purple, and shades of bright yellow either thickly applied, as on the girl's skirt, or applied as a thin wash. Flesh pink is derived from mixing a buff color with very minor iron red. This range of colors is somewhat similar to the palette displayed on many early Bow phosphatic wares.

Figure 3 Side view of bowl illustrated in fig. 1. (Photo, Erin O'Brien.) This vignette, *Youth Sliding on the Ice,* is located on the reverse side of the bowl and is also derived from James Cole's *The Second Part of Youthful Diversions,* 1739.

scenes could be traced back to a series of engravings detailing children's pastimes that were printed and sold by James Cole. In the first set of engravings, inscribed, "The Second Part of Youthful Diverfions . . . Published According to Act of Parliament 7th May 1739 & Sold by J. Cole Engraver in Great Kirby Street, Hatton Garden," Charleston and Mallet were able to identify three of the scenes—two on the bowl (*Swinging on the Rope* [fig. 2] and *Youth Sliding on the Ice* [fig. 3]) and one on the cover (*Youth Playing at Cricket* [fig. 4]).[15]

The fourth scene, *Throwing at Cocks* (fig. 5), which appears on the cover of the bowl, shows a group of children with a cock tied by its leg. Charleston and Mallet have traced this scene to an engraving in another series of children's pursuits inscribed "Published According to an Act of Parliament of October 24th, 1740 by James Cole, engraver at ye Crown in Great Kirby Street Hatton Garden." Charleston and Mallet were able to trace these scenes to a further group of prints titled *Jeux,* part of a series called *Petits cahiers d'images pour les enfants,* now in the Bibliothèque Nationale, Paris. They deduced that the author was Hubert-François Bourguignon, called Gravelot (1699–1773), who was in London probably from 1732 or 1733 until 1745, when he returned to France. Gravelot, a former pupil of the history painter Jean Restout II and a student in the studio of François Boucher in 1732, was a highly talented engraver, painter, and designer. He is regarded as having had a significant influence on English illustration and is believed to have supplied various illustrations to English publishers.

The scene showing the cricket game (fig. 4) is found reversed in *Le Jeu de la Crosse,* an engraving signed "Gravelot inv." and "Bachelet sculps." Charleston and Mallet suggest that *Le Jeu de la Crosse* was created in England about 1739 (presumably by Gravelot while he was associated with the St. Martin's Lane Academy) and then reproduced in the reverse after his return to France. In view of the deduced association between Gravelot's drawings and the decoration on the covered bowl, it might appear that there was indeed some verisimilitude in the prophetic comments by the engraver George Vertue that Gravelot would "furnish this Nation with many things . . . of a much better taste."[16] The shop of the engraver John Boydell, whose sign was that of a cricket bat, was apparently located near the academy, in Duke's Court, St. Martin's Lane.[17]

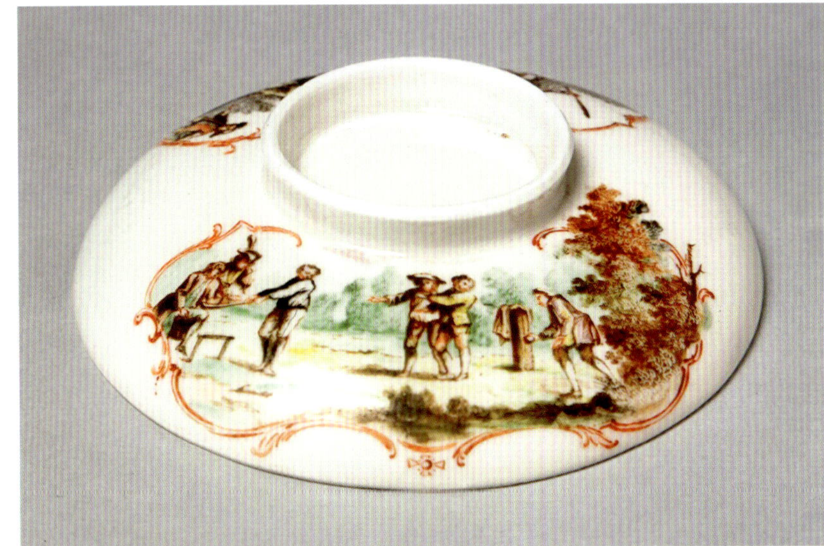

Figure 4 Cover of bowl illustrated in fig. 1. (Photo, Erin O'Brien.) Diam. 4⅞". This scene, inscribed "*YOUTH PLAYING AT CRICKET*," is derived from James Cole's *The Second Part of Youthful Diversions*, 1739, and proved to be one of the main factors that led Charleston and Mallet in 1971 to propose a British rather than Continental origin for the A-marked group of porcelains.

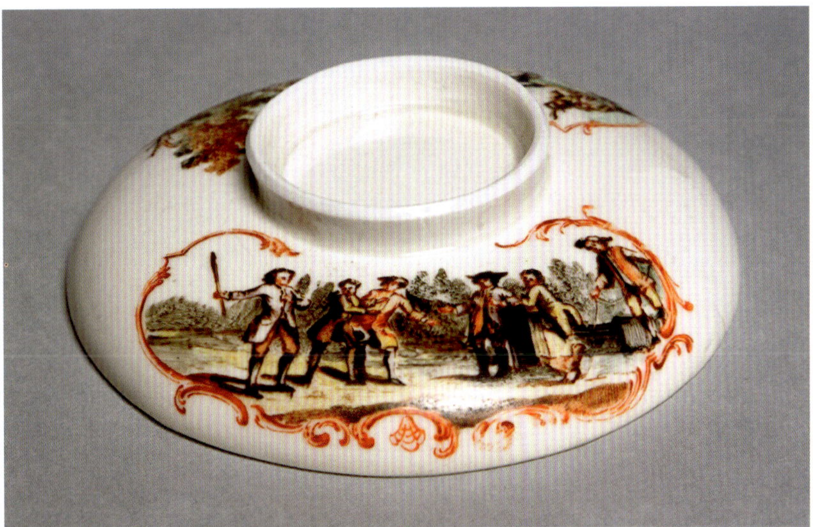

Figure 5 Cover of bowl illustrated in fig. 1. (Photo, Erin O'Brien.) View of the vignette *Throwing at Cocks* derived from *Youthful Amusements*, published by James Cole, 1740.

The identity of the artist who painted the on-glaze enamel scenes on the bowl and cover has been the subject of debate. Bouwman speculates that the scenes could be the work of Francis Hayman, who knew Gravelot and was himself a lover of cricket and a member of the St. Martin's Lane Academy.[18] Moreover, he is generally regarded as a pioneer of the application of the French rococo art style into the English idiom. Errol Manners comments:

> Whilst I cannot point out a stylistic link, it is apparent that the quality of painting is so unusually high and ambitious for English porcelain that it was clearly done by no ordinary china decorator, but by an accomplished artist. Frye being versatile enough to work as an oil painter, a miniaturist, and a mezzotint artist would have found it difficult to resist applying his talents to such a novel and exciting medium. Furthermore he was the only one of the partners who was an artist and both his daughters became painters at Bow and both married china painters. It is interesting to read the entry on the Melbourne Cricket Club "A"-marked bowl in the catalogue "Glorious Innings, Treasures from the Melbourne Cricket Club," by Richard Bouwman, p. 13, where they discuss that the style of painting

> is typical of an oil painter and they suggest Francis Hayman as the possible artist because he knew Gravelot, from whose print the design [on the bowl] was taken. However Bow also used Gravelot prints and as Frye would have mixed in the same circle, that argument could equally have applied to Frye. This line of argument finds some modest support in Frye's epitaph published in the *Gentleman's Magazine,* 1764, where it states of Frye that, "He spent fifteen years among the furnaces till his health was nearly destroyed," so we know that he was a "hands on" manager.[19]

Both the cover and bowl have a warm, creamy, gray-white color with a thin, tight-fitting, clear glaze that shows minimal evidence of running or pooling. The glaze has a very fine, "orange skin" texture. Present are blemishes and pits evidenced by fine black to brownish spots. These blemishes most likely relate to remnant biotite or breakdown products, such as hydromica and chlorite, derived from precursor garnet as recorded in *unaker,* or china clay from Macon County, North Carolina.[20]

Underglaze tears are present in the body, especially on the lid. Judging by the light postglaze grinding of the footrim and the outer margin of the lid, the bowl and lid were fired upright. Both the footrim and the inverted footrim have been lightly faceted or ground; the latter, however, was ground prior to the application of the glaze. The palette comprises an iron red, brown grading into black, purple, blue-green, blue, and yellow. Admixtures of these colors have yielded additional hues, including flesh pink, pinkish orange, turquoise green, and varying shades of yellow resulting from a thickly applied to a thin yellow wash. This latter color, along with the green, appears to have been among those applied last. The blue appears to have taken well where applied directly on the glaze, but has bubbled and blistered where painted over the brown. The background foliage in brown, brownish black, and green, or russet brown and green, is delicately painted with texture that was applied through subsequent fine scratching of the enamel in hook-shaped or wavy patterns. A remarkable ghosting technique on some of the background foliage has given a good sense of depth. In *Swinging on the Rope* (see fig. 2) a light green wash was applied over a portion of the sgraffitoed tree foliage. Translucency is a grayish white; contraction of the body during firing resulted in a poorly fitting lid. The base of the bowl contains the letter A, which was quickly drawn using three brush strokes in underglaze blue. This letter, which gives the group its name, shows little resemblance to the "Argyll A."[21]

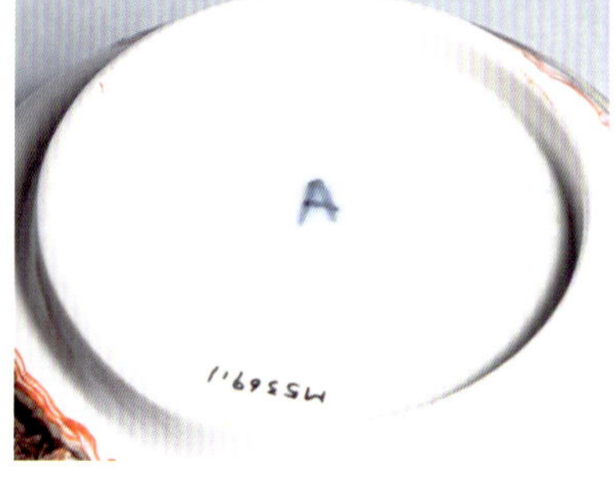

Figure 6 Base of the bowl illustrated in fig. 1. (Photo, Erin O'Brien.) View of the "A mark," which was painted in underglaze blue. It is the occurrence of this letter, either painted or incised, that characterizes the A-marked group. One line of thought has suggested that the A stands for the third duke of Argyll, who was a known patron of the arts at this time and had close links with the Bow manufactory. A more recent, alternative view is that the A commemorates Alderman George Arnold, who is generally regarded as being the financial supporter of the Bow manufactory during its infant years and, by inference, its supporter during the phase of manufacture of these porcelains.

The factory source has been ascribed to continental Europe by Lane; to Vauxhall or Gorgie out of Edinburgh by Charleston and Mallet; to Kentish Town, Stourbridge, or Gorgie by Mallet; and to Scotland, Chelsea, or Italy by John and Margaret Cushion.[22] Ian Freestone, while noting the strong correspondence between determined A-marked compositions and the recipe contained in the 1744 Heylyn and Frye ceramic patent, appears to have favored a Pomona or Limehouse attribution.[23] Subsequently he noted that the relationship between A-marked wares and other products of the mid-eighteenth century remains unclear, although he recognized the distinct possibility that the A-marked porcelain utilized an imported North American clay as specified by Heylyn and Frye's 1744 patent.[24] More

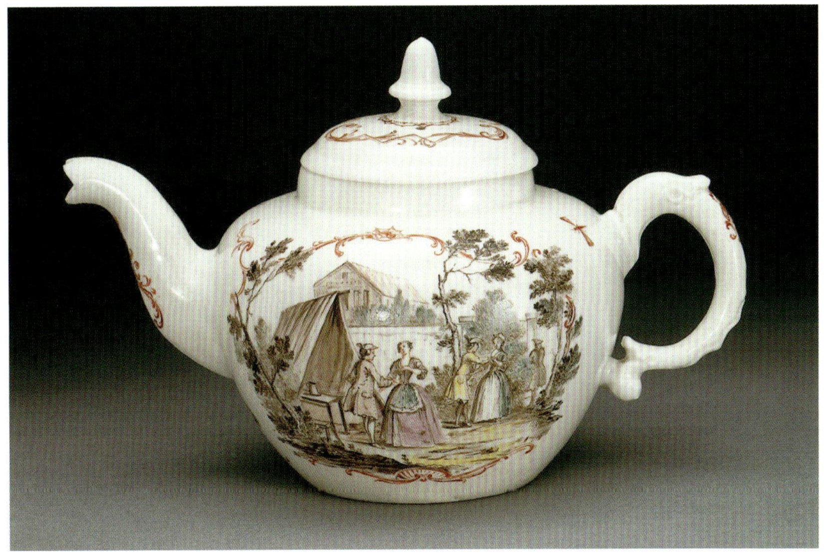

Figure 7 Teapot and cover, East London, England, ca. 1744. Porcelain, decorated in enamels and marked with an underglaze "A" in blue. H. 4½". (Courtesy, V&A Picture Library.) The scene shown on the teapot is taken from an engraving by George Bickham Jr. after Gravelot. This was based on the operetta *Flora* by John Hippisley, first produced on April 17, 1729.

recently, Ramsay, Gabszewicz, and Ramsay suggested that this group of porcelains in fact represents the "long lost" representatives of the patent.[25]

Chemical Analysis of Body and Glaze

A small amount of the clear, thin, tight-fitting glaze and the underlying porcelain body were lightly abraded from the inside of the basal footrim of the MCC bowl using a portable high-speed dental drill with drill bits tipped with diamonds set in a stainless steel matrix. Approximately 0.4 mg of ceramic powder and 0.2 mg of glaze were collected, mounted in epoxy resin, polished, and subjected to quantitative chemical analysis using a scanning electron microscope (SEM) with an energy dispersive attachment. Operating conditions are given in the Appendix. The chemical compositions so obtained for both body and glaze are presented in Table 1.

Table 1 presents two analyses of the covered bowl, one for the body and the other for the glaze. The analysis from the porcelain body compares with a previous analysis taken from the flange of the lid from a teapot in the Victoria and Albert Museum (V&A) that also belongs to the so-called high-style group.[26] Previous analyses of A-marked wares, both published and in preparation, have shown considerable variation in the glass-to-clay ratio and in the composition of the glass used. In this example, however, there is close chemical agreement with the V&A teapot.[27] Both examples demonstrate virtually identical SiO_2-to-Al_2O_3 ratios. Likewise there is reasonable agreement with regard to CaO, with the covered bowl having slightly higher amounts (7.3 wt %) than the teapot (5.9 wt %). K_2O and MgO are both lower in the covered bowl, indicating some variability in the glass composition used. The similarity in chemical composition (and, hence, recipe) between the MCC covered bowl and the V&A teapot suggests that the paste composition had become more or less standardized in the production of these two representatives of the high style. This more uniform recipe with a closely comparable $SiO_2 : Al_2O_3$ ratio ~ 2.2, together with the remarkable enameling, suggests that these examples were made

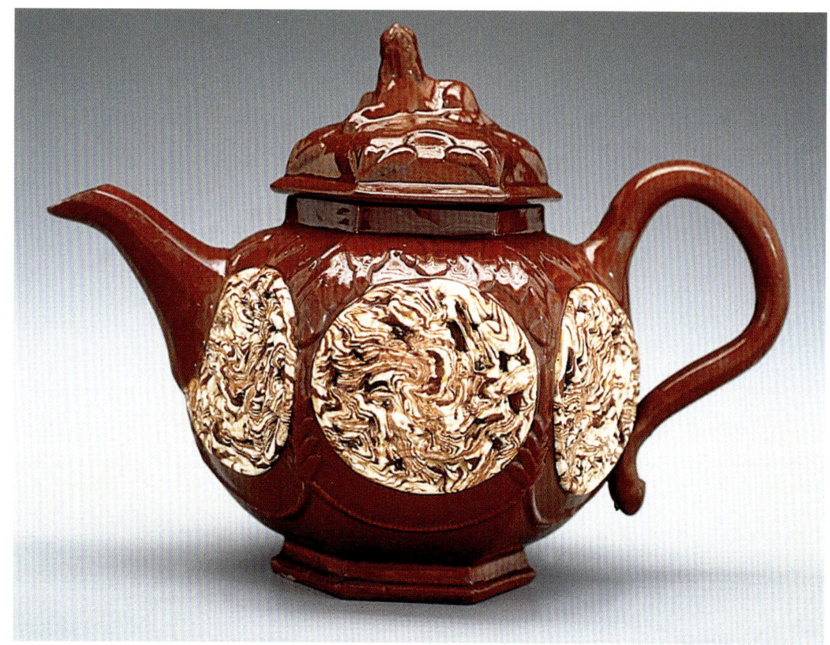

Figure 8 Hexagonal teapot, Staffordshire, ca. 1730–1745. Lead-glazed redware with agate panels. H. 3⅞". (Chipstone Foundation; photo, Gavin Ashworth.) This slip-cast hexagonal teapot exhibits applied press-molded agate panels of the Chinese-boy-in-a-tree design. A lion finial tops the lid. Examples such as this teapot suggest possible links between some A-marked forms (see fig. 12) and potters derived from Staffordshire.

using a higher proportion of scarce, imported clay, and probably were made toward the end of the A-marked porcelain output period, possibly dating from the mid- to latter half of 1744.

The chemical composition of the porcelain bowl strongly suggests that it is composed of a mixture of residual or primary kaolinite clay (as judged by the very low FeO and below-detection-level amounts of TiO_2) and a calciferous alkali-glass. Such low levels of these elements are a feature of primary kaolinite or china clays, such as those found in the Franklin-Sylva district of North Carolina.[28] J. Victor Owen has noted that low to nonexistent levels of these two elements either indicates the presence of a well-washed and screened secondary clay or suggests that the clay used in the paste was initially relatively free of these impurities, as would be expected in a primary kaolinite clay.[29] One of the most common sources of ball clay for mid-eighteenth-century London and Staffordshire potters was the mid-Eocene Broadstone Sequence in the Wareham Basin, Dorset. Average analyses of this clay unit demonstrate TiO_2 levels of 1.30 wt % and Fe_2O_3 of 1.30 wt %.[30] Judging by analyses of wares from other contemporaneous factories, there is no evidence that proprietors in England at that time had the ability to wash completely and remove these colorant oxides from the secondary clays used.[31] Consequently the clay used in the MCC sugar bowl—and in all other A-marked items analyzed to date—must have been a primary, residual kaolinite clay.[32] Mineralogical analysis of this clay from the most likely source mine (Iotla mine) in the Little Tennessee River catchment north of Franklin in Macon County, North Carolina, demonstrates that the clay comprises 90 percent halloysite and 10 percent kaolinite. This use of a primary residual kaolinite clay contrasts with most mid-eighteenth-century English porcelains, which comprise variable amounts of ball or pipe clay with distinctly higher levels of titanium and iron. The notable exception to this are the hard paste porcelains made by Richard Champion

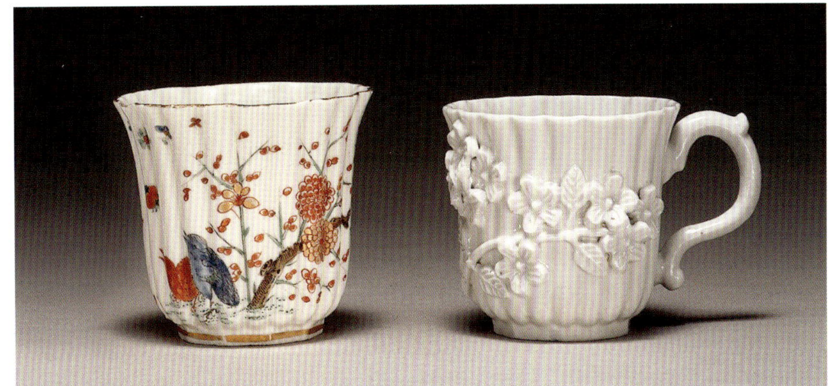

Figure 9 Fluted cups, East London, England, ca. 1744. Porcelain. H. 2⅝" and 2⅜". (Courtesy, Seattle Art Museum, Dorthy Condon Falknor Collection of European Ceramics; photo, Susan Dirk.) The cup on the left is marked with an incised "A" and enameled in the Japanese Kakiemon-style quail pattern, which was used by Meissen, Bow, and, less commonly, by several other early English factories. The form of this slip-cast cup, with its twenty flutes originating from a decagonal low footrim, is a feature of A-marked cups. The white fluted cup on the right, with a somewhat primitive use of applied prunus blossom, leaf, and twig decoration, is one of two examples found occurring in the white and is inspired by a Chinese *blanc de chine* example. A feature characteristic of but not exclusive to early Bow phosphatic wares is the use of applied prunus blossom. Note the S-shaped handle originating after European silver-derived forms.

and William Cookworthy (Plymouth and Bristol) dating from the mid- to late 1760s onward.

The calculated recipe used for the MCC sugar bowl is given in Table 2; the clay:glass ratio is approximately 60 percent clay (hydrous) to 40 percent glass. These features—the high clay content, the deduced use of a primary kaolinite clay, the use of a lead-free alkali-lime glass frit, the typical absence of remnant ground-quartz or flint particles, and the composition of the glaze containing a clay component and lacking PbO—confirm that the bowl belongs to the A-marked group of porcelains, as initially proposed by Charleston and Mallet.[33] Moreover, the body and glaze compositions closely reflect the chemical compositions as reconstructed from the 1744 patent.[34]

The high aluminum content in the body of the MCC bowl (27.7 wt % Al_2O_3) indicates that the recipe used was a high-clay-content recipe, a feature reflected in the products from three factories operating at that time—namely Pomona or Newcastle-under-Lyme, Limehouse, and the maker of the A-marked wares.[35] Ian Freestone and Ramsay et al. have discussed the key chemical features that distinguish A-marked porcelains from Pomona and Limehouse wares.[36]

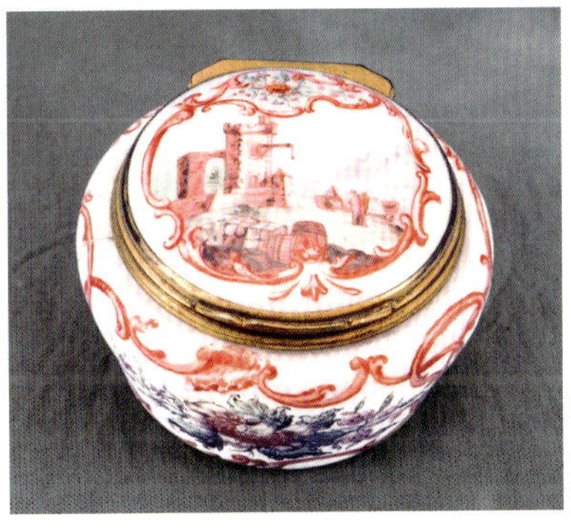

Figure 10 Snuff box, East London, England, ca. 1744. Porcelain. Diam. 2$\frac{5}{16}$". (© National Museums and Galleries of Wales, De Winton Collection of Continental Porcelain, acc. no. D.W. 552.) Enameled with an incised "A" or "V." A scene set within a scrolled cartouche is depicted on the lid. The body is decorated with various flowers and leaves associated with intertwined scrolls.

The glaze analysis indicates a composition more siliceous and less clay-rich than the body, comparable to other glaze compositions obtained from A-marked wares in that it is lead-free and highly calciferous with a distinct clay component, as deduced from the Al_2O_3 levels in the glaze. This glaze composition appears to be unique for mid-eighteenth-century English porcelains and conforms to the expected composition, as deduced from the glaze recipe contained in the 1744 patent.[37]

From the above it is reasonable to conclude that the kaolinite clay used in both the body and glaze was most likely derived from North America as specified in the 1744 patent. The source was possibly the Iotla mine or the Guerny mine, some five miles north of Franklin.[38] Other potential sources of such primary kaolinite clay include Cornwall, the Bohemian Massif, and China. There is no apparent evidence of Chinese or Eastern European primary kaolinite clay being imported into England at this time. Although William Cookworthy might have been aware of the kaolinite deposits at Tregonning Hill in Cornwall by about 1745–1746, there is no indication that porcelains were being made using Cornish kaolinite until the mid- to late 1760s, when Cookworthy took out a patent (1768).[39]

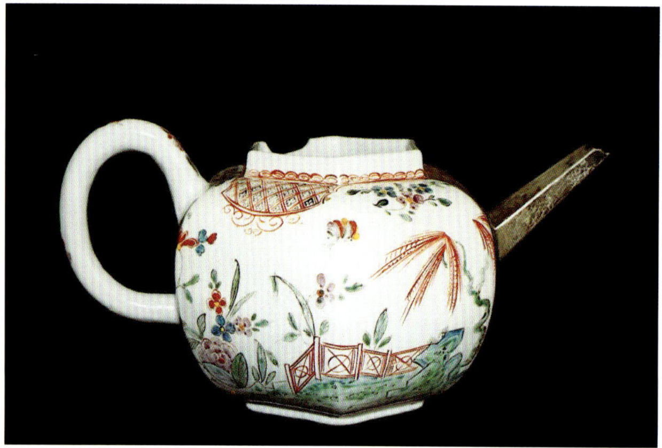

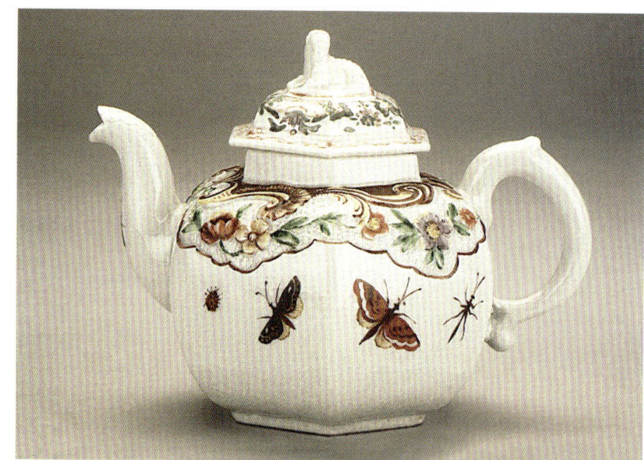

Figure 11 Hexagonal teapot, East London, England, ca. 1744. Porcelain. H. 3⅛". (Private collection.) Enameled in the Kakiemon style with an incised "A," this teapot has a replacement silver spout. The palette shows many similarities to the covered bowl and comprises iron red, bluish green, vibrant mid-blue, bright yellow, and mauve. Note that much of the design was initially outlined in thin black and subsequently filled in.

Figure 12 Hexagonal teapot and cover, East London, England, ca. 1743. Porcelain. H. 4$\frac{1}{16}$". (Courtesy, © Copyright British Museum.) Both the base of the pot and the inside of the cover are marked with "A" in underglaze blue; the pot is enameled with molded shoulder decoration. The form of this teapot, together with its lion finial, suggest derivation from an unglazed stoneware or a salt-glazed prototype, possibly from Staffordshire or even South London.

Conclusions

A series of landmark papers and an authoritative book on the Bow factory and its products have significantly influenced our current understanding of the Bow porcelain manufactory and the proprietors who managed and financed the concern.[40] In his 1963 paper Hugh Tait made the following points:

- Andrew Duché found clay "somewhere in the remote hinterland in the territory of the Chirokee Indians";
- this clay was the essential ingredient for making porcelain;
- Duché made porcelain using that clay;
- Duché brought both clay and porcelain to London;
- the granting of the Heylyn-Frye patent coincided with Duché's arrival in London;
- Duché returned to America to dig clay; and
- Frye was a painter who was attracted to porcelain making.

Tait concluded that the two driving forces behind the Bow manufactory were Thomas Frye and George Arnold: Frye was the genius who discovered the secret to making porcelain, and Arnold was the businessman whose financial backing and faith in Frye made this pioneering venture possible. Tait also stated that the Bow manufactory was far more British, far more free from foreign influences and dominance, than either Chelsea or Derby.[41] These views were based largely on the fact that the 1744 patent was applied for by, and granted to, Heylyn and Frye, as well as on the wording in Frye's epitaph, published in *Gentleman's Magazine* in 1764, which stated that Thomas Frye was the inventor and first manufacturer of porcelain in England.[42]

The weakness in this series of proposals is that while Frye was actively involved in painting and mezzotint engravings on one side of the Atlantic Ocean during the late 1730s and early 1740s, on the other side of the Atlantic, Duché was experimenting with the secrets of making porcelain. In fact, there is reasonable evidence that he was experimenting with *unaker* clay, the very clay deduced to have been used in the manufacture of A-marked porcelains by May 1741.[43] Frye in effect attested to this himself, when in his 1744 patent he listed his profession not as "ceramic experimentalist" or "potter" but as "painter." Tait acknowledged this weakness by admitting that it was not known why Frye was attracted to porcelain making.[44] Frank Hurlbutt also commented on this problem, suggesting, "It may have been due to his helping Brooks [an Irish colleague] in his experiments in printing on enamel and porcelain that Thomas Frye was first led to experiment with bodies and glazes for making porcelain itself."[45]

Based on a study of the MCC's A-marked covered bowl, our conclusion is that the bowl is made of a mixture of kaolinite clay and lime alkali-glass in the general proportions of 60 percent clay (hydrous) to 40 percent glass by weight, a recipe unique to A-marked porcelains, and conforms to the reconstructed 1744 patent of Heylyn and Frye.[46]

We suggest that the most reasonable deduction is that the kaolinite group clay utilized was sourced from the Cherokee Nation, as stated in the 1744 patent. Moreover, we support previous suggestions that the most likely supplier of this remarkably white clay mixture was Andrew Duché himself. We cannot accept the long-held notion that Duché supplied this clay to the Bow proprietors, provided examples of his experimental porcellaneous wares, and then passively returned to America to continue digging clay, thus allowing Thomas Frye to discover the secret of porcelain making.

While not in any way diminishing Thomas Frye's qualities of skill, energy, and imagination in developing the large-scale success of the Bow manufactory, we suggest that for too long several aspects have been ignored or overlooked: the vital contribution from colonial America in the form of the raw clay; the recognition of its ceramic potential; the entrepreneurial enterprise associated with the transportation of that clay to London; and almost certainly a significant component of the associated technology required to make porcelain. While we accept that Duché would have been influenced by Chinese and early European porcelain examples obtained through imports and supplied to him by the Countess of Egmont, his recognition of the ceramic potential of Cherokee clay, his initial transportation of samples of that clay (most likely down the Savannah River), and his experimental firings in Savannah were done largely in isolation.

We suggest that Andrew Duché acted as a vital catalyst in attracting Arnold and Heylyn to develop what we now believe to be England's earliest quality porcelains, the A-marked wares.[47] We contend that Alderman George Arnold's faith in apparently investing financially in this early venture was based not so much on Frye's undoubted ability to paint but rather on Andrew Duché's entrepreneurial ability, his stunning white clay, his porcellaneous samples (which we accept he brought to England with him), and his knowledge of firing porcellaneous wares gained during his time in Savannah. We accept that the potting of the MCC bowl and the remarkable enameling on it were almost certainly of English derivation.

Likewise, the general impression one gains from the current literature is that early porcelain production in America is viewed as largely the result of an Asiatic-European endowment in the form of technology and artistic conception.[48] Hood and Adams and Redstone have commented on the influence of the European tradition and the Bow factory on initial porcelain manufacture in the American colonies.[49] Possibly the best summary of current thinking has been expressed by Terrence Lockett:

> The principal reason for such an extensive trade was the lack of any indigenous American fine earthenware (or porcelain) industry before the Revolution. There were potters in America, but on the whole with the exceptions of Bartlem in South Carolina and Bonnin and Morris in Philadelphia, only relatively coarse wares for local consumption were produced.[50]

In one sense we agree with Lockett in that Duché chose to develop and promote his white *unaker* clay and his technology in London, not in America. Yet some twenty-five years prior to the establishment of Bonnin and Morris (American China Factory), we would suggest that it was the Bow manufactory in East London and its proprietors who were indebted to the raw materials, to the considerable enterprise, and possibly to some technology transfer from America. It was this ceramic tradition, developed initially in Philadelphia by potters such as Anthony Duché and then in Savannah, Georgia, by his son, that was to play such an important role in the initial porcelain production of the Heylyn and Frye manufactory. These A-marked wares, most likely containing Cherokee clay, appear to be the earliest quality porcelains to have been made in Britain, dating from at least 1743, according to current evidence. This ceramic concern subsequently grew into the specially built manufactory (New Canton), which in turn greatly influenced Bonnin and Morris in Philadelphia a quarter of a century later. While ceramic historians have emphasized the influence that Bow and the European tradition had on Bonnin and Morris, little attention has been afforded the "Philadelphia ceramic tradition" and its prior influence on English porcelains.

In summary we note, with regard to Graham Hood's article on the career of Andrew Duché,[51] that Andrew Duché is in fact a pivotal figure in English and American ceramics, and that the contribution by colonial America to the fledgling English porcelain and subsequent bone china industry needs to be reevaluated. We suggest that Duché did make experimental wares of a porcellaneous nature in Savannah of sufficient quality that, together with his remarkably white clay, attracted the attention of Arnold and Heylyn. The identification of A-marked porcelains—with their assumed content of Cherokee clay or *unaker*—as the likely "long-lost" representatives of the 1744 Heylyn and Frye patent now constitutes very good circumstantial evidence that Andrew Duché had a significant if not seminal connection with both the Bow manufactory and its proprietors. While the initial European discovery of the Cherokee clay deposits was probably by metalliferous prospectors en route through the Iotla Valley and over the Nantahala Ranges to the Nantahala Valley in western North Carolina, it was Duché who recognized the ceramic potential of these residual clays and it was he who was actively experimenting with this clay by mid-1741. There is now very reasonable evidence that this clay, "the produce of the Chirokee nation," was being used in the limited commercial—

not experimental—production of highly sophisticated porcelains in East London by at least 1743 or 1744. Such developments owed a great deal to American enterprise, which to date has been largely overlooked.[52]

Future lines of research include the identification of the initial kiln site, assumed to have been located in East London, and the possible recovery of A-marked wasters. An important question yet to be addressed is whether Andrew Duché made contact with Arnold and Heylyn prior to embarkation for London in 1743 or whether, on hearing rumors of Duché's experimental porcelain firings in Savannah, they sought him out first. We note that the genius—if that is the correct word—required to discover the secret to making porcelain might lie more with Andrew Duché than with Thomas Frye. If wasters of A-marked porcelain are ever uncovered on which multi-element chemical analysis can be conducted, thus allowing conclusive sourcing of the primary clay used in the porcelain body to North Carolina, then we suggest that there would be a basis for proposing that Andrew Duché, a first-generation Philadelphian, be recognized as one of the founding fathers of the English and American porcelain industry.

ACKNOWLEDGMENTS Funding for travel to North Carolina to collect samples was made to the senior author by the Research Office, Deakin University, and by Professor N. W. Archbold from research funding to the interim Priority Research Area, Global Change, Deakin University. Both contributions were invaluable and we offer our sincere thanks. Jo Ann and Frank Meeks of "The Centre," Rose Creek, North Carolina, and Gloria Durfey contributed greatly to the visit to North Carolina by providing accommodation, information, and trips to see the local geology. Robert Douglas, Monash University, provided expert polished specimen preparation, Steve Swenser undertook the SEM analyses, and Erin O'Brien kindly carried out the photography. John Mallet, Anton Gabszewicz, and Barry Taylor provided helpful comments and advice and were always willing to share their knowledge and collections. Special acknowledgment is made of Gillian Brewster, manager, Museums Department, Melbourne Cricket Club, who gave permission to sample and photograph the covered bowl. Three internal reviewers, Maurice Hillis, Errol Manners, and an anonymous reviewer, kindly commented on a draft version of the manuscript and offered valuable advice.

Interested readers may contact the authors through Gael Ramsay at <gaelramsay@ballarat.vic.gov.au>.

This paper is dedicated to David C. D. Cooke, formerly of 99 Shortland Street, who first kindled an interest in antiques in the senior author.

Appendix

Samples of abraded ceramic powder and glaze were mounted in PVC, polished, and subjected to chemical analysis using a JEOL 840A scanning electron microscope (SEM) equipped with an Oxford Instruments ATW X-Ray Energy Dispersive Spectrometer (XEDS). Each sample was coated with a film of amorphous carbon (<3nm) to prevent charge buildup. Each spectrum was counted for 120 seconds with the microscope at high-tension at 40 kV, the probe current set at 6nA, and a nominal working distance of 39nm. Internal standards were employed and accuracy was ± 5 percent. For areal analyses, spectra were acquired while the beam was set to raster slowly over square areas 2.3 x 2.3 mm. Glaze analyses were by spot analysis. Results were expressed as oxide percents with O by difference.

TABLE 1: *Chemical Analysis (wt %) for Body and Glaze Composition*

	Body of MCC bowl	V&A teapot	Glaze composition of MCC bowl	Calculated glass frit composition (MCC bowl body)
SiO_2	59.7	59.5	74.4	68.3
TiO_2	bdl	na	bdl	
Al_2O_3	27.7	26.4	8.3	
P_2O_5	bdl	na	bdl	
FeO	0.1	na	0.4	
MgO	0.3	1.2	1.5	0.8
CaO	7.3	5.8	10.7	18.5
Na_2O	3.7	3.8	2.2	9.4
K_2O	1.2	2.8	2.5	3.0
PbO	bdl	na	bdl	
Total	100.0	99.5	100.0	100.0

bdl = below detection level
na = not analyzed

TABLE 2: *Theoretical Paste Recipe Used in Producing the MCC Bowl**

	weight % (hydrous)
Kaolinite (*unaker* clay)	59.0
Soda ash	5.3
Potash	1.5
Limestone	10.3
Dolomite**	1.2
Quartz / flint***	22.7

* Method calculates volatiles (CO_2 and H_2O) and recasts to 100 percent; after J. Victor Owen, "Antique Porcelain 101: A Primer on the Chemical Analysis and Interpretation of Eighteenth-Century British Wares," *Ceramics in America,* edited by Rob Hunter (Hanover, N.H.: University Press of New England for the Chipstone Foundation, 2002): 39–61.

** Although dolomite is suggested as the source of MgO, various vegetable ashes of the day could have been the source for magnesium.
*** This quartz and/or flint would have been incorporated in the glass frit used and would not have been a separate phase.

1. On October 9, 2002, an unrecorded fluted cup—closely comparable to figure 1 in W.R.H. Ramsay, Anton Gabszewicz, and E. G. Ramsay, "The Chemistry of 'A'-Marked Porcelain and Its Relation to the Heylyn and Frye Patent of 1744," *Transactions of the English Ceramic Circle* 18, pt. 2 (2003): 264–83—but more densely enameled and with a brown painted rim, was auctioned by Dreweatt Neate, Newbury, lot 376. See also J.V.G. Mallet, "The 'A' Marked Porcelains Revisited," *English Ceramic Circle Transactions* 15 (1994): 240–57.

2. Arthur Lane, "Unidentified Italian or English Porcelains: The A Marked Group," *Mitteilungsblatt* (Keramik-Freunde der Schweiz), no. 43 (1958): 25.

3. Lane, "Unidentified Italian or English Porcelains," pp. 15–18; Robert J. Charleston and J.V.G. Mallet, "A Problematical Group of Eighteenth-Century Porcelains," *English Ceramic Circle Transactions* 8, pt. 1 (1971): 80–121; Mallet, "'A' Marked Porcelains Revisited," pp. 240–57.

4. Lane, "Unidentified Italian or English Porcelains"; Charleston and Mallet, "Problematical Group of Eighteenth-Century Porcelains"; Mallet, "'A' Marked Porcelains Revisited."

5. Hilary Young, *English Porcelain 1745–95: Its Makers, Design, Marketing and Consumption,* Victoria and Albert Museum Studies in the History of Art and Design (London: Victoria and Albert Museum, 1999), p. 229.

6. Maurice Hillis, "An Introduction to Ceramic Raw Materials, Bodies and Glazes," *Journal of the Northern Ceramic Society* 18 (2001): 77–111.

7. B. L. Rauschenberg, "Andrew Duché: A Potter 'A Little Too Much Addicted to Politicks,'" *Journal of Early Southern Decorative Arts* 7, no. 1 (1991): 1–101.

8. Graham Hood, "The Career of Andrew Duché," *Art Quarterly* 31 (1968): 168–84.

9. Rauschenberg, "Andrew Duché."

10. W.R.H. Ramsay, Anton Gabszewicz, and E. G. Ramsay, "'Unaker' or Cherokee Clay and Its Relationship to the 'Bow' Porcelain Manufactory," *English Ceramic Circle Transactions* 17, pt. 3 (2001): 473–99.

11. Ibid.

12. Ibid., p. 492.

13. Richard Bouwman, *Glorious Innings: Treasures from the Melbourne Cricket Club Collection* (Melbourne: Hutchinson Australia, 1987), p. 131.

14. For example, see the Ch'ien Lung famille rose bowl and cover from The Metropolitan Museum of Art illustrated in Warren E. Cox, *The Book of Pottery and Porcelain* (New York: Crown Publishers, 1970), 2: 1158, and a Ch'ing dynasty bowl and cover illustrated in W.B.R. Neave-Hill, *Chinese Ceramics* (Edinburgh and London: John Bartholomew and Sons, 1975), p. 176.

15. Charleston and Mallet, "Problematical Group of Eighteenth-Century Porcelains," pp. 80–121.

16. Quoted in William Vaughan, *Gainsborough* (London: Thames and Hudson, 2002), p. 224.

17. Robin Simon and Alistar Smart, *The Art of Cricket* (London: Secker and Warburg, 1983).

18. Bouwman, *Glorious Innings,* p. 131.

19. Errol Manners, personal communication, May 2002.

20. W. S. Bayley, "The Kaolins of North Carolina," *North Carolina Geological and Economic Survey, Bulletin* 29 (1925): 132.

21. Nancy Valpy, "'A'-Marked Porcelain: 'A' for Argyll?," *English Ceramic Circle Transactions* 13, pt. 1 (1987): 96–107.

22. John P. Cushion and Margaret Cushion, *A Collector's History of British Porcelain* (Woodbridge, Suffolk, Eng.: Antique Collectors' Club, 1992), p. 448.

23. Ian C. Freestone, "A-Marked Porcelain: Some Recent Scientific Work," *English Ceramic Circle Transactions* 16, pt. 1 (1996): 76–84.

24. Ian C. Freestone, "The Science of Early English Porcelain," in *The Sixth Conference and Exhibition of the European Ceramic Society, 20–24 June 1999, Brighton Conference Centre, UK: Abstracts; British Ceramic Proceedings,* no. 60 (London: IOM Communications, 1999), 1: 11–17;

Ian C. Freestone, "The Mineralogy and Chemistry of Early British Porcelain," *Mineralogical Society Bulletin* (July 1999): 3–7.

25. Ramsay, Gabszewicz, and Ramsay, "'Unaker' or Cherokee Clay"; Ramsay, Gabszewicz, and Ramsay, "Chemistry of 'A'-Marked Porcelain."

26. Mavis Bimson and Michael J. Hughes in Charleston and Mallet, "Problematical Group of Eighteenth-Century Porcelains," pp. 80–121. The teapot and cover (V&A C.207 and A-1937) are illustrated in ibid., pl. 65b.

27. Bimson and Hughes in Charleston and Mallet, "Problematical Group of Eighteenth-Century Porcelains"; Freestone, "A-Marked Porcelain"; Ramsay, Gabszewicz, and Ramsay, "Chemistry of 'A'-Marked Porcelain."

28. Freestone, "A-Marked Porcelain"; Ramsay, Gabszewicz, and Ramsay, "'Unaker' or Cherokee Clay."

29. J. Victor Owen, "Geochemical and Mineralogical Distinctions between Bonnin and Morris (Philadelphia, 1770–1772) Porcelain and Some Contemporary British Phosphatic Wares," *Geoarchaeology* 16, no. 7 (2001): 785–802.

30. Andrew Deeming, personal communication, January 2003.

31. Ramsay, Gabszewicz, and Ramsay, "Chemistry of 'A'-Marked Porcelain"; Freestone, "A-Marked Porcelain."

32. Freestone, "A-Marked Porcelain"; Ramsay, Gabszewicz, and Ramsay, "Chemistry of 'A'-Marked Porcelain"; W.R.H. Ramsay, G. Hill, and E. G. Ramsay, "Re-creation of the 1744 Heylyn and Frye Ceramic Patent Wares Using Cherokee Clay: Implications for Raw Materials, Kiln Conditions, and the Earliest English Porcelain Production," *Geoarchaeology*, in press.

33. Ramsay, Gabszewicz, and Ramsay, "Chemistry of 'A'-Marked Porcelain"; Charleston and Mallet, "Problematical Group of Eighteenth-Century Porcelains."

34. Ramsay, Gabszewicz, and Ramsay, "'Unaker' or Cherokee Clay"; Ramsay, Gabszewicz, and Ramsay, "Chemistry of 'A'-Marked Porcelain."

35. Freestone, "Science of Early English Porcelain," and Freestone, "Mineralogy and Chemistry of Early British Porcelain."

36. Freestone, "A-Marked Porcelain"; Ramsay, Gabszewicz, and Ramsay, "Chemistry of 'A'-Marked Porcelain."

37. Ramsay, Gabszewicz, and Ramsay, "Chemistry of 'A'-Marked Porcelain."

38. Ramsay, Gabszewicz, and Ramsay, "'Unaker' or Cherokee Clay."

39. Bernard Watney, *English Blue and White Porcelain of the 18th Century* (London: Faber and Faber, 1973), p. 145; Hillis, "Introduction to Ceramic Raw Materials, Bodies and Glazes," pp. 77–111.

40. Hugh Tait, *Bow Porcelain, 1744–1776: A Special Exhibition of Documentary Material to Commemorate the Bi-centenary of the Retirement of Thomas Frye, Manager of the Factory and "inventor and first manufacturer of porcelain in England,"* exh. cat., British Museum, London, October 1959–April 1960 (London: Trustees of the British Museum, 1959); Hugh Tait, "The Bow Factory under Alderman Arnold and Thomas Frye (1747–1759)," *English Ceramic Circle Transactions* 5, pt. 4 (1963): 195–216; Hugh Tait, "Bow," in *English Porcelain, 1745–1850*, edited by R. J. Charleston (London: E. Benn, 1965), pp. 42–52; Elizabeth Adams and David Redstone, *Bow Porcelain* (London: Faber and Faber, 1981), p. 251.

41. See Tait, *Bow Porcelain, 1744–1776*, fig. 1, and Tait, "Bow Factory under Alderman Arnold and Thomas Frye," p. 195.

42. The epitaph is quoted in full in Adams and Redstone, *Bow Porcelain*.

43. Ramsay, Gabszewicz, and Ramsay, "'Unaker' or Cherokee Clay."

44. Tait, "Bow Factory under Alderman and Thomas Frye."

45. Frank Hurlbutt, *Bow Porcelain* (London: G. Bell and Sons, 1926).

46. Ramsay, Gabszewicz, and Ramsay, "Chemistry of 'A'-Marked Porcelain."

47. See Tait, "Bow," p. 43.

48. Graham Hood, *Bonnin and Morris of Philadelphia: The First American Porcelain Factory, 1770–1772* (Chapel Hill: University of North Carolina Press, 1972); Garrison Stradling, "American Ceramics and the Philadelphia Centennial," *Antiques* 110 (July 1976), pp. 146–58; Graham Hood, "The American China," in *The American Craftsman and the European Tradition, 1620–1820*, edited by Francis J. Puig and Michael Conforti (Minneapolis: Minneapolis Institute of Arts, 1989), pp. 240–55; Garrison Stradling, "American Porcelains," in *Sotheby's Concise Encyclopedia of Porcelain*, edited by David Battie (Boston: Little, Brown and Company, 1990), pp. 182–83; Morrison H. Heckscher and Leslie Greene Bowman, *American Rococo, 1750–1775: Elegance in Ornament*, exh. cat., Metropolitan Museum of Art, New York, January 26–

May 17, 1992; Los Angeles County Museum of Art, July 5–September 27, 1992 (New York: Metropolitan Museum of Art, 1992), p. 288.

49. Hood, *Bonnin and Morris of Philadelphia*; Adams and Redstone, *Bow Porcelain*.

50. Terrance Lockett, "English Porcelain and Colonial America," *English Ceramic Circle Transactions* 16, pt. 3 (1998): 283–97.

51. Hood, "Career of Andrew Duché."

52. Tait, *Bow Porcelain, 1744–1776*; Watney, *English Blue and White Porcelain*.

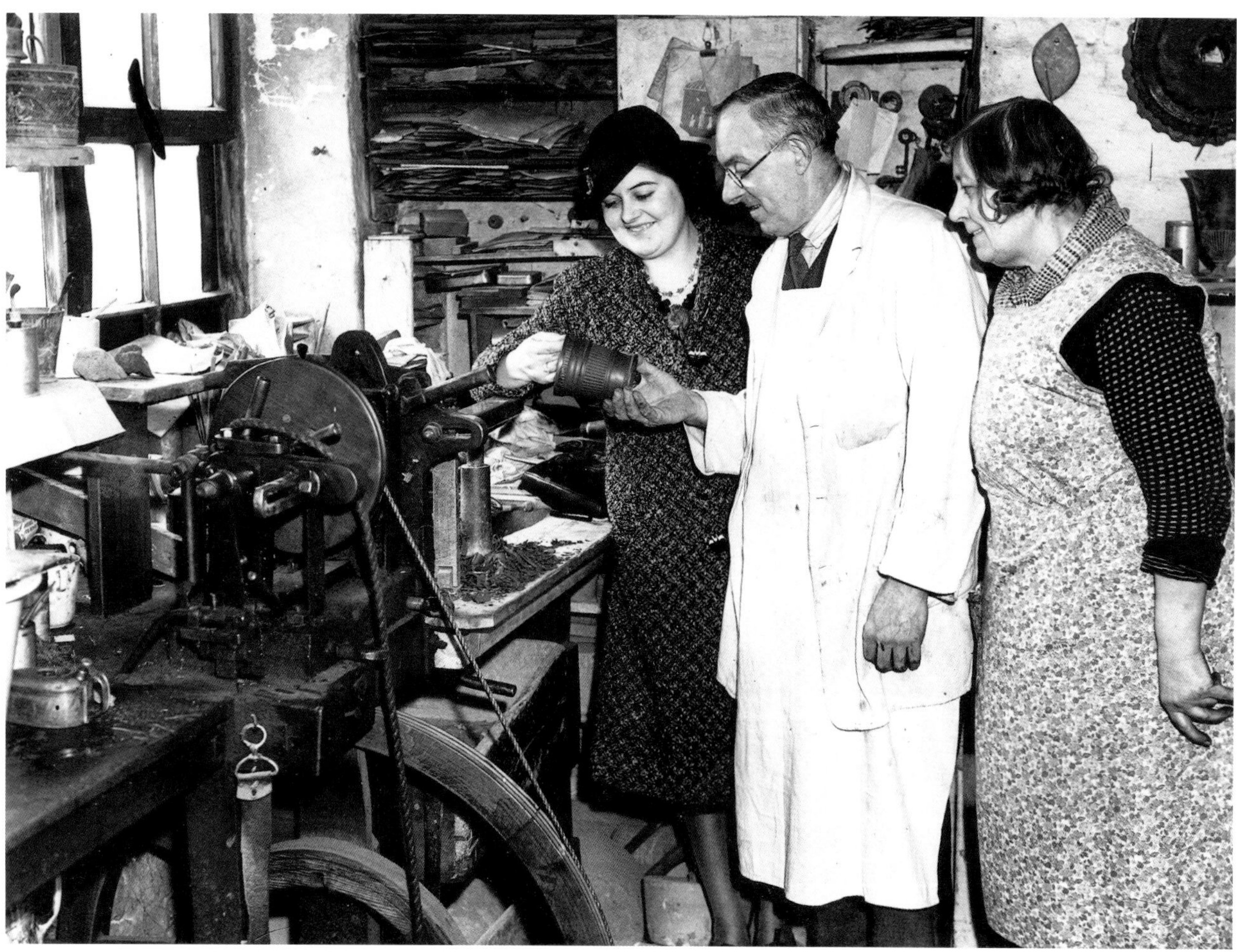

Figure 1 Archival photograph of the ornamental engine-turning lathe in the basalt room at the Wedgwood Etruria factory, 1941. *Left to right:* Mrs. Warrilow, Tom Simpson, and Mary Thornton. (Courtesy, The Warrilow Collection, Keele University Library, Newcastle-under-Lyme, Staffordshire.) In the 1950s this nineteenth-century lathe was moved to the Wedgwood Museum in Barlaston, where it is today. This photograph shows the lathe essentially as it was built; later it was highly modified.

Jonathan Rickard

and

Donald Carpentier

The Little Engine That Could: Adaptation of the Engine-Turning Lathe in the Pottery Industry

▼ SOMETIME PRIOR TO 1770 a complicated machine known as the engine-turning lathe began to be used to produce surface decorations on earthenware and stoneware in England. By cutting shallow regular patterns into the leather-hard surface of pots as they rotated slowly on this machine, turners in the potteries embellished wares with remarkable precision. This ingenious machine produced extraordinary, geometrically exact flutes and ribs as well as graphically exciting patterns visible through the play of light or by the contrast of colored slips.

We can attribute the development of engine-turned earthenwares and stonewares to Josiah Wedgwood based on surviving letters he sent to his friend and eventual partner, Thomas Bentley. Wedgwood was fascinated by the engine-turning lathe he had seen at Matthew Boulton's Soho metalworking facility in Birmingham in 1763. He was intrigued by the possibilities that such a machine might hold for use on pottery.[1] In a letter to John Wedgwood dated July 6, 1765, Josiah Wedgwood wrote that "I shall be very proud of the honour of sending a box of patt^{ns} to the Queen, amongst which I intend sending two setts of Vases, Creamcolour engine turn'd, & printed."[2]

Recently, evidence has been published of the even earlier use of an engine-turning lathe on porcelain in London at the Chelsea factory.[3] The Chelsea objects under discussion were probably press-molded using molds created by incorporating engine-turned segments in the original master model, rather than by the process described in this paper. The lathe used for creating those components was significantly different from the lathe described here and was not designed for ceramic production. The possibility remains that another potter (or potters) was involved in similar explorations before or even during Wedgwood's experiments. If there are any written notations, letters, or other documents regarding those explorations, they have not come to light.

The engine-turning lathe used with wood and metal differs in its construction and operation from the lathe adapted for ceramic use under Wedgwood's direction. Simple turning lathes had been used for the production of pottery since the early 1700s. By the 1730s virtually all hollow wares (mugs, jugs, cups, bowls, and so forth) were being lathe-turned to shape and thin the bodies. The engine-turning lathe further provided the ability to cut regular patterns in the clay bodies to create decorative elements.

City directories for the Staffordshire potteries district of the five towns (now known as Stoke-on-Trent) in the late eighteenth and early nineteenth

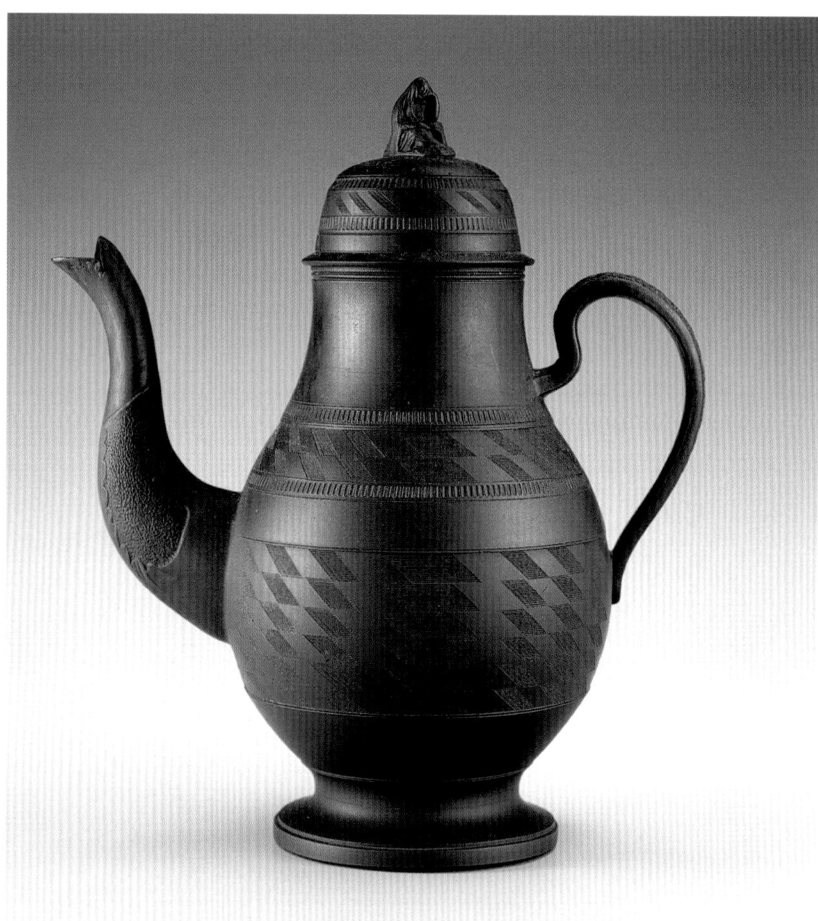

Figure 2 Coffee pot and cover, England, ca. 1800. Black basalt. H. 9⅛". The engine-turned surface of this coffee pot and cover was created with the edge (rose) cam. (All objects from the Jonathan Rickard Collection unless otherwise noted; photo, Gavin Ashworth.)

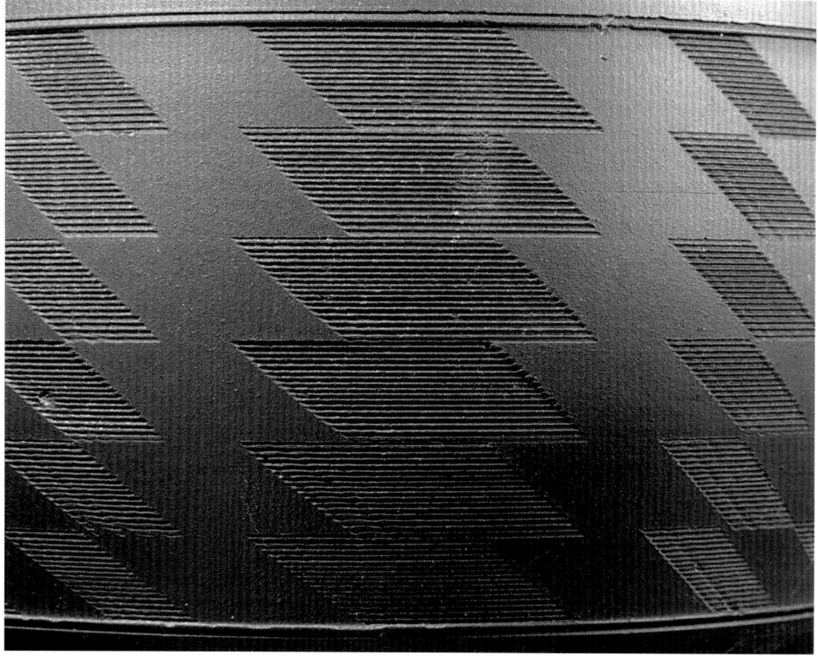

Figure 3 Detail of the coffee pot illustrated in fig. 2.

Figure 4 Jug, England, ca. 1775. Red stoneware. H. 7½". (Photo, Jack McConnell.) The engine-turned surface of this baluster-form jug with press-molded masque snip or pouring lip was created with the end (crown) cam.

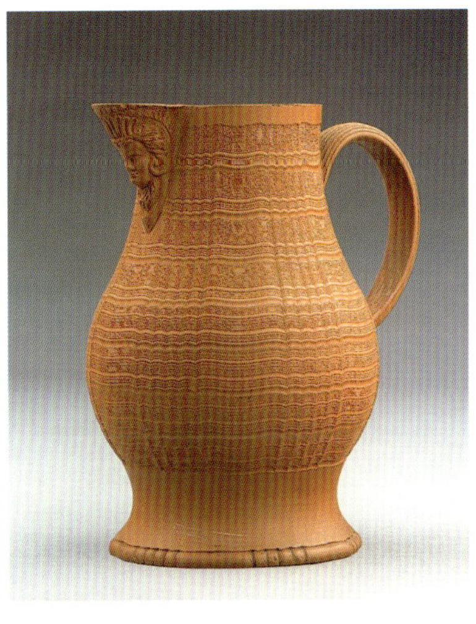

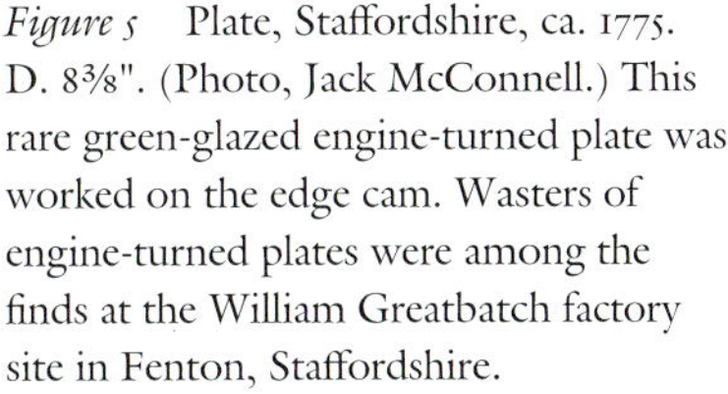

Figure 5 Plate, Staffordshire, ca. 1775. D. 8⅜". (Photo, Jack McConnell.) This rare green-glazed engine-turned plate was worked on the edge cam. Wasters of engine-turned plates were among the finds at the William Greatbatch factory site in Fenton, Staffordshire.

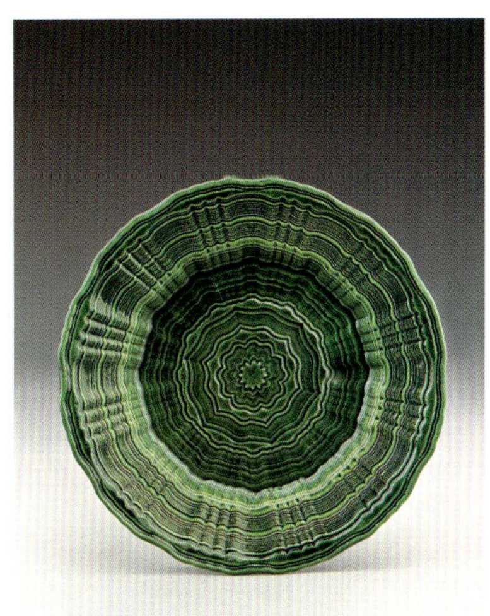

Figure 6 Mug, England, ca. 1800. Lead-glazed creamware. H. 3½". (Photo, Jack McConnell.) The decoration at the rim of this mug with extruded strap handle with foliate terminals is rouletted and slip-filled, above a reeded band colored in the glaze with either antimony or uranium to produce the brilliant translucent yellow. The two ochre slip bands bracket a field of horizontal black slip bands cut through vertically using the edge cam.

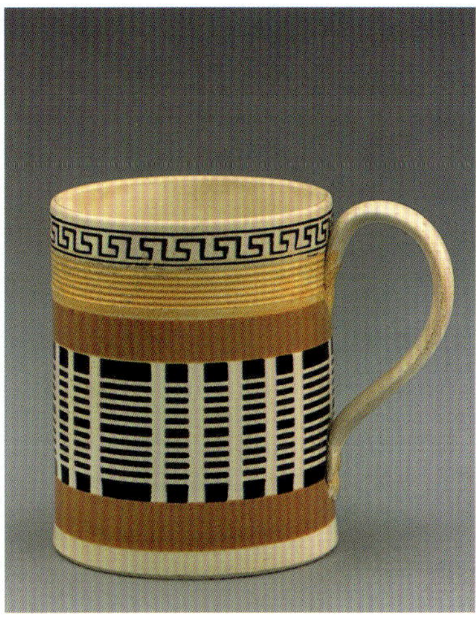

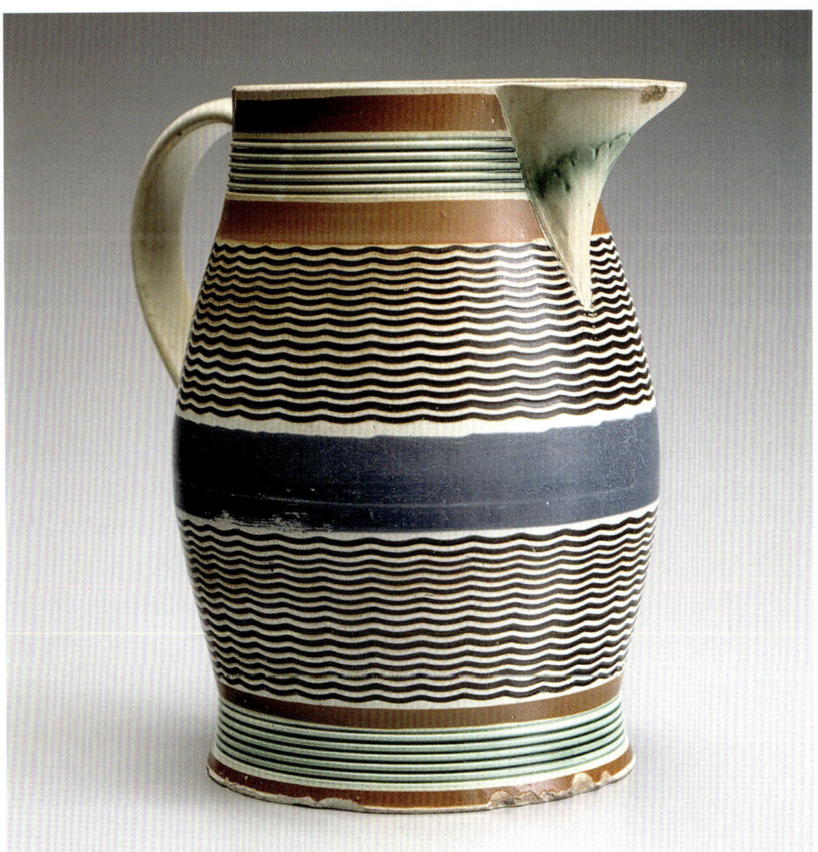

Figure 7 Jug, England, ca. 1790. Lead-glazed pearlware. H. 7". (Photo, Gavin Ashworth.) Baluster-form jug with slip banding, green-glazed (copper oxide brushed into the lead glaze) reeded bands brushed with a concentrated glaze mixture containing copper oxide, and black slip-filled engine-turned pattern cut using the end cam.

Figure 8 Detail of the engine-turned pattern on the jug illustrated in fig. 7.

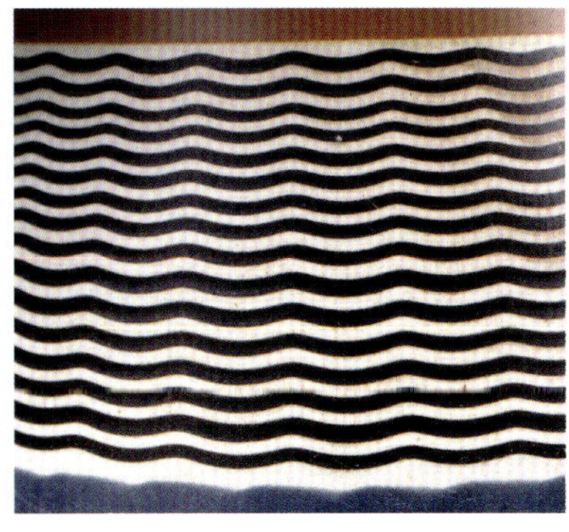

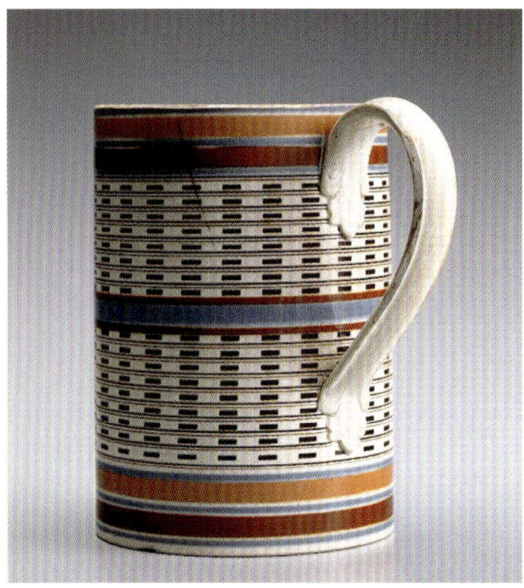

Figure 9 Mug, attributed to the Leeds Pottery, Yorkshire, ca. 1790. Pearlware. H. 6". (Photo, Gavin Ashworth.) Quart-capacity mug with slip banding and a black slip-filled pattern cut with the edge cam. The pattern appears in watercolor drawings in the Leeds Pottery pattern books in the Print Room of the Victoria and Albert Museum.

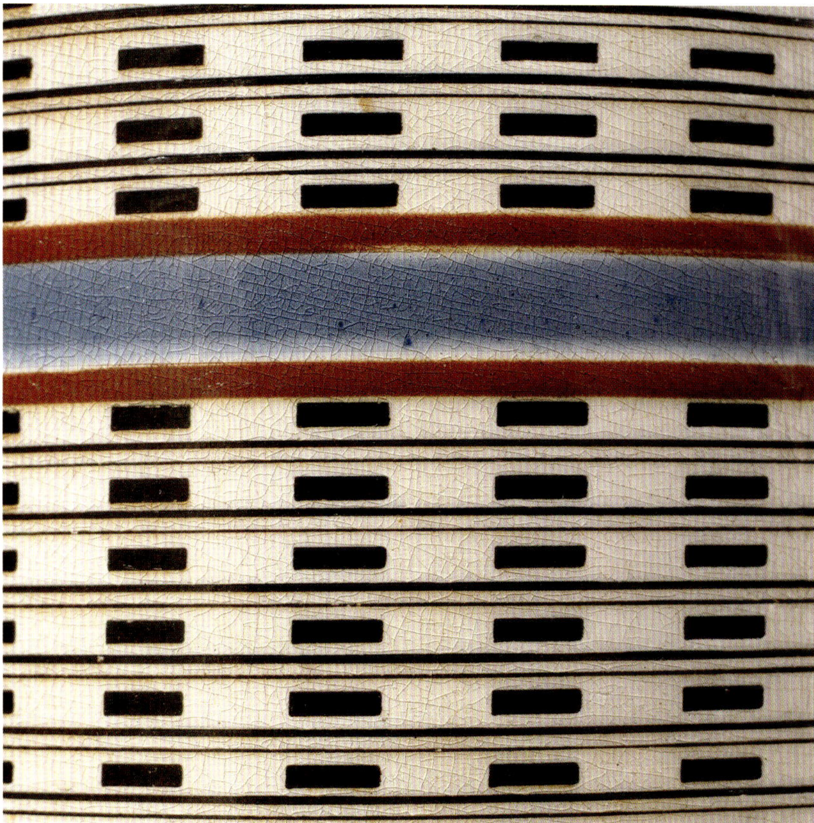

Figure 10 Detail of the engine-turned pattern on the mug illustrated in fig. 9.

centuries list numerous lathe makers; however, no individuals are identified as engine lathe makers. We look to Wedgwood's surviving daybooks and correspondence for a hint of the name of the man who first constructed or adapted an engine-turning lathe that met with Wedgwood's approval.

The history of the use of engine-turning lathes in the ceramic industry during this period is complicated by the rise in popularity of engine turning as a gentleman's hobby. A company developed by the Holtzapffel family in late-eighteenth-century London manufactured and sold engine-turning lathes for use by people of means who turned ivory and wood into intricate objects having no particular function other than amusement. The Holtzapffel firm maintained a registry of its lathes, recording the names of purchasers and the dates of their transactions.

In an unpublished history of the company Warren Greene Ogden Jr. lists a number of tantalizing customer names, but unfortunately none has anything to do with the ceramics industry. For example: "Mr. Baddeley bought Number 645 on March 6, 1809," and on November 9, 1810, a Thomas Wedgwood is listed as purchasing "Number 792, a 5 screw mandrel." While these are names familiar to students of the Staffordshire pottery industry, in neither case were the customers involved in the manufacture of pottery.[4]

In 1878 the ceramic historian Llewellynn Jewitt wrote of a lathe maker named William Baddeley:

> About 1720 William Baddeley (an old name in the district) commenced making brown ware at Eastwood, Hanley [Staffordshire]. About 1740, having invented an engine-lathe, he began to make turned articles in cane

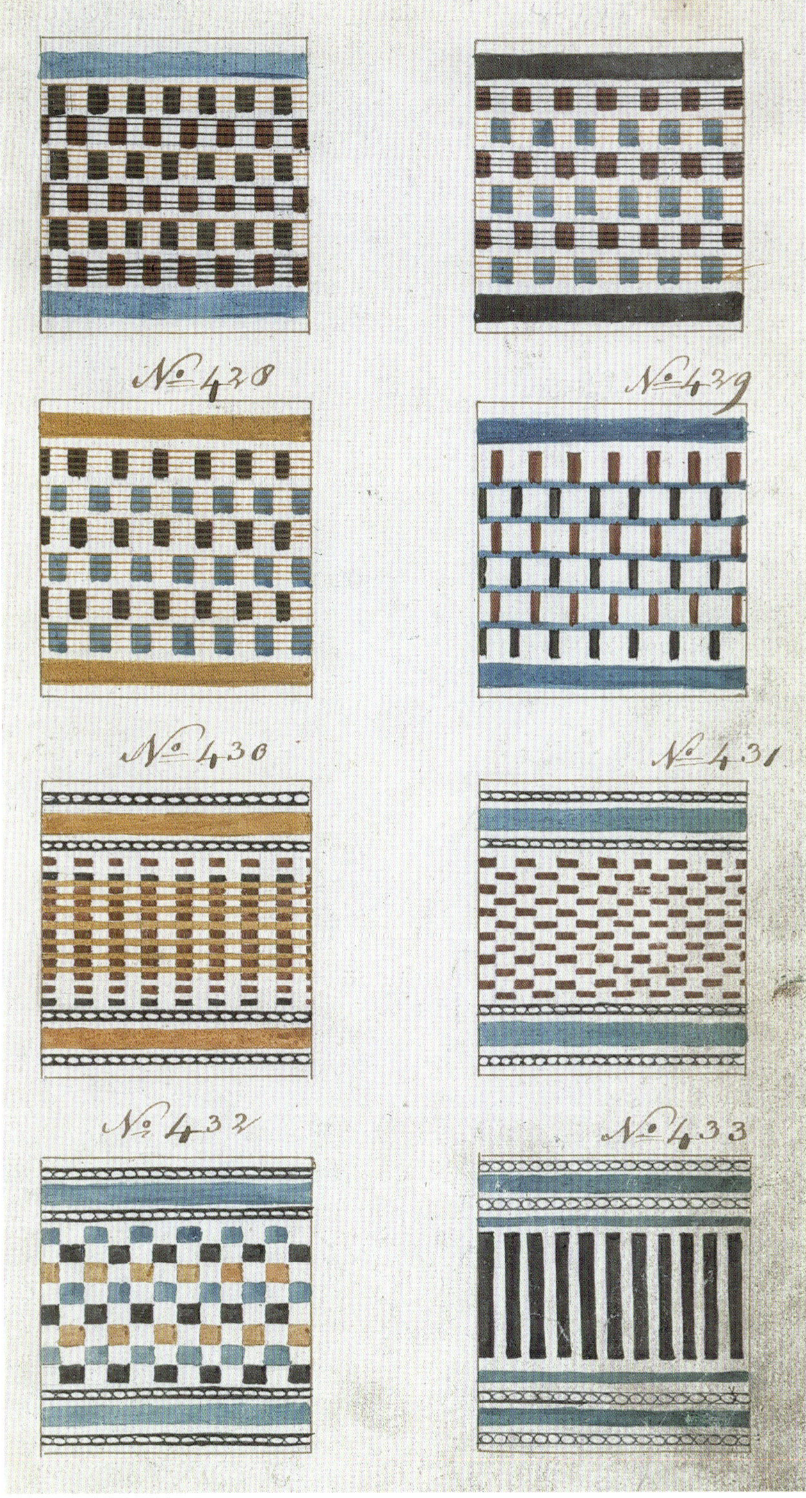

Figure 11 A page from the Leeds Pottery Pattern Book No. 3 showing a variety of engine-turned designs. (Courtesy, V&A Picture Library.)

and brown ware. He was succeeded in the pottery by his son William Baddeley, his other son, John Baddeley, taking the business of lathe-making, by which he acquired a competancy [*sic*], and died in 1841, aged 85. This second William Baddeley made many improvements in the ware and attempted both by an imitation of the body of his vitreous wares and by his mark, to palm off some of his goods as Wedgwood's. His mark was the word "EASTWOOD" impressed on the ware, but he contrived always

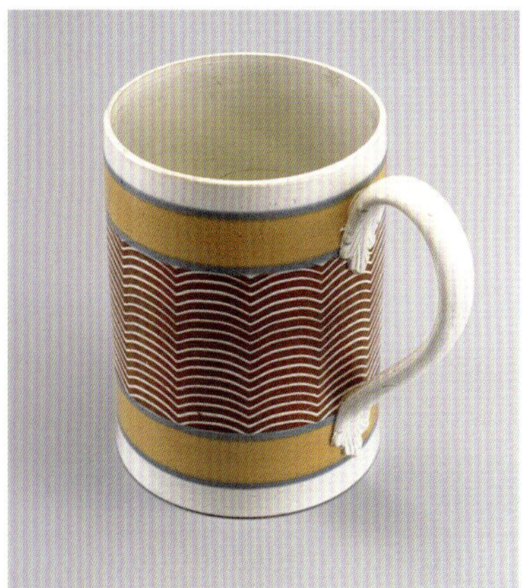

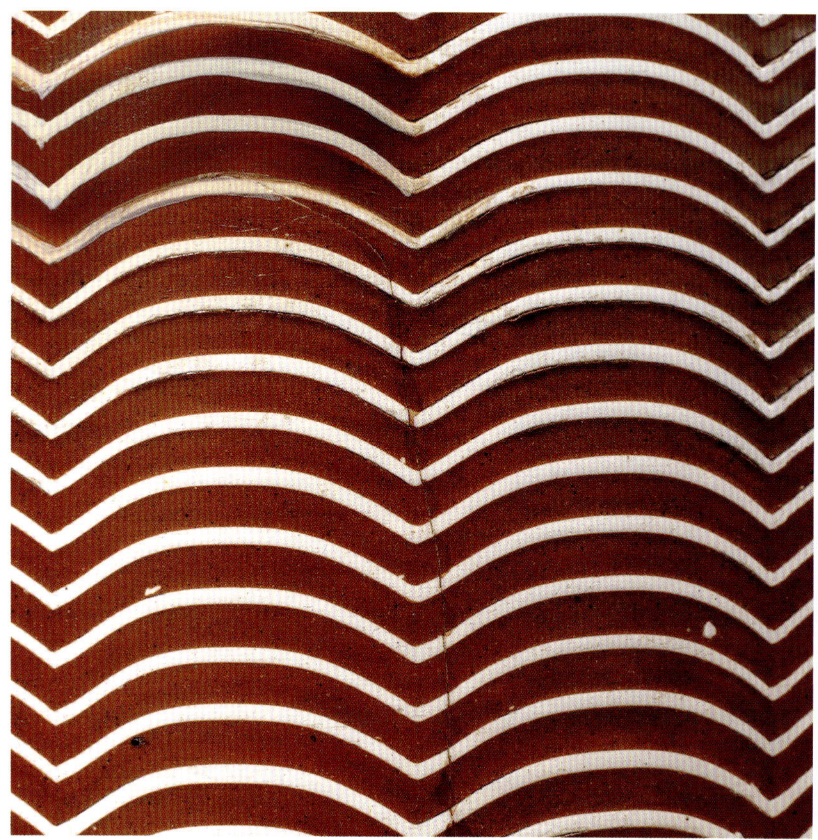

Figure 12 Mug, England, ca. 1800. Pearlware. H. 5⅞". (Photo, Gavin Ashworth.) Quart-capacity mug, slip-banded with red slip-filled engine-turned decoration cut with the end cam.

Figure 13 Detail of the engine-turned pattern on the mug illustrated in fig. 12. The mug is shown at an angle, illustrating the trompe l'oeil effect of a faceted surface.

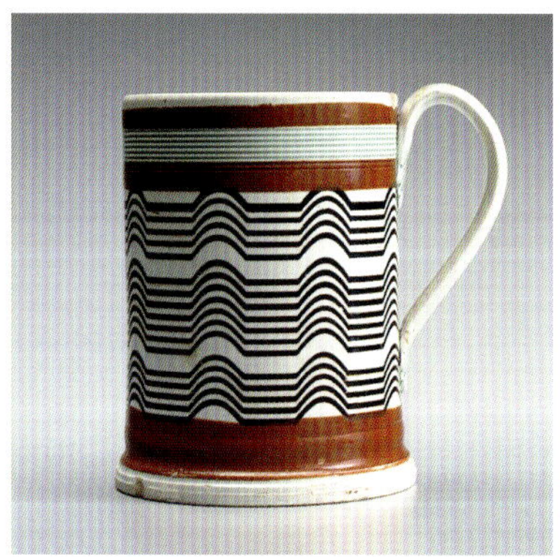

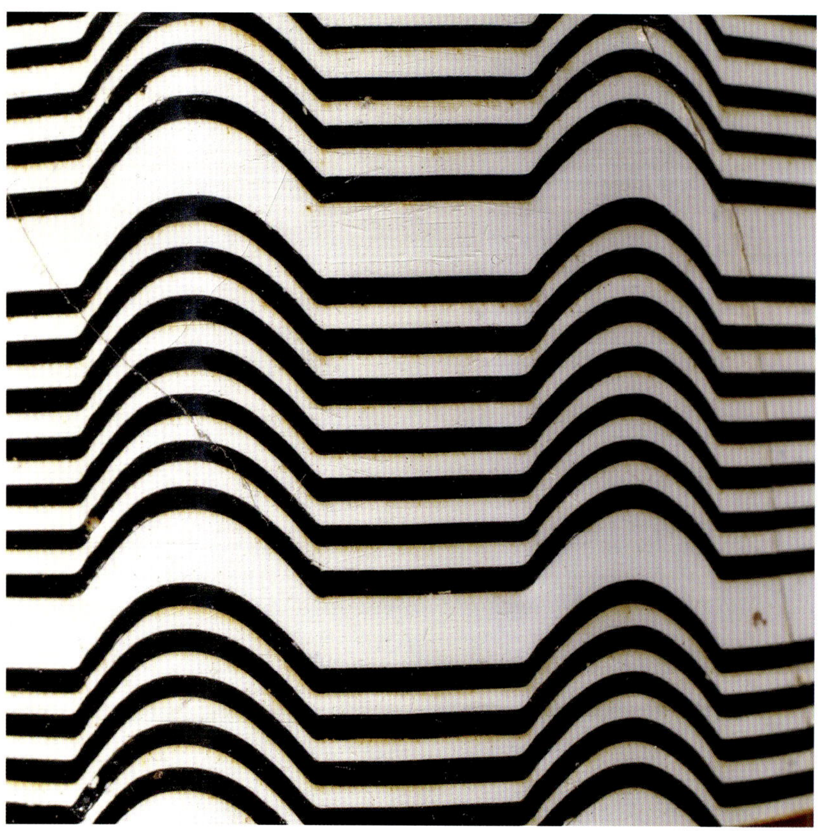

Figure 14 Mug, England, ca. 1830. Pearlware. H. 4⅝". (Photo, Gavin Ashworth.) A pint-capacity mug with slip banding and a green-glazed reeded band with a black slip-filled engine-turned pattern cut with the end cam. Wasters of vessels with similar patterns were found in an accumulation from the James and Ralph Clews manufactory, Cobridge, Staffordshire, 1818–1834.

Figure 15 Detail of the engine-turned pattern on the mug illustrated in fig. 14.

> to have EAST indistinct and WOOD clear; thus hoping to catch the unwary by the latter syllable. He died at an advanced age, and the works at Eastwood, having been sold, his son William Baddeley commenced on Queen Street, Hanley, for the manufacture of terra cotta articles, and a large trade was carried on in earthenware knobs for tin and japanned tea and coffee pots.[5]

Warren Ogden apparently had read these words and concluded thus: "It appears that an Eastwood potter by the name of William Baddeley was the person responsible for introducing engine turning to the Staffordshire potters. Apparently John Baddeley was the individual who first equipped the firm of Josiah Wedgwood for Rose Engine work."[6]

No city directories for the potteries district are known prior to 1781. Several subsequent directories list lathe makers and the Baddeley name is amongst them. *Allbuts Directory* for the year 1800, for example, lists:

> Samuel Allen, machine-maker, Burslem
> Thomas Ball, lathe-maker, Burslem
> John Baddeley, lathe-maker, Fields, Hanley
> William Lees, lathe-maker and white-smith, Lane End[7]

The normally reliable Mr. Jewitt, by the use of one word, has most likely further confused researchers looking for the origin of engine turning in the Staffordshire potteries. By employing the term "engine-lathe," Jewitt suggests a very early date of 1740 for the introduction of this machine.[8] It is more likely, however, that the "engine-lathe" he refers to is what we now know as a simple turning lathe. Archaeological findings at the Shelton Farm site of John Astbury confirm that turning lathes were in general use prior to the middle of the eighteenth century, yet no evidence, archaeological or otherwise, suggests the use of engine turning in the Staffordshire potteries prior to the late 1760s.[9]

Perhaps more to the point is the following, published in 1829 by Simeon Shaw:

> About 1765, Thomas Greatbatch, turner, at Mr. Palmer's, Hanley, suggested the movements which form the Engine Lathe, to the noted lathe maker, Mr. John Baddeley, of Eastwood; and worked upon it some years afterwards. Mr. Wedgwood offered eighty guineas each for six, provided Mr. B. would not sell any under that price to other persons. This was not accepted; Charles Chatterly had two made, on one of which were turned several ornamental vases, &c. given to the author by his father-in-law, after he had carefully preserved them more than forty years. Mr. W. engaged Mr. Cox, of Birmingham, to make his; and on the first of his productions, worked old James Bourne, at the Bell Works, about 1766; at any rate, before the commencement of erecting the present Etruria.[10]

The Mr. Palmer referred to is presumed to be the potter Humphrey Palmer of the Church Works, Hanley.

Referring to Wedgwood's own notations, we find that his initial trials, working with a man named John Taylor, a machine-maker from Birmingham, began in 1763.[11] These first attempts were based on the engravings in a French book published in 1701, *L'art de tourner* by Plumier.[12] The Plumier-based lathe proved to have both limitations and liabilities. It utilized a two-edged, small-diameter barrel cam combining the features of what the two

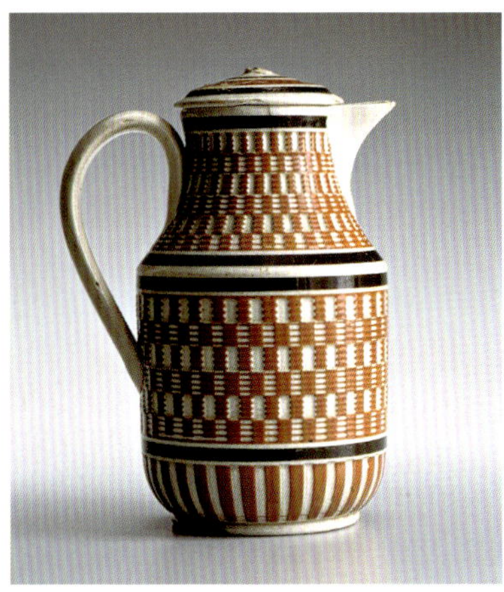

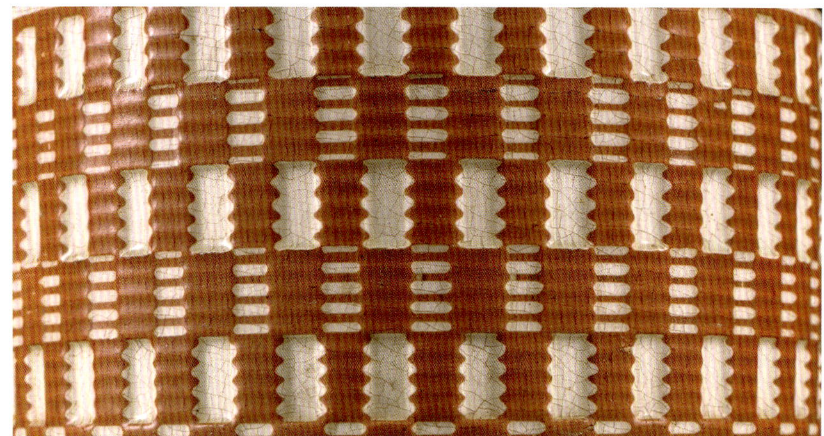

Figure 16 Cream jug and cover, Leeds Pottery, Yorkshire, ca. 1790. Creamware. H. 5½". (Photo, Gavin Ashworth.) The engine-turned decoration cut through the slip field with a matched set of checkering cams. The extruded strap handle has foliate terminals, and the cover knop is missing. This object was found in Russia. Impressed on the bottom is "LEEDS POTTERY." A related teapot and cover with the same mark are in the collection of the Victoria and Albert Museum.

Figure 17 Detail of the engine-turned pattern on the jug illustrated in fig. 16.

cams of Wedgwood's later lathe offered. This made it much too difficult to function in ways that were necessary for ceramic production, primarily in that changing patterns other than the small number of patterns on the barrel required the virtual dismantling of the machine. Wedgwood deserves credit for what is essentially a reinvention of Plumier's original design to facilitate the production of ceramics.

Wedgwood's most obvious engine-turned products are his jasperwares, but he applied this new technology to his creamwares, canewares, basalts, and red stonewares, too. Based on further correspondence to Bentley, we can infer that real production of his engine-turned wares began about 1767.[13] Following his lead, other potters within the district began similar production shortly thereafter, and in an amazingly short time potters as far away as Bovey Tracey in Devonshire followed suit, probably acquiring machinery from makers in Staffordshire.

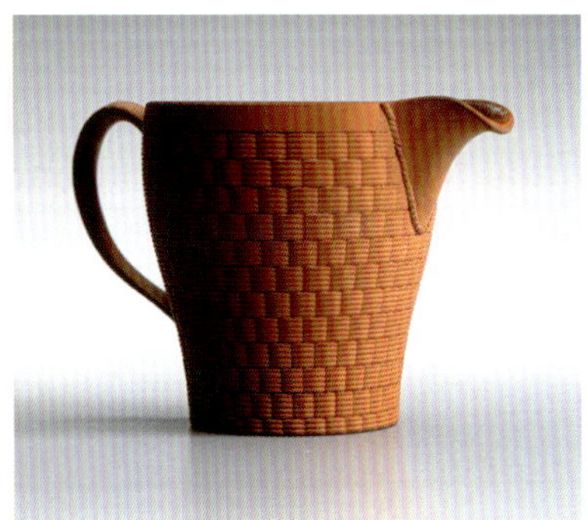

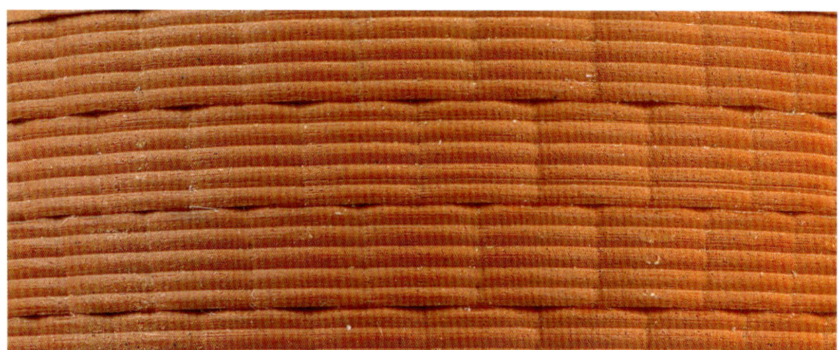

Figure 18 Cream jug, Wedgwood, Staffordshire, ca. 1820. Red stoneware. H. 3¼". (Photo, Gavin Ashworth.) The engine-turned basketweave pattern of this cream jug with glazed interior was cut using a double-edge cam. It has the impress "WEDGWOOD" on the bottom.

Figure 19 Detail of the engine-turned pattern on the cream jug illustrated in fig. 18.

The reference by Warren Ogden to "Rose Engine work" cited previously requires explanation. The type of engine-turning lathe developed and used by Wedgwood is known as a "rose and crown lathe." The *rose* refers to the edge cam and the *crown* to the end cam. It is likely that most engine lathes were made with only the edge cam (also known as a dicing lathe), whereas the larger, more successful potteries employed the more expensive and more complicated rose and crown version.[14]

With all three remaining engine-turning lathes residing in the Wedgwood Museum in Barlaston, one being nineteenth-century and the others

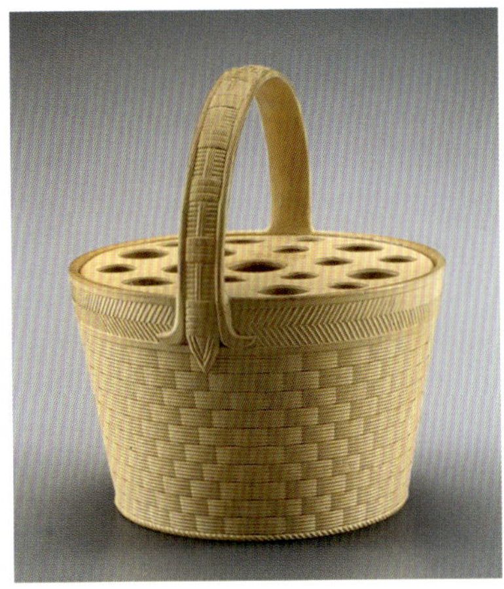

Figure 20 Potpourri basket, Wedgwood, Staffordshire, ca. 1810. Caneware. H. 5". (Photo, Gavin Ashworth.) The caneware body has the same engine-turned pattern as the redware creamware jug illustrated in figs. 18, 19.

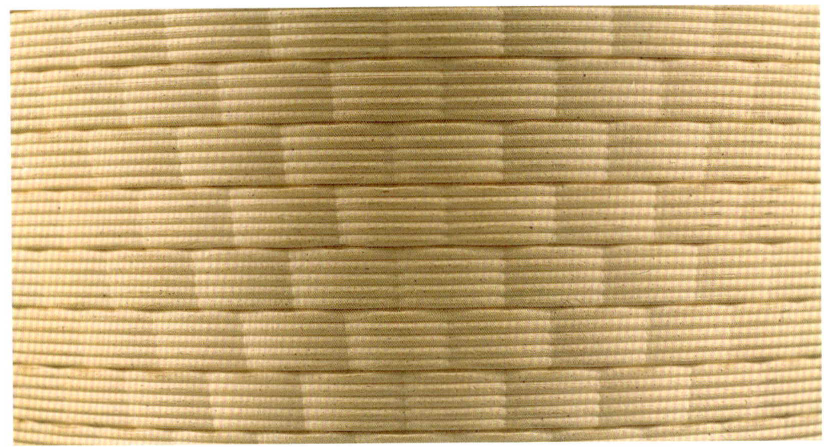

Figure 21 Detail of the engine-turned pattern on the basket illustrated in fig. 20.

twentieth-century copies, it became a matter of conjecture as to just how the original machine worked. Years of speculation made matters more confusing. The only way to understand fully the operation and details of the engine-turning lathe was to build one.

It turns out that two working potters on opposite sides of the Atlantic were at the same point of discovery, each having begun the process of reinvention. Nicholas Mosse of Bennettsbridge, Kilkenny, Ireland, and Donald Carpentier of Eastfield Village, near Albany, New York, had reached similar points in development when they first met in New York City in January 2000. Considerable discussion ensued, with both of the men sharing their hard-won knowledge.

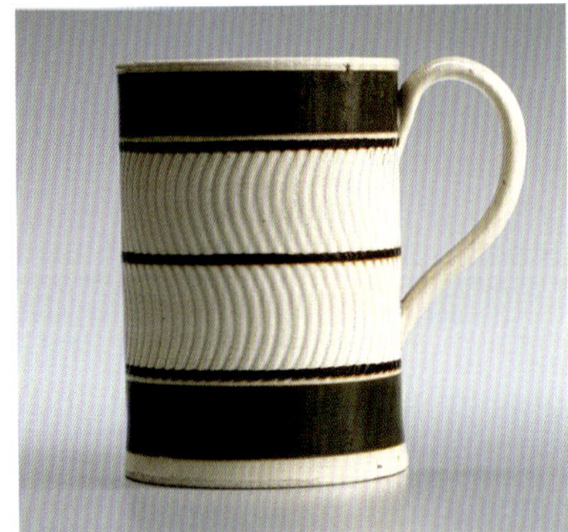

Figure 22 Mug, England, ca. 1800. Pearlware. H. 3¾". (Photo, Gavin Ashworth.) A half-pint-capacity mug, slip-banded and cut using a standard edge cam used for vertical reeding, but with a curved blade.

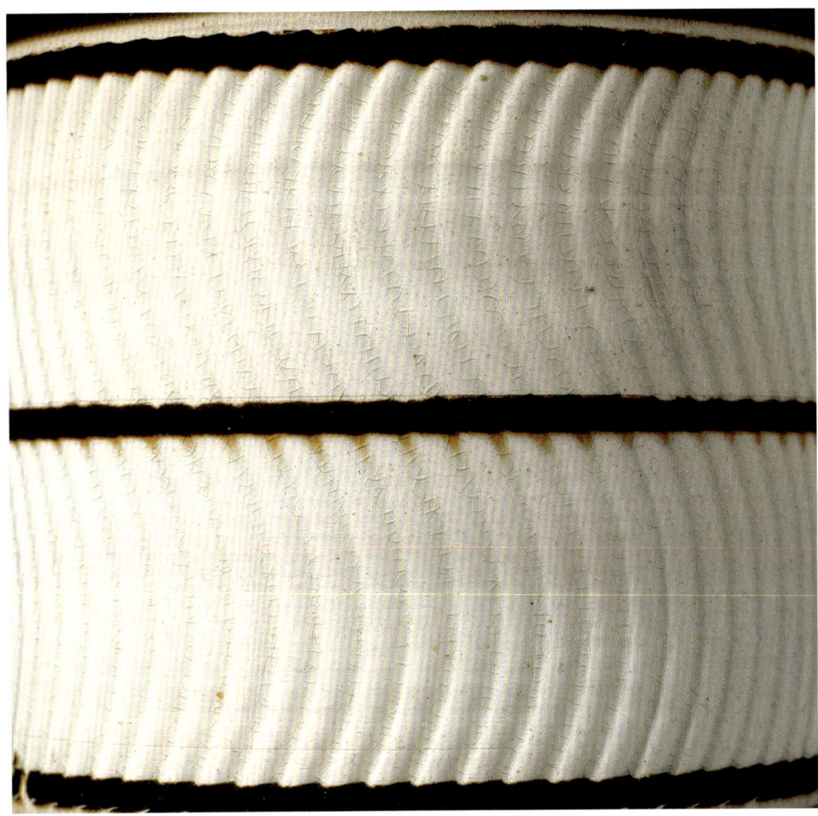

Figure 23 Detail of the engine-turned pattern on the mug illustrated in fig. 22.

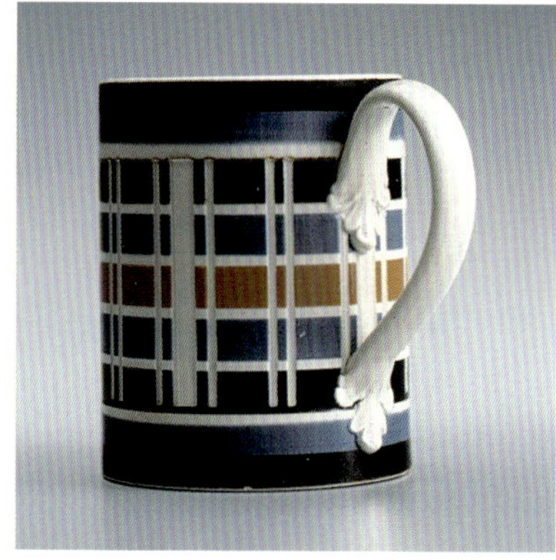

Figure 24 Mug, attributed to Wood & Caldwell, Burslem, Staffordshire, 1797–1818. Pearlware. H. 3¾". (Photo, Gavin Ashworth.) A half-pint-capacity mug, slip-banded with vertical cuts through the slip using the edge cam.

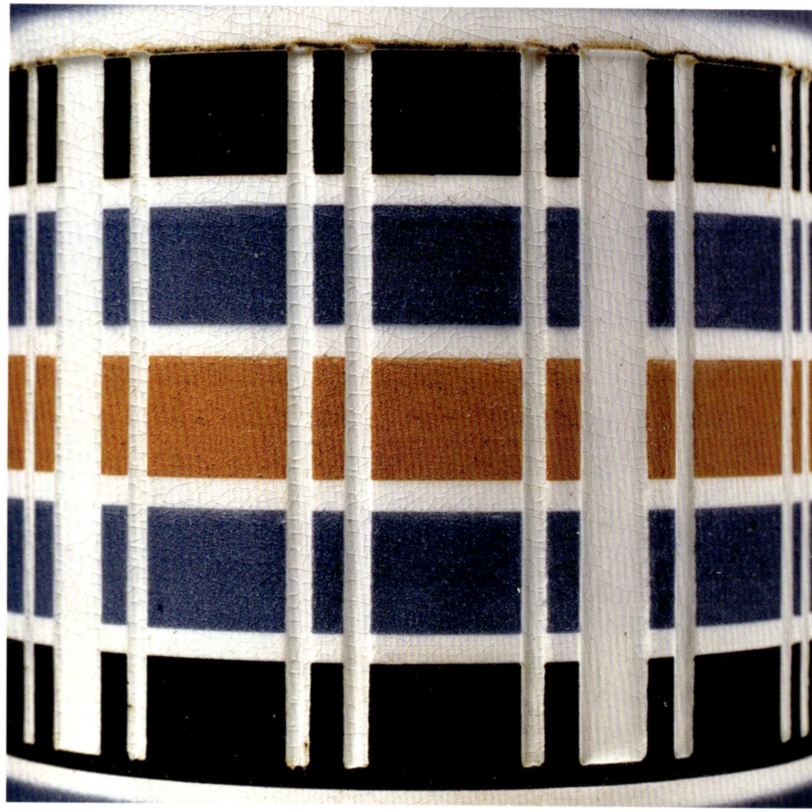

Figure 25 Detail of the engine-turned pattern on the mug illustrated in fig. 24.

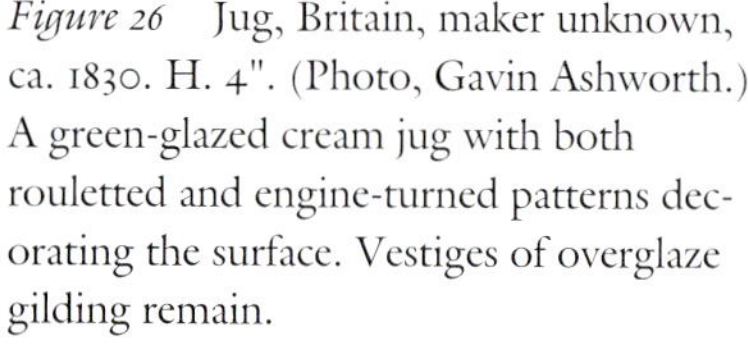

Figure 26 Jug, Britain, maker unknown, ca. 1830. H. 4". (Photo, Gavin Ashworth.) A green-glazed cream jug with both rouletted and engine-turned patterns decorating the surface. Vestiges of overglaze gilding remain.

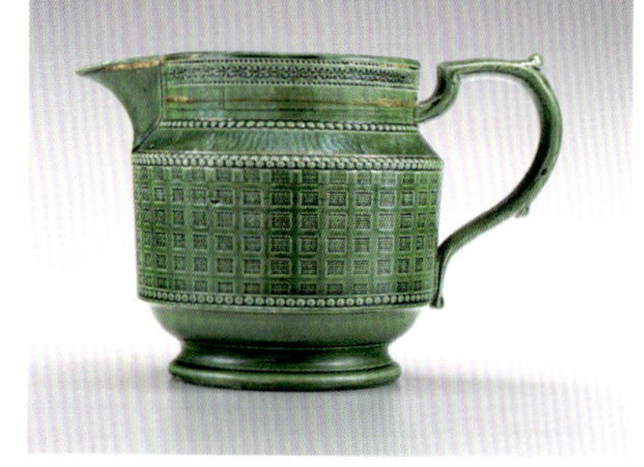

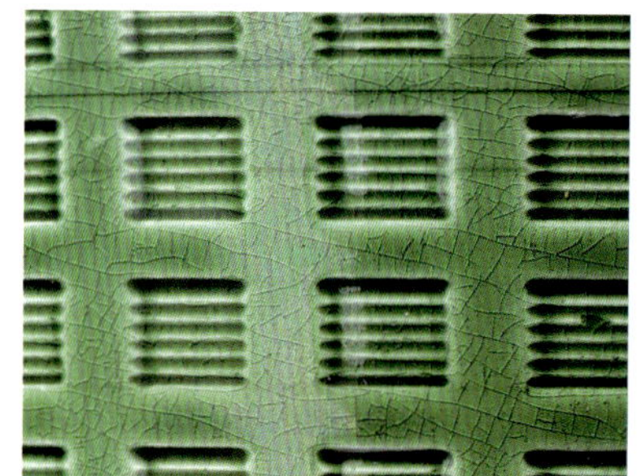

Figure 27 Detail of the engine-turned pattern on the jug illustrated in fig. 26.

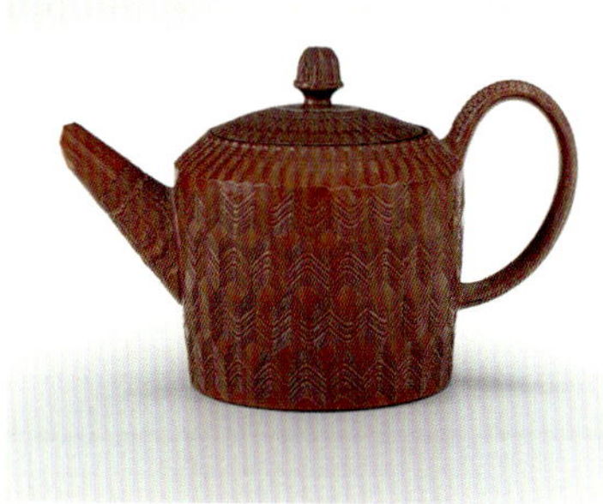

Figure 28 Teapot and cover, England, ca. 1790. Lead-glazed red earthenware. H. 4". (Photo, Gavin Ashworth.) The spout and vertical sides of the body were cut with the end cam, whereas the cover and the pot's shoulder patterns required the edge cam.

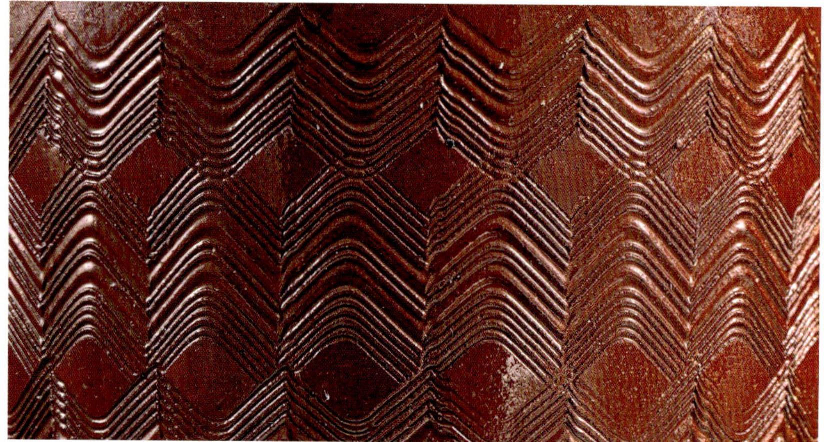

Figure 29 Detail of the engine-turned pattern on the teapot illustrated in fig. 28.

Figure 30 Teapot and cover, Davenport, Longport, Staffordshire, ca. 1810. Caneware. H. 4½". (Photo, Gavin Ashworth.) Enamel decorated with engine-turned dicing on the body and cover, this example has the impressed mark "DAVENPORT" on the bottom.

Figure 31 Detail of the engine-turned pattern on the teapot illustrated in fig. 30.

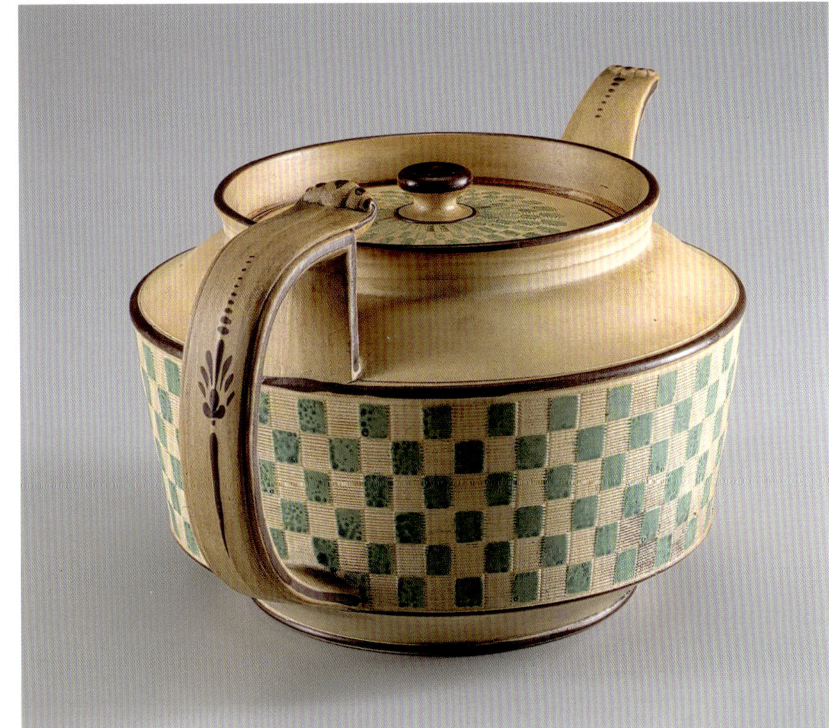

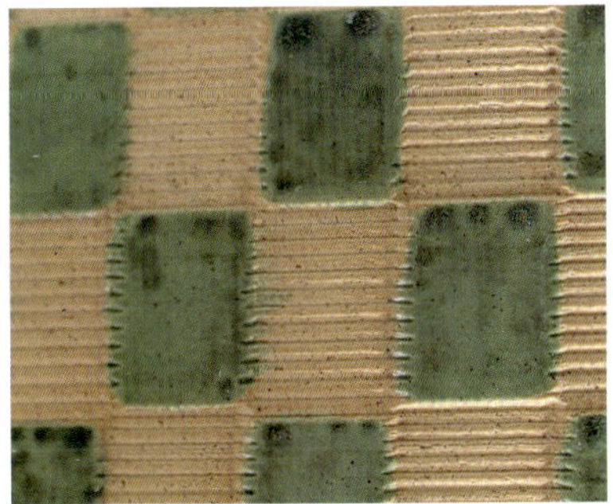

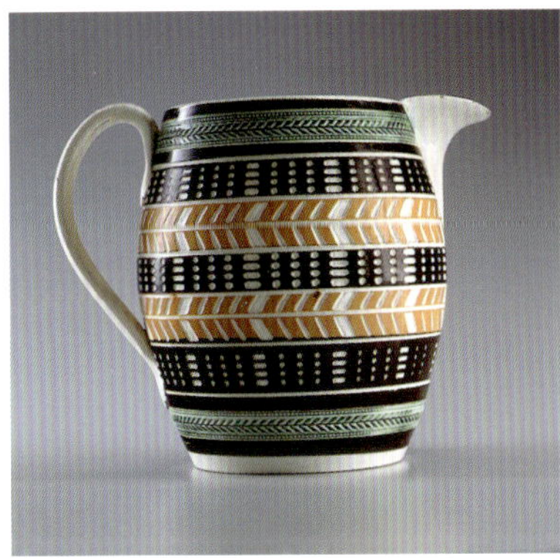

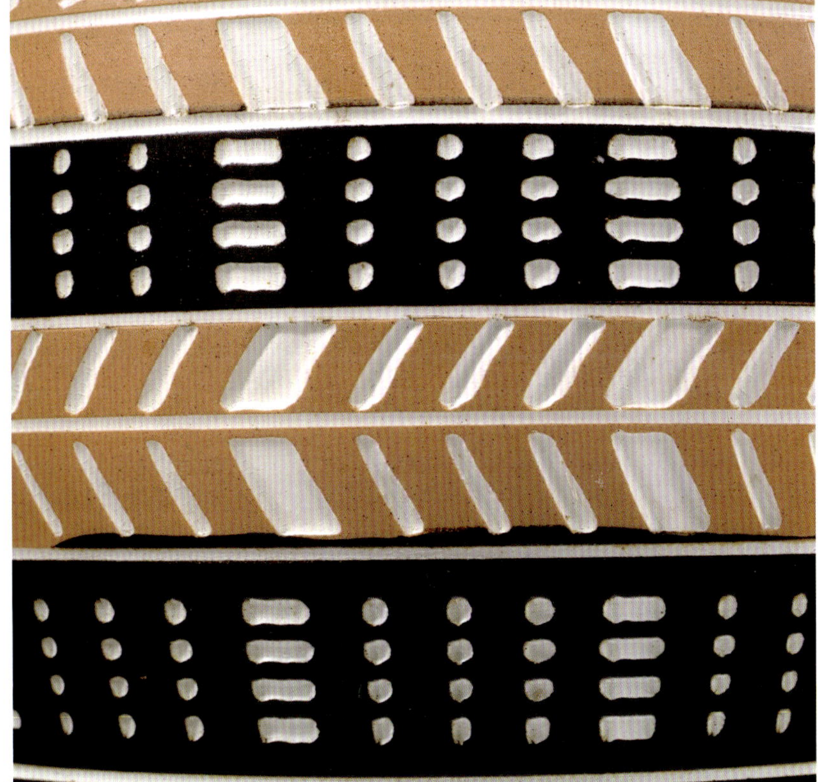

Figure 32 Jug, Britain, ca. 1820. Pearlware. H. 7½". (Photo, Gavin Ashworth.) A barrel-form jug banded with black and ochre-colored slip, engine turned with the edge cam through the slip to reveal the white body. Green-glazed rouletted bands bracket the engine-turned surface cut with two different blades, the chevron pattern requiring a V-shaped blade.

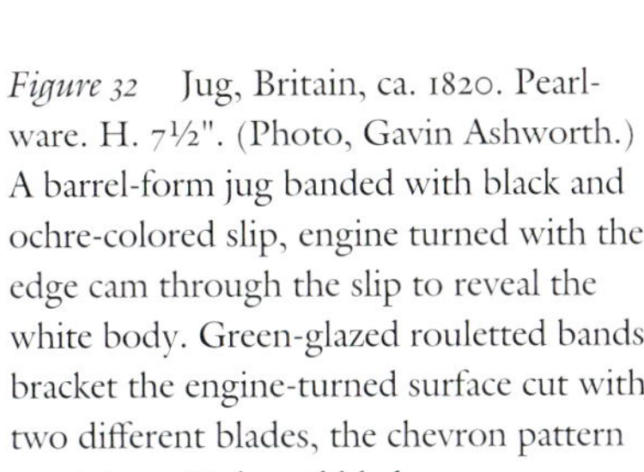

Figure 33 Detail of the engine-turned pattern on the jug illustrated in fig. 32.

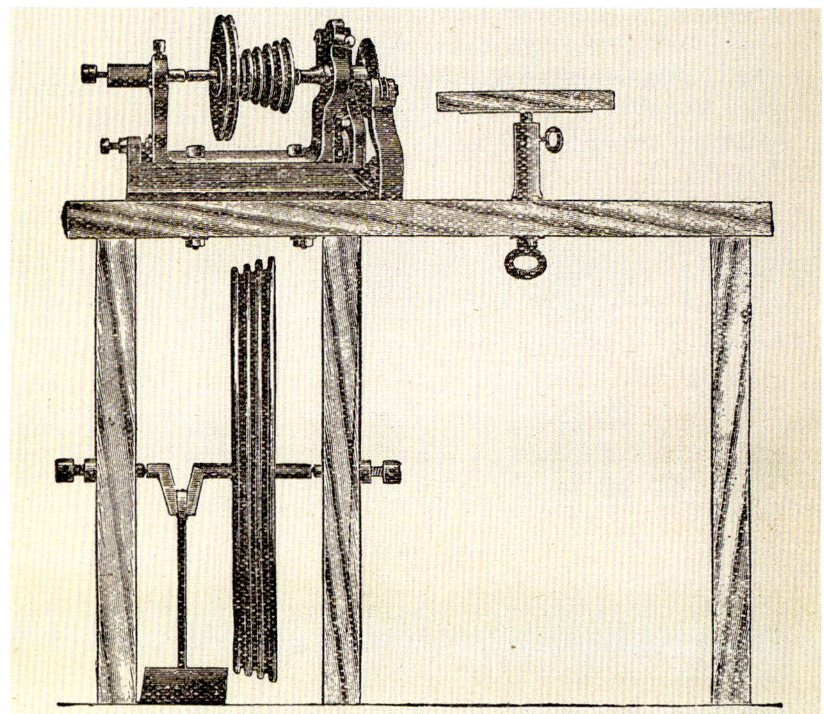

Figure 34 A line engraving that depicts a simple dicing lathe, reproduced in Ernest Albert Sandeman, *Notes on the Manufacture of Earthenware* (London: H. Virtue and Company, 1901).

The following explanation of the processes involved is based on the Carpentier lathe. Whereas the eighteenth-century examples were powered by children or women working foot treadles, this lathe runs on electricity. The cutting tools employed on the original machines were handheld or clamped in place; here they are alternately handheld or magnetically held in place. Since Carpentier's lathe is used to produce pottery for sale, it uses some modern technology to speed production. However, it still closely parallels the original as its function is essentially the same as its eighteenth-century forebears.

The newly constructed engine-turning lathe uses a steel frame to support a central axle on which can be mounted the *crown cam* (also known as the end cam), the *rose cam* (or edge cam), and the *chum* or *mandrel* (the plaster or wooden devices to which the pot is affixed). Chums must be custom designed for various forms and sizes of pots. The roses and crowns are also designed to produce different patterns.

In a typical factory setting, as many as fifty types of these three components could have been used. Patterns may have been further varied by employing various cutting blades, each producing a new pattern when combined with different cams. Another example of the flexibility of the machine involves the placement of the pulley, or *tudicle* (Wedgwood's term); when the pulley is in one position, reeding is produced, but when it is reversed, fluting results. Attempts at using both cams simultaneously proved unsuccessful, however, which Wedgwood's own experiments apparently confirmed.

Adjacent to the placement of the mandrel is the rest on which is mounted the cutting blade. The axle has the capacity to move a short distance from end to end (pumping action) when the crown cam is employed. When this

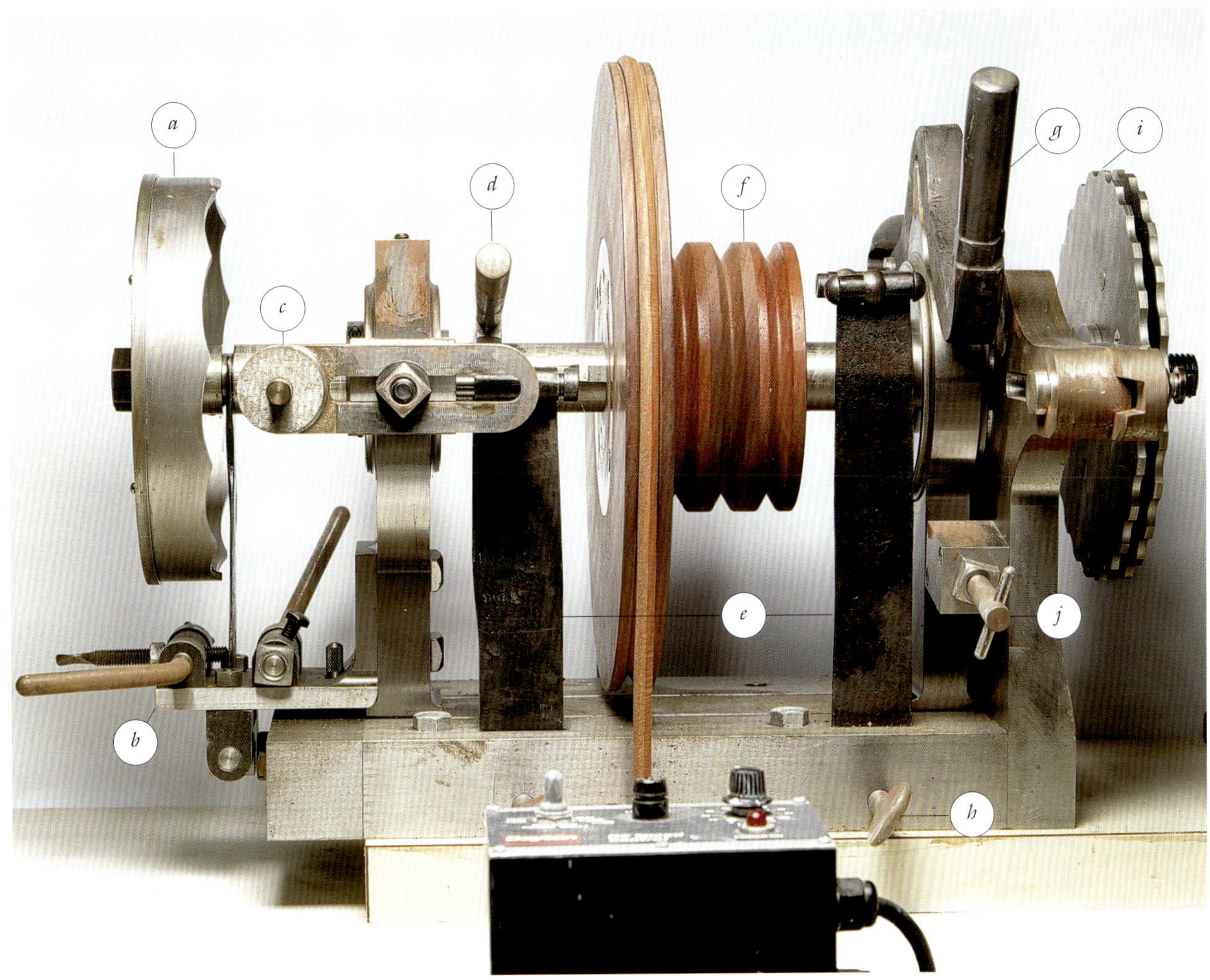

Figure 35 Side view of the Carpentier engine lathe showing the basic working components. (*a*) The crown (end) cam: left and right edges can be cut with patterns. (*b*) Double-action, crown-cam spring assembly: allows crown cam to be followed on left or right edge and creates spring tension for the sideways pumping action. Josiah Wedgwood describes making this addition to his redesigned lathe in a 1768 letter. (*c*) Crown-cam follower. (*d*) Lock to keep main shaft from moving sideways. (*e*) Main springs: put pressure against pivoting main frame as it follows the edge cams and produces a rocking motion. (*f*) Wooden pulleys: using a large pulley slows the motion and using a small pulley increases it. (*g*) Mainframe locking arm (seen in the down position): prevents the front-to-rear rocking action. (*h*) Spring tensioner: increases pressure on main springs, either forward or backward. (*i*) Edge cams: can be changed simply by removing a nut and sliding another cam on or off. Like the double-action, crown-cam spring assembly, this appears to have been invented by Wedgwood for use on his 1768 redesigned lathe. (*j*) Depth stop: controls the depth of cut the knives make in the body. (All demonstration photos by Gavin Ashworth.)

Figure 36 The end cam on Carpentier's lathe. At the lower left is the follower. At right is a portion of the wooden flywheel.

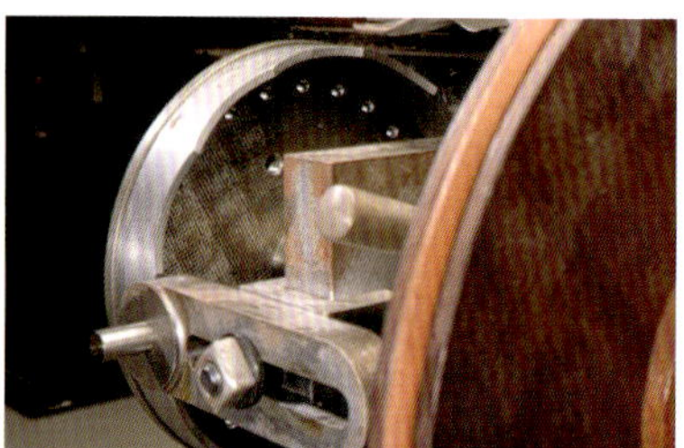

Figure 37 The edge cam on Carpentier's lathe. At lower left center is the follower; the flywheel appears in the background.

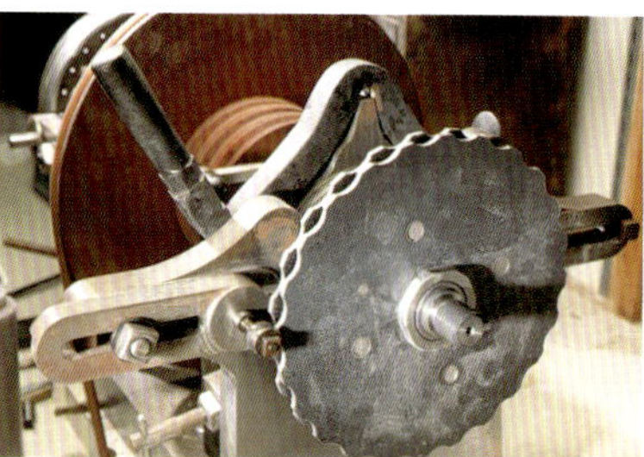

Figure 38 Detail of the follower mounted against one of two attached edge cams used, in this configuration, to create checkered patterns. For this application, alternating patterns are cut with one of the edge cams, then the offset patterns are cut with the other.

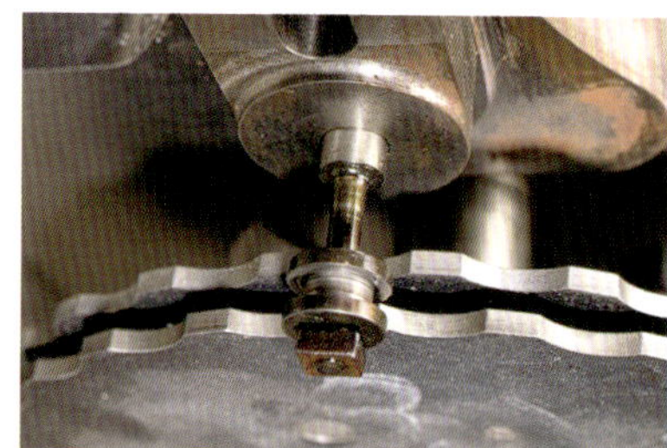

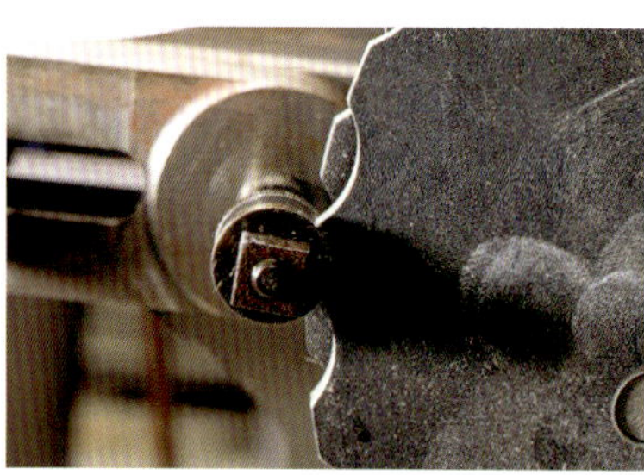

Figure 39 Another view of the follower and an edge cam. The follower's size can be changed depending on the size and intricacy of the pattern needed to be run against on the edge cam.

Figure 40 Don Carpentier at his lathe. *Left to right:* a leather-hard pot mounted on a plaster chum, or mandrel; the edge cam; clamp; and the wooden flywheel.

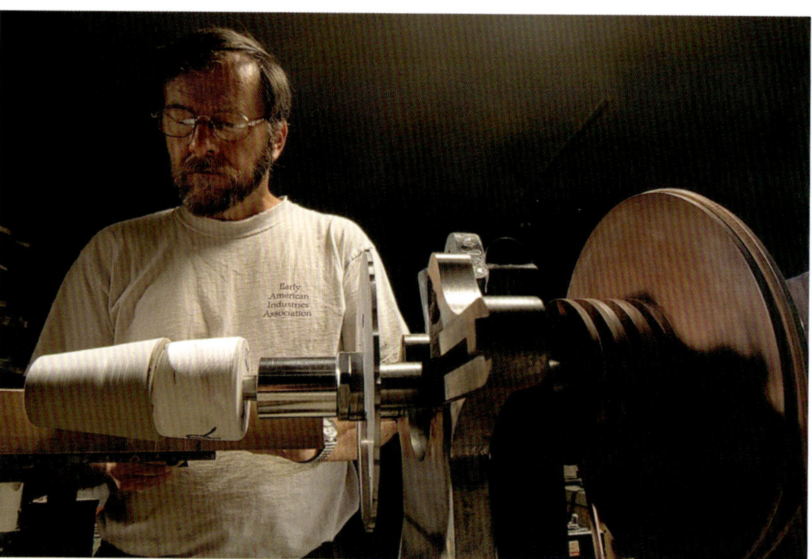

Figure 41 To illustrate the pantographic effect of the cam in relation to the pattern cut on a pot, Don devised this arrangement of an edge cam with a period mug. The white lines on the cam show the reduction of the edge pattern to the final cut. The larger the cam, the more spread out the pattern became, thus increasing the ease of following the pattern. (Collection of Donald Carpentier.)

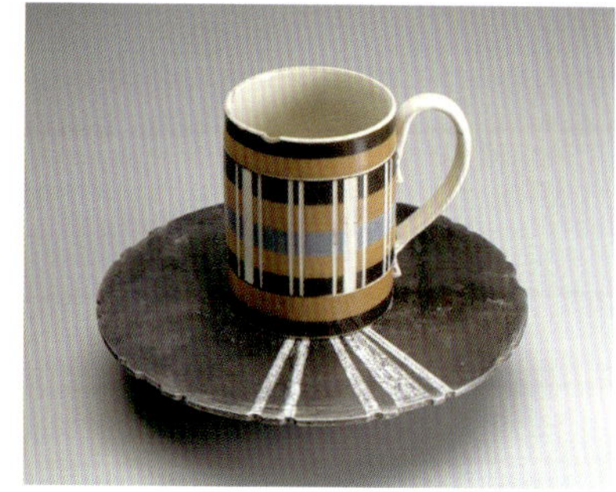

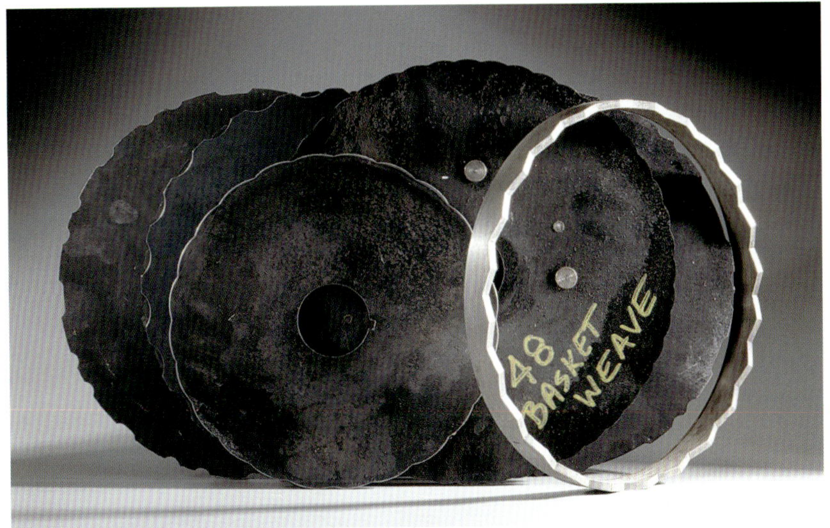

Figure 42 An assortment of end and edge cams, each of which is capable of many patterns depending on the blades chosen.

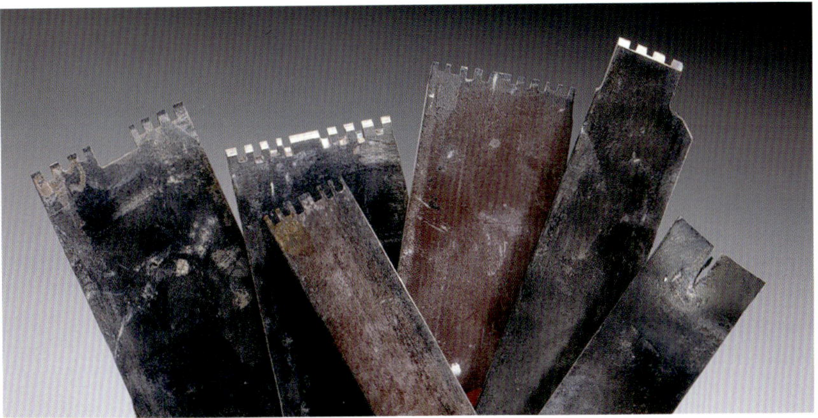

Figure 43 An assortment of cutting blades.

Figure 44 A group of engine-turned vessels having a variety of decorations. (Collection of Donald Carpentier; photo, Gavin Ashworth.) All of these pieces were cut using one or both sides of a checking cam, similar to the one seen in the center of the illustration. Most of the variations were created by changing either the slip colors or the patterns on the ends of the cutting blades.

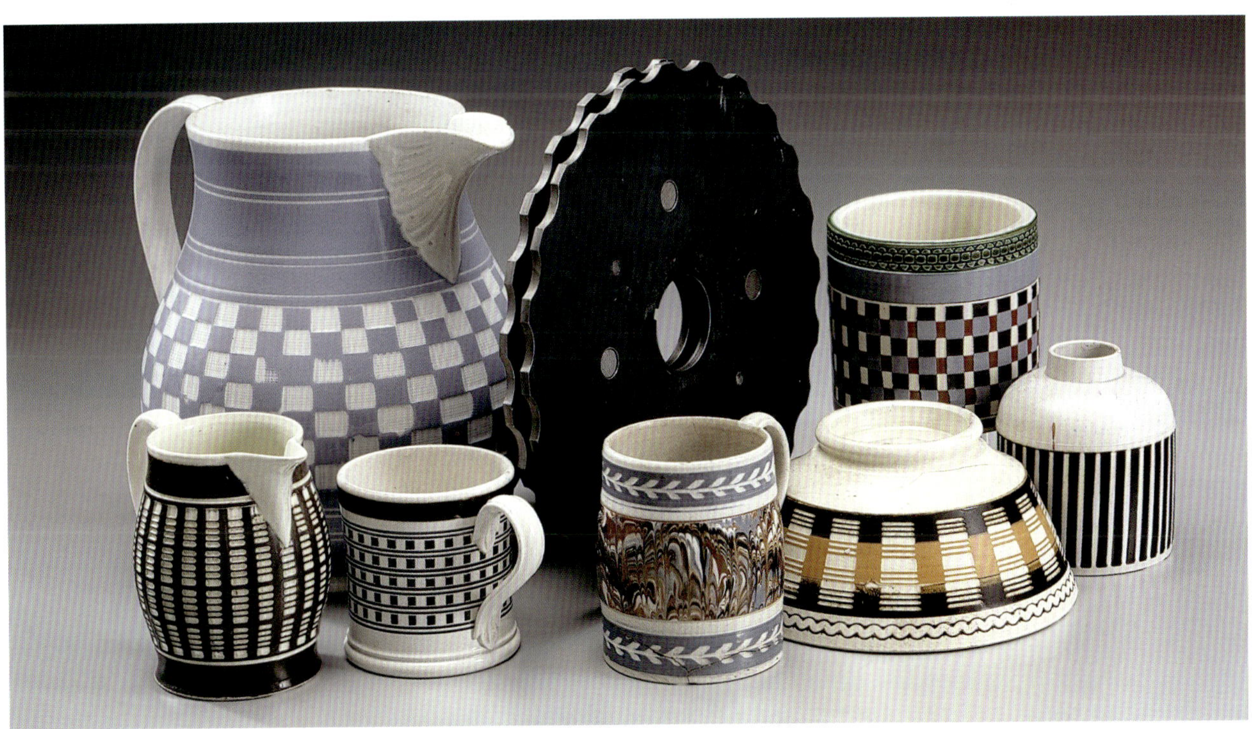

Figure 45 Beginning the process of cutting a pattern into a quart-mug's surface using the end cam. The pot revolves as the blade gradually begins to cut into the surface.

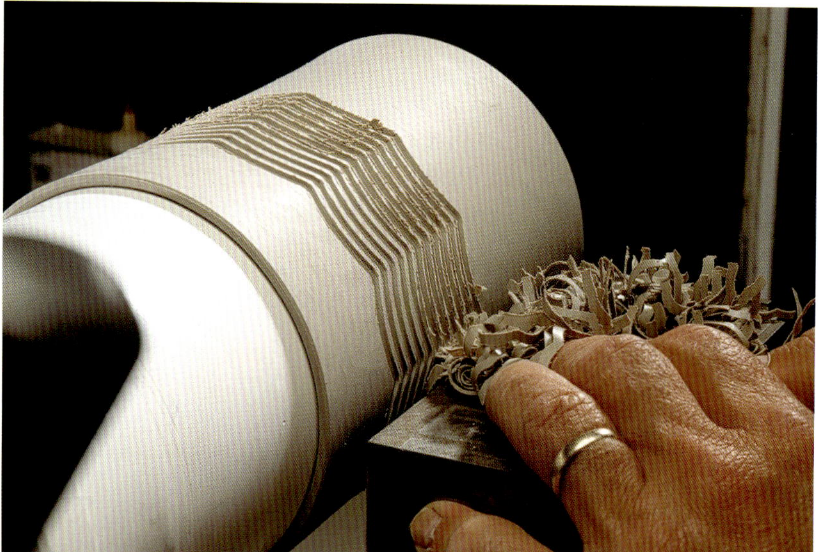

Figure 46 With the pattern completely cut in, the surface is flooded with colored slip and set aside to dry.

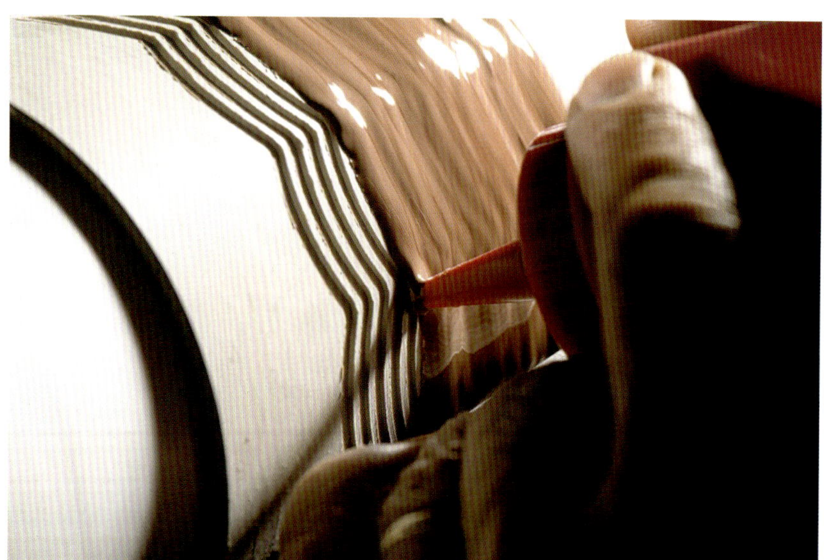

Figure 47 After drying, the excess slip is turned away with a flat blade, exposing both the white body of the pot and the red clay inlay.

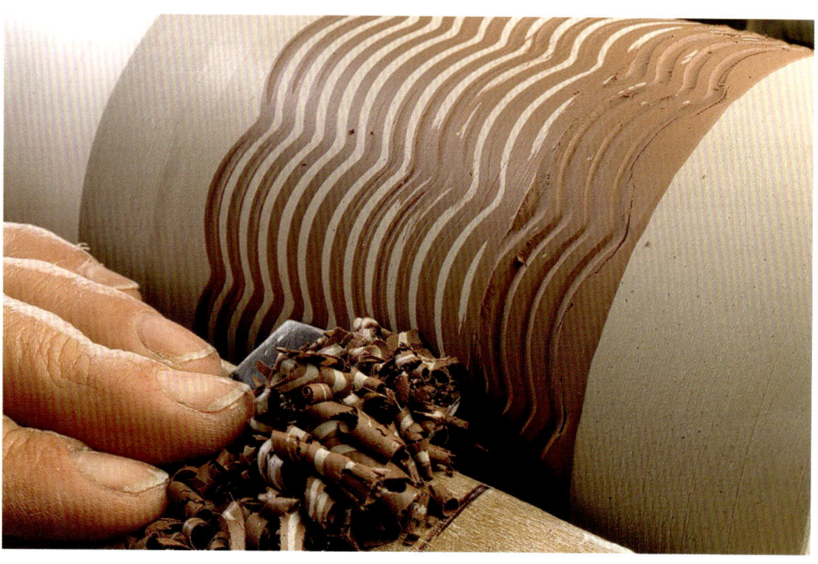

Figure 48 Detail of the inlaid slip pattern prior to the biscuit firing.

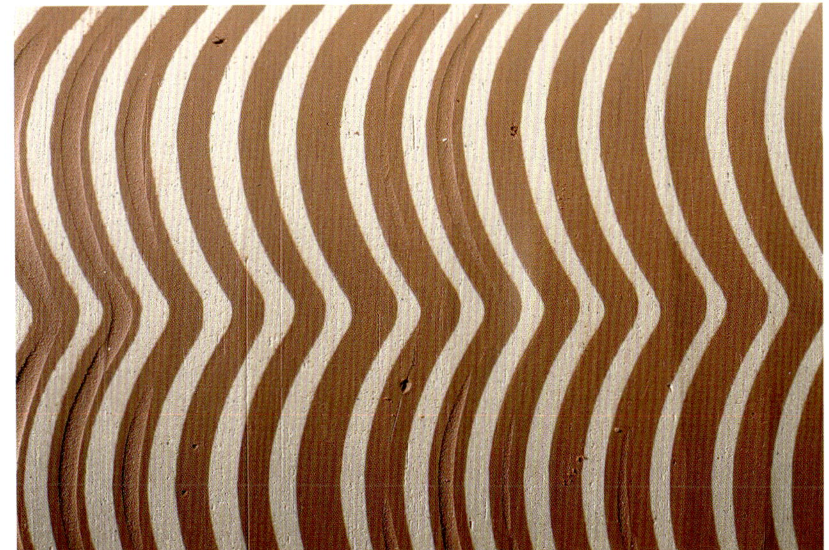

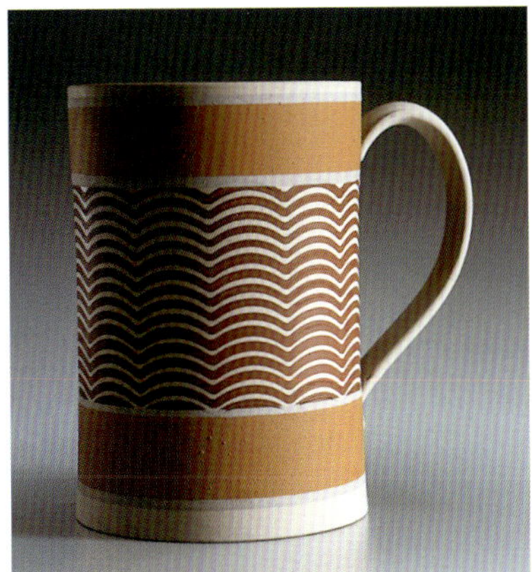

Figure 49 The completed mug prior to biscuit firing. As these modern pots are intended to be used, non-leaded glazes are applied. Carpentier discovered that lead was an integral component in producing the colors of the glazes. Consequently, he had to develop his own clay sources and color recipes to achieve the look of the original lead-glazed products.

action takes place, the blades cut continuously in a pattern, resulting in an up-and-down appearance, either angled or curved, depending on the design of the crown.

When the rose is employed, the blades cut an intermittent pattern, as the entire frame of the lathe is rocked back and forth by the shape of the rose, the rose being followed by a tudicle or follower, which stays in constant contact with the edge of the cam. As the tudicle follows the edge into a recess, the spring-loaded frame and its mounted vessel rock into contact with the blades, causing the blades to dig into the surface of the clay body, and, as the follower rises onto a high point, it pushes the pot away from the cutting blades.

There are two devices built into the design that function as locking clamps, preventing either of the two movements. When the rose is employed, the crown clamp is locked to prevent the end-to-end movement of the axle. When the crown is employed, the main locking arm clamp is engaged to prevent the frame from rocking. Both clamps act in opposition to powerful forged steel springs. The axle's rotation is controlled by an electric motor running leather belts connected to a broad wooden flywheel. The entire lathe is bolted to a countertop work surface. In rose action practice, the axle rotates at a slow speed, with the unit making a regular clicking noise while it rocks back and forth against the cams as the pot is making and breaking contact with the blades.

The blades are also custom-made for each pattern and size desired. In general design some are similar to a comb with, for example, six identical, regularly spaced teeth that do the cutting. The patterns produced rely on a play of light and shade for appearance but also have tactile properties. In the case of dipped wares, where contrasting color patterns result, the appearance is greatly enhanced. Wedgwood and a number of his competitors produced colorful geometric patterns on jasperware while, at a generally lower price level, many potteries throughout Great Britain produced engine-turned, slip-decorated utilitarian earthenwares. These products

Figure 50 Jug, British, ca. 1820. Pearlware. H. 7¾". (Collection of Donald Carpentier; photo, Gavin Ashworth.) A barrel-form jug, slip-banded with black slip-filled rouletted decoration. Rouletted decoration such as this illustrates the imprecise geometric patterns achieved by hand, as opposed to the regular patterns found on engine-turned wares. The use of the end cam seems to have diminished by the 1830s, but edge-cam work continued to the end of the nineteenth century. By the early nineteenth century the much simpler and less expensive dicing lathes were available as stock items. Cams were also available in standard sets, obvious from sherds found on various factory sites. The only known period engine-lathe cams are at the Wedgwood factory in Barlaston, Staffordshire.

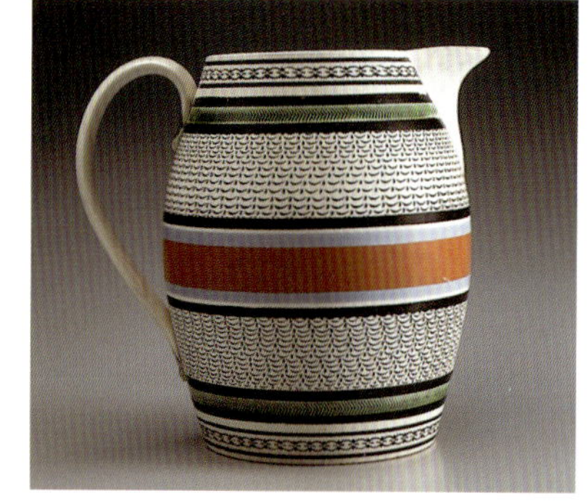

Figure 51 Detail of a rouletted inlay in three different patterns, together with a rouletting wheel in one of those patterns (three different roulettes were used). Many factories were too small or too under-capitalized to afford even a dicing lathe, and they had few options available in order to compete. One of those options was to become very creative with the practice of inlaid rouletting. Most factories had a variety of these inexpensive and easily available patterned wheels that could be used in a variety of combinations. The surface of the pot was simply embossed using the roulette and the ornamental depression created was filled with a colored slip. Once the slip had set, the excess was trimmed away on the lathe, leaving an inlaid pattern. Many inlaid designs are similar in design to engine-turned patterns and are incorrectly attributed to engine turning by many dealers and collectors.

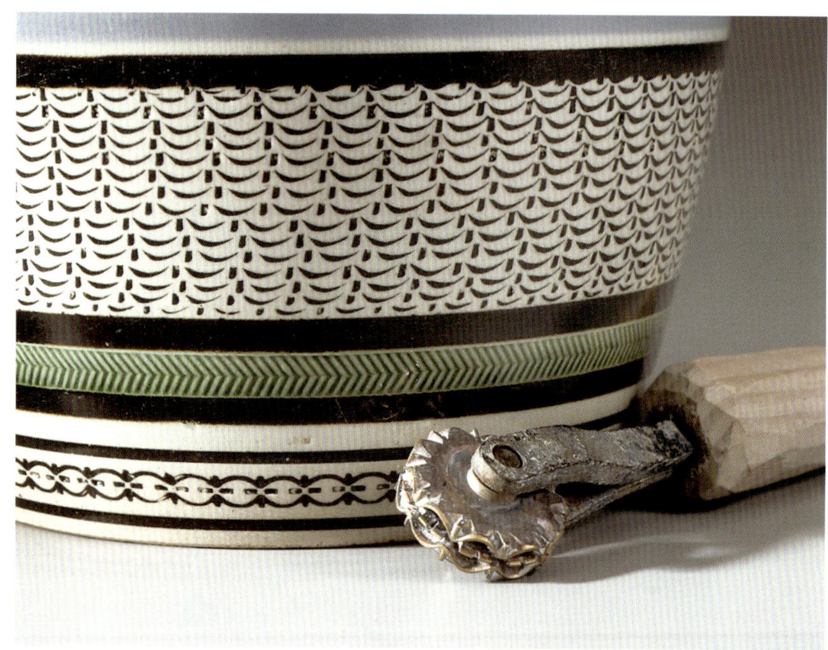

Figure 52 Teapot, Staffordshire, ca. 1770. Earthenware. H. 4⅛". (Courtesy, Skinner's.) This teapot has typical engine-turned decoration under its colorful glaze, and without close inspection one would assume that it had been cut on such a lathe. In fact, this pot was press-molded. The blocks used to produce the molds in which it was pressed were made from an original master model that was, in fact, cut on an engine lathe. Mold marks run down both the front and rear of the pot and are partially obscured by the handle and spout. This technique was one of the ways that small potteries could compete with larger firms that had expensive engine lathes.

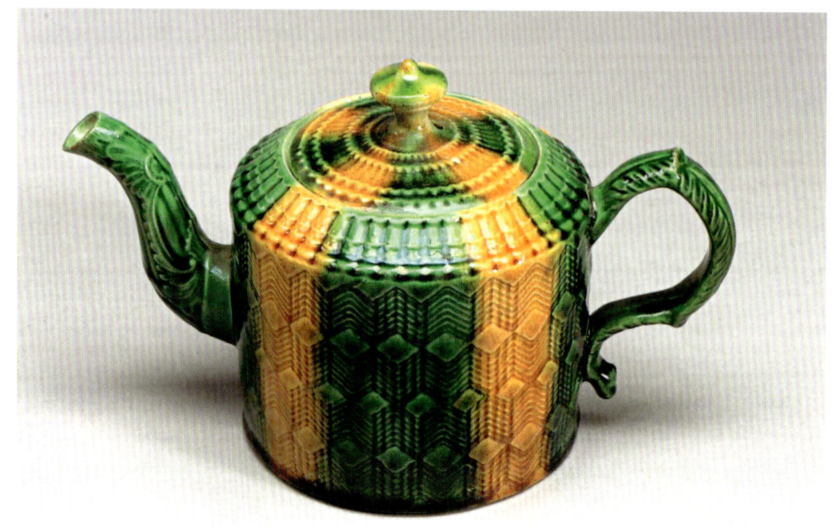

Figure 53 Beginning the process of cutting a pattern with the edge cam through firm slip on the leather-hard body of a quart mug. Because of the need for full circumferential access, the last step before biscuit firing is the application of the handle. In this pattern, chevrons are an integral part of the design, so a V-shaped rather than flat blade is used. The rouletted patterns near the rim and the foot will be brushed with a concentrated glaze mixture containing copper oxide.

Figure 54 The earliest stage of cutting the chevron pattern.

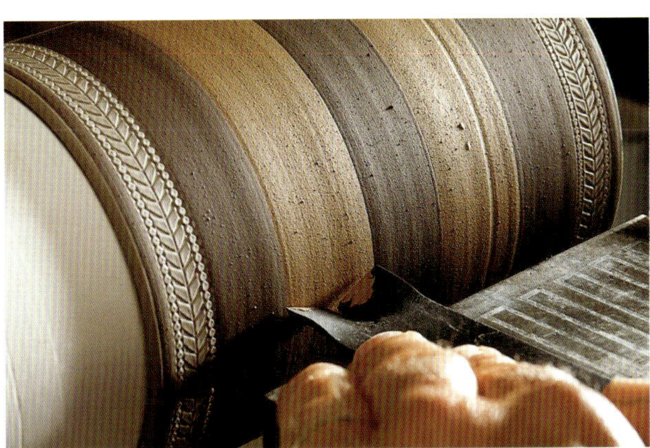

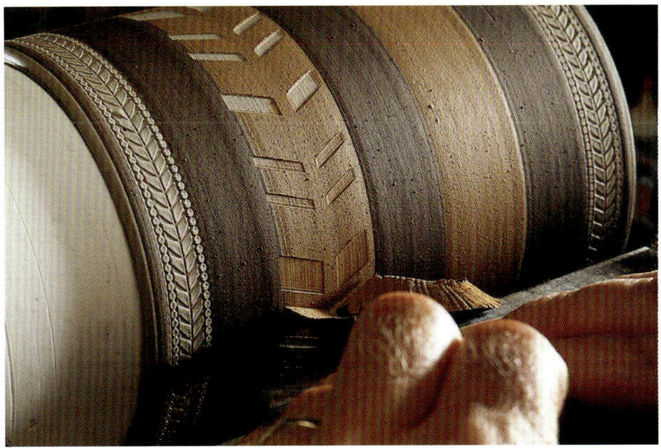

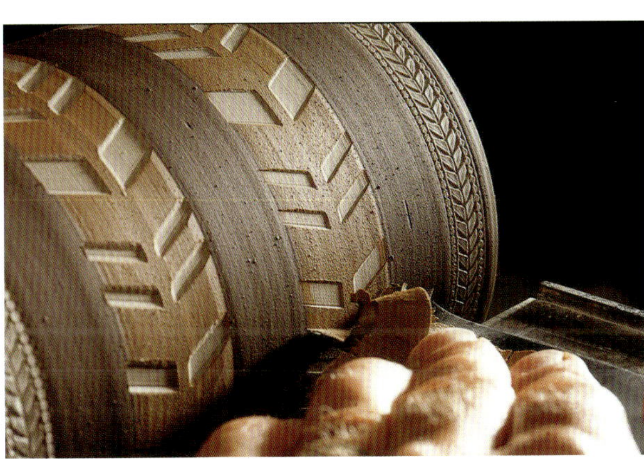

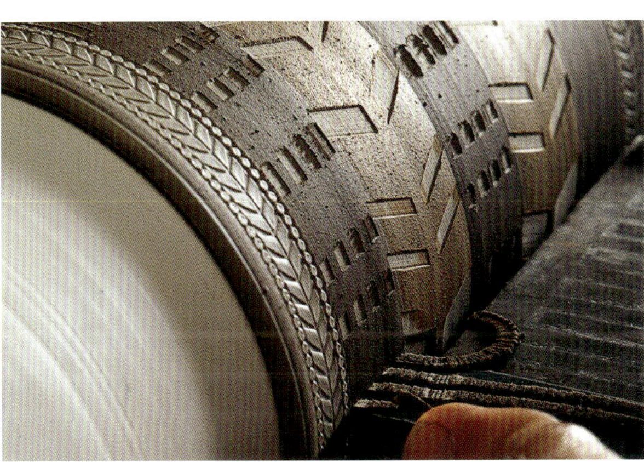

Figure 55 The pattern begins to reveal the body color beneath the slip.

Figure 56 A different blade being used to cut the short dashes through the contrasting slip band.

consisted of mugs, jugs, bowls and other functional tablewares with colors and geometric patterns that have a very modern appearance.

Unlike standard dipped or mocha wares, engine-turned items require a great amount of planning.[15] Potters were not able to just throw a random shape on the potter's wheel and then turn and decorate it on the engine lathe. The potter would have to carefully draw out and plan the size of each curve, cut, and type of ornament. Knives would be cut to fit the exact shape of large sections of the body in order to produce vertical fluting or reeding. The time needed to set up the lathe for each specific operation was considerable, and therefore economy dictated that large numbers of a specific design be made while the lathe was set up.

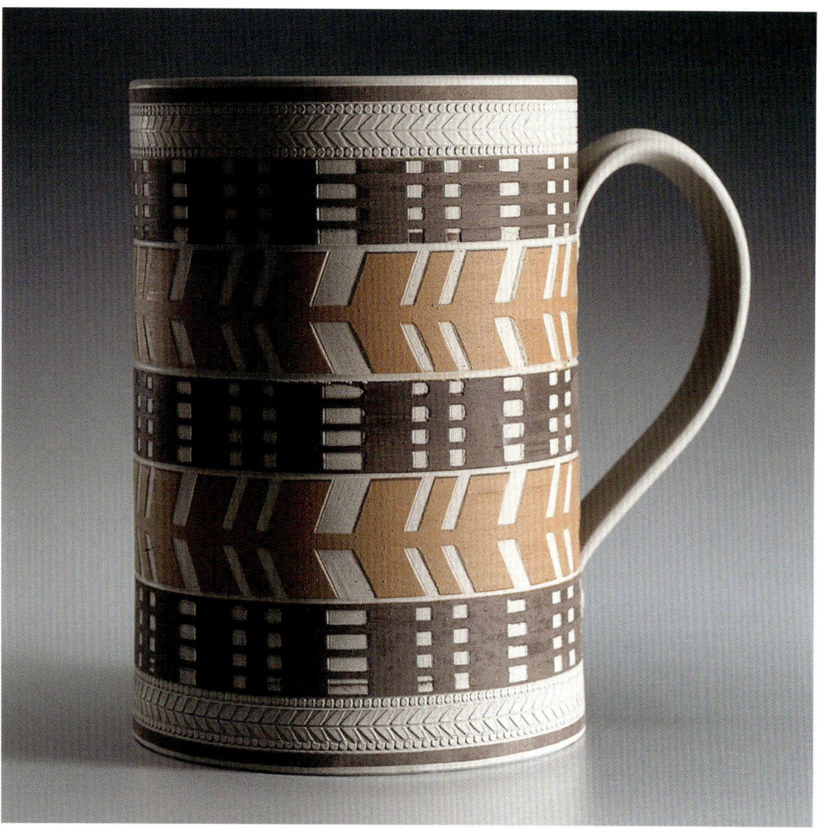

Figure 57 The completed mug prior to biscuit firing.

Two basic methods of decoration were employed in producing engine-turned dipped wares. In one, the geometric pattern was cut into the surface of the vessel, which was then dipped or flooded with slip. After the slip had been sufficiently absorbed into the pot body, the excess slip was turned away, leaving the slip remaining only in the created recesses. The other method involved cutting the pattern through a slip coating to reveal the body color in a mechanized version of sgraffito. Layering colors of slip and cutting through one or two layers—rather than through to the body itself—to reveal contrasting colors created more ambitious designs.

The most enduring application of the engine-turning lathe in potteries seems to have been with dipped wares. The more complicated patterns began to fall out of use around 1830, while simple checkered designs may be found on pots made at the very end of the nineteenth century, suggesting continuous production use of this machine at some potteries for more than a century. One late-nineteenth-century pottery making these wares in particular was at Llannelli in Wales. The popularity of these wares is attested to by the later imitations by French and German factories, with existing examples bearing the mark of Villeroy and Boch, Dresden.

1. Robin Reilly, *Wedgwood* (London: MacMillan London, 1989), 1: 201.

2. Katherine Eufemia, Lady Farrer, ed., *Wedgwood's Letters to Bentley 1762–1770* (London: Women's Printing Society, Limited [for private circulation], 1903), p. 47.

3. J.V.G. Mallet, "Engine-turning on Chelsea Porcelain, with Considerations on Its Previous Use at Meissen and Vincennes/Sèvres," *English Ceramic Circle Transactions* 17, pt. 3 (2001): 420–29. It is possible that those objects considered to have been engine-turned were pressed into a patterned mold. Segments of the block from which the plaster mold was cast conceivably

were cut on a straight-line engine lathe commonly used in the metal-working trades. Salt-glazed stonewares of the same period appear to have been produced this way, as the process of engine-turning in the round could not have been used on the marley with raised rims.

4. Warren Greene Ogden Jr., "The Pedigree of Holtzapffel Lathes" (manuscript, North Andover, Mass., 1971).

5. Llewellynn Jewitt, *The Ceramic Art of Great Britain from Pre-historic Times down to the Present Day . . .* (London: Virtue and Company, 1878), 2: 401–2.

6. Ogden, "Pedigree of Holtzapffel Lathes."

7. *Allbut's Directory, Containing an Alphabetical List of Manufacturers in the Staffordshire Potteries* (Stoke-on-Trent, 1800).

8. Jewitt, *Ceramic Art of Great Britain,* pp. 401–2.

9. Sherds from an excavation at the Shelton Farm site headed by David Barker are in the archaeological stores of the Potteries Museum, Hanley, Stoke-on-Trent. See David Barker, "'The Usual Classes of Useful Articles': Staffordshire Ceramics Reconsidered," *Ceramics in America,* edited by Robert Hunter (Hanover, N.H.: University of New England Press for the Chipstone Foundation, 2001): 84.

10. Simeon Shaw, *History of the Staffordshire Potteries* (Hanley: Printed for the author by G. Jackson, 1829; reprint, New York: Praeger Publishers, 1970), p. 183.

11. Farrer, *Wedgwood's Letters,* pp. 142–43, "London, May 23, 1767," referring to Matthew Boulton: "He is I believe the first—or most complete manufacturer in England, in metal. He is very ingenious, Philosophical, & Agreeable. You must be acquainted with him, he has promised to come to Burslem, & wod. attend our congress (we are to have one immediately on my return remember on many accts.) but this year he is too much immers'd in business to indulge he says in anything else. There is a vast difference betwixt the spirit of this Man & the Great Taylor, though both of them have behaved exceeding liberally to me in offering me every improvement they could furnish me with." Taylor is identified here as a Birmingham manufacturer of buttons, buckles, etc. Preceding this passage is a note referring to Wedgwood's having seen an ingenious lathe at Boulton's Soho factory.

12. Charles Plumier, *L'art de tourner, ou de faire en perfection toutes sortes d'ouvrages au tour,* 2d ed., expanded by Charles-Antoine Jombert (Lyons: J. Carte, 1701; Paris: C.-A. Jombert, 1749). See also Farrer, *Wedgwood's Letters,* p. 113, February 1767: "We shall want the book on Engine turning with us . . ."; and R[ichard] B[entley], *Thomas Bentley, 1730–1780, of Liverpool, Etruria, and London* (Guildford: Billing and Sons, 1927; reprint, New York: Wedgwood Society of New York, 1975), p. 56.

13. Farrer, *Wedgwood's Letters,* p. 177, between October 12 and 24, 1767: "Inclos'd are Engine Turning, Antiquitys, Plans &c, & first, Engine Turning. I think you will meet with nothing very curious 'till you come to part the third, but I suppose you will skim the other part over. I hope you will read with a pen in your hand, & some sheets of blotting paper before you to enter the memorand^{ms}, as they occur to you & let me have the Identical sheets on which such memorand^{ms} are made. You will readily conceive which of the Machines may, or may not be applicable to a Potter . . ."; p. 203, Burslem, February 22, 1768: "We have an ingenious & indefatigable smith amongst us, who has ever since Engine Lathes were first introduc'd here, been constantly employd in that business, & he promises me very faithfully that whatever improvements I may instruct him in, he will make them for no one else . . ."; p. 222, Burslem, July 14, 1768: "I have accidentally met with another Artist who is like enough to stick by me if you can send me a good sober honest account of him. He is a Mathematical instrument maker, a Wooden-leg maker, a Caster of Printers types, & in short a Jack of all trades. His name is Brown & he wears a wooden leg, at present he is making me some legs, [Wedgwood was an amputee] but as he can forge Iron and file extremely well, & cast in various metals, I sho^{d}. employ him in making & repairing Engine Lathes, punches, & tools of all sorts"; p. 266, by July 1769: "You both want Vases,—you both want flowerpots, and you both want *Engin'd ware* of various kinds, & we have but two turners & an half for both our works, & for all these things which would employ six or eight."

14. One illustrated example (see fig. 52) indicates that some potteries manufactured items that appeared to be engine turned but were not. Instead, it appears that block-makers used an engine-turning lathe to create geometric patterns on the block from which molds were made and sold to factories that did not have an engine lathe.

15. See Donald Carpentier and Jonathan Rickard, "Slip Decoration in the Age of Industrialization," in *Ceramics in America,* edited by Robert Hunter (Hanover, N.H.: University of New England Press for the Chipstone Foundation, 2001): 115–34.

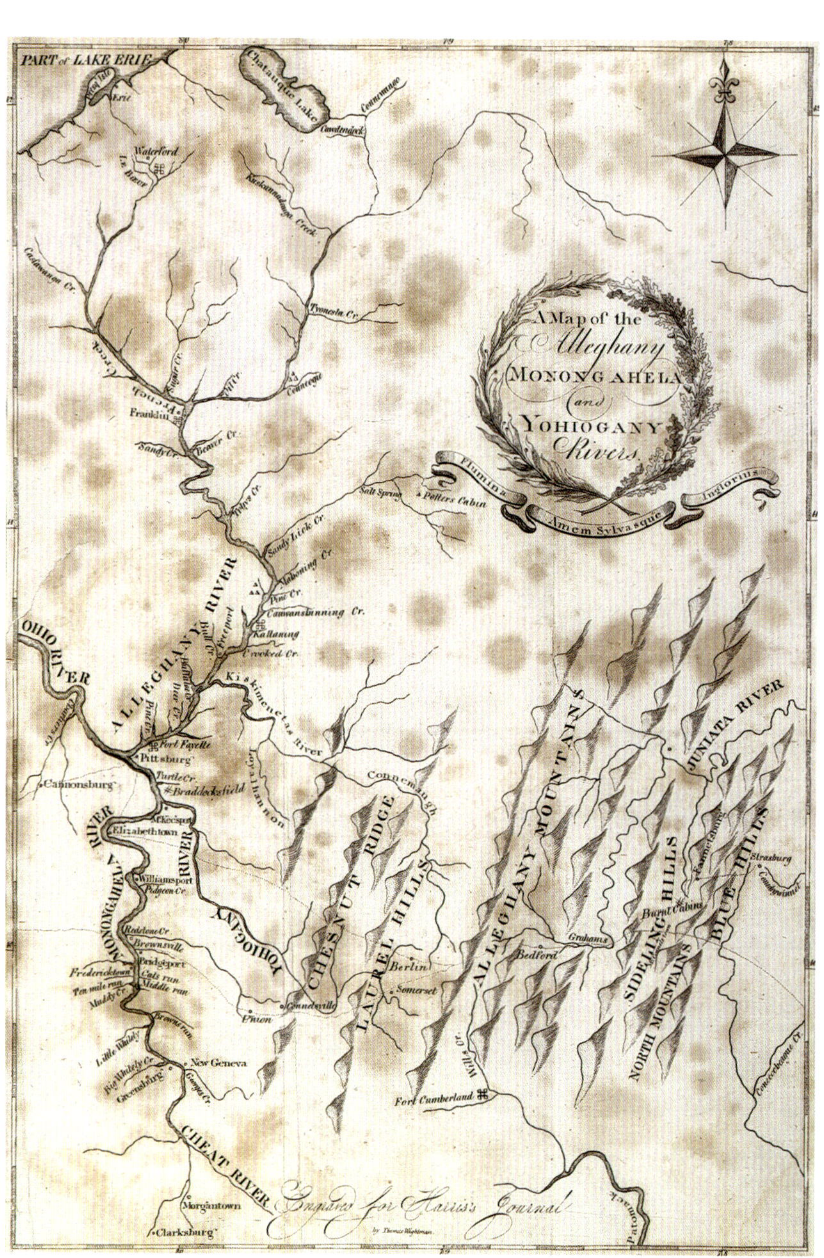

Figure 1 Thomas Wightman, "A Map of the Alleghany, Monongahela and Yohiogany Rivers," 1805. This map is from the *Journal of a Tour in the Territory Northwest of the Alleghany Mountains Made in the Spring of the Year 1803* by Thaddeus Mason Harris. It shows the Monongahela Valley, Clarksburg, Morgantown, Greensboro, New Geneva, and Pittsburgh. (Duez Collection.)

Don Horvath and Richard Duez

The Potters and Pottery of Morgan's Town, Virginia: The Earthenware Years, Circa 1796–1854

▼ THE POTTERY PRODUCED in what is now Morgantown, West Virginia, is remarkable in several ways. Its decorative elements are diverse and often innovative, as are some of its forms. Its history is recorded more fully than that of most American pottery. And, through the efforts of Dr. Walter Hough, a Morgantown native who became an assistant curator of the Division of Ethnology at the U.S. National Museum, many early specimens, including potter tools, were collected in the nineteenth century and donated to the Smithsonian Institution in Washington, D.C.

There are several other publications that treat some aspect of the Morgantown potteries, the most important being Hough's seminal history, "An Early West Virginia Pottery."[1] This article examines the production and development of the earthenware in greater detail and incorporates findings from three episodes of "backhoe archaeology" within the past decade. The first excavation took place in the basement of Morgantown's Old Stone House, as well as in a trench in front of this late-eighteenth-century building; the second occurred on the property designated as Lot 88, where the potter's kiln was located; the third, which yielded a large number of sherds, was at a satellite pottery in Clarksburg, West Virginia.

The Setting

Rapid population growth in Virginia's eastern region spurred inland exploration after 1700. By the second half of the eighteenth century settlers were streaming westward (although the population of the Morgantown area remained sparse until General "Mad Anthony" Wayne's victory over the Indians resulted in the signing of a peace treaty at Greenville, Ohio, in 1795).

In a 1768 land office lottery, Col. Zackquill Morgan won a settlement right to land adjoining the Monongahela River and Decker's Creek (fig. 1), although he waited until 1772 before moving from his farm in Bedford, Pennsylvania. Originally called Morgan's Town, the settlement was laid out by Maj. William Haymond in 1783/84. By that time, Thomas Laidley, who was recruited to the area by entrepreneur Albert Gallatin, had opened a mercantile store.

According to family history James Thompson Sr. of Bel Air, Maryland, came to the area when he was chosen to assist his Revolutionary War commander, Capt. Samuel Hanway, in the task of surveying Monongalia County. In 1787 Thompson took up permanent residence in Morgantown, where three of his sons and three of his grandsons would become potters.[2]

Potters gained a secure foothold in the area because the entire region of southwestern Pennsylvania, mideastern Ohio, and north-central Virginia once lay at the bottom of an extensive lake created by a glacial dam. Over time, fine clay particles settled in layers of considerable depth on the lake bottom. The clays, which included significant amounts of kaolin (porcelain clay), would—millennia hence, in the nineteenth and twentieth centuries—support the region's large-scale stoneware potteries.

These clays, as well as the high cost of imported pottery, the cheap land, and the prospect of shipping wares downriver to larger markets, encouraged potters to move to Morgantown, the head of navigation.[3] However, downstream competition developed at nearby Greensboro, Pennsylvania, in the early 1800s. This competition may explain why many of the Morgantown examples found in the twentieth century came from areas south and east of Morgantown, rather than to its north. Moreover, by 1815 there were yellow ware potters in Pittsburgh, and Pittsburgh dealers were also importing English queensware via the Mississippi and Ohio Rivers.[4]

The First Anglo-European Potters

In his report for the U.S. National Museum, Hough stated that a pottery was in existence in Morgantown "before 1785" and was operated by "Master Foulk." However, ceramic historian Gene Comstock has shown that Jacob Foulk Jr. was in Frederick County, Virginia, at least in the early part of 1801.[5] The most direct evidence of Morgantown's eighteenth-century potting activity is Hugh McNeely's sale of "the pottery kiln lot," the south half of Lot 7 (fig. 2), to John Scott, occupation not given, in

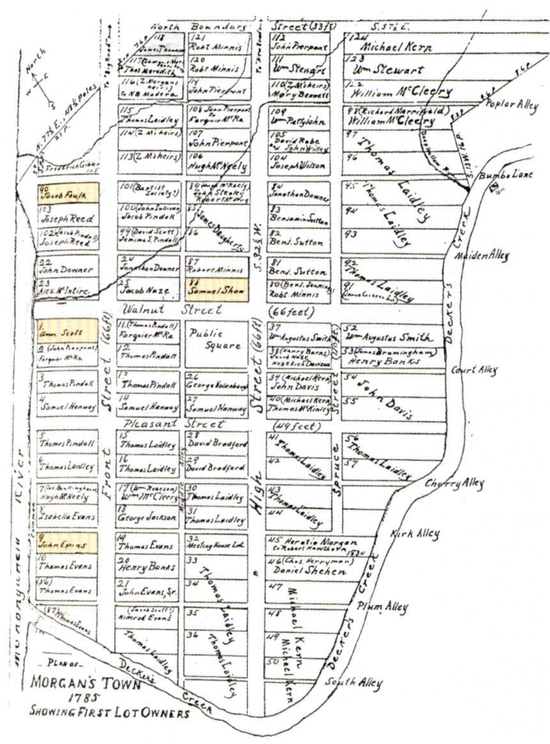

Figure 2 James M. Callahan, *History of the Making of Morgantown, West Virginia* (Morgantown: West Virginia University Studies in History, 1926). Reconstructed by county clerk Evans after loss of the court records in a 1796 fire.

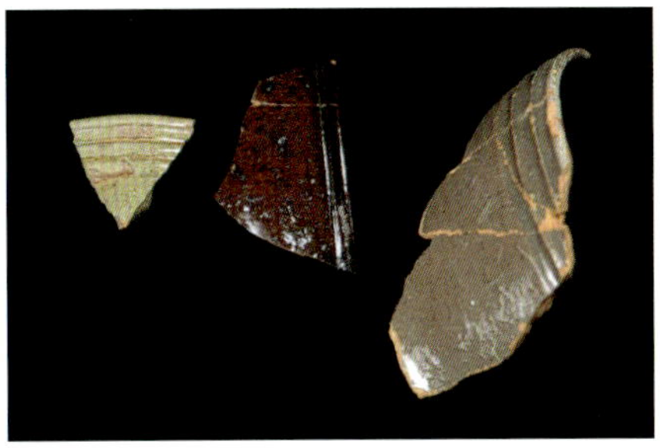

Figure 3 Sherds, Morgantown, West Virginia, ca. 1810. Earthenware. (Photo, Gavin Ashworth.) These fragments were recovered from the basement of the Old Stone House in Morgantown. (The town was still part of Virginia at the time they were made, as West Virginia did not become a state until 1863.) The very thin walls, which are approximately ⅛" thick, may be evidence of the production of "fine" tablewares during the Jefferson Embargo period. Several sherds with piercing (not shown) also suggest attempts at producing fine tablewares.

1800.[6] Historian James Callahan was convinced that Scott was a potter, but we have not found court records that confirm this.[7] (In any event, potting by Scott would have ceased in 1807 when he was sentenced to five years in jail for stealing a horse.[8]) Callahan also believed that Francis Billingsley was a potter. Billingsley did own Lot 7 from 1814 to 1827 and shared it with Foulk beginning in 1815.[9]

Some of Hough's dates for particular earthenware pieces do not agree with current research, but his overall timeline for the glazes and forms of wares deserves attention. He states that the "first ware made at Morgantown was porous terra-cotta covered with a yellow lead glaze," although later he offers conflicting color information: "Terra-cotta covered with glaze giving the reddish-brown color which is said to have been the color of the earliest ware made at Morgantown."[10]

The difference in color may distinguish the fine tableware from the more utilitarian wares. Hough continues,

> During the War of 1812, as [potter] William Boughner of Greensboro, Pennsylvania informs me, "the yellow glazed ware was in good demand. . . . cups and saucers sold at a dollar the set." Previously the [Morgantown] wares were of the commoner forms for domestic use, such as milk pans, preserve jars, jugs, etc. . . . Teapots, cups, saucers, dishes, and other tableware were turned out [in Morgantown] . . . fragments from the site of the old pottery show its character [fig. 3].[11]

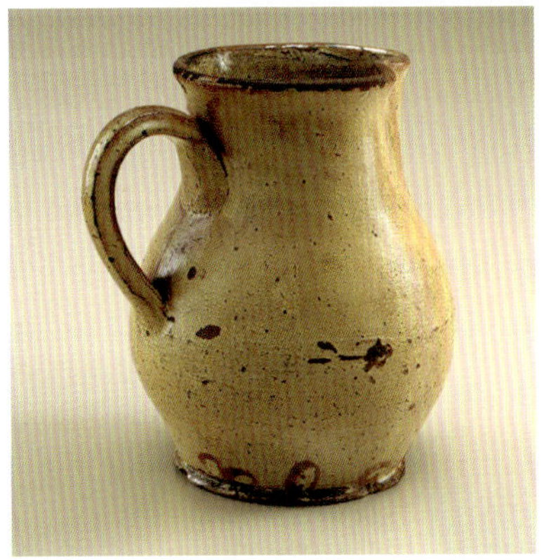

Figure 4 Pitcher, Morgantown, West Virginia, ca. 1810. Earthenware. H. 7¼". (Private collection; photo, Gavin Ashworth.) This straw-colored pitcher is finely formed and finished, and although it is not thin-walled it may be what Hough called "yellow tableware" of the Jefferson Embargo period. Its handle has the chamfered-edge cross section noted under jugs. The pitcher has a capacity slightly less than one quart. It was found in a Morgantown yard sale.

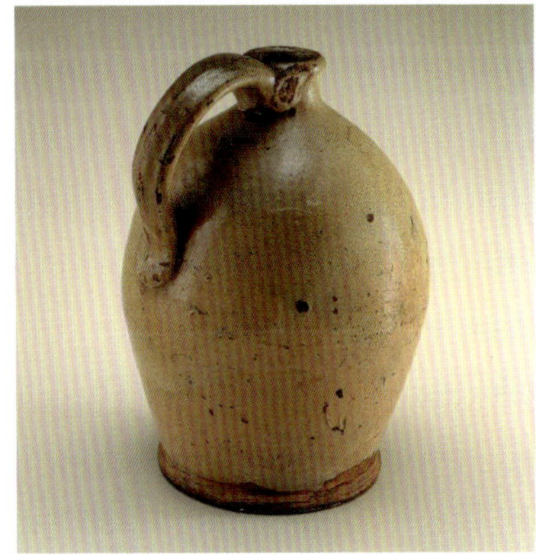

Figure 5 Jug, probably Morgantown, West Virginia, ca. 1810. Earthenware. H. 8⅝". (Private collection; photo, Gavin Ashworth.)

It is probable that Hough's "yellow glazed ware" was a thin white clay slip rendered yellow by traces of iron. Several extant straw-colored pieces may be what he described (figs. 4–6). Hough then describes the next phase: "'redware,' or terra-cotta, covered with transparent lead glaze. In the period around 1800 a number of glazes began to be used, such as dark-

Figure 6 Milk pan, probably Morgantown, West Virginia, ca. 1830. Earthenware. D. 14¾". (Private collection; photo, Gavin Ashworth.)

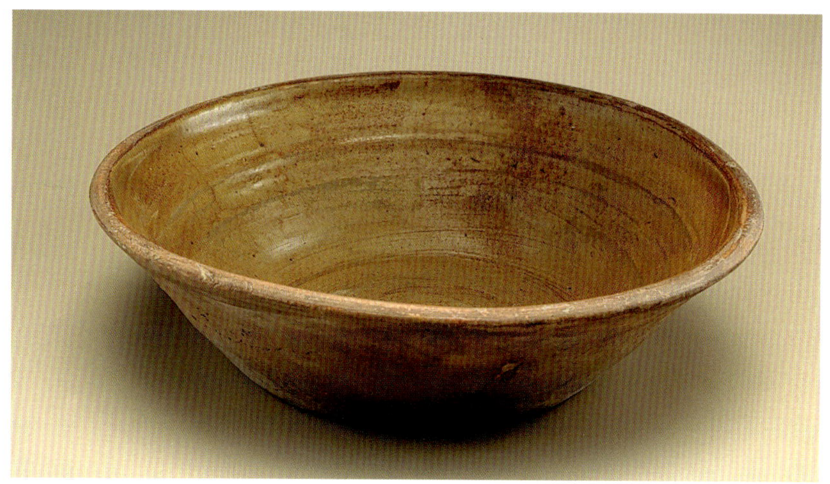

brown lead glaze, black iron or manganese glaze, [Flemish] gray 'china glaze,' greenish-gray [also called china glaze by the potters] and white, the surviving specimens being interesting and beautiful."[12] Many key examples of these ceramic types—gifts to the Smithsonian Institution principally from Mrs. Dorcas Haymond, daughter of nineteenth-century potter John W. Thompson—are featured in black and white photographs published in Hough's history. The names of glazes are presumably those used by Thompson and his sons.

Chronological Account of the Morgantown Potters

JACOB FOULK JR. (FOUKE, FOLK, FULK), CA. 1764–AFTER 1817

Even though two "Jacob Foulks" appear in the 1801 Taxables List for Monongalia County, it is known that Jacob Foulk Jr. and his slaves, Reuben and Samuel, moved to Morgantown in 1801.[13] In 1804 father and son are distinguished in the records, and Jacob Jr., recorded as having three white males above sixteen years in his household, apparently was a builder as well as a potter. He offered to build a brick house for Nicholas Madeira and to supply the bricks.[14] One might have expected him to keep his slaves for digging and pugging clay and making bricks while he did the skilled work. However, evidently he had sold Reuben and Samuel soon after arriving in Morgantown, as no slaves with those names appear in the records nor were blacks declared in his tax entries.

Over the years, he did acquire other help. In 1803 he engaged Charles Snodgrass Jr. as his first recorded Morgantown apprentice. Around 1804 John W. Thompson was his second recorded apprentice.

Payments in pottery were common for Jacob Jr. "Earthenware at the said Foulk's Pothouse in Morgantown" was his method of paying for land. In the contract for a land purchase in 1804, for example, Jacob Jr. agreed to pay with $600 in crockery for each of two six-month periods. This arrangement hints at the production output of his pottery and also provides some insight into his financial well-being. In 1804 Foulk's land still was not paid for, however, and the crockery payment was deferred for another year.

Whatever Foulk's financial status, it could not have been helped by his frequent legal difficulties. Foulk is somewhat remarkable for the number of court cases in which he appears. Charges against him include slander, resisting execution "by force and arms" (he threatened to strike the constable with "an earthen pott"), assault and battery, trespass and battery, wife beating, suing to avoid paying $50 owed for a bet on a horse race, suing to restrain his father-in-law, Elihu Horton, from providing shelter for Horton's battered daughter, perjury, and two instances of fathering a baseborn child. He was even sued by his father for debts. Hough reports that in order to make lead glaze, Foulk stripped the lead liner from tea chests and oxidized the lead in an open iron pan.[15] It is tempting to suggest that lead poisoning from this practice contributed to his egregious behavior.

In 1803 both John Scott and Foulk were charged by "Margaret ———" with bastardy and each paid $50. This suggests that the two men knew each other. Two years earlier Scott may have leased the kiln site on Lot 7 to Foulk.[16] Were this the case, it would be circumstantial evidence that Scott also worked there and was a potter. If Scott had agreed to lease the pottery from businessman Hugh McNeely until he could purchase it outright, this would answer the question of Scott's trade. As postmaster, keeper of an "ordinary" (tavern), and also owner of a brewery, McNeely would have had the resources to build the pottery as a source of rent or of "shares" income.[17] The fact that Scott was residing with Patrick Johnson in the 1786 Taxables List suggests that he was not then in a position to acquire property in Morgantown proper. In 1770 he had been granted land in Union District "on Decker's Creek,"[18] but this was probably "undeveloped" forest that was of little value at the time. Scott did purchase the south half of Lot 7 for $100 in May 1800, but he sold it to Ralph Berkshire in 1806.

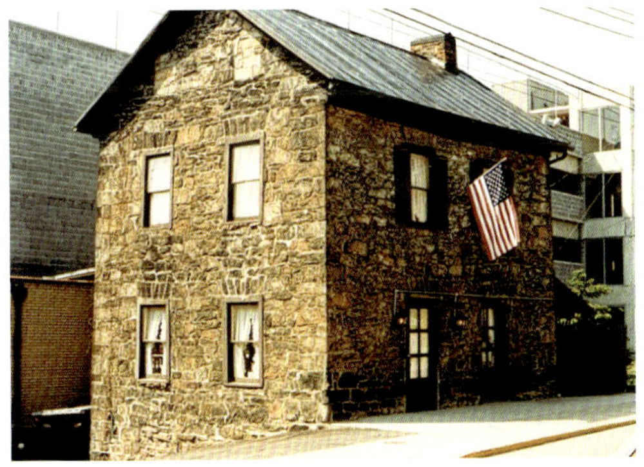

Figure 7 Old Stone House, Morgantown, West Virginia. (Photo, Richard Duez.) This building, on the north half of Lot 25, was owned by Jacob Foulk Jr. from 1807 to 1809, when it passed to James Goff, who then sold it to John W. Thompson in August 1810. Thompson kept it until May 1813. The earthenware floor of the basement contained several wheelbarrow loads of clay—more orange clay than white clay—and some earthenware sherds. A stone-lined drain capped with stone ran from the front to the back. It is now the home of the Morgantown Service League and is on the National Register of Historic Places.

The year 1805 was the last in which two Jacob Foulks were found in the Monongalia County Taxables List; only Jacob Jr. appears through 1813. In 1807 Foulk purchased the north half of Lot 25, near the kiln site on Lot 88. In 1810 the property passed from James Goff to John W. Thompson. Clay that was removed from the basement of the house on Lot 25 (fig. 7) may represent potting activity, which would have been conveniently located to the kiln across Middle Alley. It also is possible that the clay was simply stored where it would not freeze during winter.

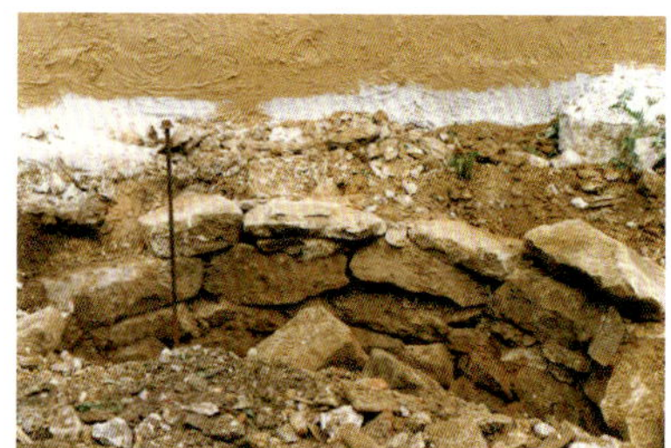

Figure 8 The kiln used jointly by Jacob Foulk Jr. and John W. Thompson. (Photo, Don Horvath.) Located on Lot 88, the kiln operated from about 1812 to 1830. It was uncovered in 1992, when a later structure built over it was partially burned and subsequently removed. When first seen, there were several courses of dense, dark-red bricks atop a sandstone foundation approximately 1 foot thick and 3½ feet above a consolidated floor. The stones were irregular and there was little or no mortar bonding them.

The west end of the chamber was a somewhat flattened half circle with an inner radius of approximately 2 feet. This merged with two parallel sides 5 feet apart running about 6 or 8 feet to the east wall. The latter had an opening about 3 feet wide from which two parallel walls extended a short distance farther east. At the time of the photo the eastern end was already reburied, in preparation for paving a parking lot that same day. Note the remnants of red bricks in the center foreground. There were considerable accumulations of unfired, mostly orange, clay containing some sherds close to the mouth of the kiln.

In 1812 Jacob Jr. bought the Lot 88 kiln site (fig. 8). The same year he conveyed it to Thompson, who returned it in 1814. Such frequent property transfers suggest cash flow problems.

In 1815 Jacob Jr. entered into a property sharing agreement with Francis Billingsley for the joint operation of the pottery on Lot 7, and in 1817 his name appears jointly with Billingsley's in a suit initiated by William Gallahue. However, Jacob Jr. may have been absent from Morgantown by this time. He is said to have gone to Brooke County, Virginia, in 1817,[19] although in 1820 he collected an 1817 debt from Joseph Allen in Monongalia County Court. Neither father nor son is mentioned in any of the wills recorded in Brooke County, Virginia, and there are apparently no "Cemetery Readings" from Brooke County.

Jacob Jr.'s name has not been found on any pottery, but there are slip-decorated sherds (fig. 9) and several intact pieces (figs. 10–12) that we believe are his work.[20] They share slight irregularities in the contours of the walls but are significantly better than those we attribute to John W. Thompson (fig. 13). Jacob Jr.'s putative pieces have a lustrous and viscous dark trailed slip, creating three-dimensional, finely tapered stems supporting two-dimensional brushed slip leaves. Some of the jars display

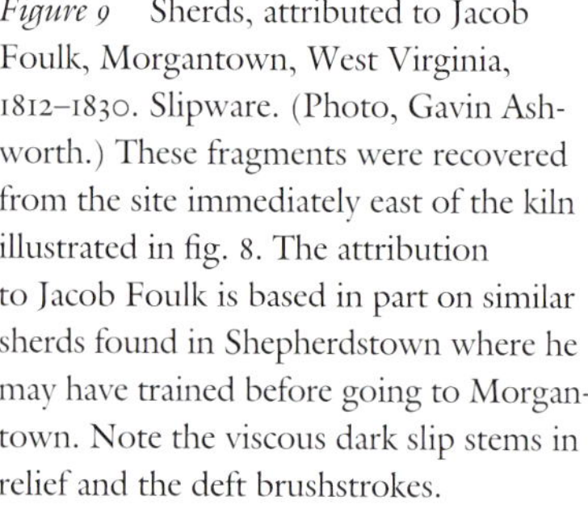

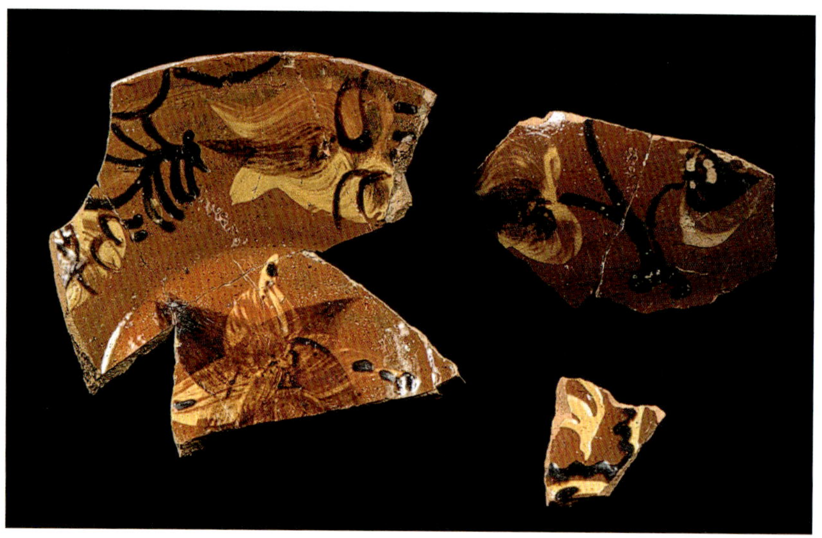

Figure 9 Sherds, attributed to Jacob Foulk, Morgantown, West Virginia, 1812–1830. Slipware. (Photo, Gavin Ashworth.) These fragments were recovered from the site immediately east of the kiln illustrated in fig. 8. The attribution to Jacob Foulk is based in part on similar sherds found in Shepherdstown where he may have trained before going to Morgantown. Note the viscous dark slip stems in relief and the deft brushstrokes.

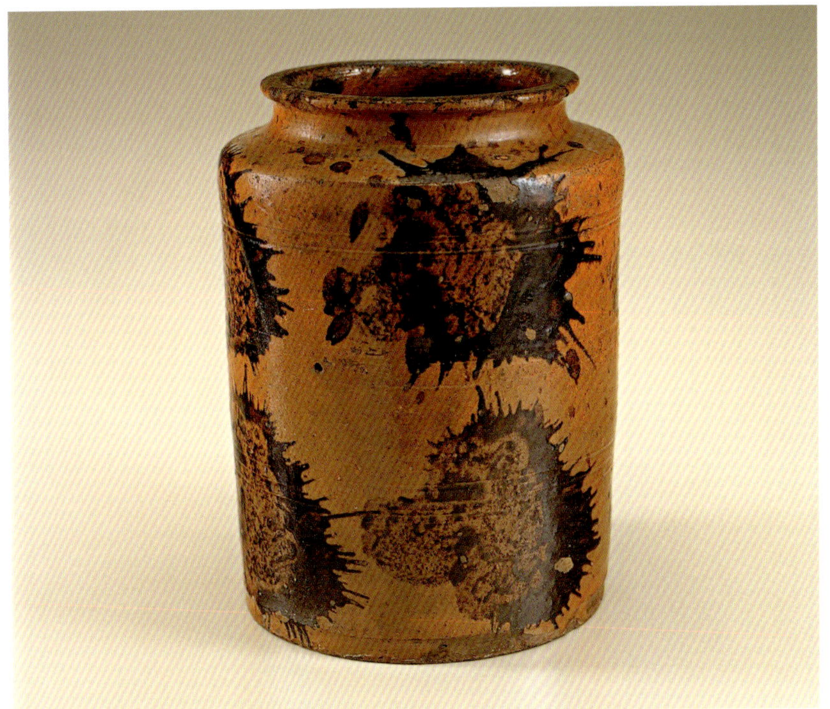

Figure 10 Jar, attributed to Jacob Foulk, Morgantown, West Virginia, 1802–1817. Earthenware. H. 8⅛". (Private collection; photo, Gavin Ashworth.) Earthenware cylindrical storage jar with bold sponged decoration. This has a less red color on the base than some we attribute to Foulk and Thompson, but there are others of this shade with Morgantown provenance.

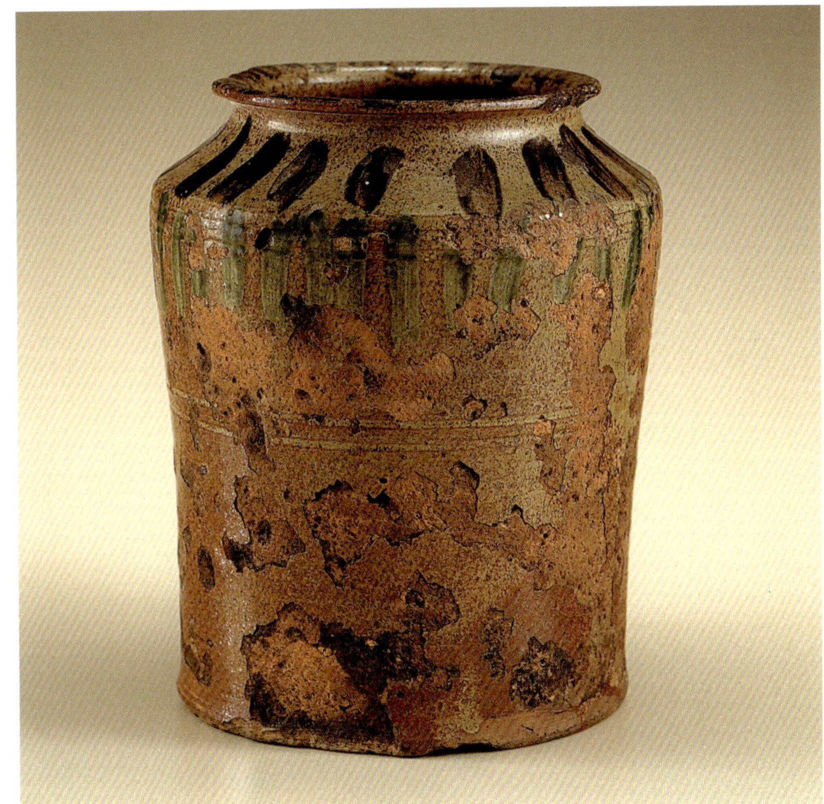

Figure 11 Jar, attributed to Jacob Foulk, Morgantown, West Virginia, ca. 1802–1817. Earthenware. H. 7¾". (Private collection; photo, Gavin Ashworth.) This cylindrical string-tie storage jar has green and black brushed slip decoration. The rim has narrow black brushed slip stripes. All of these appear to be more hurried than the other brushed slip examples. Note that the green is brighter than usual when applied directly to a red body. The slip probably included white clay as a substitute for engobe.

cuprous green brushed on top of white slip, thereby masking the dark background clay. Applying the green leaves over the white ones is a de facto use of engobe. However, there is no engobe on the storage jar with green strokes (see fig. 11) nor on the small leaflets of figure 12. It is probable that

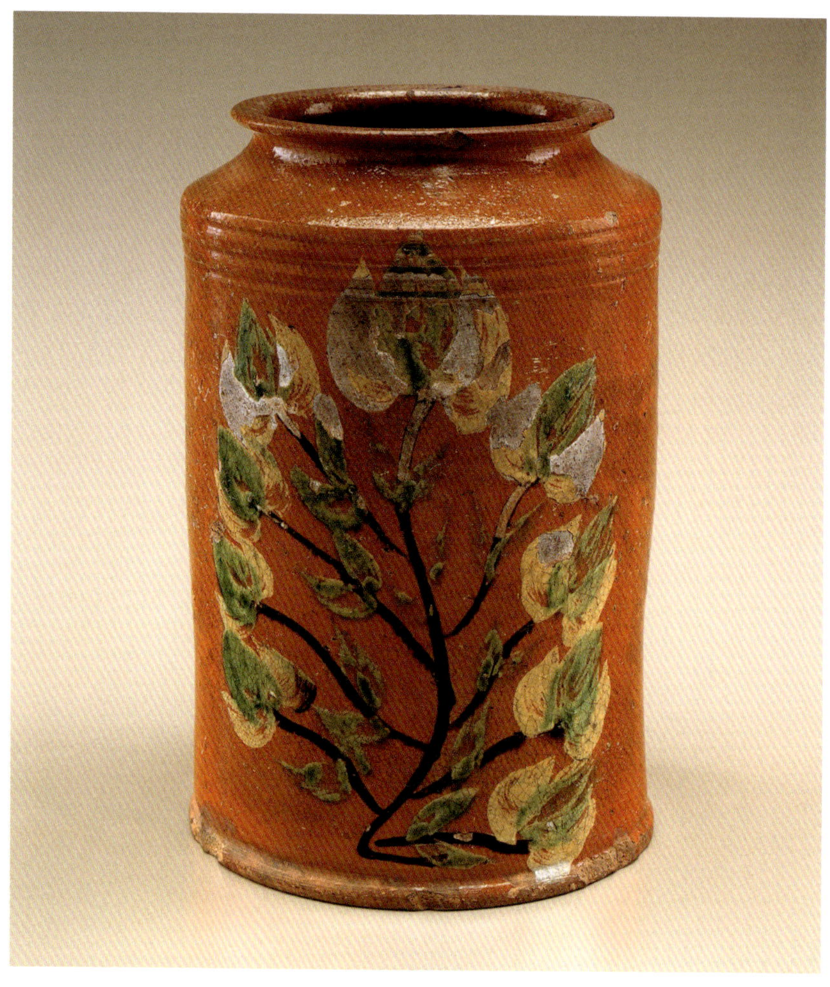

Figure 12 Jar, attributed to Jacob Foulk, Morgantown, West Virginia, ca. 1802–1817. Earthenware. H. 8". (Private collection; photo, Gavin Ashworth.) This cylindrical string-tie storage jar shows trailed viscous dark slip and brushed white and green slip. The white slip is a de facto engobe, but the green slip appears to incorporate some white slip, as evidenced in the small leaflets.

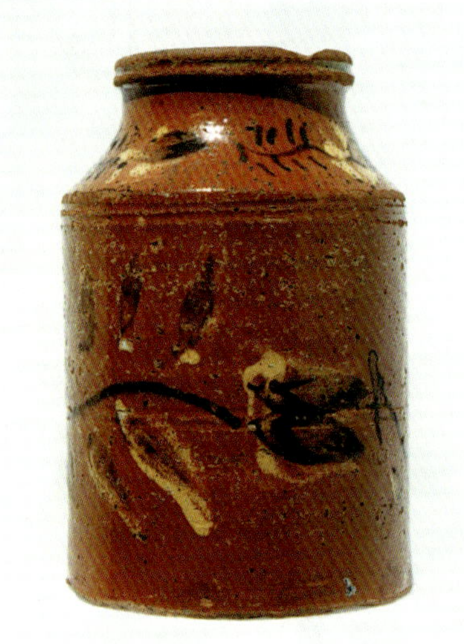

Figure 13 Jar, possibly John Wood Thompson, Morgantown, West Virginia, ca. 1810–1830. Earthenware. H. 7¾". (Courtesy, George R. Allen.) The slip decoration is looser than in the examples illustrated in figs. 9–12.

the copper was premixed into a white slip or the green would have been much darker.[21] It is partly this distinction among contrasting greens that led us to attribute the cylindrical storage jar in the Smithsonian's collection to Samuel Butter, another of Foulk's former apprentices (figs. 14, 15). A further distinction of Foulk's work is his "fuller" use of available space.

Charles Snodgrass Jr., b. ca. 1787

Charles Snodgrass Jr. was apprenticed to Jacob Foulk Jr. in Morgantown in 1803, when he was "upwards of sixteen years of age." He married Jacob's daughter, Sarah, the same year. The couple later moved to Trumbull County in northeastern Ohio.

We have no further information concerning him or his wares.

Francis Billingsley (Billingsly, Billings), dates unknown

Francis Billingsley first appears in the 1801 Taxables List but could have been settled in the area as early as 1788 since the intervening records are lost. Based on information from several records, Billingsley was believed to have been involved in the pottery business, and Callahan implied that he was, in fact, a potter.[22] However, Billingsley may also have been content to let others do the actual potting. In his 1815 contract with Jacob Foulk Jr. for

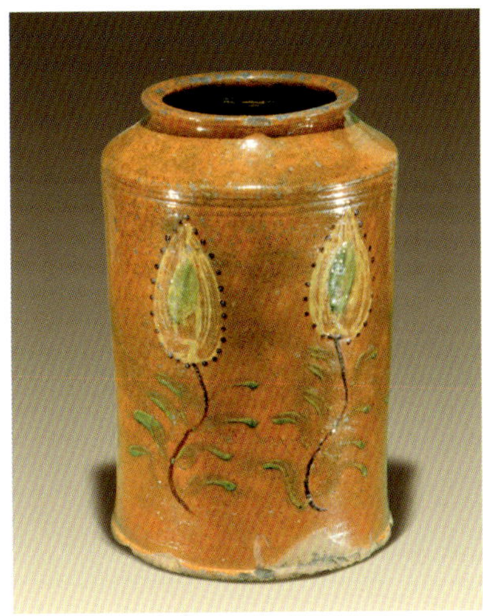

Figure 14 Jar, probably Samuel Butter, Clarksburg, West Virginia, ca. 1820. Earthenware. H. 10¼". (Courtesy, Ceramics and Glass Collection, National Museum of American History.) This cylindrical string-tie storage jar has trailed viscous dark slip and brushed white and green slip. The decoration resembles that on the sherds illustrated in fig. 9.

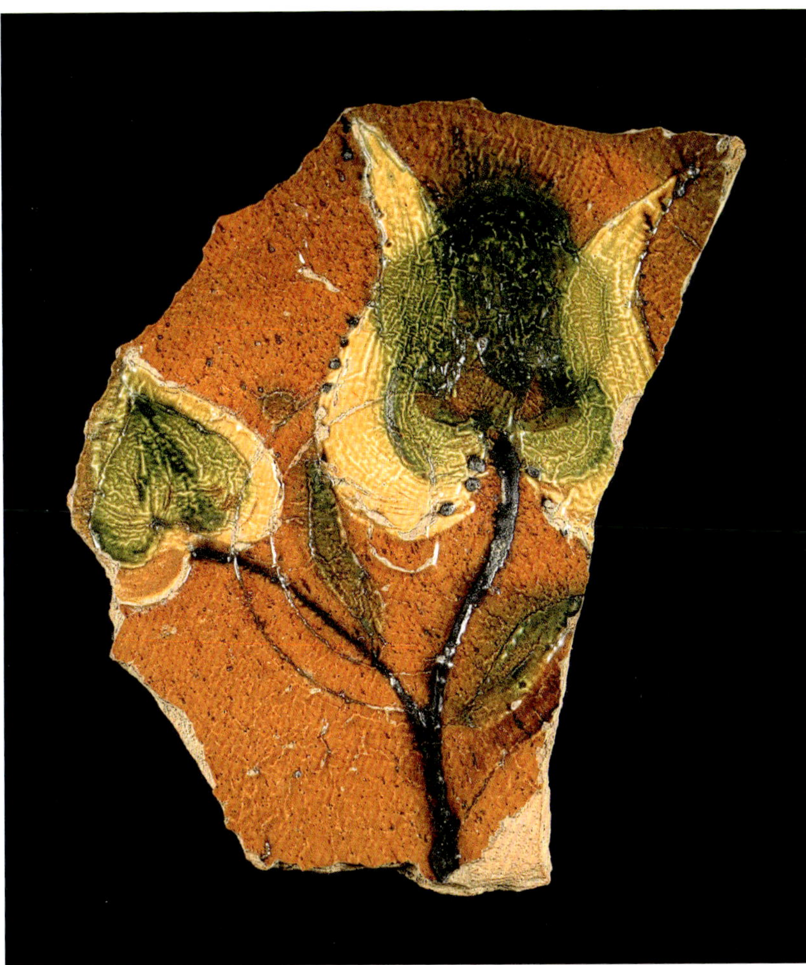

Figure 15 Sherd, Samuel Butter, Clarkburg, West Virginia. Slipware. (Private collection; photo, Gavin Ashworth.)

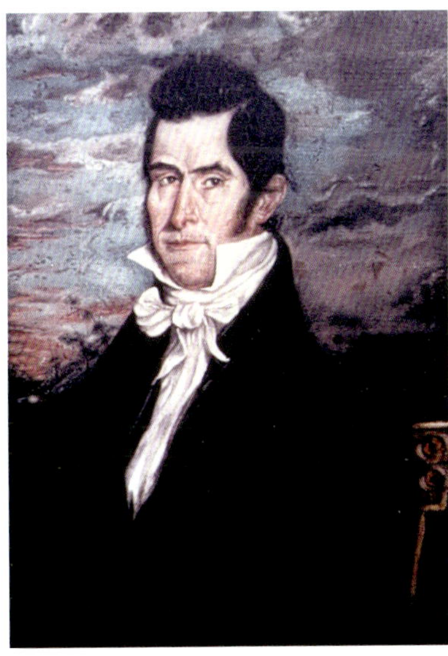

Figure 16 Portrait of John W. Thompson, Baltimore, probably painted in Baltimore, ca. 1830. (Courtesy, R. Crommett.)

the joint operation on Lot 7, which he had purchased from Ralph Berkshire in 1814, Billingsley agreed to provide all materials necessary "for the prosecution of the said business" as well as the venue, and to have "half the wares made and finished in the said shop."[23] Foulk was also to keep one wheel going half the year and a second wheel the entire year. Billingsley had other interests to pursue; he became a magistrate, legislator, and tavern owner.

We know of no examples of his work.

John W. Thompson, 1782–November 1863

John Wood Thompson (fig. 16) was the son of James M. Thompson Sr. (1732–1809) and Sarah Dorcas Wood (b. 1738). The couple is said to have moved to Dorsey's Fort (just south of Morgantown) from Bel Air, Maryland, "about 1785" when John W. was "four years old"[24]—family history indicates the year was 1787. John W.'s father was a boot maker and a Methodist preacher who is said to have been granted over 1,000 acres in Ross County, Ohio.[25] He had sufficient resources to purchase Lot 118 in 1790 and to build "the fifth house" in Morgantown.[26] This house would pass first to John W., then to David G. Thompson.

In 1803 John W.'s first known venture was a tailoring business "in all its branches." Since he advertised for a "journeyman tailor," it is probable that he was an entrepreneur, not an accomplished tailor.[27] The apparent failure of this endeavor may account for his apprenticeship agreement in 1805, when he was twenty-two or twenty-three, with Jacob Foulk Jr. It is possible he began his new career a year earlier, however, since he, his father, and his younger brother, James M. Thompson Jr., were summoned to appear in court in 1804 to testify in a case regarding Foulk's debt to Davis Shockley. Shockley had agreed to board "one of Foulk's said boys for one year for two hundred dollars." The boy was probably apprentice Charles Snodgrass Jr.

John W. was first recorded in the Taxables List for Monongalia County in 1806 as having one white male above the age of sixteen, no slaves, and no horses. In 1810 he purchased Jacob Foulk Jr.'s house (now 313 Chestnut Street) on the north half of Lots 24 and 25 (see fig. 2), a short distance from the pottery kiln on Lot 88. The basement of that house yielded a quantity of clay, both orange and gray-white, and some glazed earthenware sherds (see fig. 3). A later excavation of the street in front of the house yielded numerous additional sherds, which probably are wasters that were used to fill potholes.

In 1812 John W. married his first wife, Mary Webb. Mary had a difficult delivery of twins at the end of her first pregnancy in 1812 or 1813. The daughter, Charlotte, survived, but the boy and Mary did not. That same year none other than Jacob Foulk Jr. sued John W. for assault and battery. Significantly, John W. is said to have advertised "Pottery Ware" for sale under his own name at this time.

In 1815 Foulk conveyed part of the kiln on Lot 88 to John W. but retained use of two-thirds of the pottery for four years, as well as the right to erect two wheels and to "burn or fire" his wares. The deed also required John W. to erect a new pottery within four years. Since Foulk was already engaged in a joint operation with Francis Billingsley, he now had up to four wheels operating simultaneously. If we add at least one wheel for John W., Morgantown was becoming a significant source of pottery.

Figure 17 Advertisement of John W. Thompson's pottery in the 1825 *Monongalia Chronicle*.

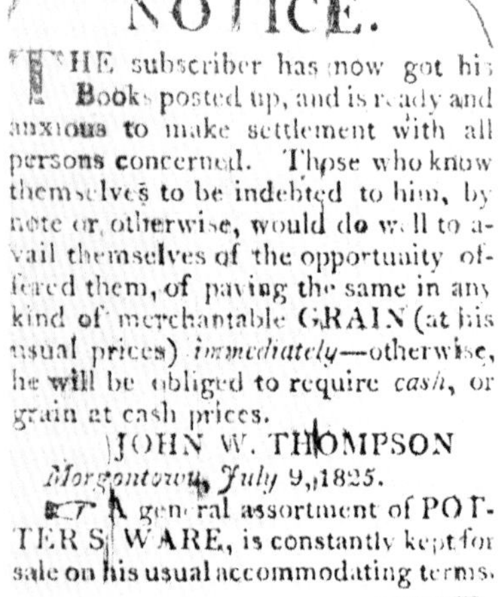

NOTICE.

THE subscriber has now got his Books posted up, and is ready and anxious to make settlement with all persons concerned. Those who know themselves to be indebted to him, by note or otherwise, would do well to avail themselves of the opportunity offered them, of paying the same in any kind of merchantable GRAIN (at his usual prices) *immediately*—otherwise, he will be obliged to require *cash*, or grain at cash prices.

JOHN W. THOMPSON

Morgantown, July 9, 1825.

☞ A general assortment of POTTERS WARE, is constantly kept for sale on his usual accommodating terms.

In the 1816 U.S. Census, John W. Thompson's household had three white males above sixteen years of age. He owned seven horses and paid sixty cents in taxes. We do not know if all the men noted were potters, but one may have been his younger brother James M. Thompson Jr. (b. 1786), who was a potter. Some of the horses might have been used to power pug mills to prepare clay, but most were probably bought on speculation since John W., like Foulk, also speculated in land.

By 1821 Thompson's resources had expanded to include four white males above the age of sixteen years, one slave above twelve years and another above sixteen years, and one horse. In 1824 or 1827 he purchased Billingsley's pottery,[28] and in 1825 he advertised "POTTER'S WARE" (fig. 17), noting that merchantable grain "at his usual prices" was the only alternative to cash payments.

In 1826 his household included one carriage, two horses, one slave above the age of sixteen years, and six white males above the age of sixteen. He paid $2.71 in taxes. Ownership of a carriage reflects growing wealth, and it

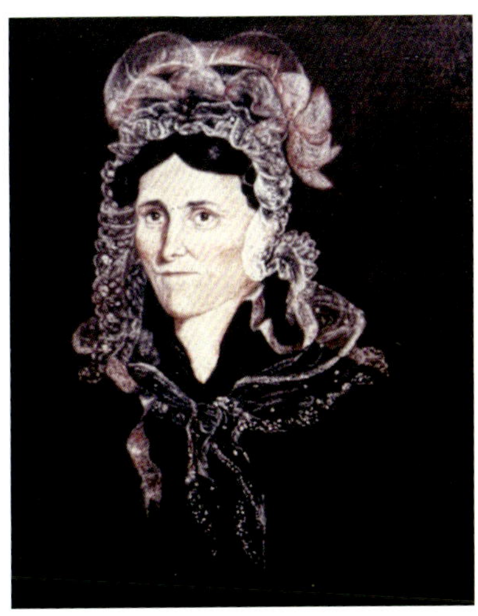

Figure 18 Portrait of Deborah Vance Thompson. (Courtesy, R. Crommett.)

may be that this was the period in which he commissioned a portrait of himself. The portrait of his second wife, Deborah Vance Thompson (fig. 18) was probably made after 1850. In both portraits husband and wife are elegantly attired, reminding us of Thompson's earlier interest in tailoring. The portraits set him apart from most provincial tradesmen of the period and certainly indicate a lifestyle dramatically different from that of his former master. Historian Samuel Wiley examined early Morgantown advertisements and noted that in 1829 and 1830 Thompson was engaged in "the mercantile business."[29] Perhaps he was not actively potting.

In 1830, however, Thompson's wife was seriously ill and, by most accounts, that was the year the pottery on Lot 88 burned, a loss of $1,600.[30] On September 15, 1830, Thompson established a new pottery on Lot 1, next to the wharf at the bottom of Walnut Street.[31] It would be converted to steam power sometime after 1853, when his son, James J. Thompson, took over its management in 1853.[32]

Thompson may have retired from managing the pottery business before the 1854 conversion of the pottery from earthenware to stoneware production. However, three of his four sons continued the new stoneware business. The 1850 U.S. Census provides insight into the last years of his known involvement.[33]

	Age	*Sex*	*Trade*	*Value of Property*	*Birthplace*
John W. Thompson	64	M	Potter	$200	Maryland
Deborah (Vance)	60	F	– – –		Maryland
David Greenland	30	M	Potter		Virginia
George B	29	M	Carpenter		Virginia
Francis (Frank)	45	M	Potter	$300	Virginia

John W. Thompson's mark appears on several extant earthenware objects. A number of these marked wares are neither well thrown nor well finished and they are relatively common forms (figs. 19–22). They have no decoration other than ribbing and, on the inkwells (figs. 23–25), fine cogging. By way of comparing quality, the inkwell signed by Samuel Butter

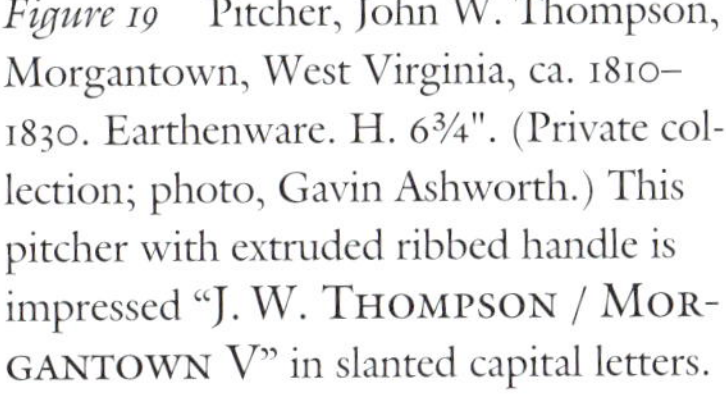

Figure 19 Pitcher, John W. Thompson, Morgantown, West Virginia, ca. 1810–1830. Earthenware. H. 6¾". (Private collection; photo, Gavin Ashworth.) This pitcher with extruded ribbed handle is impressed "J. W. THOMPSON / MORGANTOWN V" in slanted capital letters.

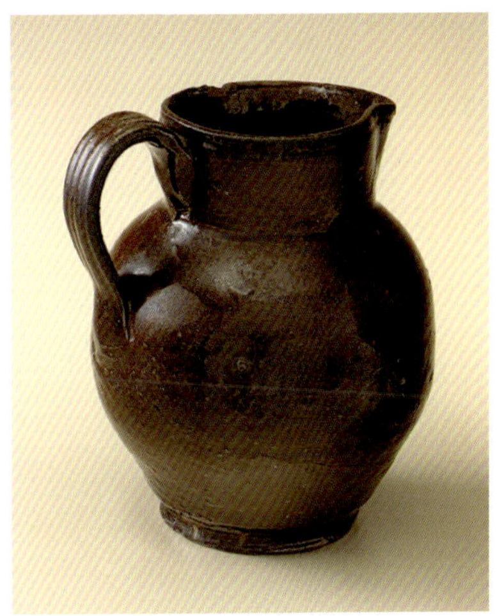

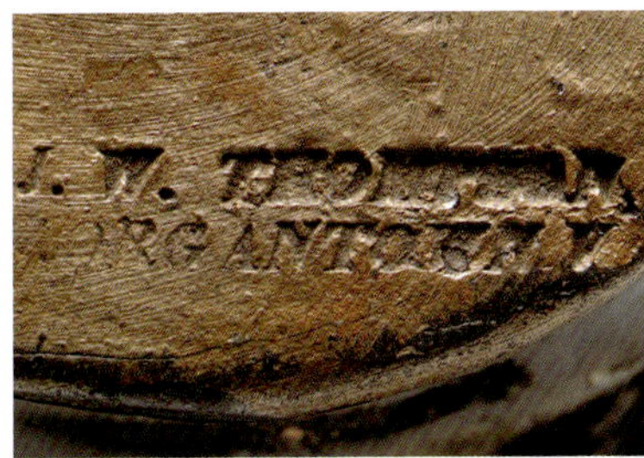

Figure 20 Detail of the mark on the pitcher illustrated in fig. 19. This mark was also found among Lot 88 sherds.

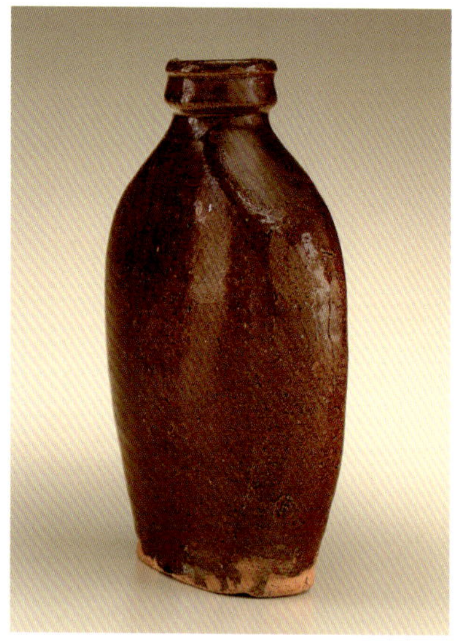

Figure 21 Flask, John W. Thompson, Morgantown, West Virginia, ca. 1810–1825. Earthenware. H. 7". (Private collection; photo, Gavin Ashworth.) This flask is stamped "Thompson" on the base. Note that the treatment of the spout lip and the definition of the neck/shoulder transition differ from the signed example illustrated in fig. 22.

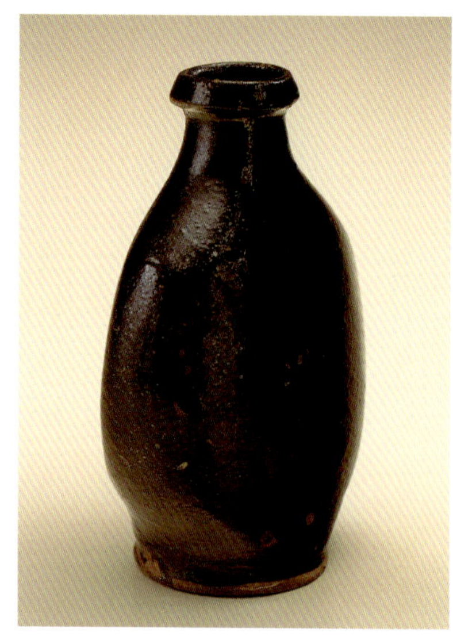

Figure 22 Flask, John W. Thompson, Morgantown, West Virginia, ca. 1820–1840. Earthenware. H. 6¾". (Private collection; photo, Gavin Ashworth.) This flask, impressed "Thompson," has a beveled lip that was used extensively in Morgantown. A third example of a Morgantown flask, showing a simpler lip, is in the Smithsonian Institution and is labeled a "tickler," or pint flask.

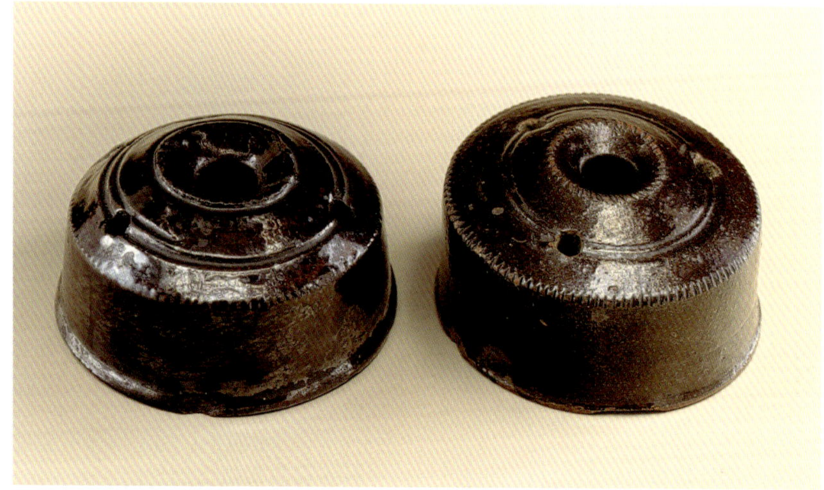

Figure 23 Inkwells, John W. Thompson, Morgantown, West Virginia, ca. 1830–1854. Earthenware. H. 2" and 2¼". (Private collection; photo, Gavin Ashworth.) The inkwell at left is impressed "J.W. THOMPSON / MORGANTOWN, VA."; the one at right is impressed "Thompson." Three signed inkwells by Thompson are known. This pair differs slightly in shape but has the same fine coggling at the edge of the shoulders. These examples can be compared with the more carefully finished example by Samuel Butter illustrated in fig. 26. The third example, not shown, is signed by Thompson; it is about 50 percent larger and displays a moderately dark, slightly yellow, shade of green.

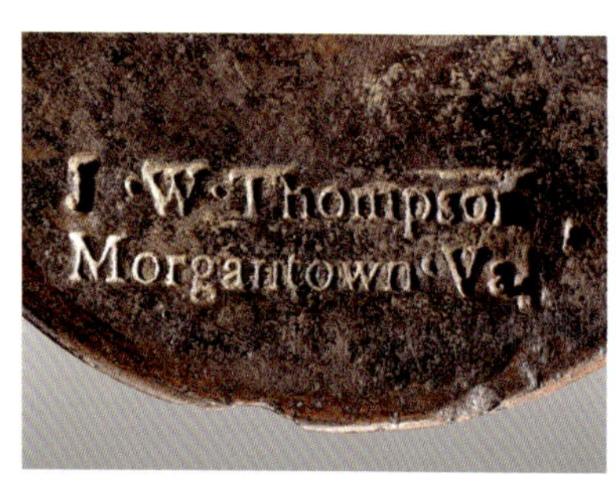

Figure 24 Detail of the mark on the inkwell at left illustrated in fig. 23.

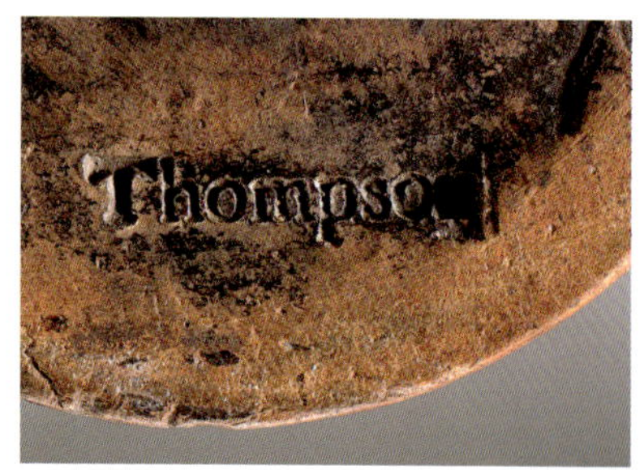

Figure 25 Detail of the mark on the inkwell at right illustrated in fig. 23.

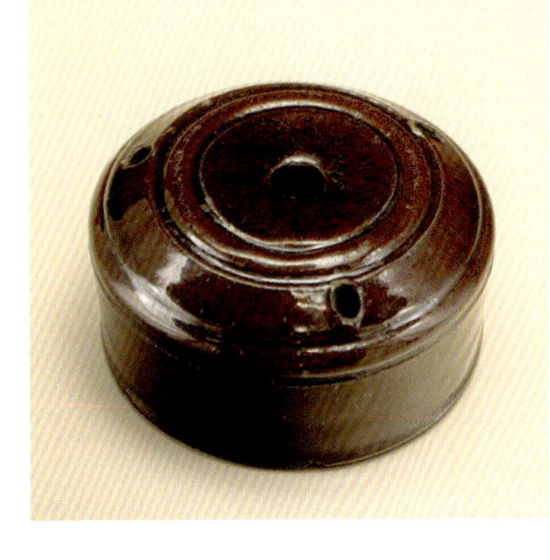

Figure 26 Inkwell, Samuel Butter, Clarksburg, West Virginia, ca. 1820. Earthenware. H. 2½". (Courtesy, Hardy Collection; photo, Gavin Ashworth.) Note that the glaze appears thicker and more lustrous than on the Thompson examples illustrated in fig. 23.

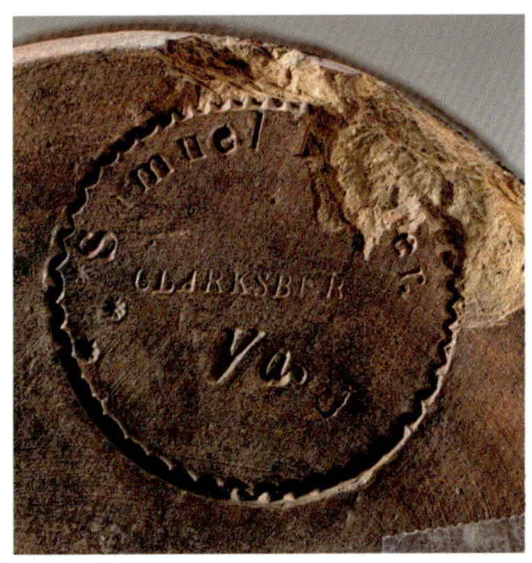

Figure 27 Detail of the mark on the bottom of the inkwell illustrated in fig. 26. Note the lack of the final "s" in Butter's last name and the absence of "& Co," which appears in his later marks (see fig. 64).

(figs. 26, 27) is more skillfully thrown and glazed than Thompson's, even though both of these potters were trained by Foulk. Similarly, a signed Samuel Butter jug (fig. 28) is more refined than other jugs attributed to Thompson and other Morgantown potters (figs. 29–31). Based on body shape and handle attachments the jugs appear to have been made by several hands, yet four of these, plus one not shown, have similar extruded handle cross sections. One jug bears a brushed manganese slip decoration that is attributed to Thompson (fig. 32). The same decoration also occurs on a molasses jar (fig. 33).

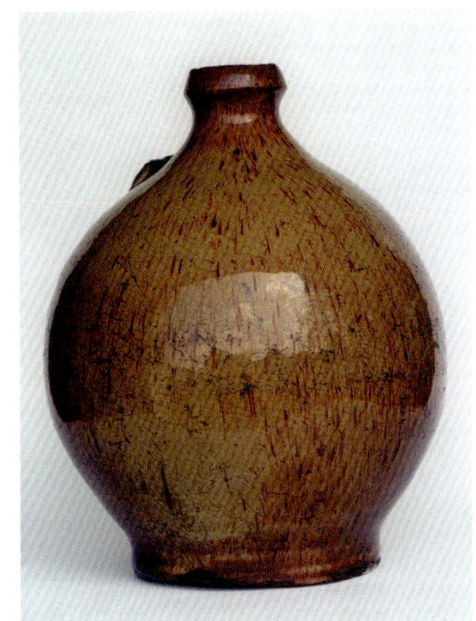

Figure 28 Jug, Samuel Butter, Clarksburg, West Virginia, ca. 1820–1850. Earthenware. H. 6⅜". (Photo, Richard Duez.) Signed on the bottom, this bulbous jug has a high luster lead glaze over a straw-colored slip. Found in southern Harrison County, West Virginia.

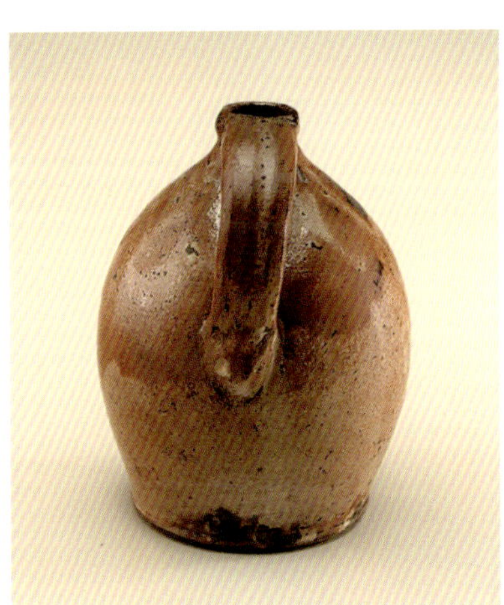

Figure 29 Jug, probably Morgantown, West Virginia, ca. 1805–1840. Earthenware. H. 6¾". (Private collection; photo, Gavin Ashworth.) The thin straw glaze on this jug reveals much of the red clay body.

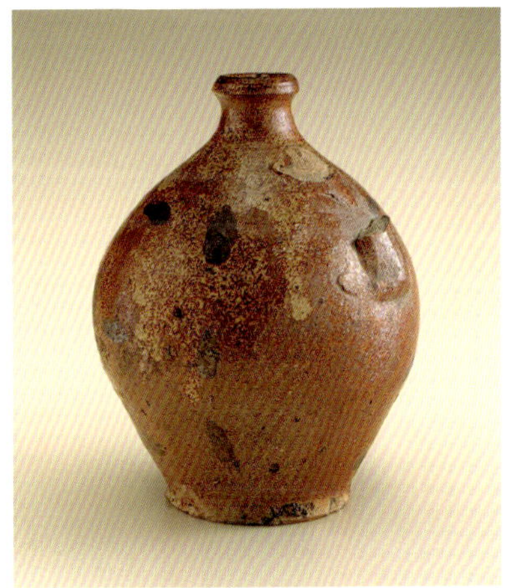

Figure 30 Jug, probably Morgantown, West Virginia, ca. 1805–1840. Earthenware. H. 6¾". (Private collection; photo, Gavin Ashworth.) This jug is decorated with alternating spots of manganese in a grid-like pattern.

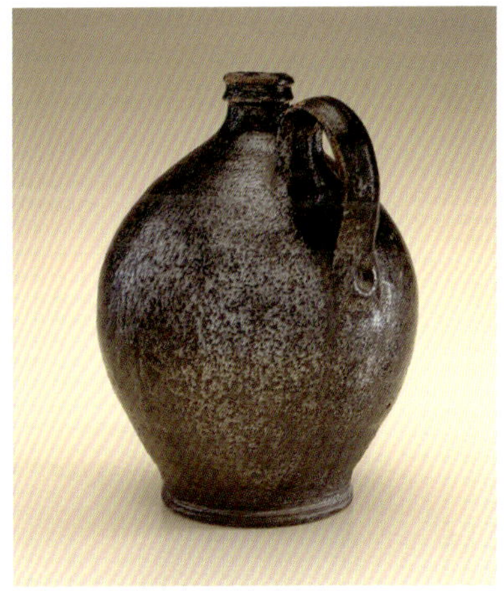

Figure 31 Jug, probably Morgantown, West Virginia, ca. 1820 –1850. Earthenware. H. 8⅝". (Private collection; photo, Gavin Ashworth.) The spout rim of this jug resembles that of the flask illustrated in fig. 21.

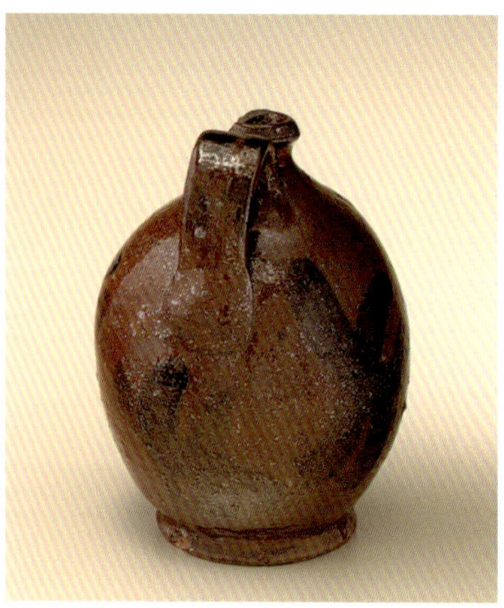

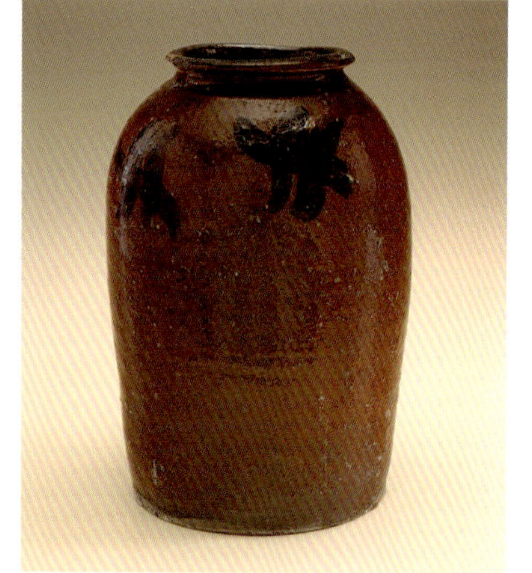

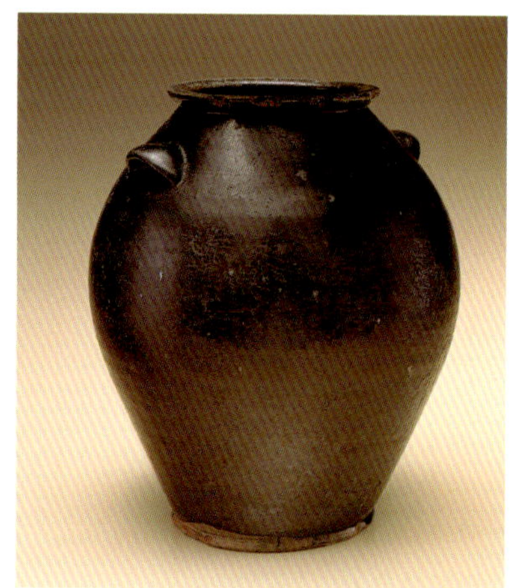

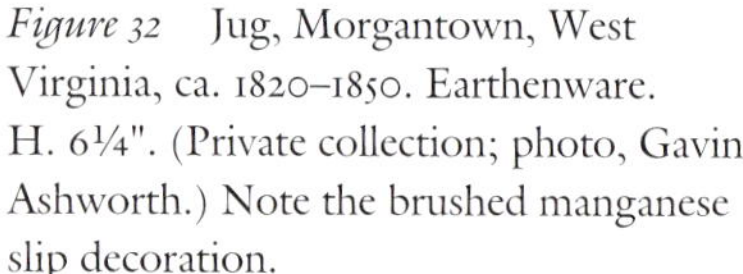

Figure 32 Jug, Morgantown, West Virginia, ca. 1820–1850. Earthenware. H. 6¼". (Private collection; photo, Gavin Ashworth.) Note the brushed manganese slip decoration.

Figure 33 Jar, Morgantown, West Virginia, ca. 1820–1850. Earthenware. H. 11¾". (Private collection; photo, Gavin Ashworth.) Brushed manganese slip decoration adorns this early molasses jar. (Molasses was uncrystallized maple sugar.) Several spalls reveal gravel in the body.

Figure 34 Jar, Morgantown, West Virginia, ca. 1820–1854. H. 11½". (Private collection; photo, Gavin Ashworth.) Two similar examples are illustrated in Walter Hough, "An Early West Virginia Pottery," pl. 2, fig. 1, where they are referred to as "Molasses Jars."

Figure 35 Jar, Morgantown, West Virginia, 1840–1854. Earthenware. H. 7¼". (Duez collection; photo, Gavin Ashworth.) Although this jar appears primarily black, in bright daylight highlights of green and yellow are visible throughout the glaze.

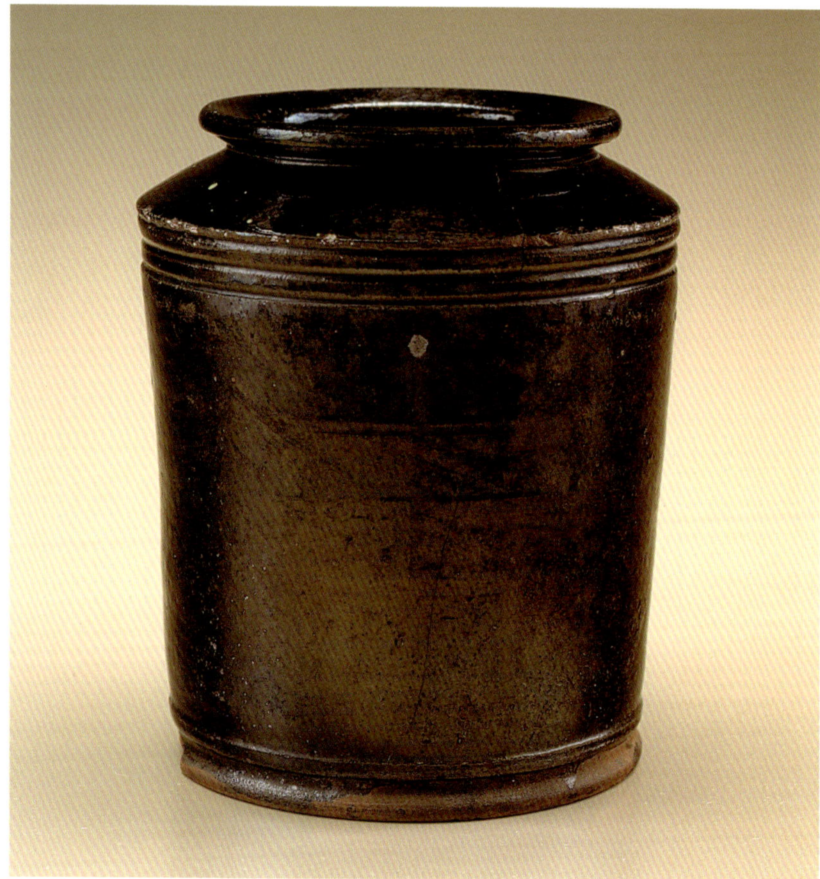

There are more storage jars in the study group than there are other earthenware forms (figs. 34–37). They were probably made over a longer period. These jars often have roulette decoration work (see, for example, fig. 37), and existing roulettes and other tools in the Smithsonian's collection can be matched to these jars (figs. 38–41). These roulettes were also used during the stoneware period of production (post-1854) at Thompson's pottery.

Another distinctive group of cylindrical storage jars that can be attributed to the Thompson pottery is characterized by distinctive "splotch" or

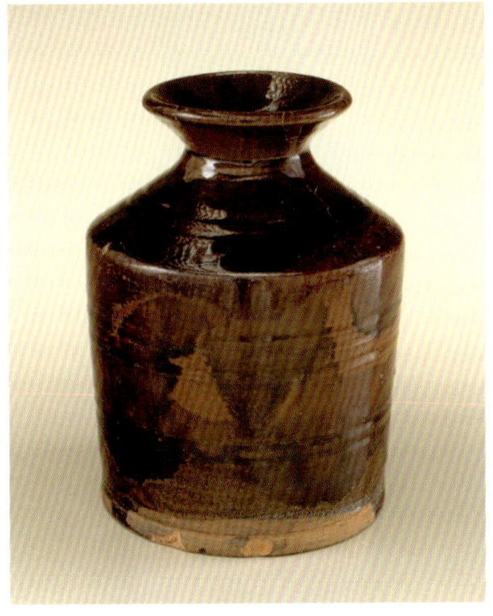

Figure 36 Bottle, Morgantown, West Virginia, ca. 1850. Earthenware. H. 5¼". (Duez Collection; photo, Gavin Ashworth.) This bottle was perhaps for ink or boot blacking. It was found in a basement next door to the Lot 88 kiln site.

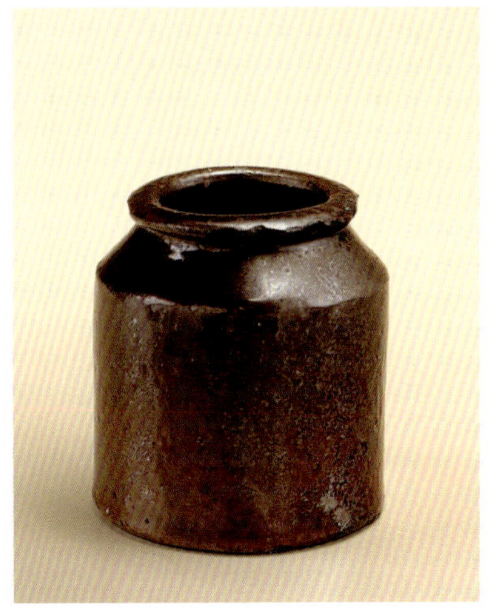

Figure 37 Jar, Morgantown, West Virginia, ca. 1830. Earthenware. H. 1⅞". (Duez Collection; photo, Gavin Ashworth.) This miniature cylindrical string-tie storage vessel is possibly an ink or ointment jar. It was found in Morgantown.

Figure 38 Jar, Morgantown, West Virginia, ca. 1840–1854. Earthenware. H. 7¼". (Private collection; photo, Gavin Ashworth.) This cylindrical string-tie storage jar has an impressed geometric design created by a roulette that is now in the Smithsonian Institution. This same roulette was used in Morgantown's stoneware period, which began in September 1854. They probably were made near the end of the earthenware period, since roulettes flourished in the early stoneware period. Competition from glassmakers—Albert Gallatin's glass plant at nearby New Geneva, Pennsylvania, began production in 1807—may have forced potters to speed up production to cut costs. Roulette decoration could be completed in one quick rotation of the jar, whereas carefully placed daubs or strokes of slip involved more time and additional material.

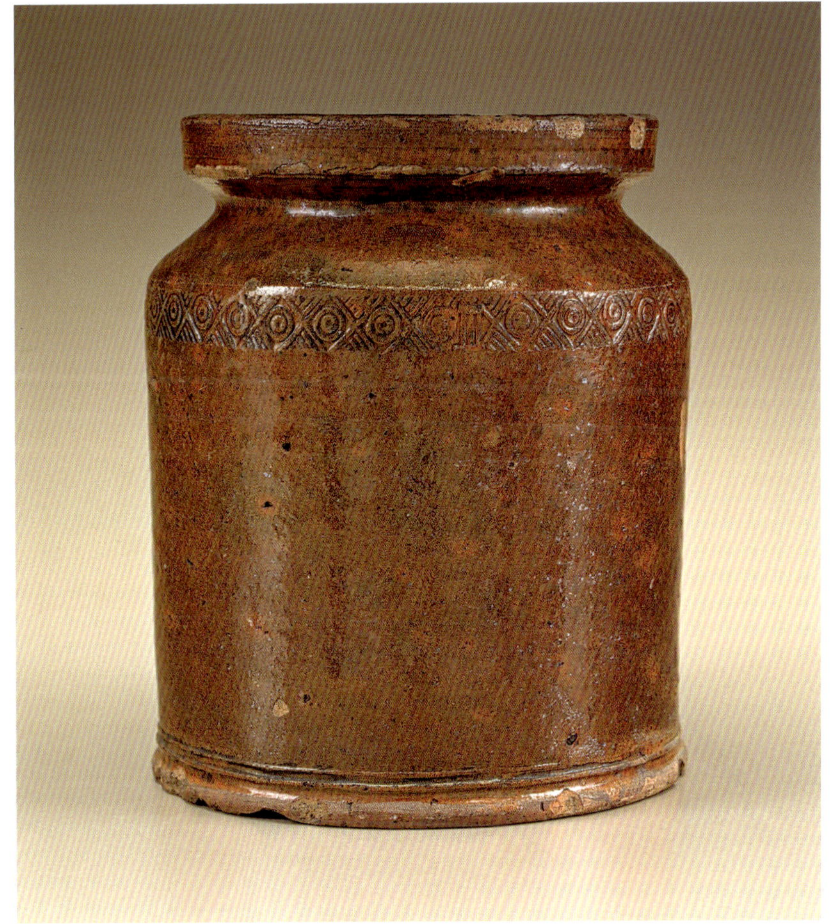

Figure 39 Detail of the roulette design on the jar illustrated in fig. 38.

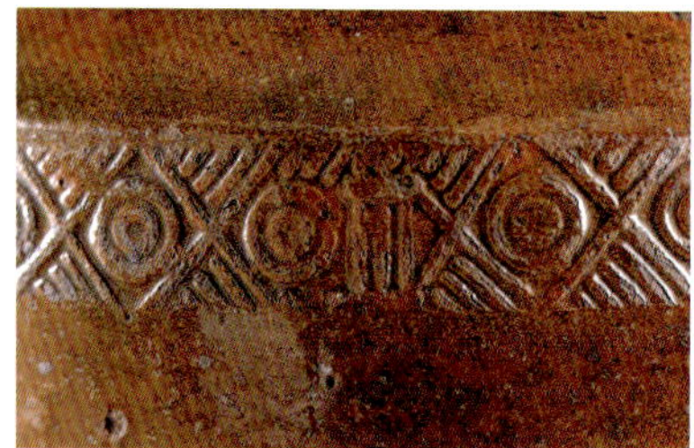

Figure 40 Rouletting tool, Morgantown, West Virginia, ca. 1840–1854. The roulette is a fired clay disk. (Courtesy, National Museum of American History; photo, Gavin Ashworth.)

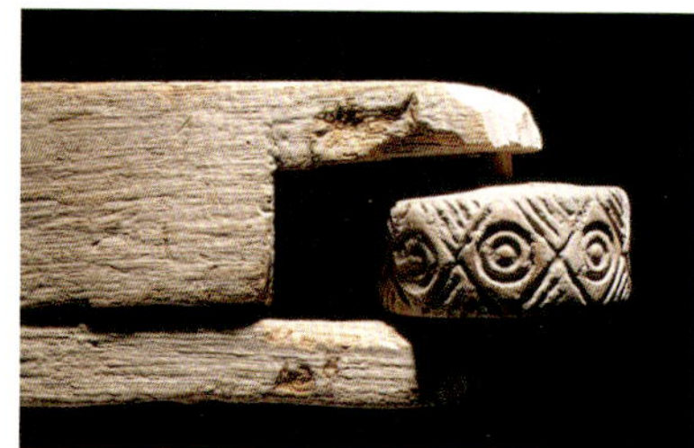

Figure 41 Jar, Morgantown, West Virginia, ca. 1840–1854. Earthenware. H. 7½". (Duez Collection; photo, Gavin Ashworth.) The geometric roulette design on this cylindrical string-tie storage jar differs from that illustrated in fig. 38. The roulette that made this design is also in the Smithsonian Institution. This roulette was also used on Morgantown stoneware.

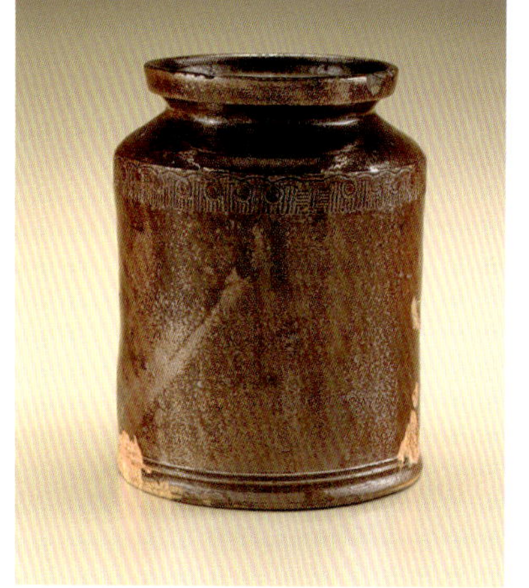

Figure 42 Wooden rib, Morgantown, West Virginia, ca. 1840–1854. (Courtesy, National Museum of American History; photo, Gavin Ashworth.) This rib is one of several that are preserved in the Smithsonian Institution. The tool was used to form the contours of the lip and neck of storage jar forms.

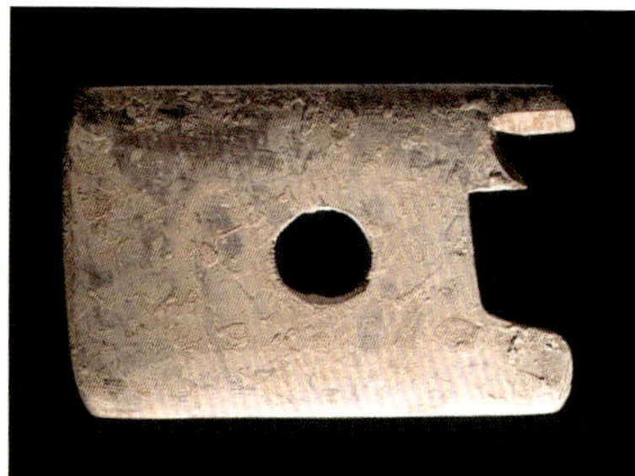

"polka dot" slip decoration (figs. 43, 44). It is unclear who to credit with this innovative decoration. It may have been introduced by John Thompson or possibly his son David Greenland Thompson (discussed below). This type of decoration, as well as others occurring on both earthenware and stoneware forms, helps provide some dating evidence for the sequence of forms from those of John W. Thompson to those of his sons.

Figure 43 Jars, Morgantown, West Virginia. *Left:* ca. 1855. Stoneware. H. 5¾". *Right:* ca. 1830–1854. Earthenware. H. 7". (Private collection; photo, Gavin Ashworth.) Note that this earthenware form carried over to the stoneware period; we attribute the innovative decoration to David Greenland Thompson.

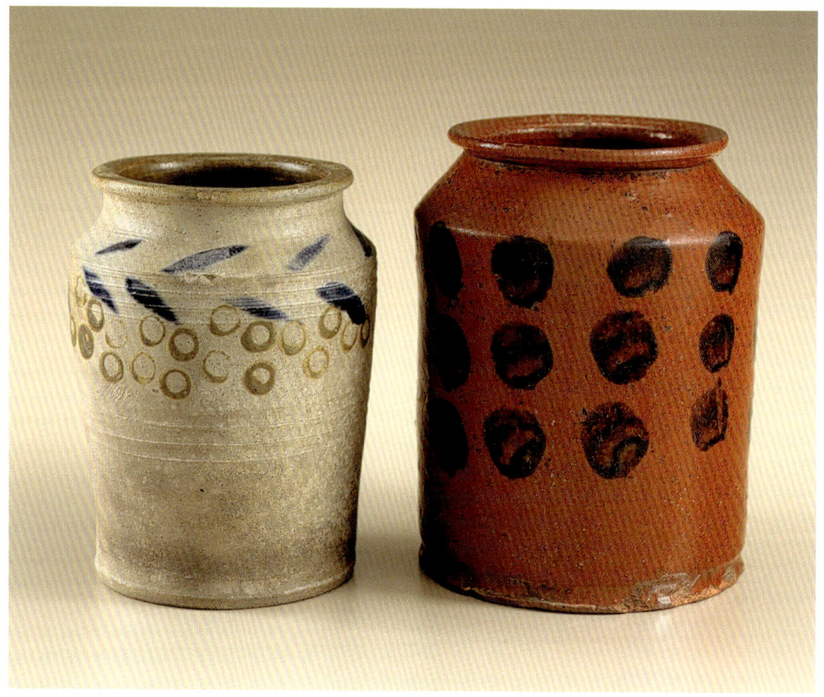

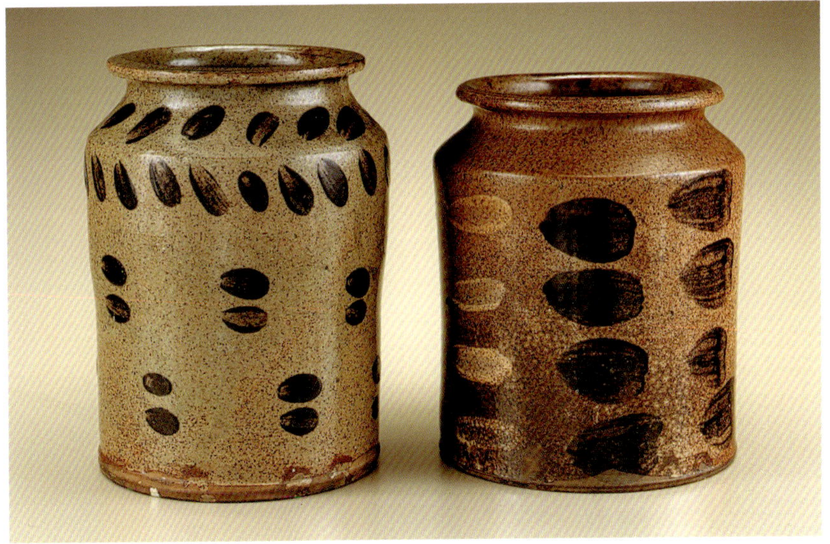

Figure 44 Jars, Morgantown, West Virginia, ca. 1820–1854. Earthenware. H. 7½" and 7". (Duez Collection; photo, Gavin Ashworth.) These jars were found together in a house some seventeen miles upstream from Morgantown.

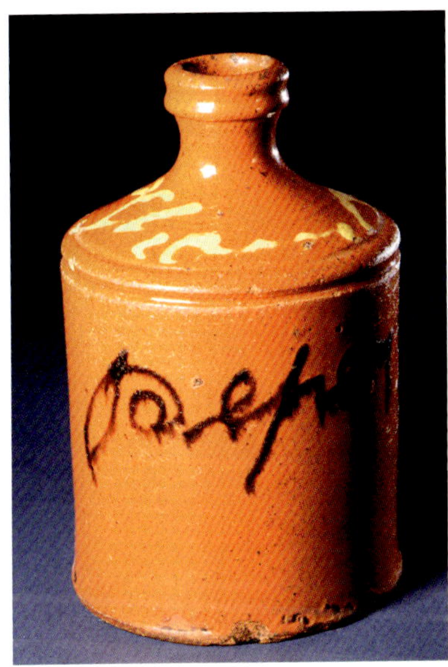

Figure 45 Spice ("Peper") bottle, David G. Thompson, Morgantown, West Virginia, ca. 1840–1854. Earthenware. H. 5½". (Courtesy, Ceramics and Glass Collection, National Museum of American History.)

David Greenland Thompson, 1820–1890

David Thompson, often referred to by his middle name, is listed in the 1850 U.S. Census as living with his father, John W. Thompson, and would have trained in his father's pottery. Although he passed the Virginia bar examination in 1845, he remained a potter.

At least two earthenware vessels, spice bottles that are illustrated in Hough, can be directly associated with David—one has "D. Thompson" in slip, the other has his name incised on the bottle's base (fig. 45).[34] Apparently he did not use a stamp on the earthenware pieces as he later did on stoneware.

David may be responsible for introducing the roulette wheel decoration as previously illustrated in the earthenware storage jars. He also may have initiated the controlled "polka dot" slip decoration found on several surviving earthenware pieces (see figs. 43, 44), although there may be earlier precedents.

Another form that reflects a crossover between the earthenware and stoneware operations is the conical shape earthenware churn illustrated in Hough (fig. 46).[35] This conical form, as well as a number of stoneware wax

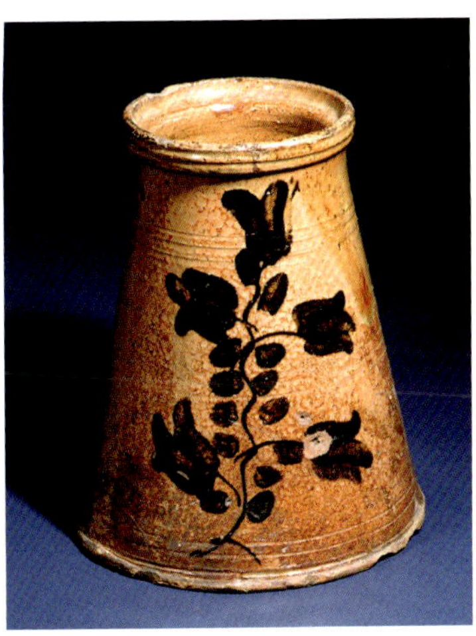

Figure 46 Churn, Thompson pottery, Morgantown, West Virginia, ca. 1840–1854. Earthenware. H. 9¾". (Courtesy, Ceramics and Glass Collection, National Museum of American History.)

sealers, appears on various stoneware pitchers attributed to David. The churn shows freehand decoration that his father and Foulk, so far as we know, did not employ. David probably was also instrumental in the adoption of stamps and molds for applied decoration. His role in several of the most remarkable items in the Smithsonian's collection needs further examination. Moreover, the amazing polka-dot pitcher appears to have little precedent in American earthenware (fig. 47). Its Morgantown origin is clear even though its maker remains unknown. The slip decoration is related to the various storage jars attributed to David.

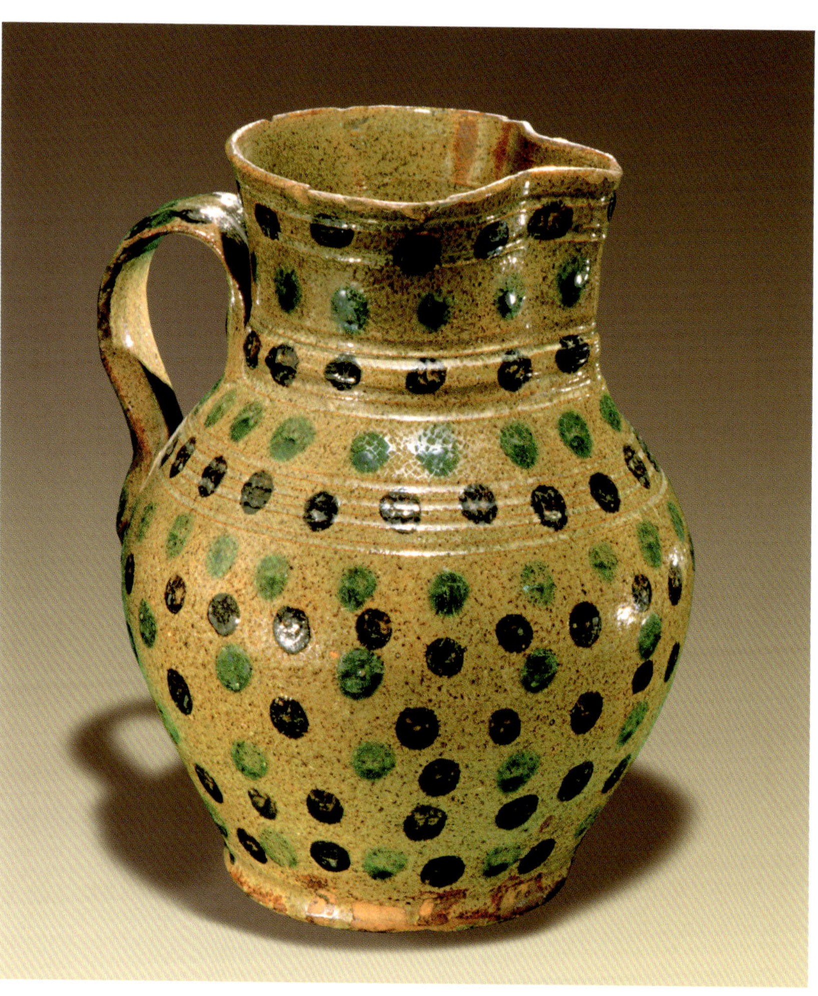

Figure 47 Pitcher, Thompson pottery, Morgantown, West Virginia, ca. 1820–1840. Earthenware. H. 9¾". (Courtesy, Ceramics and Glass Collection, National Museum of American History.)

Another important pitcher linked to the Thompsons is a large bisqued but unglazed example at the Smithsonian (fig. 48). A number of related molds and other tools must represent the best-documented example of a nineteenth-century American potter's toolkit (figs. 49–52).

Hough remarked that "the work of Greenland Thompson was not appreciated." Based on extant examples of his earthenware and stoneware, we feel that David Greenland Thompson was more absorbed by potting than managing the business. Further, we believe he was a much more skillful potter than his father—though, as later years will attest, not as skillful an entrepreneur—and that he used clay and glazes as a poet uses words.

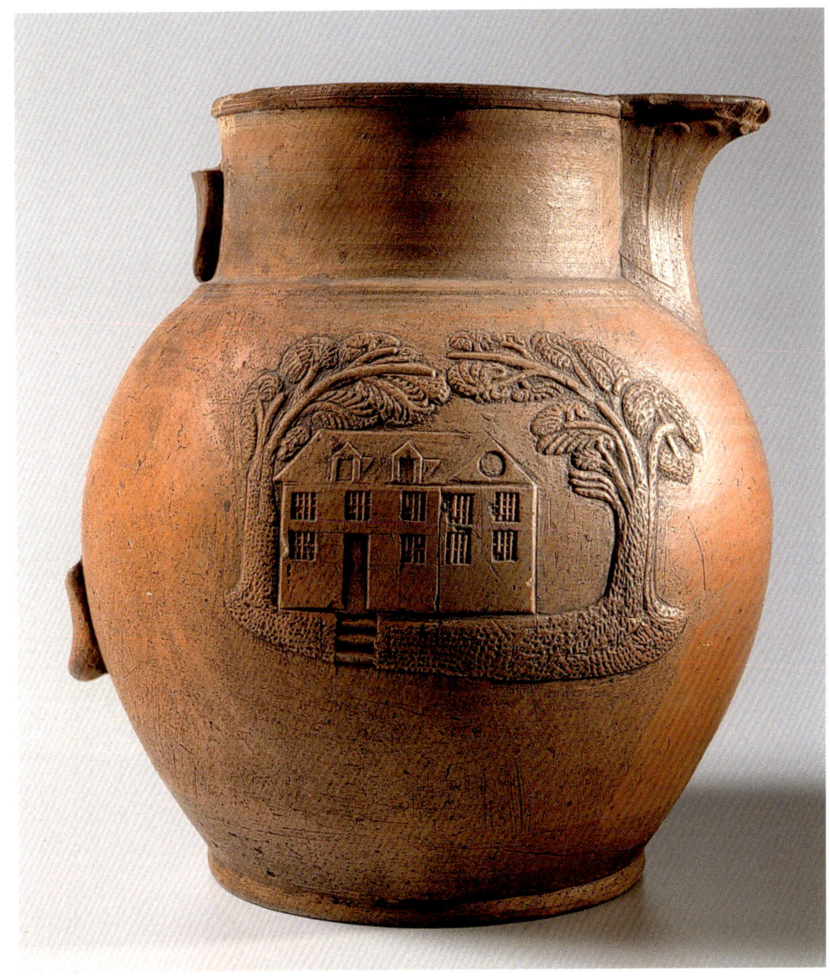

Figure 48 Pitcher, attributed to the Thompson pottery, Morgantown, West Virginia, ca. 1850. Earthenware. H. 9¾". (Courtesy, National Museum of American History; photo, Gavin Ashworth.) The molded spout is the only surviving provincial earthenware example known to us. The molds in the Smithsonian include similar spout designs as well as smaller versions of houses. Molded spouts occur on Staffordshire pottery, and in the 1830s and 1840s Staffordshire potters were moving into East Liverpool, Ohio. A craftsman there might have supplied the Thompsons with molds, although no examples have been seen in that city's excellent ceramics museum. It is also possible that Thompson employed a Baltimore mold maker, as he maintained contact with this city.

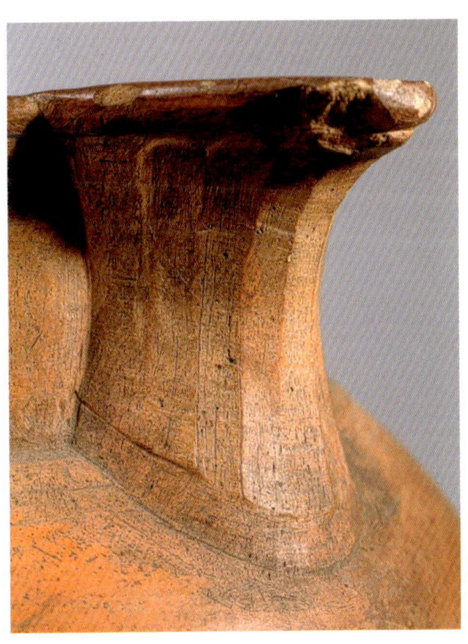

Figure 49 Detail of the spout on the pitcher illustrated in fig. 48.

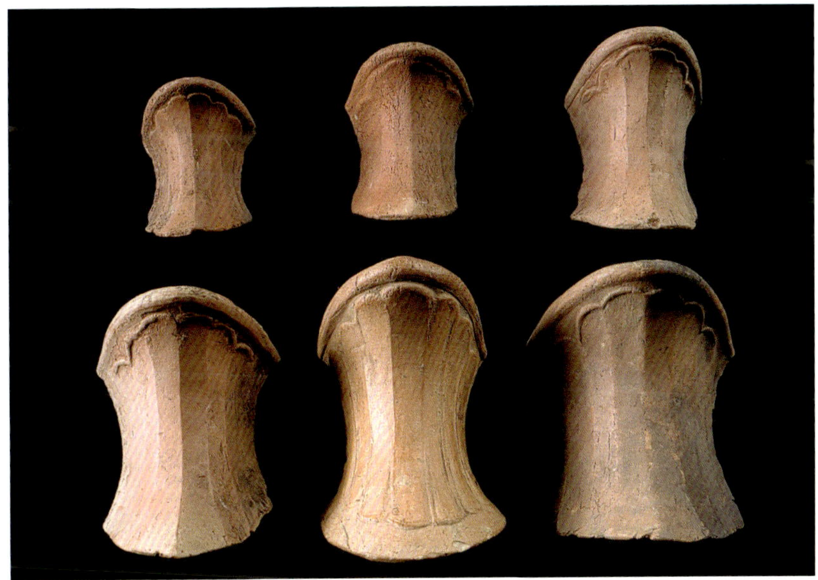

Figure 50 Spout molds, Thompson pottery, Morgantown, West Virginia. (Courtesy, National Museum of American History; photo, Gavin Ashworth.) This collection of graduated molds suggests that a range of sizes may have been produced at the Thompson pottery.

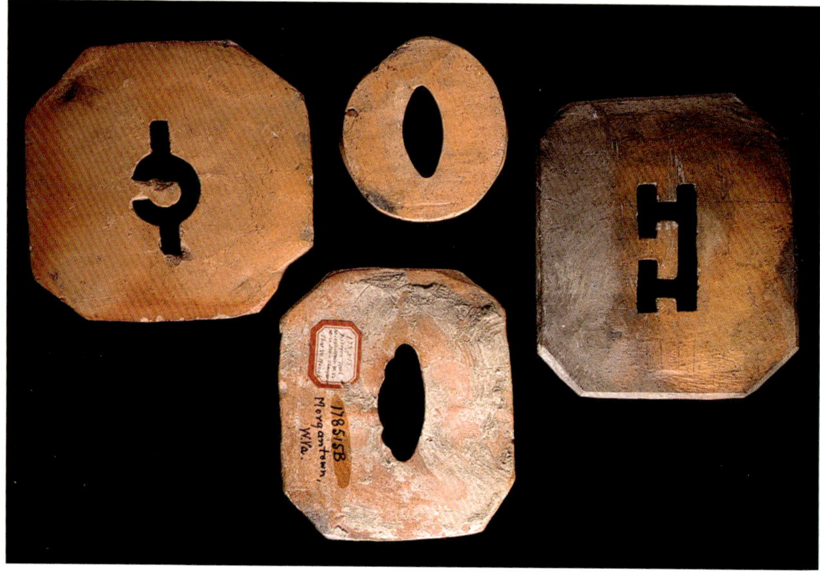

Figure 51 Extrusion dies. (Courtesy, National Museum of American History; photo, Gavin Ashworth.) An assortment of dies used in conjunction with an extruder to produce various handle shapes and profiles.

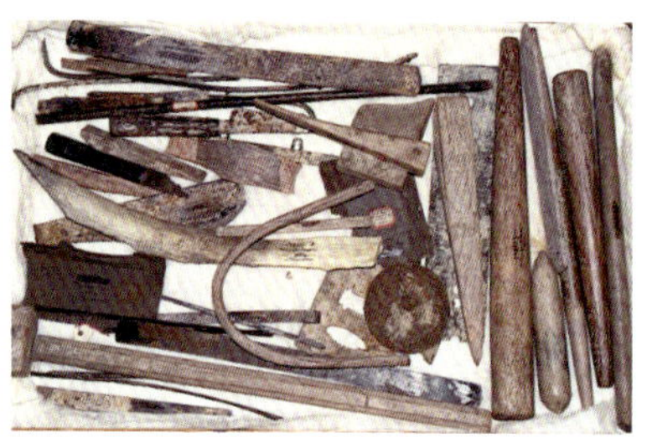

Figure 52 Tools, Thompson pottery, Morgantown, West Virginia, nineteenth century. (Courtesy, National Museum of American History; photo, Robert Hunter.) A snapshot of some of the common potting tools, such as ribs, scrapers, and finishing implements. The amazing variety of surviving tools collected by Hough, particularly the roulettes and molds, is to our knowledge unmatched by that from any other American provincial pottery of the early to mid-nineteenth century. They are a wonderful, but dismaying, reminder of what has been lost from other potteries.

Abner Greenland, 1783–1830

In 1800 Abner Greenland entered into an apprenticeship agreement with the potter Eli Haines in Cecil County, Maryland. Abner probably arrived in Morgantown no later than 1805 since he married Jane Thompson (1790–1842), John W. Thompson's sister, on January 5, 1806. Abner appears in two Monongalia County court cases in the same year. In the first, *David Bayles v. Jacob Foulk,* he and John W. appeared as witnesses in a case regarding a debt due by deed of trust. Later that year, in the second case, Jacob Foulk was the witness when Abner and John W., as co-plaintiffs, sued Davis Shockley for a debt due by note. Since Abner does not appear on the Monongalia County Taxables List, it is likely he was the "white male above sixteen years" residing with John W. Thompson. By 1810 Abner and Jane had moved to nearby Uniontown, Fayette County, Pennsylvania. Their first son, John, "born in Virginia," became a potter, as did their other sons, Garrett and Norval. It is reasonable to assume that Abner worked as a journeyman potter with Jacob Foulk Jr. and/or John W. Thompson.

We have not been able to identify any earthenware turned by Abner.

John Sloneker (Slonaker), 1798–after 1825

John Sloneker, journeyman potter, agreed on May 21, 1815, to work for Jacob Foulk Jr. for " $11.00 per mo. and board and lodge." It is probably not a coincidence that on May 10 of the same year, Foulk agreed to operate Francis Billingsley's pottery. John Sloneker appears next in the records

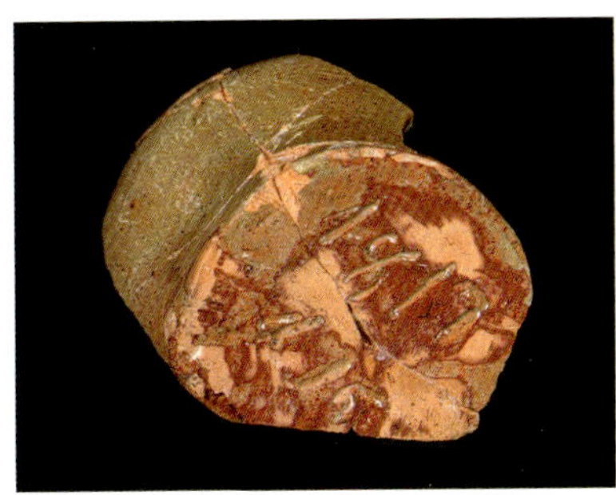

Figure 53 Slip cup fragment, attributed to John Sloneker, Morgantown, West Virginia, 1817. Earthenware. (Photo, Gavin Ashworth.)

of Bullskin Township, Fayette County, Pennsylvania, from 1817 to 1825. Sloneker may have made the dated slip cup (fig. 53) found near the kiln on Lot 88, because when Foulk deeded it to John W. Thompson, he retained the right to use part of that pottery until 1819.

We do not know where Sloneker was trained, nor do we know of any signed examples of his work.

James M. Thompson Jr., 1786–after 1850

James M. Thompson Jr., younger brother of John W. Thompson, almost certainly had begun training with Jacob Foulk Jr. about 1804 (recall his part in a court case against Foulk in that year), although no apprentice papers have been located. In 1810 his older brother deeded to him sixty-three acres on Scott's Run in Maidsville, Virginia, across the Monongahela River. This was probably part of a group of properties deeded in 1809 to John W. by his father, James M. Thompson Sr., in apparent anticipation of the latter's death. John W. was evidently the de facto administrator of his father's estate.

The 1850 U.S. Census for Mt. Pleasant Township, Madison County, Ohio, shows James M. Thompson Jr., potter, age sixty-four, born in Virginia, as was his wife, Sarah. We believe this to be John W.'s younger brother. We know of no examples of his work, but he may have been a more experienced potter than his older brother since he apprenticed at a younger age.[36]

Francis M. Thompson, b. 1805

Francis M. Thompson, potter, and younger brother of John W. and James M. Thompson, was listed as residing with John W. in the 1850 U.S. Census. He also owned property valued at $300. We have no specific information concerning his potting career.

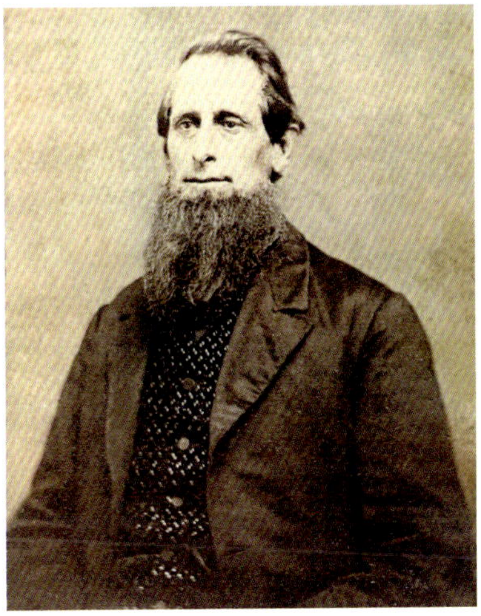

Figure 54 James J. Thompson, potter. (Courtesy, R. Crommett.)

James J. Thompson, 1826–1899

Capt. James J. Thompson's middle name, Jackson, is in honor of the father of Thomas "Stonewall" Jackson, to whom James J. (fig. 54) was related by marriage. James J. was the second of John W. Thompson's sons to become a potter. He would have trained about 1840 to 1845. In 1853 management of the new pottery on Lot 1 would be turned over to him by his father, although Core places Col. Frank W. Thompson, a younger brother, in charge.[37] One might have expected David G. Thompson to have been the manager, but he was probably too introspective.

No pieces by him are known.

Francis "Frank" W. Thompson, 1828–1900

Col. Frank W. Thompson (fig. 55) was the fourth son of John W. Thompson and the third to become a potter. He left home for "the West" about 1850 and from 1852 to 1855 served with the Oregon Mounted Volunteers in campaigns against the Yakima and other Indian peoples. In 1859 he was listed as potter in Thurston's *Directory of the Monongahela and Youghiogheny*

Valleys.[38] He then served on the Union side in the Civil War, rising to the rank of lieutenant colonel. There is no mention of him in the 1870 U.S. Census of Manufacturing, but David Greenland Thompson, who filed the census report, was paying wages to someone, and there is one crock impressed "F. W. Thompson." In 1873 Frank W. opened the first steam-powered flour mill in the borough at the Walnut Street pottery lot at the wharf.[39] This new operation probably ended his involvement in the pottery business. By 1880 he was a justice of the peace and he eventually became mayor of Morgantown.

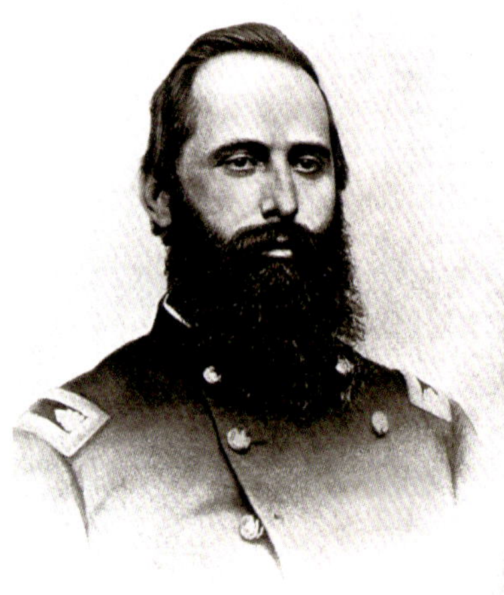

Figure 55 Francis W. Thompson, potter. (Courtesy, R. Crommett.)

William C. Crichfield (Crickfield, Crihfield, Christfield, Schrichfield), 1784–1863

William C. Crichfield, who was born in New Jersey, moved with his family to Greene County, Pennsylvania, before 1816, when his father, Absolam, died. In 1821 William Crichfield, potter, was taxed in Whitely Township, Greene County, Pennsylvania.[40] At that time he was almost certainly an earthenware potter. Whitely is ten to fifteen miles from Maidsville, (now West) Virginia, where Crichfield is buried in his family's cemetery across the river from Morgantown.[41] Hough states that William Crichfield was an employee of the Thompson pottery but does not indicate when.[42] He refers to a salt-glazed jar bearing "Home manufacture. Independence. High tariff. William Crihfield. August 1844." in cobalt blue brush work. In 1842 the Whig administration passed a protective tariff act. Tariffs were a principal

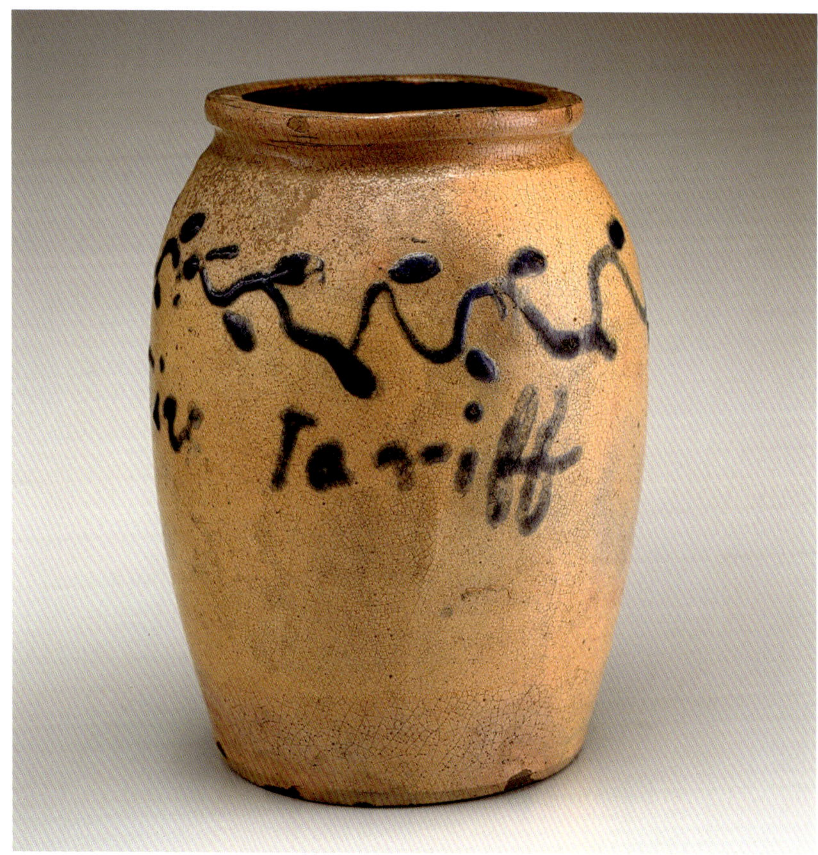

Figure 56 Jar, attributed to William Crichfield, Greene County, Pennsylvania. Stoneware. H. 8". (Duez Collection; photo, Gavin Ashworth.) The body of this jar is covered in a buff-colored slip and decorated with trailed and brushed cobalt. The inscription reads: "Potectiv Tariff."

source of federal funds, and in 1844 the Democrats' campaign promise included changing the tariff to one based on valuation of imports. This salt-glazed jar reflects support for the unsuccessful Whig campaign of 1844. The jar's present location is unknown.

A slightly buff-colored, salt-glazed stoneware jar is known extolling "Potectiv Tariff" in cobalt decoration (fig. 56). It displays a sinuous vine decorated with oval leaves. This "tariff jar" may also have been made by Crichfield. Although we have no clear evidence of Crichfield's earthenware products, there is another possible clue. A so-called sugar purifier that is inscribed "JFC" is illustrated in Hough.[43] The purifier may have been made for Crichfield's younger brother, John, who died in Doddridge County, West Virginia, in 1865. However, as we have not learned John's middle name, this remains speculation.

Crichfield does appear in minor court records in Monongalia County from 1841 to 1852, and Wiley states that Crichfield established his own pottery a few miles downstream at [West] Van Voorhis (Collin's Ferry), but does not give a date.[44] It is possible that he produced stoneware there, as stoneware production had begun by 1824 by J. Bower of nearby Frederick Town.[45] The Boughners had attempted stoneware production as well, but the first results were "desultory." Hough states that William Boughner had informed him that their first (successful) stoneware production was in 1849. Crichfield does not appear in the 1850 census and is listed as "farmer" in the 1860 census.

The Clarksburg Pottery

Samuel Butter (Butters), 1798–1863

Members of the Butter family appear in the Taxables List of Monongalia County as early as 1806. Samuel Butter was born in Pennsylvania, the son of a miller who apprenticed him in Morgantown before moving to Ohio. According to the original town plan, Butter had established Clarksburg's first documented earthenware pottery by 1819. It was located on the north side of Main Street on the upper or western half of Lot 20. The earliest reference to the pottery is in a deed dated November 6, 1819, which describes this lot as the one "on which the Potter's shop now stands."

John G. Jackson, Clarksburg's leading entrepreneur, bought Lot 20 in 1807 for $250. Jackson then leased the property to Thomas Synott, shoemaker, who was to pay $25 annually. After ten years, by which time the principal presumably would have been paid off, Synott divided the lot and sold the half with the pottery. The likely interpretation is that Jackson arranged for the pottery to be built and, just as they had helped other tradesmen, Synott, George Towers, and the buyer were silent partners with Jackson in establishing the pottery in Clarksburg. By the 1850 census, Samuel Butter, fifty-one years old, listed his occupation as miller. He had two sons, Samuel Jr., age fifteen, and John, age twenty-one, whose occupations are not given. Butter died in 1863 from a gunshot injury. While tending his nearby grist mill/saw mill, a revolver slipped from his pocket and went off.

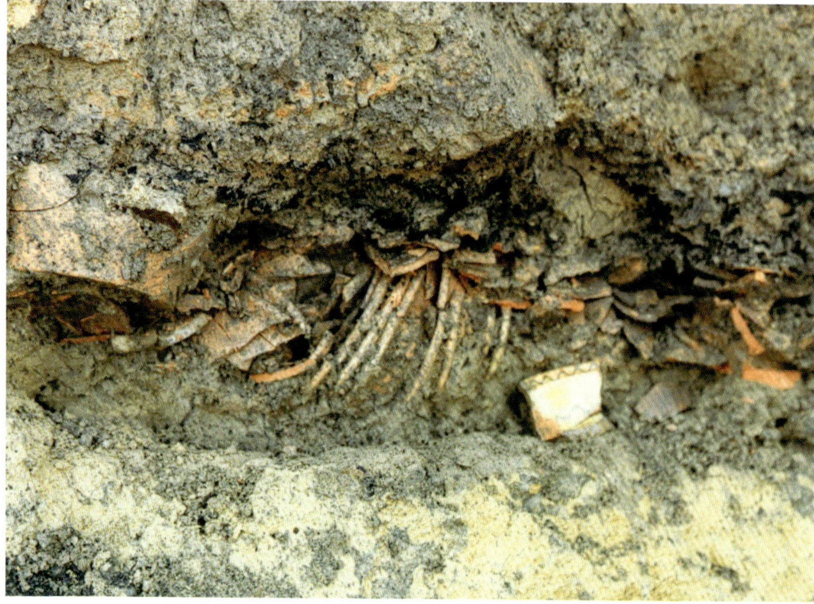

Figure 57 Salvage excavation at the Samuel Butter pottery, Clarksburg, West Virginia. (Photo, Don Horvath.) A hurried and limited opportunity to observe the remains of the Butter pottery came during construction activities on the site. This illustration shows two stacks of slip decorated plates and dishes unearthed during excavation.

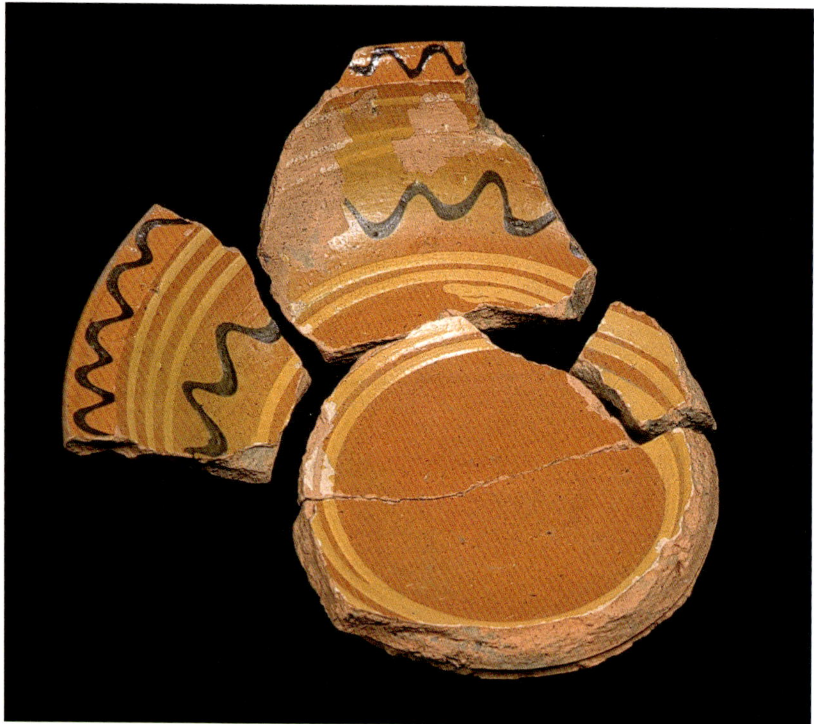

Figure 58 Dish fragments, Samuel Butter, Clarksburg, West Virginia, ca. 1820–1850. Slipware. (Photo, Gavin Ashworth.) This plate shows the use of concentric white slip bands accented with a black slip trailing.

We do not know the names of his potting assistants nor the final date of his potting activity. A signed ring jug with an orange-hued glaze is known, as is the sophisticated jug in figure 28. Two stacks of broken plates (fig. 57), revealed during construction and subsequent excavation at the Clarksburg site, show a variety of trailed slip lines (figs. 58–62) that include the type of viscous dark slip used by Foulk in Morgantown. However, some of the compositions are rather random and appear trite compared with those found on the Butter's sherd (see fig. 15) and the putative Foulk sherds (see fig. 9) discovered next to the kiln on Lot 88 in Morgantown.

Figure 59 Dish fragments, Samuel Butter, Clarksburg, West Virginia, ca. 1820–1850. Slipware. (Photo, Gavin Ashworth.)

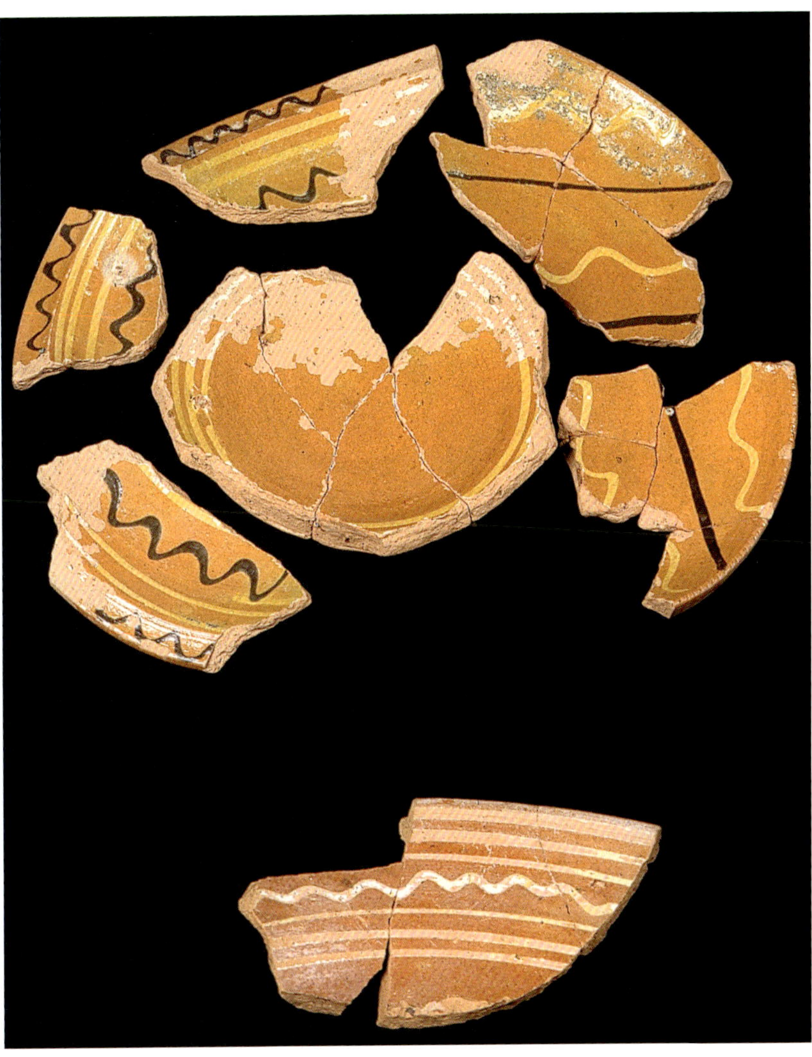

Figure 60 Dish fragment, Samuel Butter, Clarksburg, West Virginia, ca. 1820–1850. Slipware. (Photo, Gavin Ashworth.) This plate has a coggled rim and a more spontaneous use of black and white slip trailing to form the decoration.

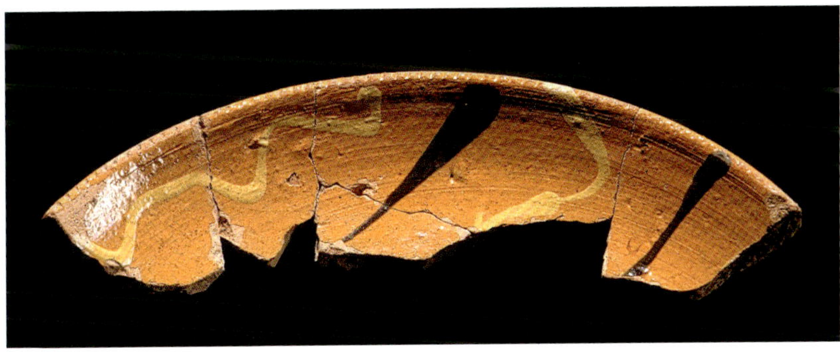

Interestingly, few of the plate sherds at either site have coggled edges. A single example of an agate or "scroddled" lay body was found (fig. 63). Several examples of stamped "Butter" and "Butters" marks (figs. 64, 65) were recovered along with a sherd (fig. 65) that displays carefully trailed "yellow" slip forming reciprocal, separate S scrolls which, when viewed from a distance, create a helical border. There is also a sherd (not shown) with white slip disks that are bordered with dark beads and centered with dark slip disks.

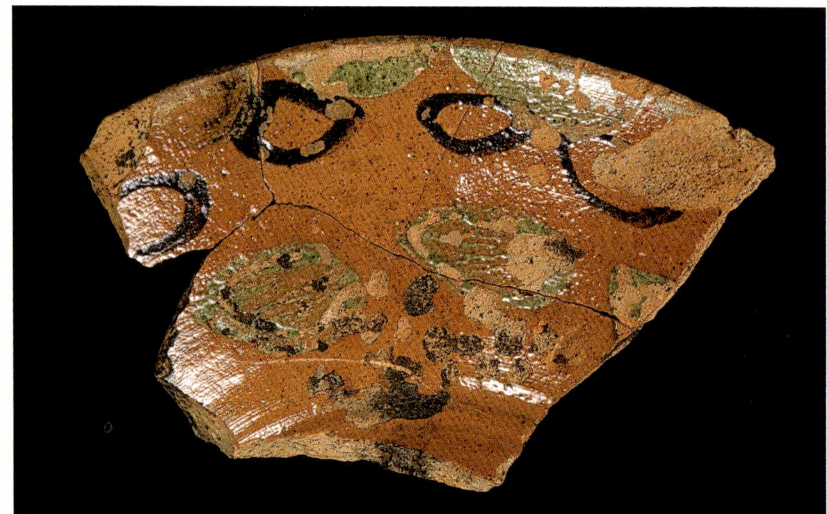

Figure 61 Dish fragment, Samuel Butter, Clarksburg, West Virginia, ca. 1820–1850. Slipware. (Photo, Gavin Ashworth.)

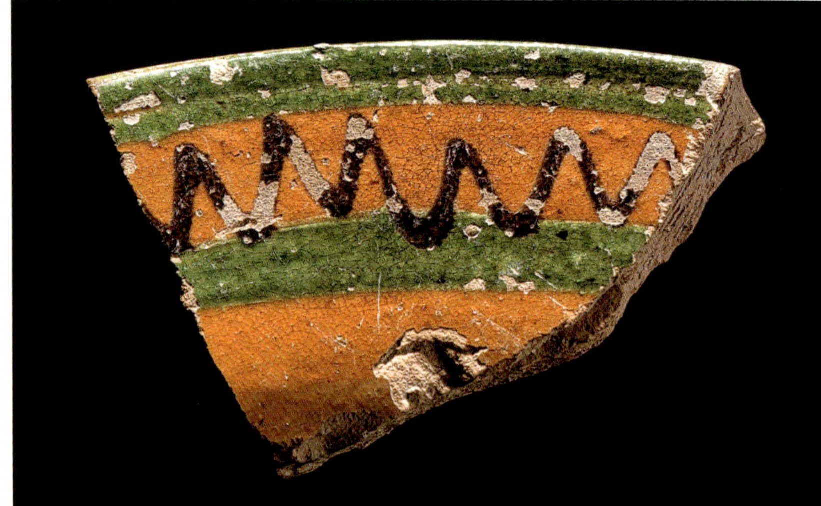

Figure 62 Dish fragment, Samuel Butter, Clarksburg, West Virginia, ca. 1820–1850. Slipware. (Photo, Gavin Ashworth.)

Figure 63 Sherd, Samuel Butter, Clarksburg, West Virginia, ca. 1820–1850. Agateware. (Photo, Gavin Ashworth.) This sherd of an agate red and white clay body, sometime referred to as *scroddle ware,* is the only known example from the Butter pottery.

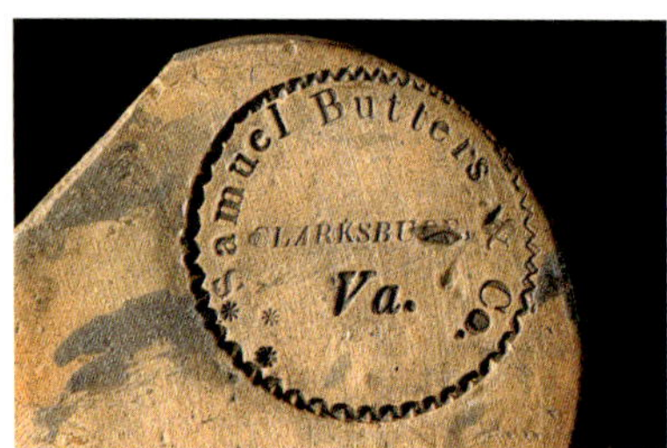

Figure 64 Sherd, Samuel Butter, Clarksburg, West Virginia, ca. 1820–1850. Earthenware. (Photo, Gavin Ashworth.) Note the presence of a final "s" in his last name and the addition of "& Co." Compare this example with the mark illustrated in fig. 27.

Bearing in mind that there are limited numbers of sherds and intact wares available for comparison, some observations are offered: Butter appears to have acquired more of Foulk's vocabulary than had John W. Thompson; Foulk was deft and fast, whereas several of Butter's early pieces are more labored and show more careful control; unlike Foulk, Butter did not use engobe under portions of his green slip or apparently much white slip in his cuprous slip, thus rendering the green in those portions much darker than Foulk's greens; and the finish on Butter's inkwell in figure 26, the jug in figure 28, the sherd illustrated in figure 15, and a ring jug (not shown),

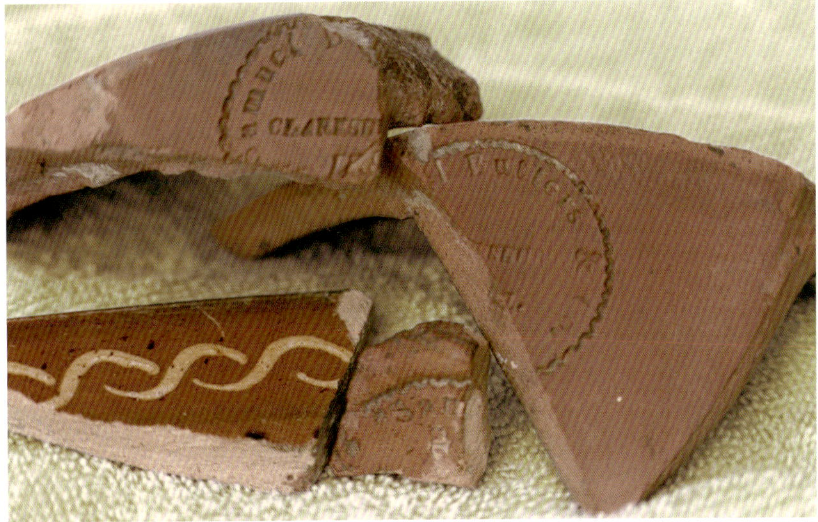

Figure 65 Sherds, Samuel Butter, Clarksburg, West Virginia, ca. 1820–1850. Earthenware. (Photo, Richard Duez.)

are superior to John W. Thompson's surviving signed wares. (Admittedly, the irregularity of the surfaces of the underlying clay in John W. Thompson's wares prejudices the impression made by the brushed slip and the glaze.) Also, Butter's use of raised bead outlining is not seen in Morgantown wares.

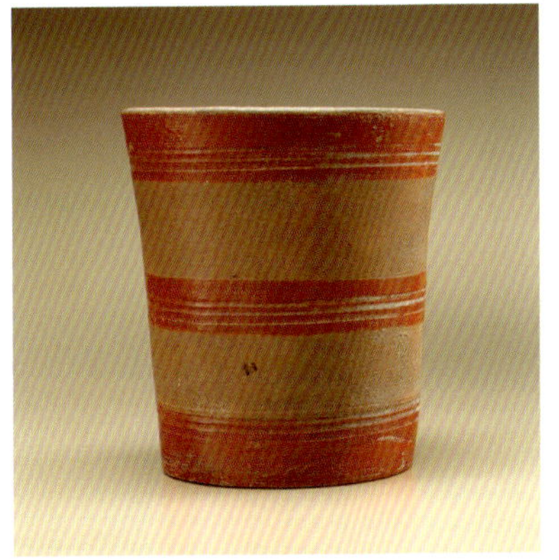

Figure 66 Tumbler, Pennsylvania or West Virginia, nineteenth century. H. 4". (Private collection; photo, Gavin Ashworth.) From a Morgantown family said to have a potter in its family history. This unglazed example resembles New Geneva tanware though it is less "dry." Decorated with incised lines and a red slip, the body is very dense and finely finished.

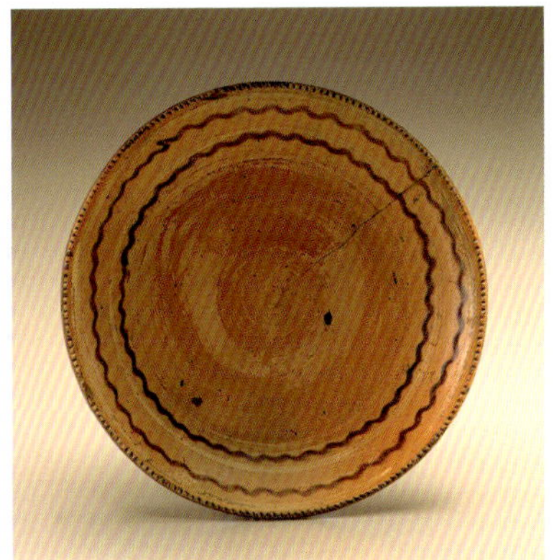

Figure 67 Plate, probably Morgantown, West Virginia, ca. 1800. Earthenware. D. 9". (Private collection; photo, Gavin Ashworth.) This coggled-edge slip-trailed earthenware plate was obtained from an "old" family on Grand Street in Morgantown. Morgantown and Clarksburg potters occasionally coggled plate edges.

Conclusion

As with any investigation into regional ceramic typologies, much research remains to be done. While many of the attributions in this article are based on years of experience in collecting examples found locally, there are always pieces that defy firm identification (figs. 66, 67). This overview of Morgantown earthenwares provides a glimpse into the range and diversity of this manufactory. As a companion to this article, a future article will examine the manufacture of stoneware in Morgantown beginning in 1854 and will discuss and illustrate some of the most unusual forms and decorative devices in America.

ACKNOWLEDGMENTS The authors wish to acknowledge the efforts of Ron Chrislip, who prepared an educational display of Morgantown pottery at the Old Stone House and presented a program at the Historical Society in Clarksburg, West Virginia.

1. Walter Hough, "An Early West Virginia Pottery," in *Report of the National Museum* (Washington, D.C.: Government Printing Office, 1901), pp. 513–22.

2. James Thompson took the oath of loyalty in 1776, at age sixteen, in Harford County, Maryland. George Washington mentions visiting Hanway's surveying office at Pierponts (just east of Morgantown) in 1784 while looking for possible routes for a canal to connect the Potomac to the Monongahela River.

3. The early Morgantown potters faced local competition for their well-to-do customers in the form of Ralph Berkshire's 1806 advertisement for "china" wares. See James M. Callahan, *History on the Making of Morgantown, West Virginia* (Morgantown, W.V.: West Virginia University Studies in History, 1926), p. 136. Berkshire also sought some of Jacob Foulk Jr.'s wares to resell (see note 8 below), but had to go to court in 1809 in an attempt to obtain the wares due to him. By 1806 Berkshire owned both halves of Lot 7, having bought the kiln portion from John Scott in 1803. Perhaps Foulk had an unrecorded lease arrangement for use of this kiln and was to pay in crockery ware rather than money. The first steamboat reached the wharf in Morgantown in April 1826 but service would have been seasonal. See Samuel T. Wiley, *History of Monongalia County, West Virginia: From Its First Settlements to the Present Time . . .* (Kingwood, W.V.: Preston Publishing Company, 1883), p. 541.

4. Diana Stradling and J. Garrison Stradling, "American Queensware: The Louisville Experience, 1829–1837," in *Ceramics in America*, edited by Robert Hunter (Hanover, N.H.: University Press of New England for the Chipstone Foundation, 2001): 165–66.

5. Hough, "Early West Virginia Pottery," p. 513; H. E. Comstock, *Pottery of the Shenandoah Valley Region* (Winston-Salem, N.C.: Museum of Early Southern Decorative Arts, 1994), p. 13.

6. Earthenware potters were working in nearby Pennsylvania, particularly in northern Fayette County, by 1791. The term "potter" had another definition in the eighteenth century, "a maker of metal pots," hence it may refer to laborers working in the iron foundries springing up locally. This confounds the records. The following are believed to be late-eighteenth-century earthenware potters: Christian Tarr, 1791, Uniontown, who also built a pottery in Waynesburg that was operated in 1799 by Nicholas Hager (see James Hadden, *A History of Uniontown: The County Seat of Fayette County, Pennsylvania* [Akron, Ohio: New Werner Company, 1913], p. 808); Edward Bittle, 1794–1800, Cumberland Township, Greene County; Henry Tarr, 1794–1811, Washington; John Bower, 1795–1828, Frederick Town; Jacob Webb, 1797, Bridgeport (South Brownsville), Fayette County; and John Baners, who in 1798 paid for milling at Heaton's mill, near Carmichaels, with earthenware (see Helen Elizabeth Vogt, *Westward of Ye Laurall Hills, 1750–1850* [Parsons, W.V.: McClain Printing Company, 1976], p. 363). There was also an Adam Funk potter/pottery merchant, 1785–1800, in Pittsburgh. Data without citation sources are from James B. Whisker, *Pennsylvania Potters: 1660–1900* (Lewiston, N.Y.: Edwin Mellen Press, 1993), which refutes Hough's conjecture that Morgantown had the first pottery west of the Appalachian Mountains.

7. Callahan, *Making of Morgantown*, p. 130.

8. Of the principal candidates for "first potter," only John Scott's name appears before 1801. He was on the 1786 Taxables List residing with Patrick Johnson. The years 1788 to 1800 are missing, but the 1801 list includes Francis Billingsley, who acquired Lot 7 in 1814 and conveyed it to John W. Thompson in 1827. Jacob Foulk Jr. was in Morgantown in 1801 and purchased Lot 90, which is described as "Foulk's Pottery on the S.W. corner of Front St. and Bumbo Lane." The "appurtenances" on Lot 90 are not named in the deed to Foulk. The deed from John and Nicey Evans was made out to Nicholas Madeira but his name is crossed out and Foulk's name written in above it. This is the same lot on which Foulk would offer to build a brick house for Nicholas Madeira. After several suits and countersuits Foulk sold it to Christian Madeira in 1806—the same year that Berkshire bought Lot 7. For a fuller account of his tangled transactions with the Madeira brothers, see Comstock, *Pottery of the Shenandoah Valley Region*, pp. 405–6.

The most accessible chronology of deeds to Morgantown lots is contained in the appendix of Callahan's *Making of Morgantown*. This is the source of all subsequent references to lots.

9. Callahan, *Making of Morgantown*, p. 309.

10. Hough, "Early West Virginia Pottery," p. 515.

11. Ibid., pp. 514–15.

12. Ibid., p. 515.

13. Comstock, *Pottery of the Shenandoah Valley Region*, p. 404.

14. Lot 112, the "vacant brick kiln lot," is on the southeast corner of High and North Boundary Streets, not far from Lot 90. However, Foulk may have used a pottery kiln for firing bricks.

15. Hough, "Early West Virginia Pottery," pp. 414–15.

16. Wiley (*History of Monongalia County,* p. 260) states that Foulk had a pottery on Lot 90, which he owned until 1806. The clearest evidence is Foulk's offer of his house in Morgantown—"where he had his pottery kiln"—as security to William Tingle, who was assisting Foulk in the acquisition of land on the Cheat River. We do not know whether Foulk was able to use the kiln after the sale of Lot 90 to Christian Madeira. He may have made an unrecorded arrangement with Ralph Berkshire to use the pottery on Lot 7.

17. Ibid., pp. 579, 586; Callahan, *Making of Morgantown,* p. 121.

18. Wiley, *History of Monongalia County,* pp. 39, 669.

19. Comstock, *Pottery of the Shenandoah Valley Region,* p. 406.

20. A comparison of early Morgantown sherds with those on display in the Hagar House Museum in Hagerstown, Maryland, reveals very little similarity and casts doubt on suggestions that Foulk trained in Hagerstown. There is a closer relationship to Shepherdstown sherds formally owned by Mr. J. Wimer. Shepherdstown lies in the northeast corner of Jefferson County, West Virginia, formerly Frederick County, Virginia, where his name appears in court records.

21. There is a large green inkwell (not shown) that is signed John W. Thompson, but its green glaze is less bright than the green seen in the pieces attributed to Foulk.

22. Callahan, *Making of Morgantown,* p. 130.

23. Billingsley also may have started a pottery on Mrs. Kelly's lot, probably Lot 12, and later sold it to John W. Thompson, perhaps in 1824. However, Thompson's only known purchase within this time frame was Lot 7.

24. Hough, "Early West Virginia Pottery," p. 513.

25. Glen A. Thompson, <glent@gte.net>, March 16, 1999, entry s-1.

26. Hough, "Early West Virginia Pottery," p. 513.

27. Earl L. Core (*The Monongalia Story: A Bicentennial History,* 5 vols. [Parsons, W.V.: McClain Printing Company, 1974–1984], 3: 311–12) implies that John W.'s tailor shop was successful, but his turn to potting casts doubts on this.

28. Callahan, *Making of Morgantown,* p. 360.

29. Wiley, *History of Monongalia County,* p. 580.

30. Callahan (*Making of Morgantown,* p. 130n) placed the fire in 1830.

31. Wiley, *History of Monongalia County,* p. 260.

32. Core (*Monongalia Story,* 3: 51) states that John W. operated the pottery until 1853, when his son, Capt. James Thompson, "came into possession [and] afterwards attached steam to it. . . ." The potter's steam engine was only 5 hp; 1870 Industrial Census.

33. There were three other residents: Charlotte (Webb) Sears, Dorcas S. Thompson, and twelve-year-old Henry C. Madeira, who may have been an apprentice. Dorcas Thompson Haymond would later donate many of the pottery's remaining tools to the National Museum. When the Thompson home burned in 1909, any remaining ledgers and correspondence were lost. The portraits were virtually all that was rescued.

34. See Hough, "Early West Virginia Pottery," pl. 1, fig. 5, and pl. 5, fig. 1, respectively.

35. Ibid., pl. 5, fig. 3.

36. The authors would welcome photos of his Ohio products for a planned article on Morgantown's stoneware era.

37. Wiley, *History of Monongalia County,* pp. 467, 468; Core, *Monongalia Story,* 3: 405.

38. George H. Thurston, *Directory of the Monongahela and Youghiogheny Valleys: Containing Brief Historical Sketches of the Various Towns Located on Them . . .* (Pittsburgh, Pa.: A. A. Anderson, 1859).

39. Wiley, *History of Monongalia County,* p. 579. One reference calls it a corn mill. However, corn originally was defined as the principal grain of a region, and in this case the principal grain was wheat. Wiley calls it the first flouring mill in the borough limits and states that Col. Francis Thompson had installed a 56-hp steam engine in 1873.

40. Whisker, *Pennsylvania Potters,* p. 83.

41. Monongalia Cemetery Readings, Dille collection, West Virginia Regional History Collection, Morgantown.

42. Hough, "Early West Virginia Pottery," p. 516.

43. Ibid., p. 2, fig. 2.

44. Wiley, *History of Monongalia County,* p. 260.

45. See Phil Schaltenbrand, *Stoneware of Southwestern Pennsylvania* (Pittsburgh, Pa.: University of Pittsburgh Press, 1996), pp. 11, 12; and Phil Schaltenbrand, personal communication, September 2003.

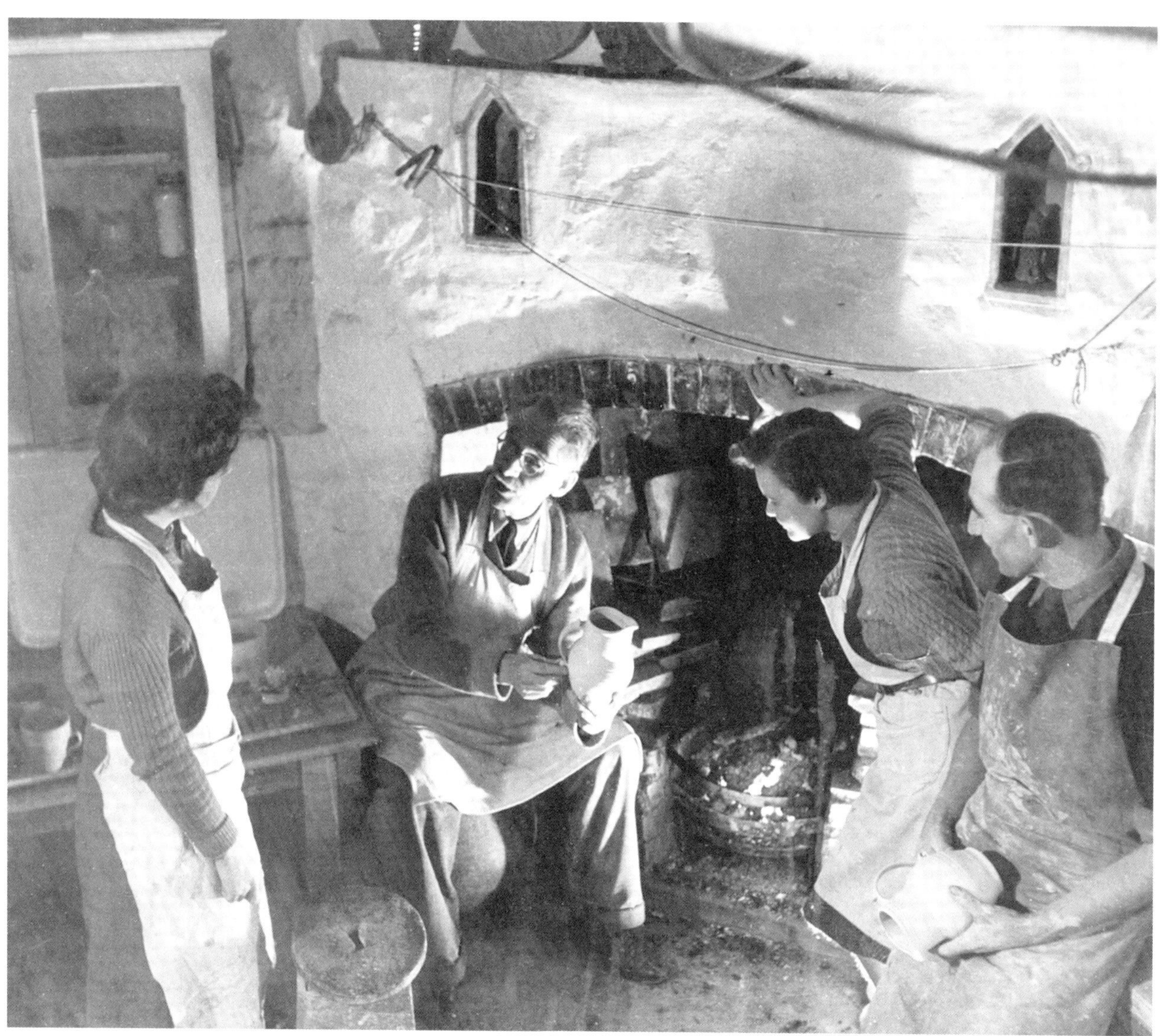

Figure 1 Bernard Leach, David Leach, and students at the Leach Pottery, St. Ives, Cornwall, ca. 1945. (Courtesy, Leach Archive, Crafts Study Centre, Surrey, England.)

Emmanuel Cooper

Bernard Leach in America

▼ POTTER, ARTIST, WRITER, POET, and one of the great figures of twentieth-century art, Bernard Howell Leach (1887–1979) played a crucial pioneering role in creating an identity for artist potters in Britain and around the world.[1] After studying to be a potter in Japan in the early decades of the twentieth century, in 1920, with the help of Japanese potter Shoji Hamada, he set up his pottery at St. Ives, Cornwall (fig. 1). They built an Asian climbing kiln for high-temperature firing—the first in the West—and a small, round updraft kiln for earthenware and oxidized raku, introducing this technique to the West.[2] Alongside individual pots that were a synthesis of oriental and western influences (fig. 2), Leach first made tableware in earthenware and, later, with the help of his son David, in stoneware. A great admirer of Korean ceramics, Leach made important visits to Korea in 1918 and 1935. In 1934–1935 he toured and worked at country potteries in Japan, which further inspired his understanding of pottery. In 1940 he published his most important text, *A Potter's Book,* which combined an aesthetic approach to appreciating pottery (advocating the "Sung standard") with practical instructions on preparing clays, making pots, mixing glazes, and firing kilns.[3] Popular for its notion of the indivisibility of work and leisure in the life of a potter, the book rapidly assumed the status of a potter's bible.

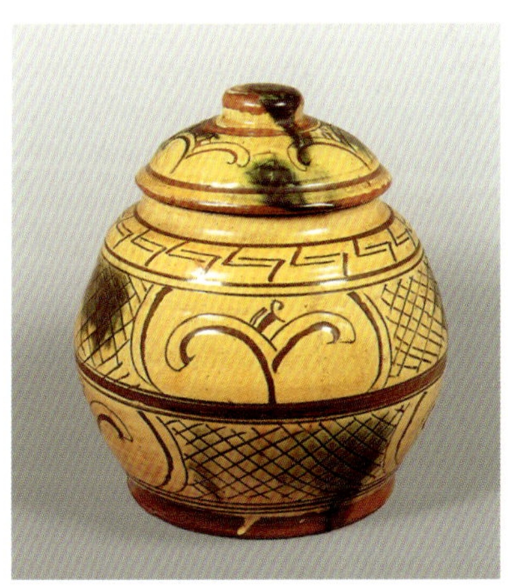

Figure 2 Bernard Leach, covered jar, 1924. Slipware. H. 9⅞". (Ohara Museum of Art, Kurashiki, Japan.)

In the postwar years Leach felt that he had a mission to travel and introduce his ideas abroad. In 1950, after a successful visit to Scandinavia the previous year, he embarked on the first of three major tours of America. All were concerned with presenting his work and ideas to potters, curators, enthusiasts, educators, and collectors. Although prewar exhibitions of his pots in the United States had met with little success, Leach was encouraged by visitors to St. Ives and, more particularly, by Robert Richman, director of the Institute of Contemporary Art in Washington, D.C., who arranged the itinerary. An ambitious ten-week lecture and demonstration tour was planned, spanning twelve thousand miles and including about one hundred seminars. Independently, an exhibition of 200–300 of Leach's pots toured to various museums.

In February 1950 Leach set sail on the much-lauded brand-new liner SS *Ile De France*. His first major stop was at Alfred University, New York State College of Ceramics, the leading institution for both industrial and studio techniques, where Charles Harder (1889–1959) had arranged a full program of practical sessions in the morning and talks and lectures in the afternoon (fig. 3).[4] Most members of the predominantly male student body,

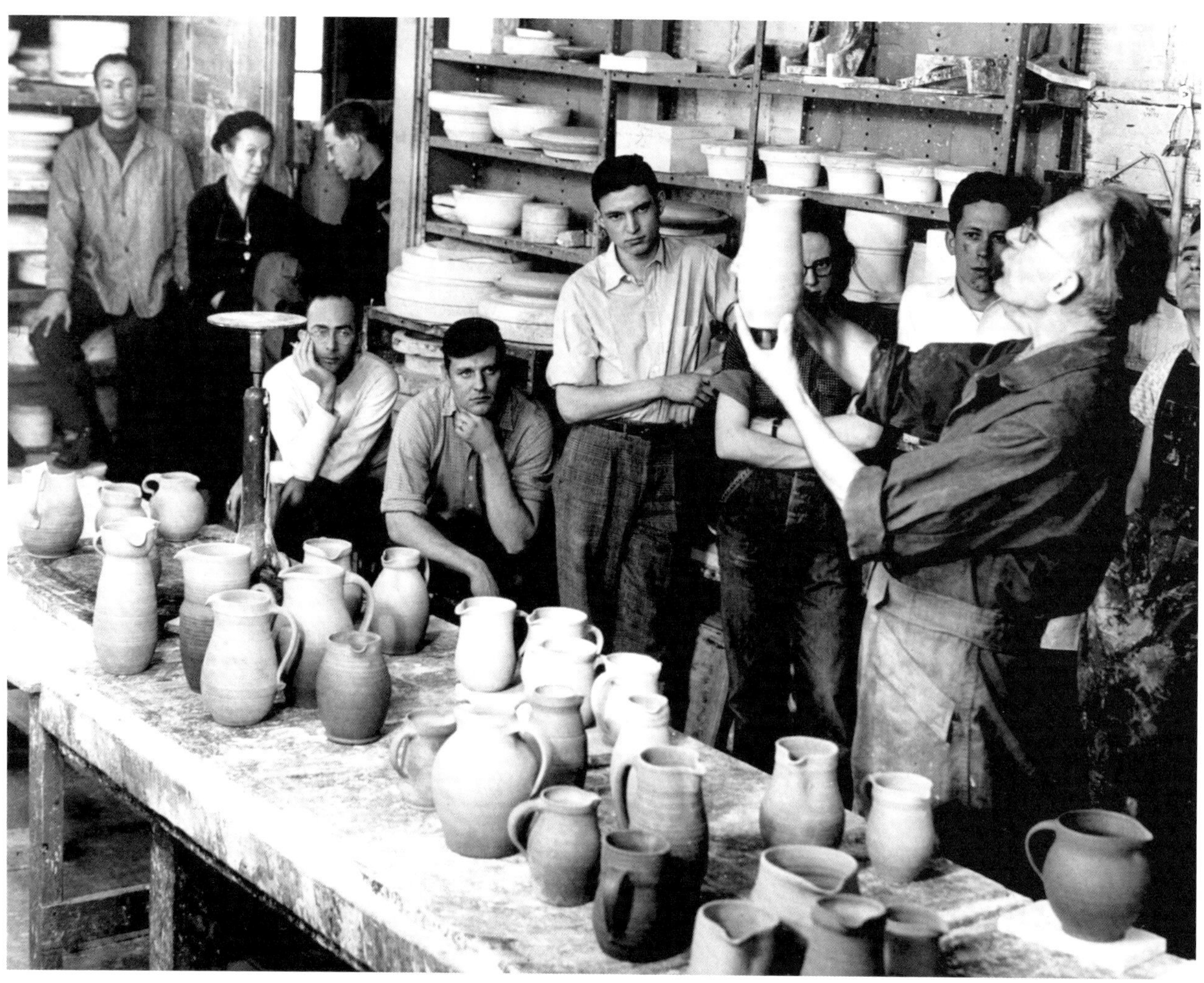

Figure 3 Bernard Leach discussing the merits of thrown pots with students at Alfred University, 1950. (Courtesy, College Archives, New York State College of Ceramics at Alfred University.)

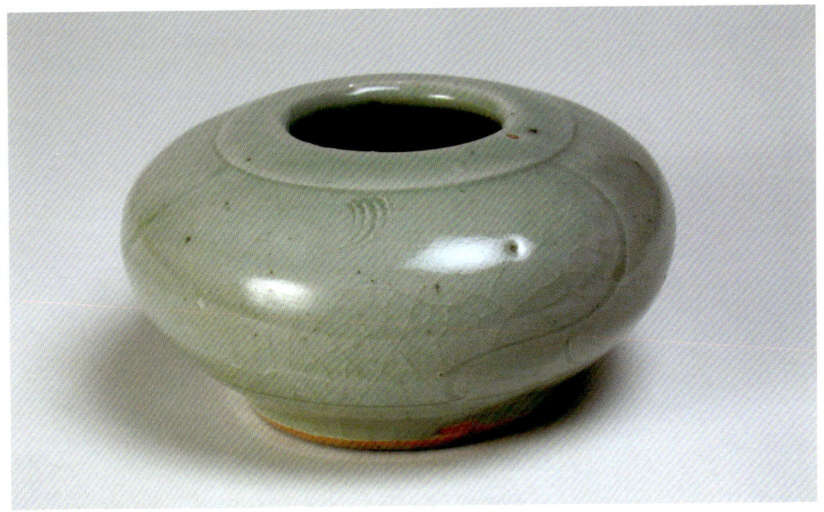

Figure 4 Bernard Leach, jar, St. Ives, Cornwall, ca. 1920–1948. Stoneware. H. 1¾". (Courtesy, Henry Bergen Collection, Potteries Museum and Art Gallery, Stoke-on-Trent.) Thrown and turned with a celadon glaze.

however, had served in the war and, wanting to get on with their own projects, did not take kindly to the disruption, though they did enjoy Leach's comments on their thrown pots.[5] He also introduced raku.

The visit was a mixed success. Some thought he spoke directly about their work, about the pleasure of the well-made object, and about the quietness and contemplative qualities of high-fired wares within an oriental aesthetic (fig. 4). Many, however, were more attracted by colorful Scandinavian pots and the ideas of the Bauhaus, and did not see his ideas as having much relevance. Nevertheless, he was able to convey the concept of wholeness, particularly the idea that "the pot is the man."

Leach was greatly honored when the American Ceramics Society presented him with the Binns Medal for Ceramics, the highest such award in the country. The fact that the medal, usually awarded for industrial production, was given for his studio pottery tickled him.

Curious to see as much as possible, both by way of pots and institutions, Leach was pleased to be entertained in New York by Aileen Osborn Webb (1892–1979), a "tall, authoritative, yet strangely shy" figure who was a great patron of modern crafts and who combined a regal presence with genuine humility and an idealistic commitment to the crafts.[6] She helped to found the American Crafts Council and served as chairman of its board of managers; she also served as director of the School for American Craftsmen and was president of the American Craftsmen's Cooperative Council, Inc., which published the magazine *Craft Horizons*. Her enthusiasm was in sharp contrast to Leach's experience in England, where private patronage was modest at best.

For Leach, the biggest challenge was in trying to conceal his disapproval of the pots he saw on his tour. He soon missed the "old, tap-rooted inbred intimacies of a small country," and described the United States as the "land of money and speed and gadgetry." Whether in Washington, D.C., San Francisco, or New York, he was not averse to speaking his mind on the subject of pots—often with more than a hint of missionary zeal.[7] The pieces he saw, in his opinion, were often badly conceived. One example, a round, full, balloonlike shape with a tiny neck, a form that was made by several potters in different variations, stretched the shape to the point of distortion. Practical criticisms included "handles which are obviously stuck on and do not grow from within as branches grow from a tree-trunk" and "jug lips which will not pour without dripping; teapot spouts which are either goiterous or camel-like; hollow knobs on covered pots which contradict the formal rhythms of the rest of the shape."[8] These observations confirmed his belief in the need for education and enlightenment.

By the same token, some American commentators were less than enthusiastic about Leach and his achievements. The innovative potter and teacher Daniel Rhodes (1911–1989), while acknowledging Leach's importance in "turning the attention of potters to Chinese and Japanese values in pottery," thought that in his own work Leach had not developed "a truly personal style, or a pottery which seems in keeping with any dynamic Western tradition" (figs. 5–8).[9] Despite this criticism, Leach, an interested visitor, found the tour invigorating and worthwhile.

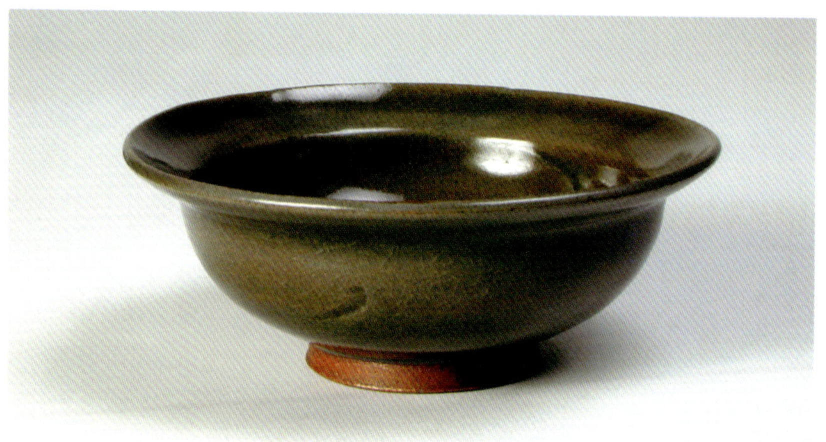

Figure 5 Bernard Leach, bowl, St. Ives, Cornwall, ca. 1920–1948. Stoneware. H. 1¾". (Courtesy, Henry Bergen Collection, Potteries Museum and Art Gallery, Stoke-on-Trent.) Thrown and turned with a celadon glaze.

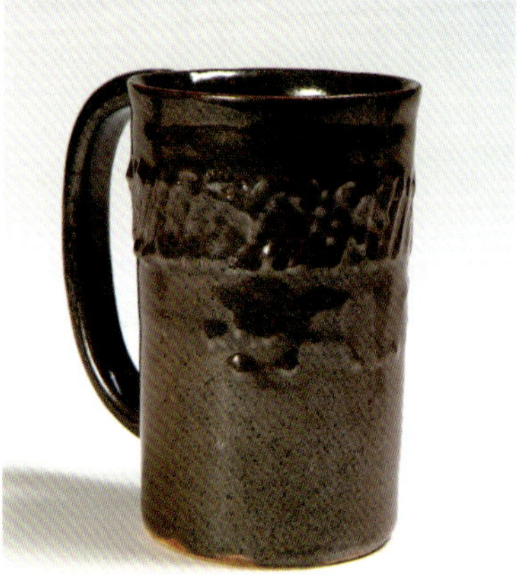

Figure 6 Bernard Leach, mug, St. Ives, Cornwall, ca. 1920–1948. Stoneware. H. 4⅞". (Courtesy, Henry Bergen Collection, Potteries Museum and Art Gallery, Stoke-on-Trent.) This is a so-called trellis mug with pulled handle and slip-trailed trellis decoration, and the word "ALE" below.

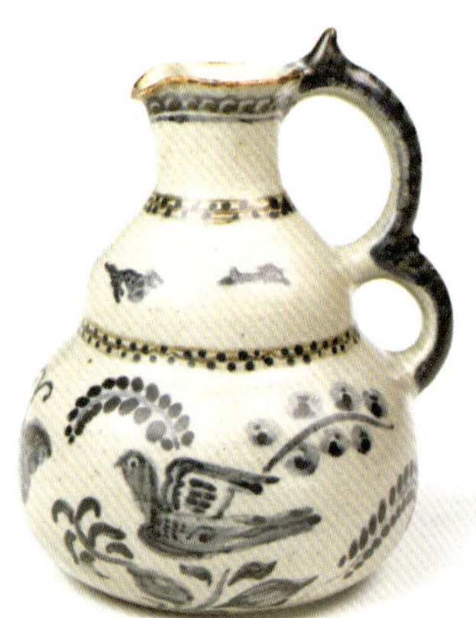

Figure 7 Bernard Leach, jug, 1912–1913. Stoneware. H. 5⅝". (Courtesy, Leach Archive, Crafts Study Centre, Surrey, England.)

In Minneapolis, where he gave lectures and demonstrations before flying to San Francisco, Leach stayed with Warren and Alix MacKenzie, two potters who had visited him in St. Ives. An example of Warren MacKenzie's pottery is illustrated in figure 9.

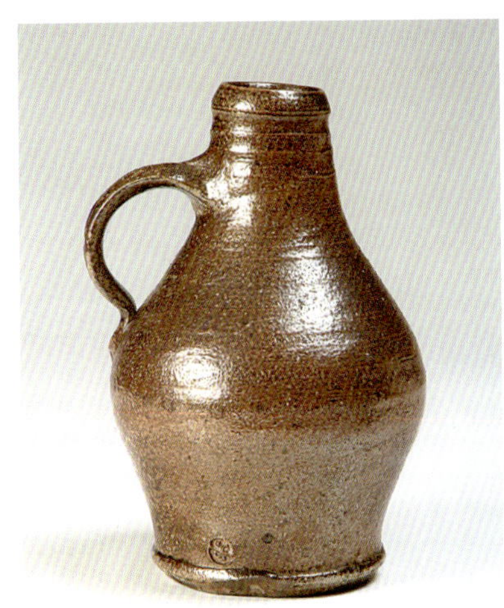

Figure 8 Bernard Leach, bottle, St. Ives, Cornwall, ca. 1920–1948. Stoneware. H. 7½". (Courtesy, Henry Bergen Collection, Potteries Museum and Art Gallery, Stoke-on-Trent.) Thrown with a pulled handle.

Leach also spent two weeks in Seattle with his old friend, fellow Bahá'í and abstract expressionist painter Mark Tobey and Tobey's partner, Pehr Hallsten, an artist working in a naive style. In Tobey's opinion Hallsten painted "wonderful attractive little paintings" and had "a remarkable natural color sense."[10] Their relationship was a complex combination of love and aggression, in which affection was interspersed with much snarling and snapping. It was fully accepted by Leach, though to what extent he recognized its homosexual nature is not clear. (What he did find difficult was Tobey's obsession with endless shopping expeditions, which left Leach so exhausted that at one point he sat on the pavement and demanded to be left alone.)

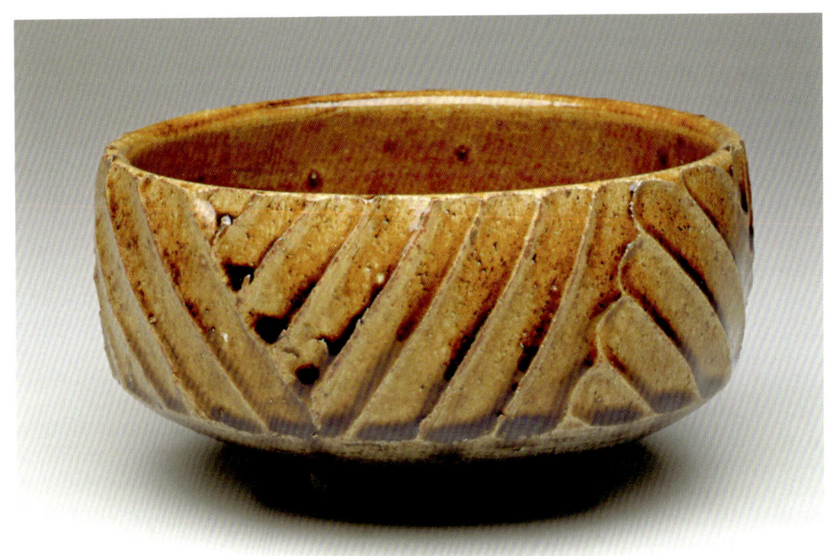

Figure 9 Warren MacKenzie, bowl, ca. 1969–1970. Stoneware. D. 6¼". (Courtesy, Minneapolis Institute of Arts, gift of Rev. Richard L. Hillstrom.)

The Three Musketeers

In 1952 Leach, Shoji Hamada, and the Japanese critic and philosopher Soetsu Yanagi set out on a four-month coast-to-coast tour (fig. 10). Having held the highly successful International Craft Conference on Pottery and Weaving at Dartington in Devon, England, "the three Musketeers" (as they were dubbed by Leach in a letter to Lucie Rie) set sail for America in October on the SS *Mauritania*.[11] Their first stop was Washington, D.C., where they stayed with Robert Richman, and after sorting out a muddle over financial arrangements they traveled to their inaugural, two-week seminar at the experimental, interdisciplinary Black Mountain College in Asheville, North Carolina. At an elevation of 2,500 feet, the setting was magnificent. The mountains were clad in brilliant autumn colors, and black swallowtail butterflies with their blue sheen flitted amongst the trees and falling leaves, seemingly undisturbed by the great highways and fast traffic.

Thirty-five enthusiastic students and potters had enrolled in the program, which was to consist of films, slides, demonstrations, and lectures, as well as parties, excursions, and social events. All three lecturers quickly fell into roles they were to retain throughout the tour. Leach, the "articulator, the innovator . . . who coupled standards with form," talked

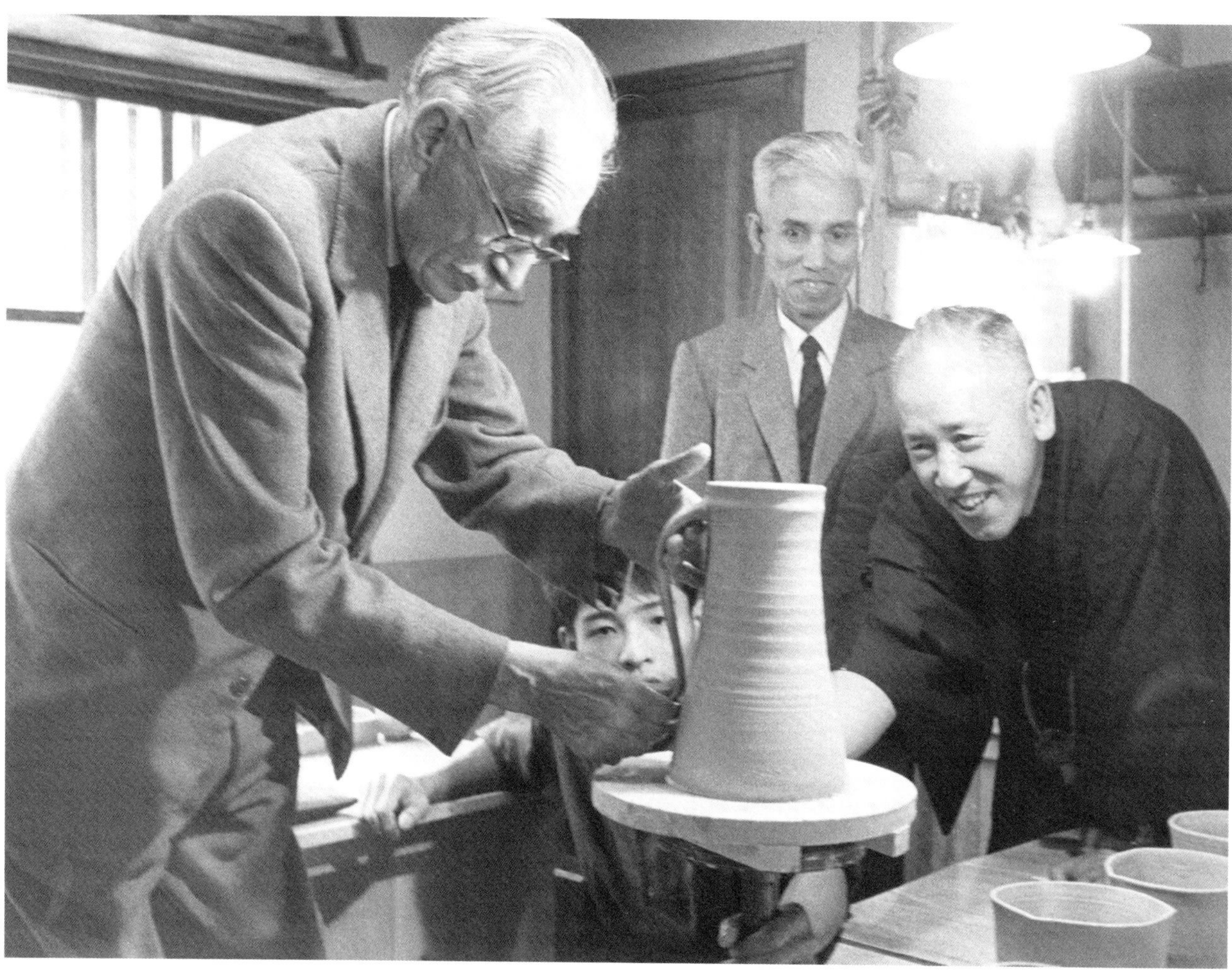

Figure 10 *Left to right:* Bernard Leach, Soetsu Yanagi, Shoji Hamada, and Tea-master Sato at Toyama, Japan, 1961. (Courtesy, Leach Archive, Crafts Study Centre, Surrey, England.)

endlessly, gesticulated freely, and made a few pots.[12] Hamada, the doer, who "wrote in visual language" and who spoke only Japanese despite having good English, silently threw on the wheel and assembled a teapot in a matter of minutes. Yanagi, "the master of Zen aesthetics," lectured on Buddhist theories of beauty and Zen and Shin—"the road of the few and the road of the many"—difficult concepts that often went over the heads of their audience.[13]

Three successful stoneware and earthenware firings were held. A high manganese glaze was used over black and white slips for the earthenware, and the stoneware body was enlivened by adding a local iron-bearing sand. One Leach pot, about seven inches tall, had a typical willow tree design (see, for example, fig. 11) incised through a dark slip under a white glaze.[14] The pieces produced by Leach and Hamada were sold for a total of $235, which the potters donated to the badly depleted college funds.

The twin themes of tradition and theory dominated discussions at Black Mountain—as they did, indeed, throughout the tour. With crusading passion Leach, Hamada, and Yanagi freely criticized attitudes to the craft as well as pots in an endeavor to enlighten, inform, and provoke. Although they stressed the need to understand rather than ape the broad base of their aesthetic ideas and philosophical approach, from the outset there was

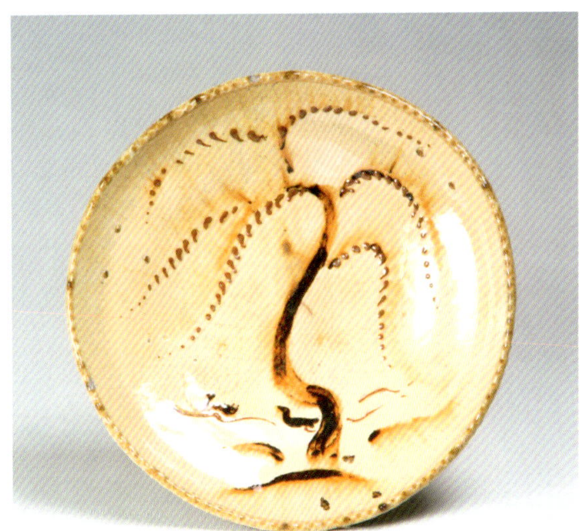

Figure 11 Bernard Leach, dish, St. Ives, Cornwall, ca. 1920–1948. Slipware. D. 13". (Courtesy, Henry Bergen Collection, Potteries Museum and Art Gallery, Stoke-on-Trent.)

mixed response to their preference for soft, muted earth colors and harmonious shapes. Students seemed to prefer "recipes, tricks and dodges" over serious discussion about pots and pottery making. As a way of demystifying their approach, Hamada explained how attractive stoneware glazes could be made from combinations of rock and wood ash, and demonstrated how bundles of grass could be bound to make useful brushes.

The need for a tradition, or "tap root," a topic articulated by Leach at great length two years earlier, was regularly discussed. "America as a new amalgam of races does not provide a craftsman with traditions of right making born on its own soil," was Leach's authoritative view.[15] Few students responded to such observations, and many dismissed his analysis as a failure to understand the nature of American culture. Susan Peterson, the potter in charge at the Chouinard Art Institute, Los Angeles, thought that "none of the three men could comprehend the melting pot nature of the United States."[16]

At Black Mountain Leach's most significant meeting was with the Texas-born potter Janet Darnell (1919–1997), for it was the start of a relationship that was to continue throughout his life. Having read and been impressed by the sense of wholeness and unity expressed in *A Potter's Book,* and having heard Leach lecture two years earlier in New York, Darnell wanted to know more about his approach and philosophy. She traveled seven hundred miles from New York State to attend his workshop.[17] Strong-minded and determined, she had a clear vision of her needs and capabilities. With her striking angular features and a mop of dark, curly hair, she is remembered by Susan Peterson as "wiry, boney, thin with deep-set eyes . . . fun-loving and happy."[18]

After Black Mountain the tour took Leach, Hamada, and Yanagi to Boston, Worcester, Ann Arbor, Detroit, St. Paul (again staying with the MacKenzies), and to the Archie Bray Foundation in Helena, Montana (fig. 12), where they met the gifted young potters Peter Voulkos (fig. 13) and Rudy Autio (fig. 14).[19] Voulkos, kicking the wheel for Hamada, admired his easy technique and relaxed brushwork, which he thought

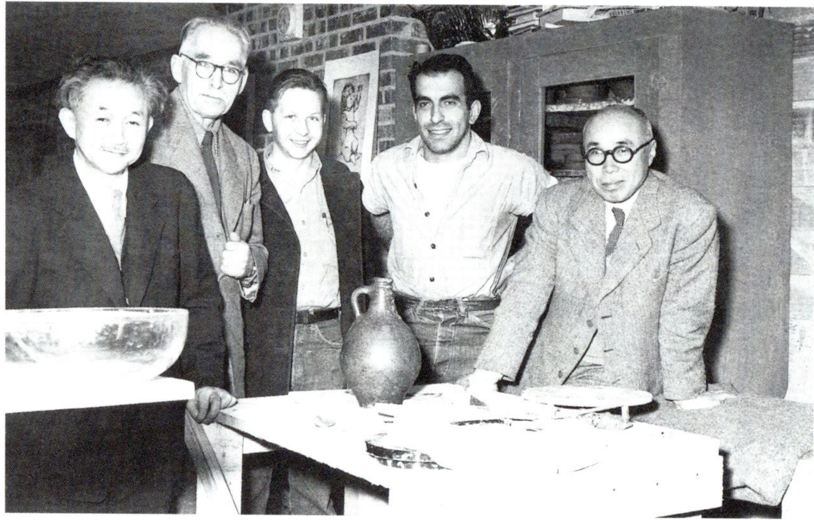

Figure 12 Workshop at the Archie Bray Foundation, 1952. *Left to right:* Soetsu Yanagi, Bernard Leach, Rudy Autio, Peter Voulkos, Shoji Hamada. (Courtesy, Archie Bray Foundation for the Ceramic Arts, Helena, Montana.)

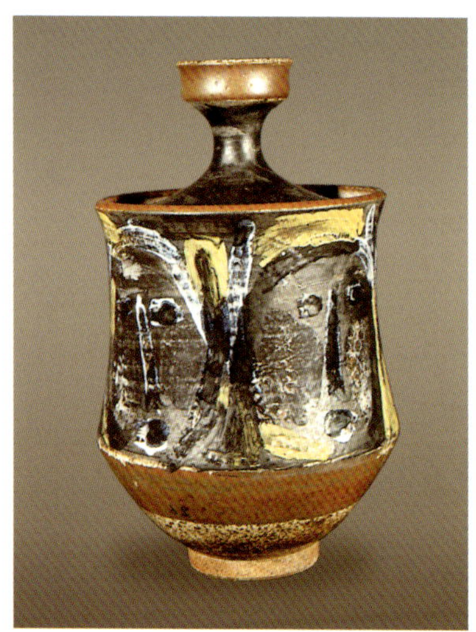

Figure 13 Peter Voulkos, covered jar, ca. 1954. Stoneware. H. 14". (Courtesy, Montana Museum of Art and Culture. Gift of Lela and Rudy Autio.) This jar was refired with low-fire imagery in 1958.

"rhythmical and dance like in movement and gesture."[20] Visitors, however, were highly critical of Voulkos's functional tableware for being too decorative. With a powerful sense of his own strong, simple forms but already concerned with pushing the boundaries of conventional craft, Voulkos was taken more by their ideas than by their opinion of his pots.

In search of American Indian pottery, Leach, Hamada, and Yanagi flew to Santa Fe, New Mexico, to admire old handmade pots, woven and printed textiles, and genuine primitive Spanish religious paintings. At San Ildefonso they met the renowned potter Maria Martinez (1884–1980), who, when they found her, was raking pots out of the ash heap. Black and shiny from being fired with horse dung, the pots gleamed and sparkled and—for once—all three nodded their approval. For their lectures and demonstrations at the International Museum of Folk Crafts, Maria Martinez honored them by wearing her best blankets and necklaces of coral, jet, silver, and turquoise. Appropriately, Leach's subject was the "Integration of the Craftsman," a theme also taken up by Yanagi, who spoke on the "Responsibility of the Craftsman."

Traveling around the countryside Leach marveled at the dramatic landscape—extinct volcanoes, ancient lava flows, gigantic ramparts of rock, erosion, scrub, and slopes dotted with evergreen piñon—enthusing, "I have never seen a place which excited me more."[21] The mile-deep, many-colored Grand Canyon was all they had imagined and appeared even more impressive under a light covering of snow. Its "scintillating opalescent light and incredible formations of ramparts, pinnacles, castles, bastions and slopes of water-worn rocks and far, far below glimpses of the thin thread of the Colorado River" for once overawed Leach.[22] Leach captured in a few deft lines the quality of the Arizona desert in a pen-and-ink wash (1952; Victoria and Albert Museum, London), evoking the vastness, heat, and drama of the landscape. The sepia-colored study contrasts with *Snow and Pines, USA* (1950; Mingeikan, Tokyo), a drawing in black ink wash that simplifies the hills and trees to great effect.

The final leg of their tour was Los Angeles and the Pacific Palisades,

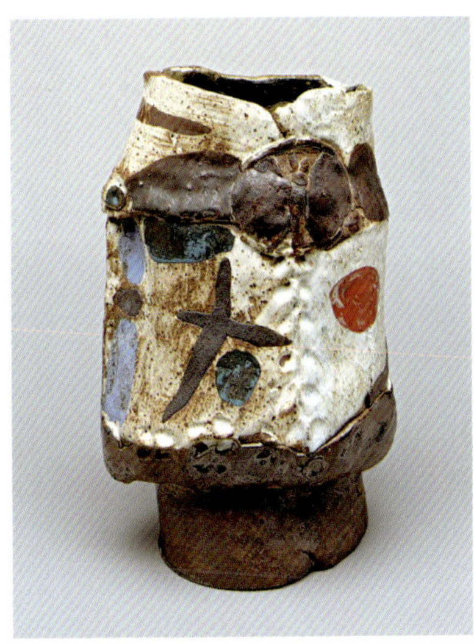

Figure 14 Rudy Autio, vessel, ca. 1965. H. 12". (Milwaukee Art Museum, Gift of Ruth and Robert Vogele, photo, John R. Glembin, acc. no. M2002.43.)

where Hamada stood on the cliffs gazing longingly over the Pacific toward Japan. The last stops were Scripps College, Claremont, and a two-week workshop with Susan Peterson at the Chouinard Art Institute. The audiences watched respectfully as Leach and Hamada threw several score of pots, ranging from modest marmalade jars to large urns. Again Hamada neatly assembled a teapot with a few rapid motions to an audience of one hundred students and four movie cameras. In San Francisco, as guests of the Japanese consul general, they stayed in his "posh and ugly" house overlooking the Golden Gate Bridge; the massive six-hundred-yard structure made a great impression. One remarkable night was spent at a snow-covered gorge in Yosemite to see the four-thousand-year-old redwoods, *Sequoia gigantea,* and the magnificent granite masonry of Half Dome.

While in California Leach and Hamada, both great admirers of the innovative American designer Charles Eames (1907–1978), visited him and his wife, Ray (1912–1988).[23] Eames's openness to both hand- and machine work and his readiness—"open hearted, accepting and recreative"—to respond to East and West about furniture and design in general, successfully combined the traditional and the new. His radical molded fiberglass chair, exhibited to wide acclaim at the Museum of Modern Art, New York, seemed so far from Leach and Hamada's handcrafted pots, both in spirit and appearance, that it is difficult at first to see the connection.

Accounts of their tour in *Ceramics Monthly* singled out Leach and Hamada's unenthusiastic response to American ceramics, quoting Leach's view that "strong digestive capacities" were required to absorb influences as diverse as pre-Columbian Indian and the contemporary abstract idiom, a feat that Leach thought few could achieve.[24] Various correspondents strongly rejected what they saw as the potters' patronizing attitude. Far from respecting Leach's work, one described his pots as "stuffy, heavy; and mid Victorian . . . and incredibly dull."[25] In *Craft Horizons* Marguerite Wildenhain joined the many critical voices, contending that Leach and Hamada were starting from the wrong premise. Wildenhain insisted that to look for a single root was misconceived; the country had many cultures and, in fact, therein "lies its uniqueness, its grandeur."[26]

The Third Visit

Leach's third major visit to the United States, in 1961, was with his wife, Janet Darnell Leach, the potter he had met in America, got to know in Japan, and married in England in 1956. The trip was both a cementing of their relationship and an opportunity for talks, demonstrations, and sales. It was Janet who arranged their eight-week lecture and exhibition tour, which included seminars in thirteen different centers. They bought a large Ford station wagon, to allow for easier travel and to avoid expensive airfares, and Leach devised a scheme of first drawing and then making pots of a certain type so those sold could be replaced. At the suggestion of the Canadian potter John Reeve, then working in St. Ives, Leach read *Dharma Bums,* by the American beat writer Jack Kerouac, to give him an alternative view of the country.

The tour began with an exhibition at the small but exclusive department store Bonniers in New York. Meetings and events in the city ranged from public talks to what seemed like an endless round of dinner parties, including one at Aileen Webb's handsome penthouse flat. At the Museum of Indian Art they had lunch with the "sophisticated, but sincere, daughter of one of the Sioux chiefs and her American husband" and talked about pots.[27] More controversial was Peter Voulkos's exhibition of painting and sculpture at the Museum of Modern Art. The large, bold, energetic sculptural pieces with their references to abstract expressionism, though technically skilled, were not to the taste of Leach and his wife, and they were convinced that had Voulkos made pots rather than semiabstract forms, his work would not have been shown at all. "Where has pottery failed this man?" Janet wondered.[28]

On two occasions they were invited to lunch by Miss Gordon, editor of *House Beautiful,* at the Four Seasons, thought to be the world's most expensive restaurant, where "glass icicles fell from a heaven 50' above in cascades, the carpets were thick and silent, the food very good."[29] Miss Gordon had "caught Zen and *shibui*" and, after devoting the August 1960 edition of the magazine to those ideas, wanted to hear more about them. "It astonishes me," Leach wrote, "that a popular magazine in America should have the insight and courage to attempt to bring the austerities of Zen Buddhist taste to the multitudes of the West. Straw, straw, where blows thy wind?"[30]

As he had hoped, Leach discovered more about Janet and her life in America during this trip. They were received warmly at Threefold Farm, where she had worked as a potter, despite residual resentment at what some perceived as her disloyalty in abandoning the Steiner community.[31] From New York they went to Baltimore for a two-day stop to teach "29 nice, normal, eager beaver amateur but keen women students," then drove 1,850 miles to Dallas and Grand Saline to stay with Janet's parents and meet her relatives.[32] Although her mother disapproved of the marriage, she got on well with Leach, and he enjoyed watching Janet play dominoes with her father—both of whom, he noted, soon reverted to their private, well-established language.

"A lanky old man in a baggy tweed suit" was how a student in Dallas described Leach.[33] Leach proudly explained, however, that his outfit had belonged to his father, demonstrating his belief that the old was neither bad nor useless. He further impressed his audience by producing, prior to his demonstration, a handsome wooden lacquer toolbox "embedded with a sort of mosaic of colored bits of eggshells."[34] Although well smattered with clay, the box possessed an element of finesse and style. During lectures he spoke enthusiastically about the work of potters like Cardew and Hamada and their awareness of tradition. This "warm, affable and opinionated potter-draftsman-philosopher" went over well, even when Leach told one would-be potter that his pot looked like "a top-heavy ballerina about to tip over on a too narrow foot."[35]

At the University of Michigan in Ann Arbor they stayed with Jim Plumer

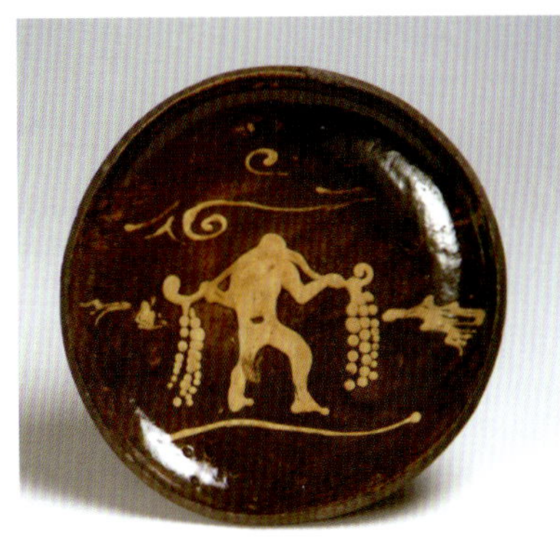

Figure 15 Bernard Leach, dish, St. Ives, Cornwall, ca. 1920–1948. Slipware. D. 13". (Courtesy, Henry Bergen Collection, Potteries Museum and Art Gallery, Stoke-on-Trent.)

and interviewed an earnest young potter named Byron Temple (1933–2002), who had written for permission to work at Leach's pottery.[36] At St. Paul they stayed with the MacKenzies, though Leach's habit of treating them as students rather than mature potters continued to grate. He was particularly critical of what he saw as Alix's lack of understanding of pattern. "Decor, rhythm, repeat pattern," he pointed out, "are secondary to the pattern idea—the little dance—the little melody which picks up the form of a pot and completes it" (fig. 15).[37] Alix thought it typical of Leach that he made no effort to appreciate her experimental exploration of design.

The ten-thousand-mile journey, which would have taxed a man half Leach's age, was a success in most ways. Critical reception was respectful, although, as Janet observed, they did not "meet many of the leading potters," and she could not help noticing that audiences tended to be enthusiasts rather than respected professionals.[38] Sales, however, were excellent, and Janet, on territory, felt at ease despite driving vast distances and making innumerable arrangements. She and Leach were together virtually without a break, and it seemed to work.

While many visitors may have found New York's "man-made canyons of architecture" or the vast open spaces and huge distances daunting, for Leach they were a challenge, part of what he saw as "a crusade from coast to coast."[39] And if the pots he saw failed to gain his approval, the people he found on all his visits were, almost without exception, polite and charming, generous in their hospitality, and greatly enthusiastic for the craft. Across the length and breadth of America he felt that he was met with every conceivable kindness, experiencing firsthand the life of prosperous Americans. But he did not accept America easily, suspicious of its modernity and consumer-oriented values. Janet, like many others, thought Leach made no real attempt to appreciate either the American way of life or their approach to making pots. But for many he spoke about values at a time of profound change, and, if not offering specific solutions, he did put forward a way of thinking about pots that was far from doctrinaire, and one that, as he often said, involved the "head, heart, and hand."

1. Emmanuel Cooper is a potter, writer, critic, and editor of *Ceramic Review: The International Magazine of Ceramic Art and Craft*. This article is adapted from his biography of Bernard Leach, *Bernard Leach: Life and Work* (New Haven and London: Yale University Press, 2003).

2. When Leach took pots from the kiln he allowed them to cool rapidly in the open air. The glaze invariably crazed, but the colors were often bright. Post-firing reduction, a technique developed in America and one not used by Leach, was achieved by taking the pot directly from the kiln and placing it in an airtight container with a combustible material such as sawdust, leaves, or newspapers. The heat of the pot would cause the combustible to smoulder, resulting in blackened bodies and luster glazes.

3. Bernard Leach, *A Potter's Book* (London: Faber and Faber, 1940).

4. Charles Harder, head of the design department, made salt-glazed domestic stoneware.

5. See Susan Peterson, "Reflections: Part 1—Leach at Alfred," *The Studio Potter* 9, no. 2 (June 1981).

6. The American Crafts Council grew out of Aileen Webb's efforts during the Depression. She was also involved with America House (est. 1940), the School for American Craftsmen, the Museum of Contemporary Craft (1956), and the World Craft Council (1964). For accounts of Aileen Osborn Webb, see Rose Slivka, "Our Aileen Osborn Webb," *Craft Horizons*

(June 1977): 10–13, and Rose Slivka, "Aileen Osborn Webb, David Campbell: A Reminiscence," *Craft Horizons* (August–September 1993): 133–41.

7. Slivka, "Our Aileen Osborn Webb," pp. 10–13.

8. Bernard Leach, "American Impressions," *Craft Horizons* 10, no. 4 (winter 1950).

9. Daniel Rhodes, *Stoneware and Porcelain: The Art of High Fired Pottery* (1959; reprint, London: Pitman Publishing, 1978), p. 39.

10. Mark Tobey, letter to Bernard Leach, April 4, 1958, Leach Archive, no. 12239.

11. Bernard Leach, letter to Lucie Rie, November 4, 1952, Rie archives.

12. Susan Peterson, "Bernard Leach: Two Recollections," *The Studio Potter* 8, no. 1 (1979–1980): 3.

13. Bernard Leach, "The American Journey with Yanagi and Hamada," n.d., private collection.

14. This piece is now in the collection of the Mingeikan (Japan Folk Crafts Art Museum), Tokyo.

15. Bernard Leach, *A Potter in Japan* (London: Faber and Faber, 1960), p. 34.

16. Peterson, "Bernard Leach: Two Recollections," p. 3.

17. Leach, *Potter's Book*.

18. Interview with the author, March 21, 1997.

19. The foundation had been set up by Archie Bray on the property of the Western Clay Manufacturing Company two years earlier to provide facilities and advanced ceramic studies within the state. Voulkos (1924–2002) was one of the most influential and significant potters of postwar America. Autio (b. 1926) remained at Archie Bray until 1956. Glenn Adamson's review of Louana M. Lackey's book *Rudy Autio* (2002) appears in this issue of *Ceramics in America*.

20. Quoted in Rose Slivka and Karen Tsujimoto, *The Art of Peter Voulkos* (Tokyo: Kodansha International, 1995). This was a turning point in Voulkos's life, as shortly afterward he was invited to teach at Black Mountain College, where he came into contact with the ideas of the abstract expressionist painters. The connection stimulated him to produce more abstract sculptural forms in ceramics.

21. Leach, "American Journey with Yanagi and Hamada," p. 6.

22. Ibid., p. 8.

23. The couple often worked as a team and together developed many ideas.

24. E. James Brownson, "Midwest Craftsmen's Seminar," *Ceramics Monthly* (March 1953): 10, 28.

25. *Ceramics Monthly* (March–April 1953); Leach Archive, no. 1728.

26. Marguerite Wildenhain, letter to the editor, *Craft Horizons* (May–June 1953): 43–44.

27. Bernard Leach, letter to Lucie Rie, March 16, 1960, Rie archives.

28. Janet Leach, "A Few Impressions of Current American Pottery," *Pottery Quarterly: A Review of Ceramic Art* 7, no. 25 (1961): 12–16.

29. Bernard Leach, letter to Lucie Rie, March 16, 1960, Rie archives.

30. Bernard Leach, letter to Warren MacKenzie, March 16, 1960, private collection.

31. Rudolph Steiner (1861–1925) is the Austrian founder of anthroposophy. He evolved a study of spiritual concerns opposed to conventional occultism, and his educational theories of using the arts therapeutically were widely influential.

32. Bernard Leach, letter to Lucie Rie, March 16, 1960, Rie archives.

33. John P. McElroy, "A Visit from Bernard Leach," *The Studio Potter* 27, no. 1 (December 1958): 18–19.

34. Ibid.

35. Ibid.

36. Byron Temple worked at the Leach Pottery from 1959 to 1962, and again from 1978 to 1979. He also made pots at Lambertville, New Jersey.

37. Bernard Leach, letter to Warren MacKenzie, May 16, 1960, private collection.

38. Leach, "Current American Pottery," pp. 12–16.

39. Bernard Leach, letter to Lucie Rie, March 10, 1950, Rie archives.

Luke Zipp

Henry Remmey & Son, Late of New York: A Rediscovery of a Master Potter's Lost Years

▼ THE REMMEYS STAND in American decorative arts history as arguably the most influential family of stoneware potters. Although the history of their potteries in Manhattan and Philadelphia has been sufficiently fleshed out, their potting activity in Baltimore remains largely undocumented. Based on the scant mention of the name Remmey in Baltimore business directories and the rarity of extant examples of stoneware signed "H. REMMEY / BALTIMORE," it has long been assumed that Henry Remmey Jr. briefly operated a pottery in Baltimore but returned to his father's successful Philadelphia manufactory when his Baltimore experiment failed. As a result, his tenure in Baltimore exists as a footnote and a failure in the history of the Remmeys. However, new research has revealed that both Henry Remmey Sr. and Henry Remmey Jr. worked in Baltimore, and their impact there was, in fact, far greater than previously thought.[1]

Remmey Sr. was born around 1770 and inherited an American stoneware potting tradition handed down by his grandfather, John Remmey I, who arrived in New York in 1735. John's family had been practicing in France and Germany for centuries when he set up his shop in New York, and the stoneware that he and his descendants produced in Manhattan was recognized as the finest in the country. In 1793 Henry took over operation of the pottery with his brother, John Remmey III, but his association with the shop did not last long; he left his brother in 1796 and began a series of independent business ventures.[2]

In 1806, however, Henry Remmey's fortunes in New York changed. Louis Zukofsky, in his Depression-era radio script entitled "Remmey and Crolius Stoneware," describes the dramatic turn of events:

> In 1803, [Henry Remmey] had been appointed to the position of Superintendent of City Scavengers—street cleaners we call them today—and when three [years] later the office was abolished, he was found guilty of appropriating city funds. He begged, "on account of the distressed state of his family," to be excused from repaying the money which he had collected during his term of office. But the Council refused.[3]

Unable to comply with the council's ruling, Remmey took his family and fled New York City.[4]

Henry Remmey arrived in Baltimore in the summer or early fall of 1812.[5] Although the colonies had won their independence, the emerging United States remained financially bound to Britain and American consumers continued to crave British products. It was not until events leading up to the War of 1812 halted trade relations with England that America began to

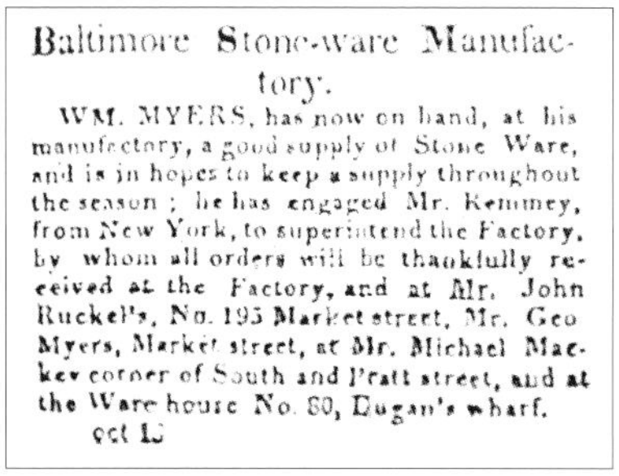

Baltimore Stone-ware Manufactory.

WM. MYERS, has now on hand, at his manufactory, a good supply of Stone Ware, and is in hopes to keep a supply throughout the season; he has engaged Mr. Remmey, from New York, to superintend the Factory, by whom all orders will be thankfully received at the Factory, and at Mr. John Ruckel's, No. 193 Market street, Mr. Geo Myers, Market street, at Mr. Michael Macker corner of South and Pratt street, and at the Ware house No. 80, Dugan's wharf.

oct 13

Figure 1 Newspaper advertisement for china merchant William Myers's Baltimore Stoneware Manufactory, October 13, 1812. This is the first known reference to Henry Remmey in Baltimore.

respect its homegrown artisans for their skills, and in the realm of American stoneware no potters were respected more than those from New York City.

In June 1812 William Myers, a Baltimore china merchant, decided to manufacture his own pottery when he "purchased of Mr. James Johnson, his well known Manufactory of stone ware" on Bond Street, north of Pitt Street, and retained Johnson to superintend the operation. Initially Myers supplemented his inventory with superior stone- and earthenware produced in Hartford, Connecticut, while he made plans to expand the manufactory. He added new materials and workers and renamed the business "Baltimore Stone Ware Manufactory."[6] But his chief aim was to produce stoneware of the highest possible quality, and for that he hired a new manager. On October 13, 1812, he announced that he had "engaged Mr. [Henry] Remmey, from New York, to superintend the Factory . . ." (fig. 1).[7]

The arrangement between Myers and Remmey benefited both men. With Remmey's help Myers anticipated manufacturing stoneware that rivaled the best New York products. Myers's mention that his new pottery superintendent was from New York surely carried implications of quality to Baltimore consumers. As an impoverished fugitive, Henry Remmey was undoubtedly delighted to manage a large pottery without having to own it and to enjoy status as a master craftsman in a city that had a dearth of them. Moreover, Myers seems to have compensated Remmey well for his skill; in addition to a fair daily wage, Remmey eventually was given a house to live in rent-free.[8]

Remmey Sr.'s arrival in 1812 represents a major turning point in Baltimore's stoneware products. Baltimore merchants relished the opportunity to offer stoneware from Manhattan. Myers clearly knew the value of the Remmey family name, as he referred to it for more than three straight months in Baltimore newspapers. As manager of the manufactory, Remmey Sr. not only produced a large amount of high-quality stoneware for Myers to sell, he also ensured superior products by the workers under his charge. And his position as superintendent gave him added status, which led to the improvement of the Baltimore potting school in general.[9]

The documentary evidence for Remmey Sr.'s early years in Baltimore remains sparse. He does not appear in the Baltimore business directories until 1817, he does not appear in Baltimore land records as a purchaser or lessee of property, and he is absent from Baltimore court records. Presumably this lack of information is related to his problems in New York; as a fugitive with known financial problems, he would not have wanted to make his whereabouts widely known, and he did not—probably could not—purchase property. As a result, little about his activity for much of the 1810s is known.

We do know that he worked at the Baltimore Stoneware Manufactory between October 13, 1812, and January 20, 1813, based on Myers's newspaper ads. And he was definitely potting at the Baltimore Stoneware Manufactory with his son Remmey Jr. in April 1818, because an advertisement placed that month by Jacob Myers (presumably William's brother), who owned the manufactory by then, states that Myers's "Stone Ware is manu-

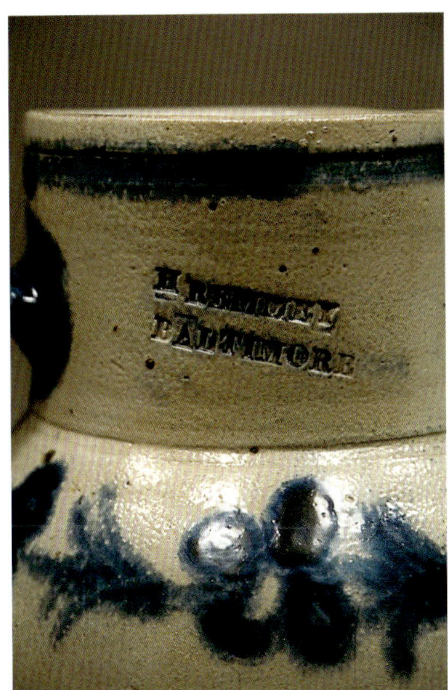

Figure 2 Henry Remmey's Baltimore maker's mark. (All photos, Luke Zipp.) Since Remmey never owned his own stoneware pottery in Baltimore, he probably produced stoneware bearing this mark at the Baltimore Stoneware Manufactory under Jacob Myers, 1818–1821, although an earlier date for this stoneware is possible.

factured by *Henry Remmey & Son,* of New-York, and is inferior to none in the United States, they being regularly brought up to the business. . . ."[10] Between 1815 and 1818, however, there is virtually no evidence concerning the whereabouts of Remmey Sr., though it is quite possible he never left the Baltimore Stoneware Manufactory despite changes in ownership.

By June 1815 William Myers wanted to expand his potting establishment to keep up with demand. He placed a newspaper advertisement that announced, "Two or more potters are wanted at the stoneware manufactory as journeymen."[11] He also sought a partner who could help finance the expansion. (Remmey Sr., of course, would not have qualified.) That month, potter Elisha Parr came to the manufactory and became William Myers's business partner.

Elisha Parr remained a partner in the Baltimore Stoneware Manufactory until March 1818, when he opened his own stone- and earthenware pottery a couple of blocks west, on Pitt Street. In the intervening three years, William Myers left the stoneware business, selling out to Jacob Myers. When Parr left, Jacob attempted to sell the business but changed his mind, instead advertising in April of that year that he "continues manufacturing Stone Ware, at his factory, upper end of Pitt street, old town." He refers to "Henry Remmey & Son, of New-York" in the ad, which, along with other evidence discussed below, supports a contention that extant stoneware impressed "H. REMMEY / BALTIMORE" (see, for example, fig. 2) was manufactured at the Baltimore Stoneware Manufactory under the ownership of Jacob Myers.[12]

Jacob Myers owned the manufactory until November 1, 1821, when, at age sixty-three, he passed the business to his son, Henry.[13] Under Henry's ownership the manufactory produced vessels impressed "H. MYERS" (fig. 3); a significant number of them survive.

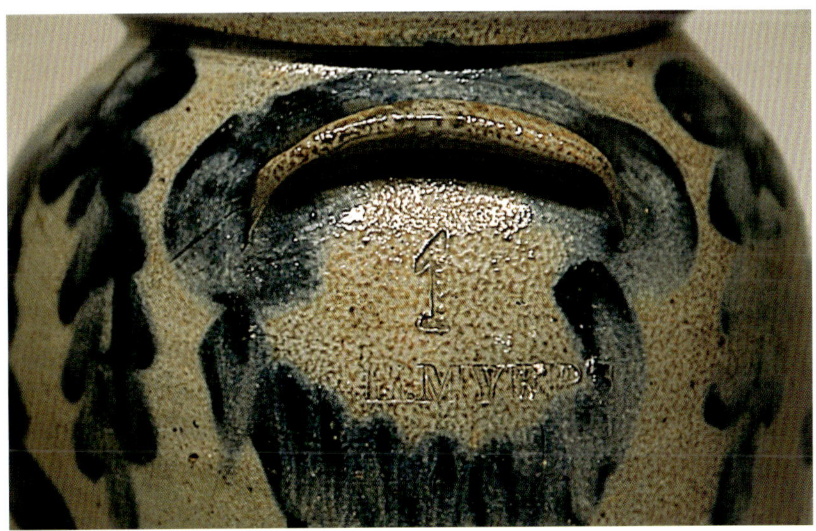

Figure 3 Mark used on stoneware made at the Baltimore Stoneware Manufactory under Henry Myers's ownership. Henry Remmey superintended the manufactory from 1821 to 1829.

In his first year of business, Henry Myers advertised his stoneware price list in the Baltimore newspapers (fig. 4) and, like his father before him, notified the public, "My Stoneware establishment is conducted by HENRY

REMMEY & SON, late of New York, and in the manufacturing of the above article they are not inferior to any in the United States."[14] That same year the Baltimore business directory lists Remmey as working at a stoneware factory on the northwest corner of Bond and Pitt Streets (the Myers pottery). Other directory listings place Remmey Sr. continuously at the Baltimore Stoneware Manufactory through 1829, the year he probably left the city altogether.[15]

Since Remmey Sr. worked for Henry Myers for approximately seven years, a large portion of the extant "H. MYERS" pieces were probably manufactured by Remmey Sr. himself, or at least under his direct supervision. Since extant stoneware from New York and Baltimore signed by Remmey Sr. is rare, his most significant representation in the American stoneware record is probably vessels marked "H. MYERS." Myers stoneware reflects a combination of skill and efficient production uncommon for stoneware in 1820s Baltimore.[16] Remmey Sr. ended his forty-year career working at Henry Myers's pottery in 1829, when he retired to live in Philadelphia with Remmey Jr., who two years earlier had established a pottery there.

Surprisingly little documentary evidence exists about Remmey Sr.'s Baltimore activities. Earlier assumptions about the Remmeys are based on an entry in an 1824 business directory that lists Remmey Jr. as living at Pitt and Bond Streets and working at a stoneware factory on Wilk Street. Since Remmey Sr. is not mentioned, scholars have interpreted this record to mean that only Remmey Jr. worked in Baltimore. Furthermore, it had been assumed that Remmey Jr. owned the pottery. Remmey Jr.'s purchase, along with Enoch Burnett, of Branch Green's Philadelphia pottery in May 1827, just three years after the beginning of the Wilk Street pottery, led many to assume Remmey Jr. had failed at his first attempt at pottery ownership.[17]

In actuality, Remmey Jr. worked with his father at the Baltimore Stoneware Manufactory until 1824, when he was hired away from Myers to be the main potter for another merchant-owned operation. George Earnest, a Baltimore china merchant, followed in the footsteps of the Myers family by attempting to manufacture his own stoneware. His initial announcement of his pottery (fig. 5) stated that he had "erected extensive buildings . . . for

STONEWARE

MANUFACTURED BY HENRY MYERS,
No. 53 MARKET STREET, BALTIMORE.

Where may be had a general assortment of STONEWARE, at the following reduced prices, deliveredin any part of the city free of cartage:

1-8 gall.	Jugs,	Pots or	Pitchers,		55 cts	per	doz
1-4	do	do	do	do	$1 00	do	do
1-2	do	do	do	do	2 25	do	do
1	do	do	do	do	3 25	do	do
1½	do	do	do	do	4 00	do	do
2	do	do	do	do	5 00	do	do
3	do	do	do	do	7 00	do	do
Milk Pans,	½	gallon			2 00	do	do
Do	1	do			2 75	do	do
Do	1½	do			4 00	do	do

Pans with lids, Spicket Jugs, Inkstands, Porrengers, &c. various prices

Wares of any size or shape will be made without any delay, to order

[My Stoneware establishment is conducted by HENRY REMMEY & SON, late of New York, and in the manufacturing of the above article they are not inferior to any in the United States.]

Also, the subscriber still continues importing CHINA, GLASS and QUEENSWARE, which will be sold by the original invoice, or repacked to ensure safe carriage—Country merchants and the public generally are respectfully invited to call, where they may depend on having their wares of the best quality and at the lowest Baltimore prices

NB. *PINE WOOD* of a good quality would be taken in exchange for wares. de 3

Figure 4 Newspaper advertisement and price list for merchant Henry Myers's stoneware manufactory, July 3, 1823. Not only does this advertisement serve as proof that Henry Remmey and Henry Remmey Jr. manufactured "H. MYERS" stoneware, but it also clarifies the types of stoneware they produced for Myers.

Baltimore Stone Ware Pottery.

COOKING FURNACES

The subscriber has erected extensive buildings on Wilk street, Fell's Point, for the manufacture of STONEWARE, and has now on hand at his *Store* in Calvert street, a large and general assortment. The ware is manufactured by Henry Remmy, jr.

He has also commenced the manufacture of *Cooking Furnaces*, and is constantly supplied with all the sizes. They are made of good materials and *warranted to stand the fire*. A large discount made to country dealers. Also on hand as above, a complete assortment of *china, glass, and Queen's ware*, which will be repacked or sold by the original package.

GEO. EARNEST,
29 Calvert st.

12—eo4t CGP

Figure 5 Newspaper advertisement announcing the opening of merchant George Earnest's stoneware manufactory, August 14, 1824. According to this ad, Earnest secured Henry Remmey Jr. as the superintendent of his new pottery.

the manufacture of STONEWARE." And, as a testament to the quality of stoneware produced by his new establishment, Earnest declared, "The ware is manufactured by Henry Remmy, Jr."[18]

Since Earnest, who catered to southern markets, infrequently advertised his pottery establishment in local publications, this manufactory has been recognized for its short-lived association with Remmey Jr. The manufactory, which eventually passed to Earnest's heirs, did last more than thirty years, which could be credited to Remmey Jr.'s early management. Certainly, when Remmey Jr. moved to Philadelphia in 1827, the stoneware manufactory he purchased would dominate the city's potting industry into the twentieth century.

The Remmeys' Baltimore Wares

Remmey Baltimore stoneware is well thrown and evenly fired. Most is decorated with cobalt oxide. Enough examples of signed or definitively attributable Remmey Baltimore stoneware exist to qualitatively judge the potters' abilities, and these pieces reveal a mastery of forming, decorating, and firing. A few surviving vessels bear ornate incised decoration attributable to Remmey Sr.'s skill. All of the stoneware discussed in this section was made by Remmey Sr. (or under his supervision), with the exception of a flowerpot that is attributed to his son.

The stoneware impressed "H. REMMEY / BALTIMORE" that Remmey Sr. produced during part or all of the period 1812–1821 more clearly resembles products in the Manhattan style. His Baltimore pots look nearly identical to early Manhattan pots, with loop handles, high-neck collars, and incised lines below the rim. He certainly produced the stoneware bearing his name at the Baltimore Stoneware Manufactory, and there is no documentary evidence linking him to any other manufactory (and we know the Remmeys did not own a shop of their own in Baltimore). Furthermore, the same one-and-one-half-gallon capacity mark found on a marked Remmey Baltimore pitcher is found on "H. MYERS" vessels as well, further suggesting that these articles were made at the same shop.[19]

Figure 6 Jar, Henry Remmey, Baltimore, 1812–1821. Salt-glazed stoneware. H. 15". (Private collection.) Impressed "H. REMMEY / BALTIMORE," this storage jar has a form identical to examples made in Manhattan in the early nineteenth century. The cobalt decoration is typical of Remmey's earlier Baltimore work.

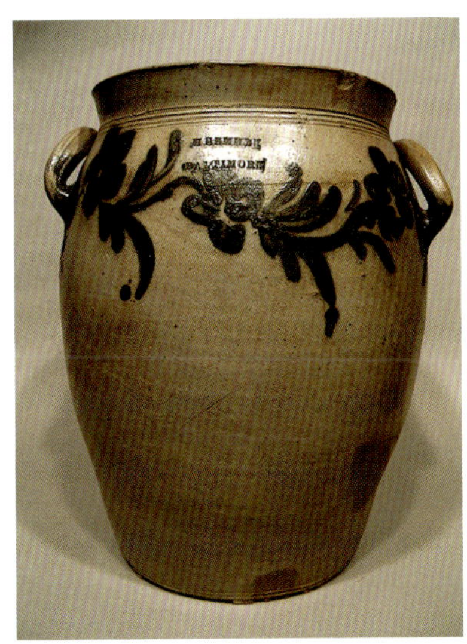

It is unusual for a pottery owner to encourage an employee to mark the stoneware he produced with his own name, but Remmey Sr. and Remmey Jr. were unusually skilled potters and had particular eminence in the context of Baltimore pottery. While it is possible that Remmey Sr. produced stoneware marked with his name at the Baltimore Stoneware Manufactory under both William and Jacob Myers, it is more likely that the "H. REMMEY / BALTIMORE" stoneware was produced between 1818 and 1821, when Jacob Myers was the sole owner of the manufactory. No other Baltimore stoneware producer used an impressed maker's mark until after the War of 1812, when resumed trade with Britain spurred local craftsmen to market their products, and the Myers family probably held to this pattern as well.[20]

While not representative of the evenly fired clay and vibrant cobalt decoration of Remmey Baltimore stoneware, a large, four-gallon stoneware pot marked "H. REMMEY / BALTIMORE" (fig. 6) does demonstrate the

Manhattan form Remmey Sr. used in his earlier pots.[21] A tall collar, a series of incised lines below the collar and at the base, loop handles, and ovoid shape typify early-nineteenth-century production in New York City by the Remmeys, Croliuses, and others. Remmey Sr. decorated this pot with the same motif (horizontal vine with four-petal flowers) that he used on his "H. REMMEY / BALTIMORE" stoneware.

Two vessels attributed to Henry Remmey, Baltimore—a marked one-and-one-half-gallon pitcher (fig. 7) and a wine keg (fig. 8)—are decorated with variations of this floral motif. Both exhibit the evenly fired gray clay and

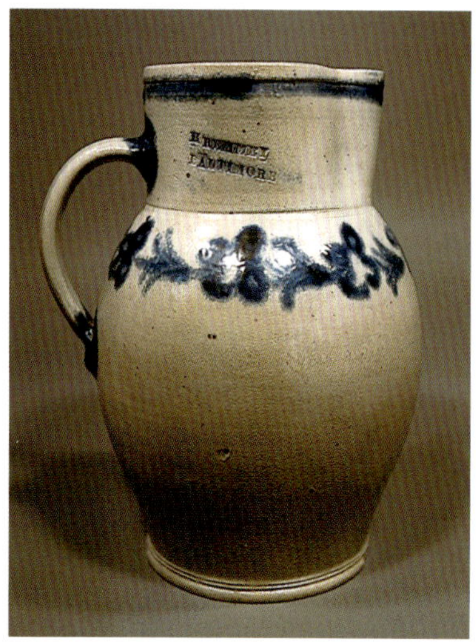

Figure 7 Pitcher, Henry Remmey, Baltimore, 1812–1821. Salt-glazed stoneware. H. 11½". (Private collection.) The pitcher's decorative motif, vibrant cobalt, and pure gray clay are typical of Remmey's Baltimore stoneware. The impressed "H. REMMEY / BALTIMORE" mark is illustrated in fig. 2.

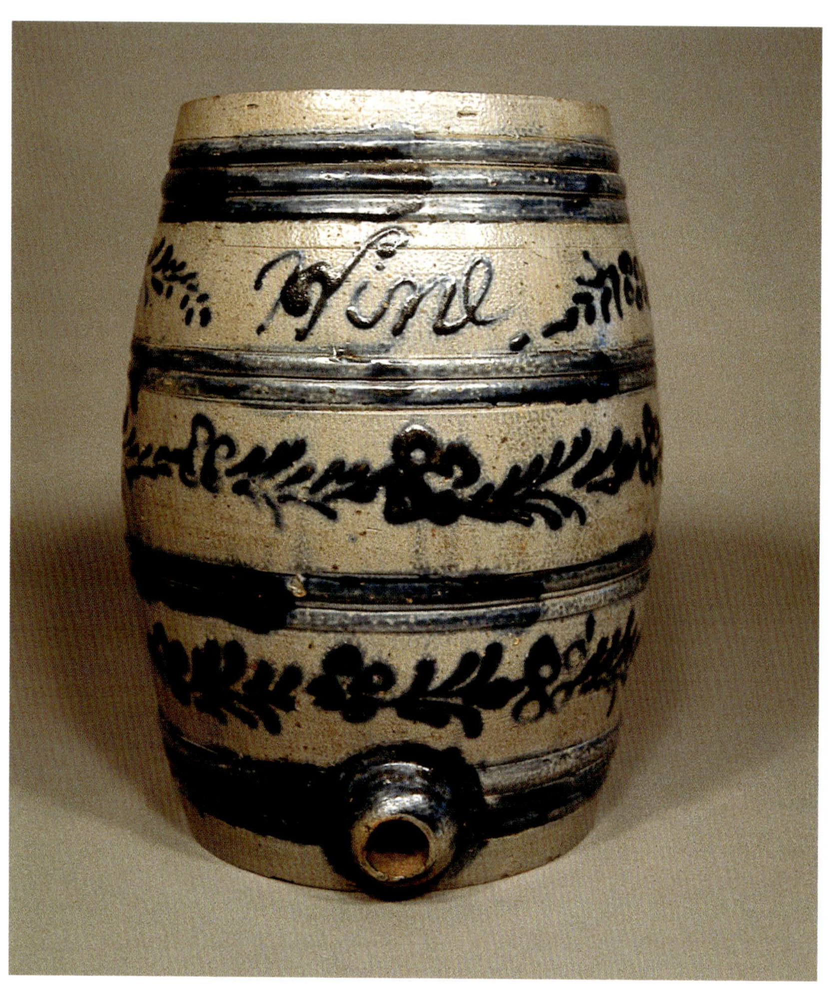

Figure 8 Wine cooler, Baltimore, ca. 1815. Salt-glazed stoneware. H. 11". (Private collection.) Although unsigned, this keg was almost certainly made by Henry Remmey in Baltimore. The keg form is rarely seen in Baltimore stoneware but is not uncommon in Manhattan stoneware.

bright cobalt-oxide slip characteristic of Remmey Sr.'s Baltimore work. The unsigned wine cooler is easily attributed based on these attributes and its Baltimore-area provenance. The cooler or keg form, common in Manhattan, is virtually unknown to stoneware production south of Pennsylvania. The extravagant use of cobalt slip and the word "Wine" in script are features more typical of Remmey Sr. than any other Baltimore potter at the time.[22]

Baltimore pitchers marked by Remmey do not exhibit many common characteristics. Although they all are fashioned with ovoid bodies with footed bases and ribbed handles, the collars vary sharply in style. The collar on the pitcher in figure 7 seems fairly typical of most nineteenth-century

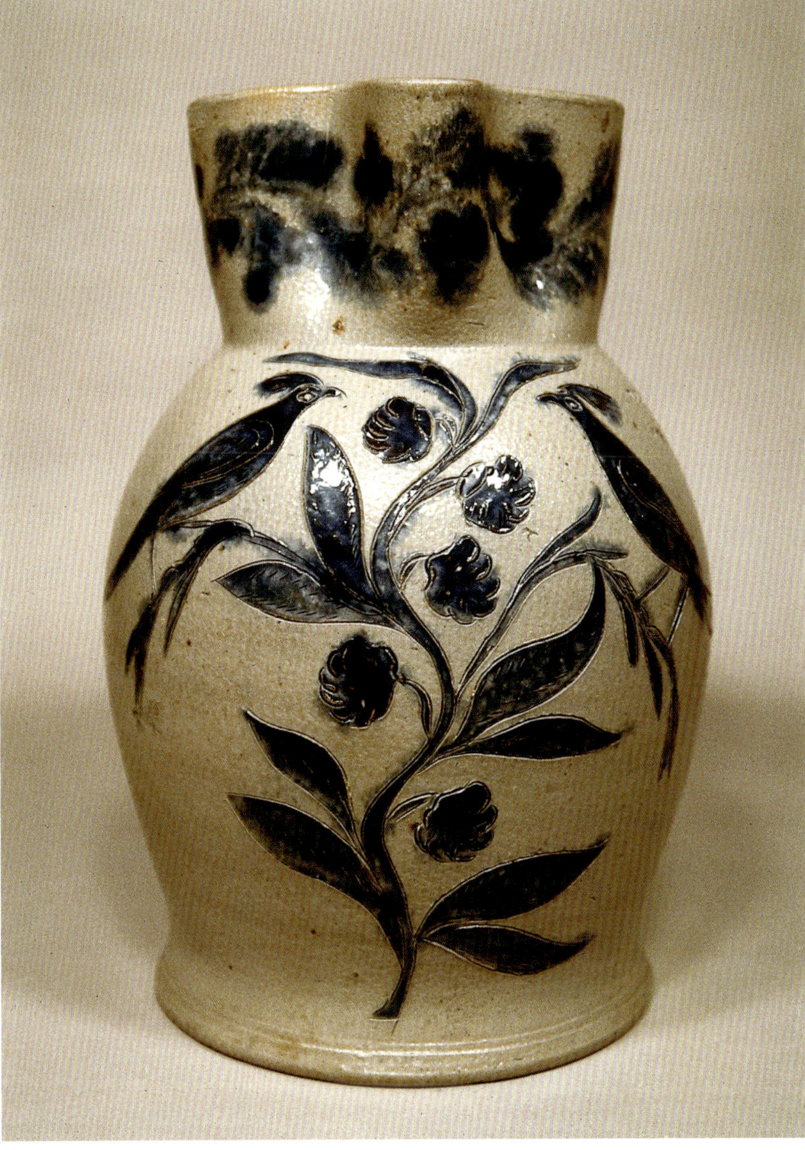

Figure 9 Pitcher, Henry Remmey, Baltimore, 1812–1821. Salt-glazed stoneware. H. 11". (Private collection.) Impressed "H. REMMEY / BALTIMORE," this pitcher, with its incised bird decoration, displays Remmey's command of incising. He included fine details of the birds and flowering trees, and washed the decoration with vibrant cobalt confined almost entirely within the incised lines.

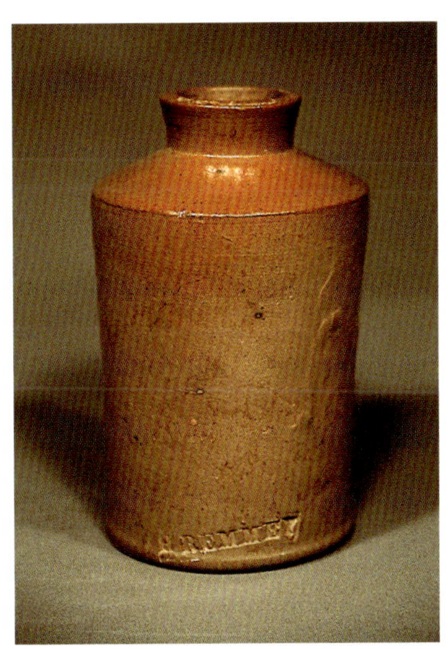

Figure 10 Ink bottle, Henry Remmey, Baltimore, 1812–1821. Salt-glazed stoneware. H. 5". (Private collection.) The type used in the "H. REMMEY" mark on this bottle is the same as that used on the "H. REMMEY / BALTIMORE" stamp. This comparison, combined with the clay color of the bottle, confirms a Baltimore attribution.

examples, with a short spout and single incised line at the top. A signed "H. REMMEY / BALTIMORE" pitcher with incised decoration in the Henry Ford Museum, Dearborn, Michigan (acc. no. 57.65.21) has a collar with an extremely elongated spout, reminiscent of period silver forms. The form of a one-gallon pitcher signed "H. REMMEY / BALTIMORE" and with incised bird decoration (fig. 9) is not nearly as exaggerated as the pitcher in figure 7. The decoration around the collar is blurred but resembles the potter's characteristic vine-and-flower decoration. Remmey Sr. used a fine implement to incise the details into the clay—the wings, feathers, and eyes of the birds, and even the veins of the leaves. He carefully applied thick cobalt slip, keeping it within the incised decorations.[23]

Highly decorative vessels are not all that bear Remmey's mark, however (a jug signed by him only uses cobalt decoration to highlight his name). And the diversity of his forms is indicated by a stoneware ink bottle (fig. 10). Although not listed in any of Myers's price lists, the ink bottle form was

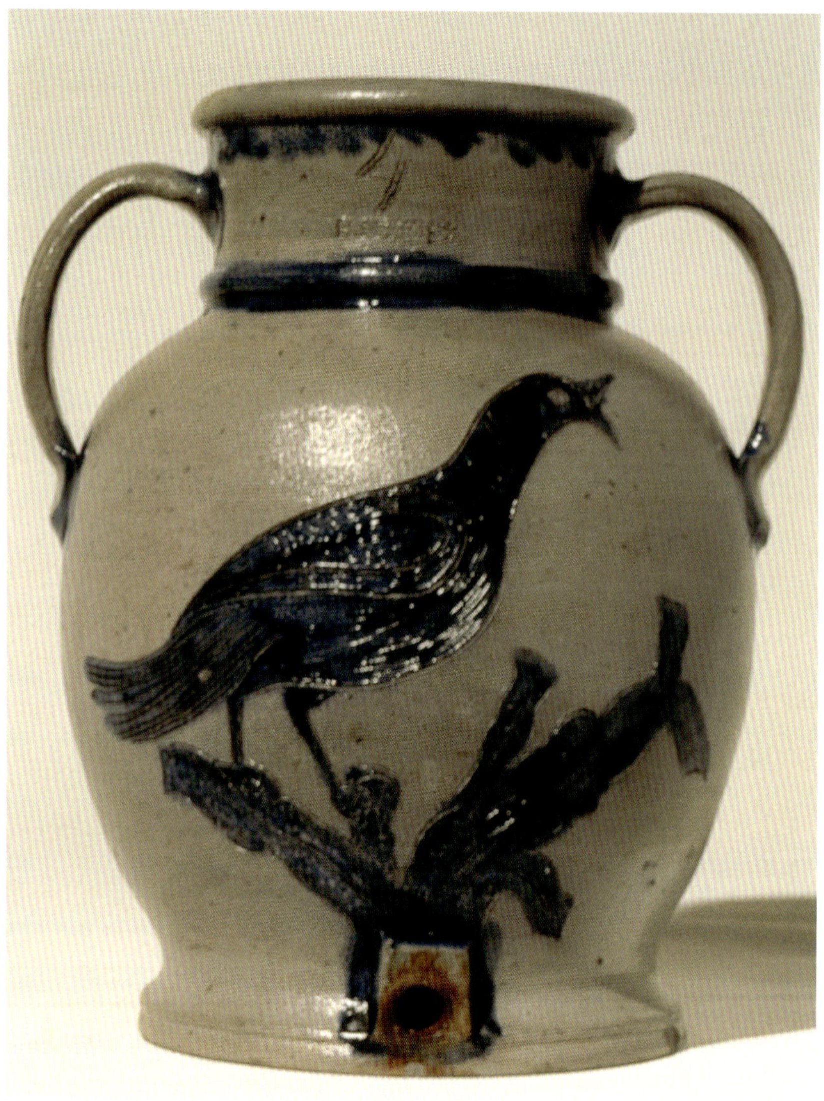

Figure 11 Cooler, Henry Myers, Baltimore, 1821–1829. Salt-glazed stoneware. H. 16". (Courtesy, Olde Hope Antiques, Inc.) Impressed "H. MYERS," this incised bird-decorated vessel is referred to as a "Spicket Jug" in Myers's price lists. Certainly made by Remmey while working for Myers, the close link between the decoration on this piece and "H. REMMEY / BALTIMORE" stoneware suggests that this cooler was probably made by Remmey toward the beginning of Henry Myers's tenure. The form of the bird as well as the quality of incising are similar to the pitcher illustrated in fig. 9. A fine flowering-vine decoration on the reverse of the cooler matches Remmey's early decorative motifs.

probably one of Remmey's regular production items, because another, virtually identical bottle exists. However, neither is decorated with the cobalt oxide or heavy salt glaze characteristic of Remmey's Baltimore wares.[24]

The "H. MYERS" stoneware example most similar to Remmey's signed Baltimore work is a four-gallon water cooler with incised bird decoration (fig. 11). An uncommon form for early Baltimore, this water cooler is related to the "Spicket Jugs" listed on Henry Myers's 1822–1823 stoneware price list. Remmey Sr. decorated the reverse of this cooler with his typical vine-and-floral motif. The overall form—ovoid shape and footed base—resembles that of "H. REMMEY / BALTIMORE" pitchers. The clay color, even salt glaze, and vibrant cobalt-oxide decoration are all typical of Remmey Sr.'s Baltimore work. The incised grouse-on-branches decoration covering the front of the cooler highlights Remmey's command of the incising technique.[25] The form and decorative detail of this bird closely match the birds on the pitcher illustrated in figure 9. Given the similarities between this water cooler and the piece marked "H. REMMEY / BALTIMORE," the

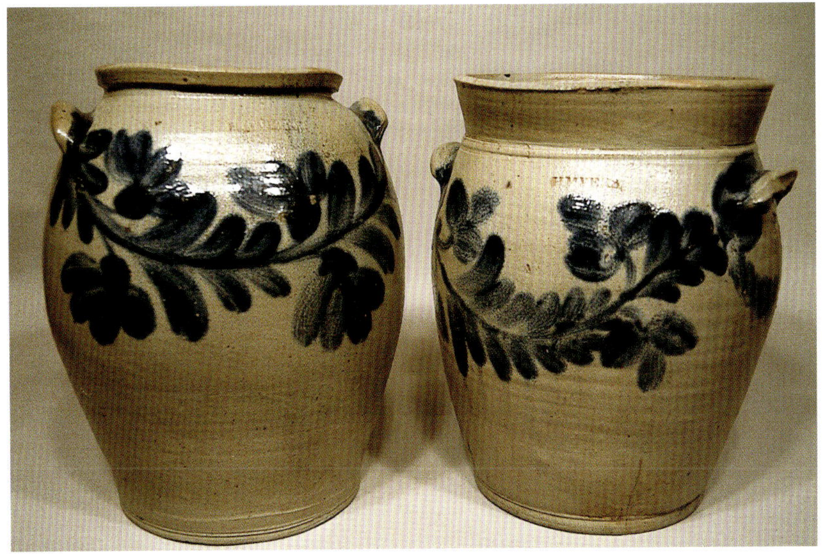

Figure 12 Jars, Henry Myers, Baltimore, 1821–1829. Salt-glazed stoneware. H. 15". (Private collection.) These impressed "H. MYERS" jars were manufactured while Henry Remmey worked for Myers and reflect Remmey's shift toward mass production. The forms are simpler than those seen in his earlier wares and the decoration is less finely executed.

cooler was probably manufactured by Remmey Sr. at the Baltimore Stoneware Manufactory shortly after Henry Myers took over ownership from his father.

Other extant "H. MYERS" stoneware articles have Remmey attributes. In the seven years that Remmey Sr. potted for Henry Myers, the form and decoration of his vessels changed, perhaps due a greater emphasis on mass production at the pottery.[26] Delicate freehand details, including open flower petals and berries, are replaced by broader, rapidly applied brushstrokes, resulting in a thicker band of decoration. But Remmey Sr.'s decoration of Myers's stoneware retains similarities to his earlier decorations, continuing, for example, the motif of flowers rising and falling from a central horizontal vine that surrounds the entire vessel.

Remmey Sr. also altered the forms of his "H. MYERS" stoneware to promote mass production. Instead of loop handles, all Myers pots are adorned with smaller, tablike handles. Instead of high-neck collars, many Myers pots have short rims. Nevertheless, the overall decorative appeal of Remmey Sr.'s stoneware from this manufactory remains, and artistic decoration, vibrant blue, evenly fired gray clay, and ovoid forms characterize his late pieces. For example, in figure 12 the pot on the left, which holds three gallons,[27] has a high-neck collar similar to those on Remmey Sr.'s earlier Baltimore pots and early Manhattan stoneware, and he incised lines at the base of both of these pots, as he had in his early days in Baltimore. The decorations on both pots is very similar, with horizontal flowering garlands surrounding the body. However, these vessels are adorned with tab ears, and Remmey left out the series of incised lines beneath the collar. To create the flower heads, he made a series of thick brushstrokes instead of outlining four petals, as he had on his "H. REMMEY / BALTIMORE" stoneware.

Remmey's "H. MYERS" stoneware pitchers are much more consistent in form than his early examples. A side-by-side comparison of two signed "H. MYERS" pitchers (fig. 13), a one-gallon and a half-gallon,[28] reveals this standardization. Both have slightly ovoid bodies, incised lines at their

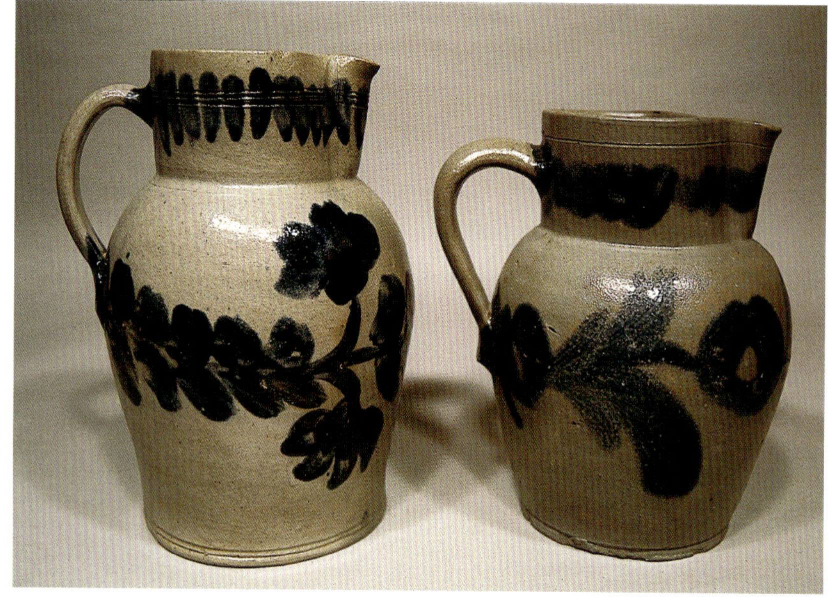

Figure 13 Pitchers, Henry Myers, Baltimore, 1821–1829. Salt-glazed stoneware. H. 10½". (Private collection.) Both of these pitchers are impressed "H. MYERS" and reflect Remmey's standardization of this form under Henry Myers. The pitcher on the left displays Remmey's standard "H. MYERS" brushed cobalt decoration. The decoration on the pitcher at right shows up on Remmey Philadelphia stoneware and possibly was made by Henry Remmey Jr.

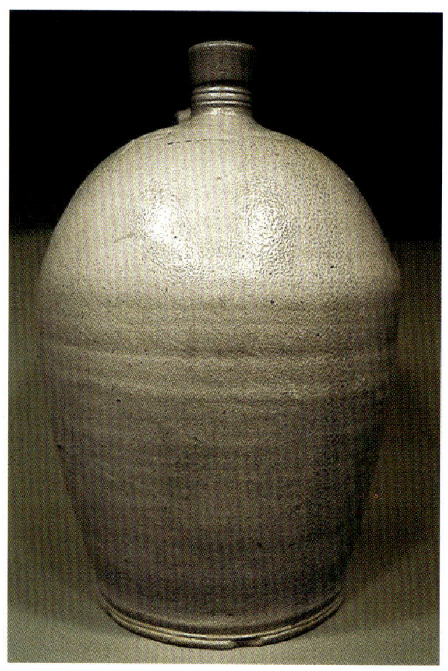

Figure 14 Jug, Henry Myers, Baltimore, 1821–1829. Salt-glazed stoneware. H. 15". (Private collection.) Although undecorated, this impressed "H. MYERS" jug is elaborate for its form. An ovoid shape and incising at the base and neck add to the visual appeal of this vessel.

bases, vertical collars with incised lines bisecting each collar, and slightly drooping pouring spouts. (The handle on the half-gallon pitcher, at right, is a modern restoration, so the variation in the forms of these handles probably did not exist when these pitchers were manufactured.) The decoration on the one-gallon pitcher, at left, is an example of Remmey Sr.'s standard stoneware decoration under Henry Myers. The decoration on the half-gallon pitcher, at right, appears on Remmey Philadelphia stoneware, suggesting that it may have been decorated by Remmey Jr.

The few extant signed Myers jugs do not display much deviation from the earlier signed Remmey jug form. A two-gallon "H. MYERS" jug (fig. 14) illustrates what was most likely the typical jug form Remmey used under Henry Myers.[29] Incised lines accentuate a foot at the jug's base, and a series of incised lines cover the jug's neck, supporting a wider mouth. There is no cobalt decoration.

In addition to jugs, pots, and pitchers ranging in capacity from one pint to three gallons, Remmey produced other unusual forms, according to Myers's 1822–1823 price list. He made "spicket jugs," inkstands, porringers, pans with lids, and milk pans. A surviving "H. MYERS" one-and-one-half-gallon milk pan (fig. 15) bears his standard decoration.[30]

Remmey also produced stoneware forms not advertised by Myers. A one-and-one-half-gallon churn (fig. 16), impressed "H. MYERS" and decorated with Remmey's vine-and-flower motif, survives. Although this form is not mentioned on the manufactory's price list, the presence of other Baltimore stoneware churns from roughly the same period reveals the popularity of the form in Baltimore. And the mention at the bottom of the price list that "Wares of any size or shape will be made without any delay, to order," indicates that Remmey made stoneware forms that were not typical production items.[31]

Judging by Philadelphia stoneware bearing his name, Remmey Jr. unquestionably had great skill in forming, decorating, and firing stoneware.

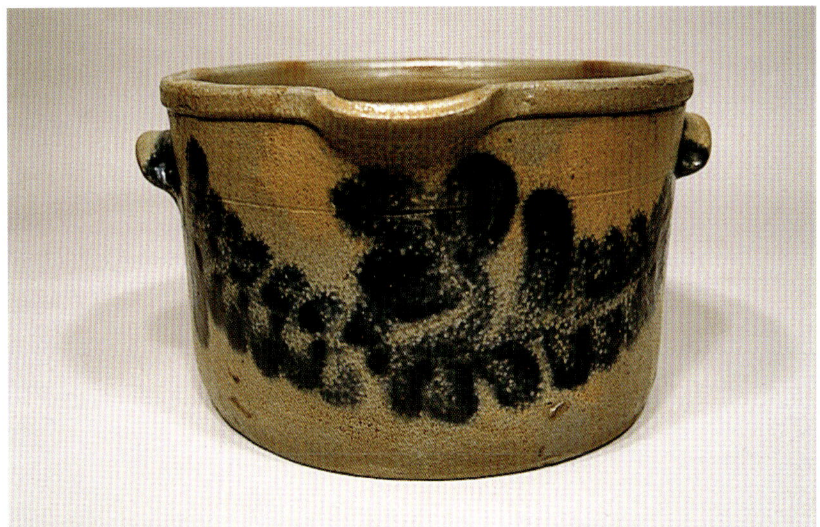

Figure 15 Milk pan, Henry Myers, Baltimore, 1821–1829. Salt-glazed stoneware. D. 9¾". (Private collection.) This milk pan, impressed "H. MYERS," bears a variation of Remmey's standard decoration.

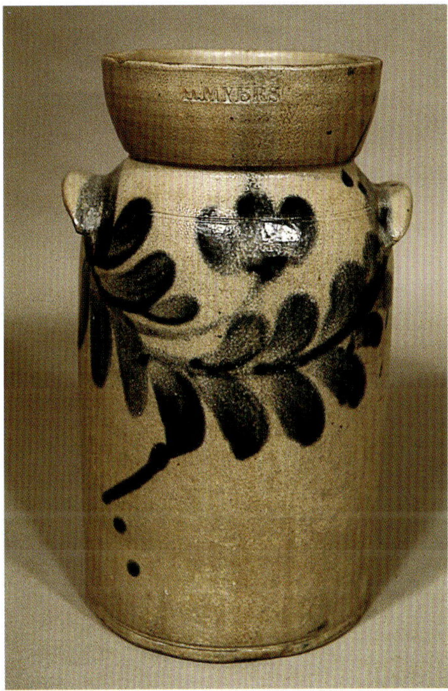

Figure 16 Churn, Henry Myers, Baltimore, 1821–1829. Salt-glazed stoneware. H. 12½". (Private collection.) Impressed "H. MYERS." Although not a standard production item at the Henry Myers pottery, stoneware churns are not unusual in Baltimore stoneware.

However, while we know that stoneware from Philadelphia signed "Henry Remmey" can only be the work of Remmey Jr., Baltimore vessels signed "H. REMMEY / BALTIMORE" and "H. MYERS" were made by or under the supervision of his father. Remmey Jr. could have made some of the vessels discussed herein, but his influence at the Baltimore Stoneware Manufactory was secondary to his father's and his presence at the Myers pottery did not last as long. Unfortunately, no known Baltimore stoneware exists that was personally signed by him, nor is there surviving stoneware signed George Earnest, whose pottery Remmey Jr. superintended. Therefore, any discussion of Remmey Jr.'s Baltimore stoneware would rely heavily on speculation.

One piece, a heavily incised stoneware flowerpot with bird-and-flower decoration (fig. 17), was almost certainly made by Remmey Jr. while in

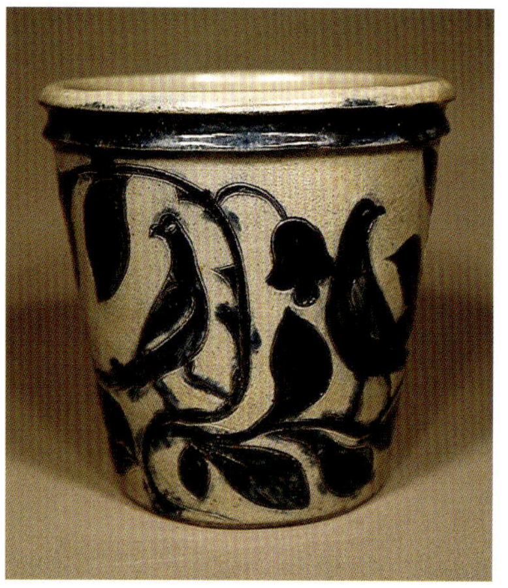

Figure 17 Flowerpot, Baltimore, ca. 1820. Salt-glazed stoneware. H. 7". (Private collection.) Excavated in Baltimore City (part of the bird at left has been restored), this incised bird-decorated flowerpot was almost certainly made by Henry Remmey Jr. in Baltimore. While its clay and cobalt color substantiate its Baltimore origin, the flowerpot's incising is very similar to incising found on Remmey Jr.'s Philadelphia stoneware.

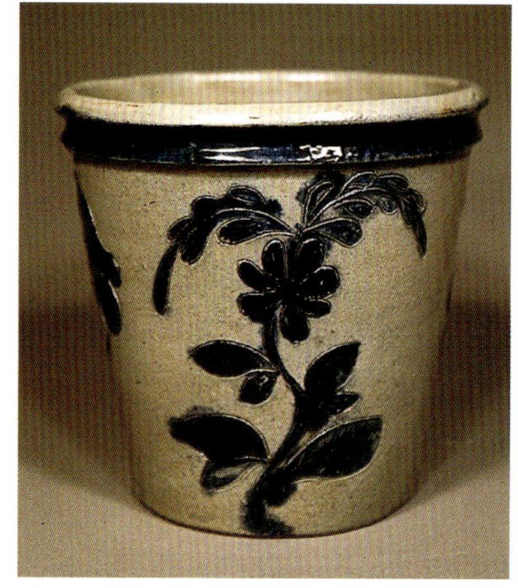

Figure 18 Reverse of the flowerpot illustrated in fig. 17.

Baltimore, however. Although unsigned, the flowerpot's Baltimore attribution is definite, given its clay and cobalt color and the fact that it was excavated in an early-nineteenth-century Baltimore privy. And of all potters in Baltimore at that time, only the Remmeys could have achieved the high quality of the incised decoration. Remmey Jr. would have made the flowerpot either at the Baltimore Stoneware Manufactory or at George Earnest's Wilk Street manufactory.[32] The deeply incised decoration is good, and, although Henry Remmey Jr.'s potting abilities were not equal to those of his father, they unquestionably were superior to the rest of his Baltimore peers.

Before Henry Remmey Sr. arrived in Baltimore in 1812, the quality of stoneware production in the city was such that William Myers chose to import from Hartford rather than sell local wares in his shop. But Remmey Sr. changed the whole dynamic of Baltimore stoneware, producing pottery for the Baltimore Stoneware Manufactory that was without parallel. The expertly formed, decorated, and fired Remmey Baltimore stoneware adequately testifies that Henry Myers was no mere braggart when he stated that the stoneware potters Henry Remmey & Son, late of New York, were "not inferior to any in the United States."[33]

1. W. Oakley Raymond expresses the common belief about the Remmeys in Baltimore: "Evidence drawn from the Baltimore directories makes it certain that Henry Remmey, founder of the Philadelphia works, sought to command two profitable markets by placing his son Henry Harrison [Henry Remmey Jr.] in charge of a Baltimore branch. . . . Whatever the father's purpose in entering the Baltimore market, he either found, or presently developed, plenty of local competition. . . . This may help to explain why by September 25, 1835 . . . we find [Henry Remmey Jr.] in Philadelphia." W. Oakley Raymond, "Remmey Family: American Potters, Part II," *Antiques* 32 (1937), quoted in Diana Stradling and J. Garrison Stradling, *The Art of the Potter* (New York: Main Street/Universe Books, 1977), p. 116.

2. Stradling and Stradling, *Art of the Potter,* pp. 114–16.

3. Louis Zukofsky, *A Useful Art: Essays and Radio Scripts on American Design* (Middletown, Conn.: Wesleyan University Press, 2003), p. 197. This script was penned for the Works Progress Administration.

4. Stradling and Stradling, *Art of the Potter,* p. 116.

5. Henry Remmey Jr., who was by then eighteen years old, almost certainly accompanied his father to Baltimore. He potted with him from 1812 until he gained enough experience to be recognized as a highly skilled potter in his own right.

6. *American & Commercial Daily Advertiser,* July 4, 1812, p. 1; *American,* July 3, 1812, p. 4.

7. *American,* October 15, 1812, p. 2.

8. The evidence that supports a rent-free arrangement is persuasive. Remmey does not appear in Maryland land records as leasing or purchasing property in Baltimore. In 1817–1818 he is listed as living at the north end of Happy Alley, which was near the Baltimore Stoneware Manufactory (although it was also close to other stoneware potteries, notably the Pitt and Green Street pottery of Morgan and Amoss, and the Eden Street pottery of Parr and Burland). The records of 1822–1823, 1824, and 1829 show Remmey living on Bond Street. From an 1838 newspaper listing for the trustee's sale of the property of Henry Myers (Jacob Myers's son) we know that the Myers family owned on Bond Street "a small dwelling . . . heretofore occupied by the person who has conducted [the] pottery." This dwelling presumably is where Remmey lived in the 1820s. *The Baltimore Directory for 1817–18* (Baltimore, Md.: Printed by James Kennedy, 1817), p. 157; *The Baltimore Directory for 1822–23* (Baltimore, Md.: Printed by R. J. Matchett, 1822), p. 231; *Matchett's Baltimore Directory for 1824* (Baltimore, Md.: Printed by R. J. Matchett, 1824), p. 253; *Matchett's Baltimore Directory for 1829* (Baltimore, Md.: Printed by R. J. Matchett, 1829), p. 265; *American,* September 11, 1838, p. 3.

9. It is interesting to note, however, that he never took a formal apprentice in Baltimore. Information concerning Baltimore stoneware prior to 1812 is sketchy, but the fact that William Myers needed to import Hartford stoneware in 1812 (*American,* July 4, 1812, p. 1.) is a strong indication that Baltimore-manufactured stoneware was of inferior quality. A stoneware pitcher excavated from a Baltimore privy dating to the early 1800s is probably an example of the type of stoneware produced in Baltimore before Remmey's arrival. Its form is not much different from the form of Remmey's pitchers, but it is decorated with only a small amount of cobalt. Also, it has a very light salt glaze and its clay has an uneven, blotchy appearance. Known examples of Baltimore stoneware dating after Remmey's arrival are of much higher quality, especially in terms of decoration and glaze.

10. *Baltimore Directory for 1817–18,* pp. 129, 146, 157 (emphasis added); *Supplement to the American,* April 28, 1818, p. 1.

11. *American,* June 8, 1815, p. 4.

12. *American,* December 23, 1815, p. 4; *Supplement to the American,* March 27, 1816, p. 1; *American,* March 7, 1818, p. 4; *American,* July 2, 1818, p. 4; *Supplement to the American,* April 28, 1818, p. 1.

13. *American,* September 25, 1822, p. 2. This issue of the *American* lists the obituary for Jacob Myers, who died less than a year after passing his business to Henry Myers.

14. *American,* July 3, 1823, p. 1.

15. *Baltimore Directory for 1822–23,* p. 231; *Matchett's Baltimore Directory for 1824,* p. 253; *Matchett's Baltimore Directory for 1829,* p. 265. It is clear that Remmey Sr. was still working for Myers in 1824, because a directory listing places his son, Henry Harrison Remmey (Henry Remmey Jr.), at another pottery at the time. The directory gives Remmey Jr.'s dwelling at the corner of Pitt and Bond; undoubtedly he lived there with his father, since we know that Henry Myers owned a house adjacent to the pottery for the use of the manufactory's superintendent (see n. 8). In 1829 the business directory still lists Remmey Sr.'s residence as being at Pitt and Bond.

16. The forms, standardized decorations, and even firing exhibited in "H. MYERS" stoneware are more typical of stoneware produced circa 1840 and later in Baltimore and Virginia.

17. *Matchett's Baltimore Directory for 1824,* p. 253; Philadelphia County Recorder of Deeds, 1827, vol. GWR 17, p. 250.

18. *American,* August 14, 1824, p. 1.

19. Capacity-mark stamps were part of the tools of a shop, and pieces bearing identical capacity marks usually were manufactured at the same shop.

20. David Parr began marking his stoneware no earlier than 1815, Elisha Parr marked his no earlier than 1818, and William Morgan began marking his stoneware with incised signatures circa 1819.

21. This pot is an example of the largest size stoneware on Myers's price lists. In 1815 it retailed for $1.25. *American,* October 23, 1815, p. 4.

22. In 1815 a one-and-one-half-gallon stoneware pitcher retailed at Myers's shop for $.62½. Kegs, water coolers, and similar forms do not appear on Baltimore price lists for the 1810s. Ibid.

23. This pitcher is the only signed "H. REMMEY / BALTIMORE" vessel with a different maker's mark. While the mark on other Remmey pieces consists of movable letters arranged to form the words, the mark on this pitcher is created from two stamps of permanently affixed letters, one for "H. REMMEY" and one for "BALTIMORE."

24. Although not explicitly signed "BALTIMORE," the clay color and the fact that the mark is identical to the top half of Remmey's Baltimore mark clearly identify this piece as of Baltimore manufacture.

25. A surviving stoneware pocket flask incised "Made by Henry Remmy / New York / . . . 1789" was made by Remmey at his father's Manhattan stoneware pottery when he was approximately nineteen years old. Although not elaborately decorated, this flask does feature a large incised "R" filled in with cobalt above the inscription, revealing that Remmey was incising stoneware as early as 1789. Donald Blake Webster, *Decorated Stoneware Pottery of North America* (Rutland, Vt.: Charles E. Tuttle Company, 1980), p. 201.

26. Of the approximately twenty-five pieces of "H. MYERS" stoneware I have seen, the only piece with vine-and floral-decoration close to that on "H. REMMEY / BALTIMORE" stoneware is the water cooler with incised bird decoration. Since Remmey was the head potter for roughly half the duration of the "H. MYERS" mark, more than one out of twenty-five pieces must have been made by or under Remmey. Some Myers stoneware has decoration and forms that resemble those of later Baltimore stoneware, indicating that later superintendents of the manufactory made them. A significant percentage of stoneware examples from the Myers pottery have the vine-and-floral motif illustrated in this article (see, e.g., fig. 12). Since this motif seems most like Remmey's early work, I attribute these pieces to him.

27. The largest items on Henry Myers's 1822–1823 price lists were his three-gallon pots, which sold for $7 a dozen. *American,* July 3, 1823, p. 1. The pot on the right, however, holds four gallons. The number 4 is incised into the clay below one ear, suggesting that, because vessels of this size were not normal production items at the manufactory, the shop did not have a four-gallon capacity mark. The four-gallon "H. MYERS" water cooler also bears an incised capacity mark.

28. In 1822–1823 Myers sold one-gallon pitchers for $3.25 per dozen and one-half-gallon pitchers for $2.25 per dozen. Ibid.

29. In 1822–1823 Myers sold two-gallon jugs like this one for $5.00 per dozen. Ibid.

30. Remmey made milk pans in one-half-gallon, gallon, and one-and-one-half-gallon sizes. In 1822–1823 he sold milk pans like this one for $4.00 per dozen. Ibid.

31. Ibid.

32. While both Remmeys are known to have decorated stoneware with incised birds, the details of the birds and surrounding floral motif on the flowerpot closely resemble the decorations of known Remmey Jr. vessels. The shapes of the birds' bodies, beaks, and tail feathers are close to birds on a Remmey Jr. stoneware water cooler in the Philadelphia Museum of Art (acc. no. 54-85-27), which, though unsigned, has a very strong attribution to Henry Harrison Remmey, Philadelphia. Three hanging bellflowers on the flowerpot match flowers on the cooler. Also, surviving stoneware pitchers by Remmey Jr., Philadelphia, are decorated with a bird standing on a branch that curves over the bird's head, a design that is similar to the motif surrounding the bird, at right, on the flowerpot illustrated in fig. 17.

33. *American,* July 3, 1823, p. 1.

Kurt C. Russ

The Remarkable Stoneware of George N. Fulton, Circa 1856–1894

▼ HAVING ACQUIRED traditional pottery-making skills at his family's pottery business in Ohio, George N. Fulton brought meaningful training, enthusiasm, and youth to his chosen profession, qualities that were to serve him well as he made his way to Virginia for employment (fig. 1). First working in the Richmond Pottery of David Parr, then establishing a significant and long-lived operation in Alleghany County, and finally ending his career in nearby Botetourt County, Fulton's mark on the Virginia craft industry is well established.[1] As a result of his extensive output, variety of forms produced, and frequency of elaborate and unique decoration—involving brushed and slipped blue cobalt and manganese floral motifs often accompanied by either initials or a full signature—his significant and enduring contribution to Virginia's pottery tradition can now be more fully documented and explored (figs. 2–4).

The success of Fulton's quarter-of-a-century endeavor in rural Virginia must be viewed in the context of industry trends elsewhere in the state, where potters were faced with the difficult choice of either closing their operations entirely or significantly altering their character in the face of advancing industrialization.[2] It appears that Fulton embraced few, if any, of the new technologies or changing trends and yet did not have to close his business. Was it the rural nature of his operation that allowed him to avoid these dilemmas? While the location of his shop undoubtedly was relevant, his keen sense of craft, understanding of local need and demand, utilization of decoration reflecting cultural symbols shared with his customers, effective basic marketing strategies, and hands-on participation in and ultimate control over all aspects of his business were factors that combined to allow him to escape the crushing fate industrialization brought to others.

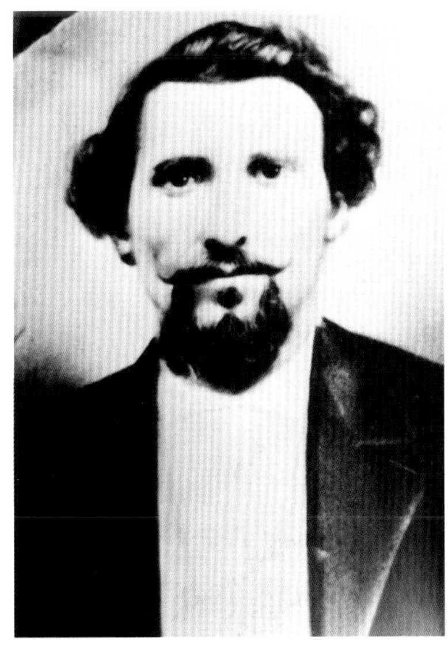

Figure 1 Photograph of George N. Fulton, ca. 1867–1875. (Courtesy, Alleghany County Historical Society, Virginia.)

Historical Overview

James Fulton, born in 1794 in Loundon County, Virginia, married his second wife, Mary Ellen Newman (from Prince Edward County, Virginia), in 1833. George W[illiam] N[ewman], their first child, was born in 1834, and by 1835 his family had moved to Fultonham in Muskingham County, Ohio. At this time the family included a stepbrother, William Henry (b. 1823), and a stepsister, Mary (b. 1823), both the product of James's first marriage (ca. 1823) to Elizabeth McGeorge, who died in 1829 in Farquier County, Virginia. By 1836 Mary gave birth to another son, Robert James Fulton, in Fultonham.[3]

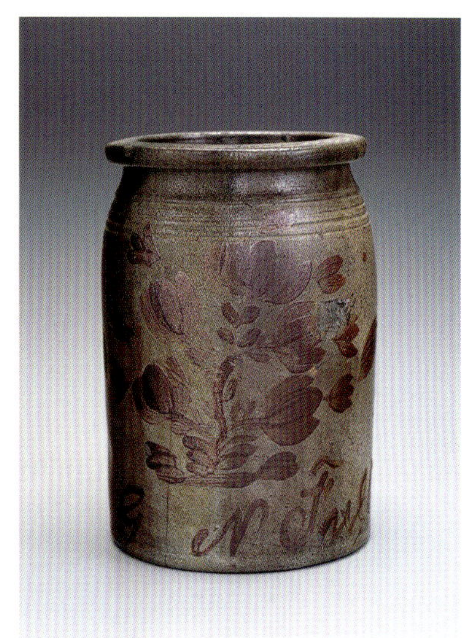

Figure 2 Storage jar, Fulton Pottery, Alleghany County, Virginia, 1867–1885. Salt-glazed stoneware. H. 10". (Unless otherwise noted, all objects are from the author's collection and photos are by Gavin Ashworth.) A one-gallon straight-sided storage jar with elaborate brushed manganese floral or tree decorative motif and signature.

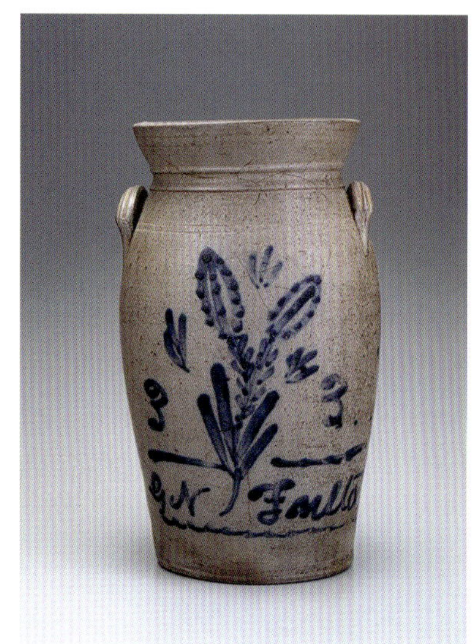

Figure 3 Churn, Fulton Pottery, Alleghany County, Virginia, 1867–1885. Salt-glazed stoneware. H. 14¾". This cobalt decorated churn is embellished with a large floral element with two upright leaves highlighted with dots, two "3" indications of vessel capacity, and a "G. N. Fulton" signature highlighted by two wavy bands. Note the similarity of this decoration and that on the jar depicted on the left in fig. 16.

Although unconfirmed, it is likely that James was a potter while in Virginia and moved to Ohio to capitalize on the industry's growth there. Not surprisingly, James's venture was successful, and he and his sons became deeply immersed in the area's thriving pottery industry. Identified historically as potters operating kilns in Marietta and Zanesville, James and his sons had a continuing impact on the industry in Ohio during its transition from a traditional craft technology to an evolving industrialized art pottery concern. Apparently Robert James operated a kiln in Marietta and later worked at the Weller pottery, while William Henry worked in Zanesville with his father.

Late in 1855 George's mastery of traditional potting skills and his intimate involvement in the Ohio pottery industry enabled him, at the age of twenty-one, to travel east to Virginia and gain employment with David Parr's thriving Richmond stoneware factory. After some six years of employment, Fulton enlisted with the Union army on July 23, 1862, at Meadowbluff, Virginia, as a private in Company E, 9th Regiment, Virginia–West Virginia Infantry. In November 1864 he was transferred to Company B, 1st Regiment, Virginia–West Virginia Infantry, with his final discharge as a private on June 14, 1865, at Parkersburg, West Virginia.[4] Although not well documented, his participation at the Parkersburg Stoneware Factory is evidenced by extant wares showing his decorative influence and, in a few cases, his signature on the otherwise standard West Virginia, and later Donaghho, forms.

After his service in the Civil War, brief employment in Parkersburg, and marriage, Fulton moved to the Potts Creek area of Alleghany County, Virginia, and established a thriving pottery business, marketing his wares locally as well as in Fincastle, Blacksburg, and as far away as Richmond. Family tradition holds that Fulton escaped to Alleghany County after being captured and taken prisoner by the Confederate army near White Sulfur Springs, West Virginia, and, while making his way back to his regiment, discovered large deposits of valuable clay in a cave in the Potts

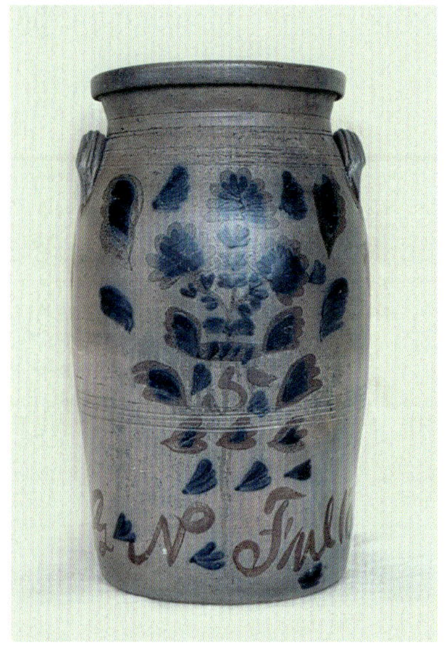

Figure 4 Churn, Fulton Pottery, Alleghany County, Virginia, 1867–1885. Salt-glazed stoneware. H. 17½". (Private collection; photo, Kurt Russ.) A five-gallon churn with elaborate brushed manganese dioxide floral decoration highlighted (or overpainted) with cobalt oxide, including a centrally placed floral spray surrounded by leaves, a "5" indicating vessel capacity, and a large signature.

Creek area.[5] Recognizing its quality, he laid out plans to return to the area, apply his pottery-making skills, and establish his own business to support his family and furnish the community with needed utilitarian vessels of "good stone body."

Fulton's Tenure at Parr's Richmond Pottery

Little is known of Fulton's role in the industry in Richmond save for family tradition—which holds that he traveled to Richmond for employment with David Parr in late 1855 and that he later established a pottery in Westmoreland County—and the survival of a spectacular piece of Virginia stoneware bearing his name.

The earliest extant piece of stoneware associated with Fulton's potting activity in Virginia is a massive twenty-gallon, salt-glazed beer or water cooler (fig. 5). It is tall, well potted, semi-ovoid, somewhat overfired, and profusely decorated, with a prominent rim, applied extruded crescent-shaped handles, and characteristic spigot receptacle. Decorative treatments (fig. 6) include an incised meandering flowering vine filled with cobalt blue draping the vessel's shoulders and an oddly shaped, incised, and blue-decorated eagle with open wings (fig. 7). Extending from the left and right

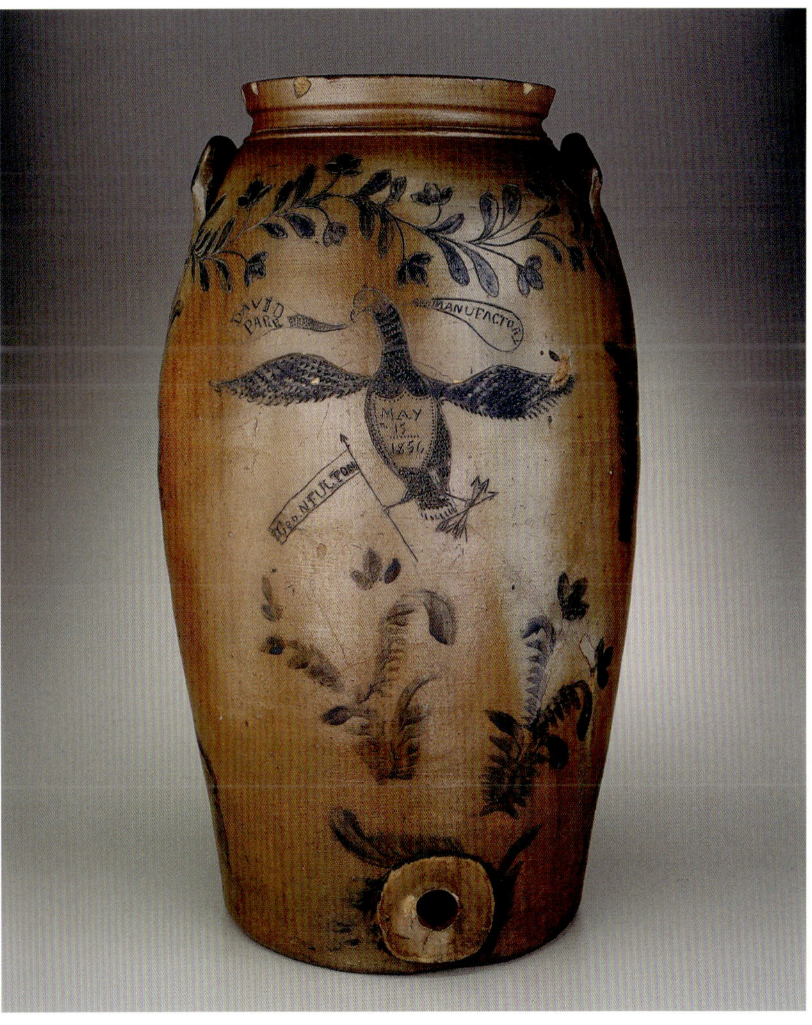

Figure 5 Beer or water cooler, George N. Fulton, David Parr's Pottery, Richmond, Virginia, 1856. Salt-glazed stoneware. H. 29¼". (Courtesy, The Greenbrier; photo, Gavin Ashworth.) A monumental twenty-gallon beer or water cooler. The incised word "Painted" appears on the vessel to the right of the arrows in the eagle's talons and strongly suggests that Fulton was involved with the vessel's decoration, if not manufacture.

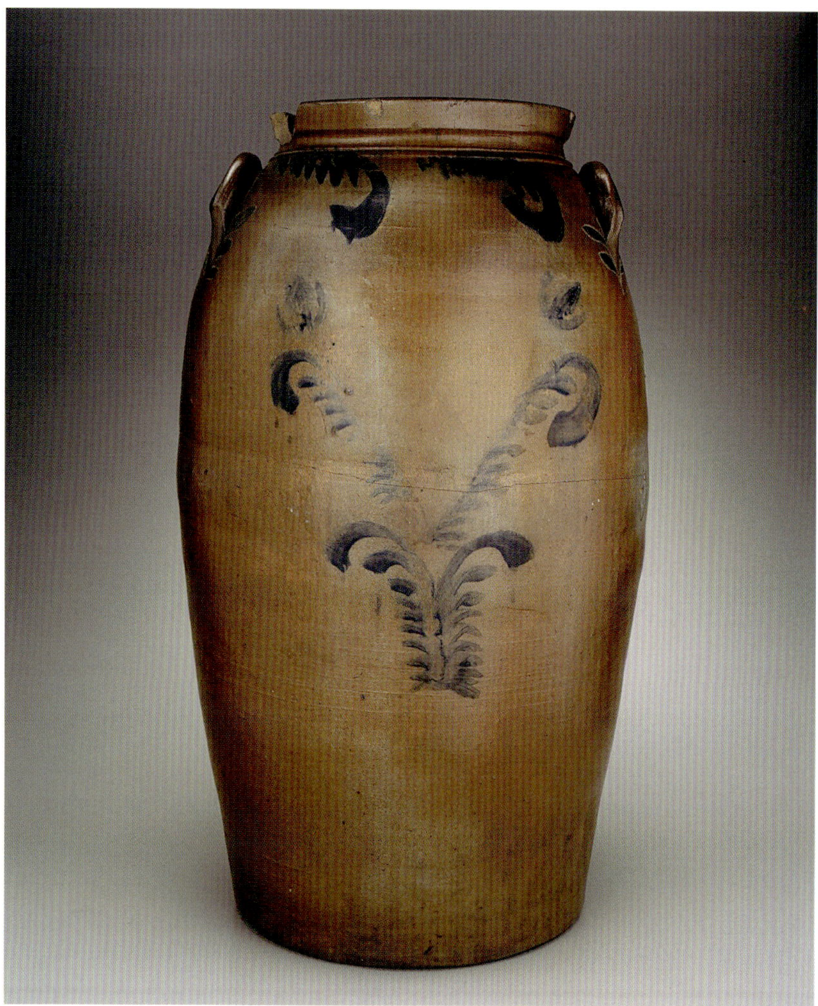

Figure 6 Reverse of the stoneware cooler illustrated in fig. 5, showing brushed blue cobalt floral decoration at the shoulder and horizontal flowers on either side. These long multipetaled, single-bloom horizontal flowers seem to characterize vessels from Parr's pottery, often appearing below the maker's stamp on the reverse of the vessel and/or beneath its handles.

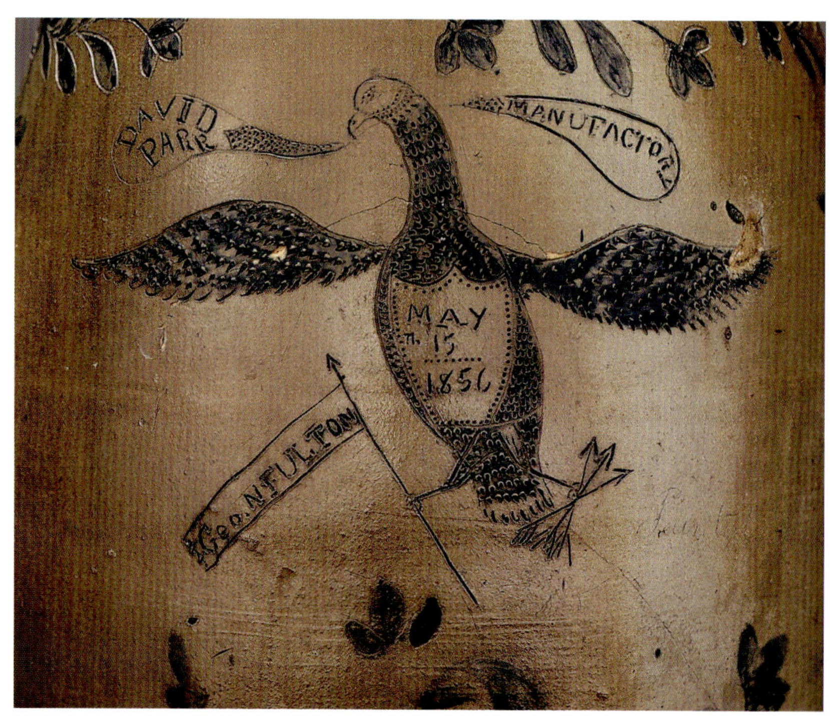

Figure 7 Detail of the cooler illustrated in fig. 5, showing an incised and cobalt-decorated eagle with spread wings and opposing banners extending from the beak reading, "DAVID PARR" and "MANUFACTORY." The shielded chest contains the date "MAY 15 1856," and the banner in its left talon reads "Geo. N FULTON."

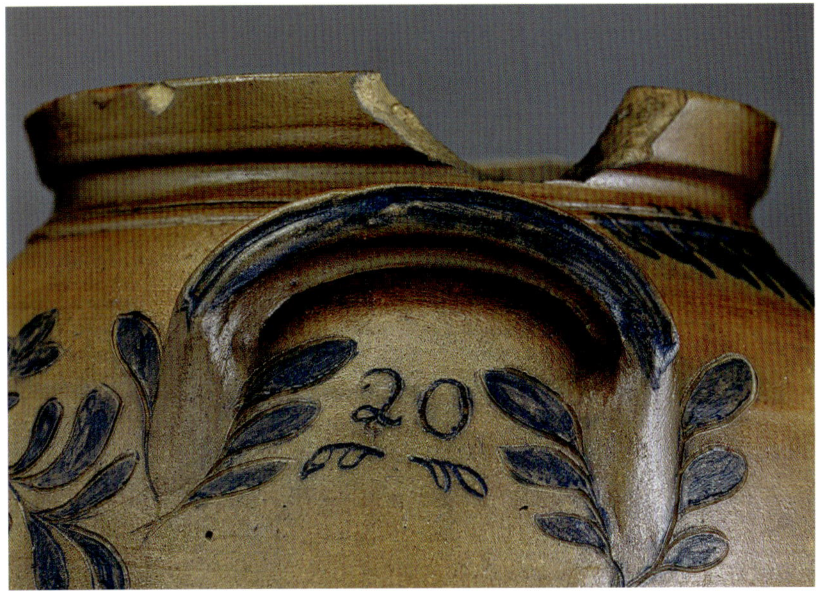

Figure 8 Detail of the stoneware cooler illustrated in fig. 5, showing the extruded crescent-shaped applied handle brushed with blue cobalt, well-formed rim, and treatment at the shoulder, as well as incised and cobalt-filled floral vines at handle terminations and an incised "20" (indicating vessel capacity) above two opposing incised leaves.

of the eagle's head are banners that read, respectively, "DAVID PARR" and "MANUFACTORY." The eagle's shielded chest bears the incised date "MAY 15 1856," and in its talons are a flaglike banner displaying the name "GEO. N FULTON" and a cluster of arrows. Brushed blue cobalt tuliplike floral sprays adorn the areas below the eagle and above the spout opening, as well as the areas below both handles (fig. 8).

Although the form and decoration of this cooler bear little resemblance to Fulton's wares produced in Alleghany County, this does not necessarily mean he was not responsible for its production. A large, ten-gallon, straight-sided vessel produced by Fulton at the Parkersburg Stoneware Factory bears little resemblance to his later Alleghany wares, despite bearing his signature. It is clear that potters employed by a pottery, especially journeyman potters, conformed their production to the factory's established forms and ware types. The incised decoration seen here is rare on Virginia pottery and even more unusual for this mid-nineteenth-century period. It is likely this special piece was commissioned by Old Crow's Tavern, Crows, Virginia, and that Fulton, eager to exhibit his mastery of the trade, responded by creating a breathtaking cooler exhibiting a full range of decorative embellishments. It is said that after the tavern closed, the piece was sold at auction for $100. It was later offered by the purchaser for the same amount to the Greenbrier, where it has remained since 1963. Now displayed in the President's Cottage at the Greenbrier Hotel in White Sulphur Springs, West Virginia, this piece can be appreciated not only by Fulton's many descendants, interested Virginia ceramic researchers and historians, but by the public as well.

Both Fulton's 1855 departure from Ohio and the 1856 date incised on this vessel establish a *terminus post quem* (earliest possible date) for Fulton's association with Parr's Richmond manufactory, while Fulton's enlistment with the Union forces in 1862 pinpoints a *terminus ante quem* (latest possible date) for his involvement with Parr. A *Richmond Whig* publication dated April 15, 1865, lists the "D. Parr earthenware manufacturer" on Carey Street as suffering from "the recent great fire," although Ketchum's indication that Parr's operation continued until 1870 suggests post–fire revitalization and successful continuation for some five years.[6]

Fulton's Return to the Parkersburg, West Virginia, Area

Fulton's discharge from the Union army places him at Parkersburg, West Virginia, on June 14, 1865. This adds credence to the family history, which indicates that about 1866 Fulton returned to his father's hometown, Fultonham, Ohio, located just across the Ohio River from Parkersburg, and worked as the captain of the Ohio riverboat *Ida,* a cargo vessel.[7] His involvement with the Parkersburg Stoneware Factory is corroborated by the identification of a few extant wares manufactured at the Donaghho Factory that were embellished with Fulton's characteristic decorations and, on one ten-gallon example, his signature in brushed blue cobalt oxide.

In addition to providing reconnection with his family and interesting employment opportunities, Parkersburg also proved to be the home of his fiancée and, hence, the perfect site for their forthcoming marriage. Family history indicates that after their union both Fulton and his wife worked aboard the *Ida,* perhaps intermittently, during 1867–1869, while preparing their move to Alleghany County.

Fulton and Waddell in Westmoreland County

Family history is unequivocal with regard to Fulton's association with a potter named Waddell (or Wadill). It is suggested that they worked together both in Westmoreland County and in Richmond, Virginia, and that they both moved to Alleghany County to work as potters after the Civil War. While it has been impossible to find historical documentation placing Fulton or Waddell in Westmoreland County as potters or establishing Waddell's association with Fulton in Richmond, it is clear that they were closely associated as potters in Alleghany County.

Fulton Pottery at Potts Creek in Alleghany County

Fulton's serendipitous discovery of that valuable clay deposit during his service with the Union army paved the way for his return to Alleghany County and the establishment of his pottery in 1867 at Arritt's near Potts Creek. Shortly before his move, Fulton married Sarah Ellen Schaffer (Shaver) in Parkersburg, West Virginia, on September 30, 1867.[8] Apparently he leased the land on which the remains of his kiln still stand from D. M. Davis, the grandfather of the land's current owner. Documentary research confirms Fulton's continuing potting activities in 1870, when Fulton recorded a homestead exemption as follows:

> I . . . hereby declare exempt . . . the following named property to wit: All of my household and kitchen furniture worth $175. All of the provisions laid in for the use of my family worth $25. All of the crockery or stoneware that I now have or may hereafter have on hand, that I have on hand being worth $175 {and $90 debts}. Signed, Dec. 7, 1870.[9]

Both his business and family grew over the next decade, so that by 1880 he had six children—four girls (Lola May, 11; Mary A., 6; Elizabeth, 2; and Amanda E., 1) and two boys (George R., 9; and John W., 4)—and had acquired two parcels of real estate: one acre on Potts Creek from the Reverend John B. Davis and his wife in 1876; and a six-acre parcel located at the confluence of Potts Creek and Mill Run, adjacent to the land of the heirs of John S. Arritt, in 1877.[10] Interestingly, Fulton produced a tombstone for the Reverend Davis and his wife to mark the grave of their two boys. The tombstone is embellished with a tree-of-life decoration in relief (fig. 9)

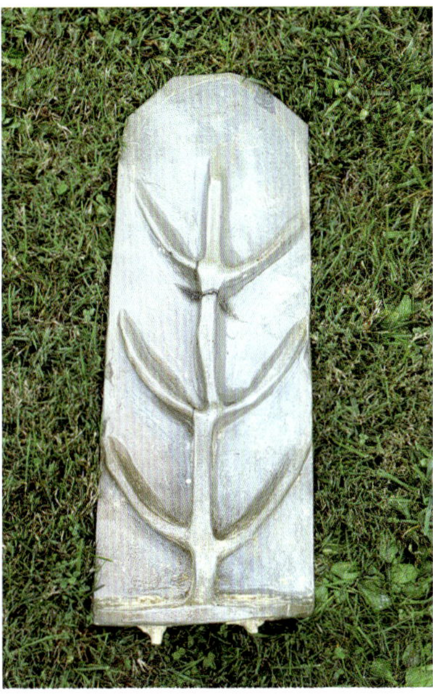

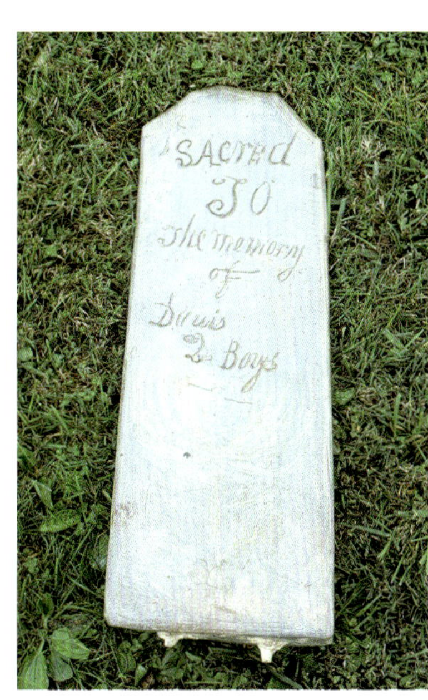

Figure 9 Grave marker or tombstone, Fulton Pottery, Alleghany County, Virginia, ca. 1874. Salt-glazed stoneware H. 42½". (Photo, Kurt Russ.) The hand-modeled stoneware tombstone contains a tree-of-life motif in relief.

Figure 10 Reverse of the grave marker illustrated in fig. 9, showing incised inscription, "Sacred to the Memory of Davis 2 Boys" and brushed manganese decoration, which is barely visible because of poor contrast with the tombstone color.

as well as brushed manganese floral decoration and, on the reverse, is inscribed "sacred to the Memory of Davis 2 boys" (fig. 10). It was on the Davis tract of land that Fulton built a log home for his family residence. At the same time he constructed a log building for making and storing his wares. As early as 1875 Fulton began utilizing another nearby clay source on land owned by Moses G. Wright located some one-and-one-half miles distant from his pottery.[11]

His post-1880 activity is evidenced by a miniature stoneware jar incised "G. N. Fulton 1881" (fig. 11) and his listing as "Geo. N. Fulton, potter located at Arritts, Alleghany County," in the 1884–1885 *Virginia Gazetteer* (Richmond).[12]

The Fulton pottery kiln is located approximately one mile south of Boiling Spring, Virginia, being situated about thirty-five yards southeast of Route 18 in a relatively flat agricultural field (fig. 12). Recorded in 1936 in conjunction with a WPA project, the pottery site was tested archaeologically in 1987 by Washington and Lee University. The site consists of the remains of a circular stoneware pottery kiln forming a mound approximately twenty feet in diameter and rising some six feet above the ground surface, as well as an associated waster pile exhibiting heavy surface concentrations of salt-glazed stoneware waster sherds and various kiln furniture fragments

Figure 11 Miniature jar, Fulton Pottery, Alleghany County, Virginia, 1881. Salt-glazed stoneware. H. 3¼". Incised "G. N. Fulton 1881."

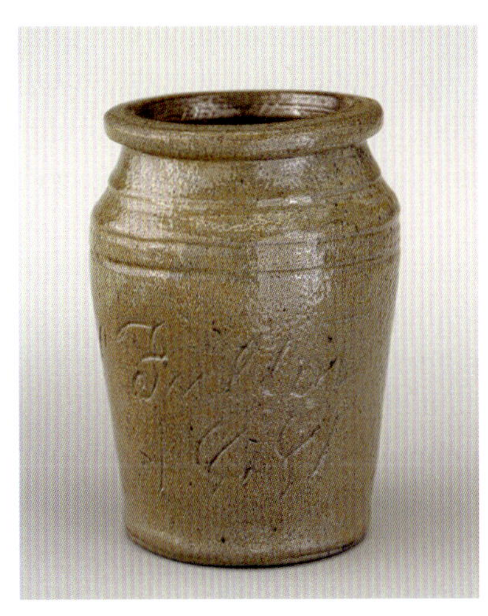

Figure 12 Map showing the location of Fulton's Pottery (44AY184) and Waddell's Pottery (44AY185) near Boiling Spring in Alleghany County, Virginia (from 7.5 minute U.S.G.S. Jordan Mines Quadrangle Map).

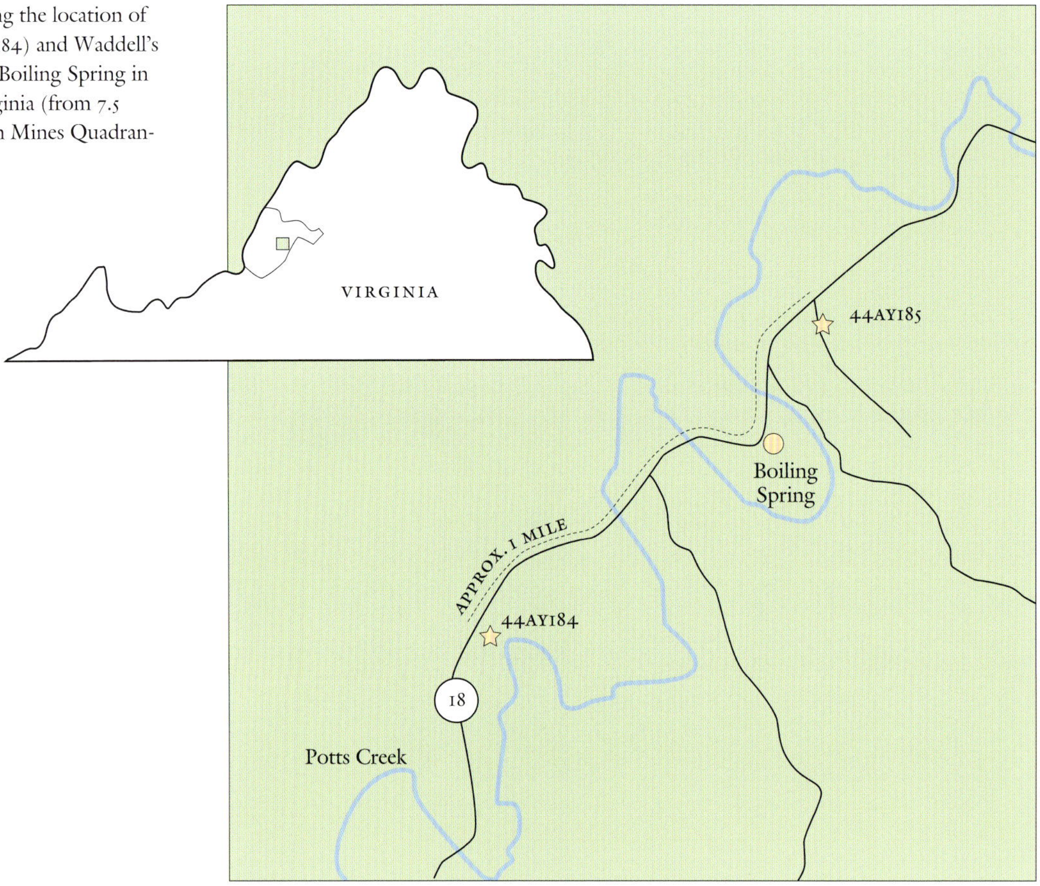

located roughly six yards northwest of the mounded kiln remains. This site is identified by the Virginia Department of Historic Resources as 44AY184, Fulton Kiln A.

In close proximity and also situated along Pott's Creek is another pottery kiln site, 44AY185, originally identified as belonging to Fulton. Documentary and archaeological research determined this was the Waddell pottery, the second of three potteries involving some five potters identified in Alleghany County during the nineteenth century. Thomas Waddell appears on the 1850, 1860, and 1870 Alleghany County census records as a potter with birthplaces listed as New York, Pennsylvania, and Virginia, respectively.[13] A land deed dated August 15, 1857, shows Waddell being granted an interest in ninety-eight acres on Christley's Run.[14] Recovered stoneware sherds from the Christley's Run site bear the stamp "T. R. Waddell, Va" and extant vessels with the same stamp are quite distinct from those produced by Fulton. The proximity of the two sites provides further evidence of the Fulton-Waddell association recorded in family history as beginning in Westmoreland County, continuing in Richmond, and ending in Alleghany County. Although dissimilar from Fulton's ware, the Waddell wares are remarkably similar to extant vessels stamped "G. A. Brown, Va" (fig. 13), attributed to a contemporaneous kiln located on the top of Potts Mountain.[15] Although no documentary evidence of the Brown pottery has been identified, the similarities of the Brown and Waddell wares suggest the

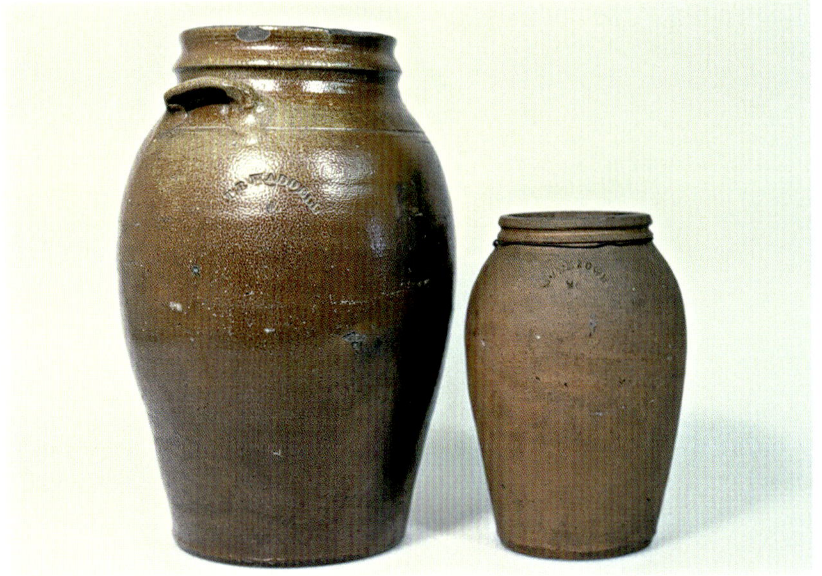

Figure 13 Examples of Alleghany County pottery. *Left*: Jar, T. R. Waddell, 1850–1870. Salt-glazed stoneware. H. 13¼". *Right*: Jar, G. A. Brown, 1850–1860. Earthenware. H. 8½". Both of these examples bear the impressed marks of their makers.

likelihood that John Brown and two of his sons, Gustavus and John W., were associated with Waddell circa 1850.[16]

Limited archaeological excavations of Fulton's kiln suggest the presence of the remains of a relatively well-preserved, nineteenth-century circular updraft kiln and recovered salt-glazed stoneware pottery sherds from a variety of vessel forms (fig. 14), some decorated with either cobalt blue or manganese dioxide floral embellishments, capacity numerals, and the signature "G. N. Fulton" or initials "G. N. F.," and numerous kiln furniture fragments, including several draw trials.

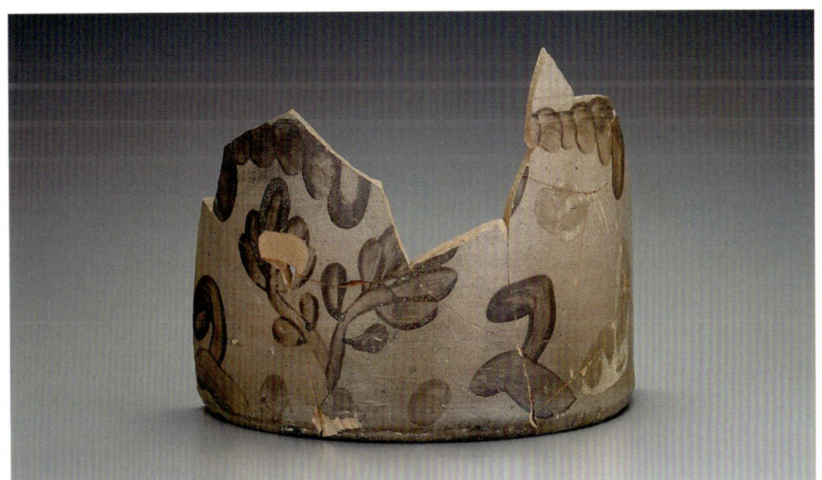

Figure 14 Fragment of a cake crock, Fulton Pottery, Alleghany County, Virginia, 1867–1885. Salt-glazed stoneware. (Courtesy, Laboratory of Archaeology, Washington and Lee University, Lexington, Virginia.) Partially reconstructed from sherds excavated at Fulton's Pottery Site (44AY184), Alleghany County, this vessel exhibits brushed manganese floral decoration and the capacity designation "2."

In 1938 Marion Rawson conducted oral history research, which recorded traditional Appalachian lifeways. Among her documentation is a remarkable interview with Daniel Arritt, who as a young man lived next door to and worked in Fulton's pottery shop. The fascinating details provide insight into not only Fulton's operation but the very nature of this traditional craft industry in Virginia during the third quarter of the nineteenth century:

You see yonder out that door where the grass looks brown just over the knoll? That's where I dug the mud and carted it a mile and a half down to Fulton's shop. He had what you call a mill standing up two feet or so from the ground and about as big as a hogshead, that was worked by an old horse at the end of a sweep; I'd throw the mud or clay in there and the knives revolving would cut it up. When it was cut up enough we took it out in blocks about a foot square—it would be about as stiff as wheat dough—and carried it to the lathe, and old man Fulton would work it round and round so, running the treadle with his foot to make the platform revolve. He'd draw it up so and so and make it like the shape he wanted it to be, sometimes using a little piece of wood to fix it right, and when it suited him he'd take a piece of wire and cut under it to loosen it so he could pick it up and carry it into the dry room. It took five days to dry and when it was dry enough he'd take his bresh and paint his name in blue across it, the full name on the big crocks, and then put some of them fancy patterns out of his head on it. He got the blue indigo at the store in a chunk and softened it with a little turpentine—yes marm. When he had enough ware—a thousand gallons—we'd set it up in the kiln.[17]

At this point Arritt stopped his narrative and explained that the kiln was about eighteen feet in diameter and approximately the same height. It was shaped like an egg, with the fire door close to the ground on one side and the only other opening being the central chimney where the smoke and flames escaped. It is inferred from his description that the kiln was of the circular updraft variety, a common nineteenth-century kiln type. He also indicated that there were four iron bars stretching across the kiln above the flues, upon which rested stones placed about eight inches apart and arranged so that the crocks and pots could be set up on them and stacked on one another, separated by little crockery plates or kiln furniture. This arrangement allowed the vessels to be exposed to equal heat on all sides. The kiln held one thousand gallons of ware, with pot quantities being computed by adding together half-pints, quarts, and gallons, represented by the various vessels to be fired.[18] Arritt continued:

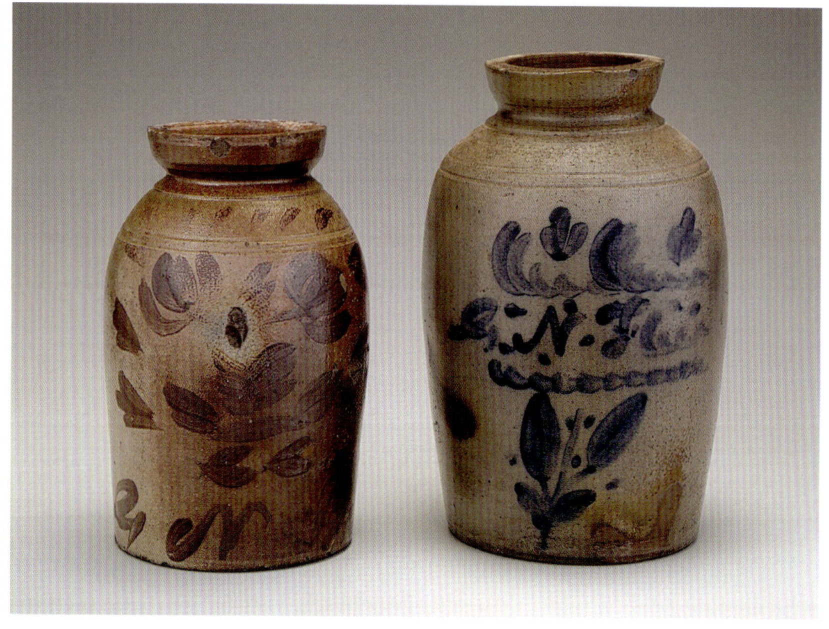

Figure 15 Canning crocks or jars (also known as wax sealers), Fulton Pottery, Alleghany County, Virginia, 1867–1885. Salt-glazed stoneware. H. 9" and 10". The quart-size jar at left is brushed with manganese floral or tree decoration and the signature "G. N. Fulton" near the base. The slightly larger jar at right is brushed with blue cobalt floral decorative motifs, including flowers, leaves, and horizontal bands enclosing the centrally placed signature.

We burnt the ware for three days and three nights and I've set up and watched many a batch and tended fire. When the ware was burnt just enough I'd go up on top of the kiln, and looking in it would seem just like a raging iron furnace, and I'd take a right smart of salt and throw it down over the ware, inside and out. You had to leave the ware where it stood for two days to cool off before you could draw it. Then it was my job to load it onto a wagon—350 gallons would make a good two-horse load—all sizes, and it brought fifty cents for a gallon and seventy-five for the bigger ones, wine crocks and water coolers.

You know, marm, this was good stoneware, not that no 'count red earthen ware. You could bile in our stoneware. I've driv the wagon many a time to Blacksburg, and there that old Waddel that sold the redware would see me coming and shout, "What you bringing that no 'count stuff to this town for?" And I'd shout back, "Yours is the no 'count stuff, aint burnt to a body. Mine's burnt to a stone body. Give me a piece of your old no 'count ware, I want to pitch it and one of mine down the road a little piece." So I pitched one of my crocks down the road twenty feet and it never broke none. His'n? He daren't give me any. He went out of business afore long. Fulton's ware was good stone body.[19]

Wares of "Good Stone Body"

A fascinating variety of wares, some unique to Virginia stoneware, characterize Fulton's production. Fulton's application of "those fancy patterns out of his head," as Arritt described his elaborate brushed and slipped blue cobalt and manganese floral trees, sprays, hearts, lines, squiggles, capacity designations, signatures, and initials, set his wares apart from those produced elsewhere in the valley during this period. Recognized forms include but are not limited to canning crocks (fig. 15), storage jars (figs. 16, 17), jugs (fig. 18), bowls (fig. 19), milk pans (fig. 20), cake crocks (fig. 21), pitchers (figs. 22, 23), churns of various sizes (figs. 24–26), miniatures, and tombstones. Family tradition holds that he was the first potter in the region to design the small-mouth crock with flaring rim and recessed interior rim/shelf that easily accommodates a wax seal (see fig. 15).[20]

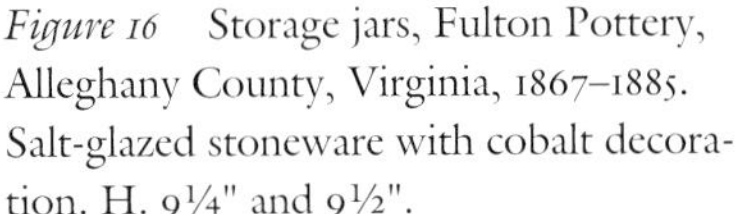

Figure 16 Storage jars, Fulton Pottery, Alleghany County, Virginia, 1867–1885. Salt-glazed stoneware with cobalt decoration. H. 9¼" and 9½".

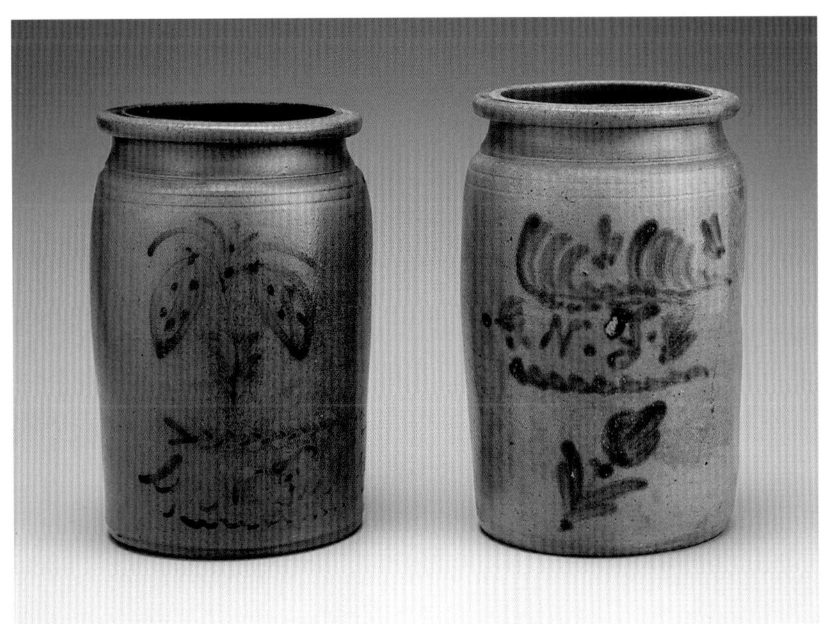

Figure 17 Storage jars, Fulton Pottery, Alleghany County, Virginia, 1867–1885. Salt-glazed stoneware with manganese brushed decoration. H. 10" and 7¼".

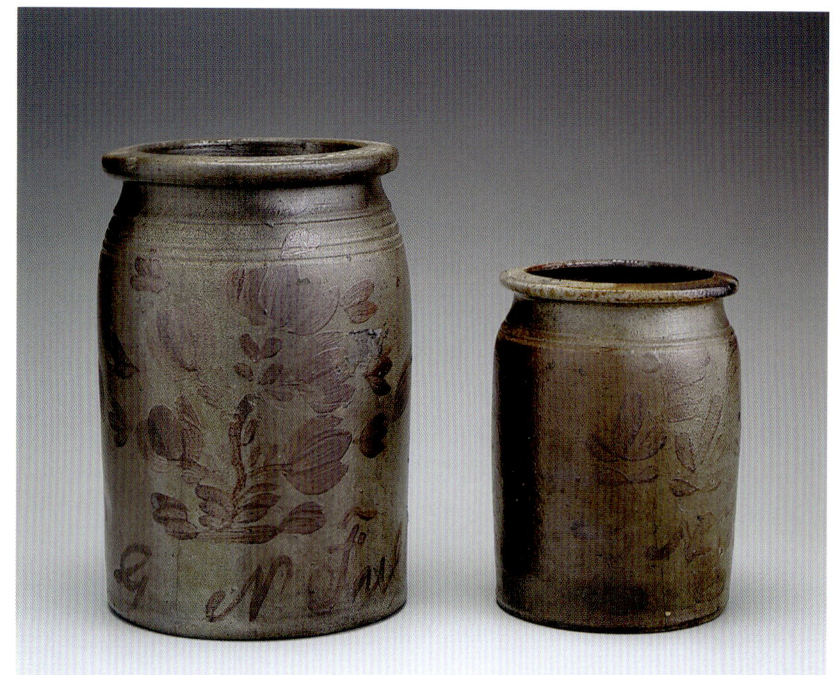

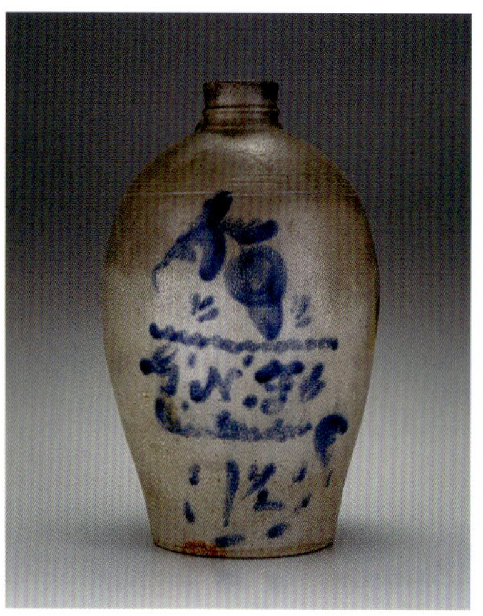

Figure 18 Jug, Fulton Pottery, Alleghany County, Virginia, 1867–1885. Salt-glazed stoneware. H. 12½". A semi-ovoid jug with brushed blue cobalt decoration, including a drooping flower, the initials "G. N. F.," and a "1½"-gallon capacity designation.

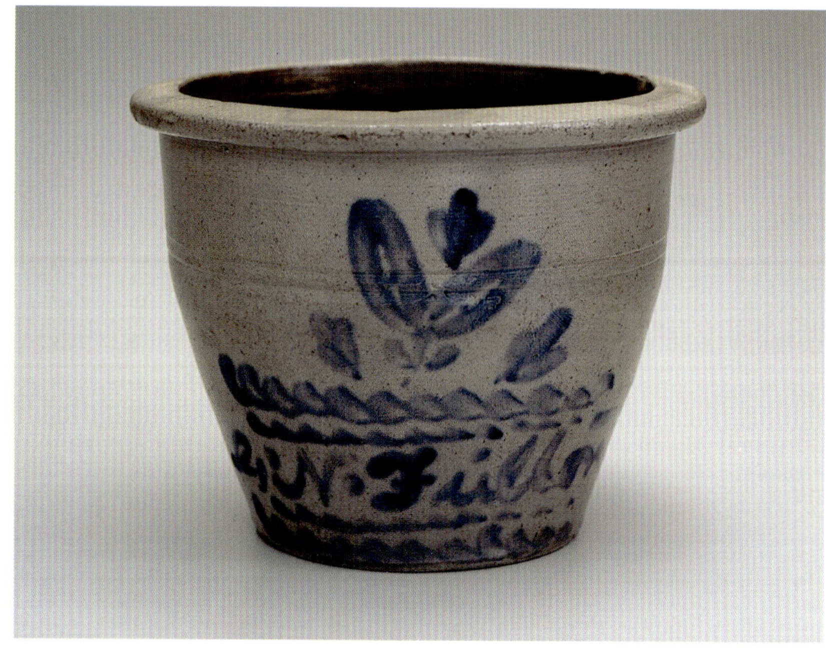

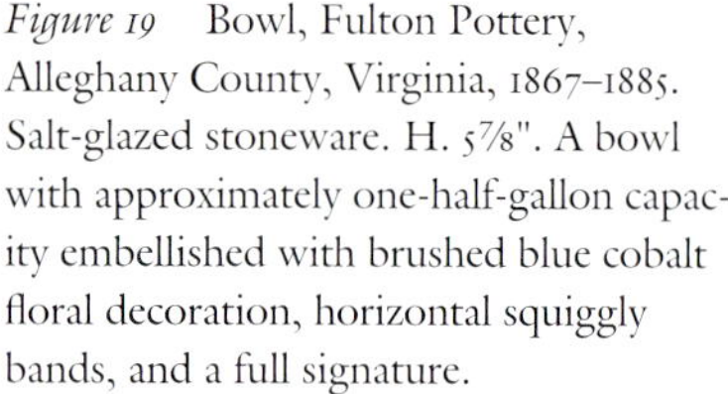

Figure 19 Bowl, Fulton Pottery, Alleghany County, Virginia, 1867–1885. Salt-glazed stoneware. H. 5⅞". A bowl with approximately one-half-gallon capacity embellished with brushed blue cobalt floral decoration, horizontal squiggly bands, and a full signature.

The frequency of decoration on his wares is high. A conservative estimate is that 75 percent of his wares were either decorated, signed, or both decorated and signed. His frequently used elaborate brushed cobalt or manganese trees covering the majority of the front of the vessel's surface contained leaves and flowers often interpreted as representing hearts. Whether the hearts were intentional is unclear, but that the decoration most commonly used by Fulton is related specifically to the Germanic-influenced tree-of-life motif, best exemplified on the tombstone discussed previously (fig.9), is unquestionable.

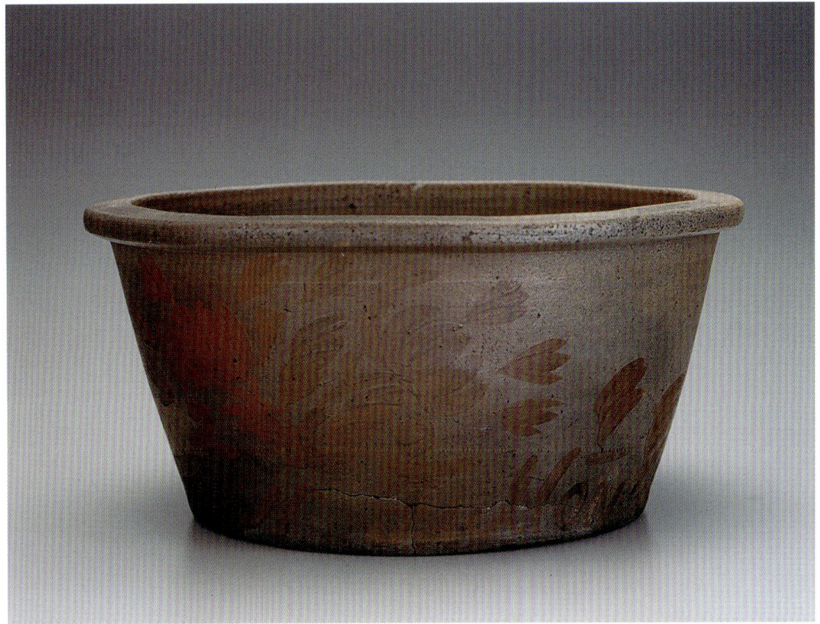

Figure 20 Milk pan or shallow bowl, Fulton Pottery, Alleghany County, Virginia, 1867–1885. Salt-glazed stoneware. H. 6⅛". This robust, wide-mouthed vessel has brushed manganese floral decoration and the signature "G. N. Fulton" above its base.

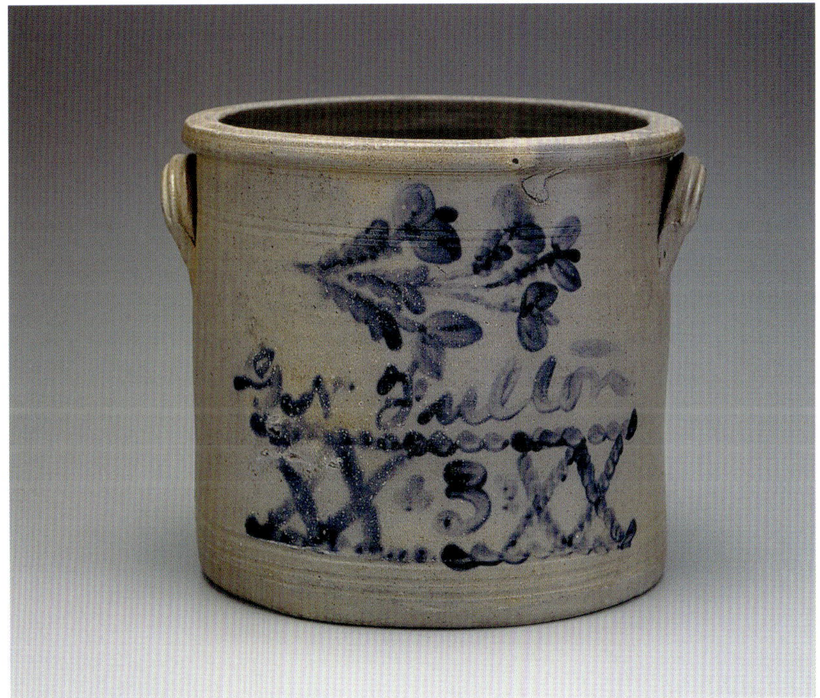

Figure 21 Cake crock, Fulton Pottery, Alleghany County, Virginia, 1867–1885. Salt-glazed stoneware. H. 9¾". This straight-sided vessel is decorated in cobalt blue with a horizontally oriented floral spray, a centrally placed signature, and, near the base, double crosshatched marks enclosed by two horizontal wavy lines with a "3"-gallon capacity designation in the center. Compare the decorative embellishment at the base with that executed in manganese on the churn illustrated in fig. 26.

Many of Fulton's surviving wares and archaeologically recovered sherds illustrate problems he faced in controlling the variables (i.e., maintaining and controlling adequate firing temperatures, application of glaze, and monitoring kiln oxygen/reduction atmospheric conditions) necessary to produce quality stoneware. The frequency of draw trials recovered from test excavations speak to this problem and show Fulton's continuing attention and attempts to both monitor and adjust the variables necessary for a successful firing, which would ensure proper vessel vitrification, even glaze application, and contrast of decoration against the vessel body.

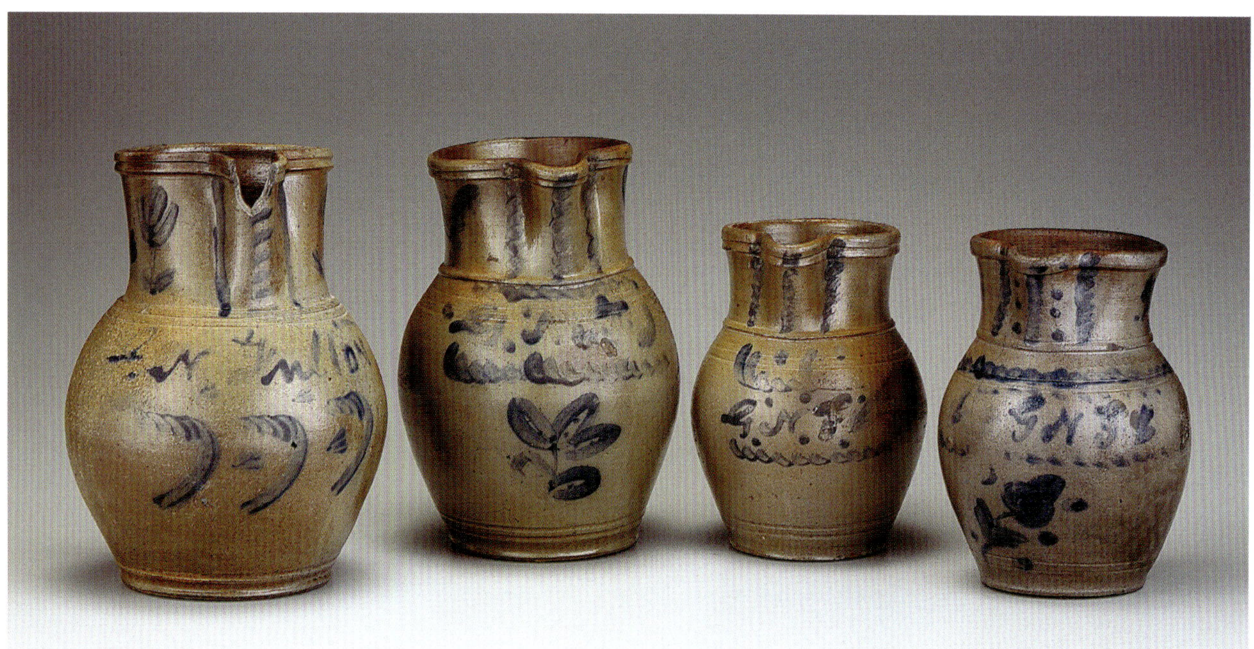

Figure 22 Pitchers, Fulton Pottery, Alleghany County, Virginia, 1867–1885. Salt-glazed stoneware. *(a)* H. 10½". A one-gallon pitcher with a well-defined beaded rim, horizontal blue lines at the spout flanked on either side by blue flowers, and the signature "G. N. Fulton" above brushed cobalt floral motifs. *(b)* H. 10". A one-gallon pitcher with a well-defined shoulder above three concentric incised bands, blue vertical lines on either side of the spout flanked by additional floral motifs, and wavy lines and floral motifs across the front of the vessel, the initials "G. N. F.," and horizontal lines on the handle. *(c)* H. 8¼". A pitcher with a prominent banded or incised rim, pronounced shoulder above two incised rings with two similar incised lines near base, and a well-defined base; cobalt decoration includes vertical stripes at spout, floral leaves, dots, and the initials "G. N. F." *(d)* H. 8½". A half-gallon pitcher with a prominent rim, well-defined shoulder, two incised concentric rings around the upper mid-section and at ½" above the base, elaborate brushed cobalt floral decoration including dots, squiggly lines, and floral motifs around the rim, with lines and the initials "G. N. F." above the floral motif.

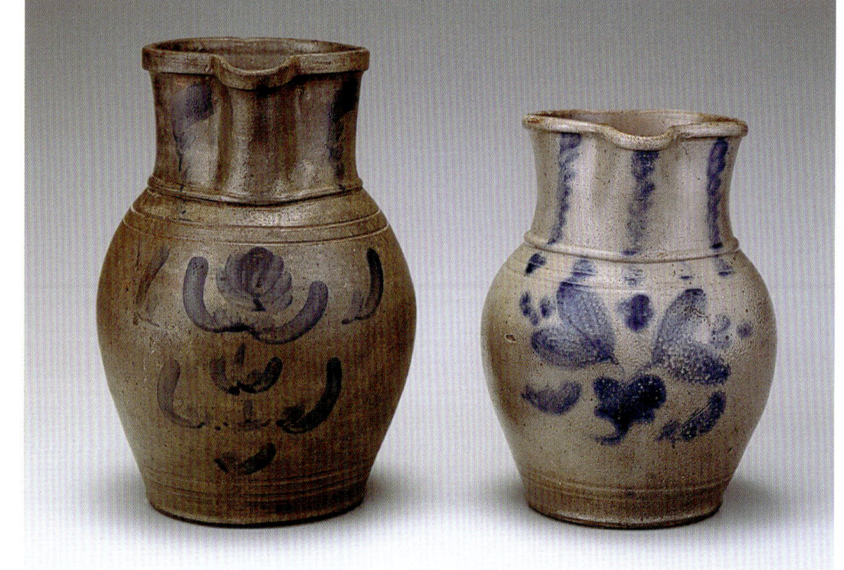

Figure 23 Pitchers, Fulton Pottery, Alleghany County, Virginia, 1867–1885. Salt-glazed stoneware. *Left*: H. 9". The thinly glazed well-potted dark gray pitcher exhibits simple curvilinear floral motifs. *Right*: H. 7⅞".The smaller, light-gray pitcher has textured salt-glaze and stylized floral motifs.

Figure 24 Churn, Fulton Pottery, Alleghany County, Virginia, 1867–1885. Salt-glazed stoneware. H. 16". This four-gallon churn is decorated with a brushed blue cobalt floral design and includes a centrally placed "palm" tree and signature.

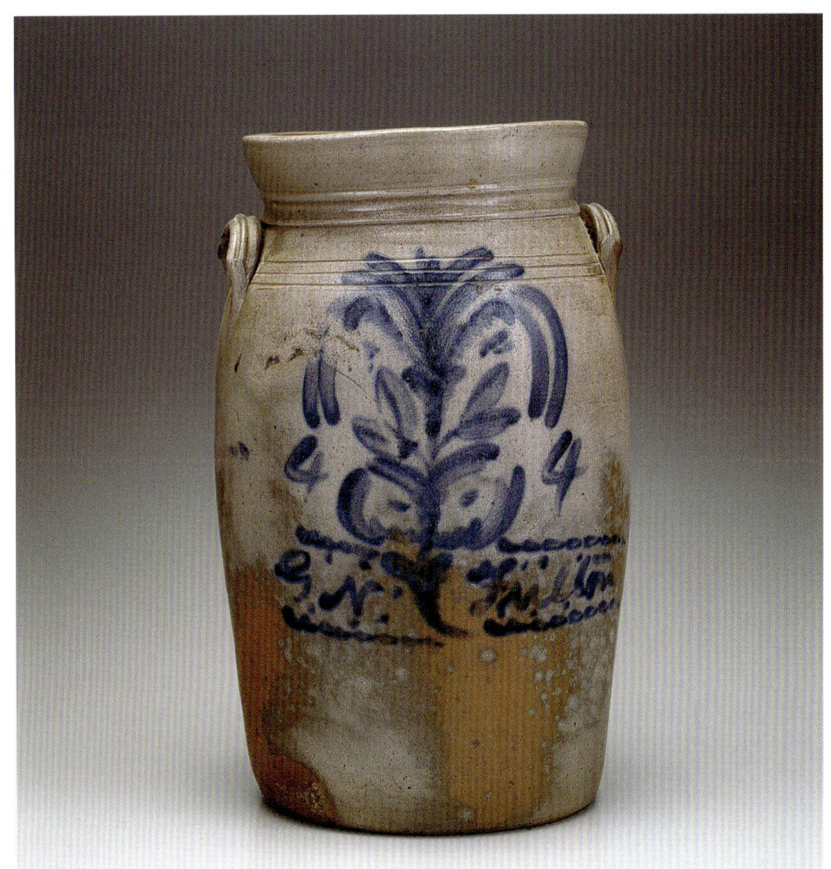

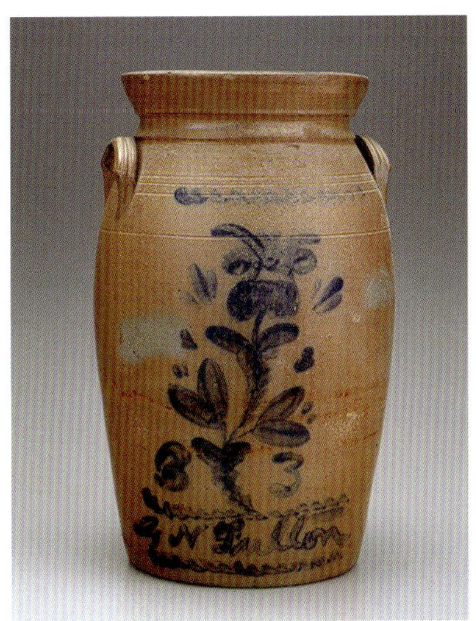

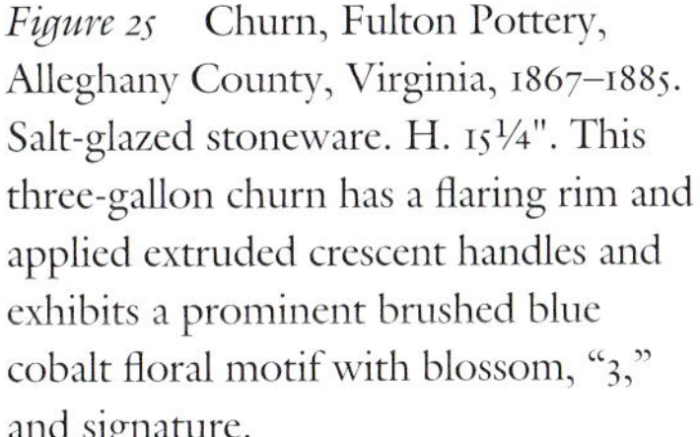

Figure 25 Churn, Fulton Pottery, Alleghany County, Virginia, 1867–1885. Salt-glazed stoneware. H. 15¼". This three-gallon churn has a flaring rim and applied extruded crescent handles and exhibits a prominent brushed blue cobalt floral motif with blossom, "3," and signature.

Figure 26 Churn, Fulton Pottery, Alleghany County, Virginia, 1867–1885. Salt-glazed stoneware. H. 17⅛". A five-gallon churn with a flaring rim, well-defined collar, and applied crescent-shaped extruded handles exhibiting elaborate brushed manganese dioxide decoration, including both horizontally and vertically oriented floral motifs, a centrally placed "5" indicating vessel capacity, and the signature "G. N. Fulton" enclosed by horizontal wavy lines. At the base a series of squares with intersecting diagonal (or 45°) lines appear to form an artificial base, or platform, for the decorative embellishment above.

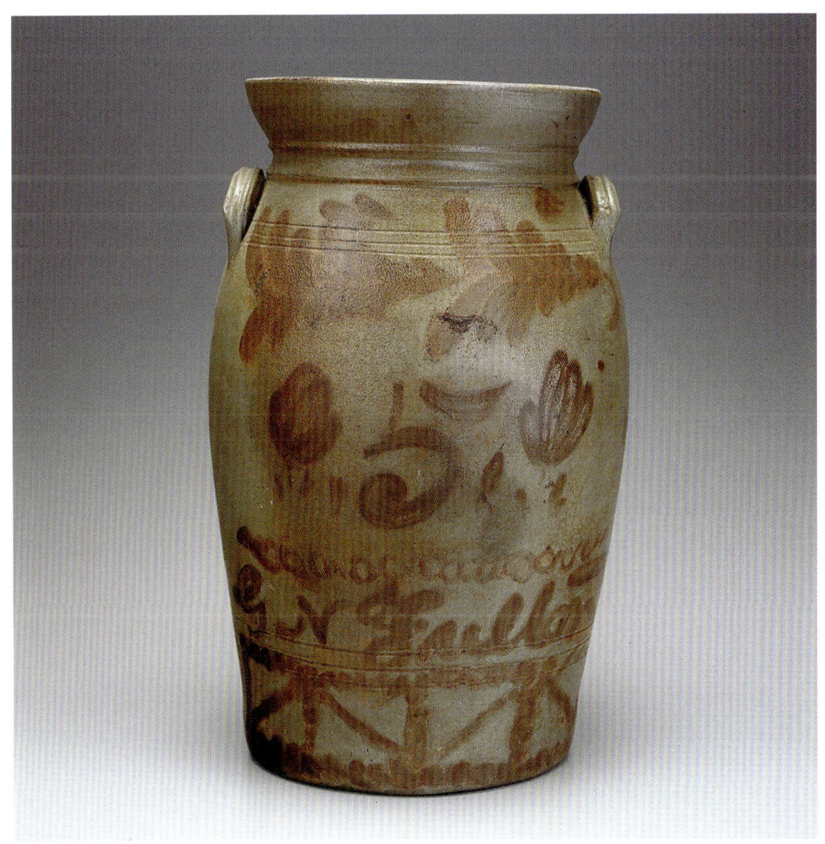

Figure 27 Jar, bowl, and pitcher, Fulton Pottery, Alleghany County, Virginia, 1867–1885. Salt-glazed stoneware. *Jar*: H. 8". A quart-size, straight-sided jar with folky manganese floral decoration, including a prominent blooming tulip resembling a musical lyre flanked by vertical floral vines on both sides. *Bowl*: H. 7⅛". An approximately one-half-gallon bowl with a flat, flaring rim, three incised concentric rings, and rather detailed floral motifs, including flowers with dotted leaves and the signature "G. N. Fulton" at the base. *Pitcher*: H. 8". A quart-size pitcher with profuse manganese floral decoration and the signature "G. N. Fulton" at the base. The color of the manganese decoration, manner of execution of the decorative motifs with small fine-line, detailed brushstrokes, and the color of the vessels with a fine, well-processed clay paste suggest that these vessels may have been made and decorated by the same hand.

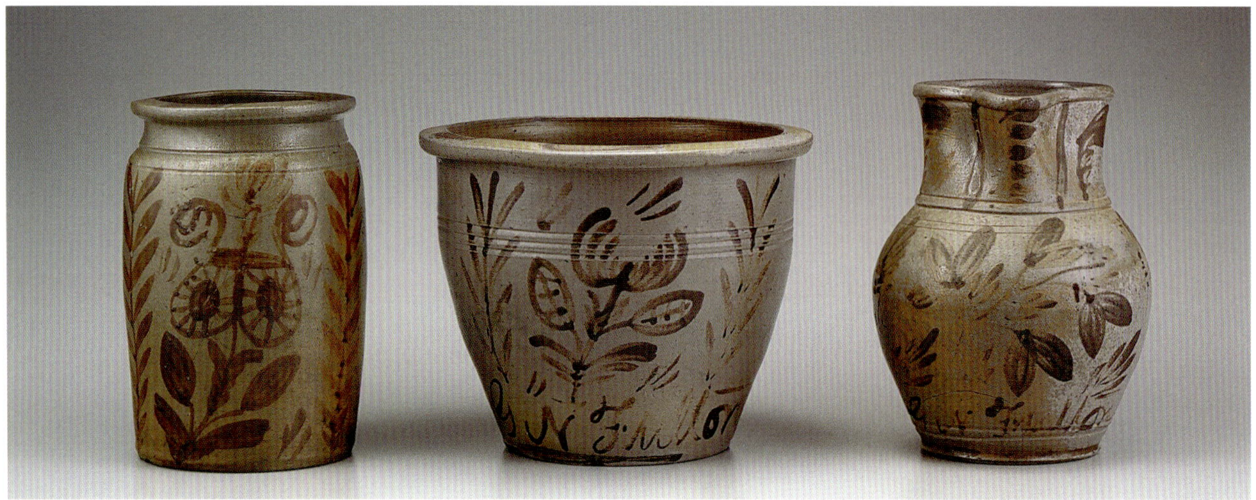

Arritt's comparison of Fulton's stone crocks with those produced by Waddell is probably in error in this descriptive account. Given Fulton's close though not well-documented association with Waddell prior to their arrival in Alleghany County, and the proximity of their stoneware kilns along Pott's Creek, it is much more likely that Arritt was referring to the redware production of Bodell's Pottery in the vicinity of Blacksburg, which is, unfortunately, even more poorly documented.

Also of particular interest is Arritt's statement that Fulton himself was responsible for decorating his wares. It is clear from comparisons of the signature on his crocks with those from surviving historical documents that the same hand was responsible for both. Variation in selected decorative motifs and the manner and detail with which they are executed is noted within the extant assemblage examined during this research, suggesting that someone else may have had a hand in decorating (fig. 27). With the exception of the cooler discussed previously (figs. 5–8), perhaps the most impressive of his decorated wares are those embellished with both cobalt and manganese decoration (fig. 28).[21]

Fulton's Final Move to Botetourt County and Retirement

Although family tradition states that Fulton moved to Botetourt County about 1875, he appears as a potter in the 1880 Alleghany County census, and, as mentioned previously, advertised himself as a potter located at "Arritts, Alleghany County" in an 1884–1885 Richmond newspaper.[22] The date ascribed to his move may relate to the assertion that he had established or was associated with a retail outlet for his pottery in Fincastle, Virginia,

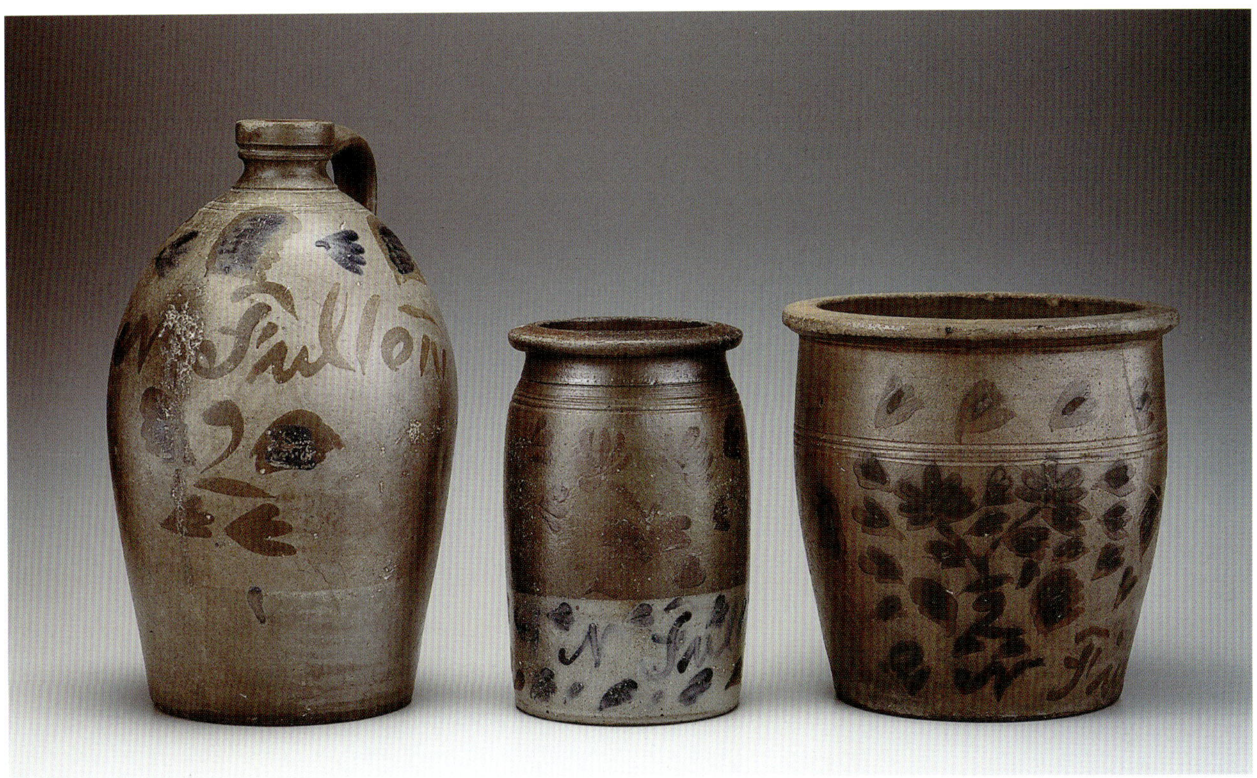

Figure 28 Jug, storage jar, and bowl, Fulton Pottery, Alleghany County, Virginia, 1867–1885. Salt-glazed stoneware. H. 14¾", 9¾", and 10". These Fulton stoneware vessels are embellished with brushed blue cobalt oxide and manganese dioxide floral decoration, and include the signature "G. N. Fulton."

during this time.[23] A document indicating that Fulton assigned a judgment against a Joseph(?) for $62 with interest from June 1, 1879—plus $8.92 in court costs previously granted to him by the Botetourt Circuit Court on May 29, 1880—to a T. M. Allen is dated September 21, 1888, and bears a signature matching that which is so frequently seen on his wares: "George N. Fulton."[24] This would suggest that as early as 1879 and certainly no later than 1888 Fulton was residing in Botetourt, although it is clear that his ties there, both in terms of family and business associations, were well established before this time.

In fact, family tradition points to an 1876 birthdate of one of Fulton's daughters in Botetourt as evidence of his even earlier residence there.[25] The historical record, however, shows that three of his daughters, Mary, Elizabeth, and Amanda, were born in Alleghany County in 1874, 1878, and 1879, respectively. Whatever the case, that he eventually made the final move to Botetourt is incontrovertible, as both he and his wife are buried in the Noftzinger family cemetery near Fincastle, Virginia.[26]

While evidence of Fulton's pottery manufacturing in Botetourt County is limited, oral history is replete with wide-ranging theories relative to his late-nineteenth-century Fincastle-area activities. These include but are not limited to the following:

1. Fulton decorated wares produced in Botetourt with blue cobalt, whereas wares produced in Alleghany County were embellished with brown or manganese dioxide. (Sherds recovered from his Alleghany pottery exhibit both cobalt and manganese decoration. No cobalt-decorated wares produced by Fulton in Botetourt have been identified.)

2. The source for the clay Fulton used in the Fincastle area resulted in the vessels made there being of a brown or red color. (While the Fincastle/Botetourt area is characterized by a strong emphasis on earthenware production, beginning in the late eighteenth century with Christian and continuing with Hinkle and Spigle, the Obenchains, and the Noftzingers into the 1880s, with their products being reddish brown in color and typically having a lead glaze, there are no known signed Fulton brown, red, or lead-glazed earthenware crocks known to have been made in Fincastle. There is, however, significant variation in the color of his wares, which relates to different sources of clay and problems in reaching and controlling proper firing temperatures for stoneware production. As a result, many of his wares may be referred to as redware and may be porous and exhibit a reddish color, but they typically will have a salt glaze, indicating his intended product was a vitreous stoneware.)

3. Fulton's potting activity in Botetourt was in association with the Noftzinger family. (It now appears that the Noftzingers' activity was limited to earthenware production with no signed vessels from their pottery having been identified. Given that the period of Fulton's residence in Botetourt was coincident with their period of operation, that their families were connected, that he and his wife are buried in the Noftzinger family cemetery, and the absence of any signed Fulton stoneware with a definite Botetourt provenance, it seems likely that any involvement Fulton had in pottery manufacturing in Botetourt concerned earthenware production in association with the Noftzingers.)

4. Fulton made and marketed his wares on Back Street in Fincastle.

5. Fulton's wares were sold at an outlet in Fincastle operated by the Lusters.[27]

That a local merchant owned or rented a building on Back Street where pottery wares were sold is well established, but Fulton's association with the shop or the marketing of his wares there remains unresolved. The well-documented history of Fincastle in the late eighteenth century identifies a pottery located along Back Street (more recently known as the Sally Douglas Home), that was operated by Israel Christian and situated across the street from his log residence (known more recently as the Becky Holmes House). An influential figure in Fincastle history, Christian had in 1770 offered some forty acres (from a larger land grant from King George III) for the establishment of a town to serve as the county seat for Botetourt. The site of the pottery operated by Christian during the late eighteenth century was purchased by the Lusters in 1878 and they were said to have offered pottery wares for sale there through 1885, while simultaneously operating a larger retail mercantile outlet on Roanoke Street.[28]

Recent examination of ceramics from local domestic sites in the Fincastle area has revealed some fascinating lead-glazed earthenware sherds with polychrome slip decoration, reflecting certain Germanic/Moravian influences, that perhaps are a product of Christian's pottery shop. Although the exact nature, extent, or duration of his activity is unknown, this is a promising area for future research. While it seems very unlikely that what once may have been an important late-eighteenth-century pottery concern remained in continuous operation for some ninety years until Fulton's involvement at retirement, it is likely that this late-eighteenth-century earthenware pottery shop of short-lived duration served, some one hundred or so years later, as an outlet for regionally produced stoneware by the Lusters, and may have included wares made by Fulton in Alleghany County or those produced by the Noftzingers, Obenchains, or others in Botetourt.[29] On the other hand, without sufficient documentary evidence, it may be that the identification of a house as the location of a pottery shop in the distant past (late eighteenth century) may have been inaccurately transposed to the more recent past (late nineteenth century) as representing, relating to, or attributed to Fulton's well-known regional pottery endeavors despite no solid documentary evidence of his involvement in pottery manufacture in Botetourt or of his pottery wares being sold at this location in the late nineteenth century.

Fulton Pottery: An Assessment

Fulton's thirty-eight-year participation in this evolving traditional craft industry and his successful establishment and continuing pottery operation in a relatively isolated rural Virginia setting for some eighteen years reflect, to a certain degree, his intimate understanding of his craft and a reliance on and strict adherence to its time-tested methods. Despite his familiarity with advancing industry technologies and shifting production methods, Fulton insightfully viewed the success of his enterprise in the context of understanding the local community's need. His utilitarian wares, embellished with a decorative aesthetic component, apparently were appreciated by

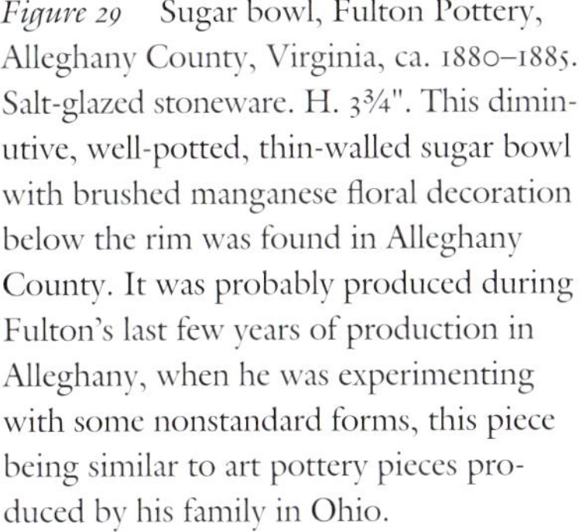

Figure 29 Sugar bowl, Fulton Pottery, Alleghany County, Virginia, ca. 1880–1885. Salt-glazed stoneware. H. 3¾". This diminutive, well-potted, thin-walled sugar bowl with brushed manganese floral decoration below the rim was found in Alleghany County. It was probably produced during Fulton's last few years of production in Alleghany, when he was experimenting with some nonstandard forms, this piece being similar to art pottery pieces produced by his family in Ohio.

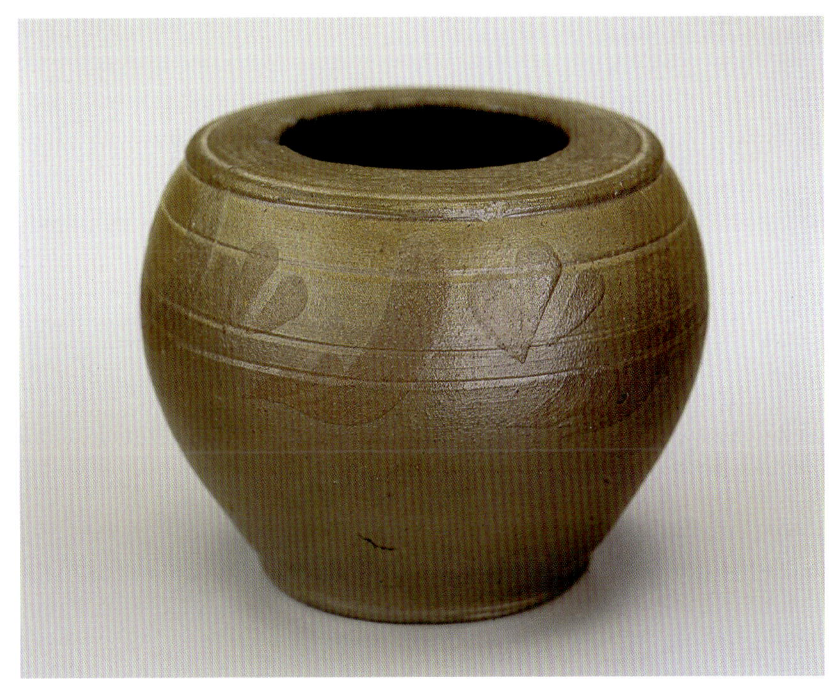

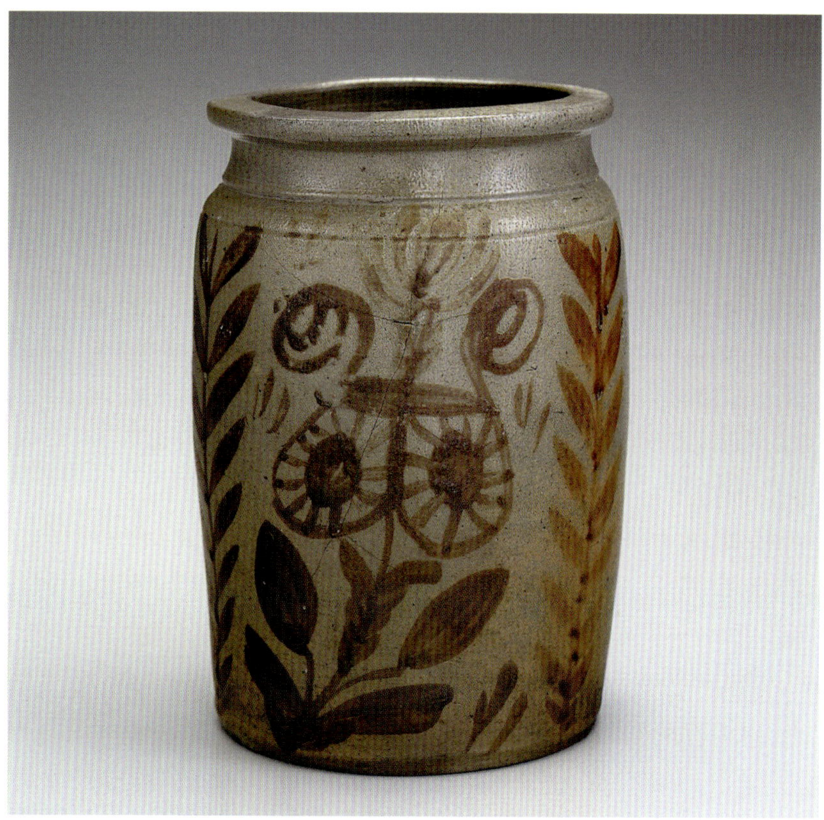

Figure 30 Jar, Fulton Pottery, Alleghany County, Virginia, 1867–1885. Salt-glazed stoneware. H. 8". Manganese floral decoration of Germanic tulip and associated leaves and vines.

consumers without a need for significant change or modification. Although he held fast to his traditional methods of production and marketing, it is obvious through an examination of both extant wares and archaeologically recovered sherds that there was some shifting in the variety and percentages of wares produced through time with some limited experimentation with more modern forms (fig. 29). These wares of "good stone body," delightfully decorated with "them fancy patterns out of his head" (fig. 30), reflect Fulton's enduring legacy as one of the Virginia highlands' most successful mid- to late-nineteenth-century traditional potters.

While the stage is set for understanding the success of his enterprise and the appeal of his wares to nineteenth-century consumers, the recent appreciation and collecting pursuit of his wares for the historic ceramic enthusiast of the twenty-first century must be viewed in the context of the enduring graphic appeal of these traditional handcrafted wares produced from the earth to fulfill a continuing utilitarian need while simultaneously reflecting the consumers' shared cultural aesthetic.

1. Gay Arritt, "Fulton Pottery," in Gay Arritt, *Historical Sketches*, (Covington, Va.: Alleghany Historical Society, 1982); Kurt C. Russ, "The Traditional Pottery Manufacturing Industry in Virginia: Examples from Botetourt and Rockbridge Counties," *Rockbridge Historical Society Proceedings* (Lexington, Va.) 10 (1990): 453–89; Kurt C. Russ, "Exploring Western Virginia Potteries," *Journal of Early Southern Decorative Arts* 21, no. 2 (1996): 98–138; Kurt C. Russ, "Making Pottery in Botetourt County," *Journal of the Roanoke Historical Society* 13, no. 2 (1996): 59–74.

2. Paul Mullins, "Historic Pottery Making in Rockingham County, Virginia" (paper presented at the Archaeological Society of Virginia Symposium, "Ceramics in Virginia 1988,"

Virginia Piedmont Community College, Charlottesville); Paul R. Mullins, "Defining Boundaries of Change: The Records of an Industrializing Potter," in *Text Aided Archaeology,* edited by Barbara J. Little (Boca Raton, Fla.: C.R.C. Press, 1992), pp. 179–93; Kurt C. Russ, "The Archaeology of Nineteenth-Century Virginia Coarsewares," in *The Transformation of Virginia from 1800 to 1900: An Archaeological Synthesis,* edited by Ted Reinhart and John Sprinkle, Special Publication No. 31 of the Archaeological Society of Virginia (Richmond, Va.: Dietz Press, 1995).

3. Brenda Fulton Booker (bbooker955@aol.com), personal communication, 2003; Nancy Pruter (bobpruter@earthlink.net), personal communication, 2003.

4. Edward F. Witsell, Major General, Dept. of the Army, September 23, 1948, to Ms. Edna Cantrell, Covington, Virginia.

5. *Virginia Fincastle Herald,* June 23, 1938; interview with Edna Cantrell, granddaughter of Fulton, by Chris Donahue, Washington and Lee University, 1987.

6. Richmond Whig publication dated April 15, 1865; William C. Ketchum, *The Pottery & Porcelain Collector's Handbook* (New York: Funk & Wagnalls, 1971), p. 191.

7. *Virginia Fincastle Herald,* June 23, 1938; Arritt, "Fulton Pottery"; interview with Edna Cantrell, 1987.

8. Wood County Marriage Record (West Virginia), no. 2, p. 35.

9. Alleghany County Deed Book 6, p. 444.

10. Alleghany County Census Records, Boiling Springs District, 1880; Alleghany County Deed Book 7, pp. 388, 554.

11. Virginia Department of Historic Resources, Richmond, Virginia, site files number 03-14 and 03-15. This is most likely the same site referred to by Mr. Arritt in his interview with Ms. Rawson as being the location where he collected the clay and transported it to Fulton's shop for processing; Marion N. Rawson, *Candleday Art* (New York: E. P. Dutton, 1938), p. 104.

12. *Virginia Gazetteer,* 1884–1885.

13. Alleghany County Census Records, 1850, 1860, 1870.

14. August 15, 1857, land deed shows Waddell was apparently granted two-and-one-half shares in this ninety-eight-acre parcel adjoining J. D. Scott's land and on which Jacob Wolfe had previously resided. Land Deeds for Alleghany County, Alleghany County Court House, Covington, Virginia.

15. Rawson, *Candleday Art,* p. 107.

16. Alleghany County Census Records (First District, July 20, 1850) list John Brown (49 years old) as being a potter born in Maryland and having a wife, Elizabeth (37 years old), five daughters, and three sons, two of whom—Gustavus A. (16 years old) and John W. (16 years old)—are listed as being born in Virginia circa 1834 and as being potters working with their father in Alleghany circa 1850.

17. Rawson, *Candleday Art*, pp. 104–5.

18. Ibid., pp. 105–6.

19. Ibid., p. 106.

20. Interview with Edna Cantrell, 1987; Owen Barnes, "George Fulton Made Pottery in Potts Creek Area," *Covington Virginian,* August 7, 1975.

21. See a similarly decorated five-gallon churn manufactured by Fulton in Russ, "Archaeology of Nineteenth-Century Virginia Coarsewares," p. 109, fig. 2.

22. *Virginia Gazetteer,* 1884–1885.

23. Dorothy Sue Simmons Kessler, *G. N. Fulton Pottery Booklet* (Fincastle, Va.: Historic Fincastle, Inc., 1987). Unfortunately, no references are provided in this booklet relative to Fulton's wares being marketed or sold on Back Street by the Lusters. In fact, the general lack of proper referencing throughout this brief consideration and the absence of citations make it impossible to know the source of the information or to whom it was originally attributed, in order to properly evaluate, investigate, and confirm or refute its accuracy. We must look to continuing thoughtful research and hope for the possibility of discovering ledgers from their (the Lusters and/or Fulton's) operations, which would surely prove enlightening.

24. Botetourt County Court House, Fincastle, Virginia. One characteristic of Fulton's signature is that the horizontal line meant to cross the "t" is typically found above the "o" and "n," having missed its intersection with the vertical line intended to form a "t."

25. Kessler, *G. N. Fulton Pottery Booklet,* pp. 7–8.

26. Fulton passed away in 1894 in Botetourt County and his wife died in 1910 in Roanoke, Virginia, but both are buried in the Noftzinger family cemetery located south of Fincastle

along Route 220 to the northeast of its intersection with Route 640, adjacent to a residence formerly owned by a Commander Ware. The Noftzinger pottery kiln was located in the same vicinity just southwest on the intersection of Route 640 with Route 602; see Kurt C. Russ, "The Fincastle Pottery (44BO304): Salvage Excavations at a Nineteenth-Century Earthenware Kiln Located in Botetourt County, Virginia," in *Technical Report Series,* no. 3 (Richmond, Va.: Department of Historic Resources, 1991); see also *Virginia Fincastle Herald,* June 23, 1938; Cantrell interview, 1987; and Russ, "Making Pottery in Botetourt County."

27. *Virginia Fincastle Herald,* June 23, 1938; Arritt, "Fulton Pottery"; Cantrell interview, 1987; Kessler, *G. N. Fulton Pottery Booklet*.

28. Katherine C. Harris, "Fincastle Building," in *Historic Fincastle 1772* (Fincastle, Va.: Historic Fincastle, Inc., 1976), pp. 6–11. Also see Harold Eads, "Town of Fincastle," in *Historic Fincastle 1772*, p. iv; and Kessler, *G. N. Fulton Pottery Booklet,* p. 9.

29. Russ, "Fincastle Pottery," pp. 59–74; Russ, "Traditional Pottery Manufacturing Industry in Virginia."

Ivor Noël Hume

A-Hunting We Will Go! from Vauxhall to Lambeth, 1700–1956

▼ FOR I MYSELF *cannot fancy a more happy frame of mind,*
Than his who rides well up to hounds, while 'care sits on behind'
There is nothing to allure him in the vanities of life;
Ambition, scandal, politics, hatred, emulation, strife,
And all those dire diseases men really good discard,
Are merged in forgetfulness when hounds are running hard.

—From an old song, pre-1860[1]

Someone once said—it may have been me—that the more you learn the less you know. That certainly is true of English brown stoneware mugs and jugs of the eighteenth to twentieth centuries. Decorated with individually molded ("sprigged") hunting scenes, they were standard tavern serving and drinking vessels as recently as the Second World War, and because many were dated they possessed the essential "keep me factor" that discouraged throwing them away. Nevertheless, it is only recently that collectors have shown an interest in the heavy-duty wares which for nigh on three hundred years have been in daily use in virtually every tavern, cottage, and kitchen. Indeed, its sprig-decorated brown stonewares are more related to, and evocative of, Britain's evolving social and political history than all others.

The hunting wares fall into three groups. The first runs from circa 1713 to 1820 and features tavern-related panels above individual hunters and quarry chasing around mugs and jugs; the second couples those sprigs with others depicting drinkers and smokers (topers), trees, windmills, and so forth, and runs from about 1792 to the 1950s; the third features a wraparound series of sprigs together creating a single hunting scene known as "The Kill." This last appeared circa 1800 and ever since has continued to decorate a variety of wares both coarse and fine.

Although decorating table wares with hunting motifs can be traced back to the red Samian wares of the Roman Empire, their stoneware story begins in the early eighteenth century.

At a meeting of the English Ceramic Circle in January 1979 ceramic scholar Mavis Bimson (later Watney) divided these wares into two groups, those whose hunts chased from left to right (clockwise) and those that pursued from right to left (counterclockwise), and assigned them to unnamed London factories "A" and "B," respectively (figs. *1a–d*).[2] Clearly, the sprig appliers were not working at the same bench, for to do so would have led to endless mold confusion. But did that mean, therefore, that the As and

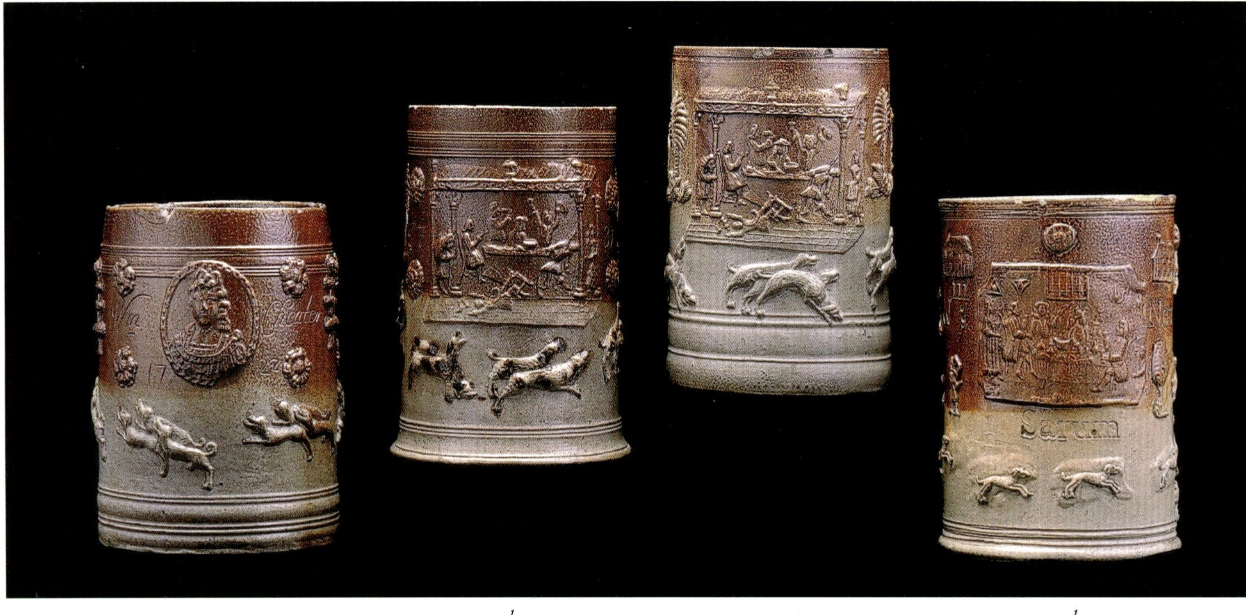

a *b* *c* *d*

Figure 1 Mugs, England. Salt-glazed stoneware. (All objects from the Noël Hume Collection unless otherwise noted; photography by Gavin Ashworth unless otherwise noted.) (*a*) Applied portrait medallion of Queen Anne, trees, clockwise hunt after stag, and a huntsman on foot, inscribed "Wm. Cheater 1722." Vauxhall. H. 8 1/16". (*b*) Counterclockwise hunt after stag, iron oxide dappled, canopied panel with Punch Party A, dated "1731." Vauxhall. H. 8 1/4". (*c*) Counterclockwise hunt after stag, canopied Punch Party A, trees, mill house sprigs, inscribed "John Sargent 1737." Vauxhall. H. 8". (*d*) Counterclockwise hunt after hare or rabbit, walking huntsman with horn, Punch Party B1, type-impressed "W^{M}; Newman / Sarum," ca. 1760, Bristol. H. 8 1/8".

Bs were from different factories, or could they be from different benches in the same shop? Those are questions still open to lively debate.

Although my purpose here is to consider the details rather than the whole, it is first necessary to review the possible manufacturing sources for the large mugs that appear to have become popular around 1710. Famed for its delftware, the Pickleherring factory in Southwark below London Bridge was heavily into stoneware production by 1699, when an inventory of its assets was recorded. Among them were:

It 12 doz pottle stone canns att	4. 8. 0
It 77 doz Quart Canns & thin Gorges att	14. 12. 0
It 13 pottle stone Canns att	8. 0
It 4 doz & half pottle Canns att	4. 10. 0
It 138 doz Quart Canns att	24. 3. 0
It 7 doz and 7 pottle stone Canns att	2 16. 0[3]

A pottle equated with half a modern gallon and the measured surviving mugs each holds an average of 5½ pints. It follows, therefore, that the Pickleherring factory was producing stoneware mugs (canns) of this capacity at the turn of the century. Unfortunately, none has been identified. Building site salvage along Vine Lane, which ran through the factory area, yielded quantities of delft wasters but no stoneware, the latter represented only by a kiln spacer and a lump of salt-caked dross.[4]

Another Thames-side factory producing both delftware and stoneware was in operation in the first quarter of the eighteenth century and was located upstream beside Gravel Lane, a site now occupied by Tate Modern (previously the Bankside Power Station). Numerous fragmentary stoneware saggers intended to house brown stonewares of various sizes and types were recovered, along with fragments of mugs and bottles. Although I was responsible for the archaeological salvage, I do not recall whether any mug wasters were found. That factory was established in 1694 and claimed to produce mugs and cans comparable to those made by John Dwight at

Fulham.[5] Through many vicissitudes the Gravel Lane factory limped along until circa 1748, when the premises were offered for sale.

Much more successful and of far longer duration were delftware and stoneware potteries located between modern Vauxhall and Lambeth Bridges. Beginning around 1697 and headed by potters from Gravel Lane, factories under several managements continued throughout the eighteenth century and most of the nineteenth—which brings us to Lambeth proper, where prodigious quantities of brown stonewares were made successively by Jones and Watts, Stephen Green, John Doulton, James Stiff, and others, until Doulton, the last of them, closed down in 1956. Farther up the Thames stood the famed Fulham stoneware factory, begun by John Dwight in 1672, which continued to make stone sanitary wares until 1956. On the south bank about two miles farther upriver (as the crow flies) lies the village of Mortlake, where delftware and stoneware were produced from the mid-1740s until the mid-1840s.

Perhaps because the English stoneware industry began with Dwight, as recently as the 1930s collectors and curators attributed all the large mugs to Fulham.[6] In truth, however, extensive excavations on the site yielded no evidence of eighteenth-century decorated mug production. As for Mortlake, only one of its two factory sites has been archaeologically explored, with similarly negative results.[7] Consequently, mugs and jugs associated with either Mortlake factory are so by reason of their date-lettered silver mounts, by a few marked examples, by their unique decoration, and by the questionable exercise of eliminating other factories whose documentary histories do not fit.

Although there is convincing evidence that most of the eighteenth-century hunting mugs were made in the London area, another contender has risen and fallen yo-yo-like over the years. Stoneware production in Bristol began around 1700 in tandem with delftware potting, a combination of effort reflective of the Pickleherring, Gravel Lane, Vauxhall, and eventually Mortlake operations. Most important of the Bristol factories was that run by Thomas and Richard Frank at Redcliff Back beginning around 1738. As their delftware business declined in the face of Staffordshire competition in white salt-glazed stoneware, creamware, and pearlware, the factory's focus shifted to utilitarian stoneware. In 1784 the Franks sold their factory to Joseph Ring who formed Ring, Taylor & Carter, listed only as potters in the *Universal British Directory* for 1793. That source listed eight potters working in Bristol, two of whom were identified as "brown potters": Earl Pearce and one Duffets, both of St. Philips Plain. As neither name appears on the standard list of Bristol potters,[8] it is easy to see how difficult it can be to determine who was making what. Another factory, that of William Powell (whose primary interest was in the glass industry), began in 1816 and earned a lasting place in the history of stoneware when in 1835 its potter Anthony Amatt invented and perfected the process known as double glazing. The resulting two-tone greenish yellow industrial wares were to dominate the Bristol stoneware industry through the second half of the nineteenth century.[9]

Known also as "Bristol glaze," the process that enabled stoneware to be made full-glazed in a single firing without the use of salt quickly spread throughout the industry and became the primary method of bottle manufacturing from the 1850s onward. Unfortunately, the process was also applied to the traditional hunting wares, thereby destroying their artistic integrity while making them much easier to clean (see figs. *9a–d*).

Based on the place-names found on eighteenth-century hunting mugs, the vast majority were centered around London, with very few from locations west of Salisbury. Nevertheless, Bristol was the source for several large examples decorated with applied bands of relief ornament at top and bottom, reminiscent of late-seventeenth-century German stoneware. One of them was signed by John Harwell in 1738, then an apprentice in the Redcliff Back factory, and therefore is indisputably a Bristol product. Ceramic historian W. W. Hamilton Foyn has made a case that none but the Harwell-type mugs were made at Bristol, a conclusion that is hard to prove.[10]

Here, then, are the potential sources for eighteenth-century decorated magnum mugs: Vauxhall and Bristol followed by Mortlake.

Now to the surviving mugs themselves: For whom were they made, and why? Most but by no means all made prior to circa 1775 bear inscriptions identifying their owners, thus making them specially ordered. By 1998 Hamilton Foyn had identified 127 dated examples, and it is fair to assume that more have come to light since then. More are undated and are attributable only on stylistic grounds. Thus, for example, we know that around 1750 inscriptions began to be impressed with printer's type rather than with a stylus. Put the dated and undated together, the surviving mugs may number 200, give or take a few. But what does that mean in terms of rarity? Their large size has led some of us to deduce that their pottle (½ gallon) capacity made them special, to be set aside for occasional celebratory use.

However, the cited entries from the 1699 Pickleherring inventory suggest that capacity alone did not make them special. In stock at that moment were 248 ready-for-sale cans of pottle capacity. In addition, listed under "Stone Clay Ware" were "175 pottle stone canns" and 53 pottle-capacity saggers wherein to fire them. There is no indication that any of these large mugs were decorated, but the list unequivocally demonstrates that although they represented a relatively small percentage of the total stock, those of pottle capacity were no rarity.

We know that hunting mugs were also made at gallon capacity, for an undated and nameless example was recently sold to an American collector.[11] On that piece, hunting and other sprigs were applied to the lower and upper wall, leaving the central area blank—important evidence that not all large hunting mugs were made as special orders. While a gallon of ale sounds excessive, such mugs were used to carry it home from the alehouse and doubtless were returnable. Journalist Ned Ward described one such carrier: She "was stepping from the ale-house to her lodgings, with a parcel of pipes in one hand, and a gallon pot of guzzle in the other."[12]

Because so many of the mugs are incised or impressed with buyers' names, the next question is whether naming and decorating developed

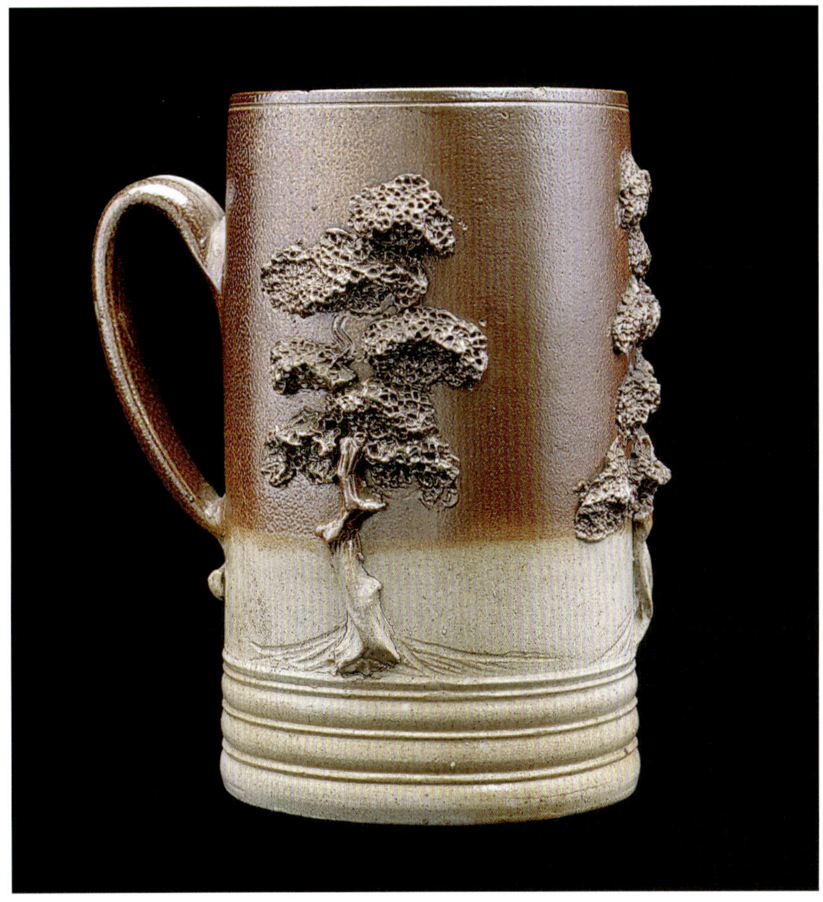

Figure 2 Mug, Vauxhall, London, ca. 1710. Salt-glazed stoneware. H. 7⅝". This quart-capacity mug shows tree trunks sprig applied and foliage created from pricked pads.

simultaneously. Figure 2 is evidence that they did not. Though of only quart capacity, the thinly potted mug is decorated with three trees whose trunks are sprig molded and applied to incised outlines of the overall design elements.[13] The foliage is applied freestyle using pads of clay pushed into shape by finger and thumb and then pricked with a nail-like tool to create the leafy effect. This dramatically decorated mug bears neither name nor date. The latter is suggested, however, by another, similarly ornamented one dated 1713.[14] That mug is of pottle capacity and exhibits the same tree application, but the trunk molds are different. In addition to the three trees, a sprig-molded hare is pursued by running hunters, making this the originator of the fully developed hunt mug.[15] The inscription reads: "John Rose Fill this with strong bear and wee will fuddle our nos^e^ 1713." So who was John Rose? It is hardly likely that he was the individual who ordered the mug to be made. More reasonable is the premise that a club that convened at John Rose's tavern kept it there to be brought out at their meetings.

In the early eighteenth century—mostly in the reign of George I—there flourished a great number of mug clubs, or more correctly *mug-house* clubs. Most were politically Whig or Tory and met regularly in specific taverns. A foreign visitor described one of them: "A harp plays all the while at the lower end of the room; and now and then some one of the company rises and entertains the rest with a song (and by the by some are good masters).

Here is nothing drunk but ale. . . ."[16] With 52 percent of the recorded mugs bearing dates between 1713 and 1730, it seems highly likely that some if not all belonged to mug-club members.[17]

Now back to that 1713 mug with its stippled foliage. A waster rim fragment from one such mug was unearthed at a Vauxhall construction site, thereby leaving little doubt that some were made there.[18] But the sherd went further; incised lettering on it proved to be bits of a long inscription found on intact mugs that read: "On Banstead Downs a hare was found which Led us all a smoking Round." Such mugs ranged in date from 1721 to 1731.[19] Four bear an owner's name, one of whom lived at Ewhurst in Sussex and another at Lewes in the same county,[20] about twenty-seven and thirty miles, respectively, from Banstead Downs. Banstead, near Epsom on the North Downs, was famed for its sporting activities, among them a memorable two-man foot race in 1663 attended by Charles II and the Duke of York, both of whom backed the loser.[21] Each of the Banstead Downs mugs bears the name of its owner or, in two instances, the triple initials of a man and his wife, suggesting that the mugs were not intended solely for use at stag parties.[22]

On occasion Londoners would descend on the countryside to raise a modicum of hell on Banstead Downs to the south or on a site near Stratford to the north named Mobs Hole or Mobs Hall. Ned Ward described the exodus: "Horses, coaches, carts, wagons and tumbrils filled the road, as if the whole town had been going to encamp; all occupied by men, women and children, rich, poor, gentle and simple, having all travelling conveniences suitable to their quality." Ward described how, on arrival, he and his companion "liquored [their] throats with two or three slender-bodied mugs of country guzzle."[23] There is, of course, no certainty that the mugs were of stoneware, but his Mobs Hall description reflects the milieu wherein the Banstead Downs mugs would have been used.

The next group belongs to much the same period, namely 1720–1734, and all are incised with variations on *This is to ye pious memory of Queen Ann. Drink all up and fill it again,* each in company with a sprig-applied bust of the queen. Similar Anne busts are present on the Banstead Downs mugs. Tying the groups more firmly together is the fact that the hand-stippled trees occur on both between 1717 and 1732. One would like this to be a straight-line progression, but it is not. Entirely sprig-applied and topiaried trees occur as early as 1719.[24] This is not surprising when one remembers that the 1713 stippled foliage trees have sprig-applied trunks. However, the massive Queen Anne example in the Noël Hume Collection dated 1722 has neither the Banstead nor the "pious memory" inscription; it does possess two varieties of sprig-applied trees: topiaried and oak (fig. 1*a*; table V.2, .3). If all these early mugs are products of the same Vauxhall factory why, we might ask, were they decorated with trees created by two entirely different processes? Unfortunately, documentation regarding factory ownership after 1712 is sparse and provides no clue to any change in production policy that might have a bearing on decorating techniques.

The predominance of Queen Anne portraits and the attendant invitations to drink to her memory can be read as a subtle nod to the old Stuart line and an unspoken rejection of the new German monarch. That likelihood is further endorsed by the occasional inclusion of the head of Charles II amid the foliage of some of the trees, a reminder of his 1651 escape from his Parliamentarian pursuers by hiding in an oak tree at Boscobel after the disastrous Battle of Worcester.[25] The symbolism would reappear on a mug dated 1744 whose sprigs include panels bearing the Royal Arms, the oak tree, and a kilted figure of Charles Stuart, the "King Over the Water." The following year would bring the Jacobite rebellion, the flight of the "Bonny Prince" to Ireland, and the dashing of any returning Stuart hopes.

By 1730 trees had become stylized, most of them looking more like palms than any English tree and rooted behind a spray of broad-leafed ground cover (table V.5, .7, .8). Although tiered topiary is found as late as 1730, a mug dated 1731 carries a clipping variation whose upper foliage is shaped like an open parasol (fig. *1b*; table V.4). Belonging to the same time span (ca. 1720–1731) are single, stemless flowers, most of them with only pistils and petals, but at least two (from 1729 and 1731) having an additional ring of anthers (table I.2). On the 1731 example, the tool made to mold the flowers was used to help secure the base of the handle (table I.5). Unfortunately, no one has yet made a wide-ranging study of early handle terminals, but when they to do, it is possible that more mugs can be attributed to this workman.[26]

Individual flowerlike devices continued to be used into the 1750s, but by then they had been reduced to scarcely recognizable blobs, often accompanied by toothed circles stamped into the wall itself (table I.3, .4). Continuing, too, were the stylized palm trees that flanked a central plaque, be it Queen Anne or some other device. So what were these plaques, and what were they saying about the mugs' purchasers?

Many small mugs, usually of pint capacity, have survived by virtue of their "keep me factor" and are decorated with panels containing tavern signs such as George and Dragon, Crossed Keys, Rose and Crown, Crown and Anchor, Bull, and Ship—invaluable designations of ownership when "ale to go" meant that bottles and mugs left the tavern premises. The practice had begun at Fulham in the Dwight era, and many examples have been found on bottles and gorges recovered from excavations on the site.[27] Beginning about 1720 and extending into the 1780s, these sprigged plaques were shaped like arched firebacks, many variations of which were probably made at Fulham.[28]

A few, indeed *very* few, among the large mugs are decorated with tavern signboards, one of them being in the Colonial Williamsburg Collection. Dated 1740, its fireback panel is that of a George and Dragon inn or tavern. Equally few in number are those bearing the badges of London livery companies such as the Watermen's and Blacksmiths'.[29] These, too, are likely to relate to taverns having those names rather than to individual members of the companies.

The most common of all the central panels are frequently lumped together as a "Punch Party," but in fact they fall into three distinct groups.

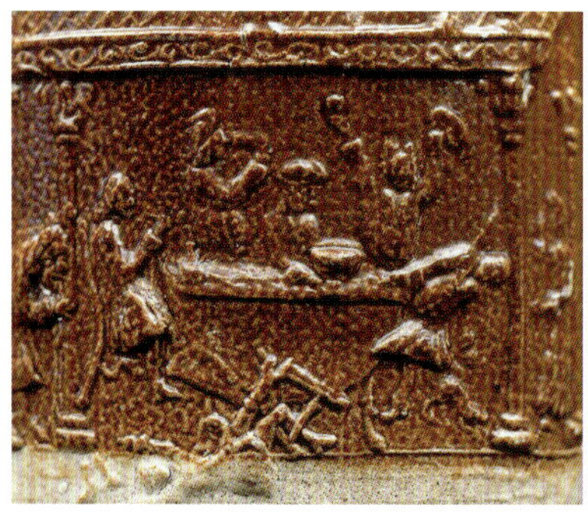

a

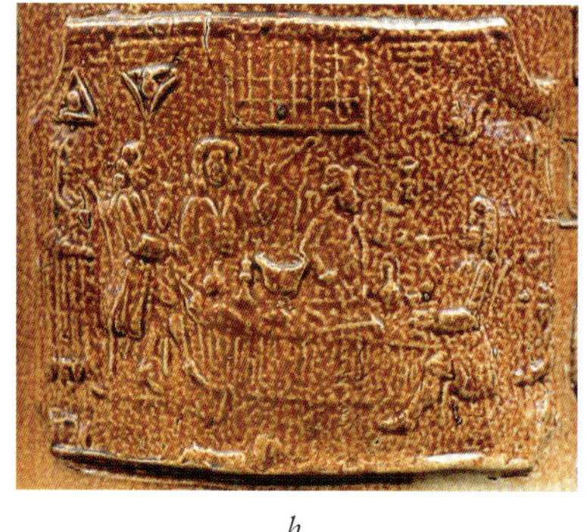

b

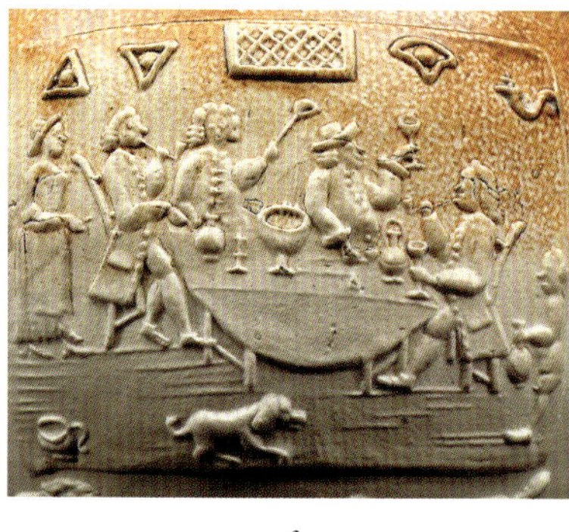

c

Figure 3 Detail of Punch Party panels. (*a*) Punch Party A, Vauxhall, 1731. (*b*) Punch Party B1, Bristol, ca. 1760. (*c*) Punch Party B2, Mortlake, ca. 1800. Note the cloth-covered table and square-paned window in B1, and the bare gate-legged table and lattice-paned window in B2.

Some authorities have classified them as variations on *A Midnight Modern Conversation,* William Hogarth's famous painting of circa 1731, widely circulated as an engraving.[30] Others who have defined them as a "Punch Party" distinguish between those with and without a canopy. For the purposes of this inquiry I am terming the canopied group "Punch Party A" and the panel with a rear-wall window "Punch Party B," with subdivision "B1" for those with a square-paned window and subdivision "B2" for those with diamond latticed windows (figs. 3*a–c*). Punch Party A equates with Vauxhall, B1 with Bristol, and B2 with Mortlake.

There can be no denying that in each case the central scene bears a resemblance to Hogarth's painting—until we realize that the illustrated example (fig. 3*a*) is dated 1731, two years before the engraving was first published. Hamilton Foyn's catalog lists them even earlier, the first dated 1728 (the latest 1761). In determining what connection the mug panels might have with Hogarth's works, we need to look in detail at his *A Midnight Modern Conversation* (fig. 4*a*).[31]

Hogarth's painting (and the engraving derived from it) satirized the excesses of the educated classes, represented by a lawyer, cleric, justice of the peace, soldier, politician, and others. Biographer John Ireland noted that it was "difficult to identify men whom the painter did not chuse (sic) to point out at the time; and near sixty years having elapsed, it becomes impossible."[32] Both painting and engraving depict eleven men around a circular, cloth-covered table. From left to right in the engraving, starting at

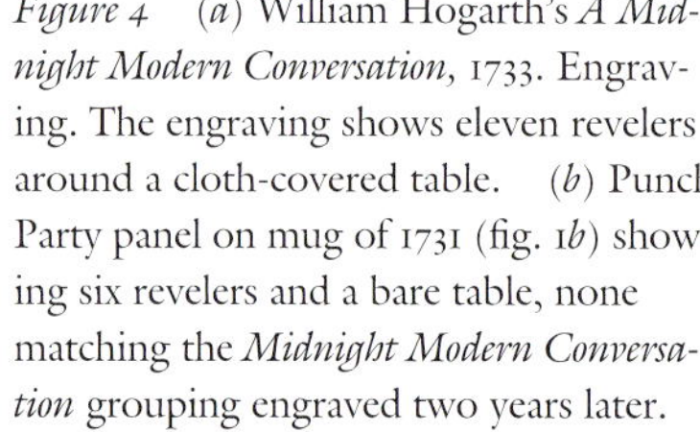

Figure 4 (*a*) William Hogarth's *A Midnight Modern Conversation,* 1733. Engraving. The engraving shows eleven revelers around a cloth-covered table. (*b*) Punch Party panel on mug of 1731 (fig. 1*b*) showing six revelers and a bare table, none matching the *Midnight Modern Conversation* grouping engraved two years later.

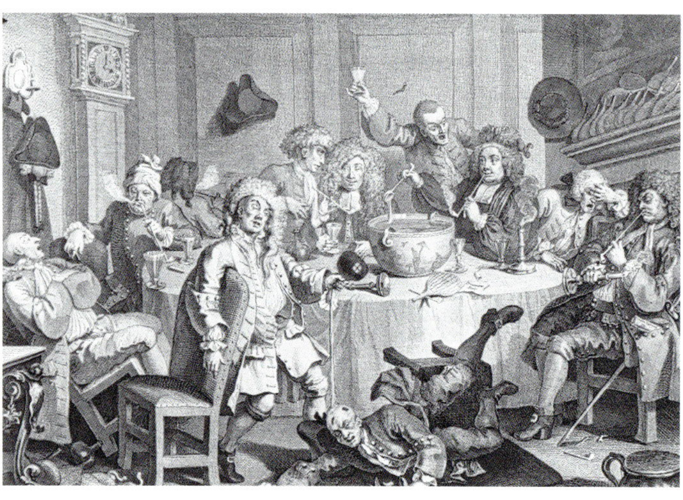

a

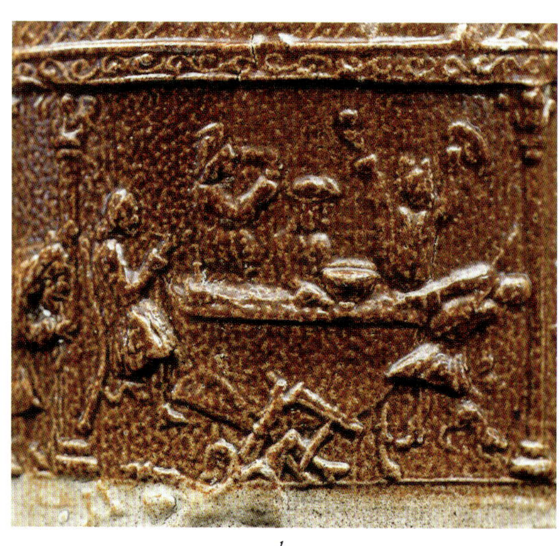

b

the back, one man leans back in his chair asleep, two more sit smoking, a fourth whispers in the ear of the fifth who wears a full wig, the next raises his glass to toast the cleric to his left who holds a pipe in his left hand while pouring punch back into the bowl from a ladle; the next has a headache and beyond him at right yet another inebriate tries to light his pipe from a candle. On the floor in front, a soldier with a shaved head and scarred scalp falls off his overturned chair and has liquor poured onto his head by the last man, whom Ireland identified as an apothecary. There is a single sconce on the left wall; two tricorn hats hang on pegs as does the cleric's round-brimmed one. A lidded chamber pot occupies the right foreground. On the table lie broken clay pipes, a wine bottle, four wineglasses in two styles, a French wicker-cased flask, two non-matching candlesticks, and the punch bowl. With all that in mind, how closely do either of the Punch Parties equate with Hogarth's alcoholic scene?

Taking the canopied and fallen chair version first (Punch Party A), the scene is reduced from eleven to six men (fig. 4*b*). The gate-legged table is uncovered and the front leaf is down. The contented smoker on the right is now on the left, next to him a drinker stands to the right holding a mug to his lips, and next to him, wearing his hat and wig, another sits and stares across the table. To his left another reveler waves his glass in one hand and what appears to be his hat in the other. To the right of the table a drunk is throwing up. Below him a dog appears to be enjoying the product. The foreground is occupied by the fallen man whose right leg is entangled in the chair's stretchers. As figure 4*b* demonstrates, only the fallen figure bears much resemblance to the revelers in Hogarth's famous engraving.

Having no relationship to *A Midnight Modern Conversation* is the bed-like canopy mounted on four possibly feather-capped columns. The floor in the foreground appears to be tiled, and to give the whole a sense of perspective, both right and left edges of the panel angle out. Between the two left columns a humpbacked man appears to be listening, while between the right columns stands a female servant.

There are at least two versions of the painting, the best of them in the Paul Mellon Collection.[33] A wide-angle view of the scene (and reversed in the engraving), has three tricorn hats on the walls and a sleeping dog in the left foreground. During restoration it became clear that Hogarth had made several changes to the picture, changes that included the removal of a door in which a servant had been standing. Was she, perhaps, the servant to the right of Punch Party A, or could she have been the woman I call the ballad singer to the left in Punch Party B1 and B2?

This very different panel is first recorded on a B1 mug dated 1754 in the Colonial Williamsburg Collection.[34] The scene comprises the ballad singer standing at left and four men seated around a cloth-covered table: the first is smoking, the second pours punch back into the bowl from a great height, the third wears a countryman's hat and holds up a wineglass, and the fourth sits with a pipe in his right hand and a glass in his left. On the table are a wine bottle, a wicker-cased and loop-handled bottle, a pedestaled punch bowl, and a clay pipe. At the extreme right a drawer enters through a doorway. Above the group two tricorn hats hang on pegs, there is a large, square-paned window, and at right a single sconce hangs on the wall. In the left foreground is a chamber pot and, in the center, a couchant dog (fig. 3*b*).

Far more sharply delineated is Punch Party B2 on a jug made at Mortlake circa 1795–1800 (fig. 3*c*; see fig. 7*c*). The overall content of this rectangular scene is the same as that of Punch Party B1 but with several significant exceptions: the window is diamond-paned, the table has no cloth and its gate-legged panel is in the down position,[35] and three rather than two hats hang on the wall.

How well, then, do these Punch Party A and B elements equate with Hogarth's *Midnight Modern* painting?

The dog parallels the sleeping animal in the *Midnight Modern* painting, as do the three hats. The single sconce is in the engraving. The pouring action into the bowl is in the engraving, albeit from a more conservative height (fig. 4*a*), but it is not in the painting. The chamber pot is in the engraving but not in the painting. The ballad singer is in neither, but she is in the Rose Tavern scene from *A Rake's Progress*. In Punch Party A the fallen man has lost his wig, but in neither the painting nor the engraving does he have one. In Plate Six of *A Rake's Progress,* however, Tom Rakewell kneels by his overturned chair and his wig lies beside it. The hat-waving man stands behind the table in neither painting nor engraving and is present only in Punch Party A.

All this interwoven evidence points to two conclusions: Punch Party A and B are derived from a single idea, and the likely source is the burin of William Hogarth, circa 1728/1729. To know whether that conclusion is reasonable, it is necessary to know what Hogarth was doing in the late 1720s.

The son of a schoolteacher, William Hogarth was first apprenticed to an engraver of copperplates. When he found that there was insufficient work in that trade, in 1712 he became an apprentice to silversmith Ellis Gamble, whose shop was in Cranbourn Alley in Leicester Fields (now Leicester Square). While still in Gamble's employ, Hogarth and several friends made a trip to Highgate and visited one of its taverns. While there, an argument between some of the beer-drinking customers led to a fight in which a small man threw a pewter pot at a larger man and "struck him in the forehead—and he sank to the floor." The man was not killed but suffered a severe gash in his forehead. According to biographer John Ireland, "his woe-begone figure . . . and the half-suppressed laugh of his surrounding friends, presented a scene too ridiculous to be resisted." Hogarth "seized his pencil, drew his first group of portraits from the life, and gave, with a strong resemblance of each, such a grotesque variety of character as evades all description. When we consider this little sketch was his coup d'essai," Ireland added, "the loss of it is much to be regretted."[36]

Indeed it is! However, it calls for no great leap of imagination to see the *Midnight Modern*'s fallen man with the scars or patches on his scalp as the offspring of the sketch made on that evening in Highgate.

Hogarth left Gamble after four years and subsequently became a pupil of his future father-in-law, Sir James Thornhill. By 1727 the still young man was eking out a living as an engraver for book illustrations, theater tickets, and any other work he could garner. Ireland wrote of "Various temporary satires of the local follies and vices of the day, which he engraved about this time . . . but have not in general much merit."[37] In short, the late 1720s found Hogarth still in search of fame and fortune, and in no position to turn down, say, an invitation to sketch a picture to slap on the sides of stoneware beer mugs. Indeed, he may have remembered that earlier grouping when circa 1731 he painted *A Club of Gentlemen* (Mellon Collection), showing them seated around a circular table, with an overturned chair in the foreground, a dog at right, and a tricorn hat hanging on the wall.[38]

If, on the basis of the surviving examples, we accept that the 1728 Punch Party A is the earlier of the two scenes, it follows that the more reserved group in B1 and B2 may reflect a changing attitude toward debauchery in the mid-century's new rococo age. That is, of course, a dangerous assumption. Earlier Punch Party B examples may yet turn up, and many more may have failed to survive.

On rare occasions Punch Party A mugs would include subsidiary panels. Thus, a 1732 example in the Colonial Williamsburg Collection exhibits rectangular plaques showing a marksman shooting at a bird while hunters on foot pursue a stag. More common, however, are individually sprigged buildings that range from a church (1722) to a manor house (?) (1729), a mill (1737), a group of buildings behind a pig, a cow, and a dog (1737), a two-story cottage (ca. 1755), and a house with a central chimney (1765). A much more prolonged comparative study of these secondary elements is needed, but with the mugs widely scattered in museums and collections in Britain and America, the task is daunting.

Although only loosely related to the Hogarthian punch parties, there is a third version which can be called "Punch Party C." It occurs through the 1760s and fits within an arched or fireback-shaped frame in the manner of previously cited tavern signboards. Six men sit around a small circular table, two of them smoking and one holding up a glass. Behind them is a closed door with an elaborate architrave, and beside it hangs a single tricorn hat. The floor is boarded and to the left a chamber pot appears to be resting on a cushion; there is no dog. Below the panel pairs of hounds pursue a stag in a counterclockwise direction. Palm trees on a 1761 example in the Northampton Museum may be from the same mold as those on the Sarum mug attributed to Bristol (fig. 1*d*). The basal cordoning is comparable to others having a likely Bristol source (fig. 5).[39]

I have deliberately left to last the element that gives "Hunt Mugs" their name, running and galloping as it does across two centuries of potting. Mavis Watney's recognition that sprig-applied huntsmen, hounds, and quarry chased clockwise or counterclockwise has become the basis for classification. An unscientific check of forty examples listed fifteen clockwise (1720–1744) and twenty-five counterclockwise (1729–1764), all of them London products.[40] In their seminal book *English Brown Stoneware 1670–1900,* Messrs. Oswald, Hildyard, and Hughes followed Mrs. Watney

Figure 5 Tankard, England, 1761. Salt-glazed stoneware. H. 10". (Courtesy, Northampton Museum and Art Gallery, No. D.1920-21-1-109.) Impressed "Thomas Triplett / 1761" and decorated with a "fireback" panel framing Punch Party C. The flanking palm trees and the crude trimming of the hound sprigs point to this mug being of Bristol origin, although the Northampton Museum attributes it to Staffordshire or London.

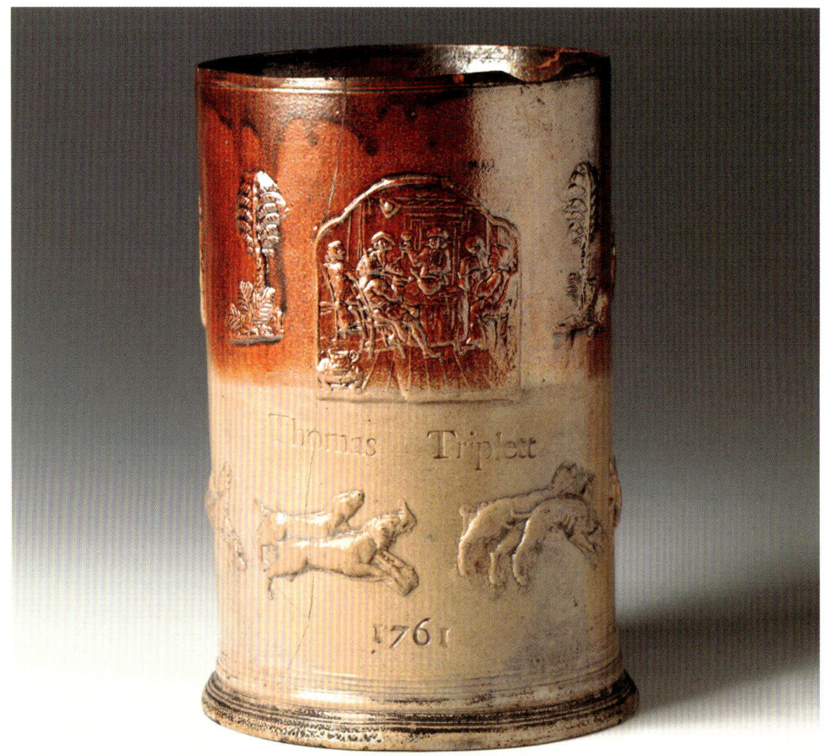

in deducing that the clockwise and counterclockwise hunts came from two, if not three, separate factories, one of them undoubtedly Vauxhall, another Vauxhall/Lambeth related, and Fulham the wild-card third.

What significance can be read into the idea of the hunt? Why hunting and not, say, horse racing or warfare? Hunting in its various forms was a sport that cut across social lines, and, more important, its elements stretched out in a continuous flow around the walls of large mugs. Is there significance in the nature of the quarry, be it rabbit, hare, stag, or fox? As previously noted, the first example, that of 1713, depicts a hare or rabbit pursued by men on foot.

The sport was described in 1725 as "a noble Game and Recreation, not only commendable for Princes and great Men, but Gentlemen and others too, there being nothing that does more recreate the Mind, strengthen the Limbs, whet the Stomach, and clear up the Spirits, so that it has merited the esteem of all Ages and nations, how barbarous soever they might otherwise have been."[41] However, the generous consumption of ale suggested by these massive mugs paints a very different picture from that of the more sedate fox hunting of the Victorian era, where insobriety among sportsmen was considered ungentlemanly. Wrote one hunting enthusiast: "There is one circumstance which might not be lost sight of. The intemperance which formerly was so frequently associated with this amusement, and gave a handle to its opponents to detract from its merits, no longer exists."[42]

As we study each sprig (and perhaps try to read into them more than is there), it is reasonable to ask whether there is anything to be deduced from these depictions of perambulatory or mounted hunting.

My 1722 (Queen Anne) mug shows a single huntsman armed with nothing more than a horn and a long staff to command and control a pack of eleven hounds; nine in full cry, one seeking the scent, and the last baying (fig. *1a*; see table VIII.1). Hunting on foot was known as "hunting under the pole," the hounds being trained to respond to gestures with the staff. The huntsman had but to "hold up or throw before [the hounds] the hunting Pole, they will stop in an instant, and hunt in full cry after you at your own Pace."[43] It is reasonable to conclude that this is the hunting technique depicted on the 1722 mug. One would be tempted, too, to suggest that this was the kind of hunting pursued on Banstead Downs—were it not for the fact that mugs so inscribed include a mounted hunter.

The usual procession, be it to right or to left, comprised a single mounted huntsman, a pack of hounds, and the quarry, which, as I have noted, could be a stag, a fox, a long-eared hare, or occasionally a rabbit. This last was not an animal that lent itself to the chase, for rabbits, unlike hares, are prone to escape into burrows.[44] Nevertheless, there were occasions when rabbits and mugs were considered in the same breath. A clockwise mug dated 1724 in the Stoke-on-Trent Museum is inscribed "Drink all out and Doe not Doubt but you shall see my Con^e^y / But if you doe you may be sure that it will cost you mony." Attached to the bottom of the interior is a model rabbit.[45] The same idea is manifest on a 1727 mug in the Victoria and Albert Museum, but this time the surprise animal is a fox while the mug belongs to the counterclockwise group. One can perhaps be forgiven for wondering whether there really is a factory difference between the two.

The hounds, like other small sprigs, deserve more careful consideration than they have hitherto enjoyed. My clockwise hunt (1722) has three groups of three hounds—all with curly tails—plus one scent seeker and another giving voice (table X.11). However, my counterclockwise mug of 1737 has its short, upturned-tailed hounds (table X.13) taken from similar molds to that of 1731 (table X.12), though the hunter and the stag were not. The 1731 dogs are dappled with manganese and the horse is similarly colored, but that is not true of the later mug. Adding to the confusion, the 1731 mug has a flaring base, which the 1737 mug does not (figs. *1a, c*).[46] Consequently, the guideline put forward by Oswald that "from the 1740s the foot-rims tended to flare" should be accepted with caution.[47]

The dogs, huntsman, and rosettes with anthers occur on a 1729 mug incised with the name "E^dw^ Smith," suggesting that the 1729 and 1731 mugs were sprigged on the same bench. However, the former has a more or less straight base above which are two pairs of cordons, whereas the latter has a flaring base and only one pair of cordons, implying that although from the same factory they were shaped by different throwers using different base-shaping templates. Yet another mug with the same huntsman as those of 1729 and 1731, this one inscribed "Jno Yeates 1729," has the same cordoning and profile as that of the former, but its flowers are from the simpler pistils-and-petals mold.[48]

All these inconsistencies and overlapping features point to a single, busy factory where pottle-capacity mugs were in regular production (as they had been in 1699 at the Pickleherring factory), and that from time to time special orders were undertaken for which an assortment of molds were extracted from their storage boxes. Ceramic authority Jonathan Horne has stated that "These massive pots were rarely used, hence their survival," adding that "they were usually made as presentation pieces or to advertise a public house."[49] In an earlier catalog, however, he stated that "very large half gallon tankards became fashionable being heavily potted with thick strap handles and intended for robust use."[50] Both statements are almost certainly true, though the survival factor may be due more to the "keep me factor" of the mugs than to their lack of use.

Not all the decorated mugs were made for special "personalized" orders, as is evidenced by the 1731 (Punch Party A) example that has no name to accompany the date (fig. 3*a*). The same is true of a 1729 tankard (Punch Party A) as well as of several of the Queen Anne and Banstead Downs mugs—though these may be read as having a collective and defined purpose. There are, of course, some that are named but undated and therefore have been of less interest to collectors. Having a lower "keep me factor" level, they were less likely to be saved. Nevertheless, these undated examples might have something to contribute—providing someone recognizes the contribution for what it is. Figure 1*d* is one of these. Impressed with printer's type, its inscription reads "W^M; Newman / Sarum," Sarum being the medieval name for Salisbury, which lies closer to Bristol than to London. It may or may not be coincidental that the first recorded stoneware pottery in Bristol was set up by "John Knight of New Sarum in the County of Wilts., Esq.," in partnership with potter Mary Orchard, a stoneware business that continued under successive ownerships until 1754.[51]

Decorated with the B1 Punch Party, the Newman mug differs from the London series in all other respects. One's immediate impression is of disorderly busyness. Each of its eight counterclockwise dogs is single sprigged and, although in sharp relief, all are backed by irregular clay pads and all are smaller than those from London (table X.14). The pack is followed by a well-dressed horseman, holding a whip, and two walking beaters, each carrying a staff and a hunting horn (table VIII.3, .4). The scene includes three varieties of tree: two are versions of the palm tree; the third, with armlike branches halfway up the trunk, is topped by a globular crown of foliage (table V.6, .8). Castings from this mold were very fragile, the resulting fragments being applied at random. Two copies of a two-story cottage with a chimney at one end flank the central panel (table I.12). Setting this mug apart from the London series is the heavy double-cordon above a rounded base. Its handle is well formed, its lower terminal wiped and then twice impressed, seemingly by a left-handed potter. How can we know that?

The fingernail impressions are to the right of each indentation, indicating that the pressure came from the left (table I.7). This detail might be dismissed as an insignificant quirk were it not that there is another mug with the same impressions formerly in the Colonial Williamsburg collection. Type-impressed "Robt; Paten / Alesbury / 1762," it has the same incuse-

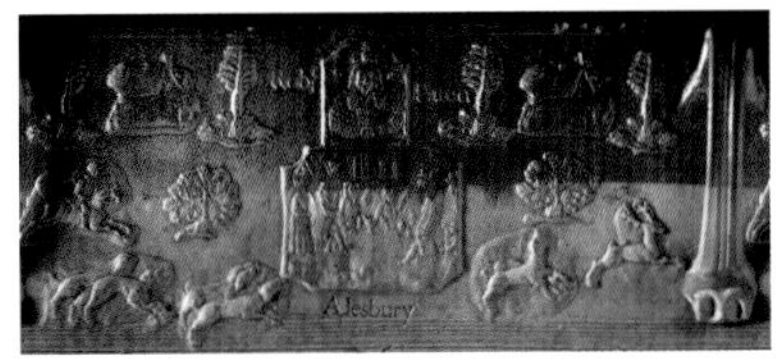

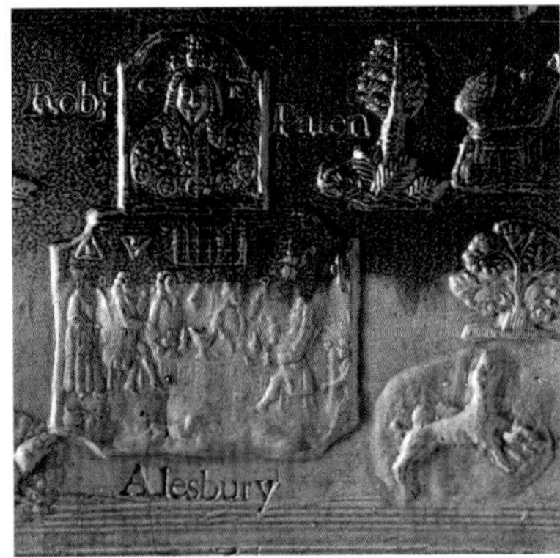

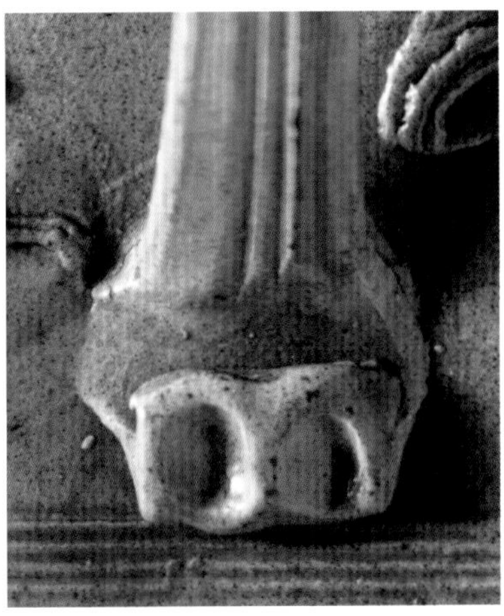

Figure 6 Mug, Bristol, England, 1762. Salt-glazed stoneware. H. 8¼". (Courtesy, Colonial Williamsburg Foundation.) The sprigs of this pottle-capacity mug feature Punch Party B1 and stag-hunting elements elevated on crude pads. A fireback panel frames a portrait of Charles I. Type-impressed ownership reads "Rob; Paten / Alesbury / 1762." The encircling photograph shows the handle terminal to have been twice pressed from the left. The whereabouts of this important mug are unknown, as it was deaccessioned by Colonial Williamsburg. Its equally important and left-hand parallel, fig. 1d (with detail in table I.7), was also deaccessioned, in 1977.

cornered B1 Punch Party panel (fig. 6). Furthermore, in abbreviating Robert a semicolon rather than a period is used in both instances. In addition, one of the tree molds is common to both mugs, as is the fact that the hounds are applied on raised, irregularly shaped clay pads. All in all, there is reason to believe that both mugs were made by the same person at about the same time. However, there are significant differences. The Newman mug has single hounds chasing a hare (or rabbit) (table X.10), whereas Paten's has pairs pursuing a stag. The basal cordoning is different, as is the huntsman and the sprigged houses. It seems likely that the thrower who applied the handles was not the craftsman who applied the sprigs and that the latter's selection of molds depended on whatever was closest at hand.

If we accept that the Newman mug was a Bristol product (as I think we can), where does that place the Alesbury mug?[52] There being no village of that name, it follows that the name is a misspelling of Aylesbury, which lies 38 miles northwest of London; Salisbury lies 83 miles southwest of it. Bristol is located 117 miles from London, which puts Salisbury much nearer to it than to London, but the reverse is true of the Alesbury mug. The obvious (but not necessarily correct) conclusion is that Robert Paten was not too far distant a customer to order a Bristol mug.[53]

Another mug with similar hounds and the weak-trunked trees of the Newman example (table V.6) is inscribed "J H /1765." The initials are believed to be those of Bristol potter John Harwell, whose name is incised into the bottom of another, much earlier mug dated 1738.[54] The weak-trunked tree also occurs on a mug impressed "C. Scott," attributed to circa 1760–1770, and on yet another, impressed "John Barnwell," which is dated 1777.[55] No wasters from these Bristol-style mugs have been excavated in the city, so the Bristol connection—until more evidence is forthcoming—begins in 1738 with John Harwell and ends in the 1770s.

In London, although the Vauxhall Pottery continued under successive ownerships until about 1865, its hunting-mug story ceased with the last of the dated series in 1775.[56] There is, however, no reason to conclude that hunting mugs had run their course. In the last years of the eighteenth century, large numbers began to be made at Mortlake, many of them of very high quality.

The Mortlake potteries brought entirely new designs and more sophisticated shapes to the hunting jug genre and may have begun to do so in the mid-1780s. Although surviving examples are relatively plentiful and without parallels, it is the plural, "potteries," that creates attributional problems. Before discussing the wares, therefore, it may be helpful to review what we know about Mortlake as a rival to Lambeth and Vauxhall in the manufacture of brown stoneware mugs and jugs.

Although considered too small and inconsequential to be listed in a 1795 national gazetteer, Mortlake was already known by that name when the *Doomsday Book* was compiled in 1086. It became famous in the 1620s as the home of emigrant Flemish weavers whose Mortlake tapestries were much prized. The looms continued to operate until 1703, when the last of the Mortlake weavers moved to London. To the south of the Thames-side village several fine eighteenth-century mansions were constructed, while in the village itself the Church of St. Ann was built in 1714 (and twice enlarged, in 1766 and 1810). A history of London published in 1806 called Mortlake "a very pleasant village, situated on the banks of the Thames about seven miles from London." As for its activities, nothing was said about the potteries, only that it was known for the "quantity of asparagus and lavender cultivated" in the parish.[57] Perhaps potting was too humble and odoriferous an activity to tarnish the description of a very pleasant village.

The first potter known to have settled in Mortlake was William Sanders, who began making delftware in 1745.[58] In 1757 "Mr Sander's pot house was burnt down, and a maidservant perished in the flames."[59] Working at the Sanders factory from 1759 to at least 1802 was its eventual manager, Benjamin Kishere. His son, Joseph, served his apprenticeship there and may have remained an employee until 1795, when he married Ann Griffin, the daughter of a relatively wealthy Westminster businessman.[60] The wedding took place on April 25 in the upscale city church of St. Martin-in-the-Fields. That may not seem to have much to do with hunting mugs, but it does suggest a relationship between one potter and another.

William Sanders died in 1784 and the factory was taken over by his son John, who took into partnership a Mr. Vernon. They sold the business to one Thomas Norris in 1794, who in turn sold it to Pressick Dodd in 1802. Two years later Dodd sold it to the owner of the Vauxhall factory, William Wagstaff. Vauxhall was making both delftware and stoneware, but with delftware rapidly declining in popularity, Wagstaff transferred its production to the old Sanders factory at Mortlake.[61] It is reasonable to deduce, therefore, that in doing so he placed little importance on Sanders's stoneware facilities. In 1795, when Wagstaff was one of ten brown stoneware producers who agreed to uniform pricing that included half-gallon (pottle) gorges at eight shillings a dozen, his output almost certainly came from Vauxhall and not from Mortlake.[62] The reference to large gorges can be presumed to relate to the straight and reeded-necked jugs akin to my figures *7a–e*. Nevertheless, Thomas Norris of Mortlake's old Sanders factory was

Figure 7 Mugs and jugs, Mortlake brown, 1792 to 1818. Salt-glazed stoneware. (*a*) Mug featuring "Two Boors Drinking" panel (table XI.1), male and female hunters pursuing a stag, trees, and classical figures, the silver rim dated 1792. H. 8 7/16". (*b*) Jug with sprigs featuring Punch Party D (table XI.2), an early Toby figure (table II.2), trees, and male hunters pursuing a stag. The silver rim carries the date letter for 1799 and the lid is engraved "E.P. 1801, R.W. 1833" and "E.J.W. 1880." H. 8 7/8". (*c*) Jug with Punch Party B2 panel, trees and classical figures (as *7a*). Silver-plated rim, ca. 1800. H. 9 3/8". (*d*) Jug with Punch Party B2 panel flanked by classical muses in ovals, trees, and male and female hunters in pursuit of a stag (tables VII.7, 8, VIII.9). Silver-plated rim, ca. 1805. H. 8 7/8". (*e*) Jug with Punch Party B2, classical figures (as *7c*), trees, windmill, and male huntsmen pursuing a hare. The silver rim bears the date letter for 1818. H. 8 3/8".

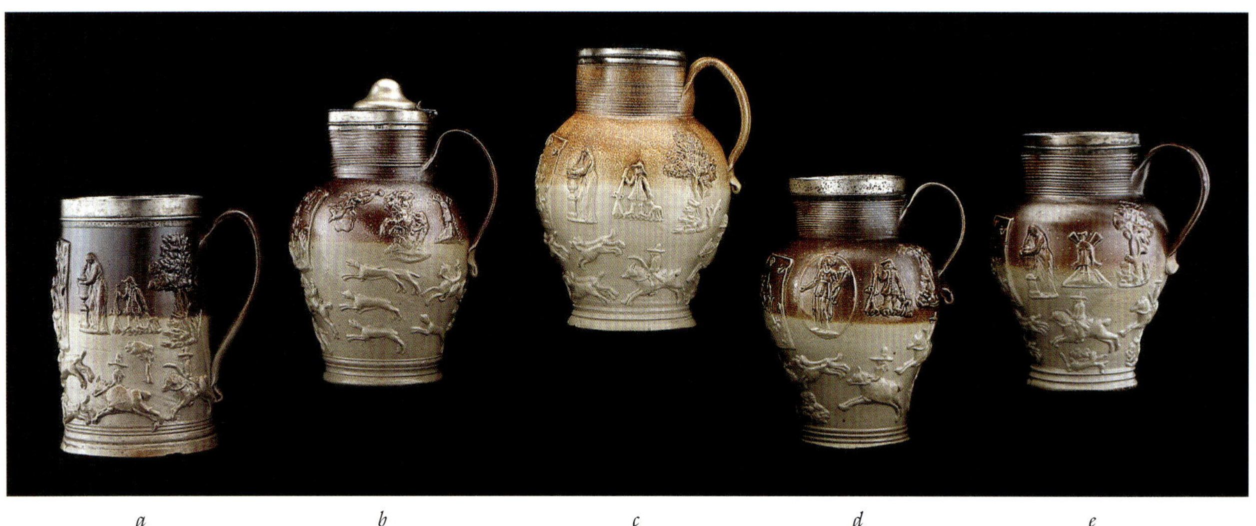

a *b* *c* *d* *e*

another of the ten 1795 signers to the list, which also included quart, pint, half pint, and quarter pint mugs. Wagstaff died in 1808, leaving the Sanders and Vauxhall factories to his nephew John Wisker who, in 1804, like Joseph Kishere before him, had been married at St. Martin-in-the-Fields.

On a surviving trade card printed for Joseph Kishere (alas, undated) he described himself as a "Brown Stone Manufacturer" in Mortlake and "Late Apprentice to Messrs Sanders and Vernon, Potters."[63] With their factory passing through several hands between 1794 and 1808, it seems unlikely that Joseph would have continued to publish the connection long after the 1794 sale—before which date he had completed his apprenticeship. Joseph Kishere was born in 1768, and given that most apprenticeships began around the age of eight and lasted for seven years, he could have been a journeyman for Sanders by 1783, though clearly he was not. But even if he had begun on that date, he would have completed his term by 1790. Joseph's card says that he served his apprenticeship during the partnership of Sanders and Vernon, which did not begin until 1784. With his father on the Wagstaff payroll until his death in 1802, it is possible that Joseph entered the craft at a relatively late age.[64] Nevertheless, it is highly likely that he was prompted to set up on his own by the sale of 1794 and the new owner's decision to focus production emphasis on delftware. There is, however, artifactual evidence that Joseph Kishere was producing his characteristic "Mortlake" wares at least two years earlier.

Oswald, Hildyard, and Hughes have written that "Delftware, and probably stoneware, continued to be made under Wisker from 1809 until the closure of the pottery in 1823."[65] However, no ceramic historian has yet identified any surviving Mortlake stonewares as being the products of either Vernon or Wisker—nor, for that matter, have any pre-1800 hunting mugs or jugs been found with Joseph Kishere's mark. Consequently, the entire class is grouped as "probably Kishere."

The Museum of London Archaeology Service's excavations on two properties belonging to the Sanders-Vernon-Wagstaff era on the north side of High Street yielded no hunting ware sherds or indeed anything resembling the many known Kishere products of the 1790s to 1840s. In light of that negative evidence it seems reasonable to deduce that Joseph Kishere's mug and jug series began at his own factory on the south side of High Street, perhaps by 1792, the date letter on the silver mount of the earliest example yet recorded (fig. 7*a*).[66]

The mug's chase sequence is characterized by hunters with very tall and wide-brimmed hats. Their hounds run clockwise in pursuit of a stag, the lead horseman waving something that resembles a limp cucumber but which is almost certainly his whip (table VIII.7). He is followed by his wife, who rides sidesaddle, a stance that accurately portrays the position of her right foot.[67] I have to confess that it was this sidesaddle image that first aroused my interest in Mortlake's hunting mugs and jugs. While excavating a well in Williamsburg, Virginia, I found the remains of such a saddle in a context of circa 1725. When my late wife published it, she drew on the knowledge of Colonial Williamsburg's master saddler, Phillip Hawk, who wrote as follows: "The two pommel side saddle was the rule until about 1830, when the addition of a third pommel enabled ladies to increase the speed of their mounts . . . and enabled women to take a more active part in sports such as fox hunting."[68] If women did not hunt to hounds until the early nineteenth century, what were these women doing in hot pursuit in the 1790s? It is true that most contemporary paintings of a riding female show her sitting sedately while a groom holds the reins, but a painting of 1755 by Judith Lewis suggests otherwise. There is, however, no doubting that the Mortlake huntress was keeping up with the pack. Perhaps, therefore, the mug is adding hitherto unnoticed information to the history of distaff equestrian hunting. It may even be significant that Joseph Kishere owned a horse and frequented racetracks, perhaps rendering him more equestrian-savvy than most potters of his era.[69]

Mortlake potters made frequent use of Punch Party B2 and did so with a level of clarity rarely, if ever, encountered among the earlier London and Bristol versions (fig. 3*c*). Indeed, it was the sight of the punch being poured back into the bowl (albeit from an alarming height) that led me to connect it to the engraved version of Hogarth's *A Midnight Modern Conversation* and eventually to the belief that it was his design for the pot panel that inspired the painting and not the other way round.

The 1792 mug possesses, in addition to the male and female hunters, a pair of trees (a four-barred gate abutting the trunk of one of them) (table V.10, .11), a gamekeeper with his musket and dog, and a pair of classical figures reminiscent of Wedgwood jasper plaques (table VII.1, .4), one holding a wreath and the other leaning on a garden urn.[70] The central panel, however, is not of Punch Party B2 but rather a high-relief composition known as "two boors drinking" (table XI.1). Backed by a brick wall, two sots relax under a tree. One sits asleep on an overturned tub, his arms resting on a table made from a cut-down barrel. At right the second man sits on a stool (?) with a mug to his lips. Beside him is a jug whose body ornament suggests a Rhenish origin.[71] Both the boors panel and Punch Party B2 appear together on a pale loving cup attributed to "Mortlake (probably Kishere), about 1800"—though how much time separates the cup and its sprigs from those of 1792 remains an open question.[72]

The boors sprig evidently had its genesis in Dutch genre art from a painter working in the style of Adriaen Brouwer, but its first English ceramic incarnation is on a creamware plaque attributed to Ralph Wood circa 1780.[73] By 1790 the same theme was to be found on pearlware jugs decorated in Pratt colors. As I shall demonstrate, several more familiar brown stoneware sprig designs were copied from transfer prints and molds created in Staffordshire for use on creamware and pearlware. Indeed, as I have noted, familiarity with those wares and the publications associated with them is an essential step in understanding the stonewares and their sprigs.

My next example (fig. 7*b*) adds a new and different Punch Party, hereafter identified as "Punch Party D" (table XI.2). The grouping comprises five men sitting, smoking, and drinking around a circular table whereon lies a pipe and a punch bowl. Behind is suspended a three-branch candelabrum or sconce, and to its right is a small, square-paned window, partially concealed by a pulled-back drape with a draw-rod below it. A dog sits in the center foreground; in the left corner there is something that might be a cat attacking a bird. To the right, in a pose similar to that sketched by Thomas Rowlandson for his watercolor *The Parsonage,* a drawer is pulling a cork.[74] What separates this Mortlake composition from all previous Punch Parties is the clothing of these men—the long coats, squat hats, and workmen's leggings of countrymen. This, clearly, is the antithesis of gentlemen carousing, and in terms of social class is much more akin to the "two boors drinking" panel of 1792. However, this jug has a silver mount bearing four different dates, the earliest being the hallmarking letter D for 1799.

Unquestionably by the same semi-skilled silversmith is a similarly mounted jug of the same date illustrated by Oswald, Hildyard, and Hughes, whose straight-tailed dogs, ground cover, and perhaps the forward huntsman are from the same molds as those used for the Punch Party B2 jug.[75] In the multidated example (Punch Party D), none of the flanking sprigs matches those of the other mugs and jugs. Prominent is a "Gabriel" with two horns—one for blowing, the other presumably for backup (table XIV.13), and an away-facing windmill that closely matches others found in contemporary woodcuts that include a weathervane on the roof and the miller mounting his steps (table XII.1). This jug also includes what may be the earliest datable version of the imbibing Toby Fillpot who would endure on hunting jugs until Doulton closed its Lambeth works (table II.2).

As I have suggested, sprigs such as Punch Party A1 owe their design origins to other media—to rough sketches, paintings, engravings, broadsheet woodcuts, and the like. Critics have argued that the people involved in the potting art would not have easy access to such sources and might also be illiterate. In interviewing often illiterate costermongers, however, Henry Mayhew painted a different picture:

> "The costermongers," said my informant, "are very fond of illustrations. I have known a man who couldn't read, buy a periodical what had an illustration . . . just that he might learn from someone, who *could* read, what it was all about. They have all heard of Cruikshank, and they think everything funny is by him. . . . "But about the picture?" they would say, and this is a very common question put by them whenever they see an engraving.[76]

There is no reason to doubt, therefore, that half a century earlier, potters—particularly those who could get married at St. Martin-in-the-Fields—would have had easy access to currently popular illustrations and would take advantage of elements familiar to jug and mug buyers and users. With that said, there can be no doubting that Mortlake's Punch Party B2 had its derivation in the much earlier Vauxhall and Bristol panels.

My third Mortlake example jug (figs. 7*c,* 3*c*) has only a Sheffield plate rim and so is undated, but an attribution to circa 1800 is reasonable.[77] Nevertheless, it provides the sharpest image available of the Punch Party B2 panel. There are distinct differences between Mortlake's Punch Party B2 and Bristol's B1 (fig. 3*b*). In the latter the rear window is square-paned, whereas the Mortlake version is diamond latticed. The Bristol singer wears a cap and a straight skirt, Mortlake's wears a hat and an apron. The Bristol drawer entering through a doorway at right is absent from the Mortlake panel. The Mortlake smoker at left wears a tight wig and has a pocket in his coat; the Bristol smoker wears a tall wig of an earlier style and has no pocket.

Other minor variations can sometimes be spotted, but more often than not they are the product of a worn mold, sloppy application, or heavy and obscuring glazing. In B1 versions an otherwise rectangular panel is incuse at its corners, a feature not found on Vauxhall or Mortlake examples. In my Bristol mug the panel has been crudely trimmed, slicing off the bottom of the chamber pot and the legs from the dog. Indeed, eighteenth-century Bristol hunt mugs were, by and large, more sloppily made than were those from London and a far cry from the precision sprigging later to be characteristic of Mortlake.[78] Although a close examination of lower-wall cordoning clearly demonstrates a difference between Bristol and Mortlake, to compare Bristol in the 1750s with Mortlake in the 1790s is as useful as comparing apples with bananas.

Another Mortlake characteristic is the method of securing the handle, whose end is drawn out into a thin tongue and then folded back on itself in the Germanic manner (table I.8). Earlier London and Bristol mugs have more robust handles, whose lower terminals were laterally smeared and their tails pushed up into a thick, thumb-impressed pad (table I.6). However, there always are exceptions to confound the rule. The handle terminal of the 1799 Mortlake Punch Party D jug was smeared laterally—meriting the cliché of "reckless abandon" (table I.9). By Mortlake standards the 1799 jug is poorly made. Its central panel had split in the drying process and some of the hounds lost their tails. Why, then, would it have merited a silver lid from the same silversmith who enriched the much better-made Punch Party B2 illustrated by Oswald, Hildyard, and Hughes? That is only the beginning of the mystery, however. In addition to the silversmith's mark on the rim, the lid is engraved with three more dates and successive owners' initials: "E. J. 1801," "R. W. 1833," and "E. J. W 1880" (fig. *7b*). Who was E. J.? If he was the jug's maker, why did he wait two years to add his initials? Who was R. W and was he related to E. J. W, whose first initials match those of 1801?

So far, I have failed to establish a connection, but with John Wisker having acquired the Sanders factory in 1808 and still being in the potting business in 1833, it is possible that the jug belonged to a member of his family. With that said, a far simpler explanation may be as follows: As would Doulton, Stiff, and others, in 1799 Joseph Kishere contracted with a journeyman silversmith to add silver or plated mounts to part of his stock. The jug remained unsold until customer E. J. bought it in 1801, at which time his initials and date were engraved. If so, the initials and dates have no bearing on the Mortlake story.

Based on the extensive documentary research by Robin Hildyard and others, those authors have concluded that in spite of changing ownership, Sanders's original Mortlake Pottery was a source of hunting jugs prior to 1795—though possibly the work of Joseph Kishere. However, ceramic historian Derek Askey has written that "about 1792 [Kishere] accumulated enough capital to establish his own pottery on the other side of the High Street."[79] If so, the previously discussed 1792 "Boors Drinking" mug may have been one of Kishere's first products. He stayed in the business until his death in 1834, leaving it to his son William, who continued until he died in 1843.

In a preliminary draft of this article, I wrote that "Joseph's elaborate hunting jugs and mugs with which he opened his factory seem to have run their course by 1810." That turned out to be untrue, as figure *7e* attests. The jug has a silver mount with the date letter for 1818. At first sight it bears a close resemblance to those of the century's opening decade, but there are minor differences, notably another version of the earlier windmill.[80] More significant, however, is the treatment of the handle terminal, which, unlike the rest, fails to be boldly upturned before being pressed to the wall. In sum, the specifically Mortlake-style hunting jug continued in production for at least twenty-six years.

Around 1810 a new hunting motif known as "The Kill" was introduced at the Kishere factory.[81] Assembled from six abutting molds, the panoramic scene begins with a tree followed by two horses, then a dismounted huntsman leaning over a broken fence through which hounds are leaping. A second huntsman reaches over a small tree to watch the next mold's four hounds savage a fox, and the scene ends with another tree. A squat and rather ugly jug so decorated is in the Museum of London's collection and marked "KISHERE MOATLAKE" [*sic*]. Robin Hildyard has attributed it to about 1810.[82]

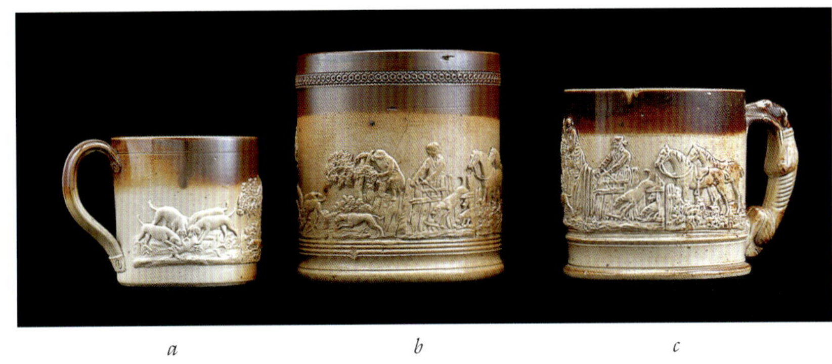

a *b* *c*

Figure 8 Mugs, England. Salt-glazed stoneware. Each of these mugs of short cylinder shape is wrapped with a four- or six-element sprig representing "The Kill." In its complete form the elements reading from left of handle comprise a tree, two saddled horses, one hound leaping over a broken fence and two more jumping through it, another hound in the foreground, one huntsman leaning over the fence, another leaning through a tree watching four hounds savaging a fox, and beyond them another tree. (*a*) Mug of yellowish buff clay black flecked, and high gloss, the handle with faux screws at top and bottom, "The Kill" reduced to four sprigs, the terminal trees at each end omitted. Derbyshire or Yorkshire, ca. 1845. H. 4¼". Paralleling handles occur on a two-handled "Kill" mug impressed "Lane End / Yorkshire / 1852." (*b*) Mug, two-tone brown exterior, with dot and V rouletting below the rim and quadruple cordoning below the six-element "Kill" sprigs. The large and heavy mug is complemented by an equally heavy handle in the form of a collarless hound. Evidence of lathe turning is visible on the base both inside and out. Bristol or Derbyshire, ca. 1840. H. 6¼". (*c*) Mug of yellowish buff clay black flecked, with four-element "Kill" sprigs and a crisply molded hound handle having white eyes, a well-defined collar, and pronounced ribs. Derbyshire, ca. 1840. H. 5¼".

As did many another sophisticated sprig decoration, the design (at least in ceramic terms) originated in Staffordshire around 1800 in the Lane End factory of John and William Turner. A segment of "The Kill" sprig sequence survives in the Turner collection of molds in the Spode Museum, so a turn-of-the-century date for the panel's introduction is likely.[83]

Almost as wide as they are tall, two of the three "Kill" sprigged mugs illustrated in figure 8 are from neither Mortlake nor Staffordshire but may be from Bristol—or more probably from Derbyshire, where brown stoneware production increased dramatically in the second quarter of the nineteenth century. Among Derbyshire's products were large mugs, some with one or more handles molded in the form of greyhounds, a feature that began around 1832 and continued through the rest of the century (fig. 18*a*).[84] Bristol factories produced numerous "Kill"-related brown stonewares through the second quarter of the nineteenth century.[85] Following the introduction of William Powell's industrial-strength Bristol glaze, his factory as well as others applied "The Kill" frieze to jugs in that ware—with increasingly unattractive results (fig. 9*a*). That this combination of old and new persisted to the end of the nineteenth century is suggested by the worn condition of the individual sprig molds. Nevertheless, in spite of its longevity, "The Kill" never achieved the popularity of the individually sprigged hunting scenes that continued to course around mugs and jugs throughout the nineteenth century, most of them products of Derbyshire factories.[86]

a

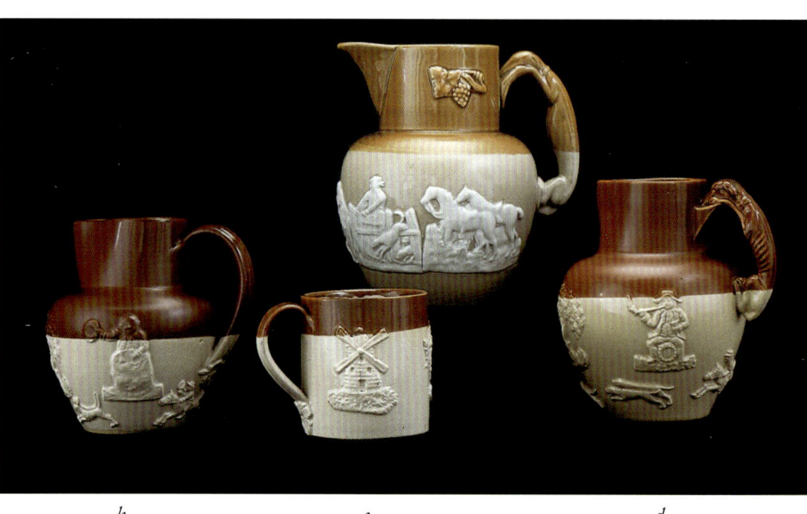

b *c* *d*

Figure 9 Examples of hunting wares with saltless "Bristol" glazing, a technique increasingly common as the second half of the nineteenth century progressed, are very hard to date: (*a*) Jug with yellow dip over a buff body, grape sprigs on the pinched spout and a four-element "Kill" in white clay below. The base is square-cut and slightly raised within it. Derbyshire or Bristol, ca. 1870. H. 6⅞". (*b*) Jug with buff body and rich brown dip, pinched spout, and traditional hunting and toper sprigs. The horn-blowing huntsman rides a "toy" horse in pursuit of a fox. His paired hounds have vertical tails. The hat-waving toper sits behind his garlanded barrel while a smoker sits astride a barrel with a glass in his left hand. The windmill is characteristic of this group, having three arched windows over an open doorway and foliage-flanked steps (see table XII.18). A lone tree has its trunk dividing into three branches (see table VI.16). The reeded handle terminates in a floral and grape sprig (table XV.10). All these features are characteristic of the Bourne factory in Derbyshire, which still makes dinner wares for the American market. A type-impressed "W" on the slightly rising base. Ca. 1870–1900. H. 5⅜". (*c*) Half-pint mug with poorly defined grape-leaf handle terminal and conventional Bourne sprigs. A type-impressed "J" on the flat base. Ca. 1890. H 3½". (*d*) Jug in typical Bourne body and slip as well as conventional toper and smoker sprigs. The paired hounds, however, have horizontal tails and the huntsman on his "toy" horse has no horn and closely resembles the sprig on an earlier Derbyshire jug (fig. 10*a* and table IX.2). The sharply defined hound handle rests its nose on a square-cut plinth, another detail characteristic of these hound-handled jugs. The emaciated hound has a collar and very thin forelegs. The flat base is type-impressed "1½ Pt." Ca. 1890. H. 6¼".

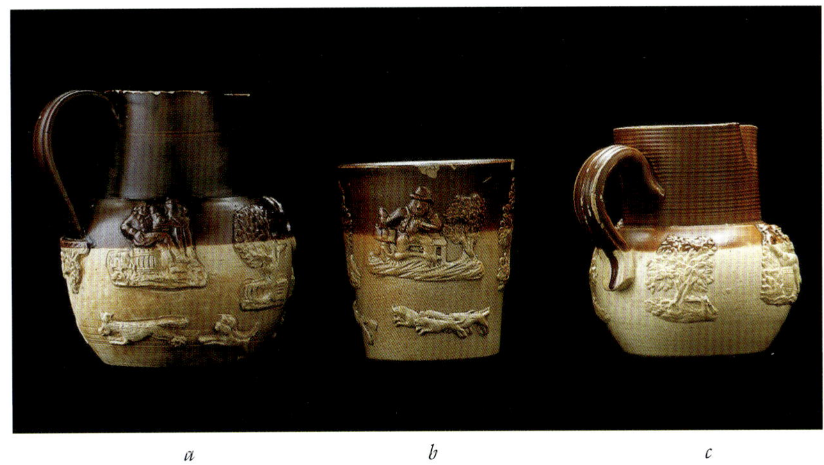

a b c

Figure 10 Jugs and beaker, England. Salt-glazed stoneware. These small, buff-bodied vessels are all solid-dipped. (*a*) Derbyshire, ca. 1835 (tables XIII.1, XV.8). H. 5". (*b*) Beaker, Mortlake, ca. 1840 (table II.4). H. 3½". (*c*) Probably Derbyshire, ca. 1830. H. 4¼".

Although Derbyshire would become the design trendsetter in the second quarter of the nineteenth century, it seems reasonable to suggest that at the turn of the century, with Fulham in decline and the Vauxhall/Lambeth industry in a period of reestablishment, Mortlake took the lead in sprig-design innovation. Toward the end of the Kishere family's operation, however, their sprig styles were following the more simplistic trend already established at Vauxhall and Lambeth, and their own early use of "Toby"-like elements on Punch Party and other paneled jugs and mugs. Nevertheless, the previous century's ubiquitous Punch Party failed to survive to the end of the Kishere family's Mortlake operation, having been replaced by individual topers in a variety of poses. Clearly not among the first, but from Mortlake nonetheless, is a quart mug with sprig-applied trees, windmill, topers, and hunt, all paralleled by a jug marked "KISHERE POTTERY MORTLAKE SURRY." A date as late as the 1840s is suggested by a colander with the same sprigs and dated 1842.[87] A half-pint hunting beaker in the Noël Hume Collection has as its principal sprig the same bowler-hatted rustic that appears on the colander—thus a Kishere product, circa 1840 (fig. 10*b*; see table II.4). One thing, as they say, leads to another.

The central character in virtually all these post-1800 wares is the semi-fictitious Toby Fillpot,[88] whose obese image was engraved and published by Carington Bowles circa 1761 along with verses telling how, when he died and returned to the earth, a potter dug the clay and "with part of fat Toby he form'd this brown jug" (table II.1). From this illustration were born an endless supply of anthropomorphic "Toby Jugs" made in creamware and pearlware by Ralph Wood, James Neale, Spode, and others. Wearing a tricorn hat that served as a spout and with a mug of ale in one hand and a pipe in the other, the figure was almost as familiar to cottage mantel shelves as those dreadful Staffordshire dogs. The date at which Toby made his first appearance as a sprig on the side of hunting mugs and jugs is uncertain, although, as already noted, he graces the wall of the 1799 Mortlake jug (fig. 7*b*; table II.2).[89] Among nine plaster molds preserved in the church at Mortlake is a Toby figure, but its exact parallel on a Kishere-era jug or mug has yet to surface.[90] A Toby mold in the Spode Museum collection is marked "Turner" and dates circa 1800–1810 (fig. 11).

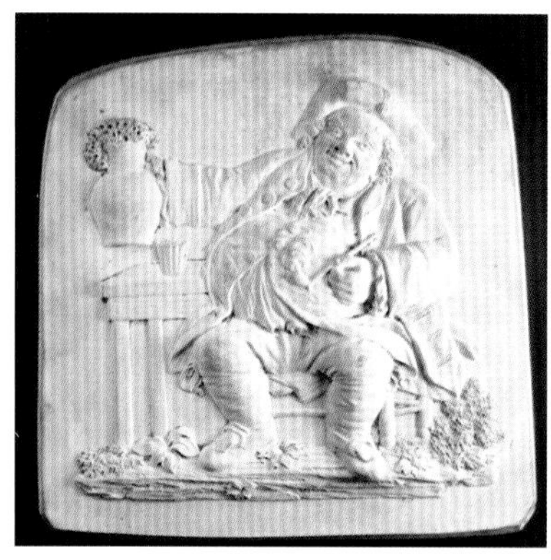

Figure 11 Master mold, impressed "Turner," ca. 1800–1810. H. 5" (figure.) (Reproduced by the kind permission of the Spode Museum Trust, Stoke-on-Trent.) Purchased by Spode in 1829, this mold for the standard Toby figure closely follows the Carington Bowles engraving of ca. 1761.

The illustrated series of Toby images (tables II, III) is by no means exhaustive but it does demonstrate the many variations on the theme, a principal division being between those with straight-legged, rectangular tables and others with single, baluster legs and circular tops. The former derived directly from the engraving and are attributable to the first half of the century, while the rest with their pedestal tables belong to the second half and later.[91]

Unfortunately, rules of thumb can be four fingers short of a hand, and this one was broken by James Stiff in Lambeth (after 1848) and C.I.C. Bailey at Fulham (after 1864), both of whom favored square tables with straight legs.

The death of William Kishere in 1843 brought an end to hunting ware production at Mortlake, and although Fulham was still in the business, the stoneware production focus had long since shifted down the Thames to its south bank, where Vauxhall and Lambeth abut. Meanwhile, Bristol stoneware manufacturing continued to flourish—and to challenge collectors to separate its sprigged wares from those of its Derbyshire and Liverpool competitors.

In my own efforts to do that I developed what I called my "hat-waver" thesis, based on my assumption that this particular sprig was a Powell innovation: the man sits behind a garlanded barrel waving his hat in his right hand (fig. 12*e*). A massive jug impressed "W. POWELL 1834" bears this sprig and was a product of William Powell, who set up business in Bristol's Thomas Street in 1816 and moved to Temple Gate circa 1830.[92] A second "hat waver" adorns another, much later Powell piece, this time a Bristol-glazed barrel stamped "ALFRED EVENS BRISTOL 1869."[93] In addition to the hat waver, both pieces include sprigs of "the contented smoker" and a young smoker facing left whose coat drapes in pleats over the side of a tub or barrel (fig. 12*f*). On the 1834 jug another sprigged figure sits on a barrel with his right arm extended holding a gorge while the left holds a short-stemmed tobacco pipe (table II.4).[94] All four figures I deduced to originate in Bristol. They occur along with four others on a puzzle jug in the Noël Hume Collection that I attributed to circa 1825–1830 (fig. 12*a*). In theory, therefore, the puzzle jug could represent the "Grail" of Bristol sprig development. But there was a problem: the jug's honey-colored ware closely resembled numerous other mugs and jugs having Derbyshire attributions and even inscriptions. It became clear that the beckoning hat waver had started his life in the hands of a Derbyshire mold maker before he and his clay companions found their way south and eventually to Lambeth in the factory of James Stiff in the 1870s (fig. 13*d*; table XIV.5).

In the second half of the nineteenth century, however, tens of thousands of hunting jugs and mugs were turned out each year in the London area alone, as previously noted major competitors were at work to the north in Derbyshire. A brown stoneware industry had begun in the 1690s at Critch in the county's center, where good clay and fuel coal were plentiful. Potting began at nearby Belper in 1737, and by the mid-century stoneware potting had extended farther north to such places as Bolsover, Chesterfield,

Figure 12 Puzzle jug and details, Brampton, England, ca. 1825–1830. Salt-glazed stoneware. H. 8¼". (*a*) This honey-colored puzzle jug is decorated with a full set of "Bristol" toper and smoke sprigs.

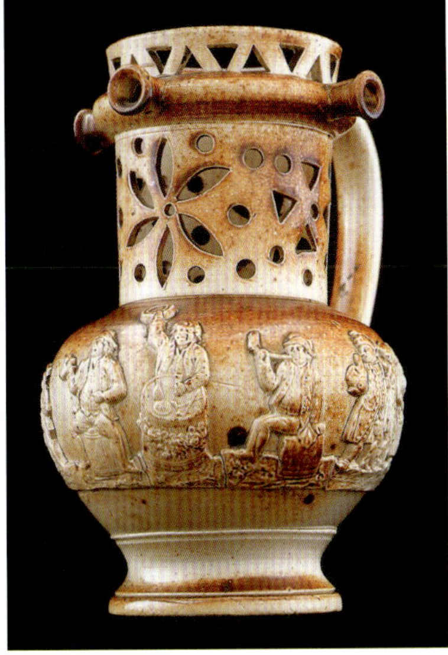

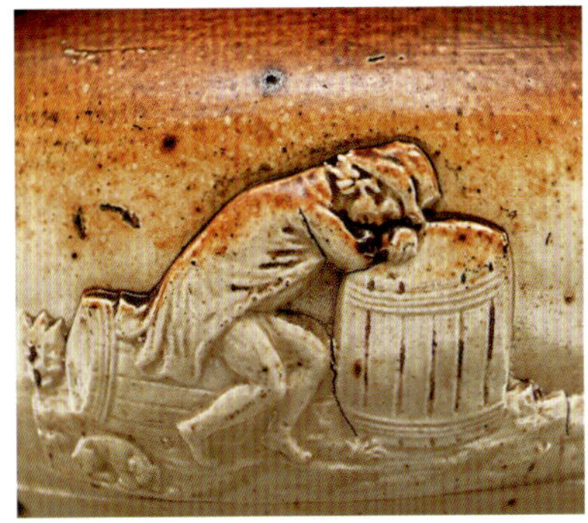

(*b*) The sleeping toper, a figure in use at Brampton in 1839.

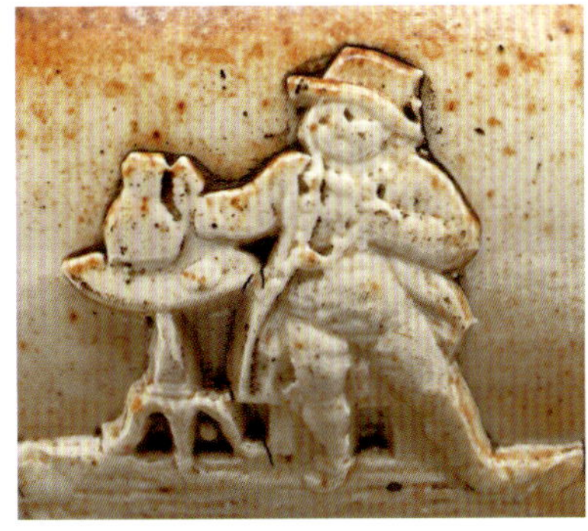

(*c*) A very different version of the Toby figure.

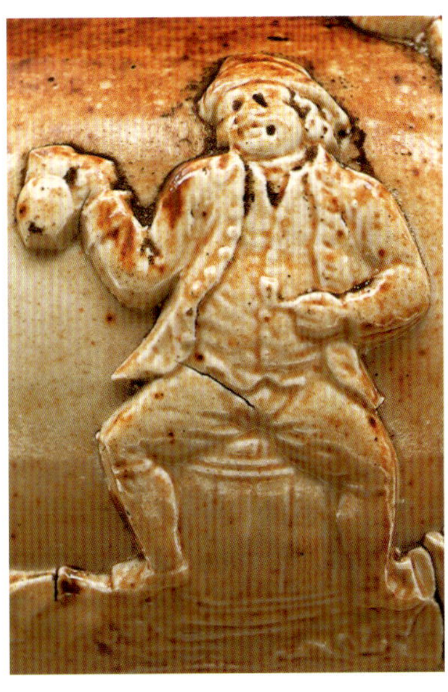

(*d*) The standard mug holder on a barrel.

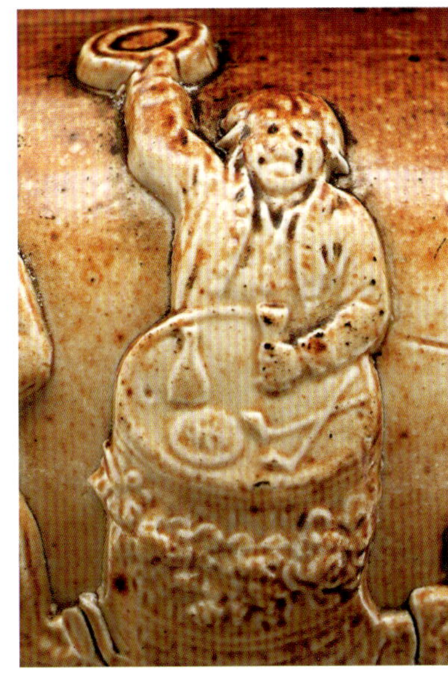

(*e*) The standard hat waver.

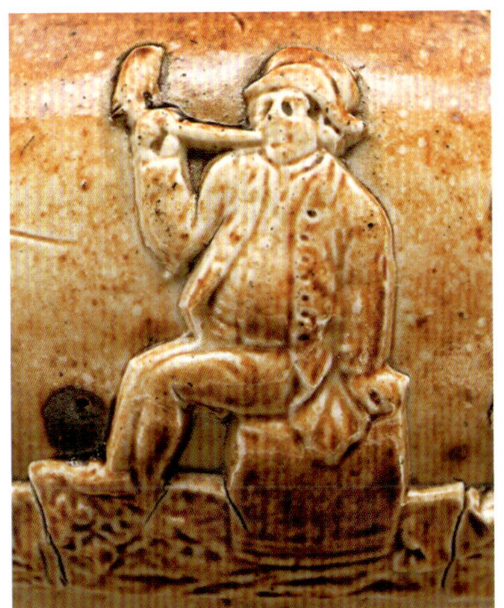

(*f*) Smoker with a pleated coat tail.

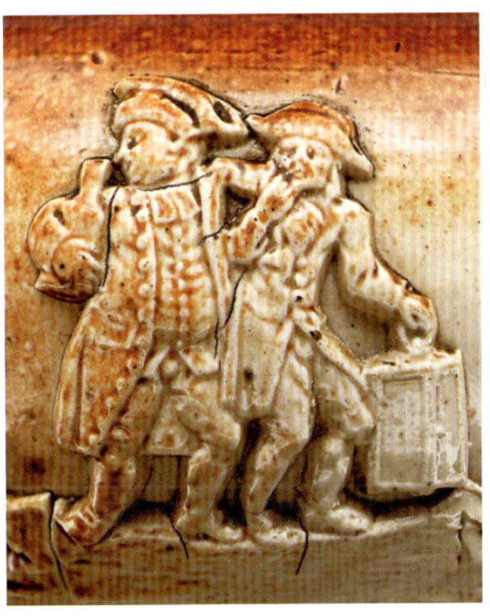

(*g*) The "Vicar and Moses" design after Ralph Wood, ca. 1790.

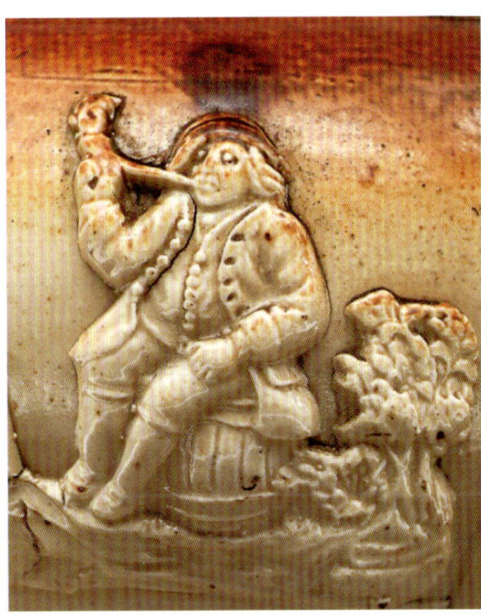

(*h*) The contented smoker.

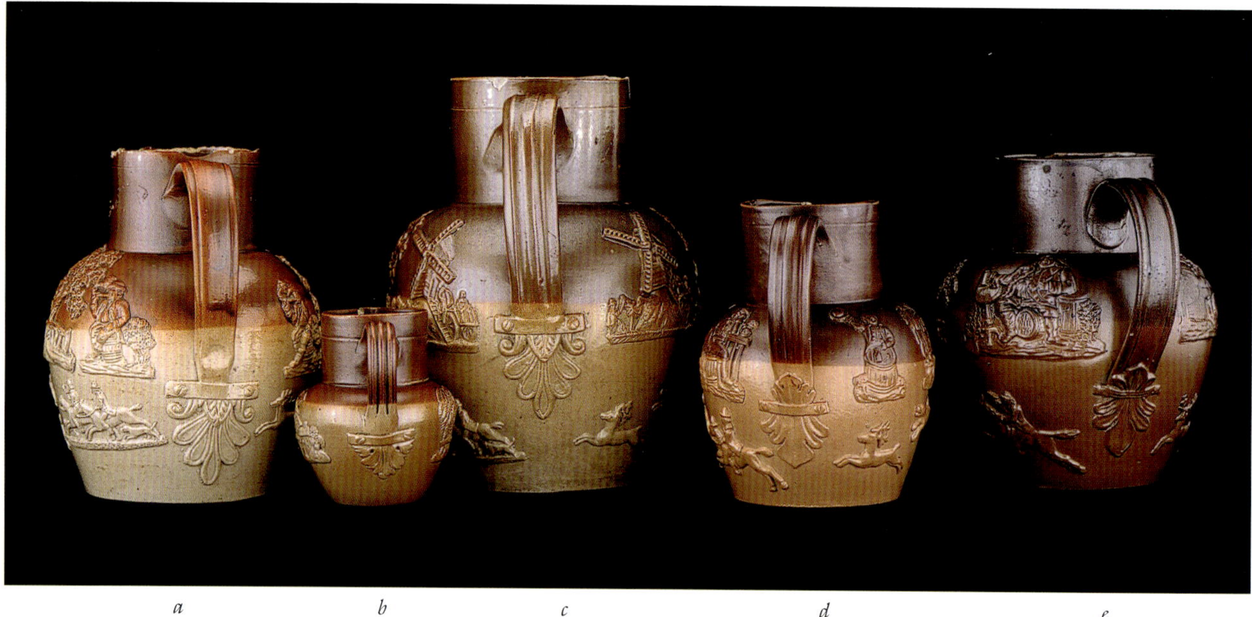

a b c d e

Figure 13 Pitchers, Derbyshire, London, and Scotland. Salt-glazed stoneware. (*a*) Derbyshire, ca. 1840. H. 8". (Table II.10). (*b*) Stiff, impressed "J Stiff & Sons / London," post-1863. H. 4¼". (*c*) Probably Derbyshire, Toby with dog akin to 13*a*, ca. 1840, H. 9⁷⁄₁₆". For windmill, see table XII.11. (*d*) Stiff, but unmarked, ca. 1880. H. 5⅜". (Tables XIV.5, XV.19). The standard Stiff windmill features among the sprigs (as fig. 13*b*), also the so-called Bristol hat waver, post-1863. (*e*) Glasgow, Scotland impressed "3PT." H. 7⅜". The central sprig group (table XI.5) occurs as early as 1828, but this jug might date as late as ca. 1860 (table XV.14).

and later to Brampton, whose several factories would burgeon in the nineteenth century and number hunting jugs among their products. My illustrated example is not of the best, but is characterized by high-relief sprigs with incised lines around each of them (table XIII.1),[95] a detail paralleled on a hunting jug attributed to the Denby Pottery in the decade 1830–1840 (fig. 10*a*).[96] The jug's handle terminal comprises a spray of grape leaves and a double cluster of fruit (table XV.8).[97] Though unrecorded, the device resembles a single bunch that Oswald, Hildyard, and Hughes have attributed to J. Bourne of Denby. But because Joseph Bourne was in the Derbyshire stoneware business from 1812 until his death in 1860, the time bracketing is less than useful.[98] Another with a slightly different spray (table XV.9) and whose sprigs include a figure of Saint George slaying the dragon (table XI.7)[99] over a somewhat compressed foxhunt is likewise attributable to Denby in the same period (fig. 16*f*). One- and two-pint and quart-capacity mugs of these proportions became fashionable in the 1830s and in Derbyshire developed a more varied and naturalistic assemblage of anthropomorphic sprigs. In this instance the flanking figures are clearly those of spirited youth and disillusioned old age (table XIV.11, .12).[100]

A smaller hound-handled mug with the same "youth" and "age" figures and almost certainly from the same Derbyshire factory also carries an unusual, trestle-mounted windmill (fig. 16*a*; see table XII.9). The same windmill decorates the wall of a Derbyshire-style loving cup in the collection of stoneware authority Mavis Watney and is inscribed with the name of one George Topham and his birth date, January 28, 1782. He was christened a month later at Crich, one of Derbyshire's earliest brown stoneware production centers. The Watney loving cup is unlikely to date any later than 1850 and might easily be attributed to Topham's fiftieth birthday in 1832.[101]

As I have noted, John Dwight's pioneering Fulham factory in London had fallen on hard times during the latter half of the eighteenth century but was regaining importance by the second quarter of the nineteenth. A gallon-

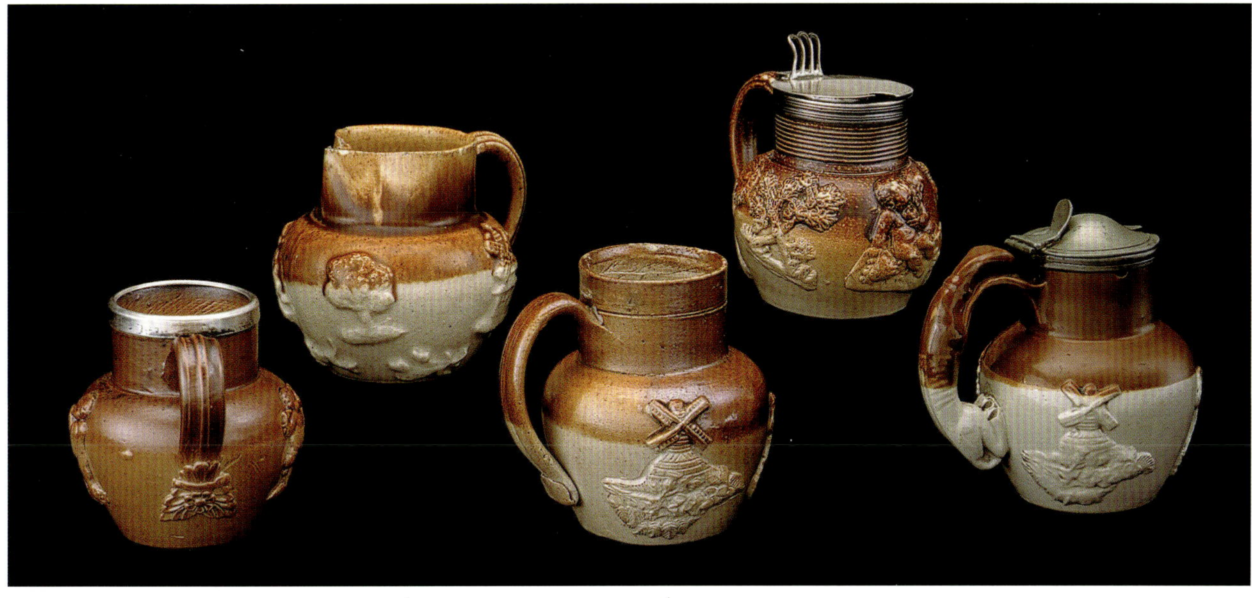

a b d c e

Figure 14 Jugs and mustard pots. Salt-glazed stoneware. (*a*) Doulton type, unmarked, with sprig-applied music-playing putti. The silver rim is hallmarked for 1880 and lightly engraved "28 1824." H. 3". (*b*) Milk pitcher with sharply reeded handle and strenuously pinched spout. A ginger-brown dip is combined with lead glaze both inside and out over a pale yellow body. Though still fired in a salt-glaze kiln, this may be an early attempt to compete with Powell's "Bristol" glaze. The sprigs include a smoker with his cat, perhaps the earliest example of Doulton's "Owl and Pussycat" motif. Unmarked, but probably from Doulton & Watts of Lambeth, ca. 1835. H. 3¹⁄₁₆". (*c*) Mustard pot sprig-decorated with trees and putti. Its reeded neck carries a silver mount stamped with the hallmark letter for 1801. Probably Mortlake (Kishere). H. 3". (Table V.13). (*d*) Mustard pot in regular, dipped brown stoneware with a simple strap handle folded at the lower terminal. The wall is decorated with three sprigs, a windmill standing atop foliate ground that includes a Scottish thistle (table XII.6), a tree with thick foliage, and Heemskerk's seated singer (table IV.5). Derbyshire or Glasgow, ca. 1845. H. 3½". (*e*) A virtual twin to fig. 14*d*, but "Bristol" glazed outside and in with a separately molded, or cast, hound handle. The sprigs are identical. The pewter mount is attached by lugs riveted through the rim, apparently after glazing but before firing. Derbyshire or Glasgow, ca. 1845. H. 3¼".

capacity jug made there in 1800 was signed by William White, whose successor, Charles Edward White, would run the business until 1859. The White jug of 1800, alas now lost, was described as being decorated with sprigs that included "Hope, Peace, women milking and a church."[102]

Unmarked but also likely to have been a William White–era product is a jug sprigged with putti, as the four seasons, flanking a portrait bust of Admiral Horatio Nelson (fig. 15*a*). This evidently dated from the year of Nelson's death (1805) and is important in that its handle terminal gives the impression of having been secured to the wall by means of two nails or screws (table XV.1). Subsequently, other potters went further and added a lateral strap to be held in place by two such faux screws. A couple of Derbyshire mugs (one with the standard "Kill" sprigs and the other with a variant called "The Chase") take the screwed-strap handle a step further, anchoring the upper terminal with two more faux screws (fig. 16*c, e*; see table XV.12).

In creating distinctive handle terminals Fulham chose a different route and developed a three-screw sprig without any reinforcing strap. A jug bearing the arms of the City of London and made to coincide with the accession of Queen Victoria in 1837 provides a documented example of a detail that would persist almost to the close of the century (fig. 15*b*; see table XV.2). Using the same terminal, but probably a few years earlier, is another Fulham jug sprig-decorated with the floral emblems of the Union (English rose, Scottish thistle, and Irish shamrock) (fig. 15*d*). The jug's Toby figure is unusual in that he has a lantern on his table and is pouring from a pitcher into a tumbler. The details are hard to see on this example, but are exactly and crisply paralleled on a Parian ware mustard pot of circa 1845 (table II.7).[103]

The characteristic Fulham three-screw terminal is to be seen on a sized pair of silver-plate mounted and lidded Fulham hunting jugs dating circa 1835–1845. These provide helpful documentation for Fulham sprigs dating to the mid-nineteenth century and parallel fragments found in excavations on the Fulham factory site (figs. 15*c, e*).[104] Like the jugs, the fragments show Toby sitting on a barrel stamped "OLD TOM" (table II.8), while the barrels of flanking figures are marked "XX" and "XXX," respectively (table XIV.1, .2). These well-defined Xs should not be confused with the single small "x" found on the upper barrel-end stave on Doulton Toby sprigs after circa 1870 and continuing into the twentieth century.[105]

The X marks on barrels serve to introduce a Scottish red herring. Factories at Glasgow (notably that at Port Dundas) produced large quantities of sprig-decorated brown stoneware hunting jugs from the 1820s through most of the century. The jugs are generally dark brown in color, have pinched spouts, and sometimes possess unusually tall necks. My illustrated example (fig. 13*e*) exhibits two sprigs that I believe are uniquely Scottish, namely a group of three men sitting around a pedestal-footed table, two of them furiously smoking and the third holding a tumbler in one hand and a jug in the other (table XI.5). An overturned tumbler on the table is decanting its contents down the leg of the left smoker. This sprig is first recorded on a massive jug in the Glasgow Museum and is inscribed "CALEDONIAN POTTERY 1828."[106] The second sprig is that of a fairly standard Toby, with one important exception: the barrel on which he sits is impressed "Old Will 1761," a detail that encourages dealers to price such jugs a century too early (table II.9). The "Old Will" Toby is found on a large spirit jar in the Glasgow Museum, attributed to the Portobello Pottery and to a date circa 1848–1870. However, the sprig also occurs on a mallet-shaped whiskey flask in the same museum but attributed to Port Dundas.[107]

In ceramic research we are always seeking connections, and the "Old Will 1761" hunting jug is a good example. Once fitted with a pewter lid, the neck had been drilled to receive four pewter pegs—a most unusual process, and arguably a characteristically Scottish method of attachment.[108] Figures 14*d* and *e* show two mustard pots, one in regular salt glaze and the other Bristol-glazed. The latter had been pre-drilled to receive two mounting pegs. The mustard pots have the same three sprigs, their windmills atop a foliate pad that includes a Scottish thistle (table XII.6).[109] The central sprig features what appears to be an old man seated on a barrel reading a book (table IV.5). The Bristol-glazed pot has a hound handle; the other has a strap handle folded back at the base. Here, therefore, we have a classic

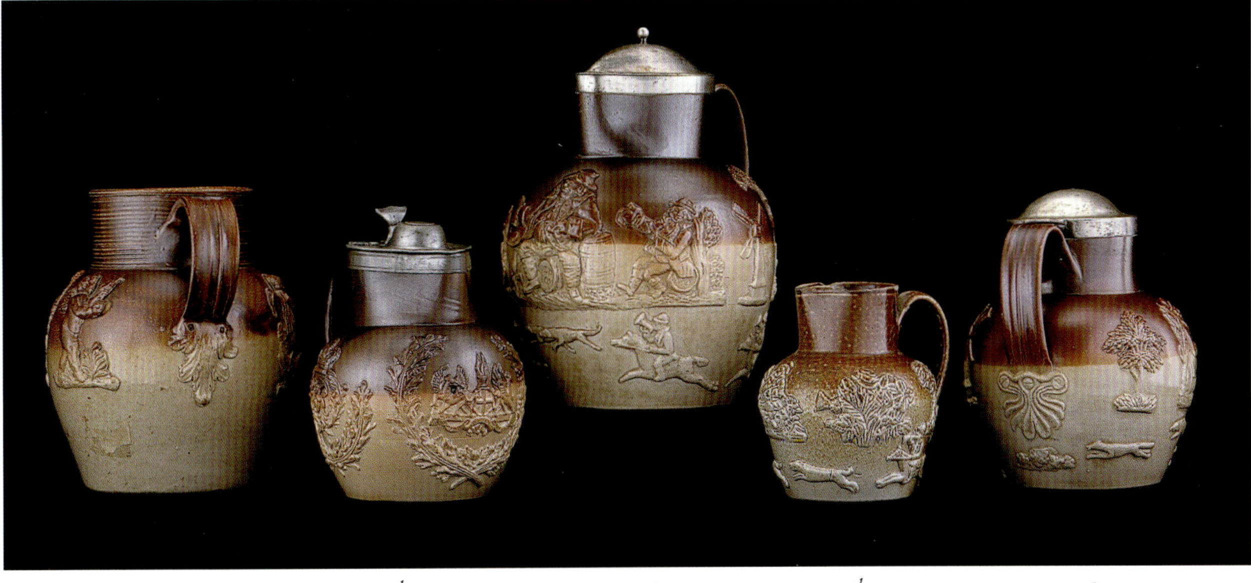

a b c d e

Figure 15 Jugs, Fulham. Salt-glazed stoneware. (*a*) Jug with reeded neck and pinched spout, decorated with putti representing the four seasons flanking a profile of Lord Nelson. The acanthus-leaf handle terminal is "secured" with two faux nails, precursors for the three screws peculiar to Fulham through much of the nineteenth century (table XV.1). Fulham or perhaps Mortlake, ca. 1805. H. 7⅝". (*b*) Jug made for the City of London, probably to celebrate Queen Victoria's first state visit there on November 9, 1837. Sprigs comprise the wreathed arms of the city flanked by similarly wreathed VR cyphers. H. 6¼". (table XV.2). (*c, e*) Jugs with a long history of being together having been found in Scotland and taken to Holland. Both are silver-plate lidded and sprig-decorated with the standard Fulham windmill (table XII.5), Toby with "Old Tom" on his barrel (table II.8), a pair of rustic topers (table XIV.1, .2), an aggressively horn-tooting huntsman (table IX.12), and the Fulham, three-screw handle terminal. Both ca. 1840. H. 8¾" (*c*), 6⅞" (*e*). (*d*) Jug with heavily mottled dip and thick greenish glaze; one rectangular stilt mark on base. Sprigs include a pair of small windswept trees, an emblematic floral device incorporating the rose of England, Scottish thistle, and Irish shamrock. The central Toby figure is unusually elaborate, with a lantern on his table as he pours from a jug into a tumbler (table II.7). The jug has the usual Fulham handle terminal. Ca. 1835. H. 5⅜". (Courtesy, Mrs. Thomas Wood, Williamsburg, Va.)

example of widely differing features conceivably from the same factory, demonstrating the difficulty of making attributions when a lone example is studied. In this instance the uncertainty grows when one realizes that the book-man sprig is a detail from a more expansive group found in the side of the large jug I have argued (unwisely) to be of Bristol manufacture (table IV.1, .2). Prominent in that group is a man playing what appear to be Celtic bagpipes. Thus, in spite of all the evidence to the contrary, it is impossible to ignore the possibility that both the Scottish group sprig and the jug's unparalleled (in my experience) handle terminal are pointing, not to Bristol, but northward toward Scotland.

Toward, but not to! Instead, the trail leads to Lane End in Staffordshire and to the series of molds made there under the direction of John Turner, their designs widely used both as stoneware sprigs and in relief on slip-cast jugs. My pursuit of the reading man and his bagpiping companion eventually (and quite accidentally) led to a print in the Colonial Williamsburg collection.[110] Titled *The Musical Club*, it was published in London by Robert Sayer of No. 53 Fleet Street on June 1, 1772, and featured the jug's convivial characters (table IV.3). The musician was indeed a bagpiper, but the elderly reader turned out to be a youth singing from a songbook. The

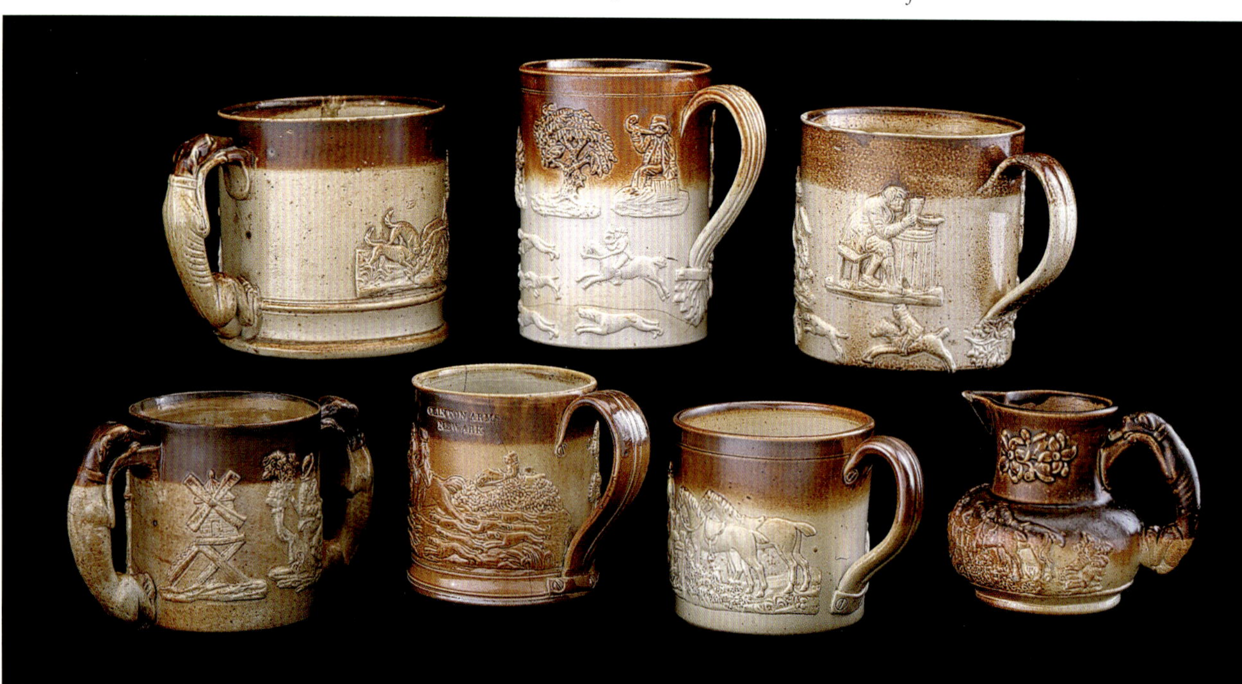

Figure 16 Mugs, Derbyshire. Salt-glazed stonewares. (*a*) Wide mug with paired hound handles, both collared, slender legged, and with open looped tails. A solid dip above four sprigs (table V.17), a pair of topers, young and old (table XIII.1, .4), and a trestle-supported windmill (table XII.9). Belper/Denby, ca. 1835. H. 4¼". (*b*) Wide mug with single, emaciated, and collared hound handle; even, solid dip spattered and with green pooling internally; and expanded, rounded and internally raised foot below a single cordon under a four-sprig version of "The Kill." Denby, ca. 1835. H. 5⅛". (*c*) Mug with a rich brown-fired body below a salt-speckled dip, the inside coated with a thin whitish slip. The strap handle is secured at top and bottom with faux screws, the latter holding an applied strap. Above a square-cut foot a single groove marks the application line for a single, wraparound sprig containing a hunting scene with four mounted riders and a plethora of hounds in pursuit of a fox. The flat base is lustrously glazed in the style of Nottingham, and the upper wall is type-impressed "Clinton Arms / Newark" (northeast of Nottingham). Denby, ca. 1850. H. 4⅜". (*d*) Tall, pale buff-bodied mug with freckled, red-brown dip, multiple-reeded handle with expanded foliate terminal under a separately applied two-screw strap (table XV.7). The wall is divided equally between a hunting scene and toper groups. Two horn-blowing huntsmen, their instruments' bells opening backward, and hounds with visible ribs singly and in pairs pursue a stag, its body pierced in application (table X.4). The topers comprise the "Bristol" hat waver with a bottle, glass, tobacco box, and two pipes on his garlanded barrel (table XIV.3), next an oak tree (table VI.9), followed by a Toby figure, his right arm extended above his straight-legged table and holding a jug of ale. There is a sharply defined tobacco box on the table (table II.5). The "contented toper" with his pleated coat tail completes the group (table XIII.14). South Derbyshire or Bristol, ca. 1820. H. 6". (*e*) Mug with strapped and "screwed" handle similar to 16*c* (table XV.11), and even brown dip over a buff body sprig-decorated with a four-part version of "The Kill." Denby, ca. 1845. H. 4¼". (*f*) Mug, buff-bodied with a pale specked dip, marks of lathe turning on the interior base. The single-grooved strap handle terminates in an elaborate vine sprig (table XV.9). The mug's hunting scene is relegated to a narrow band above the base and shows one hard-riding hunter with paired and single hounds in pursuit of an elongated fox. The central sprig comprises the dragon and Saint George wearing a Greek helmet and carrying a short spear rather than the more common sword (table XI.7). A largely defoliated palm tree (table V.18) and the young and old topers previously seen on 16*a* complete the decoration. Belper/Denby, ca. 1835. H. 5⅛". (*g*) Small jug made from a pale buff body, with a rich, mottled dip and the exterior below it a pale yellow. A collared hound provides the handle, and the straight neck is decorated with floral sprigs. The wall incurves to a small foot, above it a six-sprig version of "The Kill." Brampton, ca. 1840. H. 4¼".

engraving was attributed to Heemskerk—possibly Egbert van Heemskerk, who reputedly moved to England "from Haarlem in 1645 and became known for his paintings of drunken scenes and country life."[111] It seems likely that in 1772, along with the Heemskerk print, John Sayer published at least several engravings from Dutch sources, among them *Peasants Drink-*

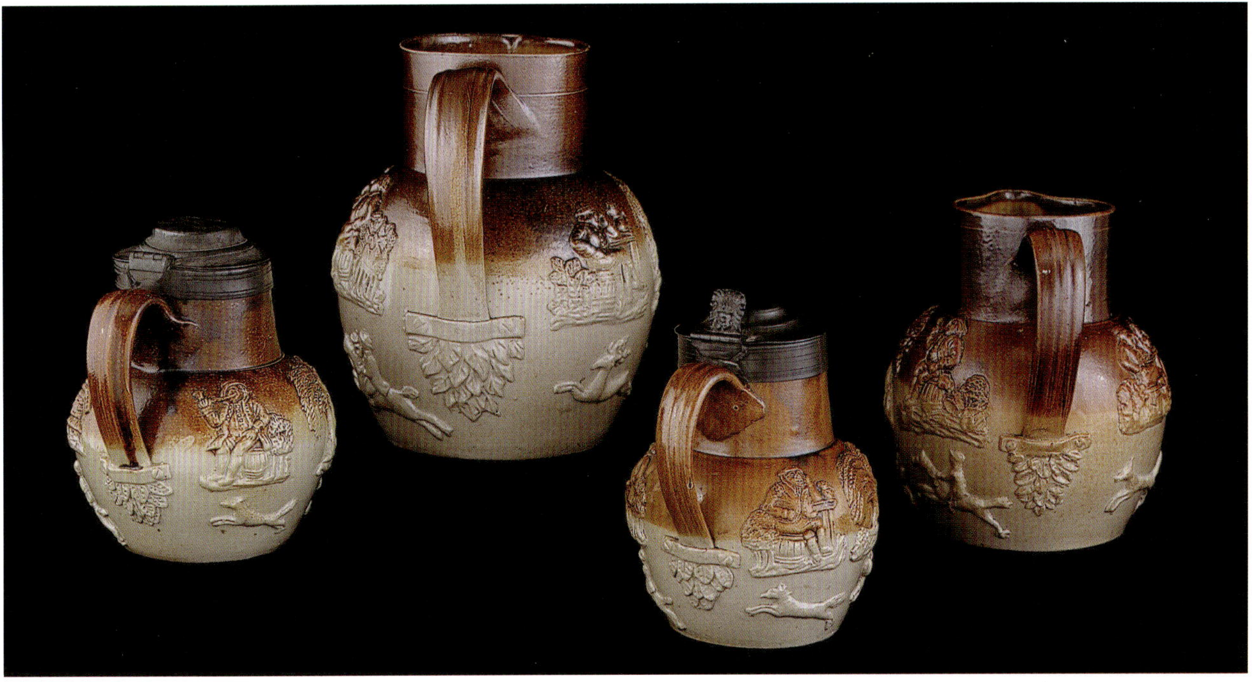

a b c d

Figure 17 Jugs and pitchers, London area. Salt-glazed stoneware. Listed by Oswald, Hildyard, and Hughes as being the "Standard early terminal, found at Mortlake, Vauxhall, etc.," the assumption may be that such details are characteristic of the London area. (*a*) Pitcher with a light reddish brown mottled dip on a body that fired a pale yellow. The single-reed handle with its leaf terminal (table XV.5) is flanked by a multitiered windmill akin to a pagoda (table XII.8), followed by a weeping willow repeated on the opposite side. Between them sits a well-defined Toby with a floppy hat and a long pipe beside a straight-legged table (table II.3). Beyond the second willow sits the "contented smoker" (e.g., fig. 12*h*). Below, paired hounds pursue a long fox, and behind them rides a hunter who appears to be wearing a jockey's cap and a short jacket. Mortlake, ca. 1830. H. 5". The pewter mount is engraved with a pair of unicorn and horse crests, one reading "Nil Temere" (not by chance) and the other "Ride Through." (*b*) Jug with reddish brown mottled dip above a pale yellow body. The lower sprig series comprises a huntsman with a twisted and upturned horn (table IX.10) following paired hounds with elevated tails in pursuit of a stag. The upper series begins with the "contented smoker" sitting beside foliage with multiple stems (table XIII.13), followed by a willow tree with one lopped limb. The Toby figure is markedly pop-eyed, sits at a straight-legged table on a chair with two stretchers and ground cover between his legs (table III.4). The willow tree is repeated and followed by the "thinking toper," whose straight-legged table supports a mug with a large handle and a tobacco pipe. Mortlake or Lambeth, ca. 1835. H. 7⅛". (*c*) Pitcher superficially similar to 17*a*. The dip is thinner and a pale ginger brown, and the handle double-reeded. However, both pitchers have the upper terminal of their handles roughly smeared from right to left. The sprigged huntsman has no horn as he follows paired hounds chasing an elongated fox. Above, the "contented smoker" is followed by a willow tree whose distinguishing feature is a ball-like hatching to the left of its ground cover (table VI.6). The Toby figure is unusual in that he has no table and his coat is voluminous and widely flowing. A small "x" is visible on the side of his mug (table III.1). He is followed by the willow tree and then by a "thinking toper" leaning on a straight-legged table whereon the mug has an incised "x." Mortlake or Lambeth, ca. 1830. H. 5". (*d*) Jug with brown mottled dip and characterized by a Toby figure with a large floppy hat and what might be construed as a mouse on a chamber pot between his legs (table III.2, .3). The upper frieze begins with the "contented smoker" and ends with the "thinking toper" (table XIII.2). Between is a heavily foliaged tree in front of a rustic fence (table VI.5). Below, the jockeylike huntsman follows large, paired hounds chasing an equally large fox. Mortlake or Lambeth, ca. 1835. H. 5⅞".

ing, a painting by David Teniers the Younger (1610–1690).[112] Only three years after Sayer published *The Musical Club,* a grouping derived from the Teniers painting would be transfer-printed onto a Liverpool delftware tile by Messrs. Sadler and Green.[113] A quarter century later Turner made molds derived from both the Heemskerk and Teniers prints, thereby enabling their convivial groups to be applied to production molds for both sides of a Liverpool pearlware jug impressed "HERCULANIUM (1796–1810)" (table IV.6, .7). Pratt ware experts John and Griselda Lewis have illustrated a fine, pale brown stoneware jug, shaped in a pearlware-style mold that they attribute to Brampton;[114] but the once "Bristol" jug is not in that class and, I believe, may now be identified as a Liverpool area product.[115]

The moral to this story is simple: Studying one ware while ignoring all others is to go through life with one eye shut. Clues and parallels may abound among the products of other contemporary factories while a constant search for pictorial sources can yield astonishing and sublime *Eureka!*-style moments.

When Dr. Richard Pococke visited Liverpool's neighboring village of Prescot in 1751, he found several potteries "where they also make the brown stoneware and work it, as they say higher with the fire than at Lambeth." Pococke added that "They make it of a mixture of two sorts of clay which they find there."[116] His observation tells us that in his day the northern stoneware potters saw Lambeth rather than Fulham or Mortlake as their competition, as indeed, it would remain for the next two hundred years. No less significant is Pococke's reference to mixed clays, suggesting that spectrographic analysis might be the key to identifying Liverpool area stonewares.

Forty-two years later Prescot was described in the *Universal British Directory* as a large market town famed for its watchmakers. Also listed were five potters: Michael Hill, Thomas Mercer, Thomas Molineux, David Sharrot, and Thomas Spencer. Unfortunately the directory did not indicate whether these were earthenware or stoneware potters.[117] Listed in the tradesmen of Liverpool, however, was but one pottery, that of John Pennington, the porcelain maker. It would seem, therefore, that in the early 1790s Liverpool could not yet lay claim to brown stoneware production.

Returning now to Fulham: The factory was bought in 1865 by C.I.C. Bailey, who took several years to remodel it. Charles Bailey had previously owned the Vauxhall factory, and on purchasing Fulham transferred Vauxhall's craftsmen and equipment to it. It may, therefore, have been as late as 1872 before Bailey was in full production. Figure 18*b* illustrates one of his hunting mugs, most of which are characterized by the use of a church sprig—possibly taken from the one used by William White in 1800 (table I.13).[118] The Bailey mug also follows another Fulham tradition, namely showing its windmills with their sails facing away from the viewer (table XII.5).[119] Bailey's modeler had also given Toby a new set of clothing, adding ornamental cuffs to his coat and a remarkably baggy woolen sweater to substitute for his usual, buttoned waistcoat (table III.11).

Bailey's predecessors, Charles Edward White (ca. 1800–1859) and Messrs. Mackintosh and Clements (1862–1865), had not been particularly successful entrepreneurs, and during their tenure at Fulham the bulk of the London area stoneware business slipped back to Vauxhall and Lambeth.

The Vauxhall Pottery had specialized in stoneware from its inception in 1697 and, as we have seen, continued to do so throughout the eighteenth century. Bought in 1793 by William Wagstaff, who also purchased William

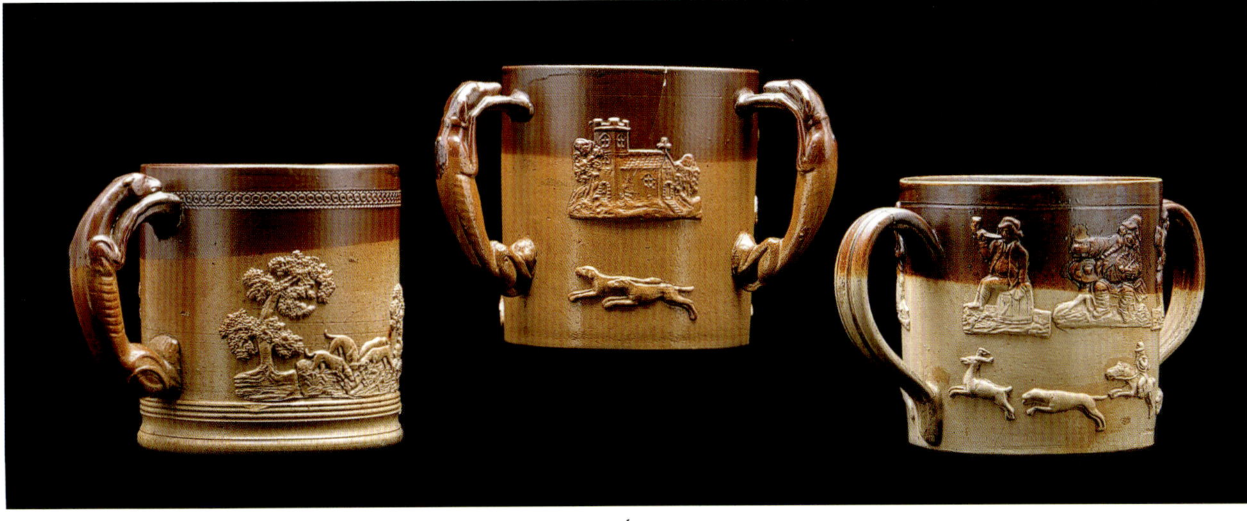

a *b* *c*

Figure 18 Large brown-dipped stoneware mugs from three different factories: (*a*) Characterized by its large, collarless hound handle and its band of doughnut and chevron rouletting below the rim. A six-element version of "The Kill" runs above the four cordons terminating at both ends with well-defined trees. Lathe chatter is visible on the base both inside and out. Bristol or Derbyshire, ca. 1840. H. 6¼". See also fig. 8*b*. (*b*) Mug with three hound handles having vestigial collars, separating an away-facing windmill (e.g., table XII.5), the standard, late Fulham church (table I.13), and Toby wearing a knitted sweater (table III.11). The base is stamped, in a circle, "Bailey & C° / Fulham," the mark of C.I.C. Bailey 1864–1889. H. 6⅝". (*c*) Mug with an unevenly applied dark brown dip over a brownish gray body. Two hunters, one with a flailing whip (table IX.4) and the other with a large, back-facing horn (e.g., table IX.6) follow single hounds in pursuit of a stag. The upper frieze is limited to the mug holder astride a barrel (as fig. 12*d*), the young smoker (as fig. 12*f*), and a well-defined Toby seated on a slender chair beside a pedestal table (table II.6). Derbyshire or Bristol, ca. 1840. H. 7".

Sanders's old Mortlake factory, Vauxhall's delft production was shifted upriver. After Wagstaff's death, both factories were inherited by John Wisker. There being no known Vauxhall hunting mugs and jugs from the Whisker era, the productivity of his plants is uncertain. It is certain, however, that new names were surfacing, among them William and Stephen Green, Martha Jones, and C. Bloodworth. In 1812 twenty-two-year-old John Doulton, who had served his apprenticeship at Fulham, obtained employment in the pottery run by Martha Jones and her foreman, John Watts.[120] Three years later Doulton invested £100 and became a partner with Jones and Watts; thus began the story of the most successful of all brown stoneware factories, one that would stay in operation at Lambeth until 1956.[121]

The widowed Martha Jones retired from the partnership in 1820, and because Doulton was a skilled potter and John Watts primarily a manager, the firm soon became Doulton & Watts. Eight years later, with their business prospering, they built two new kilns in Lambeth High Street and shortly thereafter began to mark some of their wares with both their names, occasionally adding the place name "LAMBETH." They continued to do so until Watts's retirement in 1858. Closer dating is sometimes possible. In the 1830s marks included the street address, 15 High Street, ceasing in 1838 when the number was changed from 15 to 28. From 1858 to 1910 many jugs were simply impressed "DOULTON / LAMBETH," with "ENGLAND" added in 1892. However, the most common marks found on Doulton's Victorian-era hunting mugs were set in an oval (1869–1872) with a small "x" between the words. In 1872 the mark was changed, substituting a cross formée for the "x." This new mark contained a date from 1872 to 1877 and occasionally thereafter until 1887. In 1899, still within an oval (but without crosses), the mark read "DOULTON & C°. / LIMITED / LAMBETH." Other marks occurred impressed within a circle and contained numbers whose significance has been lost.[122] In 1901 the company was granted the right to refer to itself as Royal Doulton, and thereafter a new mark was topped by a crown and lion over a circle inscribed "ROYAL DOULTON / ENGLAND."[123]

Some Doulton stonewares are impressed with marks identifying piece work by individual assistants; the base of the jug in figure 19*e* is one example. Impressed with four squares (linked in pairs) and the letter "P," it was the work of Anne Partridge (1882–1913)—thereby providing the jug with

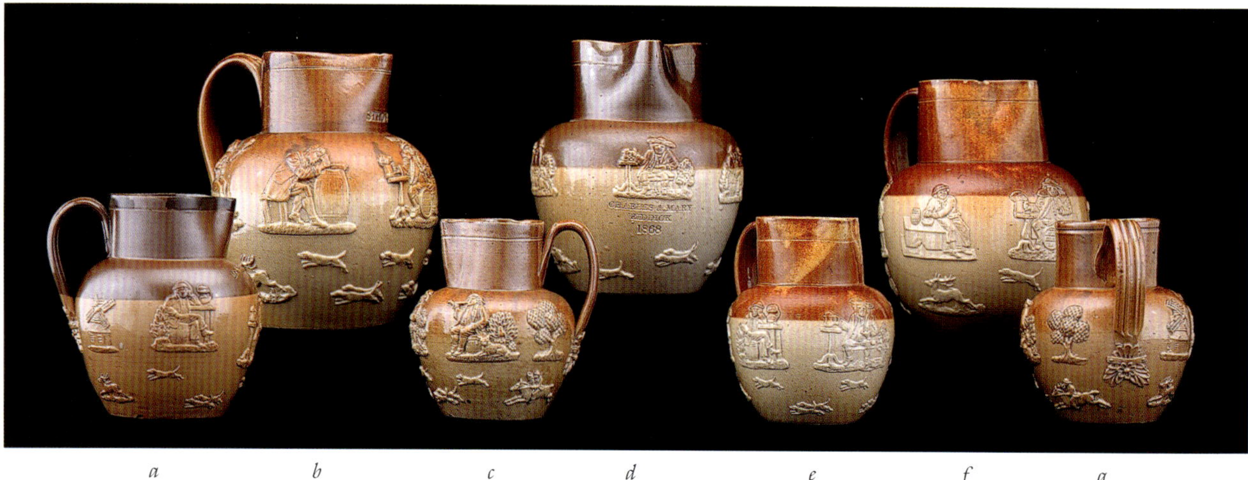

a *b* *c* *d* *e* *f* *g*

Figure 19 Dipped, brown stoneware jugs in Doulton style: (*a*) Smooth nut-brown glaze over a thin dip. The double-reeded handle is chamfered over the standard Doulton terminal (as table XV.17). The sprigs are representative of the Doulton series: The contented smoker has his cat at his feet and an owl in the bush behind him (as table XIII.10). The "thinking toper" has an owl in the bush behind him (as table XIII.9) and the front-facing windmill has two windows, one larger than the other and having six panes against four (as table XIII.15). The series is completed by a tree whose foliage is created from five hatched disks (as table VI.14). Unmarked and with three circular stilt marks on the base. Doulton, ca. 1865. H. 5½". (*b*) Jug with pale brown dip and reeded handle chamfered as 19*a* over Doulton's standard large vessel, stylized foliate terminal secured with a faux screw attaching the strap (table XV.13). The jug's sprigs feature first a black workman, wearing a heaver's cap, who has a beaker in one hand and a jug in the other; a large hog lies under his table (table XIII.16). The second sprig presents an elaborate windmill and miller's house. His wife stands at the door; a man leading a laden mule approaches and the miller makes his way into the mill. Outside the house are two chickens and a cockerel (table XII.10). Next, Toby sits astride a barrel and wears a carter's coat. He rests a straight-sided tankard on a single baluster-legged table. Below, the ground is impressed with a rouletting wheel (table III.5). Beyond Toby another black man with a short beard and curly hair leans on a barrel while holding a beaker; his cap lies on the table (table XIII.15). The last figure is a young man wearing a short jacket, sitting on a tub holding a pipe in one hand and raising a tumbler aloft with the other (table XIV.7). Like Toby, the sprig's ground is notched with a rouletting wheel. Below the frieze gallops a standard Doulton hunt. The huntsman blows an upturned horn and his hounds run singly and in pairs, pursuing a stag as it bounds toward a Doulton five-disk tree. The neck and shoulder are type-impressed "STRONG BEER." Unmarked. Doulton, ca. 1865. H. 8". (*c*) As 19*a*, showing a different view (tables XII.15, XIII.10), unmarked. Doulton, ca. 1865. H. 5½". (*d*) Jug with chocolate brown dip, the terminal of its reeded handle more stylized than that of 19*b* (table XV.15). Along with a standard cat and owl smoker, the thinker, and a Toby beside a straight-leg pedestal table, a windmill differs from the early norm by having six panes in its smaller window (table XII.16). To complete the upper series is a sharply molded family group that I have dubbed "the pig family." It comprises a hog, a child leaning on a barrel, father drinking, and mother trying to feed a small child while another, larger child sits beside her (as table XI.3). The jug is type-impressed "CHARLES & MARY / RIDDICK / 1868." Unmarked. Doulton. H. 7⅜". (*e*) Jug with apple-red dip and cream interior glaze; standard Doulton sprigs except that the windmill's windows are of matching size (as table XII.17). Base impressed "Doulton / Lambeth," with four square dots and the letter P. Ca. 1882. H. 5½". (*f*) Jug with apple-red dip and internal cream glaze. The handle reverts to the spatula terminal and to a windmill with six-pane windows of different sizes. The trees both small and large are standard Doulton, the latter in front of a gated picket fence. Toby sits astride a barrel head marked with an "x" and rests his pewter tankard on a baluster-pedestal table. Beyond him a workman sitting on a tub is filling his pipe from an open bowl that rests beside a tobacco barrel on a box-shaped bench or table (table XIII.18). The jug's base is scarred from standing on a square kiln prop and is impressed "DOULTON / LAMBETH." Ca. 1880. H. 7⅜". (*g*) Jug with chocolate brown dip over a brownish orange body and internally cream-glazed. The sprigs are standard Doulton, although Toby sits on a bench beside his straight-legged pedestal table. His tobacco pipe is short-stemmed, and his mug is globular (table III.10). The jug's shoulder is type-impressed "Mr & Mrs J. Reddick / Old Windsor / 1911" and the base is impressed with an oval "DOULTON & C° / LIMITED / LAMBETH," a mark first used in 1899. H. 6".

an undeniable *terminus post quem*.[124] The base is also marked with the old "DOULTON / LAMBETH" mark, proof that it continued in use long after the oval marks had been introduced.[125]

Unfortunately, there is little information regarding Doulton's Vauxhall Walk products (1815–1827) and no marks have been identified. Indeed, Oswald, Hildyard, and Hughes have flatly stated that Doulton stonewares were "unmarked before c. 1830, and invariably marked from c. 1870."[126]

In 1820, when Martha Jones retired, there were in Lambeth half a dozen small stoneware potteries about which very little is known. It is fair to assume, however, that like Doulton and Watts their principal output was not hunting jugs but bottles for spruce beer, ink, and carbonated waters, all in shapes that would continue in production for decades. Not until 1828 did Doulton face serious competition, specifically from Stephen Green, who three years later expanded his Imperial Potteries into stoneware production and continued in this branch until 1858.[127] Although he almost certainly included hunting jugs in his inventory, Green is most often associated with brown stoneware gin flasks, which he molded in a variety of beguiling forms, some of them hunt-related.[128]

In 1835, John Doulton's second son, Henry, joined his father as an apprentice and after serving his time became the mainstay of the company. However, Henry was primarily involved in the development and sale of industrial wares, chemical containers, crucibles, and the like. John Doulton retired in 1853, whereupon the firm's name was changed to Doulton & Co., although promotional literature and price lists continued into the 1870s under the heading of Doulton & Watts. Commenting on the 1858 change, Doulton historian Louise Irvine has stated that "almost all the wares produced before that date were undecorated industrial and domestic wares."[129] Although Doulton's 1873 catalog listed only hunting jugs, by 1880 an almost identical Doulton price list had inserted "MUGS, low shape" in pint and half-pint sizes, either plain or figured, adding that "Two and three handled Figured Mugs [were] kept in stock." By 1894 hunting-decorated kettles and coffee pots had been added to the line, but were no longer advertised as hunting vessels (figs. 21*a*–*g*). They were now called "Toby" this or that. The 1930 catalog issued by Royal Doulton Potteries offered no

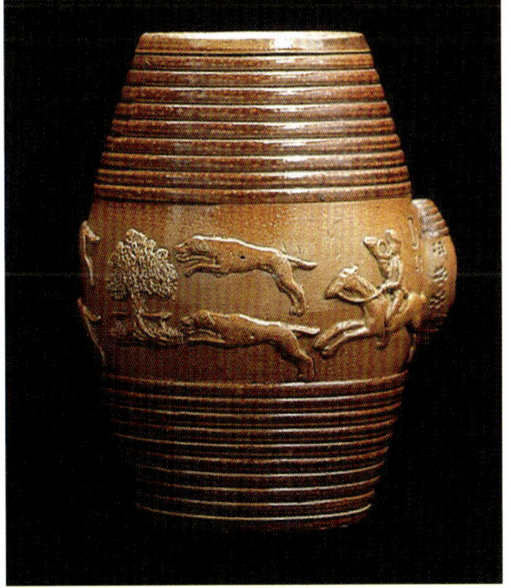

Figure 20 Barrel, Bristol, 1832. Salt-glazed stoneware. H. 5½". Barrel with applied hunting scene and type-impressed "D B / 1832," its bunghole ornamented with impressed rosettes. The short-coated huntsman blows an upturned horn as he follows single hounds past a small oak tree in pursuit of a slender but heavily antlered stag (table X.5, .16). Each sprig exhibits a small hole where a tool has been used to help it adhere.

fewer than twenty different Toby shapes with sprig-applied figures in either white or brown. Included were "Toby Jugs (White Figures)" and "Toby Jugs (Brown Figures 'Old Style')."[130] The latter continued to be made until Doulton closed its Lambeth works. A jug with a silver mount dated to 1894/99 is inscribed "TO TOBY OR NOT TO TOBY THAT IS THE QUESTION (*Hamlet Act III, Sc. I. as perverted by E. W-W.*)." Alas, E. W-W.'s identity remains a mystery,[131] but the message is clear enough: In the late Victorian era the Fillpot name had become more firmly associated with the sprigged jugs than were their previously dominant hunting features.

John Doulton's principal competitor, John Stiff, came from the Doulton factory, having served as its foreman. Stiff set up his own pottery in 1846 and continued in the business through the rest of the century. Stiff's

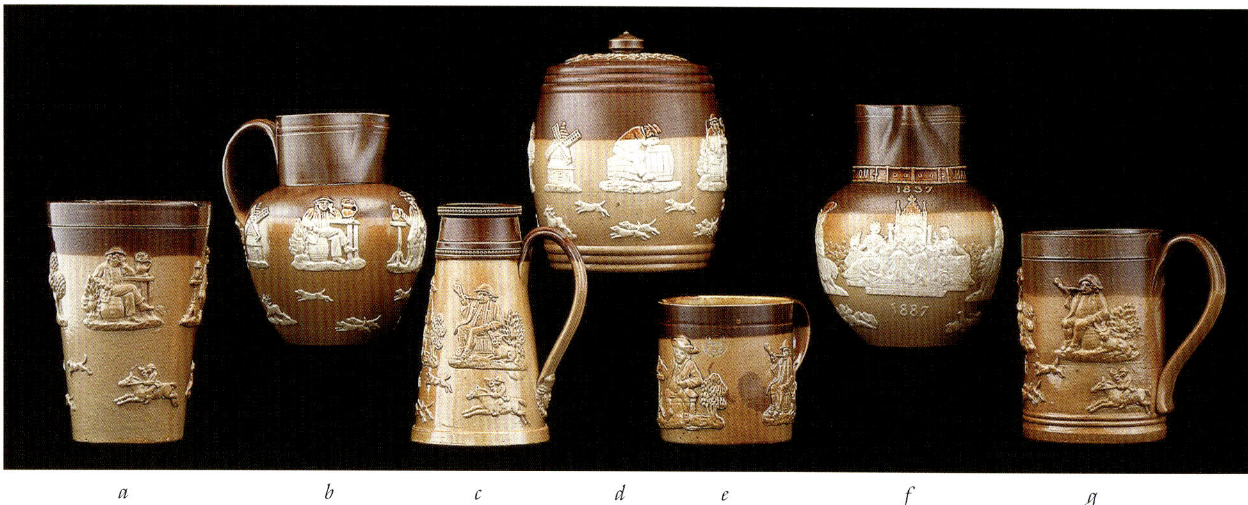

a *b* *c* *d* *e* *f* *g*

Figure 21 Various vessel forms, Doulton, ca. 1877–1910. Salt-glazed stoneware. (*a*) Brown-dipped beaker with standard Doulton sprigs and type-impressed "Gerard" below the rim. Oval mark on base "DOULTON / LAMBETH" separated by a cross formée. 1877–1887. H. 5½". (*b*) Jug with dark brown, high gloss dip and white sprigs of standard Doulton hunting wares, the only variation being that Toby sits on a bench beside a straight-legged pedestal table. Mark as 21*a*, ca. 1880. H. 5⅞". (*c*) Shaving mug with brown dip and beading around the lip and above the handle, which terminates in a face, wearing a frilled collar and resembling that of a Westminster chorister (table XV.18). Note, too, that the smoker's cat has four eyes (table XIII.11). Impressed "DOULTON / LAMBETH." Ca. 1885. H. 6¾". (*d*) Brown-dipped tobacco jar with floral sprigged lid, decorated with standard Doulton hunting and Toby sprigs; cordoned at top and bottom, the base slightly raised and impressed with the letter "f," the number "1293," and "DOULTON / LAMBETH / ENGLAND," a factory mark in use from 1891 to 1956. H. 5⅛" (without lid). (*e*) Mug, brown-dipped and internally cream-glazed, with reeded handle. No hunting elements, there being room only for the smoker and thinker, the former with his four-eyed cat. Toby sits on a bench, his face coated with the same white slip used below the rim to apply the stenciled mark reading "Half Pint" over a circle containing a crowned "GV / 522 / LCC," this last an abbreviation for the London County Council. An impressed oval mark on the base reads "DOULTON & CO / LIMITED LAMBETH." Ca. 1910. H. 3¼". (*f*) Jug with speckled brown dip but no internal glaze. The reeded handle is chamfered at its base under a floral ribbon cut into sections to be placed between white sprigged figures representing areas of British influence in the Orient, India, British Africa, and Canada. These flank a group featuring Queen Victoria, seated on her coronation throne attended by figures epitomizing peace and plenty, all above a ribbon bearing the royal motto. A belt representing the Order of the Garter circles the junction of neck and wall, and trumpet-blowing cherubs ring the base. Above the throne is the accession date 1837 and below it is the date of the queen's fiftieth Jubilee, 1887. Made to commemorate the latter event, the jug is marked on the base "DOULTON / LAMBETH" in an oval and separated by crosses formée, also with an impressed "R^{d}. 71203" and "Ho," the personal mark of either Eliza J. Hollis or Annie Horton, both of whom were working in the factory in 1882. H. 6". (*g*) Mug with brown dip over a lighter brown body, no internal glazing. The reeded handle turns outward at its lower junction immediately above two encircling cordons. A small hunting group chases a stag around the lower wall. Above are the usual owl and cat (with only two eyes) owners and a Toby figure seated on a barrel. The base is impressed with an oval reading "DOULTON / LAMBETH" separated by crosses formée. Ca. 1885. H. 4¾".

catalogs offered "Figured Hunting Jugs and Mugs" in sizes from a one-quarter pint to one gallon, "Mounted with Metal Covers if required" (figs. 13*b, d*).[132] In 1873 Doulton, still under the name Doulton & Watts Lambeth Pottery, issued a similar price list offering hunting jugs in either "Common Clay" or "Fine Clay," the latter double the price of the former.[133] Both factories also offered conical shaving mugs, either plain or hunt-decorated (fig. 21*c*).

Throughout its history from the third quarter of the nineteenth century on, Doulton consistently used the same two toper figures, one to the right of the handle accompanied by an owl (table XIII.8) and one to the left, a couchant and regardant cat with a smaller owl in the bush behind him (table XIII.10; figs. 19*a, c*). In later examples the cat often has two pairs of eyes (table XIII.11). It is axiomatic that the more examples one has to study the fewer will be one's mistakes. In an earlier stage of this study I called the animal a "cat-eared dog," but on the larger sprigs the head is manifestly feline, as is the double-bend in its tail. So now we have an owl and a pussycat together on the same jug or mug. Was it conceivable that Edward Lear's poem "The Owl and the Pussycat" was the source (perhaps an in-house joke) for these sprigs? Lear's *Nonsense Songs and Stories* was first published in 1871, so, were the connection valid, it would provide the owl and cat sprigs with a firm *terminus post quem*.[134] Proof that this also was nonsense came from an "Owl and Pussycat" jug, type-impressed "CHARLES & MARY RIDDICK 1868" (fig. 19*d*). There was, of course, the possibility that the jug was made much later, to commemorate the Riddicks' marriage anniversary. However, the ever-helpful Mormon Church records include an entry for the baptism of an infant Charles Riddick in 1870, thereby leaving no doubt as to the validity of the 1868 date. Perhaps, then, the curious relationship between owl and cat can be interpreted the other way around: Lear composing his verses after seeing the sprig on a Doulton jug. Besides providing an early date for the "Owl and Pussycat" sprigs, the 1868 jug offers dating for two more Doulton sprigs. One, which I call the "pig family," shows five human figures: three children, their parents, plus a large hog (table XI.3).[135] The other is a stylized tree whose foliage is created from five hatched, convex disks (table VI.14, .15). This globular foliage construction seems to have been used by no other factory, though a tool very like it has been used to anchor the base of a tree on a mug of almost certain London origin (table VI.6).

Attributable also to the 1860s is another Doulton jug whose intended purpose is in no doubt. Type-impressed into the neck and shoulder are the words "STRONG BEER" (fig. 19*b*). The central Toby figure is characterized by his straight-sided tankard, his pedestal-legged table, his heavy carter's coat, and his curly hair under a very flat hat (table III.5). To his left is another familiar Doulton grouping: a miller, his mill and his house, his wife feeding chickens, and a man arriving or leaving with a laden pack mule (table XII.10).[136] More surprising are the flanking toper sprigs, for both almost certainly depict black men. On the left an old, bearded, and curly-haired man leans over a barrel as though asleep, his forehead resting on the rim of his tumbler. The other man holds a glass and a jug and wears a stevedore's cap (table XIII.15, .16), and lying between the legs of his seat is the Doulton hog. Although the jug is unmarked, the black figures are paralleled on another Doulton (post-1891) example in the collection, albeit in a more refined buff-bodied ware, a fabric used from circa 1890 until the business closed. However, Louise Irvine dates a similar jug to circa 1870–1890 and a mug to circa 1880.[137] In all the post-1870 heavy-coated Toby-sprigged examples that I have seen, his curly hair has become scarecrow-straight and his hat has acquired an angular visor (table III.6).[138]

A small jug with at least superficial Doulton connections is decorated with two topers, a windmill, and realistically treated trees. But the shrub behind the imbiber at right is almost identical to Doulton's owl in the bushes (fig. 10*c*; table XIII.7). One of its trees, too, is flanked by a fence and gate that are also found on Doulton sprigs (table VI.15), but that is where the similarities end. Its windmill stands on a pad of indistinctly molded foliage, a feature found on Derbyshire products (table XII.7),[139] and its smoker at left closely parallels another on the Derbyshire puzzle jug, which could date as early as 1825 (fig. 12*h*). The jug's yellow body color and very thin ginger-brown dip also point in that direction.

Oswald, Hildyard, and Hughes took a big step forward when they provided drawn typologies of upper-level sprigs on hunting jugs, among them trees, windmills, and handle terminals, but the number of factories producing these jugs in the latter part of the nineteenth century made it inevitable that there would be as many designs missing from the lists as were included in them.[140] Making the task of identification even more difficult has been the fact that factories copied from each other. This was particularly true of Fulham, which borrowed extensively from Doulton after 1891, when George William Cheavin became manager of the Fulham Pottery.[141]

Varied though the windmills were, a few rules do apply. Thus, for example, Doulton's windmill buildings on middle-period (1860s–1870s) jugs possess a six-paned window beside a smaller, four-paned window (table XII.15).[142] On the later jugs both windows are about the same size (table XII.17). Among anomalies are the previously mentioned trestle-supported windmill (fig. 16*a*; table XII.9) and a windmill whose multitiered mill might have drawn its inspiration from the 1761 pagoda at Kew (fig. 17*a*; table XII.8). If true, the closest factory would have been William Kishere's at Mortlake.[143] If that, too, is correct, the pagoda sprig's association with the jug's strapped and multi-leaf-scaled terminal brings with it a large group of well-made hunting jugs, several of which have pewter lids and often have willow-tree sprigs (figs. 17*a*, *c*; table VI.6, .7). Oswald, Hildyard, and Hughes have called this a "standard early terminal, found at Mortlake, Vauxhall, etc."[144]

In the continuing game of "hold-the-handle" someone else decided that the job could best be done not with Fulham's third screw but with a bar spanning the terminal and secured with the original two screws. Oswald, Hildyard, and Hughes proposed a starting date at the Kishere Mortlake factory of about 1820, but no corroborating evidence is provided. Their drawn example comprises a fleur-de-lis above the bar with leaves below it capped by a flower whose petals overlie the bar at its bottom edge. That protruding petal detail occurred later on small Doulton hunting jugs beginning, perhaps, in the 1830s, but continued well into the twentieth century (table XV.17).[145] Doulton's larger jugs (quart and up) sported a more robust terminal featuring the incised strap held by two screws, securing leaf sprays, three above and five below, the central lower leaf spatula shaped (table XV.13).[146] Stiff used a similar terminal, but the leaves were more splayed and omitted the strap's lateral scoring. Stiff's smaller jugs omitted any above-the-strap decoration and the leaves were less stylized than Doulton's (fig. 13*d*).

Doulton hunting mugs (as opposed to jugs) seem never to have possessed sprig-applied handle terminals, being drawn down, thumb impressed, and squared off. Hunting-sprigged shaving mugs were an exception, their reeded handles ending in sharply molded human faces whose ruffs and caps made them resemble Elizabethan choristers (fig. 21*c*; table XV.18). Described in Doulton's 1883 catalog as "shaving pots," these mugs were available both hunt-sprigged or plain. Similar descriptions and prices had previously been supplied in the 1873 catalogs of both Doulton and Stiff.

The use of white sprigs on hunting jugs began in the late 1880s, as is demonstrated by a fine example commemorating Queen Victoria's Diamond Jubilee in 1887 (fig. 21*f*).[147] The queen sits on her throne, flanked by handmaidens and by paired figures representing aspects of her empire: Canada, British Africa, India, and the Orient. Below, where the hunt would normally be, the queen is saluted by horn-blowing flying cherubs. One might reasonably expect that by that late date Doulton's quality control would ensure that each new jug would be identical to the last, but not so. The illustrated example is impressed with a registry number (71203), but so is another whose brown slip is much paler and whose firing has turned the Canadian figures a mottled brown. More significantly, the double grooves that provide a highlight below the lip of my example are missing from the paler specimen. Together, therefore, these Jubilee jugs serve as a reminder that detail differences we might be tempted to leap upon as dating clues could be totally worthless.[148]

That is not true of the applied sprigs, which continue to provide a fertile field of evolutionary research, the attire and accoutrements of masters and their huntsmen being one such avenue.

On the earliest hunt mugs, attributable to Vauxhall in the late 1720s, the clockwise pursuit includes a very small horse with a tricorn-hatted rider with his left arm extended, urging his hounds to greater efforts (as in table VIII.5, .6). He has a hunting horn slung over his shoulder and holds the horse's reins in his right hand. As is characteristic of hunting scenes in this early period, the horse is painted with a ferruginous slip and the hounds are similarly dappled, creating a far more dramatic and realistic panorama than is found on later mugs whose animals are not highlighted (figs. 1*c*, *d*). The dappling occurs on clockwise hunts as early as 1724[149] and on counterclockwise examples as late as 1731, meaning that although the direction of hunts has been construed as indicating different factories, the coloring does nothing to bolster that thesis.[150] On the contrary, the use of it in both directions might be construed as evidence of a single source. Furthermore, if it can be proven that the application of huntsman, hounds, and quarry always began with the hunter, it is possible that sets of molds existed for the use of left- and right-handed craftsmen working in the same factory.[151]

Unlike my 1731 huntsman, whose clothing portrays no particular style, the huntsman of 1737 wears a wide-cuffed coat and knee britches (table VIII.6). On his head he wears what looks like a military cap over a ribbon-tied wig. The mid-century Bristol hunt master is equally well delineated (table VIII.4). He wears a long coat buttoned to the waist, with the wide cuffs and skirt typical of the first half of the eighteenth century. His tricorn hat is appropriate to the period, as are his short, side-curled wig and his folded-top boots. He is evidently a gentleman hunter, sitting bolt upright on his horse clutching a long whip, content to leave the tiresome activity of horn-blowing to his staff-toting and pedestrian retainers.[152] It is evident, however, that sprig molds did not keep pace with fashion. The same huntsman appears on a Bristol jug of gallon capacity and impressed "Iacob Parfons 1790."[153]

As discussed earlier, it was in the 1790s that Joseph Kishere's Mortlake Pottery began to produce hunting mugs and jugs of high quality with sharply modeled sprigging. The previously discussed male and female horse riders with their enormous hats became the poster people of this era (figs. *7a–c*; table VIII.8–.10).[154] Although wide-brimmed hats were worn at the close of the eighteenth century, I have found no parallels for the high crown. Whatever the source, there is no evidence that the style was adopted by later mold makers. Indeed, other than Mortlake's output, there are very few (if any) hunting jugs that can be attributed to dates between 1810 and 1830.[155]

If it be true that hunting jugs and mugs were out of fashion in that twenty-year period, by 1832 the idea was back in full cry (fig. 20). The barrel impressed with that date and the initials D B is almost certainly a Bristol product.[156] The hunting scene that girdles it is very sharp and introduces a new huntsman—a youthful figure wearing a short coat, boot-length trousers, and a hunting cap with its brim or bill upturned (table IX.8). He blows a French horn and follows six hounds in pairs between small trees, in pursuit of an apprehensive stag (table X.16, .5). A shape and glazing parallel is impressed "John: Evans 1797," and, as Robin Hildyard has noted, a young man of that name was apprenticed to Bristol stoneware potter John Hope.[157] Though better made, the D B barrel fits well among Lambeth flasks that exploited the taste for gin which was dispensed from the huge tuns set behind the counters of most gin shops in the 1830–1860 period. However, none of the London barrel-shaped flasks is girded with hunting scenes.[158] A possibly factory-revealing detail are single small holes in each of the sprigs. Be it huntsman, trees, hounds, or stag, all have been pressed to the wall by a pin-sized tool, either to help them adhere or to transfer the partially dried casts from worktable to wall.[159] Although uncommon and not, to my knowledge, discussed by previous writers, the application pinholes are present on my 1737 mug attributed to Vauxhall (tables VIII.6, X.13) as well as to the 1792 example from Mortlake (table VIII.7). That there is a technical link between those and the Bristol barrel made several generations later seems hard to refute.

A layman who has never applied a sprig tends to assume that the clay is pressed into individual plaster molds, like those in the collection of the Mortlake parish church, and when the clay dries and shrinks the image is transferred directly to the moistened pot wall.[160] However, in 1894 local Mortlake collector John Eustace Anderson published *A Short Account of the Mortlake Potteries,* a previously cited booklet in which he described how Joseph Kishere's daughter Susan sometimes helped by "stamping out" the hunting figures and applying them to the jugs.[161] But since Anderson was not born until 1840 it is unlikely that he ever saw sprigs applied, and, like much hearsay, what he was told he remembered incorrectly or misunderstood.

The previously illustrated gallon-capacity jug perhaps attributable to Liverpool (table IV.1) displays two hunters, one waving a whip and the other blowing a horn that is so long it goes twice around his arm before expanding into the bell (table IX.5, .7). This man wears a billed cap but the whip carrier has a hat with a small brim and rectangular crown, a detail that separates master from huntsman. Both men, along with hounds fore and aft, are to be found as a single sprig on a quart jug whose scale-decorated handle terminal has been attributed to Derbyshire (fig. 13*c*; table IX.14).[162] The neck and shoulder have been twice dipped and appear a rich reddish brown over a pale body with black (coal?) flecks. The Toby figure is large, flanked by trees, and has a dog at his feet—all in a single sprig (table II.10). Gripped in the man's large hand is what appears to be a bottle rather than a mug, and on the table is a beaker. A secondary toper sits on a barrel, smoking a pipe from which the smoke billows back to his hat (table XIV.8).[163] Another, smaller jug, more certainly attributable to Derbyshire, has its sprigged decoration in high relief and compatible with the excessive thickness of the body and base. The dry and matte-surfaced buff ware extends up to a contrastingly high gloss, dark brown washed shoulder and neck. Because the jug is small and the sprigs large, there was no room for a standard Toby figure, so a well-sculpted member of the supporting cast was substituted (fig. 10*a*). The sexton leans sideways on a small barrel, smoking a pipe in his left hand and holding a glass in his right; hanging from his wrist is a pair of large keys (table XIII.1).[164] In contrast, this jug's huntsman is small. He wears the master's flat-topped hat and possesses a formidable nose on a face registering aggressive determination; he looks like a man who would gouge his horse and beat his dogs. As is usual with hatted masters, he is not encumbered by a hunting horn (table IX.2). The jug's grape-and-leaf handle terminal makes it likely that this is a product of the Bourne factory at Denby (table XV.8), but dating is less certain—probably circa 1830–1845.

Although there may be dozens of different riders chasing round the bellies of jugs made by small and forgotten potteries, Doulton's capped huntsman remained consistent from the 1860s to the end of production at the onset of the Second World War in 1939.[165] He rode with a French horn to his lips and wearing a hat resembling a British steel helmet (table IX.11).[166] It seems fair to assume that to a Doulton mold maker a countryman's hat was a countryman's hat no matter who was wearing it. The barrel-seated figure on this jug is not our standard jolly Toby but is, rather, the previously noted individual wearing a heavy coat of the type worn by coachmen and wagoners. His hat, too, is of a kind worn by such people. To his left is another uncommon sprig, namely a working man leaning on a boxlike table while filling his pipe from a tobacco container (fig. 19*f*; table XIII.18). Beside him on the table a small barrel substitutes for the usual mug or jug of foaming ale.[167] However, the handle terminal is more typical of Doulton, although it has very small tacks rather than screws to secure the lateral strap.

Doulton's premier Lambeth competitor (and frequent copyist) James Stiff also used a single horseman, but one wearing what looks like a bowler hat and a jacket with broad, buttoned facings, and with neither a crop nor a horn in his hand (table IX.3). The jug is identified as a Stiff product (ca. 1880–1900) on the evidence of a windmill and its abutting, chimneyed miller's house, a sprig that seems to have been used only by that factory (table XII.13).[168] Stiff, however, went out of business in 1913, leaving the Lambeth stoneware field to Doulton. Figure 19*g* shows one of the last made for a named public house (1911). It retains the cat and owl sprigs, the standard Toby, the factory-identifying checkered-disk foliage, and the long-established strapped, leaf-and-bloom handle terminal.[169]

Unlike most other nineteenth-century factories, Doulton, as previously noted, resisted the urge to decorate its mug handles, being content to ensure that they were firmly pressed to the wall and slightly upturned (fig. 21*g*). Numerous examples are stamped with an oval mark stenciled in white reading "VR / 523 / L C C" (Victoria Regina—London County Council) and probably were intended for heavy-duty workhouse service. Figure 21*e* illustrates a half-pint Toby mug with a similar "L C C" stencil but made in the reign of "GV" (George V) and therefore dating no earlier than his 1910 accession.[170] Doulton also made special edition mugs to commemorate that event.[171]

Thousands of late-Doulton-type hunting mugs and jugs can still be bought at reasonable prices and provide a foundation for brown stoneware collections which, as I have tried to demonstrate, still have *eureka!* moments in store. Many avenues remain to be explored, along with a plethora of frustrating blind alleys—but therein lies the thrill of the search.

We have to keep reminding ourselves, however, that big factories copied each other as did little ones whose locations have yet to be identified, and that my illustrated details are by no means comprehensive, limited as they are to the gamut of one collection. But just as I have learned much from assembling it, I dare to hope that other collectors and curators will be inspired to come forward with rebutting or confirming examples.

In the space of the year in which I worked on this article, more than thirty new hunting jugs and mugs were added to this collection, some of them confirming previous suppositions and others consigning them to the trash can. Three last-minute additions graphically demonstrate the pitfalls that lie in wait for both the novice and the advanced collector. Like the products of all stoneware factories prior to circa 1870, the first is unmarked but has a silver mount bearing that date letter (fig. 22*a*). At first glance, this two-handled mug looks like a standard Doulton product but turns out not to be. By 1870 Doulton had settled into its standard versions of the windmill, pig, family, windmill, and so forth (table XI.4). In this instance, however, nothing quite matches: the pig family has no pig and is short a child;

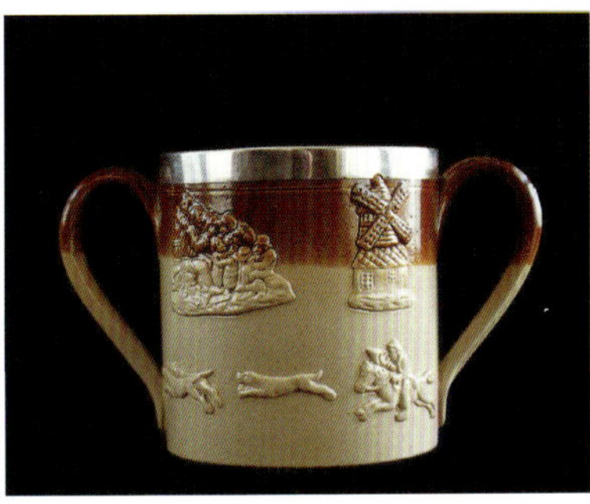

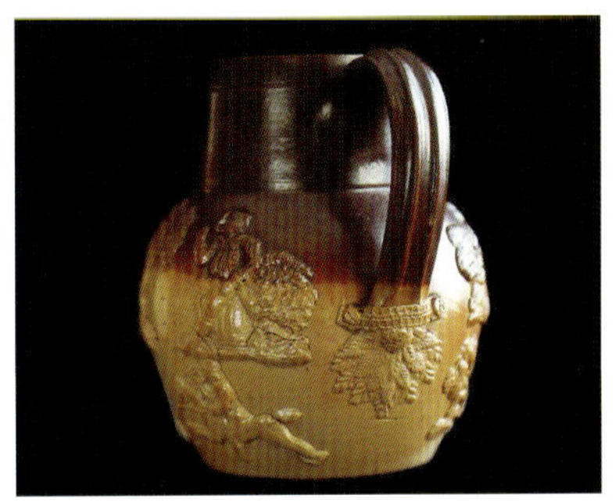

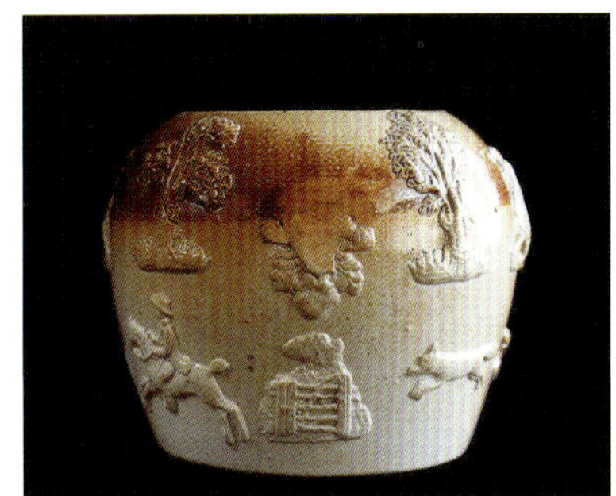

Figure 22 Late arrivals. (Photos, Ivor Noël Hume.) (*a*) Mug, double-handled, brown-dipped over an almost white body, its two handles single reeded. The principal sprigs evidently were very carelessly copied from those used by Doulton on fig. 19*f*. Included are a Toby figure seated on a crudely delineated barrel head (table III.7) beside a table with a wrythen baluster pedestal, also a version of the Doulton pig family (table XI.4). The mug is important in that its silver mount carries the hallmark letter for 1870, a date by which Doulton was already settled into its sprig designs. The mount is marked as having been made by "Lambert 12 Coventry St," thereby strongly suggesting that the mug was a London product. H. 6".

(*b*) Jug with dark brown dip and double-reed handle terminating in an elaborate foliate and floral sprig for which no parallel has been published (table XV.6). The "contented smoker" has no tobacco pipe (table XIII.17), the windmill's housing has a tiled roof (table XII.12), and the tree's foliage is stippled in the manner of Vauxhall at the beginning of the eighteenth century. London, ca. 1850. H. 6¼".

(*c*) A rare, if not unique, waster elevated to "second" status prior to firing. The neck had cracked while drying, prompting the potter to remove both it and the handle to convert a brown-dipped jug into a jar. Its expansive Toby sprig (table II.11) suggests an affinity with that of table II.10 in that both include dogs in the foreground. The other sprigs, two trees (one of them with fruit) and a windmill (table XIII.14), are unparalleled, as is the smeared handle terminal that included the usual screwed strap but also a naturalistic treatment of the foliage below it. The hunting scene augmented by a swing gate is also without a published parallel. Unknown. Ca. 1840. H. 5¾".

the carter-coated Toby has a wrythen baluster to his table, while his barrel head is flat and crudely executed; and the pipe filler lacks a pipe and appears to be breaking something into a three-footed bowl. It seems likely that the mold maker was unsure of what it was he was supposed to be copying—just as I remain unsure who made this travesty and why anyone would think it merited a silver rim. Curiously, however, the sprigs he copied are to be seen on the jug in figure 19*f*, which is impressed "DOULTON / LAMBETH," a mark for which, hitherto, there has been no dating confirmation prior to circa 1870.

The second anomalous new arrival (fig. 22*b*) provides a heretofore unrecorded handle terminal (table XV.6) and an absentminded smoker who forgot his pipe. At a wild guess it should be a London-area production from the mid-nineteenth century. The last of this nameless trio is notable by virtue of having neither neck nor handle (fig. 22*c*). The New Zealand dealer described it as a jar. However, it had not started out as such. A prime clue to its intended shape is provided by the remains of a foliate and screw-strapped handle terminal that had been finger-smeared before firing and after the handle came off. None of its tree, fence, hounds, rider, or windmill motifs is represented among the published examples (table XII.14). The closest it comes to a sprig parallel is provided by the Toby figure who, with a dog at his feet (table II.10), appears on the jug illustrated as figure 13*a* and the detail table II.11. Evidently, the neck and handle broke away while still in the leather-hard state, and rather than waste the effort put into applying the sprigs, the potter decided to fire it as a jar. It seems fair to argue, therefore, that it was the product of a small factory whose master could not afford to discard it as a "waster" and so sold it as a "second." In a belated irony, this truncated hunt jug has survived to earn pride of place in the collection.

To the dismay of all who treasure the countryside, these hunt-decorated stonewares can be classified as "commemorative," fading reminders of a soon-to-be-forgotten age. The Duke of Wellington—the Iron Duke of Waterloo renown—is reputed to have said that he "found men who followed the hounds brave and valiant soldiers." The cavalrymen who rode into battle at Balaclava, Omdurman, and on through the First World War would prove him right. But now, at the dawn of the twenty-first century, the clamor of the socialistic towns against the more conservative country may soon result in a total ban on British hunting, leaving the sport once enjoyed by every level of rural society to be memorialized on little else but antique prints and the sides of old stoneware jugs.

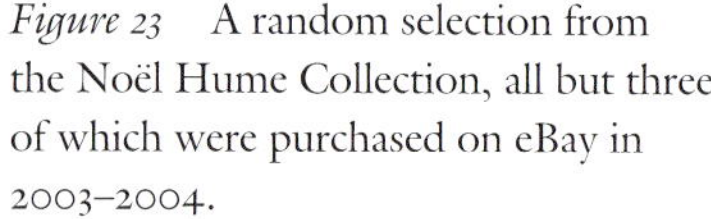
Figure 23 A random selection from the Noël Hume Collection, all but three of which were purchased on eBay in 2003–2004.

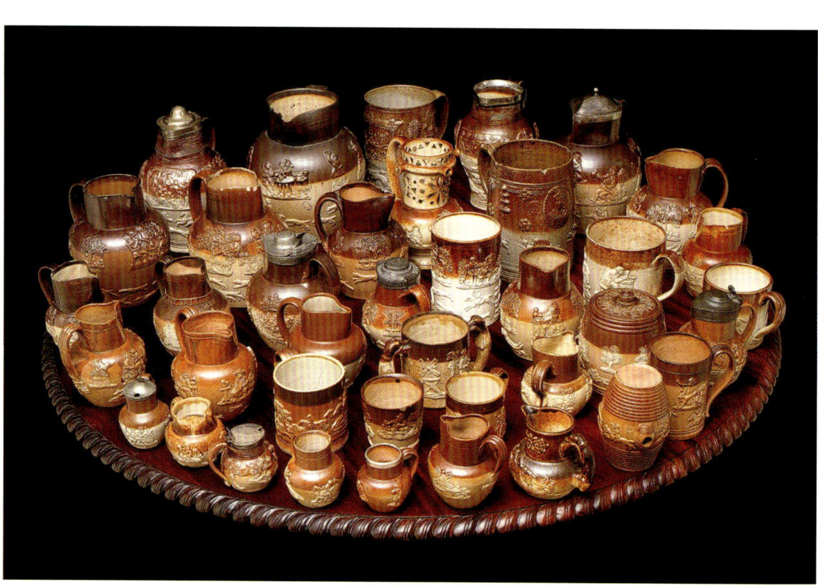

TABLE I. ENGLISH BROWN, SALT-GLAZED STONEWARE HUNTING MUG AND JUG DETAILS

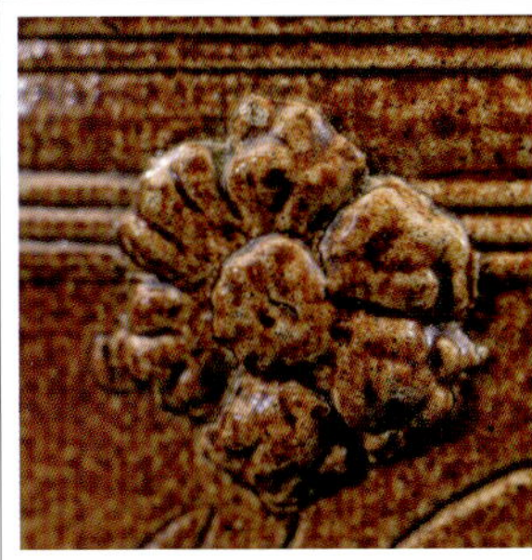

1. Flower sprig, 1722; detail of fig. *1a*

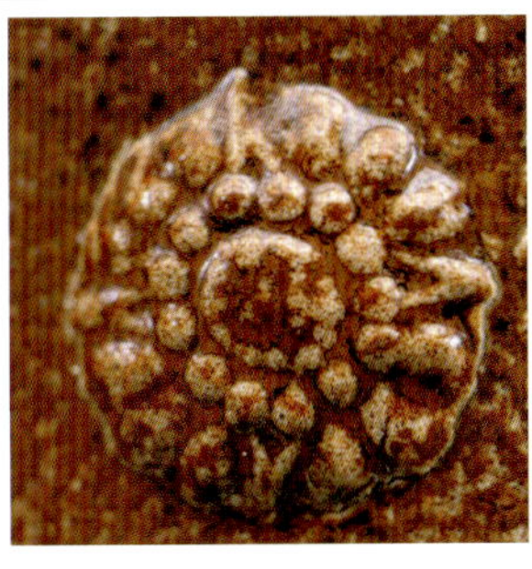

2. Flower sprig with additional anthers, 1731; detail of fig. *1b*

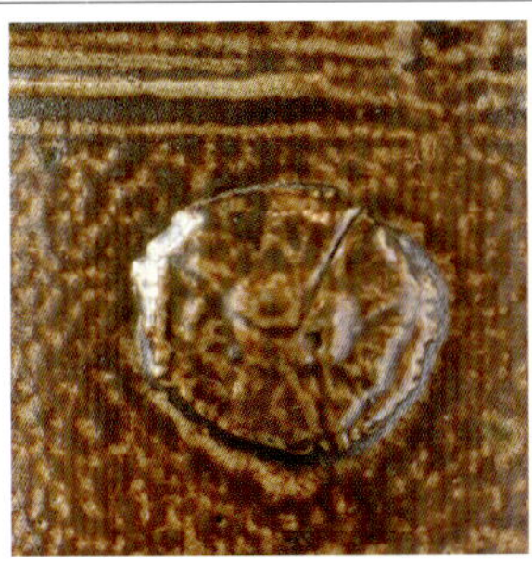

3. Flower sprig, ca. 1760; detail of fig. *1d*

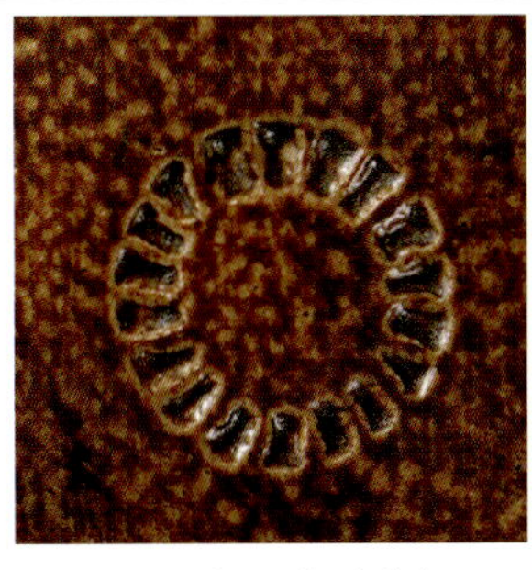

4. Impressed notched disk, ca. 1760; detail of fig. *1d*

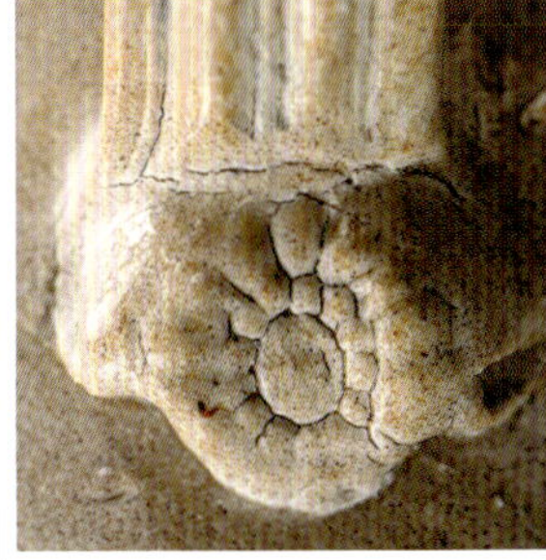

5. Flower mold used to impress handle terminal, 1731; detail of fig. *1b*

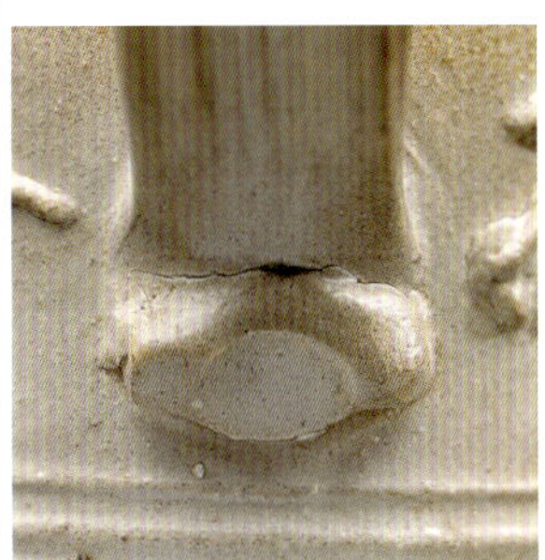

6. Thumb-impressed handle terminal, 1737; detail of fig. *1c*

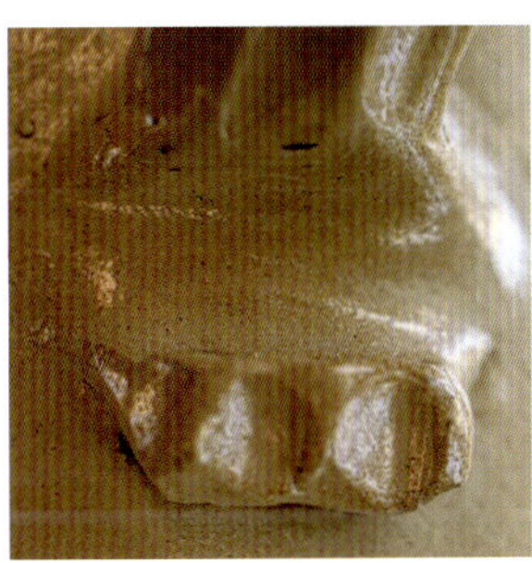

7. Left-hand finger impressions for handle, ca. 1760; detail of fig. *1d*. Note nail indentations.

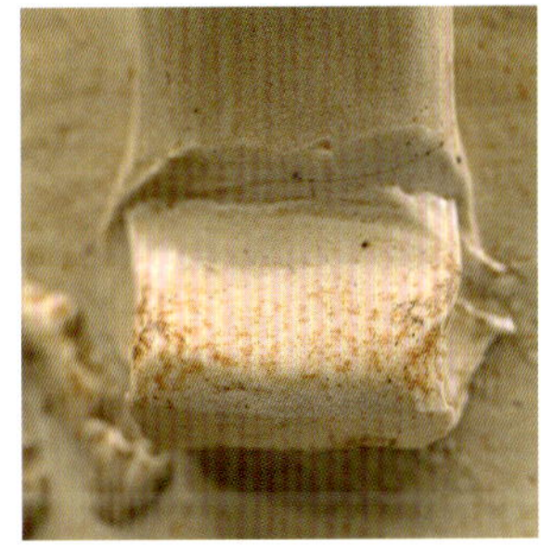

8. Folded handle terminal for Mortlake mug, 1792; detail of fig. *7a*

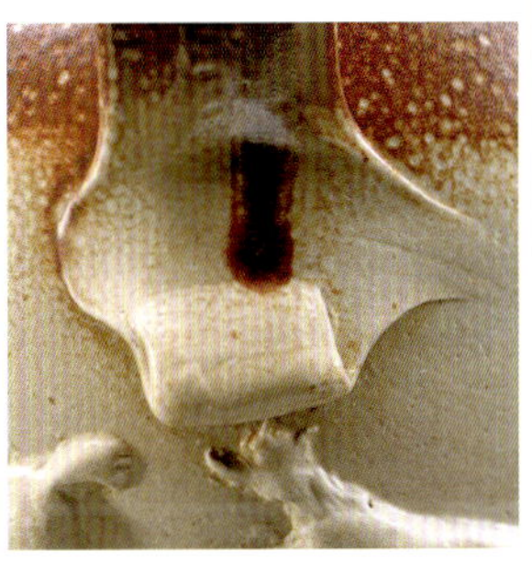

9. Smeared and folded handle terminal for Mortlake jug, 1799; detail of fig. *7b*

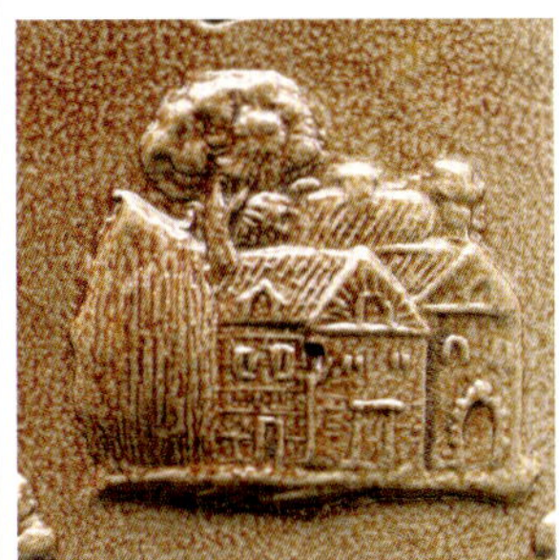

10. Mansion or mill house sprig, 1737; detail of fig. *1c*

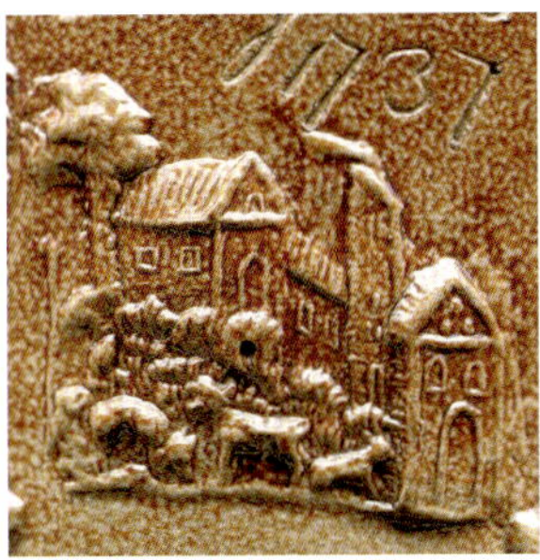

11. Town and domestic animals sprig, 1737; detail of fig. *1c*

12. Thatched house sprig, ca. 1760; detail of fig. *1d*

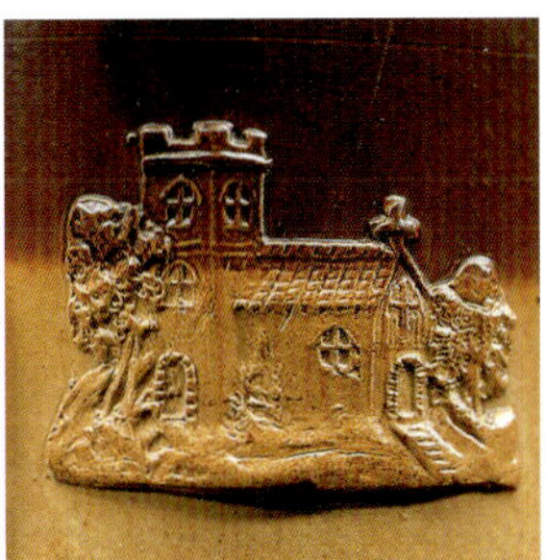

13. Church sprig, Fulham, ca. 1880; detail of fig. *18b*

TABLE II. TOBYS 1

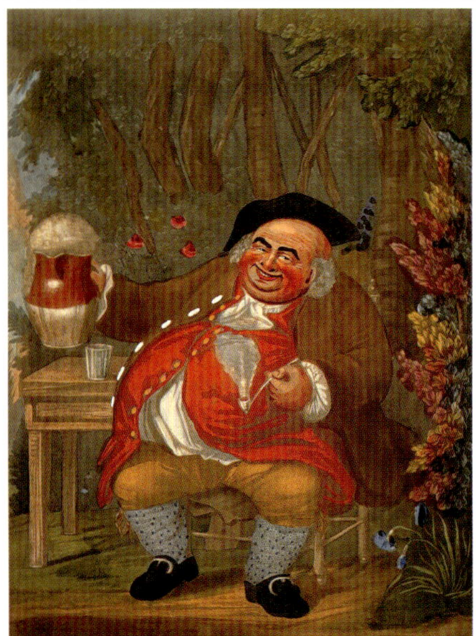

1. The source for a century of Tobys. Hand-colored engraved portrait of Toby Fillpot, printed in London, ca. 1761, for popular illustration publisher Carington Bowles. (Courtesy, Department of Prints and Drawings, British Museum.)

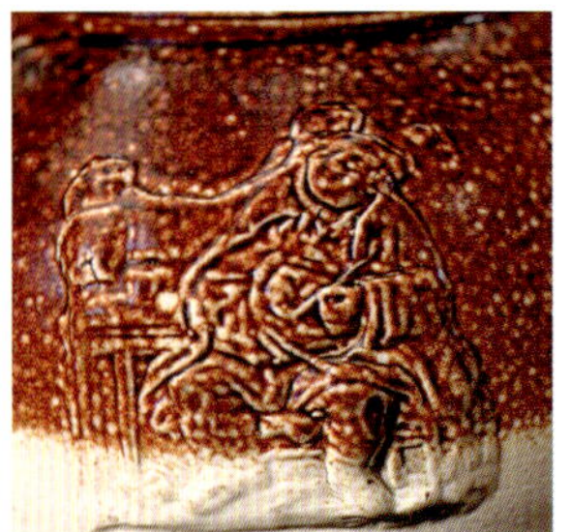

2. Mortlake, 1799; detail of fig. 7*b*

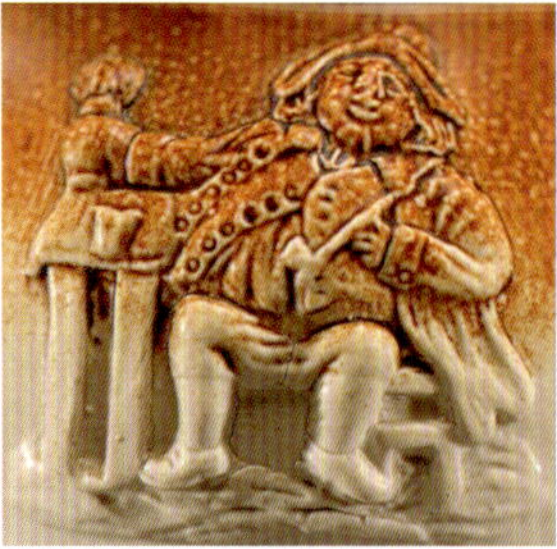

3. Mortlake, ca. 1830; detail of fig. 17*a*

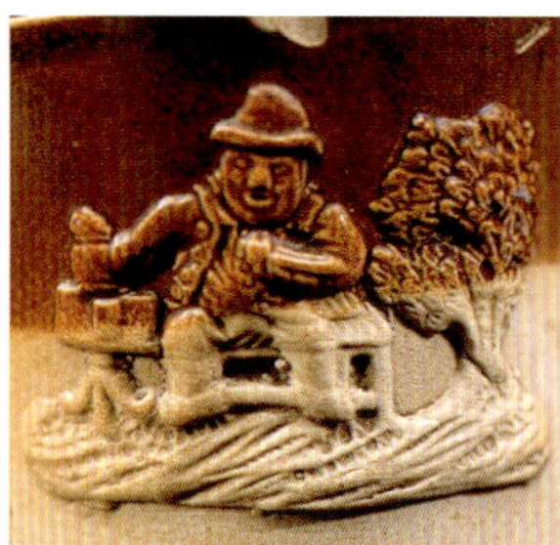

4. Mortlake, ca. 1840; detail of fig. 10*b*

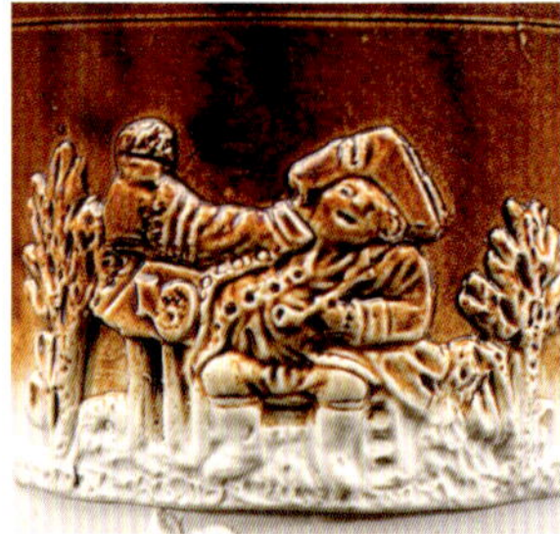

5. South Derbyshire or Bristol, ca. 1820; detail of fig. 16*d*

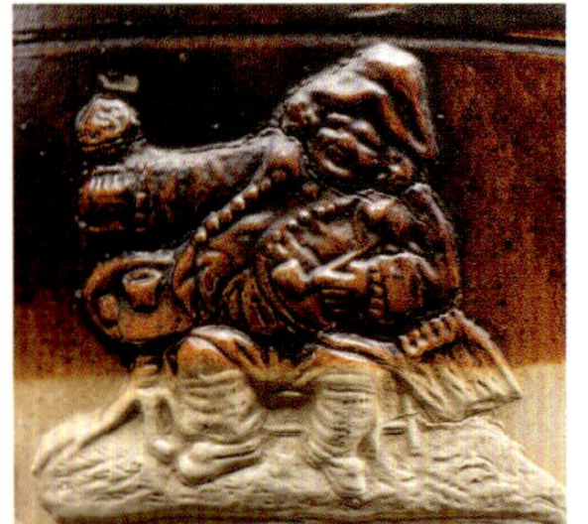

6. Derbyshire or Bristol, ca. 1840; detail of fig. 18*c*

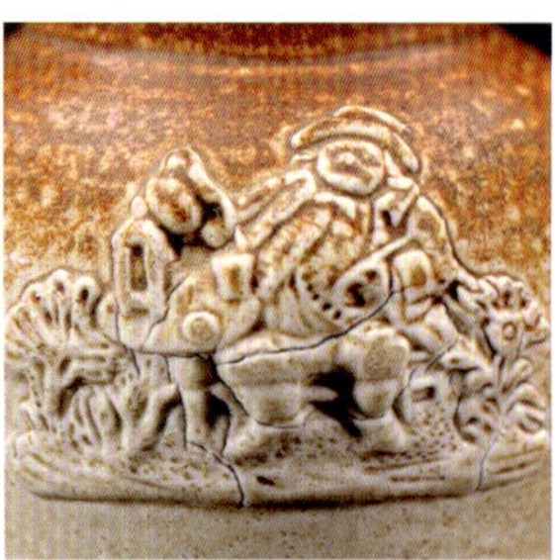

7. Fulham, ca. 1845; detail of fig. 15*d*

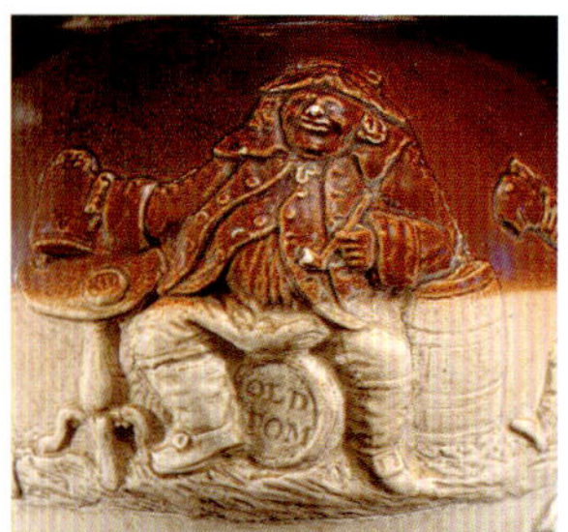

8. Fulham, ca. 1840; detail of fig. 15*c*

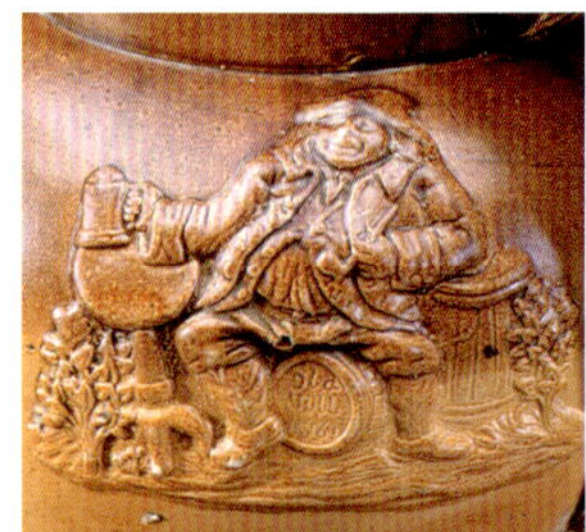

9. Glasgow, ca. 1860; detail of fig. 13*e*

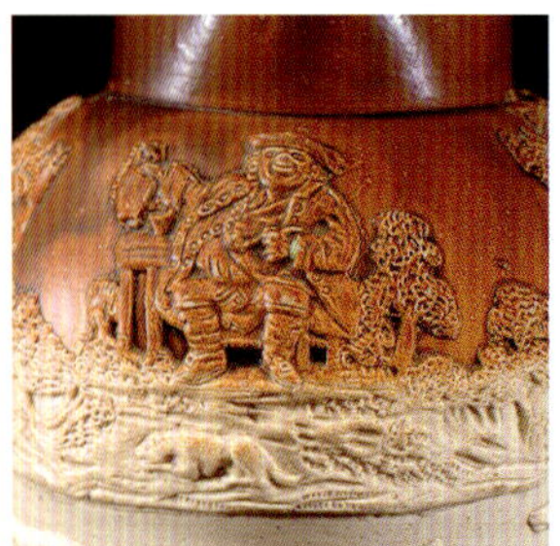

10. Derbyshire, ca. 1840; detail of fig. 13*a*

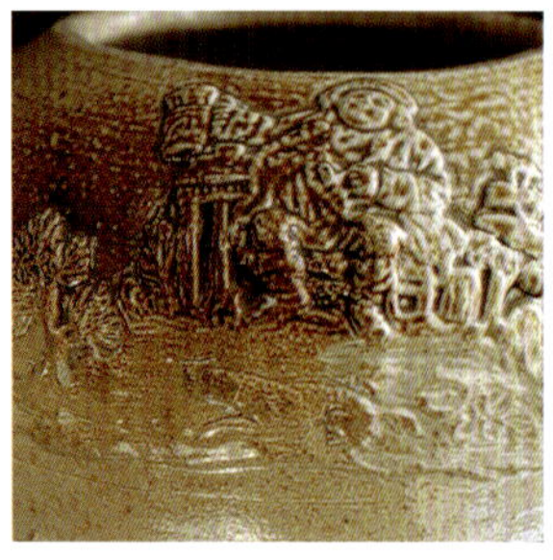

11. Unknown, ca. 1840; detail of fig. 22*c*

TABLE III. TOBYS 2

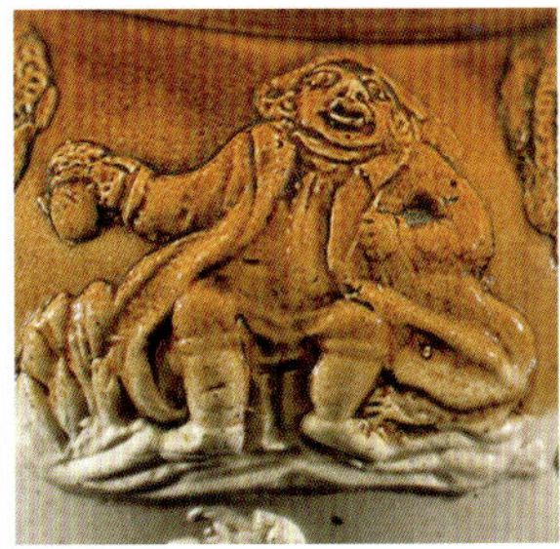

1. Mortlake or Lambeth, ca. 1830; detail of fig. 17*c*. Note absence of table.

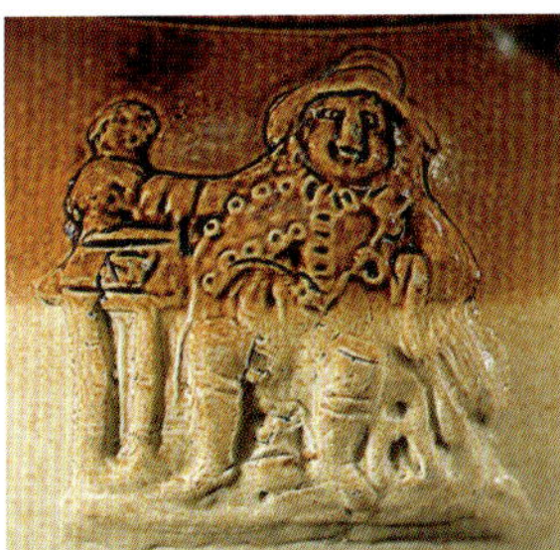

2. Mortlake or Lambeth, ca. 1835; detail of fig. 17*d*

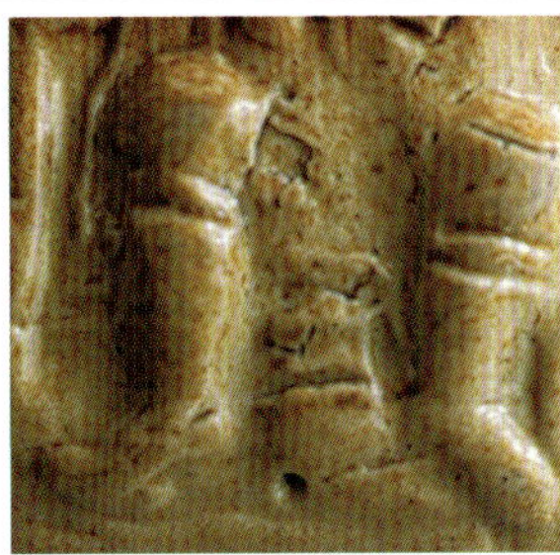

3. Detail of mouse on chamber pot between feet of Toby illustrated in table III.2

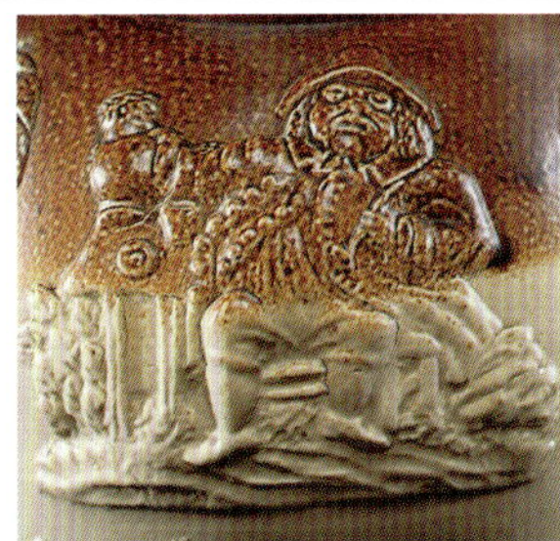

4. Mortlake or Lambeth, ca. 1835; detail of fig. 17*b*. Note foliage under seat.

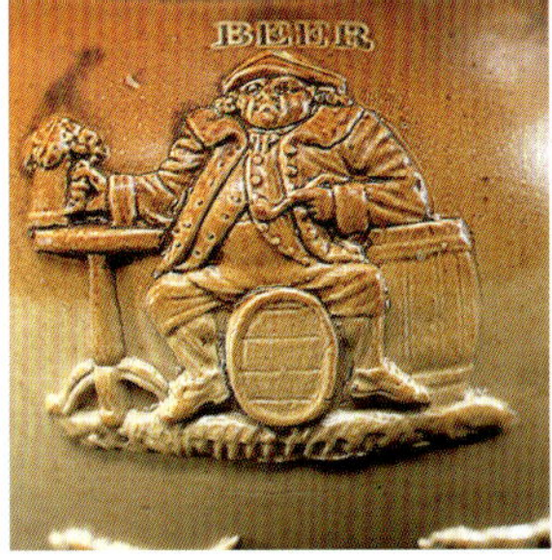

5. Doulton, ca. 1865; detail of fig. 19*b*

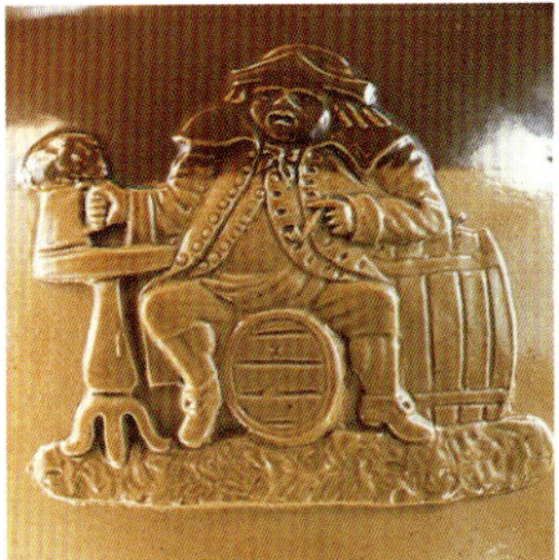

6. Doulton, ca. 1870–1890; detail of fig. 19*f*

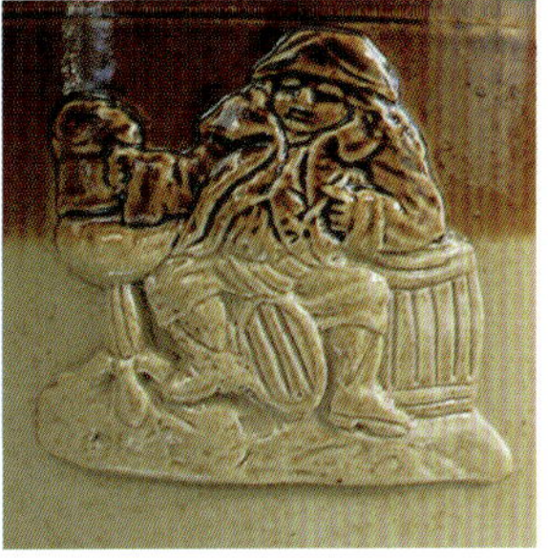

7. Vauxhall-Lambeth, 1870; detail of fig. 22*a*

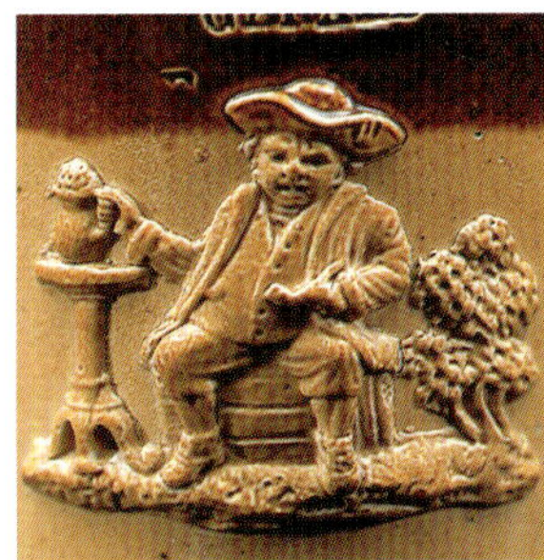

8. Doulton, 1877–1887; detail of fig. 19*a*

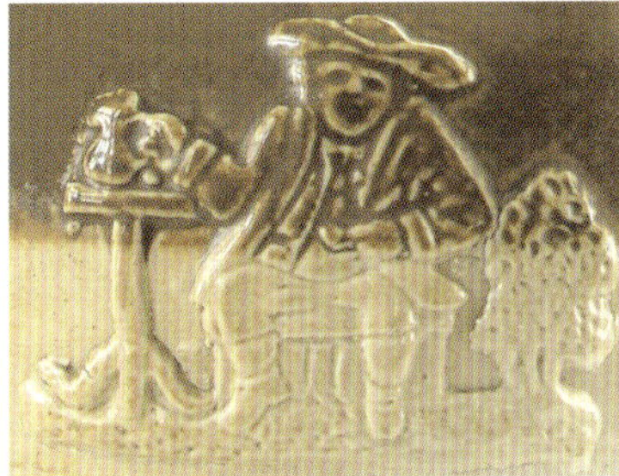

9. Doulton, 1868; detail of fig. 19*d*

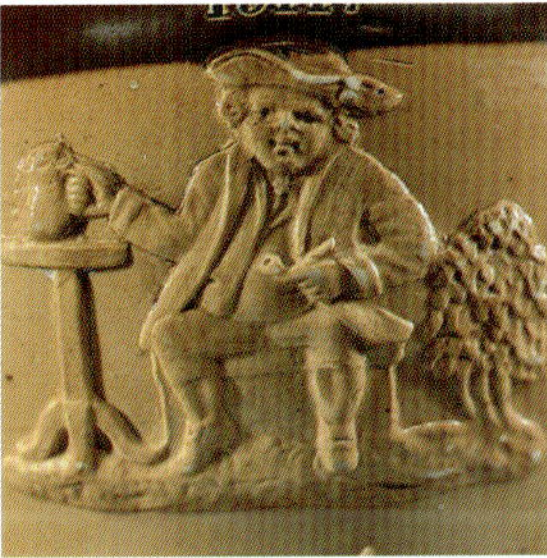

10. Doulton, 1911; detail of fig. 19*g*

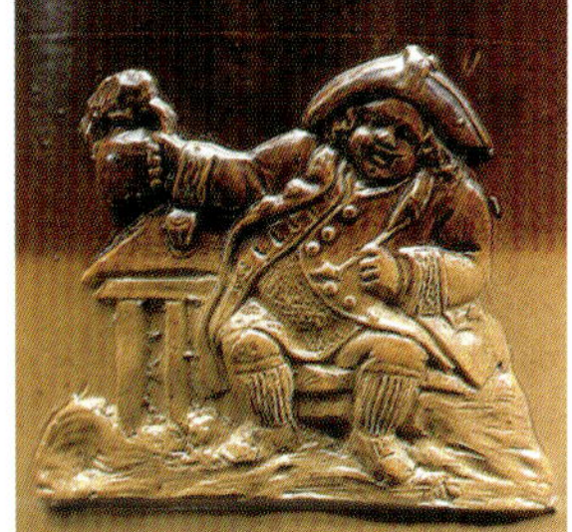

11. Fulham (Bailey), ca. 1880; detail of fig. 18*b*

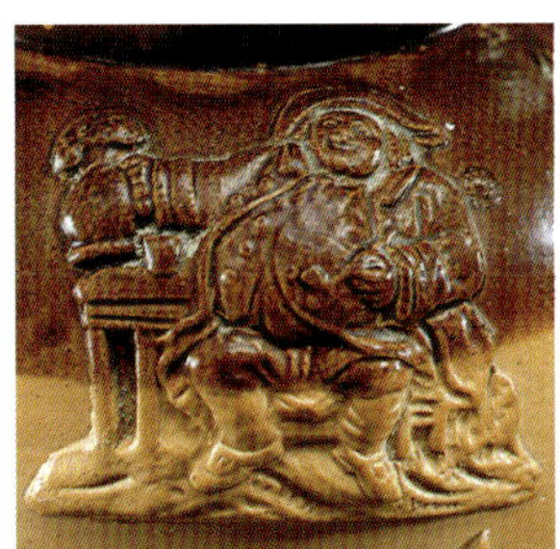

12. Stiff, post-1863; detail of fig. 13*b*

IV

TABLE IV. A DOCUMENTARY TRAIL

The hunting scene depicted on this gallon-capacity jug (IV.1) begins with a huntsman blowing something akin to a French horn and following single hounds (see table IX.7). A second huntsman (the master) rides whipping his horse after two more hounds and a small stag (see table IX.5) The upper frieze includes the "Bristol" mug waver, the young smoker, the hat waver, and sleeping toper (see table XIV.4, .5, .10). The central sprig features two men drinking and smoking seated at a circular and straight-legged table. A taproom boy arrives to their right carrying a flagon of foaming ale. Something that may be a hat lies on the floor at left. This motif has yet to be paralleled (table XI.6). However, a second large sprig (IV.2) showing people grouped round a barrel has its parallel first in a 1772 engraving (IV.3) from a ca. 1660 Dutch painting. The engraving depicts a group of singing peasants led by a seated youth reading from a song book and accompanied by a bagpiper.

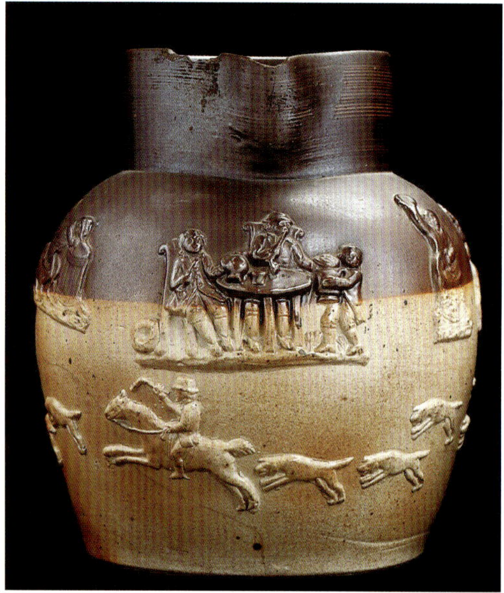

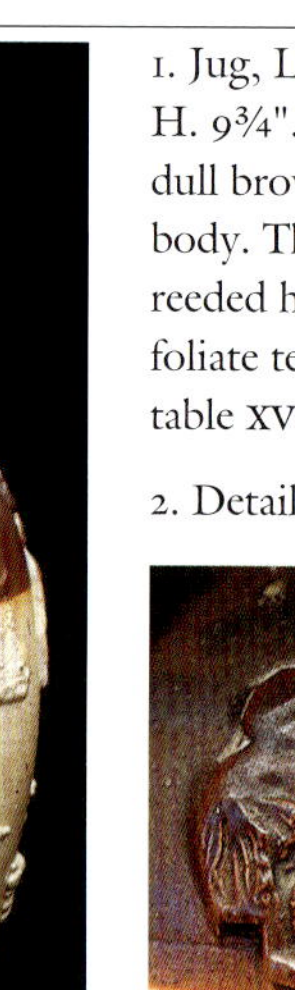

1. Jug, Liverpool or Bristol, ca. 1860. H. 9¾". Gallon-capacity jug with a dark, dull brown dip over a yellowish gray firing body. The proportionately heavy single-reeded handle ends with an extremely weak foliate terminal with a faux screw strap (see table XV.12).

2. Detail of fig. 1

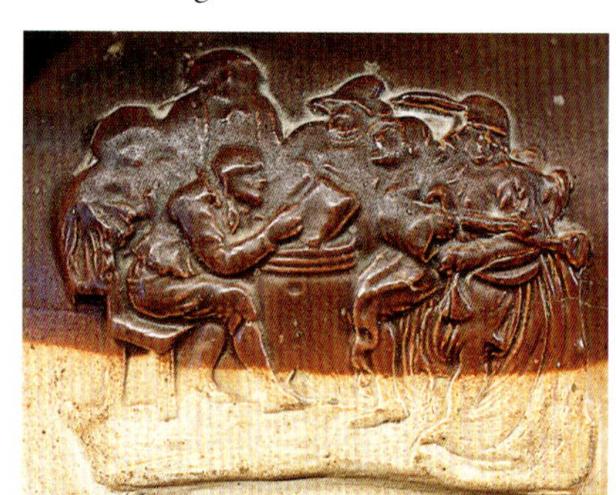

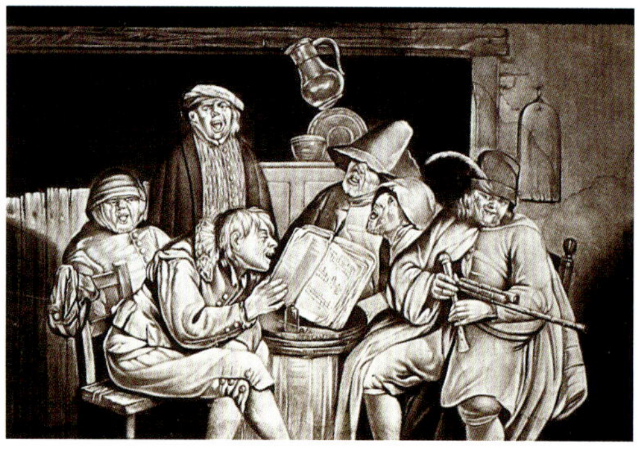

3. Engraving, attributed to [Egbert van (?)]Heemskerk, 1772. (Courtesy, Colonial Williamsburg Foundation.)

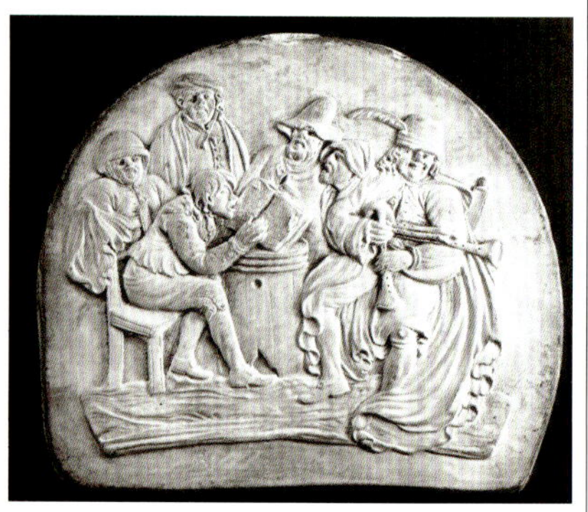

4. A master mold from the factory of John and William Turner, ca. 1810. H. 3¹³⁄₁₆". (Courtesy, Spode Museum Trust.)

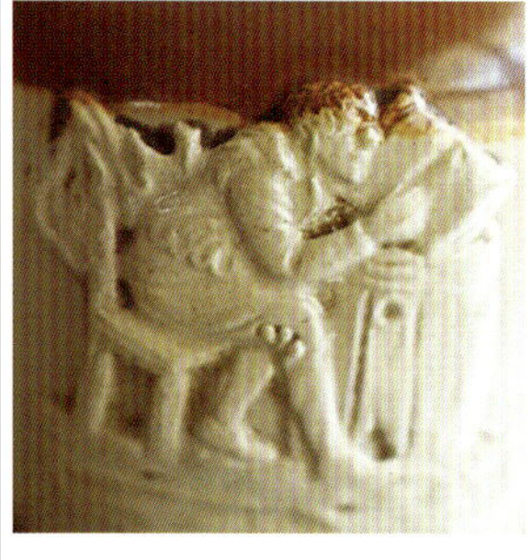

5. The central figure used as a separate sprig on the mustard pots shown in figs. 14*d* and 14*e*.

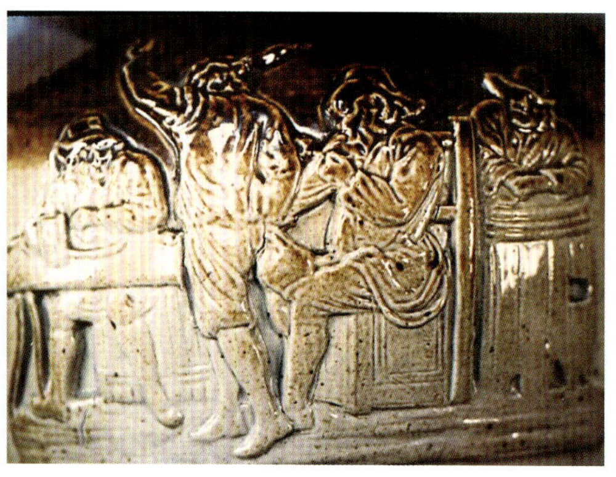

6. A companion to the Heemskerk original (IV.3), this sprig is from David Teniers the Younger (1610–1690). (Courtesy, Dr. Nicholas Johnson.)

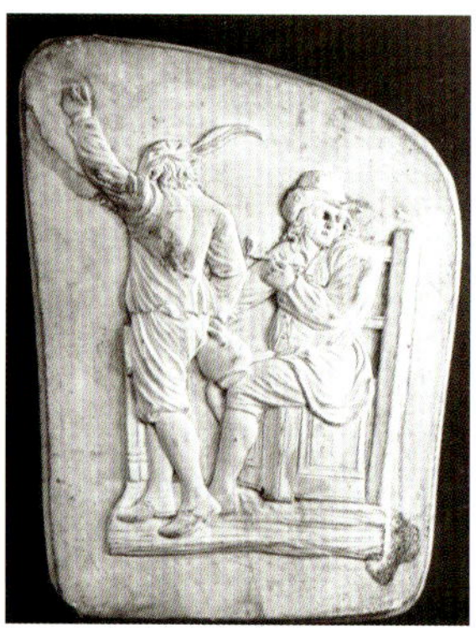

7. A ca. 1810 Turner mold for part of this group. (Courtesy, Spode Museum Trust.)

TABLE V. TREES I

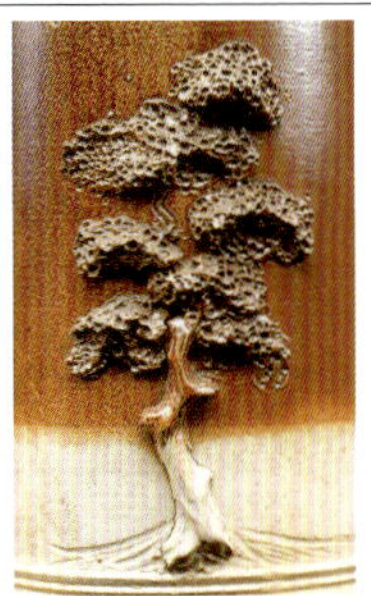
1. Vauxhall, ca. 1710; detail of fig. 2

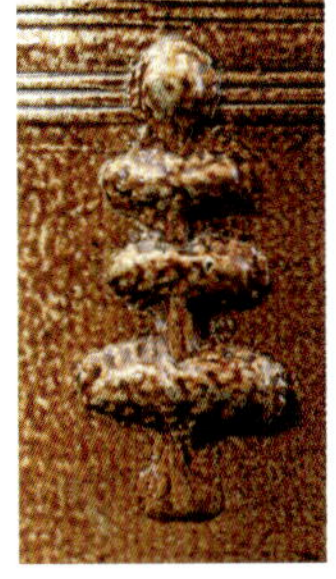
2. Vauxhall, 1722; detail of fig. *1a*

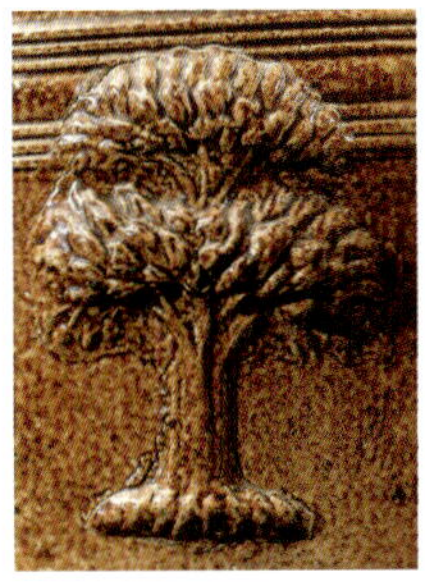
3. Vauxhall, 1722; detail of fig. *1a*

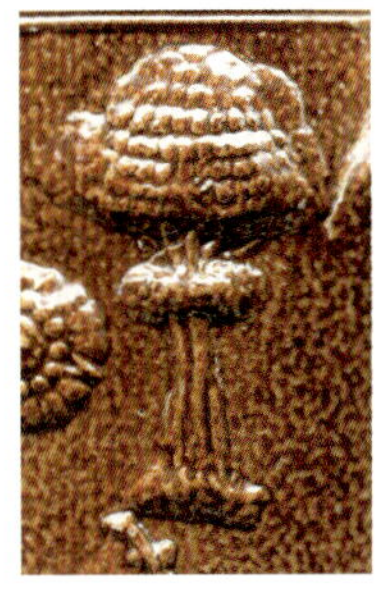
4. Vauxhall, 1731; detail of fig. *1b*

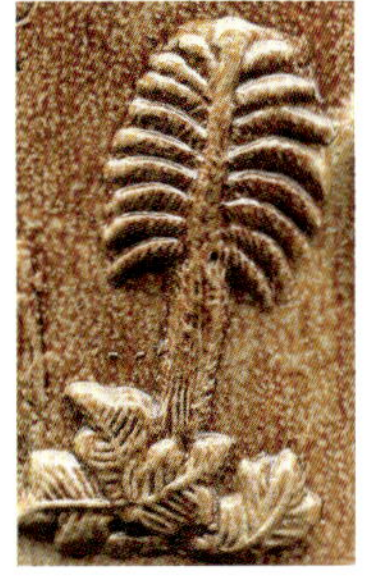
5. Vauxhall, 1737; detail of fig. *1c*

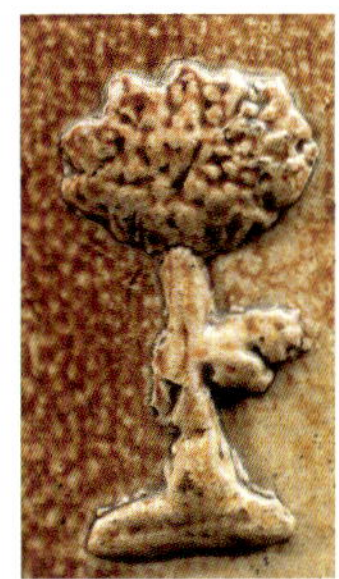
6. Bristol, ca. 1760; detail of fig. *1d*

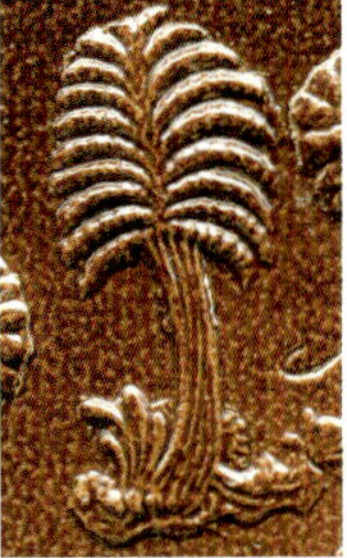
7. Vauxhall, 1731; detail of fig. *1b*

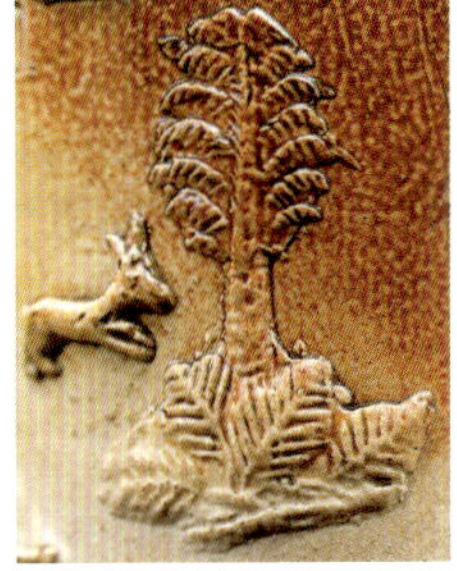
8. Bristol, ca. 1760; detail of fig. *1d*

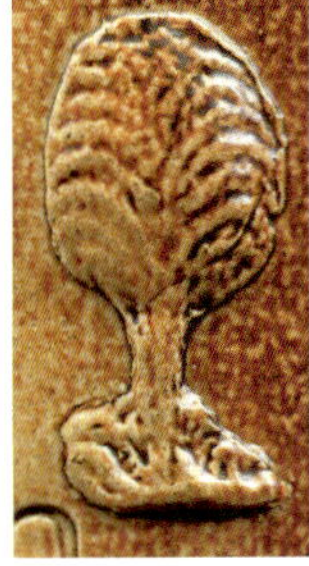
9. Bristol, ca. 1760; detail of fig. *1d*

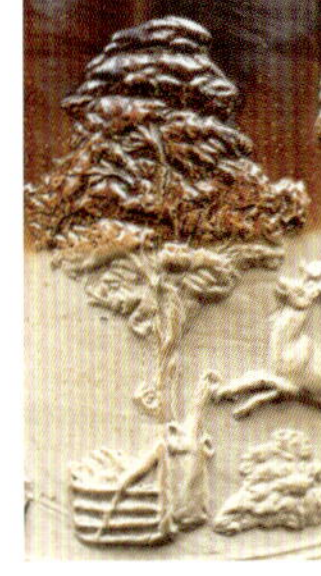
10. Mortlake, 1792; detail of fig. *7a*

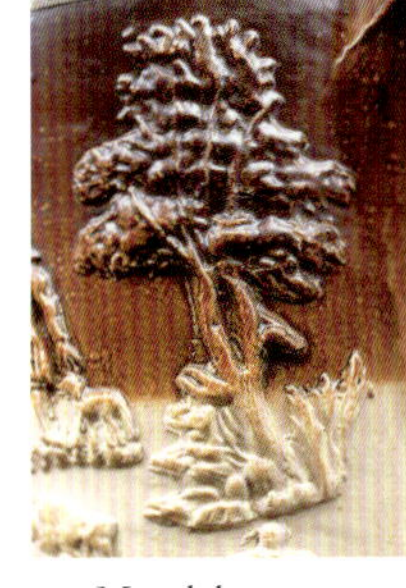
11. Mortlake, 1792; detail of fig. *7a*

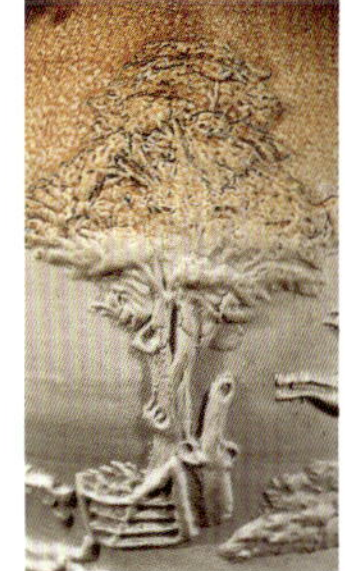
12. Mortlake, ca. 1795; detail of fig. *7c*

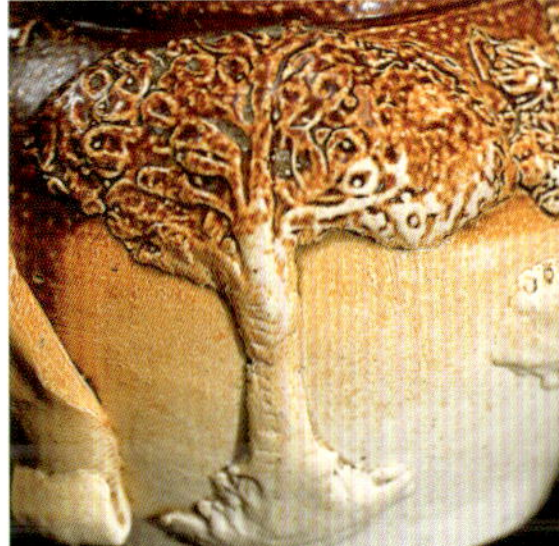
13. Mortlake, 1801; detail of fig. 14*c*

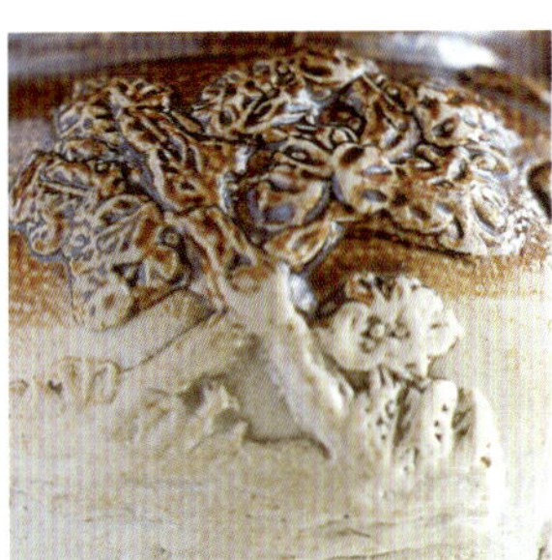
14. Mortlake, 1801; detail of fig. 14*d*

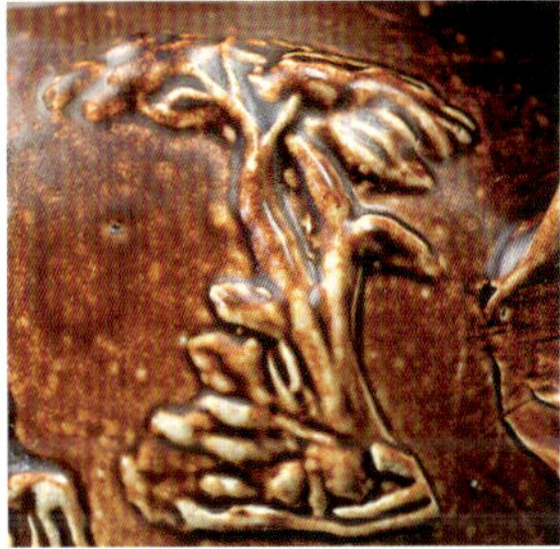
15. Mortlake, ca. 1805; detail of fig. *7d*

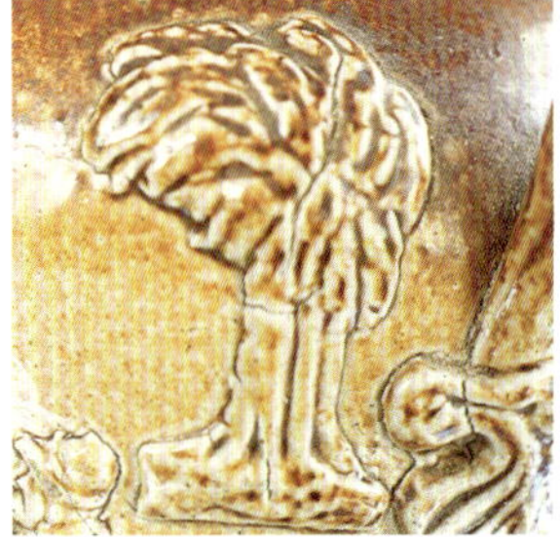
16. Fulham, ca. 1835; detail of fig. 15*d*

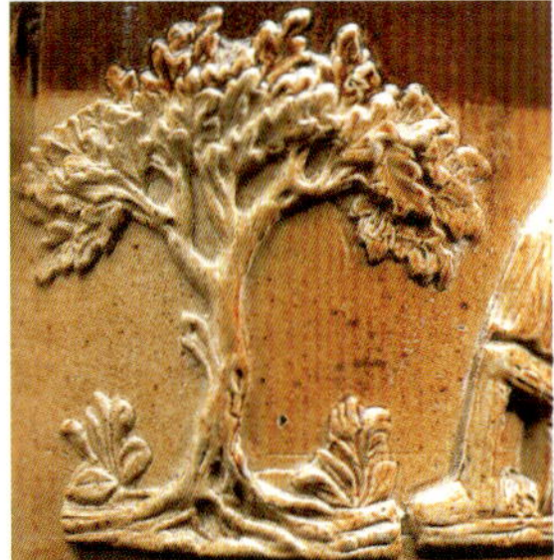
17. South Derbyshire, ca. 1835; detail of fig. 16*a*

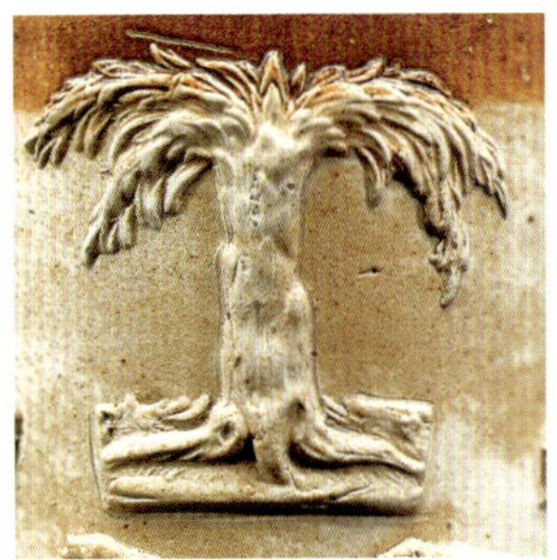
18. South Derbyshire, ca. 1835; detail of fig. 16*f*

TABLE VI. TREES 2

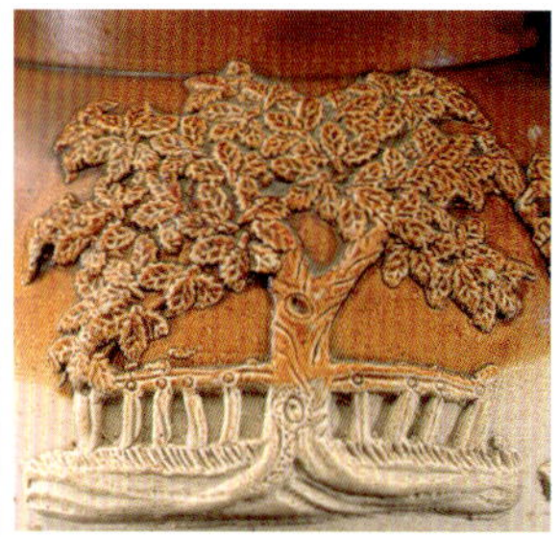
1. Derbyshire, ca. 1840; detail of fig. 13*c*

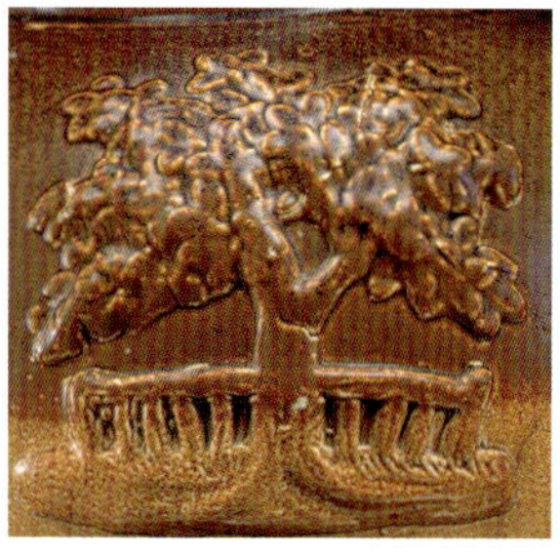
2. Derbyshire, ca. 1840; detail of fig. 13*c* (foliage variation)

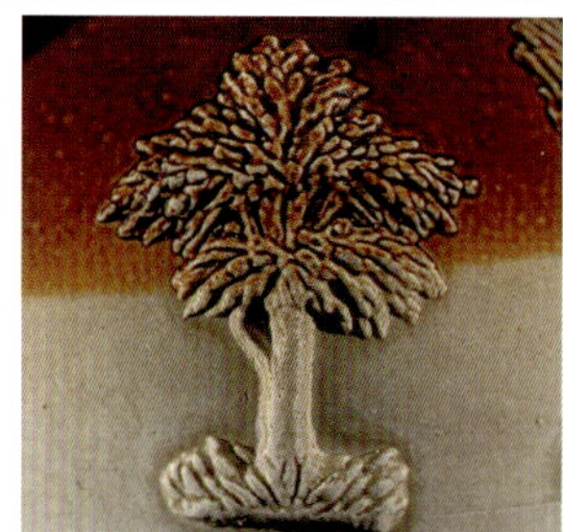
3. Fulham, ca. 1840; detail of fig. 15*c*

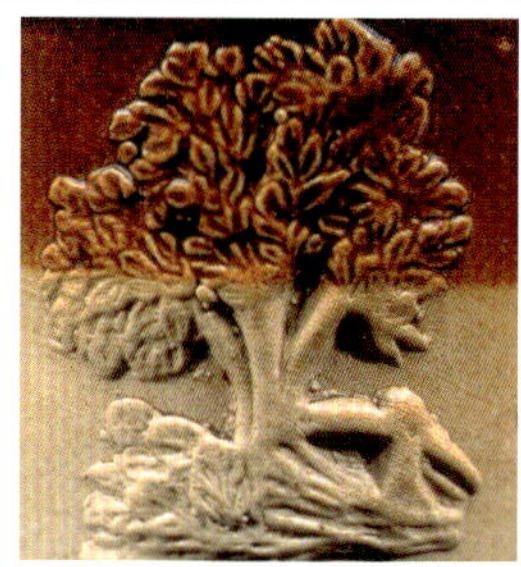
4. Mortlake or Lambeth, ca. 1840; detail of fig. 10*b*

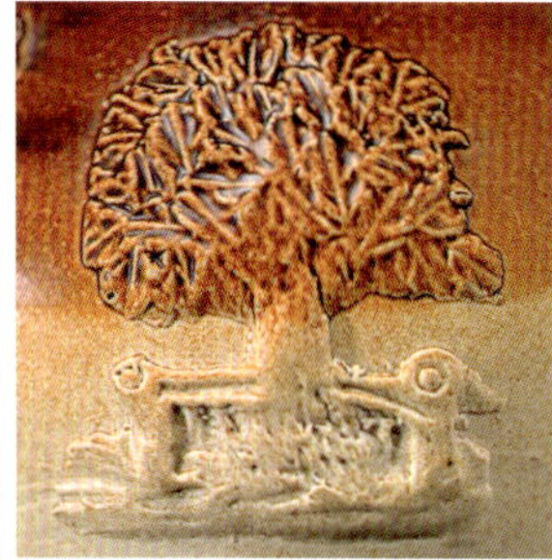
5. Mortlake or Lambeth, ca. 1835; detail of fig. 17*d*

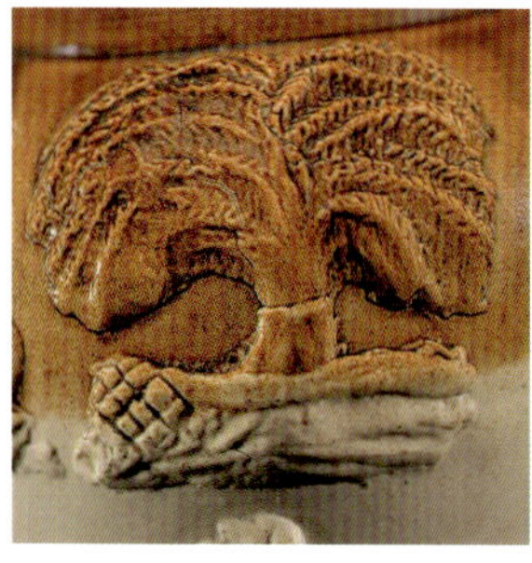
6. Mortlake or Lambeth, ca. 1830; detail of fig. 17*c*

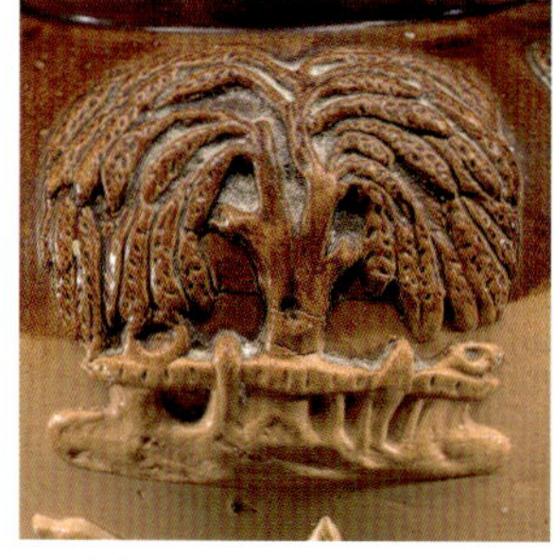
7. Stiff, Lambeth, ca. 1885; detail of fig. 13*c*

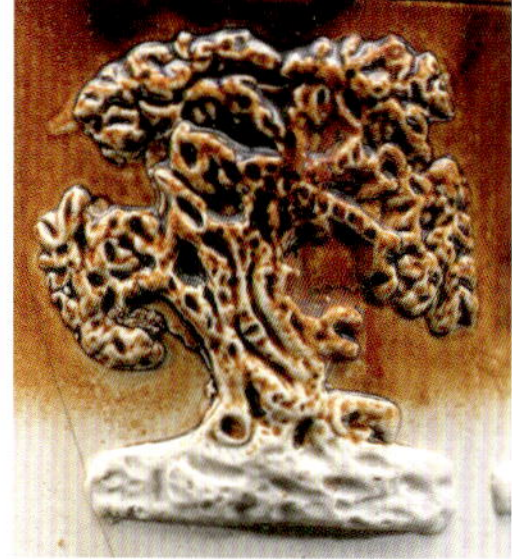
8. South Derbyshire or Bristol, ca. 1820; detail of fig. 16*d*

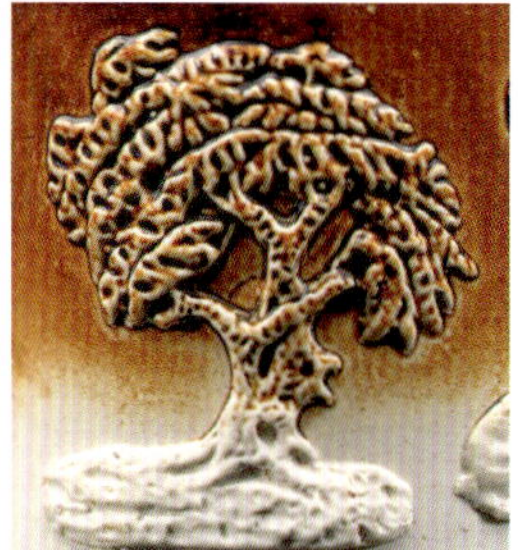
9. South Derbyshire or Bristol, ca. 1820; detail of fig. 16*d*

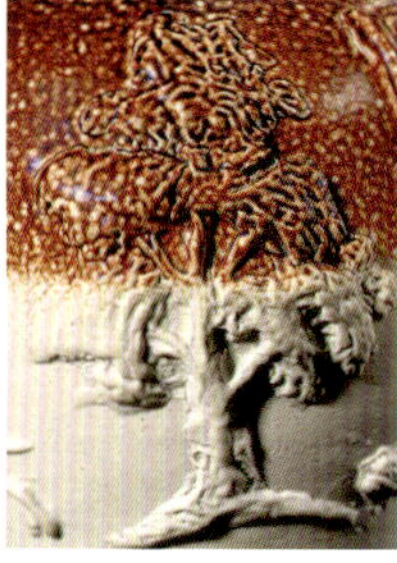
10. Mortlake, 1799; detail of fig. 7*b*

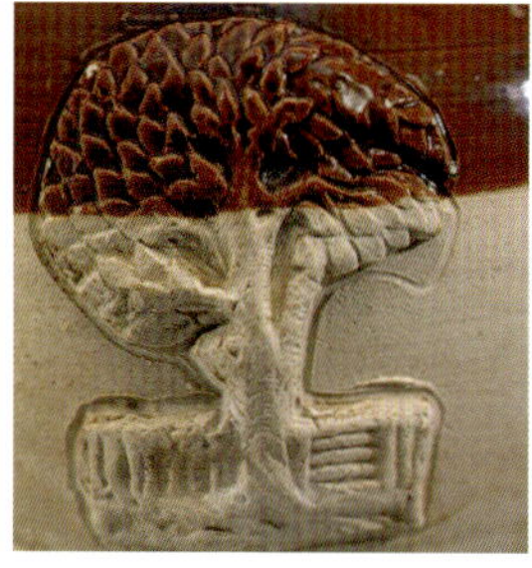
11. Derbyshire, ca. 1835; detail of fig. 10*a*

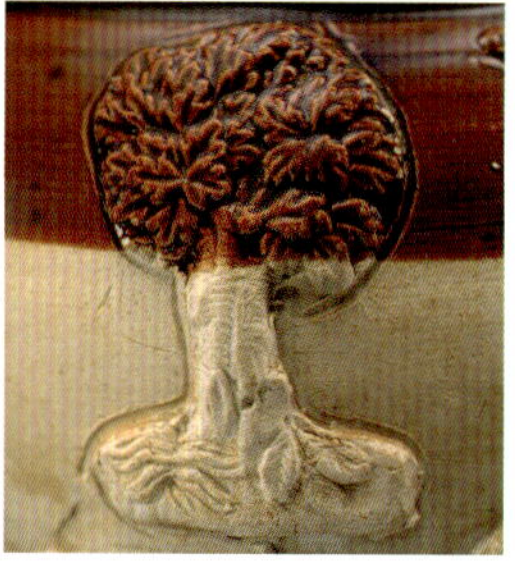
12. Derbyshire, ca. 1835; detail of fig. 10*a*

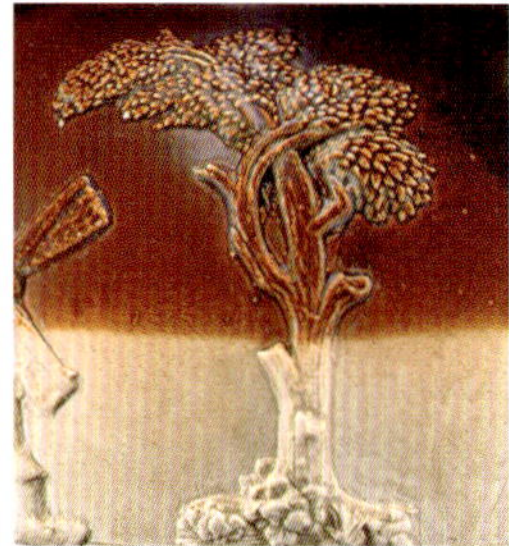
13. Doulton, ca. 1840; detail of fig. 15*c*

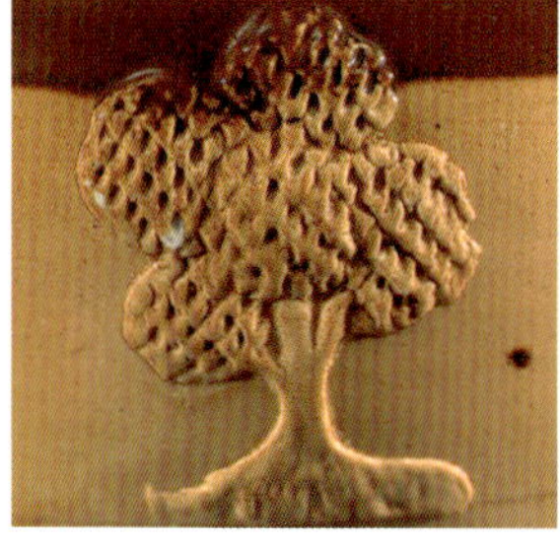
14. Doulton, ca. 1865; detail of fig. 19*c*

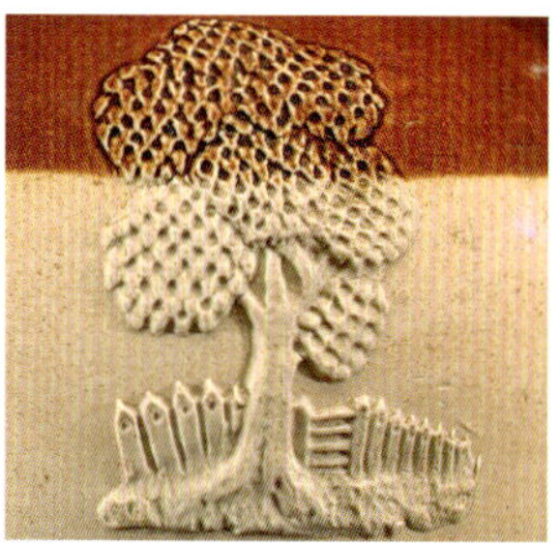
15. Doulton, ca. 1880; detail of fig. 19*f*

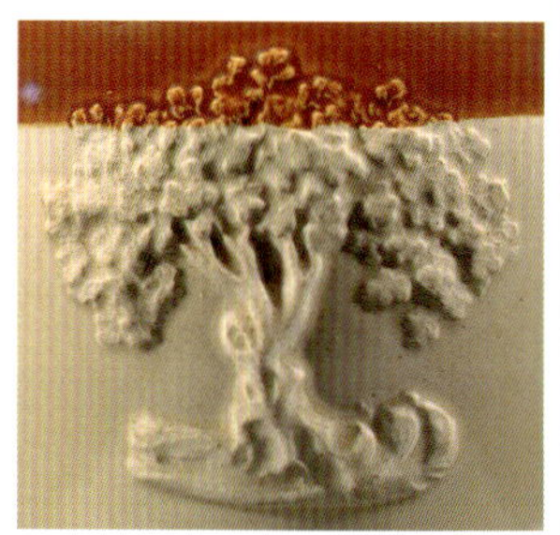
16. Bourne, ca. 1890; detail of fig. 9*c*

TABLE VII. PEOPLE

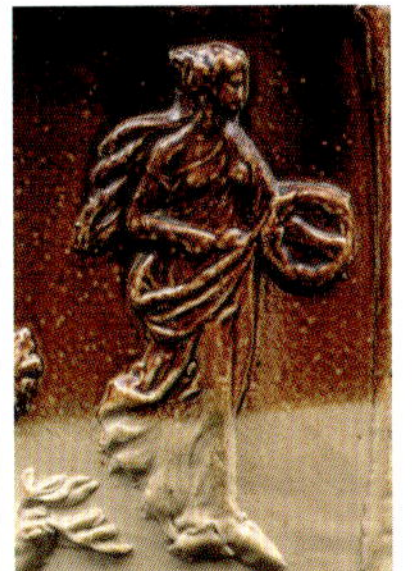

1. Mortlake, 1792; detail of fig. *7a*

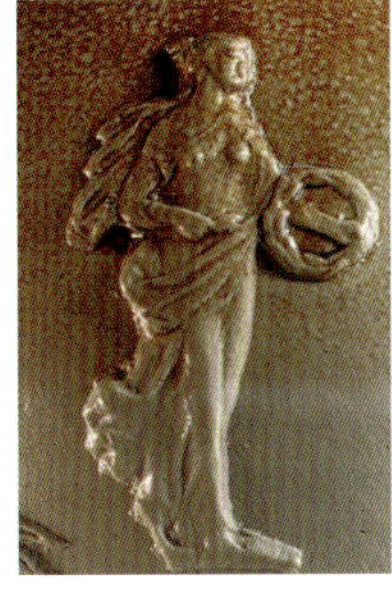

2. Mortlake, ca. 1800; detail of fig. *7c*

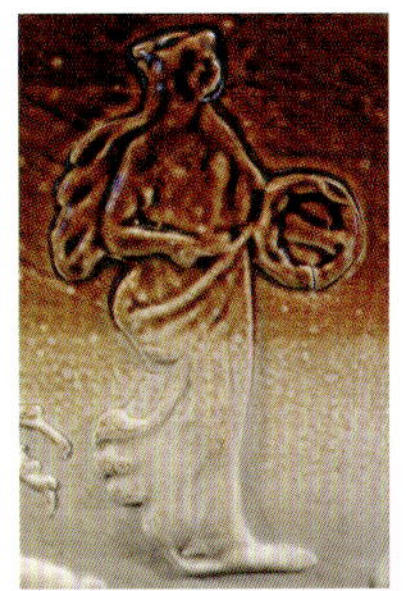

3. Mortlake, 1818; detail of fig. *7e*

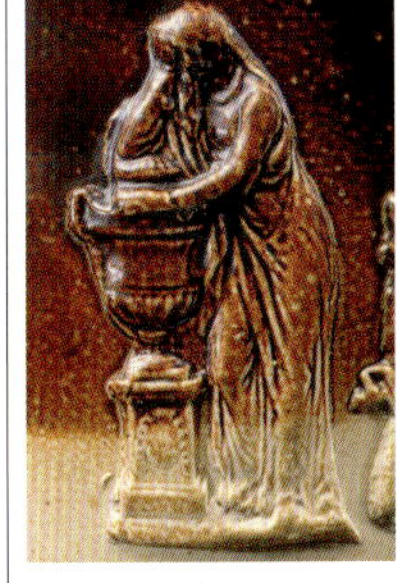

4. Mortlake, 1792; detail of fig. *7a*

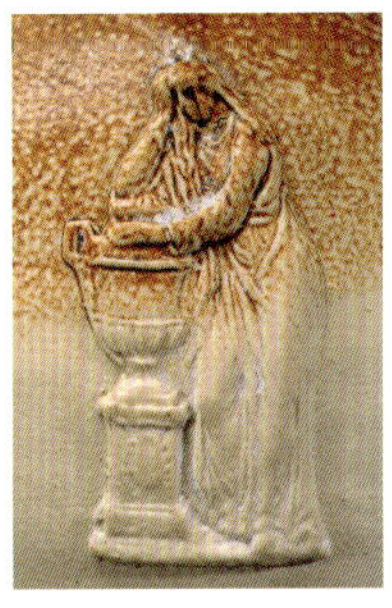

5. Mortlake, ca. 1800; detail of fig. *7c*

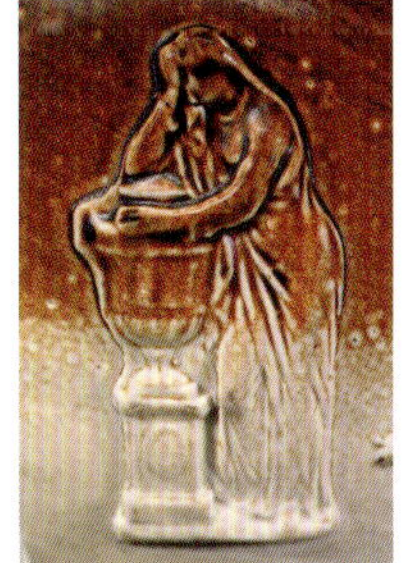

6. Mortlake, 1818; detail of fig. *7e*

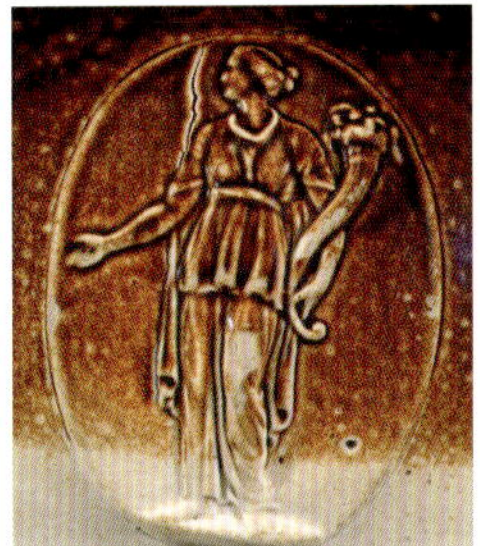

7. Mortlake, ca. 1805; detail of fig. *7d*

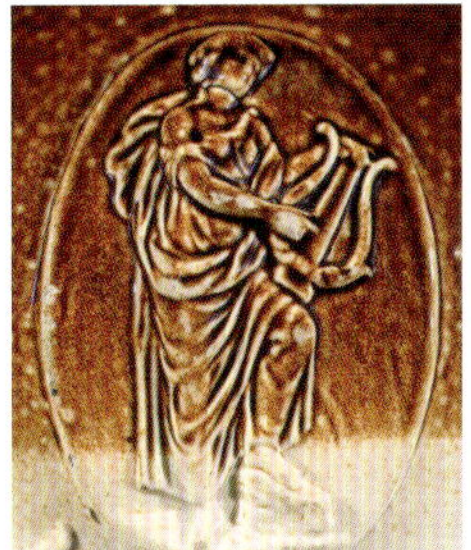

8. Mortlake, ca. 1805; detail of fig. *7d*

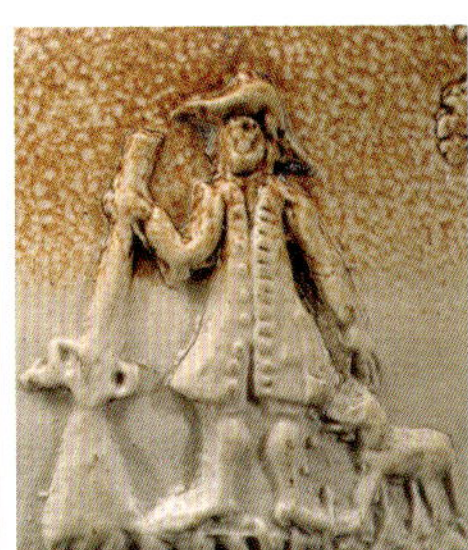

9. Mortlake, ca. 1800; detail of fig. *7c*

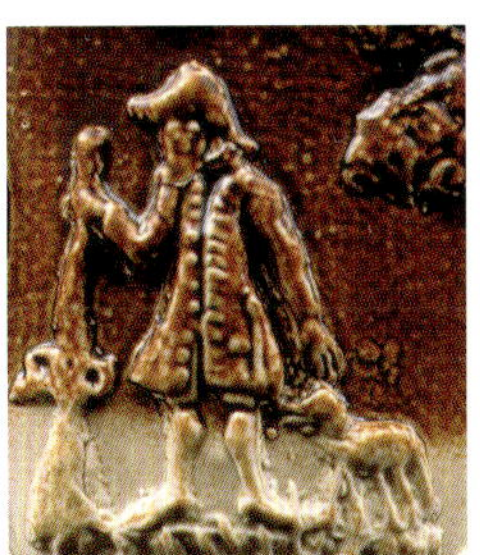

10. Mortlake, ca. 1805; detail of fig. *7d*

TABLE VIII. HUNTERS 1

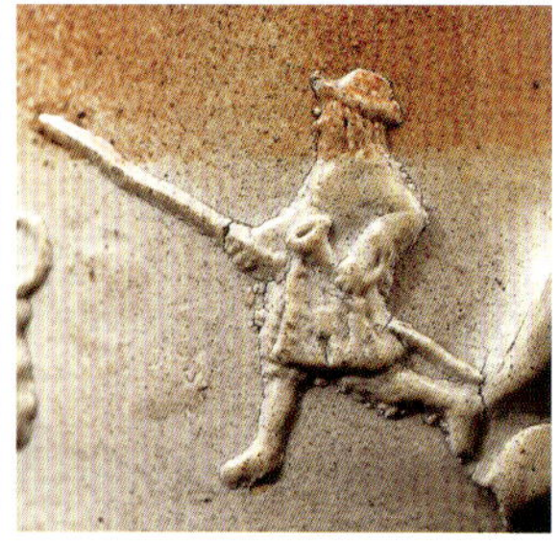

1. Vauxhall, 1722; detail of fig. *1a*

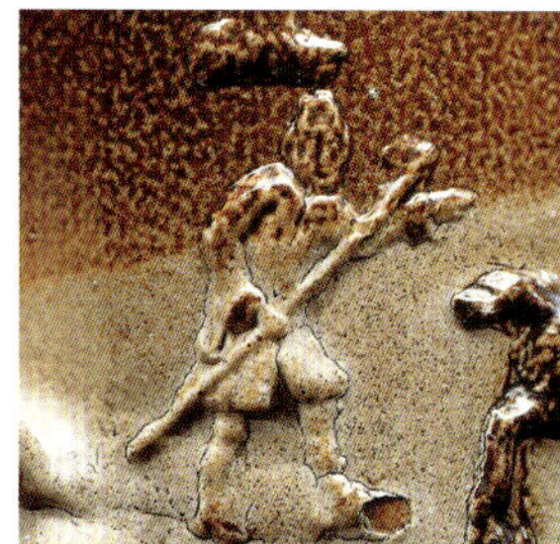

2. Vauxhall, 1731; detail of fig. *1b*

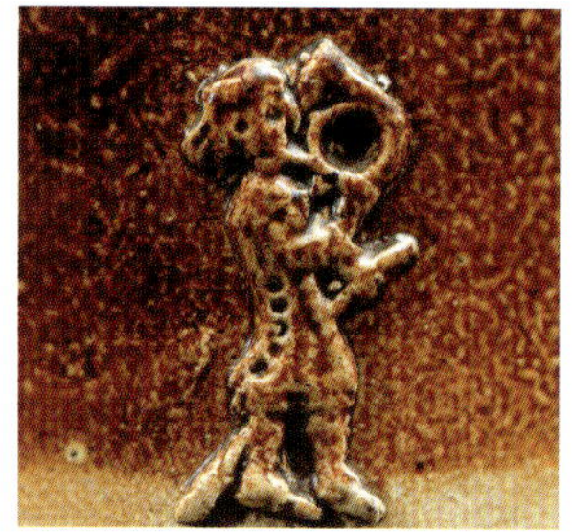

3. Bristol, ca. 1760; detail of fig. *1d*

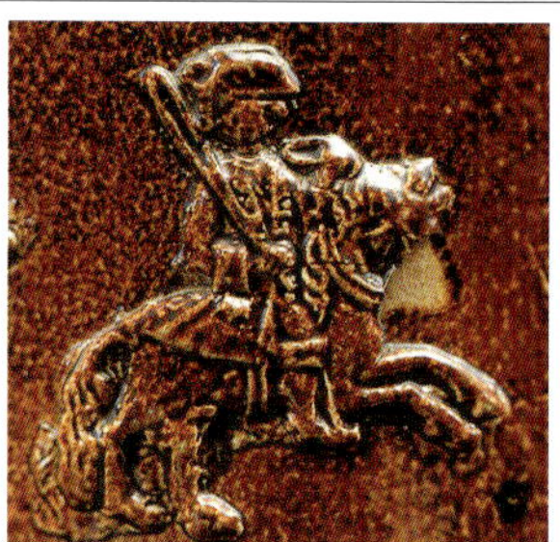

4. Bristol, ca. 1760; detail of fig. *1d*

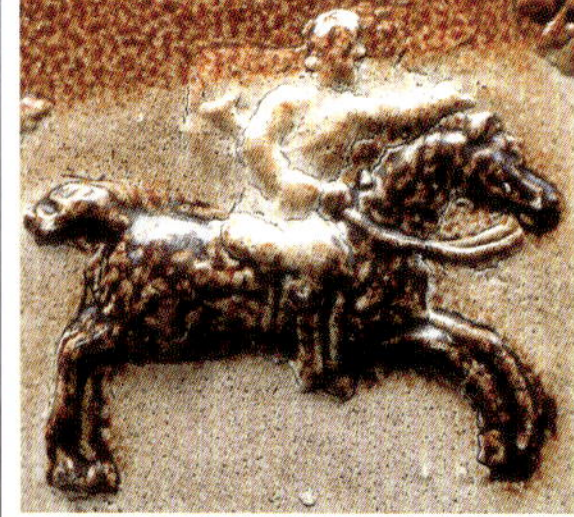

5. Vauxhall, 1731; detail of fig. *1b*

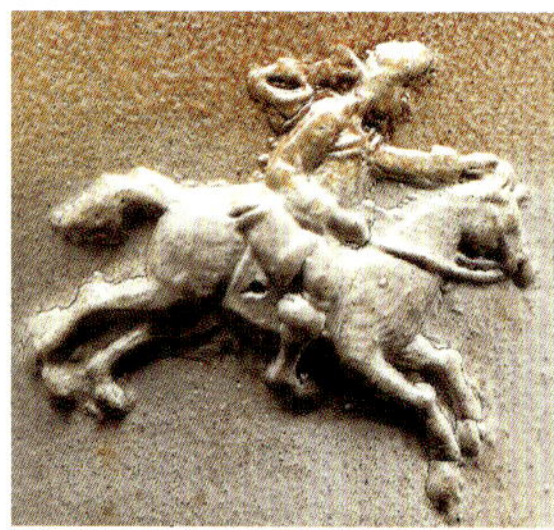

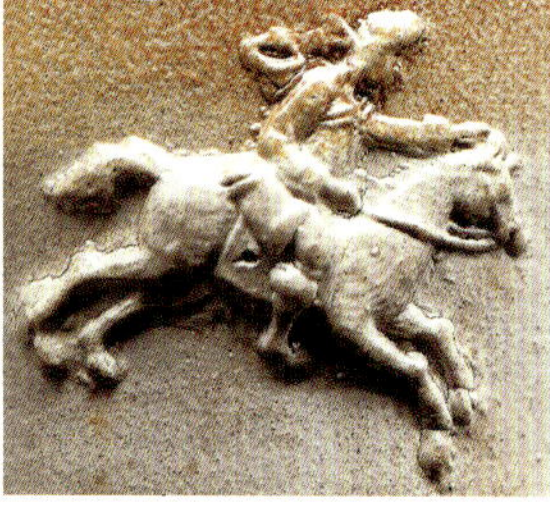

6. Vauxhall, 1737; detail of fig. *1c*

7. Mortlake, 1792; detail of fig. *7a*

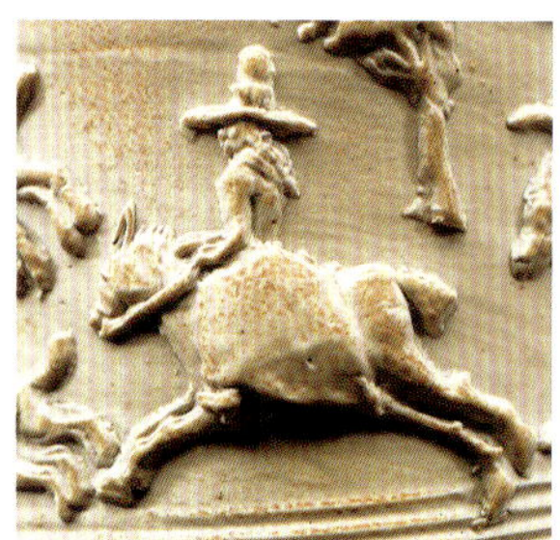

8. Mortlake, 1792; detail of fig. *7a*

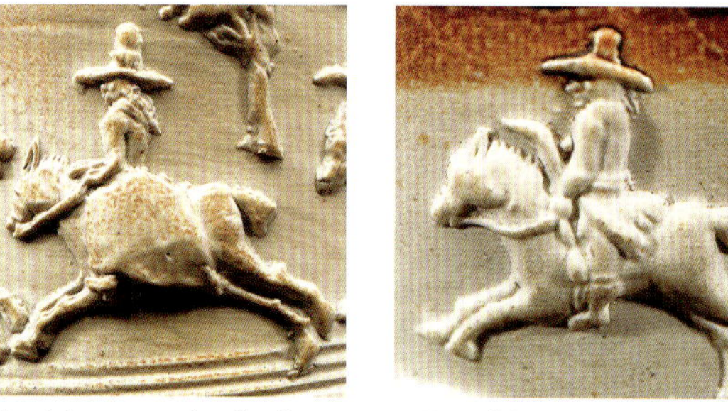

9. Mortlake, ca. 1805; detail of fig. *7d*

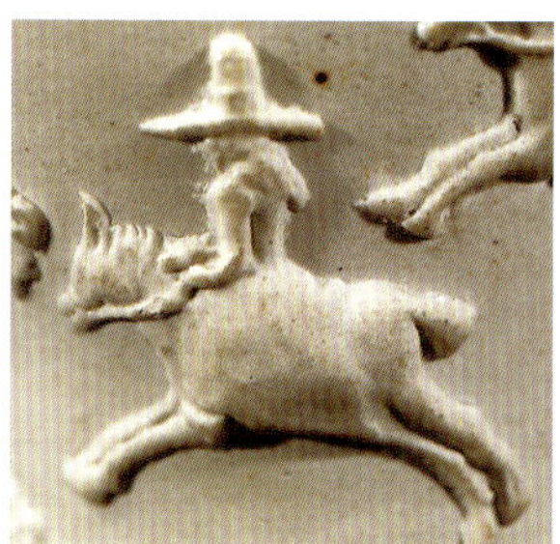

10. Mortlake, ca. 1805; detail of fig. *7d*

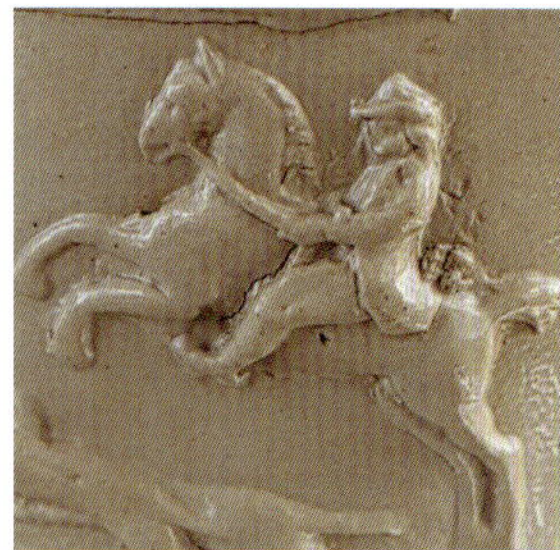

11. Mortlake, 1799; detail of fig. *7b*

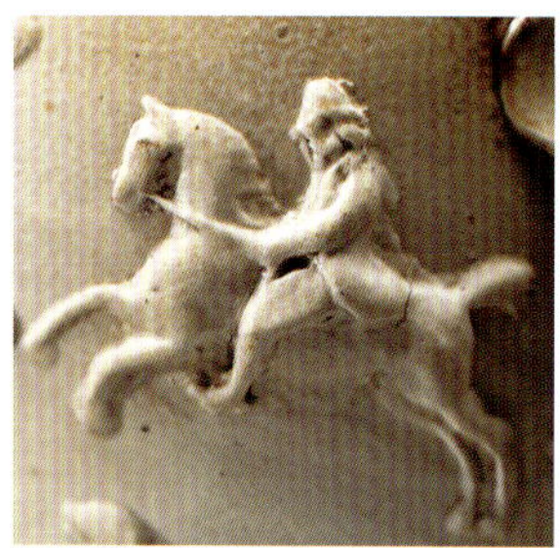

12. Mortlake, 1799; detail of fig. *7b*

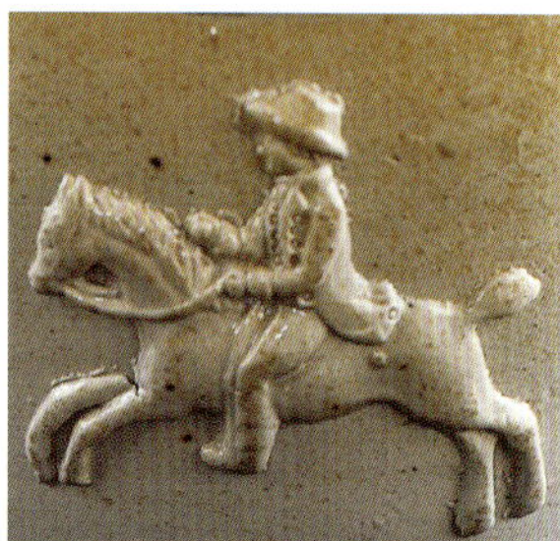

13. Unknown, ca. 1840; detail of fig. *22c*

TABLE IX. HUNTERS 2

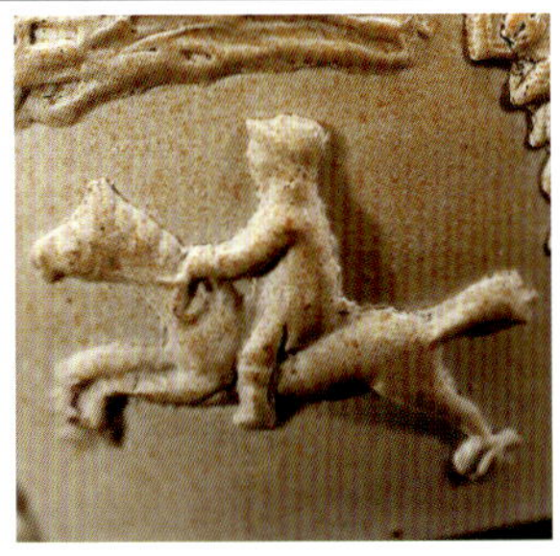
1. Mortlake or Lambeth, ca. 1835; detail of fig. 17*d*

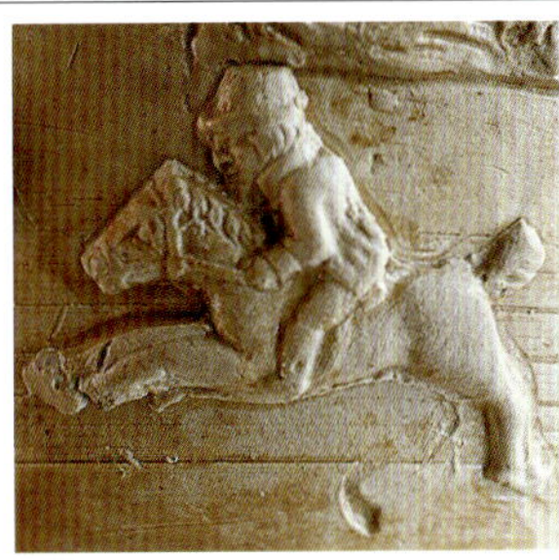
2. Derbyshire, ca. 1835; detail of fig. 10*a*

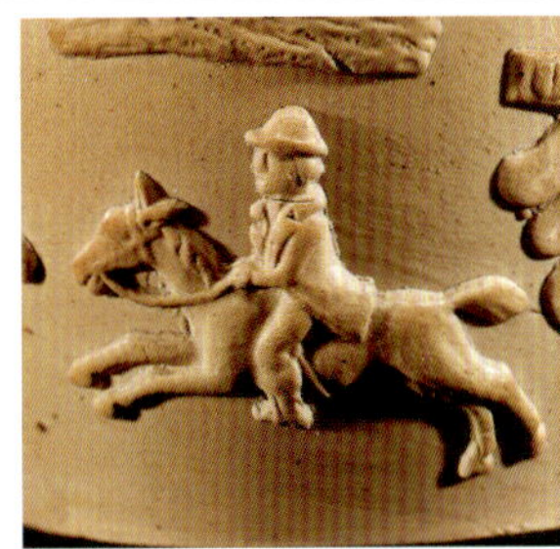
3. Stiff, Lambeth, ca. 1880; detail of fig. 13*d*

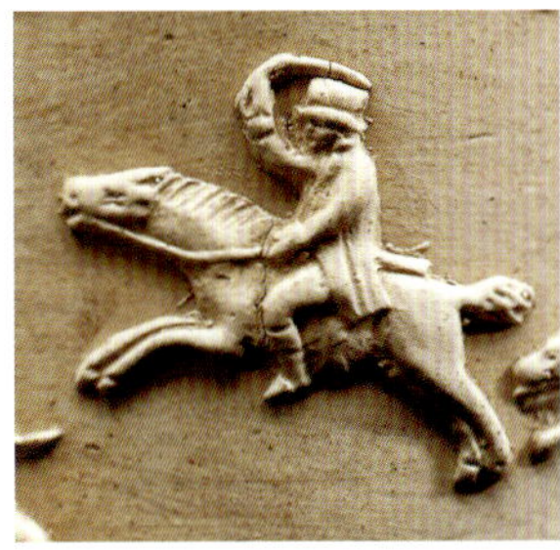
4. Derbyshire or Bristol, ca. 1840; detail of fig. 18*c*

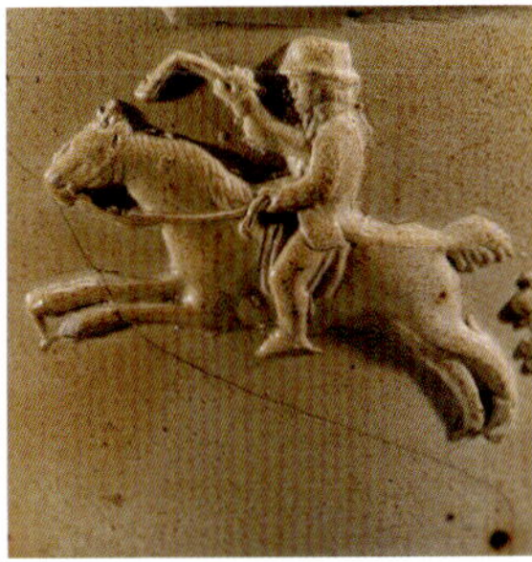
5. Liverpool?, ca. 1840; detail of table IV.1

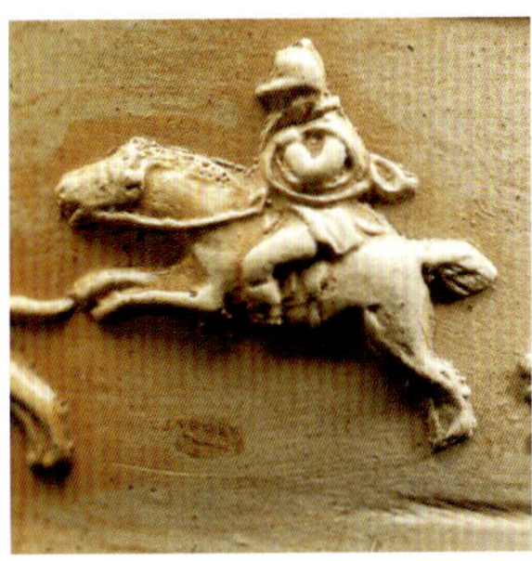
6. Derbyshire or Bristol, ca. 1840; detail of fig. 18*c*

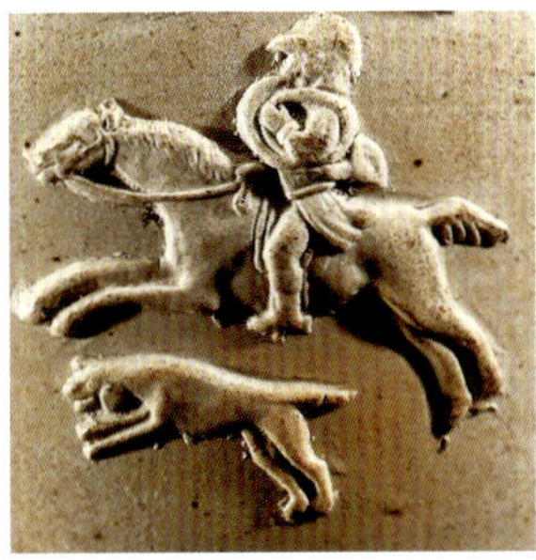
7. Liverpool?, ca. 1840; detail of table IV.1

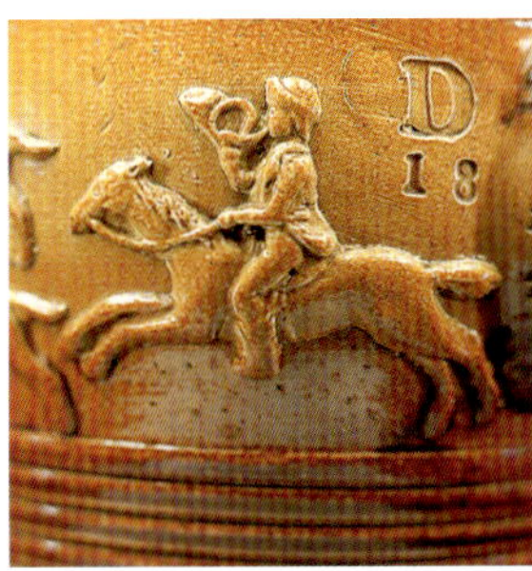

8. Bristol, 1832; detail of fig. 20

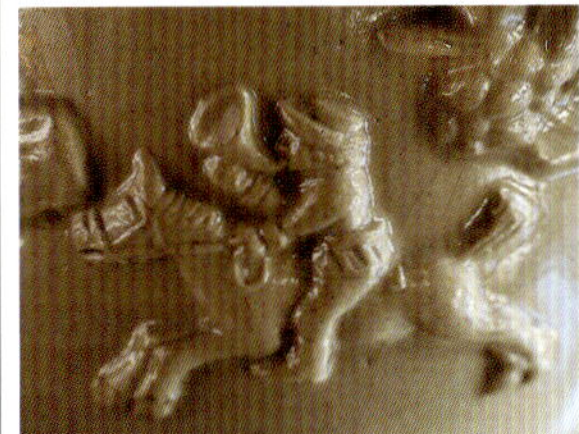
9. Bourne, ca. 1890; detail of fig. 9*d*

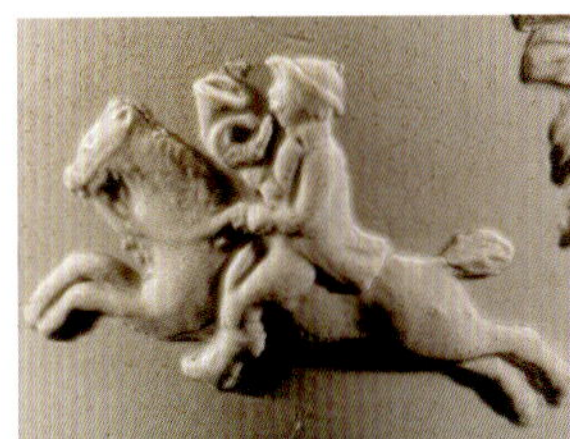
10. Mortlake or Lambeth, ca. 1835; detail of fig. 17*b*

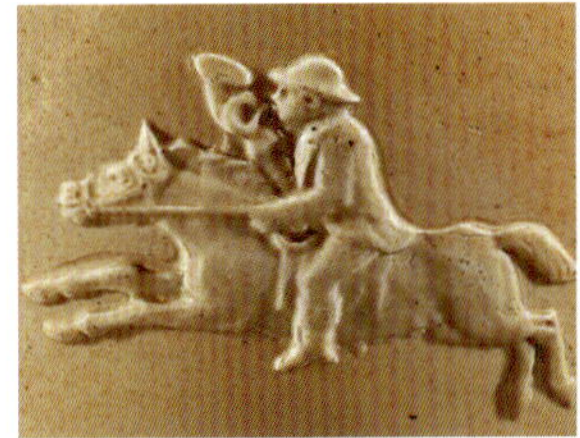
11. Doulton, ca. 1880; detail of fig. 19*f*

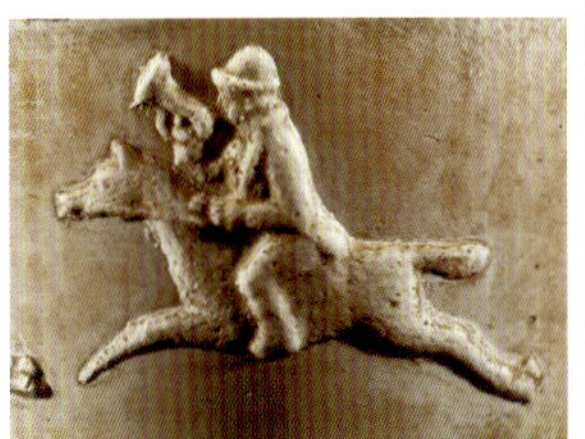
12. Fulham, ca. 1840; detail of fig. 15*c*

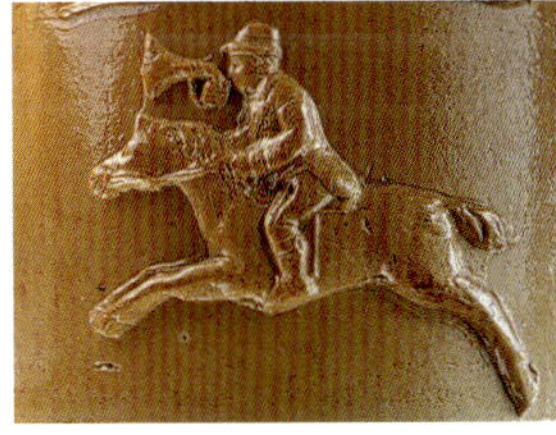
13. Fulham, ca. 1880; detail of fig. 18*b*

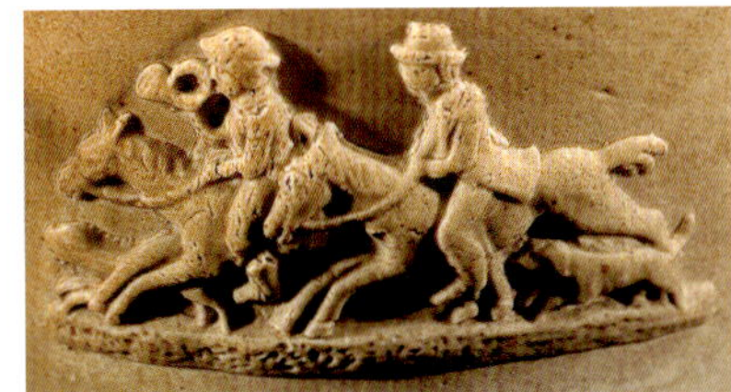
14. Derbyshire, ca. 1840; detail of fig. 13*c*

X

TABLE X. QUARRY AND HOUNDS

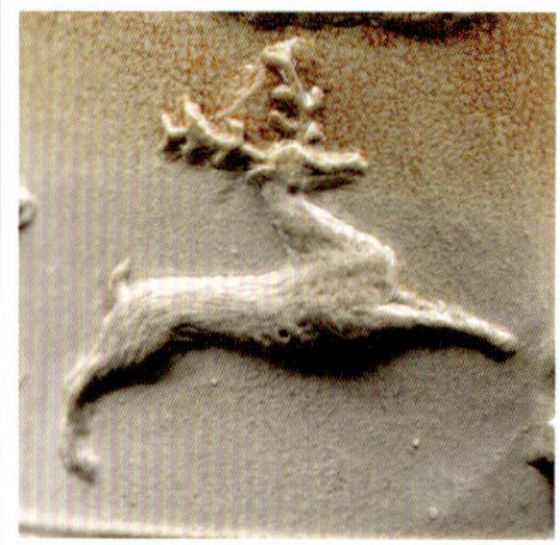

1. Vauxhall, 1737; detail of fig. 1*c*

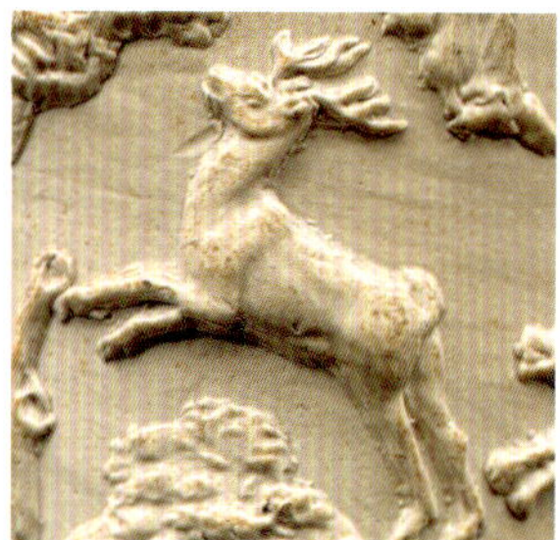

2. Mortlake, ca. 1805; detail of fig. 7*d*

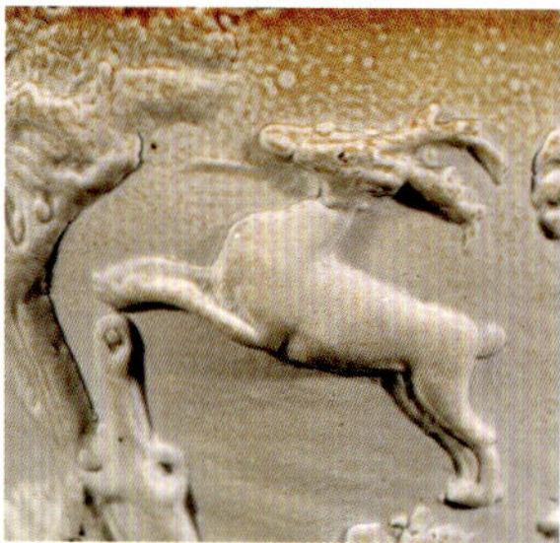

3. Mortlake, 1818; detail of fig. 7*e*

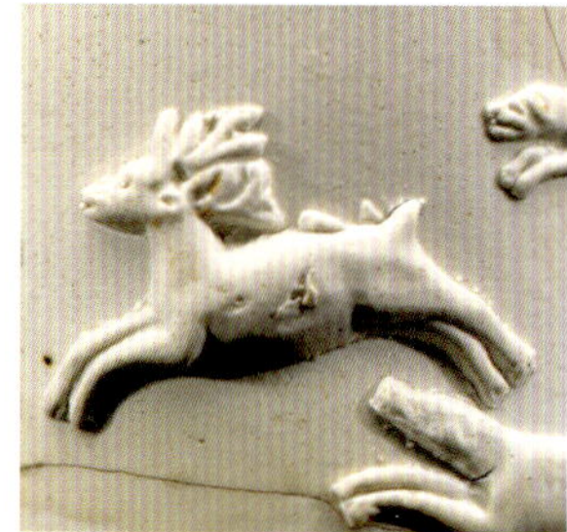

4. South Derbyshire or Bristol, ca. 1820; detail of fig. 16*d*

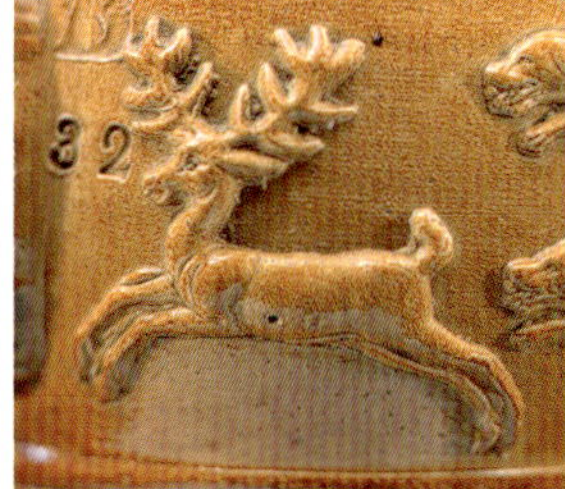

5. Bristol, 1832; detail of fig. 20

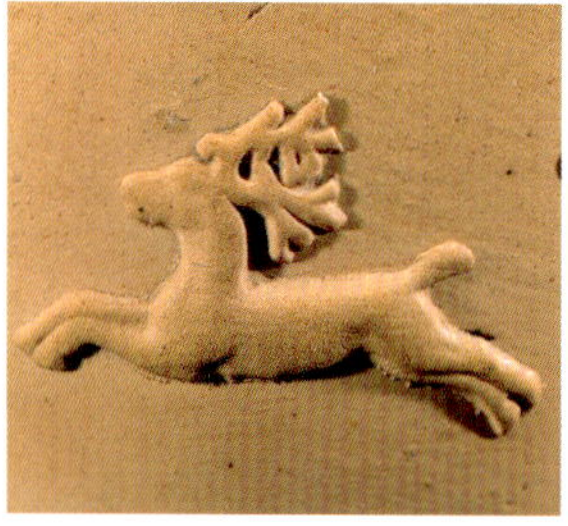

6. Stiff, Lambeth, ca. 1880; detail of fig. 13*d*

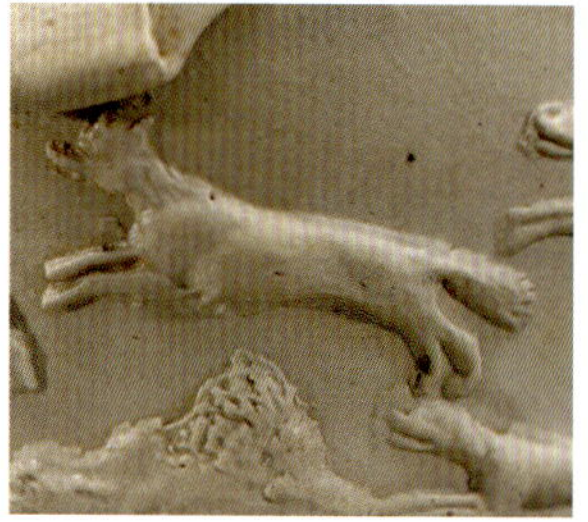

7. Mortlake, 1799; detail of fig. 7*b*

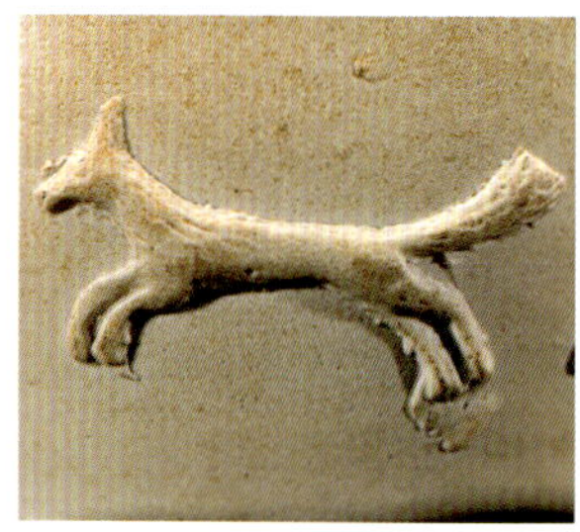

8. Mortlake or Lambeth, ca. 1835; detail of fig. 17*d*

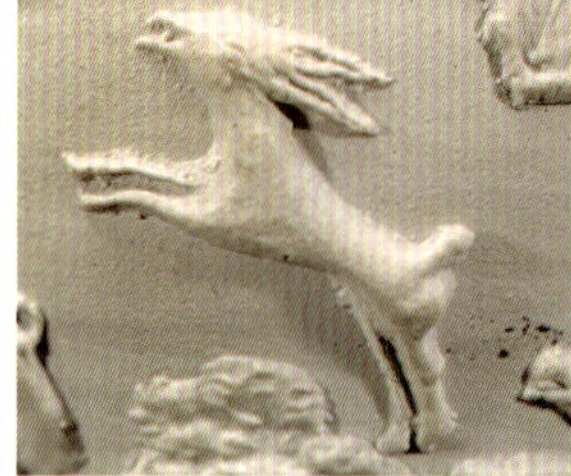

9. Mortlake, ca. 1800; detail of fig. 7*c*

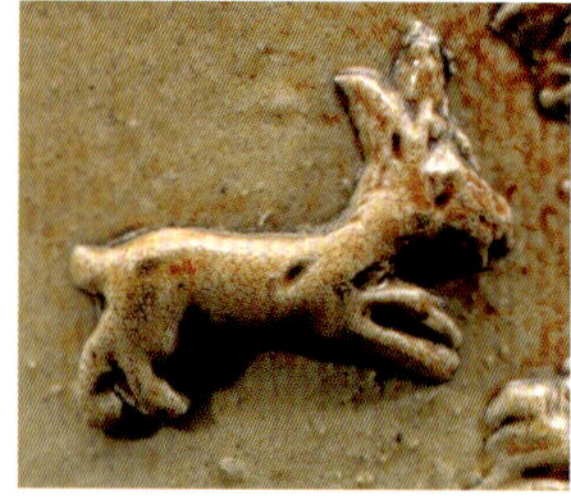
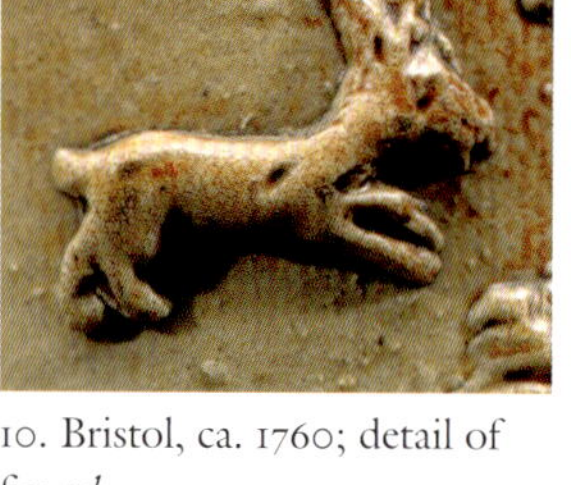

10. Bristol, ca. 1760; detail of fig. 1*d*

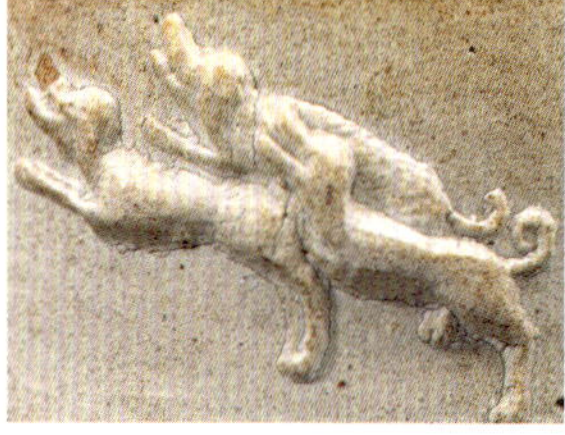

11. Vauxhall, 1722; detail of fig. 1*a*

12. Vauxhall, 1731; detail of fig. 1*b*

13. Vauxhall, 1737; detail of fig. 1*c*

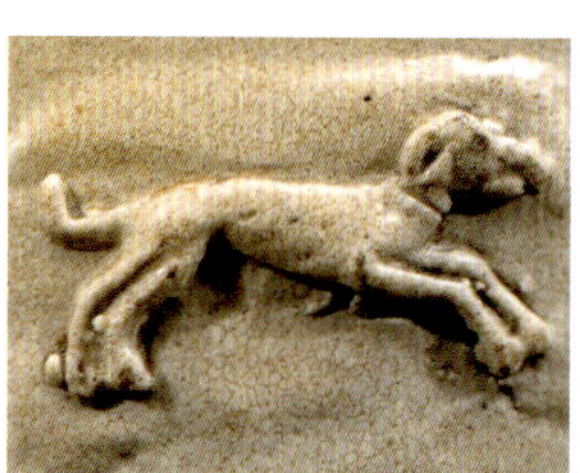

14. Bristol, ca. 1760; detail of fig. 1*d*

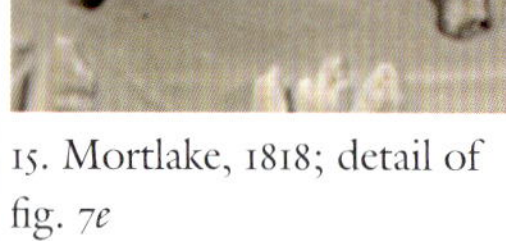

15. Mortlake, 1818; detail of fig. 7*e*

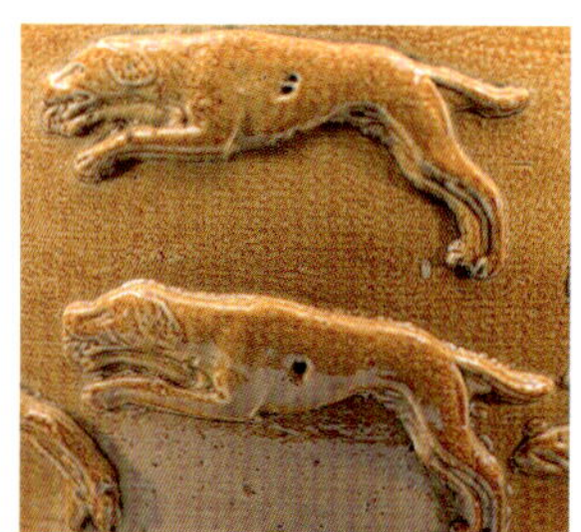

16. Bristol, 1832; detail of fig. 20

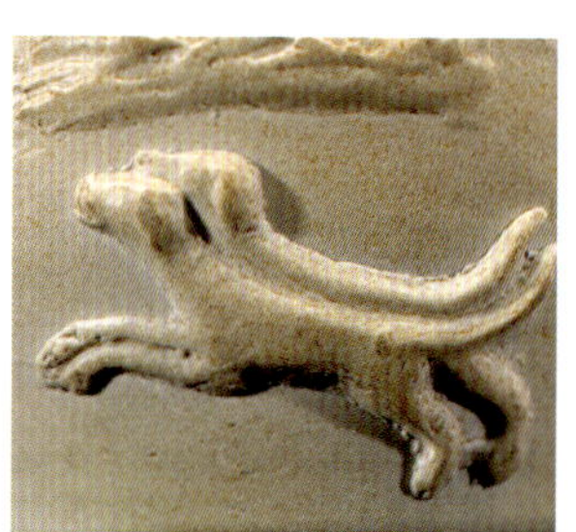

17. Mortlake or Lambeth, ca. 1835; detail of fig. 17*d*

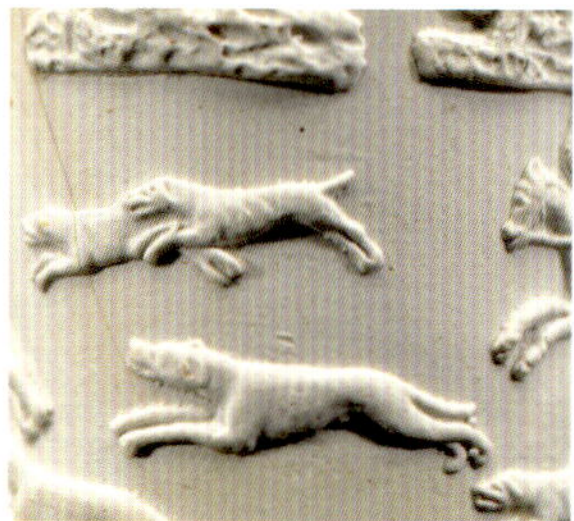

18. South Derbyshire or Bristol, ca. 1820; detail of fig. 16*d*

TABLE XI. PANELS

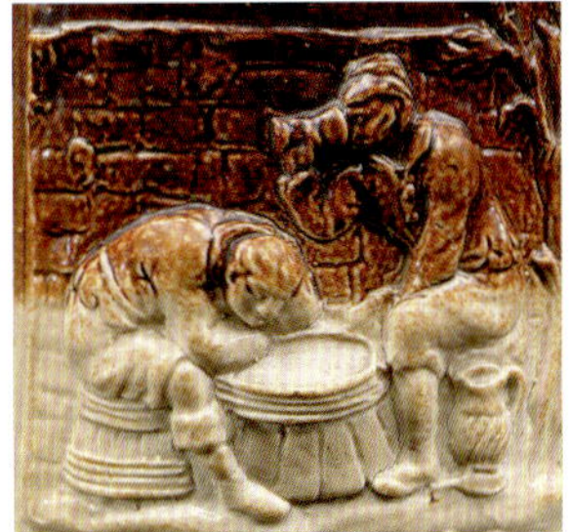
1. Mortlake, 1792; detail of fig. *7a*

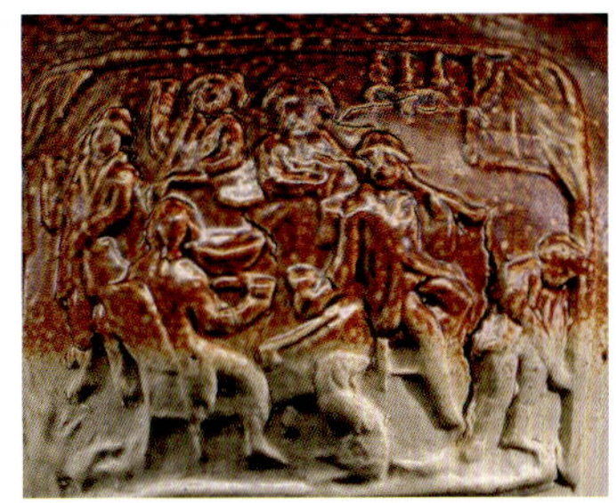
2. Mortlake, 1799; detail of fig. *7b* (Punch Party D)

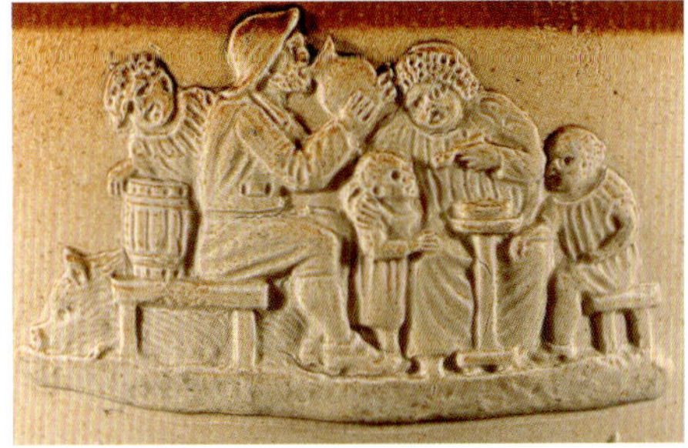
3. Doulton, ca. 1880; detail of fig. 19*f*

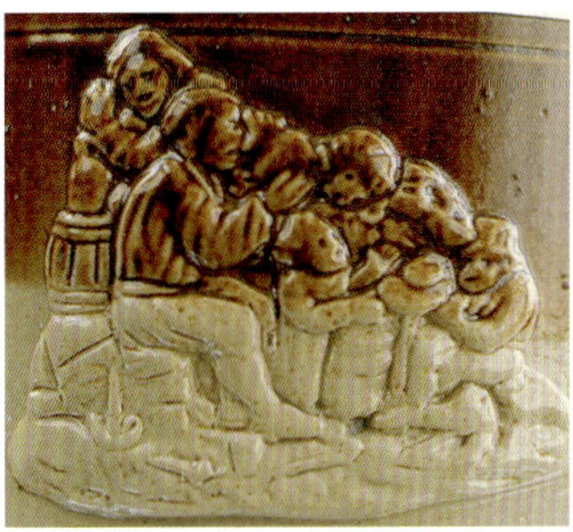
4. Lambeth, 1870; detail of fig. 22*a*

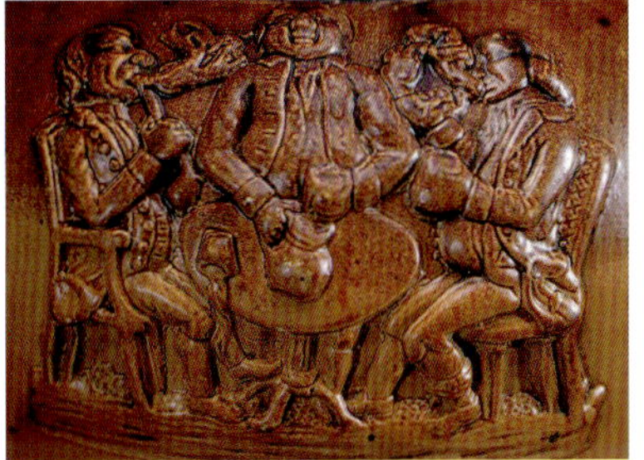
5. Glasgow, ca. 1860; detail of fig. 13*e*

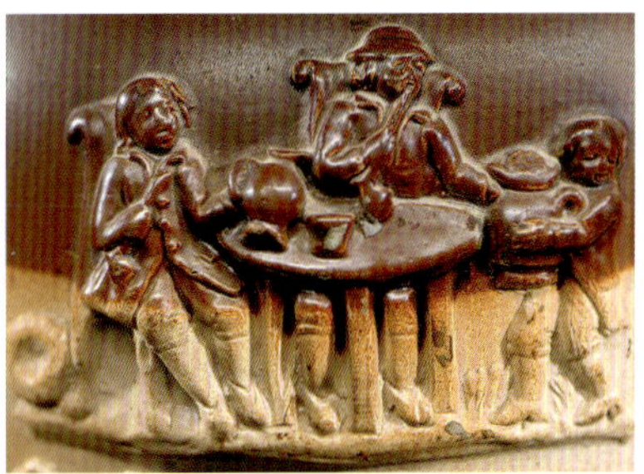
6. Liverpool?, ca. 1850; detail of table IV.1

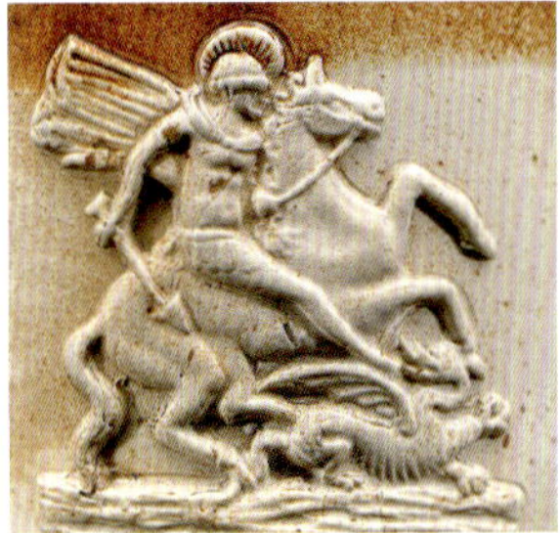
7. South Derbyshire, ca. 1835; detail of fig. 16*f*

TABLE XII. WINDMILLS

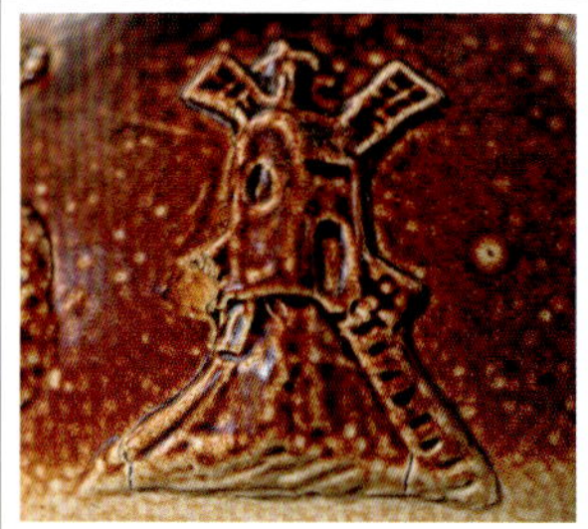

1. Mortlake, 1792; detail of fig. 7*a*

2. Mortlake, 1818; detail of fig. 7*e*

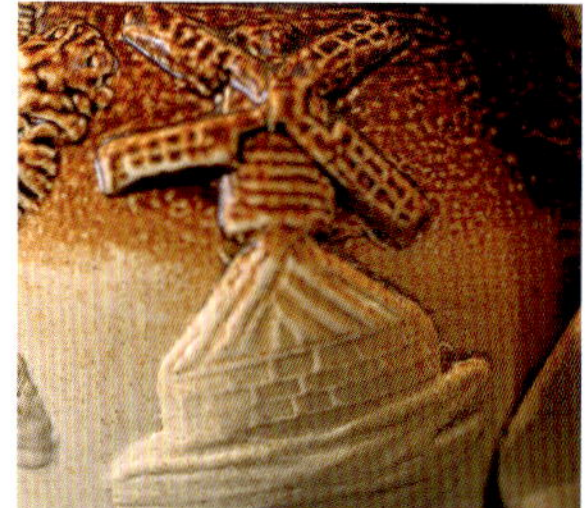

3. Mortlake, 1801; detail of fig. 14*c*

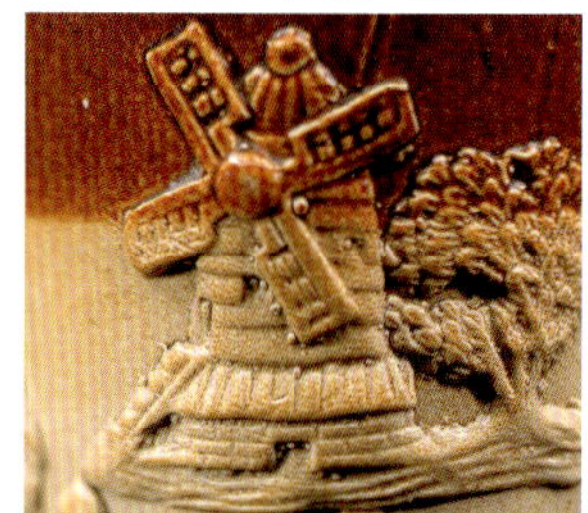

4. Mortlake, ca. 1840; detail of fig. 10*b*

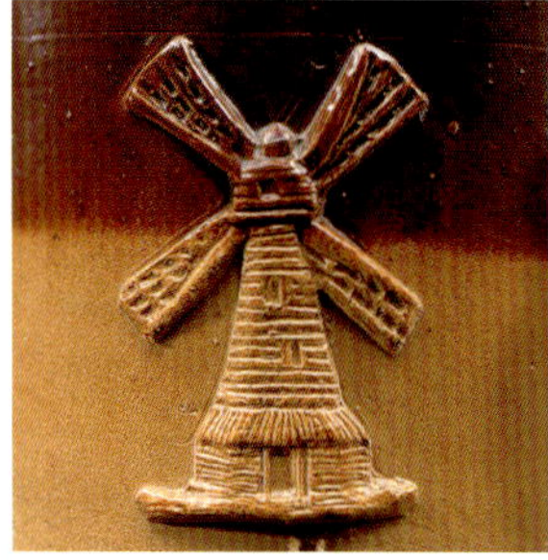

5. Fulham, ca. 1840; detail of fig. 15*c*

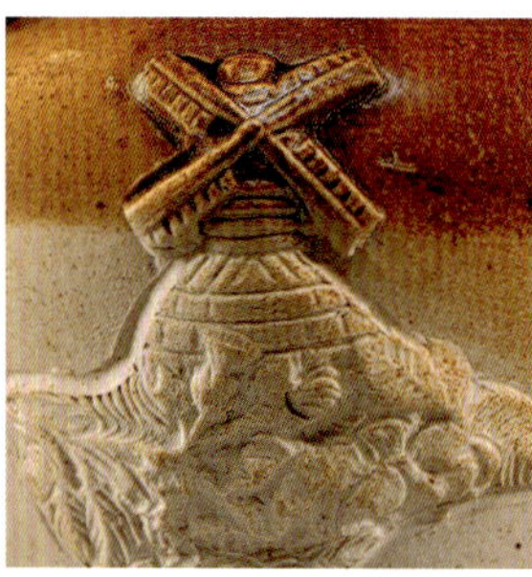

6. Derbyshire or Glasgow, ca. 1845; detail of fig. 14*d*

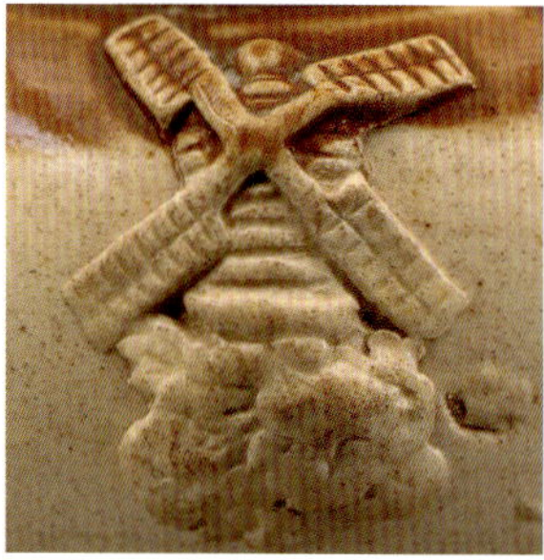

7. Derbyshire, ca. 1830; detail of fig. 10*c*

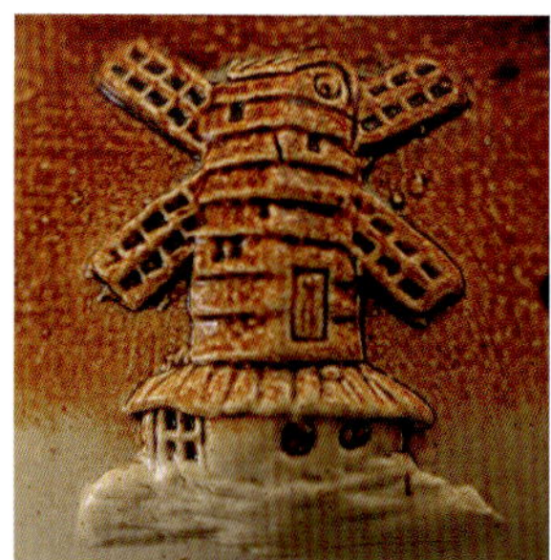

8. Mortlake or Lambeth, ca. 1830; detail of fig. 17*a*

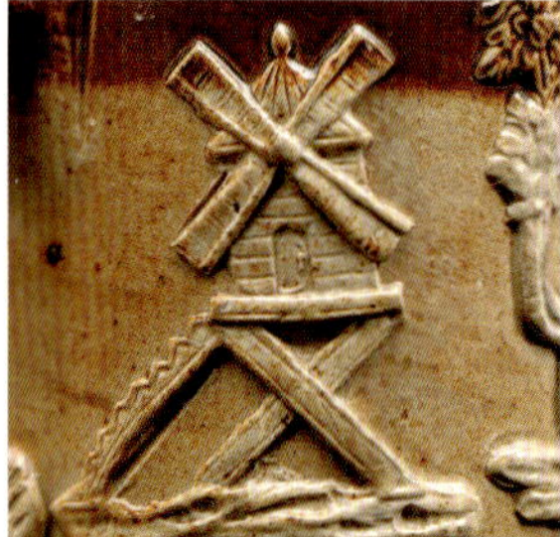

9. South Derbyshire, ca. 1835; detail of fig. 16*a*

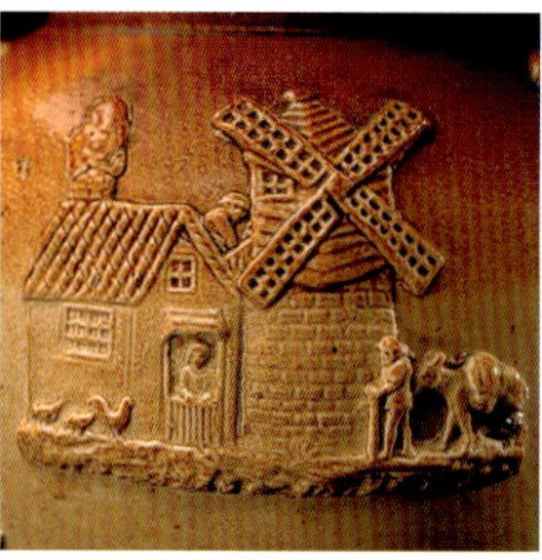

10. Doulton, ca. 1865; detail of fig. 19*b*

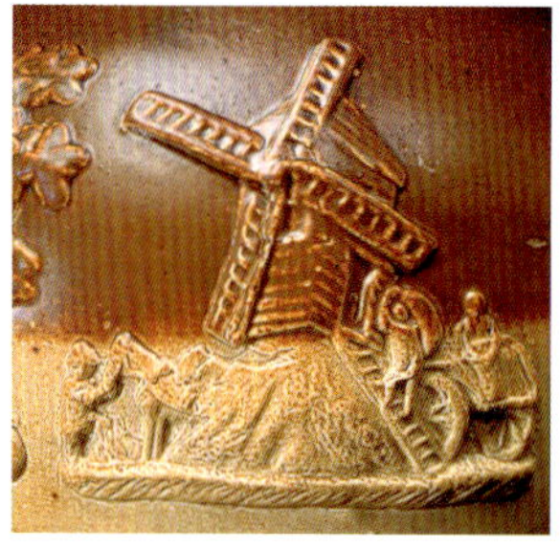

11. Derbyshire?, ca. 1840; detail of fig. 13*c*

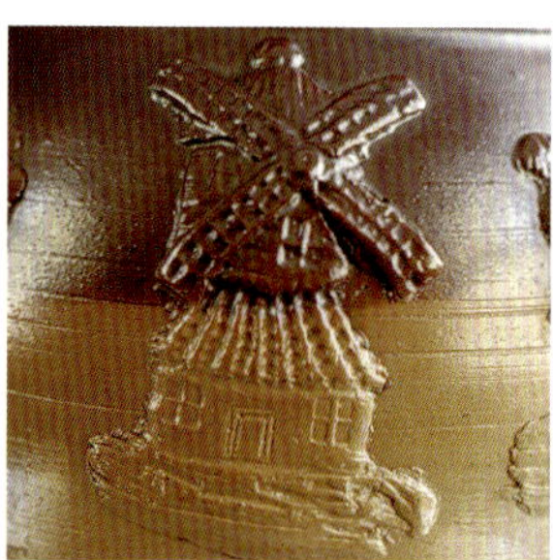

12. London, ca. 1850; detail of fig. 22*b*

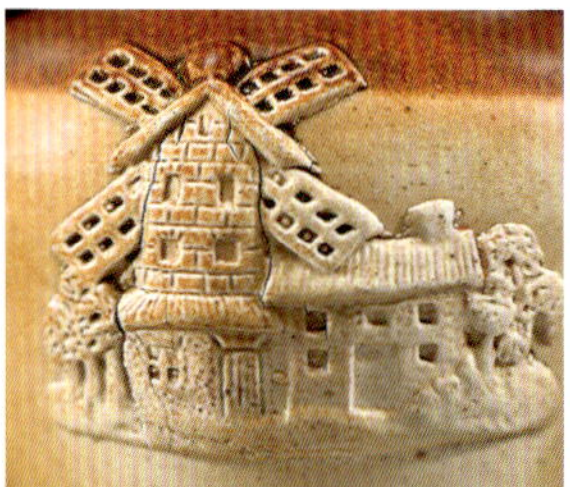

13. Stiff, Lambeth, ca. 1880; detail of fig. 13*d*

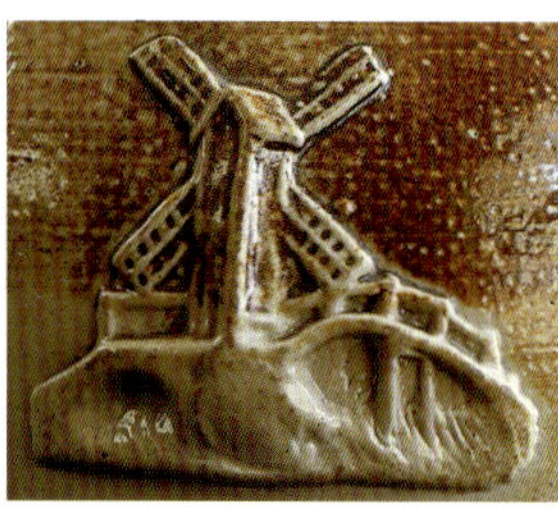

14. Unknown, ca. 1840; detail of fig. 22*c*

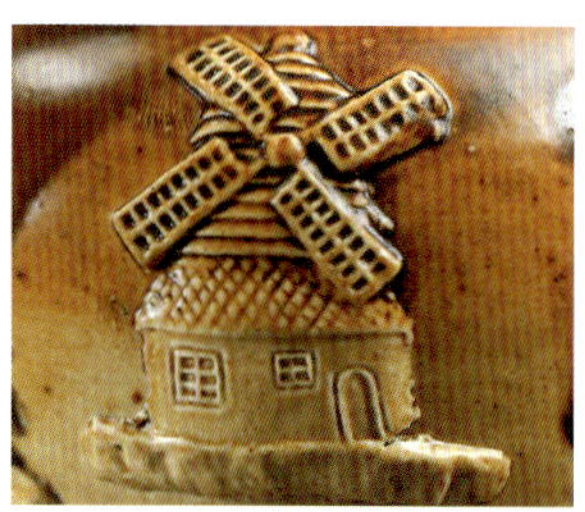

15. Doulton, ca. 1882; detail of fig. 19*e*

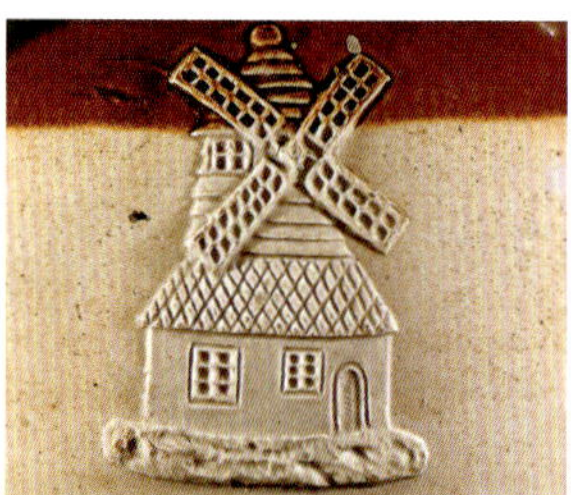

16. Doulton, ca. 1880; detail of fig. 19*f*

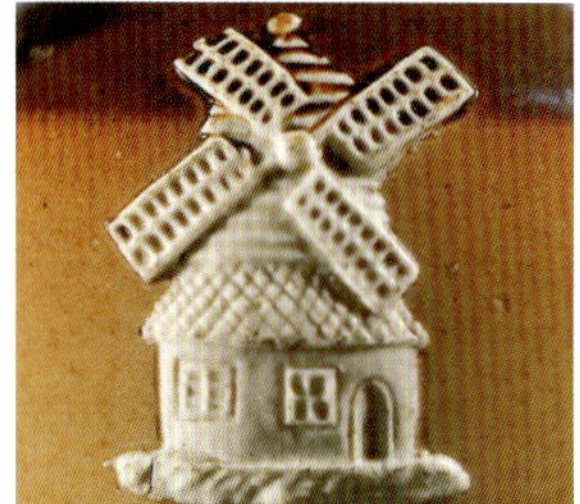

17. Doulton, ca. 1880; detail of fig. 21*b*

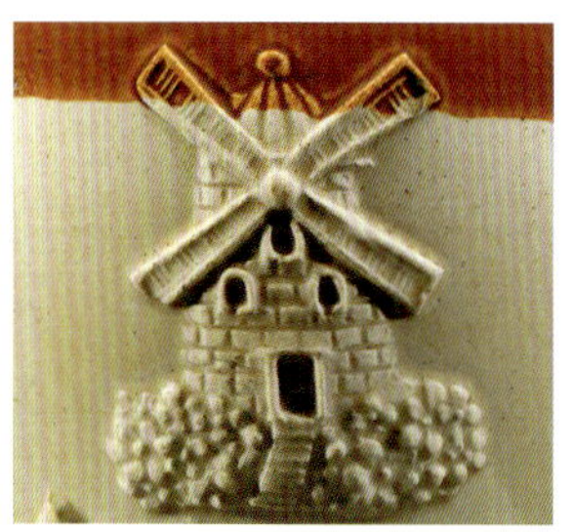

18. Bourne, Derbyshire, ca. 1890; detail of fig. 9*d*

TABLE XIII. SMOKERS AND THINKERS

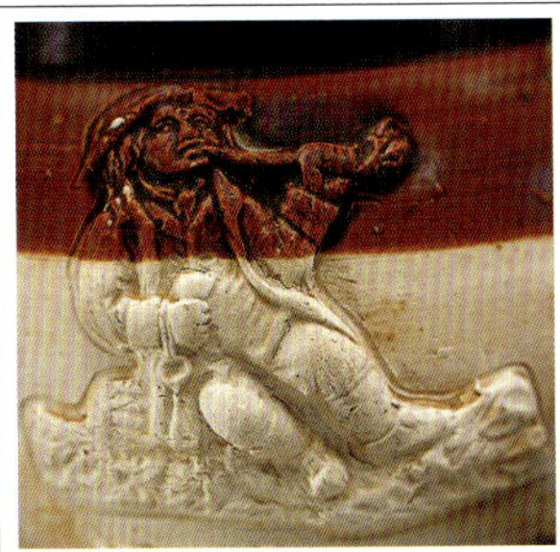
1. Derbyshire, ca. 1835; detail of fig. 10*a*

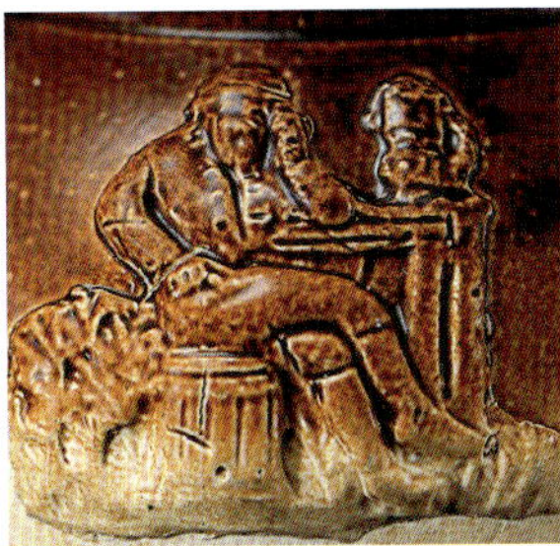
2. Mortlake or Lambeth, ca. 1835; detail of fig. 17*d*

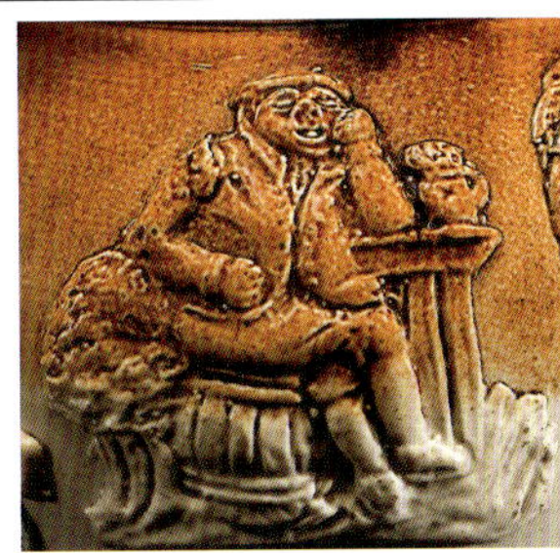
3. Mortlake or Lambeth, ca. 1830; detail of fig. 17*c*

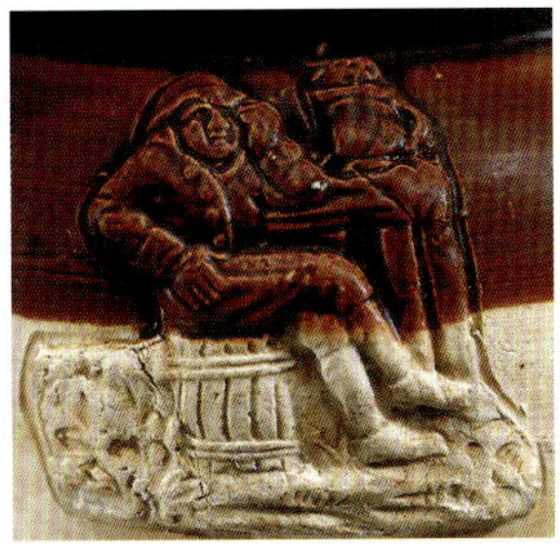
4. Derbyshire, ca. 1835; detail of fig. 10*a*

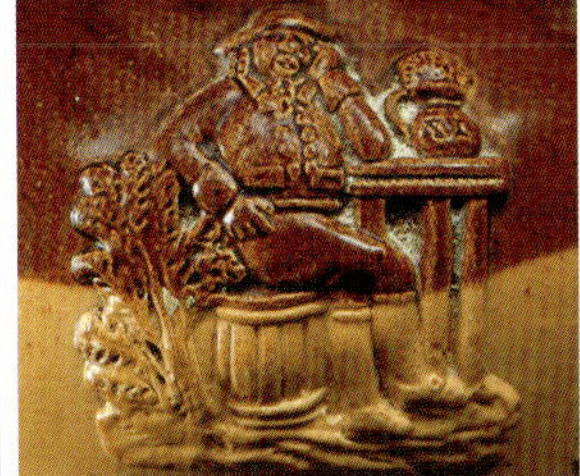
5. Stiff, Lambeth, ca. 1880; detail of fig. 13*d*

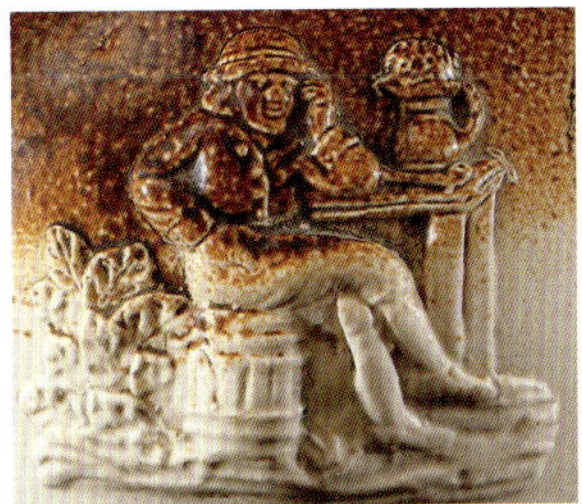
6. Mortlake or Lambeth, ca. 1835; detail of fig. 17*b*

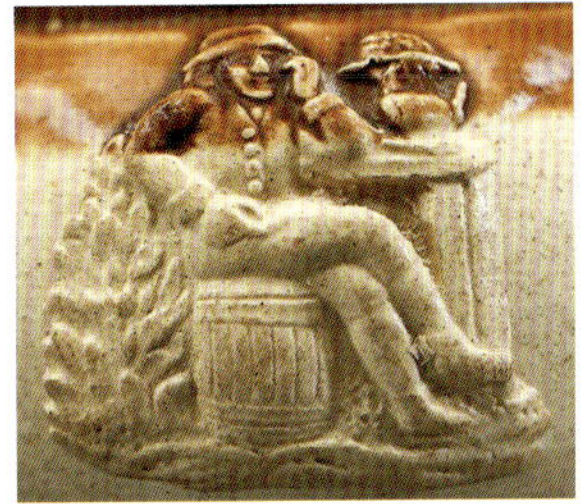
7. Derbyshire, ca. 1830; detail of fig. 10*c*

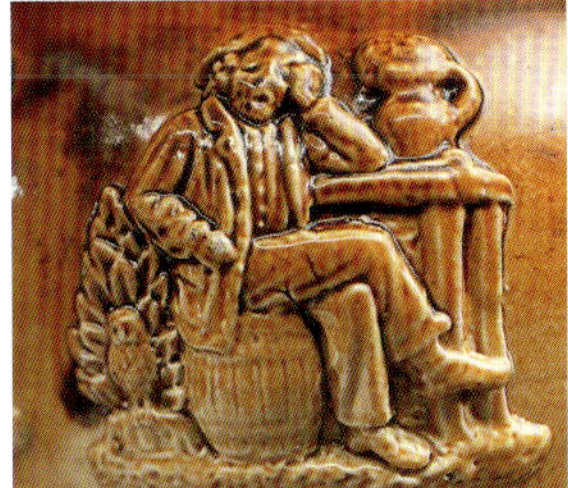
8. Doulton, ca. 1882; detail of fig. 19*e*

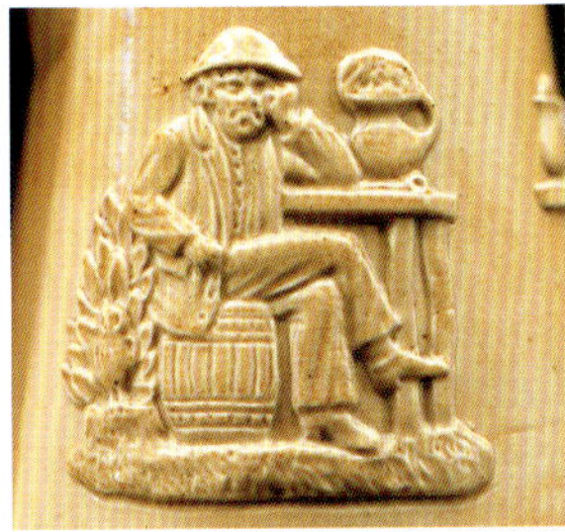
9. Doulton, ca. 1885; detail of fig. 21*c*

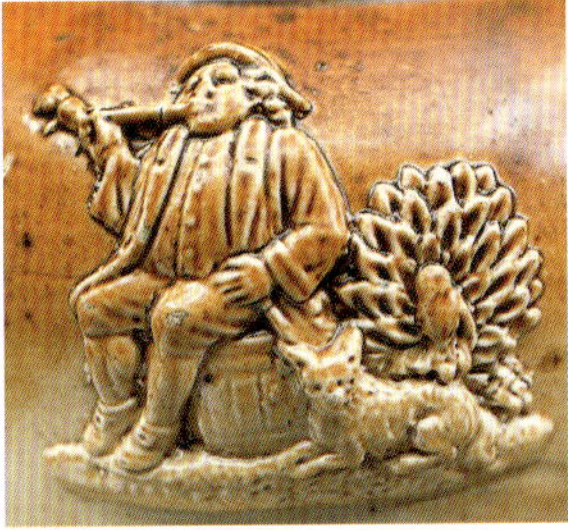
10. Doulton, ca. 1865; detail of fig. 19*c*

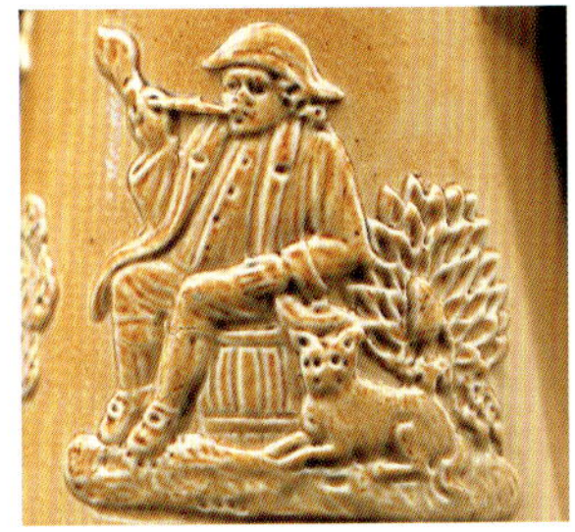
11. Doulton, ca. 1885; detail of fig. 21*c*

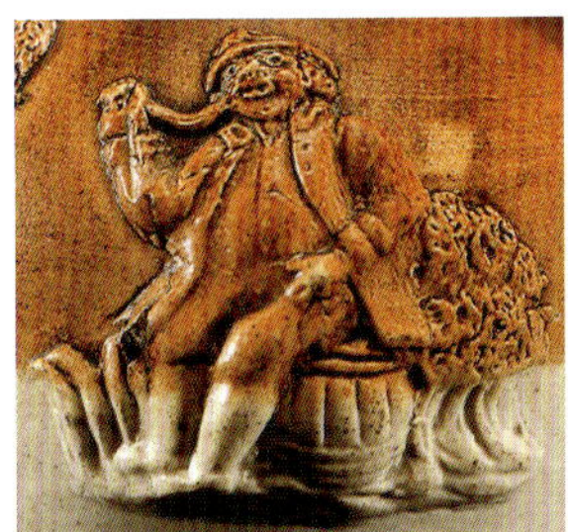
12. Mortlake or Lambeth, ca. 1830; detail of fig. 17*c*

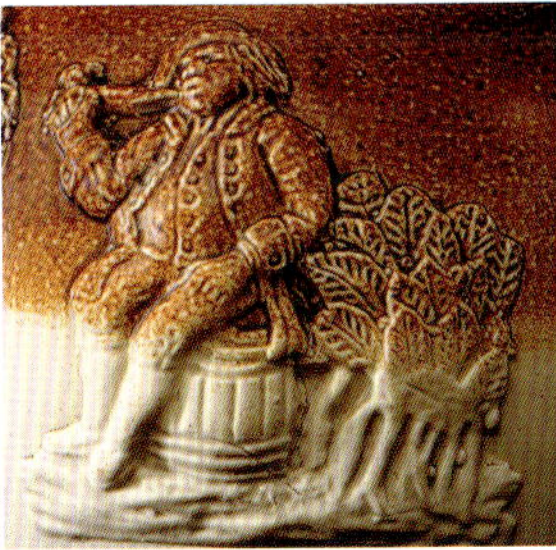
13. Mortlake or Lambeth, ca. 1835; detail of fig. 17*b*

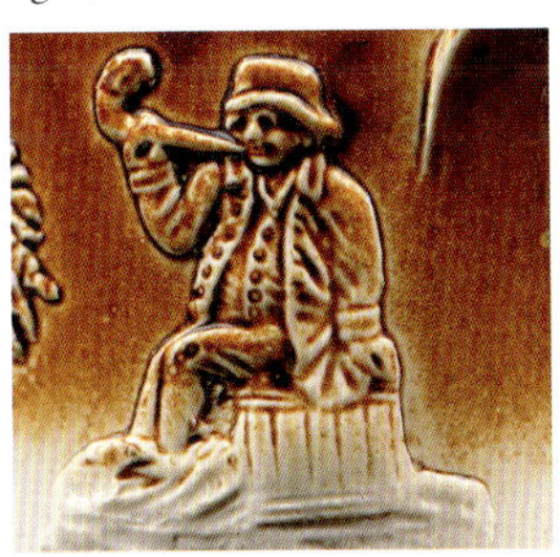
14. South Derbyshire or Bristol, ca. 1820; detail of fig. 16*d*

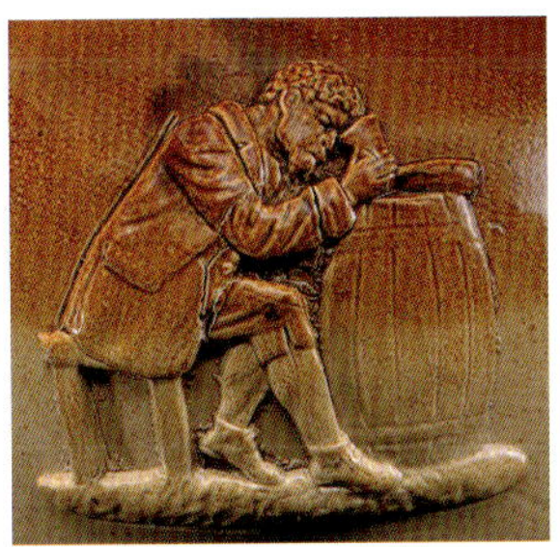
15. Doulton, ca. 1865; detail of fig. 19*b*

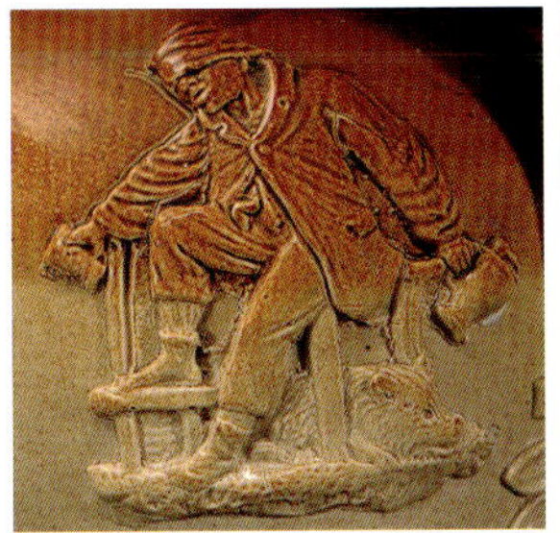
16. Doulton, ca. 1865; detail of fig. 19*b*

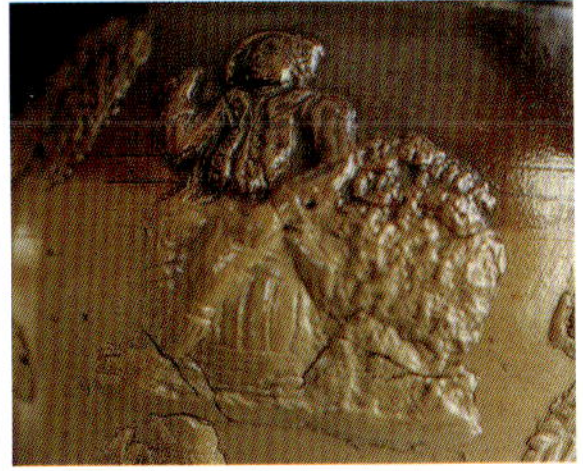
17. London, ca. 1850; detail of fig. 22*b*

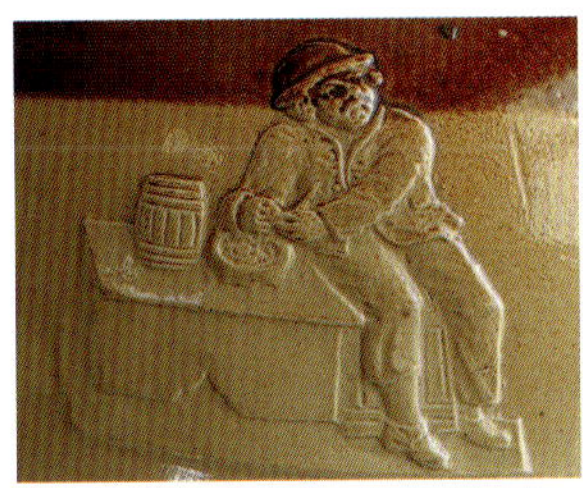
18. Doulton, ca. 1880; detail of fig. 19*f*

TABLE XIV. SMOKERS AND WAVERS

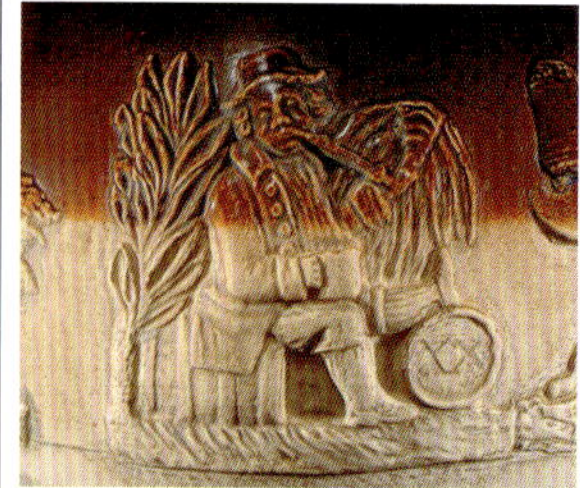

1. Fulham, ca. 1840; detail of fig. 15*c*

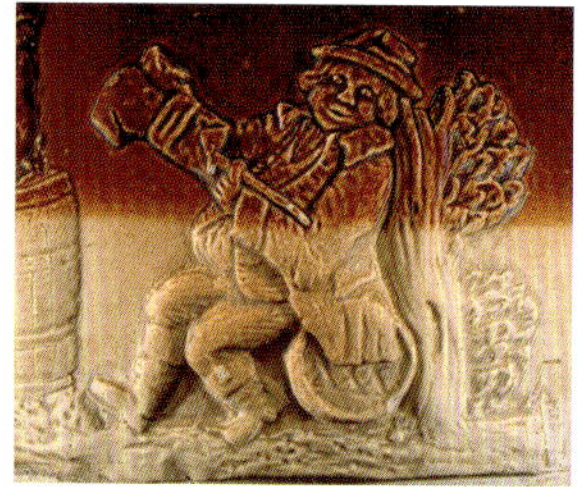

2. Fulham, ca. 1840; detail of fig. 15*c*

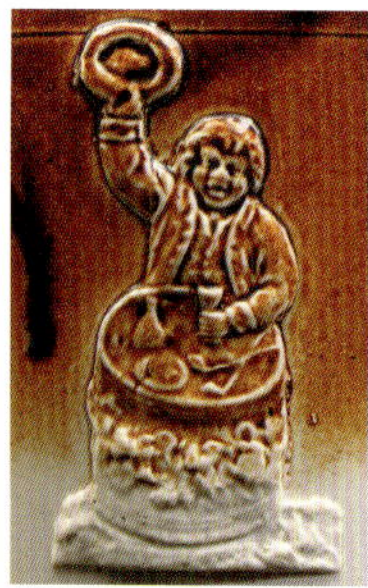

3. South Derbyshire or Bristol, ca. 1820; detail of fig. 16*d*

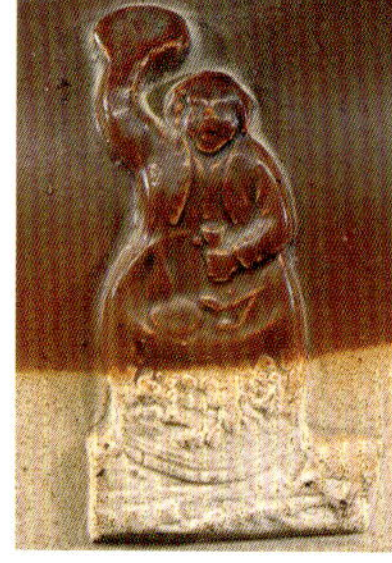

4. Liverpool or Bristol, ca. 1860; detail of table IV.1

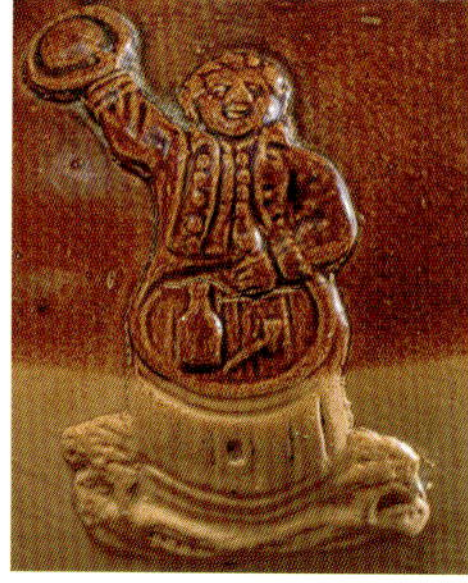

5. Stiff, Lambeth, ca. 1880; detail of fig. 13*d*

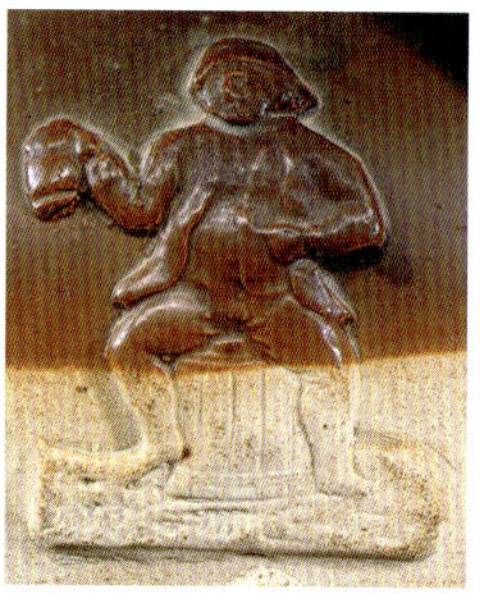

6. Liverpool or Bristol, ca. 1860; detail of table IV.1

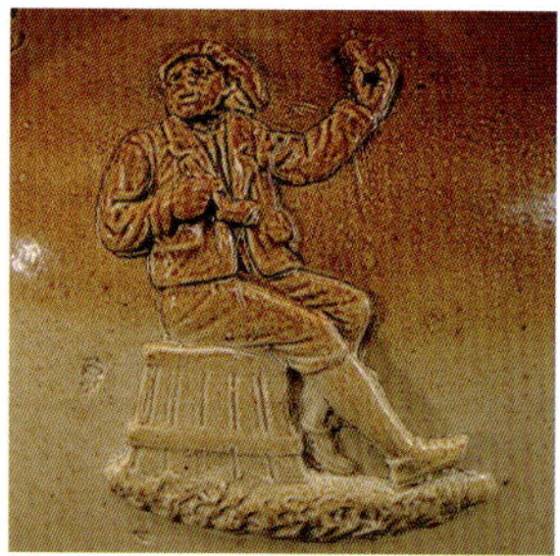

7. Doulton, ca. 1865; detail of fig. 19*b*

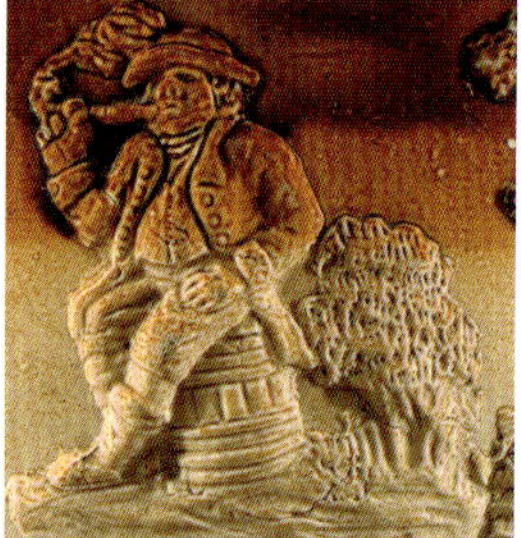

8. Derbyshire, ca. 1840; detail of fig. 13*a*

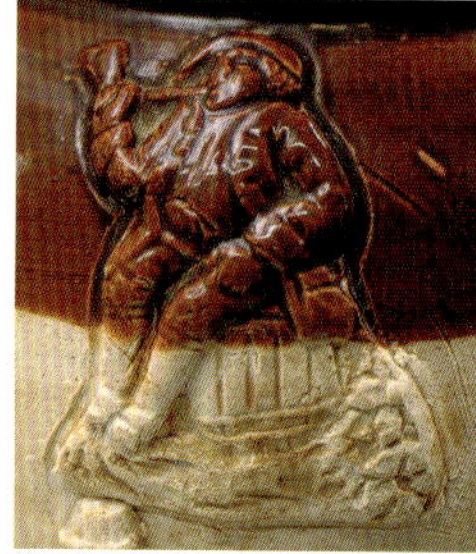

9. Derbyshire, ca. 1835; detail of fig. 10*a*

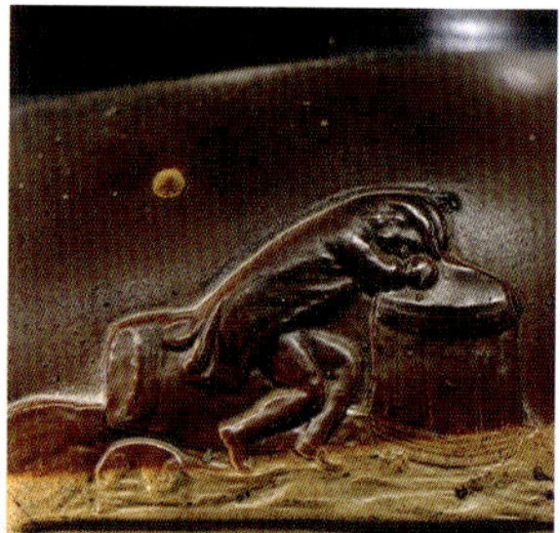

10. Liverpool or Bristol, ca. 1860; detail of table IV.1

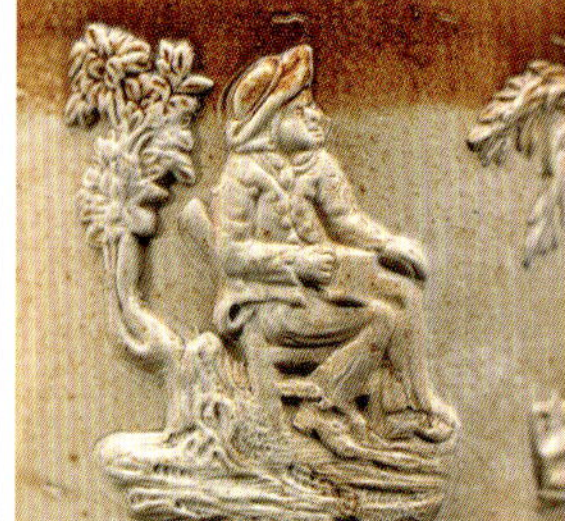

11. South Derbyshire, ca. 1835; detail of fig. 16*f*

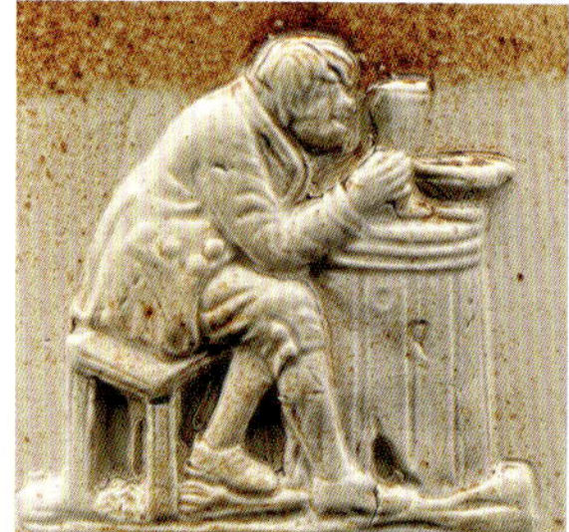

12. South Derbyshire, ca. 1835; detail of fig. 16*f*

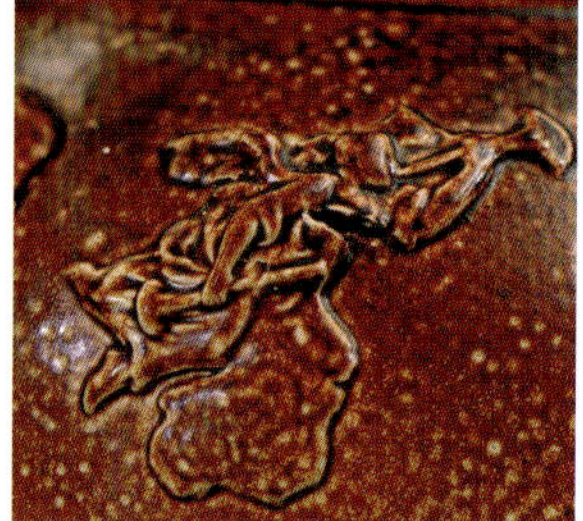

13. Mortlake, 1799; detail of fig. 7*b*

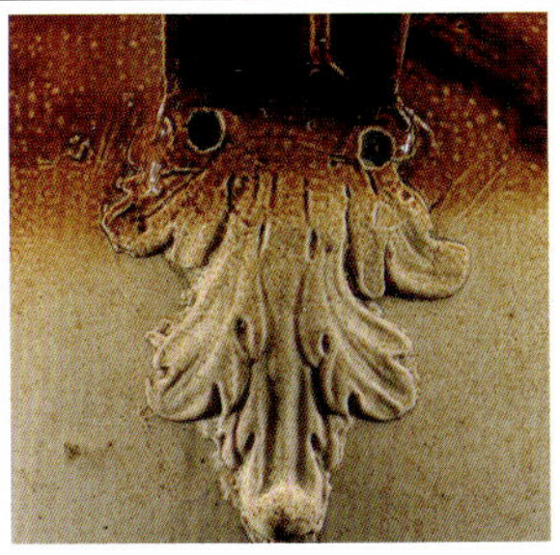

1. Fulham, ca. 1805; detail of fig. 15*a*

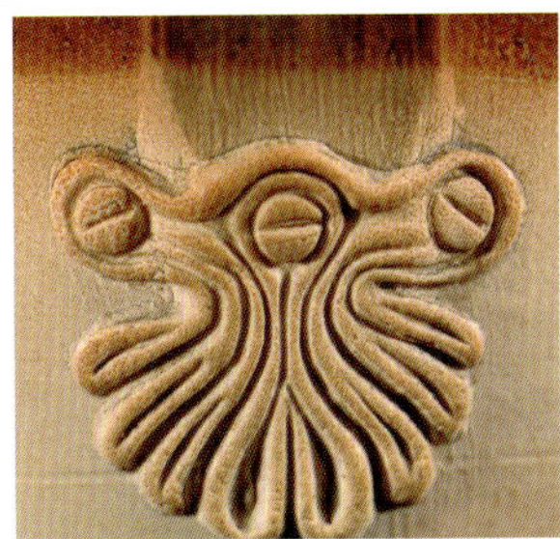

2. Fulham, ca. 1837; detail of fig. 15*b*

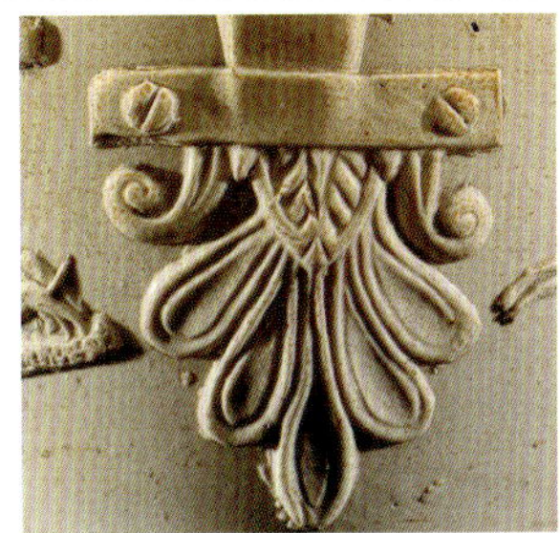

3. Derbyshire, ca. 1840; detail of fig. 13*a*

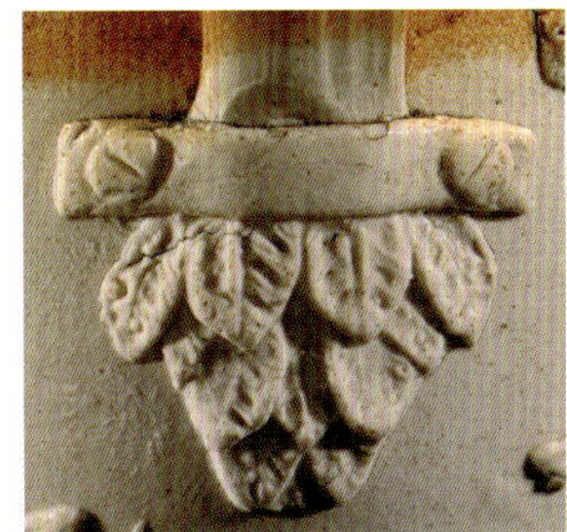

4. Mortlake or Lambeth, ca. 1830; detail of fig. 17*c*

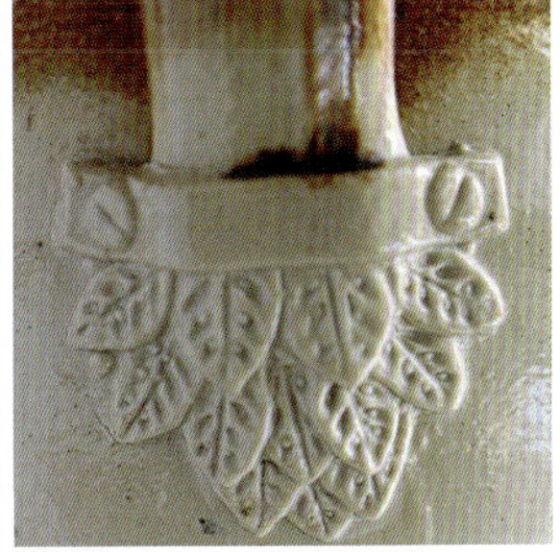

5. Mortlake or Lambeth, ca. 1830; detail of fig. 17*a*

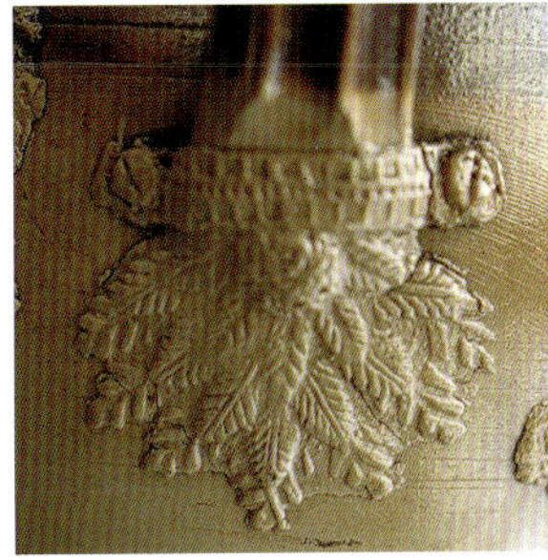

6. London, ca. 1850; detail of fig. 22*b*

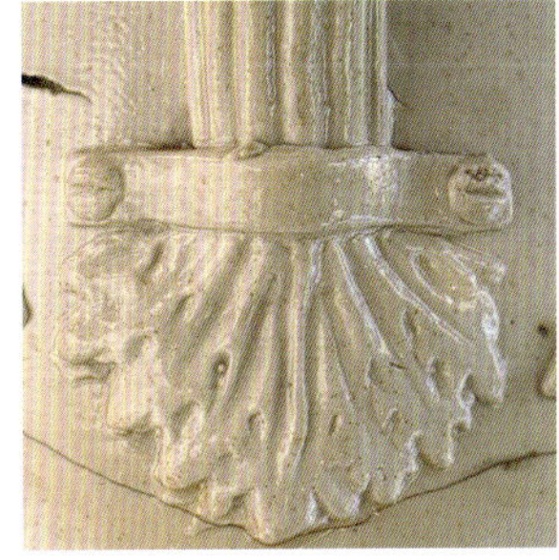

7. South Derbyshire or Bristol, ca. 1820; detail of fig. 16*d*

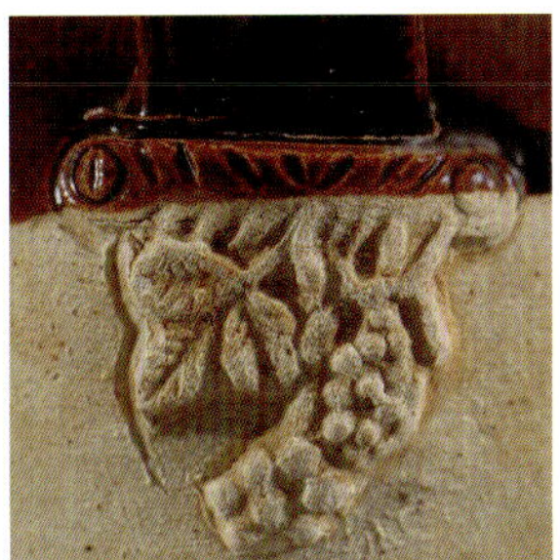

8. Derbyshire, ca. 1835; detail of fig. 10*a*

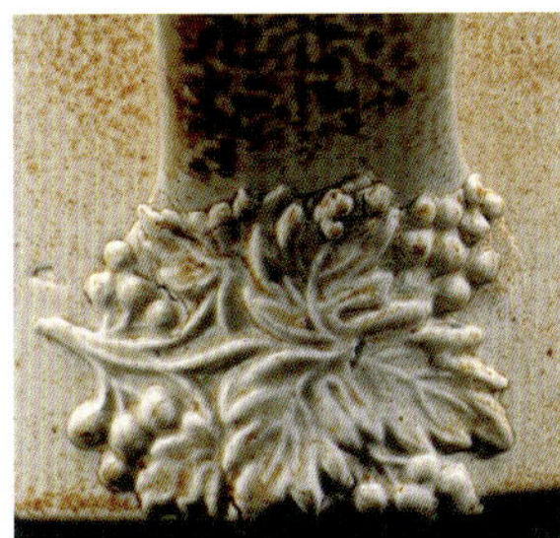

9. South Derbyshire, ca. 1835; detail of fig. 16*f*

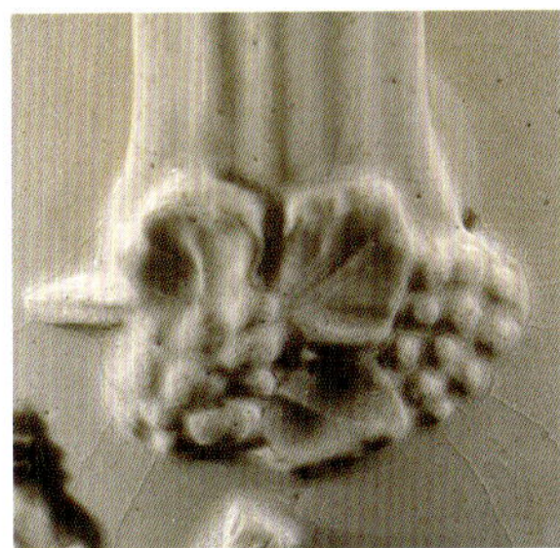

10. Bourne, ca. 1870–1900; detail of fig. 9*b*

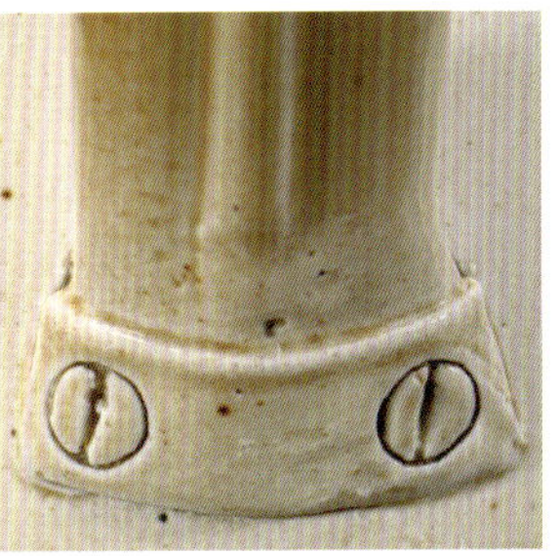

11. Derbyshire, ca. 1845; detail of fig. 16*e*

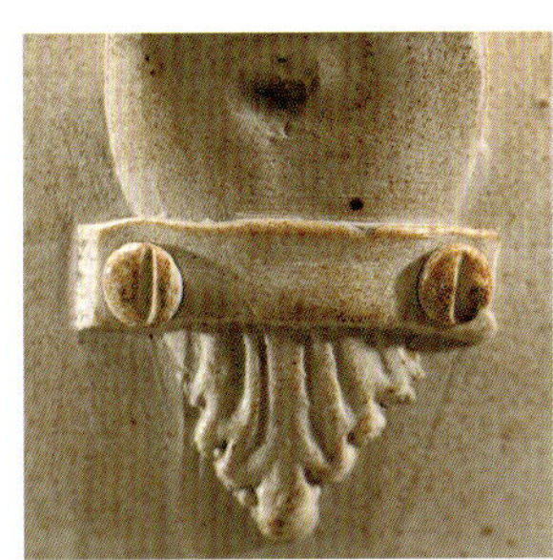

12. Liverpool?, ca. 1850; detail of table IV.1

13. Doulton, ca. 1865; detail of fig. 19*b*

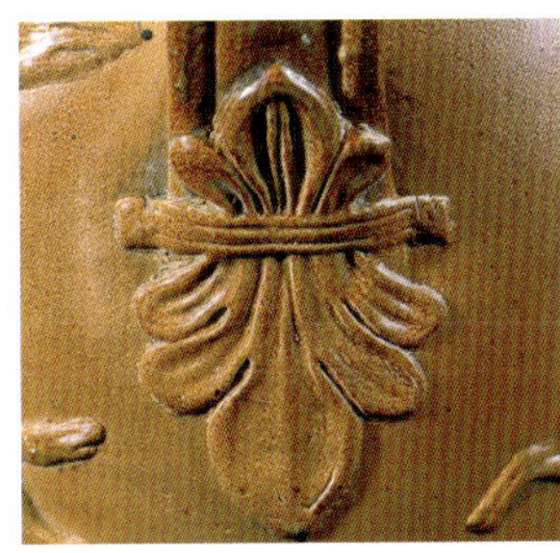

14. Glasgow, ca. 1860; detail of fig. 13*e*

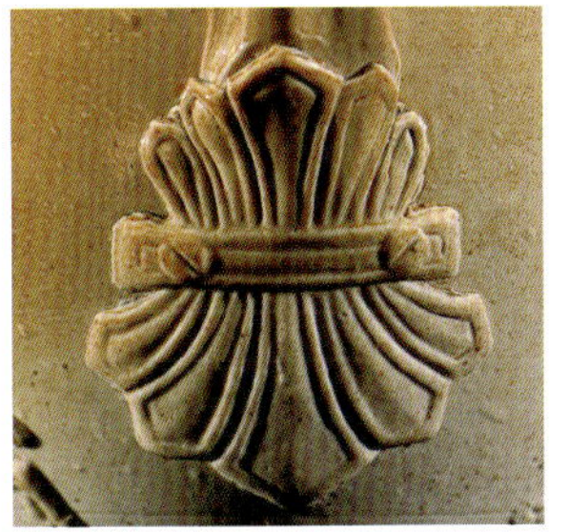

15. Doulton, 1868; detail of fig. 19*d*

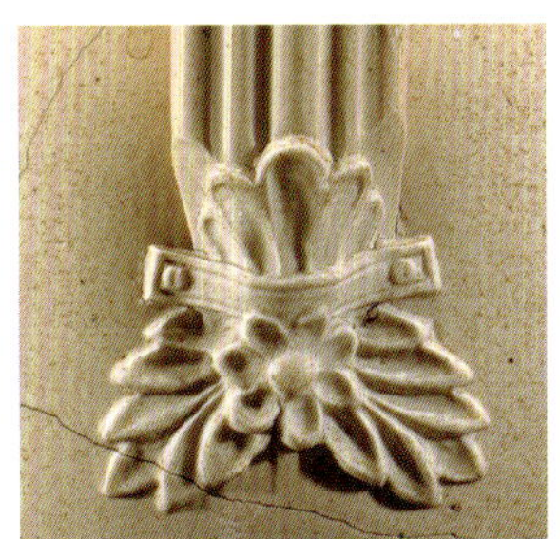

16. Doulton, ca. 1882; detail of fig. 19*e*

17. Doulton, 1911; detail of fig. 19*g*

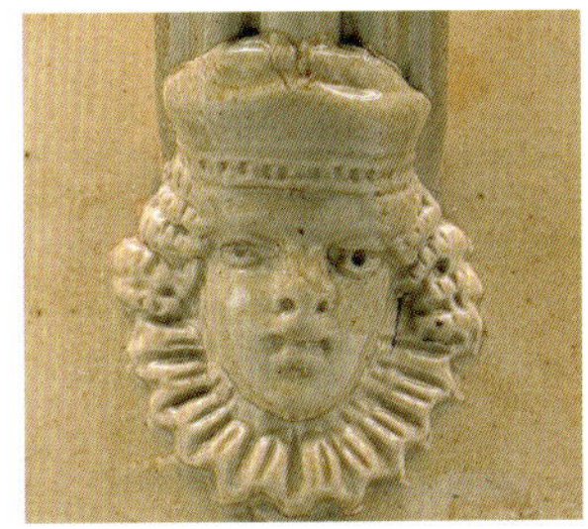

18. Doulton, ca. 1885; detail of fig. 21*c*

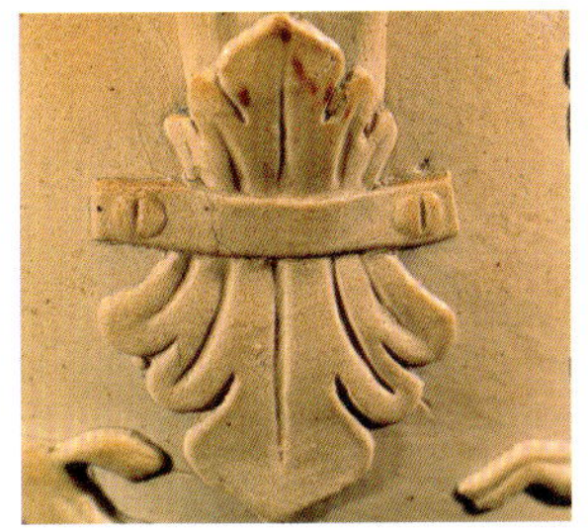

19. Stiff, Lambeth, ca. 1880; detail of fig. 13*d*

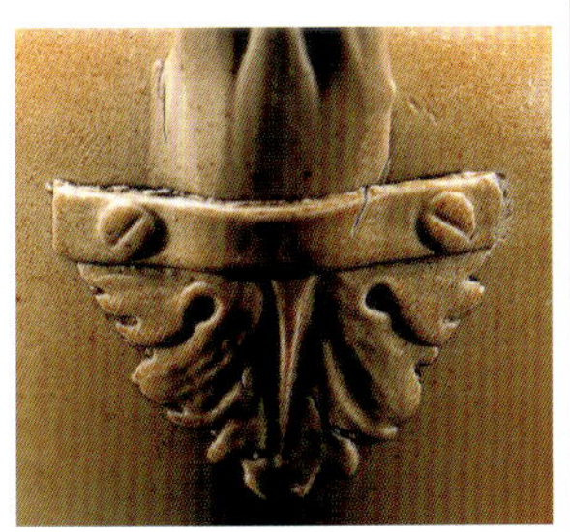

20. Stiff, Lambeth, ca. 1870; detail of fig. 13*b*

ACKNOWLEDGMENTS I am deeply indebted to all those pioneering stoneware scholars whose names and works are referenced herein, but more especially to my contemporaries, namely: American collector Nicholas Johnson; English collector and author Mavis Bimson Watney; London Museum (MoLAS) ceramic specialists Jacqueline Pearce and Roy Stephenson, and archaeologist Ian Blair; author and stoneware pioneer Derek Askey; *Ceramics in America* editor Robert Hunter; editor and collector Lance Mytton; ceramics dealers Jonathan Horne, Garry Atkins, and Rodney Harmon; and beyond all, to my career-long friend and mentor, the late Adrian Oswald. I am also indebted to Margaret Pritchard, curator of prints and drawings at Colonial Williamsburg, for her assistance in tracking the Heemskerk engraving, as well as to the Foundation's assistant curator of ceramics, Suzanne Findlen.

My circa dating throughout assumes at least a ten-year bracket, and my attributions are seated as well as they can be on the few marked parallels and the not always consistent opinions of others.

1. Sir John Eardley-Wilmot, *Reminiscences of the Late Thomas Assheton Smith* (London: John Murray, 1860), p. 299.

2. Mavis Bimson fleshed out her reasoning at the meeting, but it was not fully published. "Stoneware 16th to 20th Century," *English Ceramic Circle Transactions* 10, 1976, pt. 5 (1980): 260–62.

3. Frank Britton, "The Pickleherring Potteries; an inventory," *Post-Medieval Archaeology* 24 (1990): 61–92.

4. Ivor Noël Hume, *If These Pots Could Talk* (Milwaukee: Chipstone Foundation, 2001), p. 153.

5. A Gravel Lane factory inventory of 1726/27 lists 1,006 stone mugs. See Adrian Oswald, R. J. C. Hildyard, and R. G. Hughes, *English Brown Stoneware, 1670–1900* (London: Faber and Faber, 1982), p. 16. See also Adrian Oswald, "A London Stoneware Pottery, Recent Excavations at Bankside," *Connoisseur* (December 1950): 183–85.

6. J. F. Blacker, *The ABC of English Salt-Glaze Stoneware from Dwight to Doulton* (London: Stanley Paul & Co., 1922). Also Bernard Rackham, *Catalogue of the Glaisher Collection of Pottery & Porcelain in the Fitzwilliam Museum, Cambridge* (1935; Woodbridge, Suffolk, Eng.: Antique Collectors' Club, 1987), pp. 153–56.

7. The Museum of London Archaeology Service (MoLAS) excavated much of the oldest of the two sites (Sanders) in 1997. Barney Sloane, Stewart Hoad, John Cloake, and Jacqueline Pearce, *Early Modern Industry and Settlement: Excavations at George Street, Richmond, and High Street, Mortlake, in the London Borough of Richmond upon Thames,* MoLAS Archaeology Studies Series, no. 9 (London: Museum of London Archaeology Service, 2003).

8. Oswald, Hildyard, and Hughes, *English Brown Stoneware, 1670–1900,* pp. 96–98.

9. The process involved two glazes applied to the green ware and then fired to stoneware temperature without the infusion of salt. The formula was soon shared with Alfred Singer (successor to John Wisker) at the Vauxhall Pottery. When the Fulham Pottery was bought by Charles Bailey in 1864, he referred to "the new fashioned 'Bristol' Double glaze ware which has almost entirely superseded the Brown stone." Chris Green, *John Dwight's Fulham Pottery: Excavations 1971–79* (London: English Heritage, 1999), p. 337.

10. W. W. Hamilton Foyn, "Dated London Brown Saltglazed Hunting Mugs 1713–75," *English Ceramic Circle Transactions* 17, pt. 2 (2000): 264. W. J. Pountney, in *Old Bristol Potteries* (Bristol: J. W. Arrowsmith, 1920), pp. 250–51, quoted from *Felix Farley's Journal,* March 17, 1764, that the Tucker Street Pottery offered "all sorts of Muggs &c. at Lowest Price." Pountney also noted (p. 19) that one John Townsend "mugg-maker" had built a "mugg kiln in Tucker Street" in 1734 until it was closed by order of the city council in December 1738.

11. Illustrated in *Maine Antique Digest,* December 2002, p. 18A.

12. Edward "Ned" Ward, *The London Spy: The Vanities and Vices of the Town Exposed to View* (ca. 1705), edited by Arthur L. Hayward (London: Cassell and Company, 1927), p. 120. "Guzzle" in canting parlance meant any form of liquor.

13. The mug was still in pliable state when the tree patterns were incised, since the ground-creating scoring for one of them overlies a pad of clay used to cover a crack caused by handling at the time it was removed from the wheel. Decades later Josiah Wedgwood would describe this salvaging of a potential waster as *tinkering*.

14. Illustrated by Robin Hildyard, *Browne Muggs* (London: Victoria and Albert Museum, 1985), p. 56, no. 118.

15. Pictorial documentation for hare hunting in the seventeenth and eighteenth centuries was presented to the English Ceramic Circle in 1984. Julia Poole, "Ballads and Hunting Mugs," *English Ceramic Circle Transactions* 12, pt. 2 (1985): 156–60.

16. William Hone, *The Table Book* (London: Hunt and Clark, 1827), p. 189. The reference is to a mug-house club in London's Long Acre, ca. 1710. See Ivor Noël Hume, *All the Best Rubbish* (New York: Harper and Row, 1974), pp. 218–25, for a manuscript book of verses dated 1718 and almost certainly a relic of a London mug club.

17. It may not be entirely coincidental that in the coffee room at Boodles Club, one of London's oldest (1762), there hangs a vast painting of a stag hunt by Abraham Hondius (1671). Anthony Lejeune, *The Gentlemen's Clubs of London* (London: Dorset Press, 1984), p. 58.

18. Illustrated in Hildyard, *Browne Muggs,* p. 56, no. 119.

19. Because most if not all of the mugs with Banstead Downs inscriptions exhibit counterclockwise hunts, it is reasonable to deduce that all came from Vauxhall, thereby revealing the identity of London's Factory "A."

20. Lewes and Ewhurst are about seventeen miles apart, no great traveling distance for early-eighteenth-century gentry and merchants.

21. Samuel Pepys, *The Diary of Samuel Pepys Esquire, F.R.S.* (London: George Newnes, 1902), entry for July 30, 1663, p. 247.

22. Both are dated 1724, attributed to Vauxhall, and initialed "$\text{T}^{\text{B}}\text{E}$" and "WAW." See Hamilton Foyn, "Dated London Brown Saltglazed Hunting Mugs," p. 267. The triple initial cipher representing man and wife was commonly used by tavern keepers on their tokens in the second half of the seventeenth century. It is possible, therefore, that mugs so marked were made for tavern keepers and not their customers.

23. Ward, *London Spy,* pp. 113–14.

24. A two-handled example in the Colonial Williamsburg Collection is inscribed "Henry Bacon att Cock in Henham 1719"; see Derek Askey, *Stoneware Bottles from Bellarmines to Ginger Beers, 1500–1949* (Brighton, Eng.: Bowman Graphics, 1981), p. 40.

25. However, there were, and are, inns and taverns called the Royal Oak that used this logo.

26. There is an old potter's saying that you can always tell a craftsman by his rims and his handles.

27. Green, *John Dwight's Fulham Pottery,* pp. 112–15.

28. Ibid., pp. 149–54. See also Oswald, Hildyard, and Hughes, *English Brown Stoneware, 1670–1900,* p. 57, pl. 23, for a pickle jar dated 1752 and decorated with twenty different "fireback" tavern panels. See also James Glenn, "Brown Mugs and Jugs: A Personal Foray into the Field of Collecting," in *Ceramics in America,* edited by Robert Hunter (Hanover, N.H.: University Press of New England for the Chipstone Foundation, 2002): 171–90.

29. Hamilton Foyn cites two examples of the Blacksmiths' arms, one dated 1720 and the other 1723; "Dated London Brown Saltglazed Hunting Mugs," A8 and 22, pp. 265–66. The Watermen's Company mug in the Colonial Williamsburg Collection (1966-361) is dated 1739 and curatorially attributed to Fulham.

30. They are occasionally called a "supper party." Askey, *Stoneware Bottles,* p. 44.

31. The assumed relationship between the Punch Party A sprig and Hogarth's painting is of some longevity. In the May 19, 1871, Christie's sale of Fulham ceramics from the collection of Mr. C. W. Reynolds, lot 270 was described as "A mug with ornament in relief—the Midnight Conversation after Hogarth . . . £9.5.0. Bohn." Blacker, *ABC of English Salt-Glaze Stoneware,* p. 81.

32. John Ireland, *Hogarth Illustrated,* 2 vols. (London: J & J Boydell, 1791), 1: 97.

33. *William Hogarth,* catalog of a loan exhibition at the Virginia Museum, 1967, p. 21, no. 14.

34. Colonial Williamsburg no. 1950-26, incised initials "AP" and the date 1754.

35. In drawing the table the artist was either unsure of himself or sketching in haste and drew the table legs as they would have been had the leaf been up.

36. Ireland, *Hogarth Illustrated,* 1: xx–xxi.

37. Ibid., 1: xxxiv.

38. *William Hogarth,* p. 19, no. 12.

39. Jo Draper, *Dated Post-medieval Pottery in Northampton Museum* (Northampton: Northampton Museum and Art Gallery, 1975), p. 21, pl. 14. Type impressed "Thomas Triplett / 1761." Mus. no. D.1920-21.1-109. Hamilton Foyn lists six examples of the arched punch party dated 1760, 1761, 1764 (2), 1766, and 1767.

40. Hamilton Foyn's list has fifty-nine in the "A" column (clockwise, 1713–1744) and fifty-three in the "B" (anticlockwise, 1726–1775), plus a questionable 1791 addition. In their book *English Brown Stoneware, 1670–1900,* Messrs. Oswald, Hildyard, and Hughes provide a further classification, adding a third London/Bristol factory as "C" and Bristol as "D." See Oswald, Hildyard, and Hughes, *English Brown Stoneware, 1670–1900,* pp. 48–50.

41. M. Bradley, *Dictionaire Oeconomique, or The Family Dictionary* (London: D. Midwinter, 1725), unpaginated.

42. Eardley-Wilmot, *Reminiscences of the Late Thomas Assheton Smith,* p. 224.

43. Bradley, *Dictionaire Oeconomique*. See table XIII.1.

44. Contemporary instructions for catching rabbits were by means of snares or gin traps.

45. The invitation had a prurient double meaning and was used earlier on London delftware wine cups; see, e.g., Jonathan Horne, *English Pottery and Related Works of Art: 2001* (London: Jonathan Horne Antiques, 2001), p. 10.

46. The house sprigs on this 1737 mug are paralleled on a mug in the Colonial Williamsburg collection inscribed "John Colly / 1750. C.W. 1950–22." One wonders whether Colly's mug was postdated, perhaps as a coming-of-age gift.

47. Oswald, Hildyard, and Hughes, *English Brown Stoneware, 1670–1900,* p. 50.

48. Illustrated in Jonathan Horne's promotional material for his 1996 stoneware exhibition. Elsewhere the name is cited as *Yates,* almost certainly in error.

49. Jonathan Horne, advertisement for his 1996 exhibition.

50. Jonathan Horne, *A Catalogue of English Brown Stoneware from the 17th and 18th Centuries* (London: Jonathan Horne, 1985), p. 20.

51. Pountney, *Old Bristol Potteries,* pp. 239–44.

52. It seems unlikely that the misspelling of Aylesbury was a deliberate reference to the mug's contents. It is more likely that the lettering was the product of hearing the name pronounced.

53. Particularly if Paten had business with the port of Bristol.

54. Victoria and Albert Museum; see Oswald, Hildyard, and Hughes, *English Brown Stoneware, 1670–1900,* pp. 88–89.

55. John Barwell became a freeman in 1740 and died ca. 1772–1774. Hildyard, *Browne Muggs,* p. 78. John's son, Thomas, became a freeman potter in 1774 and continued until at least 1788.

56. Hamilton Foyn cites another with a rectangular Punch Party ("A") inscribed "WH 1791" but questions whether it may be postdated. Hamilton Foyn, "Dated London Brown Salt-glazed Hunting Mugs," p. 273.

57. B. Lambert, *The History of London and Its Environs* (London: T. Hughes, 1806), 4: 208.

58. The only known examples of Sander's products are bottles bearing the name of Edward Atthawes and the date 1755 found in excavations at Carter's Grove plantation in Virginia. Atthawes was a resident of Mortlake. He was a signatory to William Sanders's will, which named Atthawes's son Samuel as a beneficiary. See Noël Hume, *If These Pots Could Talk,* p. 170, fig. VIII.5.

59. *Lloyds Evening Post,* January 16/18, 1757.

60. David Redstone, "Kishere's Mortlake Pottery," *English Ceramic Circle Transactions* 18, pt. 1 (2002): 45.

61. Roy Stephenson, "Pottery from Mortlake," in Sloane et al., *Early Modern Industry and Settlement*. The report on excavations at 61–75 Mortlake High Street states that "stoneware became the mainstay of production in Mortlake from around 1794," but concludes that "the bulk of the stoneware production was the mundane production of leading bottles, ginger beer bottles and ink bottles." Ibid., pp. 79, 82.

62. Oswald, Hildyard, and Hughes, *English Brown Stoneware, 1670–1900,* p. 35.

63. Redstone, "Kishere's Mortlake Pottery," p. 51, fig. 8.

64. William Hogarth did not become an apprentice to silversmith Ellis Gamble until he was fifteen.

65. Oswald, Hildyard, and Hughes, *English Brown Stoneware, 1670–1900,* p. 56. John Eustace Anderson (*A Short Account of the Mortlake Potteries* [Privately printed, 1894], n.p.) gave the close date as 1827, and Llewellynn Jewitt (*The History of Ceramic Art in Great Britain,* 2 vols.

[New York: Scribner, Welford and Armstrong, 1878], 1: 160) as 1820–1821, but based on new information Oswald appears to be correct.

66. Because Joseph's father, Benjamin, managed Sanders's factory from 1759 until at least 1802, it can be speculated that his son, having completed his apprenticeship there, might have aspired to his own workshop and kiln within the old factory before moving across the street to set up on his own.

67. See table VIII.8. Note the shadow of her left leg.

68. Audrey Noël Hume, "A Group of Artifacts Recovered from an Eighteenth-Century Well in Williamsburg," *Five Artifact Studies,* Colonial Williamsburg Occasional Papers in Archaeology (Williamsburg, Va., 1973), 1: 19. The *Encyclopedia Britannica* says approximately the same thing. In his ca. 1705 description of the exodus to Mobs Hall, Ned Ward observed that "Every now and then a lady dropped from her pillion, another from her side-saddle, which though it made them blush, it made us merry." Ward, *London Spy,* p. 112. The inference is that these women were riding sidesaddle as transportation and likely to fall off if they tried to follow the hunt.

69. Blacker, *ABC of English Salt-Glaze Stoneware,* p. 125, citing John Eustace Anderson, *A Short Account of the Mortlake Potteries.*

70. The latter is to be found on a Wedgwood jasper ware wall plaque; see Geoffrey A. Godden, *An Illustrated Encyclopedia of British Pottery and Porcelain* (New York: Crown Publishers, 1966), following p. 346, upper right. The example is by Wedgwood and Bentley (ca. 1769–1780). A similar albeit more crudely executed figure occurs on a dipped stoneware goblet attributed to Derbyshire. See Oswald, Hildyard, and Hughes, *English Brown Stoneware, 1670–1900,* p. 167, no. 136.

71. The same panel and neoclassical flankers are to be seen on a two-handled loving cup illustrated by Oswald, Hildyard, and Hughes, *English Brown Stoneware, 1670–1900,* p. 61, and there attributed to ca. 1800.

72. Ibid., p. 61, fig. 26.

73. John Lewis and Griselda Lewis, *Pratt Ware: English and Scottish Relief Decorated and Underglaze Coloured Earthenware, 1780–1840,* rev. ed. (1984; Woodbridge, Suffolk, Eng.: Antique Collectors' Club, in association with Leo Kaplan Ltd., 1993), p. 196.

74. Arthur W. Heintzelman, *The Watercolor Drawings of Thomas Rowlandson* (New York: Watson-Guptill Publications, 1947), p. 85.

75. Ibid., pl. D, facing p. 113.

76. Henry Mayhew, *Mayhew's London: Being Selections from "London Labour and the London Poor,"* edited by Peter Quennell (1861; London: Spring Books, 1969), p. 66.

77. The centrally ridged Sheffield plate rim is paralleled on the ca. 1800 loving cup cited in note 71.

78. The B2 panel, when applied to small (e.g., quart) mugs, is trimmed at top and bottom, but the incorrect placement of the table legs remains the same.

79. Askey, *Stoneware Bottles,* p. 184. Although Mr. Askey has been unable to recall his source, it may have been J. F. Blacker, who in his *ABC of English Salt-Glaze Stoneware,* p. 119, stated that Joseph Kishere's factory was "established about 1792."

80. Compare table XII.1, .2.

81. "The Kill" design was to have a long life. A crude usage of this sprig series is to be seen on a hound-handled, stoneware pitcher marked "Pearson & Co, Whittington Moor Potteries, near Chesterfield" and dated 1890. Godden, *Illustrated Encyclopedia of British Pottery and Porcelain,* p. 356, no. 453. Another manifestation, this one sold on eBay, occurred on a blue jasper jardiniere made by Adams of Tunstall whose marks provided a bracket of 1896–1914.

82. Hildyard, *Browne Muggs,* p. 71, no. 177.

83. Spode Museum, SMMS/42. The mold differs from most of the sprigs found on brown stonewares in that the fence-leaping hound's rear legs are visible atop the rail. Lewis and Lewis, *Pratt Ware,* p. 115.

84. Nick Waters, "Tell-Tale Clues to Brampton Pottery," *ABC Antique Bottle Collector UK* 1 (January–February 2000): 23. The earliest hound handles have tails that formed open loops and came from well-sculpted matrices. Later, the ribcages became less prominent and the eyes and claws less sharply defined. Hound-handled jugs coated with the thick "Rockingham" glaze were in production in the United States by 1837. Arthur F. Goldberg, "Highlights in the Development of the Rockingham and Yellow Ware Industries in the United States—A Brief Review with Representative Examples," *Ceramics in America,* edited by Robert Hunter (Han-

over, N.H.: University Press of New England for the Chipstone Foundation, 2003): 37, figs. 19, 20.

85. Perhaps the earliest (silver dated) example yet found is that of 1813; this a recent addition to the collection. Another, dated 1828, is in the Museum of London Collection (London Museum cat. no. c.67). Francis Celoria, *Dated Post-medieval Pottery in the London Museum* (London: H. M. Stationery Office, 1966), p. 31. However, the design was being used by Spode as early as 1810.

86. Derbyshire is a long and thin county, with Derby to the south and Chesterfield to the north. Brown stoneware potting districts are separated along those lines, with the south Derbyshire potters in areas around Ilkeston and those to the north in the vicinity of Chesterfield.

87. Hildyard, *Browne Muggs,* p. 72, nos. 179–81. The 1842 colander is illustrated in Redstone, "Kishere's Mortlake Pottery," p. 55, fig. 22.

88. Tradition has it that the character was Henry Elwes, a Yorkshireman who reputedly consumed more than 2,000 gallons of ale.

89. Nicholas Johnson, in "The Man in the Middle," *ABC Antique Bottle Collector UK* 14 (autumn 2002): 4–5, illustrated a colored but undated version of this engraving, suggesting that the portrait was frequently reproduced and widely known.

90. Redstone, "Kishere's Mortlake Pottery," p. 51, fig. 9. The mold's defining feature is a three-tiered tree that would appear to the right of the applied sprig. Comparable molds were used for Staffordshire pearlware jugs decorated in Pratt colors ca. 1790. Lewis and Lewis, *Pratt Ware,* p. 189. One cannot allay the suspicion that the Mortlake molds in the Anderson Collection came from a variety of sources.

91. That distinction is most apparent among Doulton Tobys, the balustroidal leg being used almost exclusively from the 1850s to the 1880s, with the straight leg following thereafter.

92. Oswald, Hildyard, and Hughes, *English Brown Stoneware, 1670–1900,* p. 93, fig. 55.

93. Ibid., facing p. 192, pl. E.

94. By about 1820 the long-stemmed (average 11 inches) pipe was being replaced by those with stems of only 4 to 6 inches, a detail recognizable on later Toby and toper sprigs.

95. This smoking figure, with keys hanging from his waist, is the last in a group of three men usually described as the Parson, Clerk, and Sexton. They were used as early as 1790 on slip-cast pearlwares from factories as widely separated as Bovery Tracey in Devonshire and Delftfield in Scotland. Lewis and Lewis, *Pratt Ware,* pp. 106, 109. A similar sprig is described by Blacker, *ABC of English Brown Stoneware,* p. 120, on a jug also sprigged with St. George, in a chapter devoted to Mortlake yet illustrated as "Probably Fulham." Nicholas Johnson in "The Hunting Jug and Its Cousins, Part I," *ABC Antique Bottle Collector, UK* 15 (winter 2002/3): 5, illustrates a comparable key-toting toper and attributes him to the "London area," and another to Liverpool.

96. Hildyard, *Browne Muggs,* p. 98, no. 267.

97. Grape and vine sprigs were used as a frieze on a large goblet made at Bright's Pottery, Bristol, in 1818. See Pountney, *Old Bristol Potteries,* facing p. 254, pl. LII.

98. The Belper works had been taken over by William Bourne about 1800 and was succeeded by his son, Joseph, who in 1812 bought the neighboring Denby Pottery and moved the entire operation there in 1834. It being difficult, if not impossible, to distinguish the stonewares of one from the other, these Derbyshire wares made prior to 1834 are cautiously labeled Belper/Denby. See also n. 86 above.

99. Hildyard, in *Browne Muggs,* p. 102, notes that "Sprigs of St. George are frequently found on Denby mugs and jugs." Whether any of these belonged to an inn of that name is uncertain. The actual capacity of this "quart" mug is 36 oz.

100. Ibid., p. 98, no. 269, paralleling both youth and adjacent tree. The St. George design appears to have been taken from George IV's gold and silver coinage of 1821–1822, the principal change being the substitution of a short spear for the coins' gladius or broken lance. Although uncommon in the eighteenth century, mugs as broad as they are tall are recorded as early as 1719.

101. Mavis Watney, in a letter to the *ABC Antique Bottle Collector UK* 16 (spring 2003): 34, in which she was ready to accept that the cup was made at the Bourne pottery at Denby between 1869 and 1898. Her letter was prompted by an earlier contribution, in *ABC Antique Bottle Collector UK* 14 (autumn 2002): 33, illustrating the same windmill on a stoneware flask marked "PETTINGER / GAINSBOROUGH." Gainsborough is in Lincolnshire and a sub-port of Grimsby. It is interesting to speculate whether the strange trestle mounting was in some

way associated with the port. The *British Directory* for 1792 (vol. 3), p. 142, lists two millers and a millwright in the town.

102. Cited by Oswald, Hildyard, and Hughes, *English Brown Stoneware, 1670–1900,* p. 34 n. 45.

103. Parian stoneware (at first known as "statuary porcelain") was invented about 1845 by Copeland and Garrett at Stoke-on-Trent. The mustard pot is slip cast and therefore the Toby and smoker sprigs were applied to the master block and replicated in the two-piece mold. The rare Toby sprigs on the Parian pot are paralleled by those on a Derbyshire jug of ca. 1840 recently sold on eBay (April 2004, auction no. 3717210479).

104. Green, *John Dwight's Fulham Pottery,* p. 163.

105. Doulton's Toby figure progresses from straddling a barrel to sitting on its side, thence to a bench whose use continued at least until ca. 1930. The straddled barrel, however, goes back to ca. 1835–1840, when it is featured three dimensionally on Toby-related brown stoneware gin flasks (with and without Xs), most of which emanated from Lambeth. Noël Hume, *If These Pots Could Talk,* pp. 310, figs. XIV.14, 15. In all these instances the mark seems to relate to the contents of the barrels. A bacchanalian scene by Andrea Mantagna of Padua (1431–1506) included a small "V" on its barrel head. Ibid., p. 310.

106. Oswald, Hildyard, and Hughes, *English Brown Stoneware, 1670–1900,* pp. 224–25, fig. 171*a*.

107. Ibid., pp. 231–33, and figs. 175, 177. That two sprigs on one jug can be attributed to three potential factories suggests either that there was a great deal of mold-sharing among contemporary Glasgow factories or that much more information is needed before positive identifications are warranted.

108. But not very persuasively. Though decorated with Scottish scenes, a similarly pewter-mounted, slip-cast, pale blue stoneware pitcher in my collection is impressed "Published by / W. RIDGEWAY & Co / HANLEY / October [??] 1835." It remains possible, of course, that the lid was added after crossing the border.

109. Hildyard, *Browne Muggs,* p. 97, fig. 262, illustrates a pinched-mouthed jug with a rather similar, foliate-seated windmill but whose greenery does not include the thistle. That jug is marked "BOURNE'S Warranted" and is attributed to circa 1830. It seems likely that the same Derbyshire mold-modeler also designed the sprigs for the "Scottish" mustard pots, and that they are of comparable date.

110. I am deeply indebted to Colonial Williamsburg researcher Sue Carter for unearthing the print, albeit with no other intent than to provide its *Journal* with a tavern-related image.

111. The expanded Heemskerk information is derived from Colonial Williamsburg's catalog card for mezzotint engraving No. 1950-703, whereon the musical instrument is stated to be "a rustic flute-like instrument which perhaps is intended to be a recorder." In the 1738 edition of Ephraim Chambers's *Cyclopaedia: or, an Universal Dictionary of Arts and Sciences . . . ,* 2nd ed., 2 vols. (London: for D. Midwinter, J. Senex et al., 1738), vol. 1 (no pagination), such an instrument was more accurately defined thus: "A musical instrument of the wind-kind, chiefly used in country places, especially in the North. It consists of two principal parts; the first a leather bag, which blows up like a foot-ball, by means of a port-vent, or little tube fitted to it, and stopped by a valve. The other part consists of three pipes, or flutes. . . ."

112. The Teniers original was first published as an engraving in England by Philip Mercier (1689–1760), who had moved to London from Berlin about 1710. It is possible that twelve years after Mercier's death Sayer republished the print from his copperplate. The Heemskerk print carries the number 422, suggesting that it was but one illustration within a much larger publishing venture.

113. Alan Smith, *The Illustrated Guide to Liverpool Herculaneum Pottery, 1796–1840* (New York: Praeger Publishers, 1970), fig. 93.

114. Lewis and Lewis, *Pratt Ware,* p. 301, fig. 87.

115. I am forced to the mea culpa of confessing that in *If These Pots Could Talk* (pp. 171–72) I misidentified the jug as a product of Lambeth!

116. Quoted by Oswald, Hildyard, and Hughes, *English Brown Stoneware, 1670–1900,* p. 202.

117. None of these names is listed in Oswald, Hildyard, and Hughes, *English Brown Stoneware, 1670–1900*.

118. The mug is impressed "BAILEY & Co. / FULHAM," ergo 1872–1888.

119. Also true of early Mortlake (e.g., table XII.1, .2) and of Stiff (table XII.13).

120. Located on the street named Vauxhall Walk, close to the famed (and infamous) Vauxhall Pleasure Gardens.

121. Vauxhall Walk lies parallel to the Thames east of Vauxhall Bridge and runs into the Lambeth Walk of song renown.

122. I am greatly indebted to Doulton authority Louise Irvine for this information, as well as to her revised edition of Desmond Eyles's classic *The Doulton Lambeth Wares* (Somerset: Richard Dennis, 2002), p. 324.

123. On the accession of Edward VII the Doulton company was appointed "Potter to His Majesty."

124. An invaluable listing of the known marks and the names of the assistants is included in Eyles's work cited above, pp. 312–15. Occasionally, particularly toward the end of the Lambeth era, craftswomen's work was marked with "JA" or "SA," meaning junior or senior assistants.

125. The company's last mark (1950s) occurs in a three-line block reading "DOULTON / ENGLAND / LAMBETH."

126. Oswald, Hildyard, and Hughes, *English Brown Stoneware, 1670–1900,* p. 74.

127. The Imperial Pottery was taken over by John Cliff, who ran it until 1869, at which time he moved, like so many others, north to the fringes of the burgeoning Staffordshire industry.

128. Many more were made by Doulton & Watts, by the Fulham Pottery, and by other factories in Derbyshire from about 1830 to 1860. See Noël Hume, *If These Pots Could Talk,* pp. 303–23.

129. Eyles and Irvine, *Doulton Lambeth Wares,* p. 34.

130. Ibid., p. 23.

131. Perhaps a music-hall performer who specialized in parodying Shakespeare?

132. Green, *John Dwight's Fulham Pottery,* p. 363, illustrating pages from James Stiff's 1873 price list.

133. Ibid., p. 367.

134. The "contented smoker with cat" sprig was also used by a Doulton competitor. A shaving pot so decorated is marked "SMITH & CO / OLD KENT RD / LONDON." Stoneware manufacturer Thomas Smith was in business on the Old Kent Road from 1867 to about 1893, making hunting jugs and mugs along with chemical and other commercial wares.

135. The 1868 jug lacks any Doulton mark, but the sprigs and handle terminal leave no doubt as to its attribution. Indeed, it supports Oswald's assumption that after 1870 Doulton wares invariably were marked. A clumsy variant of "the pig family" appears on a large, double-handled mug (rim dated 1870), believed to be the product of an unidentified competitor. See fig. 22*a*, table XI.4.

136. In his article on Mortlake David Redstone illustrated an identical sprig on a "Kishere Mortlake tankard" and showed a mold from the Anderson Collection to support it. However, the mold is *not* the same and may, instead, be the product of a copier of Doulton wares in the late 1860s. See fig. 22*a*.

137. Eyles and Irvine, *Doulton Lambeth Wares,* p. 24. In the same illustration she includes the "pig family" and dates that example to ca. 1880.

138. This Toby version must have been in production prior to 1870 as he appears on an inferior copy of that date illustrated in table III.7.

139. Oswald, Hildyard, and Hughes, *English Brown Stoneware, 1670–1900,* pp. 280–81, no. 12, attribute this pad or cloudlike base to Bourne of Denby in the second quarter of the nineteenth century.

140. Ibid., pp. 280–83.

141. Cheavin managed at Fulham until 1940.

142. The smaller window sometimes has six panes. See table XII.16.

143. Unsupportive of that thesis is the existence of a freestanding stoneware pagoda made at some uncertain date by Doulton and illustrated in Blacker, *ABC of English Salt-Glaze Stoneware,* facing p. 100.

144. Oswald, Hilyard, and Hughes, *English Brown Stoneware 1670–1900,* p. 282, no. 9.

145. Ibid. In the Doulton drawing the flower is shown barely touching the bar, whereas in all examples that I have seen the overlap is distinct. The same source also attributes this terminal to Glasgow (Port Dundas).

146. Another version was used at Glasgow, but the strap detail was noticeably crude; table XV.16.

147. It can be no coincidence that Henry Doulton was knighted by his queen in her Golden Jubilee year. Eyles and Irvine, *Doulton Lambeth Wares,* p. 25, stated that "Around 1875" coffee and teapots began to be decorated with white clay sprigs, but that "by 1889 this was also the typical style for the jugs."

148. The second Jubilee jug went unsold on eBay on September 8, 2002.

149. Horne, *Catalogue of English Brown Stoneware,* p. 21, nos. 39, 40.

150. A reminder: Clockwise hunts are attributed to Factory A and counterclockwise to Factory B.

151. For what it may be worth, examples in my collection suggest a fairly standard placement of the hunter next to the handle, while the prey, be it stag or hare, is set and angled depending on the amount of space remaining.

152. This huntsman rides on quart and pottle tankards attributed to John Harwell of Bristol, ca. 1740–1750. Horne, *Catalogue of English Brown Stoneware,* p. 30, nos. 61, 62.

153. Ibid., no. 63.

154. The closest parallel for this hat type is of no help. It was worn in the sixteenth century by French peasants. See Claudia Rosoux (trans.), *The Pictorial Encyclopedia of Fashion* (London: Paul Hamlyn, 1968), p. 454, fig. 753.

155. On the collection's 1818 jug (fig. *7e*) the brims on the hunters' hats have shrunk.

156. The initials may have belonged to a family member of Temple Street potter John Bright, whose company Bright & Co. remained in business from 1798 to 1853.

157. Hope was already in business at 8, Somerset Square in 1793, but although others were listed as "stone potters" or "brown potters," his branch was not specified.

158. Hildyard, *Browne Muggs,* p. 76, no. 190. In the mid-nineteenth century farther down the Bristol Channel in Somerset, Donyatt potters were making mini-barrels. R. Coleman-Smith and T. Pearson, *Excavations in the Donyatt Potteries* (Chichester: Phillimore, 1988), pp. 122–23.

159. In the seventeenth century stoneware medallion sprigs usually were pressed to the leather-hard vessels while still in the molds. Later, the more complex sprigs were extracted from their molds and attached to the wall by hand.

160. It is important to remember that incuse plaster molds used to create the sprigs are at least a generation removed from master molds such as those in the Turner collection.

161. Cited by Redstone in "Kishere's Mortlake Pottery," p. 47.

162. Ibid., p. 282, no. 11.

163. I have yet to find a parallel for this figure. Somewhat similar is a figure on figure *22b,* who strikes the same pose but has no tobacco pipe.

164. See also note 95.

165. On some larger Doulton mug and jugs of the 1880s the horse is more reined in and the angle of its head drawn down. See Eyles and Irvine, *Doulton Lambeth Wares,* p. 24.

166. This sprig was in use by Doulton as early as 1868.

167. An unmarked but evidently Doulton jug, ca. 1865–1870, exhibits this sprig with the addition of a large dog in the foreground.

168. A very similar windmill sprig was used by Thomas Smith of the Canal Potteries in the Old Kent Road (1867–ca. 1893) but without the chimney. Oswald, Hildyard, and Hughes, *English Brown Stoneware, 1670–1900,* pp. 84, 280, no. 3.

169. In the straps' earliest Doulton form the horizontal lines are closed at the ends to create a rectangle, e.g., figure *22d* and table XV.12.

170. The London County Council was created as a result of the Local Government Act of 1888.

171. The collection includes a Doulton half-pint coronation mug made for Devonshire aristocrat Sir Robert Edgcumbe and dated June 22, 1911.

Merry Abbitt Outlaw

New Discoveries Introduction

▼ I DID NOT INTEND *to go into any detail at all, at first, but it is the failing of the true ceramiker, or the true devotee in any department of brick-a-brackery, that once he gets his tongue or his pen started on his darling theme, he cannot well stop until he drops from exhaustion. He has no more sense of the flight of time than has any other lover when talking of his sweetheart. The very "marks" on the bottom of a piece of rare crockery are able to throw me into a gibbering ecstasy; and I could forsake a drowning relative to help dispute about whether the stopple of a departed Buon Retiro scent-bottle was genuine or spurious.*

Mark Twain, *Tramp Abroad,* 1880

Charles of Bourbon (1716–1788), son of Philip V of Spain, was crowned king of Naples and Sicily in 1734. A passion for porcelain and his 1738 marriage to Maria Amalia—granddaughter of Augustus II, who in Meissen in 1710 founded the first European hard-paste porcelain factory—led to his creation of a royal porcelain factory at Capodimonte in 1743. Upon becoming king of Spain in 1759, Charles III demolished his successful factory at Capodimonte and moved craftsmen, molds, and materials to the royal porcelain factory he established at Buen Retiro, a palace outside Madrid. In production by 1760, Buen Retiro porcelain was reserved for royal use until the year after Charles III's death, and it was available to the public until the factory closed in 1808.

In *Tramp Abroad* Mark Twain (Samuel Langhorne Clemens) asserts that as a ceramics enthusiast, a debate about a piece of Buen Retiro—a stopper without the bottle, at that—caused him to abandon good judgment in the face of disaster. A painted or incised Bourbon fleur-de-lis maker's mark would not necessarily have made the identification of eighteenth-century Buen Retiro easier for him, since the mark was used previously at Charles III's earlier factory at Capodimonte.

Hence the dilemma: maker's marks often confound and fool us. Collectors, researchers, and enthusiasts must look carefully at these marks, as well as at such other identifying characteristics as shape, color, form, and decorative technique. It is crucial that important information concerning ceramics makers, wares, and places of manufacture is disseminated quickly, and the New Discoveries articles in this issue of *Ceramics in America* do just that.

Barbara Magid takes a new look at pottery recovered in 1984 during excavations of the Tildon Easton pottery kiln. Made between 1841 and 1843, the relationship of this pottery to (and differences from) stoneware produced in Alexandria, Virginia, is identified, and the mark "TILDON

EASTON" is illustrated. An earlier Alexandria potter, James Miller, is also brought to light by the careful research of Brandt Zipp and Mark Zipp. Chris Espenshade speaks to the connection among stoneware potters in Washington County, Virginia, during the second half of the nineteenth century and the ease of worker movement between shops. His research helps to account for the presence of foreign stamps on vessel sherds from the manufactory of another known maker.

In comparing two American stoneware vessels dating from the third quarter of the nineteenth century, William Liebeknecht notes their many similarities. One is stamped with the initials of Richard Clinton Remmey above "PHILA," thereby providing strong evidence for the manufacture of the other. Manufactured farther to the north, in Massachusetts, and possibly as early as the late eighteenth century, a rare jar found in Kentucky by John Kille demonstrates that, although best known for his redware, William Pecker also made decorative stamped stoneware.

Authors from both sides of the Atlantic discuss highly prized English ceramics. Jonathan Goodwin reports on recent excavations on the site of the Minton pottery factory at Stoke-on-Trent that offer new insights to the construction of "bottle"-shaped updraft pottery kilns from the mid-nineteenth to the early twentieth century. In a captivating account, Al Luckenbach links a small English stoneware jug from the second quarter of the nineteenth century, stamped "T. ROUSE / EAGLE TAVERN / CITY ROAD / MOUNTAINS," to the nursery rhyme "Pop Goes the Weasel." Robert Werowinski describes a circa 1710 Staffordshire slipware cradle in his collection that displays an unusual hood and the delightful inscription "THIS I MAD FOR YOV AND MOOM." A brief note by Robert Hunter discusses recent English ceramic acquisitions by the Chipstone Foundation as they relate to research issues published in *Ceramics in America*.

Wares produced on the other side of the Pacific are also reported in this issue. Mary Beaudry reveals her identification of Japanese Water Drop ware of the Meiji period (1868–1912). Although found in small quantities on American archaeological sites, Water Drop ware holds complex meanings for those who used and discarded them during the nineteenth-century *japonisme* craze. Combining modern technology and historical documentation, Lisa Ellis presents the detailed results of her analysis of "ghosts" and gilding on an important Kangxi-period (1662–1722) porcelain teapot, manufactured between 1662 and 1690 and now in the J. Paul Getty Museum. Also from China, and excavated in French-colonial Old Mobile, Alabama, sherds of fine Chinese Imari porcelain vessels made during the later Kangxi period probably arrived via the Manila galleon trade through Spanish settlements, according to Linda R. Shulsky. Regrettably, the underglaze blue mark on the exterior base of one sherd cannot be identified.

The final article in this lineup of New Discoveries is authored by Sara Hahn, who examines ceramics recovered from the late-eighteenth-century John Dortch archaeological site in Spanish-colonial Louisiana. In contrast to the French ceramics found on the majority of contemporary sites in the area, most of Dortch's are of English manufacture. Among these objects, a creamware jug conveying "Success to the United States of America" evocatively anticipates the eventual control of the territory by the United States.

Before I fall into "gibbering ecstasy," please read on, for the articles that follow surely will keep you captivated until you "drop from exhaustion"!

Barbara H. Magid

A New Look at Old Stoneware: The Pottery of Tildon Easton

Tildon Easton's pottery kiln was excavated in 1984, but recent information from a descendant of the potter and the Alexandria Archaeology Museum's revived focus on locally produced pottery have led to a new look at Easton and his wares. In particular, we have begun to look at ways in which Easton's pottery might be differentiated from other Alexandria stoneware.

Easton manufactured both earthenware and salt-glazed stoneware for a very short period of time, between 1841 and 1843. One of the few surviving references to his business is an announcement in the *Alexandria Gazette* on June 10, 1841, for the opening of his "New Stone and Earthen Ware Manufactory." He claims that he "has on hand, and is constantly manufacturing, STONE AND EARTHEN WARE, of every description, and of the best quality. . . ."

Tildon Easton came to Alexandria from Maryland by 1832.[1] In order to operate a pottery, he would have needed experience. He may have worked or apprenticed at the Wilkes Street pottery, which was the only one in Alexandria in the 1830s. If so, Easton would have learned his skill from Alexandria's best-known stoneware potter, B. C. Milburn, who managed the pottery for H. Smith & Co. before purchasing it in 1841. This would help to explain the similarities between Easton's cobalt-decorated stoneware and stoneware with the impressed mark of H. Smith & Co.[2]

Easton's stoneware kiln was discovered on a construction site under four feet of fill (fig. 1). All but the lowest four courses of brick had been removed in the twentieth century. The kiln base was still surrounded by the lower levels of an extensive waster dump containing kiln furniture and more than 5,000 sherds of Easton's pottery, representing at least 677 distinct vessels.

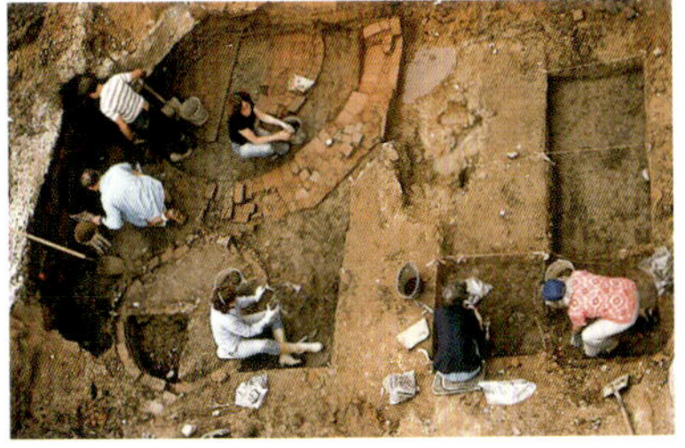

Figure 1 The base of Tildon Easton's stoneware kiln in Alexandria, Virginia, excavated in 1984 by the city archaeologists. The updraft kiln, built in 1841, measures 12' across. Volunteers are excavating the waster dump, lower right. The adjacent well (at bottom) is of a later date. (Photo, courtesy Alexandria Archaeology Museum.)

More than half of these sherds were of salt-glazed stoneware. The impressed mark "TILDON EASTON" appears on twenty vessels from the waster pile, including an ovoid flask, three jugs, two bottles, two smaller bottles, and eight cobalt-decorated milk pans (fig. 2). Four milk pans have one-and-one-half-gallon capacity marks. The same mark appears on two earthenware milk pans.

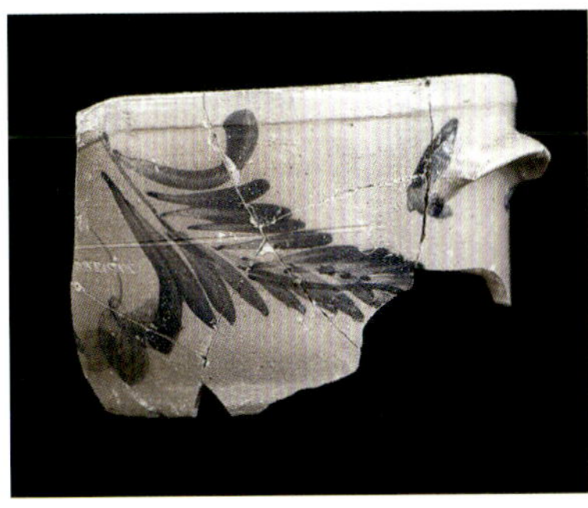

Figure 2 Milk pan, Tildon Easton, Alexandria, Virginia, 1841–1843. Salt-glazed stoneware. D. 10". This milk pan shows the typical squared rim, pouring spout, and lug handle. A version of the three-petal tulip is seen under the spout. Also under the spout is the mark "TILDON EASTON" stamped with 16-point metallic type. (All objects courtesy Alexandria Archaeology; photos by Gavin Ashworth unless otherwise noted.)

Earthenware includes over fifty flowerpots; most are unglazed but a few exhibit spots of green glaze and crimped flanges and rims. Milk pans and utilitarian pots with glaze on the interior are also common. More unusual earthenware forms are small banks and a glazed bowl like those made by Alexandria potter Henry Piercy at the turn of the nineteenth century.

Undecorated stoneware includes straight-sided bottles, small ink bottles with a greenish glazed interior, and ovoid flasks. Some of these vessels are a light buff color, which appears to be deliberate rather than an accident of firing.

Around 150 gray salt-glazed stoneware vessels have brushed cobalt decoration in rather florid floral and foliate patterns. Most are milk pans, followed by jars. All of the milk pans have a slightly sloping profile, a narrow squared rim, a pour spout, and plain lug handles. The shape is similar to some found at the Wilkes Street pottery bearing the marks of H. Smith & Co. and B. C. Milburn, although most examples from Wilkes Street have a rounder rim. Easton's jars are straight-sided, curving in below a narrow squared rim, usually with plain lug handles just below the rim. Most jars from Wilkes Street are ovoid. Straight-sided jars marked Smith or Milburn usually have no handles and either a rounded rim or a ridge below a squared rim. One pitcher rim was found, with a shape similar to those from Wilkes Street. Easton's small flowerpots have no parallels at the Wilkes Street pottery.

The decoration on Easton's stoneware shares similarities with the Wilkes Street pottery, but several differences are also evident, as noted below:

Flowers: Three-petal flowers (fig. 3) are found on twenty-four examples of Easton's stoneware. These most likely depict tulips, a common theme on both stoneware and earthenware since many potters were of German

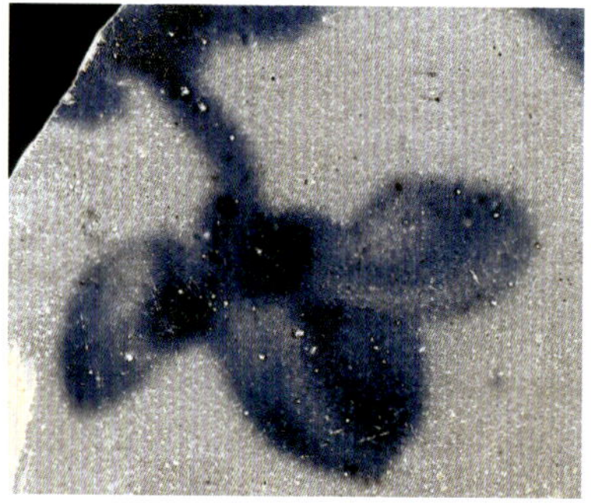

Figure 3 Detail of milk pan illustrated in fig. 4. This three-petal stylized tulip is a typical element of decoration on Easton's pottery.

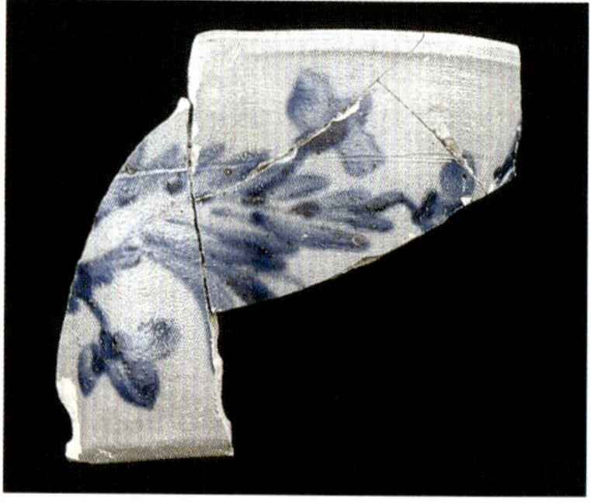

Figure 4 Milk pan, Tildon Easton, Alexandria, Virginia, 1841–1843. Salt-glazed stoneware. D. 11". The placement of the flowers, alternating above and below an undulating vine, is a common design.

origin. Easton's tulips, with outward-turned petals, closely resemble the so-called trinity tulip motif seen on Pennsylvania Dutch folk art. Several of these flowers appear on one milk pan, alternating above and below undulating foliage (fig. 4). Sometimes the flowers are in line with the foliage (fig. 5). These flowers spring from a narrow curving stem and are made up of seven brushstrokes: one at the base, and two for each petal. Sometimes there is a space within the central petal (figs. 5, 6), but there is a continuum and no clear indication that more than one decorator was employed. A three-petal tulip is seen on a few examples of Milburn's pottery, but his petals turn inward.

Figure 5 Jar, Tildon Easton, Alexandria, Virginia, 1841–1843. Salt-glazed stoneware. H. 10". The placement of the flowers in line with the foliage is less common.

Figure 6 Jar, Tildon Easton, Alexandria, Virginia, 1841–1843. Salt-glazed stoneware. D. (of rim) 7". This example shows the typical squared rim and lug handle. Leaves surround the ends of the lug handle springing from a garland of leaves, and the typical Easton flower appears on the front and sides.

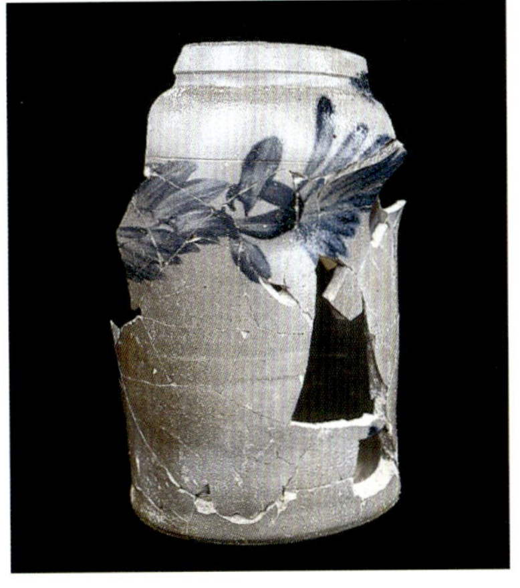

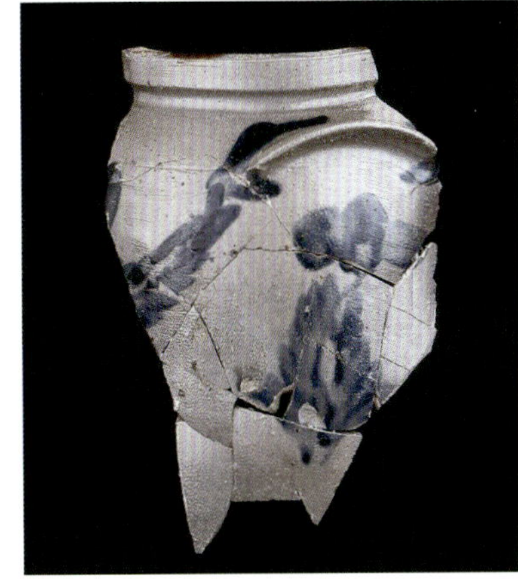

Five-petal flowers (fig. 7) are found on only two vessels. On the example shown, this flower is centrally placed on the front of the milk pan, with branches on either side. The second flower's petals are closer together and more tuliplike, but the flower's placement cannot be determined from the small fragment. One fragment from the Wilkes Street pottery has a four-petal flower similar to this.

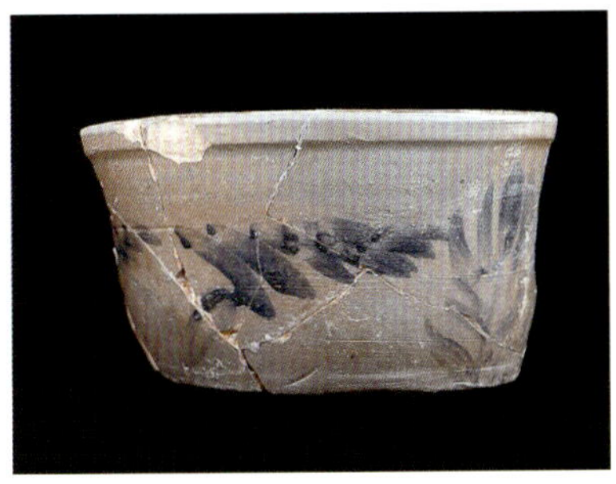

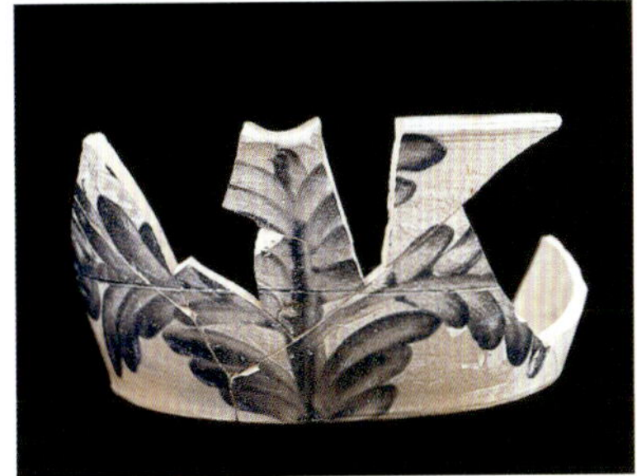

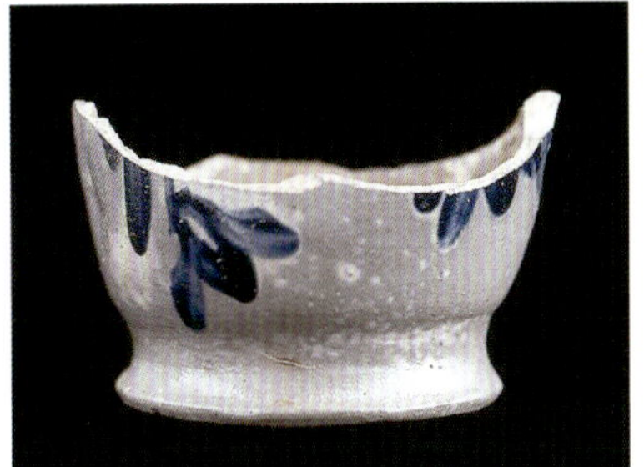

Figure 7 Milk pan, Tildon Easton, Alexandria, Virginia, 1841–1843. Salt-glazed stoneware. D. 8". The five-petal flower has been found on only two vessels.

Figure 8 Milk pan, Tildon Easton, Alexandria, Virginia, 1841–1843. Salt-glazed stoneware. D. 11". Flowers appear at the ends of the side branches in this forward-facing design.

Figure 9 Jar or vase, Tildon Easton, Alexandria, Virginia, 1841–1843. Salt-glazed stoneware. D. (of base) 3½". This unusual vessel has the typical Easton flower but an ovoid shape and flared base.

Foliage: The foliage ranges from well-executed rounded leaves (figs. 8, 9) to quickly drawn pointed leaves (fig. 7). While at first these may appear to be drawn by two different hands, there is a continuum from one style to the other.

Handles: Easton places a cobalt leaf above and below the ends of his lug handles (fig. 6). The leaves are sometimes attached to a vine and are sometimes separate. At Wilkes Street, similar treatment is found on some handles. Other Wilkes Street handles have a blue stripe above the entire handle or surrounding the handle, or sometimes the handle is undecorated.

Placement: On most of Easton's pots, lavish decoration winds around the pot (fig. 5). While a few examples have forward-facing designs with a central flower or foliate branch (fig. 7, 8), the foliage continues on the back of the pot. In contrast, most of the pots from Wilkes Street have forward-facing designs, with a central flower and only small sprigs of leaves or other small decorative elements appearing on the reverse. Even when foliage wraps around a Wilkes Street pot, there is generally a beginning and an end, with a blank area on the reverse.

Tildon Easton's wares are known almost exclusively from the archaeological finds at his kiln site. Even though some of the vessels are stamped with his name, only one surviving antique pot is known. An antique dealer discovered the marked milk pan, decorated with the typical pendant flower and large leaves, on a porch in Red Hill, Pennsylvania, in the early 1990s. He sold it to the current owners at Renninger's Antiques Market. They only just learned, through an Internet search, that this pot was from Alexandria. Perhaps the information provided here will lead to more discoveries.

Less than two years after his manufactory opened, a notice in the *Alexandria Gazette* announced that Easton was bankrupt.[3] One might speculate that he was unable to compete with Milburn's successful Wilkes Street Pottery, which had been operating under different owners for thirty years.

The last Alexandria reference to Easton is in tax records for 1846. His wife, Rebecca, continued to be listed in church records until 1849, and she and their children were listed in the 1850 census. After leaving Alexandria, Easton had a surprising change in careers: he studied the new field of dentistry at the Baltimore College of Dental Surgery. Founded in 1840, this was the first school of dentistry in the United States. Easton is listed in a Baltimore directory from 1858–1859 as "Dr. Tildon Easton, dental surgeon." By 1860 Tildon and Rebecca were living in West Virginia; they both died in 1885. Tildon's legacy lives on in the stoneware collection of the Alexandria Archaeology Museum.[4]

ACKNOWLEDGMENTS The author wishes to thank the staff and volunteers at the Alexandria Archaeology Museum for their assistance with the excavation and processing of the artifacts. Volunteer Vivienne Mitchell and genealogist Joy Talburt Biddison provided historical information about Easton.

Barbara H. Magid
Assistant Director
Alexandria Archaeology Museum
<barbara.magid@ci.Alexandria.va.us>

1. Records of the Trinity United Methodist Church, Class Membership Lists, 1802–1849.
2. Barbara H. Magid, "An Archaeological Perspective on Alexandria's Pottery Tradition," *Journal of Early Southern Decorative Arts* 21, no. 2 (winter 1995): 41–82; Suzita C. Myers, *The Potters' Art: Salt-Glazed Stoneware of 19th-Century Alexandria,* Alexandria Papers in Urban Archaeology, Museum Series, no. 1 (Alexandria, Va.: Alexandria Urban Archaeology Program, 1983).
3. *Alexandria Gazette,* February 20, 1843. He was to go to court on May 8 to discharge his debts, but the court records for that day are missing.
4. Easton's fate and more of his family history were elucidated by Joy Talburt Biddison, whose husband is a direct descendant.

Brandt Zipp and Mark Zipp

James Miller, Lost Potter of Alexandria, Virginia

Alexandria's distinction as one of the very earliest centers of stoneware manufacture in the South gives it an important place in the ceramic history of this nation. Its products are some of the most uniquely crafted and artistically rendered of all American stoneware, set apart by their elaborate and intricate cobalt designs and rotund forms. A monumental water cooler made at the pottery of Alexandria merchant H. C. Smith (now in the collection of the Smithsonian) and a large jar signed by African-American Alexandria potter David Jarbour (now at the Museum of Early Southern Decorative Arts) may be considered to be among the seminal works of American stoneware.

Historians and collectors of the 1950s and 1960s took on the task of identifying certain maker's marks found on stoneware jars, jugs, and pitchers of Alexandria origin. The marks noted by these early researchers were limited to those used at Alexandria's prolific Wilkes Street pottery; these included the marks used by potters John Swann and B. C. Milburn, as well as those used to delineate ware made for the Alexandria merchants Hugh Smith, his son H. C. Smith, and his competitor Elisha J. Miller. In the ensuing decades came the identification of other, more obscure merchant and maker's marks used in Alexandria, namely those of potters James Black and Tildon Easton, and merchant J. P. Smith. Now, with the recent discovery of stoneware vessels bearing the mark "J. MILLER / ALEX," we can add one of Alexandria's very earliest potters—James Miller—to that list.[1]

Miller was probably born circa 1780, and the first references to him in the historical record show his close association with the first generation of Alexandria master potters: Henry Piercy (the father of the Alexandria potting school) and his associates Lewis Plum, Thomas Fisher, and Thomas Hewes.[2] Piercy had been trained in the earthenware center of Philadelphia, which for years prior to his arrival had supplied Alexandria with large slip-trailed bowls, storage jars, and other vessels. He landed in Alexandria sometime in 1792, and in the years immediately following—and into the early nineteenth century—he and his associates worked side by side, competed with one another, and formed various partnerships that would lay the foundation for Alexandria's potting tradition.[3]

At the turn of the nineteenth century (and for most of his career, for that matter) James Miller was a journeyman potter. The earliest reference to him in Alexandria records appears in the 1797 city property tax assessment, where potter James Miller is listed as the last of six men associated with Henry Piercy's "Pott house" on the northeast corner of Duke and Washington streets (fig. 1). In 1800 Miller appears again in the city property tax assessment, this time working at the Lewis Plum pottery on the northwest corner of Prince and St. Asaph streets. In tiny print beneath the entry for "Lewis W. Plumb" are recorded the words, "one Man James Miller—one apprentice" (fig. 2).[4] Although in both of these references Miller's status as hired man is clear, it should be noted that no other journeyman potters appear in these early Alexandria records; the fact that Miller is listed beside these master potters attests to his importance in the potting community at that time.[5]

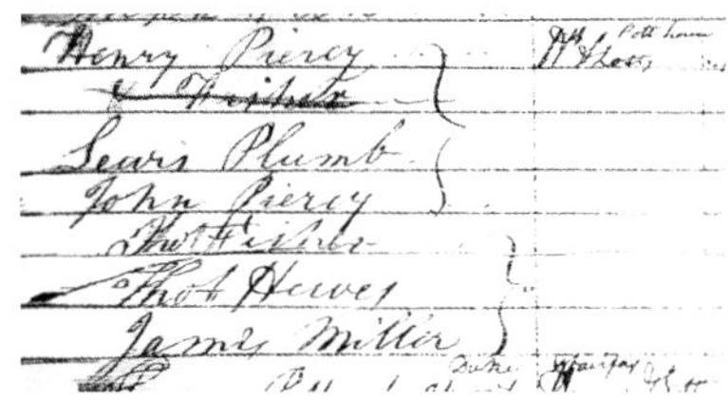
Henry Piercy
Lewis Plumb
John Piercy
Thos Hewes
James Miller

Figure 1 Property Tax Listing, Alexandria City, 1797. This entry shows James Miller's close association with Henry Piercy and other important Alexandria master potters.

Figure 2 Property Tax Listing, Alexandria City, 1800. According to this entry, Lewis Plum's small, three-man operation consisted of himself, James Miller, and an unnamed apprentice.

These two brief entries represent the entirety of concrete evidence for Miller's whereabouts pre-1820; the year 1800 marks the beginning of a twenty-year absence for him in the recorded history of Alexandria. However, the surviving vessels attributed to James Miller provide strong testament to his whereabouts during this period. While as a journeyman Miller is certain to have spent time at most, if not all, of the different potteries operating in Alexandria during these two decades, he must have had a particularly close association with those producing stoneware. The extant Miller products (produced in the early to mid-1820s) show an understanding of the stoneware potting process and of cobalt decorating techniques typical of experienced stoneware potters. Only three potters are known to have produced stoneware in Alexandria prior to 1820—Lewis Plum, William Reynolds, and John Swann. Miller's association with Plum in early tax records suggests that it was this stoneware producer with whom Miller spent much of his time during these "lost" years. However, Plum was likely not the man who schooled Miller in the art of cobalt oxide decoration; neither he nor Reynolds is known to have produced any cobalt-decorated ware. Moreover, Plum's pots are noticeably cruder than the "J. MILLER" vessels and belong to an earlier school of stoneware production.[6]

The only shop in Alexandria that possibly could have familiarized Miller with advanced stoneware production is the John Swann manufactory, which opened its doors on Wilkes Street circa 1810. Swann had learned his trade as an apprentice bound, beginning in 1803, to Lewis Plum. As an orphan Swann apparently formed a particularly close bond with his master during his years of training. It was perhaps this favored status in the eyes of Plum, coupled with what must have been exceptional skill on the young potter's part, that enabled Swann to launch his own operation immediately after the term of his apprenticeship had expired.[7]

The opening of the John Swann pottery marked the true beginning of what would become a prolific stoneware industry in Alexandria. The first decades of the nineteenth century saw a general shift by American consumers away from the previously favored earthenware toward more durable (and safer) stoneware, and it is clear that Swann well understood that trend. Whereas Plum and Reynolds had attempted only small-scale stoneware production, Swann made it his primary product; in so doing, he actively pursued a finer, more aesthetically appealing ware than other Alexandria potters had come close to achieving. Cobalt oxide, used to produce the vibrant blue decorations seen on most nineteenth-century American stoneware products, was unheard of in Alexandria before Swann introduced it to the city in the latter part of the 1810s. In 1819 advertisements in local newspapers began pointing to Swann's change in decoration from a crude brown rust solution to cobalt, and, judging from the extant "J. MILLER" products, it is likely that Miller was employed by Swann at that time.[8]

In 1820 we are able to pinpoint Miller for the first time as a potter working on his own. He had left Alexandria and established his small pottery in nearby Georgetown, where, thanks to a brief 1820 census record, we know he made stoneware. The federal Census of Manufactures of 1820 lists James Miller as a producer of "Stoneware, etc." with two hands and an annual production value of $2,000.[9] This shop clearly was operating on a much smaller scale than John Swann's pottery, where six men, three slaves, and two apprentices had manufactured the previous year's products, with a market value of about $8,000.[10]

James Miller's shop in Georgetown holds the distinction as the first stoneware pottery within the limits of today's District of Columbia.[11] It is not hard to surmise why Miller chose to leave Alexandria, an area dominated by well-established potteries like that of Swann's, and try his hand at a unique operation just up the Potomac. Financial independence as a potter could not have been easily met there. Perhaps more important, however, was the Panic of 1819, the first major economic depression in U.S. history. The depression triggered serious financial difficulties for local Alexandria craftsmen and retailers, and John Swann—at that time not only Alexandria's most prolific stoneware potter but also its most prolific potter, period—was no exception. Between July 1820 and August 1821, in advertisements placed in local newspapers, Swann repeatedly toyed with the idea of selling his pottery and moving to the western U.S. territories. Although he was able to work out an arrangement with prominent Alexandria merchant Hugh Smith that allowed him to continue operating the pottery, in 1825 Smith eventually foreclosed, putting Swann out of business.[12] In this light, Miller's decision to leave Alexandria and strike out on his own may have stemmed solely from an inability by Swann to offer Miller financial security.

When Miller's Georgetown operation began and exactly how long it lasted is unknown, but by 1824 Miller had returned to Alexandria, where he quickly became mired in protracted financial difficulties. The surviving documents related to these problems represent the most detailed record of his life as a potter.

On July 9, 1824, Miller took a significant loan, either to finance a new operation or to keep afloat his already established but struggling pottery (probably the latter). Miller's agreement with a fellow Alexandrian, Isaac Robbins, was made on the following terms: Robbins would lend Miller $437, and Miller would repay the sum within twelve months, delivering Robbins either $25 or $25 worth of stoneware (discounted 15 percent off retail price) after the drawing of each kiln. By December, however, Robbins had become dissatisfied with Miller, who had "burned and drawn six Kilns" of stoneware since the arrangement had been made but had delivered only $64.84 toward the balance owed. In order to continue using the pottery, Miller was forced to appoint a trustee to whom he assigned control of all of his property.[13] (This arrangement is strikingly similar to the one that

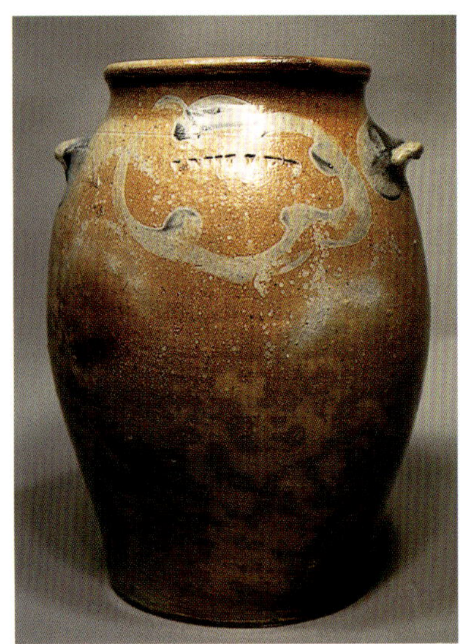

Figure 3 Jar, James Miller, Alexandria, Virginia, or Georgetown, District of Columbia, ca. 1820–1826. Salt-glazed stoneware with brushed cobalt decoration. H. 9½". (Courtesy, The Lyceum: Alexandria's History Museum; all photos by the authors.) Impressed "J. MILLER."

John Swann had made four years earlier with Hugh Smith in order to continue operating his Wilkes Street pottery.) In the document registering the assignment, Miller's property was described as follows:

> a certain lease of Fr. Peyton to the sd. James Miller of a Lot of ground in the County of Alexandria D.C. with the improvements thereon now in the occupancy of the sd. James Miller as a Pottery establishment subject to the annual rent charge of Fifty Dollars. Also a Lot of Stone-pott Clay supposed to weigh fifteen Tons. Also one sorrel Horse. Also a Lot of burnt Stone-ware, including all that is in the premises. Also a Lot of unburnt Stone-ware. . . .[14]

Six kiln loads over a five-month period was by no means a significant amount of production; the size of Miller's Alexandria operation was likely similar to that of his Georgetown pottery. It is unclear how much longer after this arrangement that Miller was able to continue using his small Alexandria shop. He was allowed to "retain possession of the said Pottery establishment together with the Clay, Horse +c." if or when Isaac Robbins ordered the sale of the property; since no record of such a sale has been found, it is possible that Miller remained there for about two more years, into 1826.[15]

It was in December of that year that Miller—with a list of creditors that had ballooned to include twenty-nine different men and institutions—found himself in debtor's prison, held at the Alexandria Gaol. On December 26, 1826, Miller appeared before Justice of the Peace William Cranch and requested his release under a federal law enacted in 1802 that provided relief for insolvent debtors living in the District of Columbia. As part of the process for his release, he was required to forfeit all of his property for the use of his creditors. Among the personal property listed in the surviving court record was "Some Potters clay, a little burnt ware, and a small quantity unburnt distrained by Francis Peyton for rent in arear," as well as "the tools and implements of potters trade." As was customary in such cases, in addition to his and his family's clothing and bedding, Miller was allowed to retain the tools of his trade. The judge ordered his release on January 29, 1827.[16]

Whether James Miller continued to pot or even remained in Alexandria following his release from prison is unclear. The last known mention of him in the historical record appears in the June 4, 1827, issue of the *Alexandria Gazette*. In the list of unclaimed letters at the Alexandria Post Office, "Jas Miller, potter" had two waiting for him.[17]

The Ware

Several examples of pottery produced by James Miller in Alexandria or Georgetown, D.C., have survived. These include two intact stoneware jars and several earthenware jar sherds impressed "J. MILLER / ALEX," as well as a jar and pitcher made of stoneware and impressed "J. MILLER" (in a slightly different typeface). There are no significant stylistic differences between those pieces that are stamped with "ALEX" and those that are not. Whereas all known Miller pieces might have been produced in Alexandria,

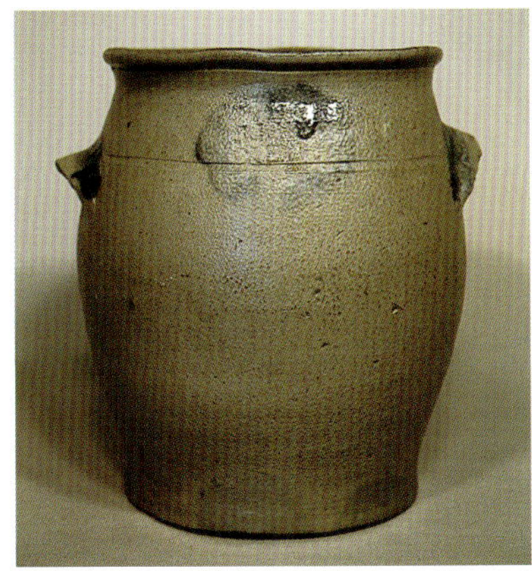

Figure 4 Jar, James Miller, Alexandria, Virginia, ca. 1824–1826. Salt-glazed stoneware with brushed cobalt decoration. H. 9". (Private collection.) Impressed "J. MILLER / ALEX."

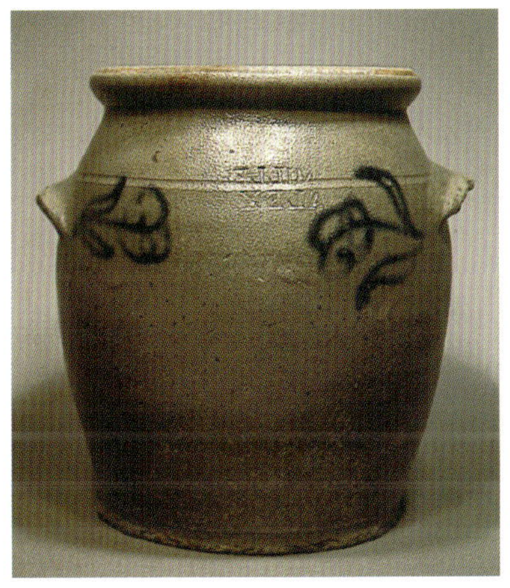

Figure 5 Jar, James Miller, Alexandria, Virginia, ca. 1824–1826. Salt-glazed stoneware with slip-trailed cobalt decoration. H. 8¾". (Private collection.) Impressed "J. MILLER / ALEX."

it is possible that those marked only "J. MILLER" can be attributed to either Alexandria or Georgetown. In these few pieces lie our greatest material evidence that Miller ever potted on his own, and our greatest understanding of how he fared as an artist and as a salesman of pots.

A salt-glazed stoneware jar stamped "J. MILLER" below the rim (fig. 3) is brush-decorated around the name and handles. Its tall form, which tapers at the base and above the handles, is consistent with pieces produced by Swann during his tenure at the Wilkes Street Pottery. The underdeveloped, tablike handles are also very similar to those found on early Wilkes Street ware, as well as on contemporary Baltimore pieces made by William Morgan and Thomas Amos and members of the Parr family.

Another salt-glazed stoneware jar with cobalt decoration, stamped "J. MILLER / ALEX" (fig. 4) below the rim, is consistent in form and handle construction with the Wilkes Street style. This ovoid form was a popular style throughout Virginia and nearby Baltimore until about 1860, although the rim construction of this jar is unique, consisting of an exceptionally thin horizontal flange. The collars of most locally made stoneware jars are more often outwardly rolled or squared, which creates a more finished appearance. The rim of this jar is one of two distinct styles noted only in Miller pottery and may be key to future attributions of his work. In addition, a peculiarity in the placement of the handles on the jar in figure 4 can be noted in all handled Miller jars: one handle is placed approximately three-fourths of an inch below the other. Such irregularities seem too obvious and too prevalent in Miller's work to be attributed to error or lack of skill. The staggered handles may have served some as yet unknown function.

A similarly shaped stoneware jar, stamped "J. MILLER / ALEX" (fig. 5), is also fitted with staggered handles and has a unique rim type. On this example, the jar is finished at the top with a thick rounded molding. This rim is of the same general form but somewhat thinner than the rims of several earthenware sugar jar fragments excavated from the Alfred Street Sugar House in the late 1980s, also stamped "J. MILLER / ALEX" (fig. 6). The unusually hefty rim and staggered placement of the handles might suggest a specialized use for this jar, but in all likelihood it was produced

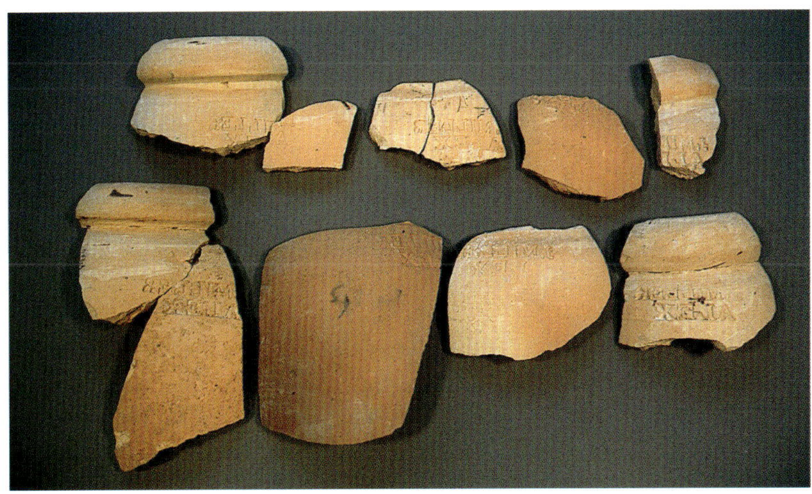

Figure 6 Fragments from a sugar jar, James Miller, Alexandria, Virginia, ca. 1824–1826. Earthenware with lead-glazed interiors. (Courtesy, Alexandria Archaeology.) Impressed "J. MILLER / ALEX." These fragments were excavated from the Alfred Street Sugar House Site, Alexandria.

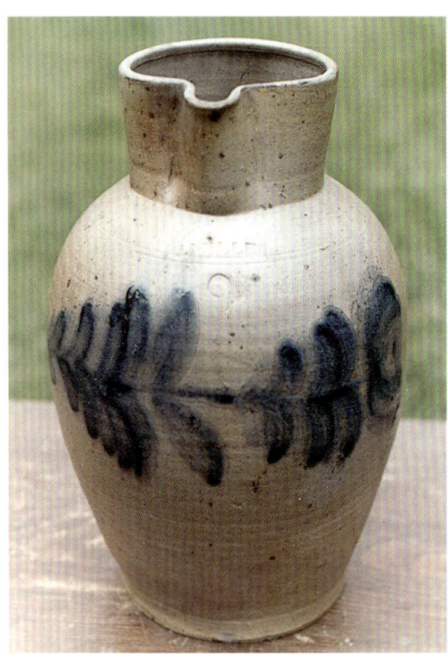

Figure 7 Pitcher, James Miller, Alexandria, Virginia, or Georgetown, District of Columbia, ca. 1820–1826. Salt-glazed stoneware with brushed cobalt decoration. (Private collection.) Impressed "J. MILLER."

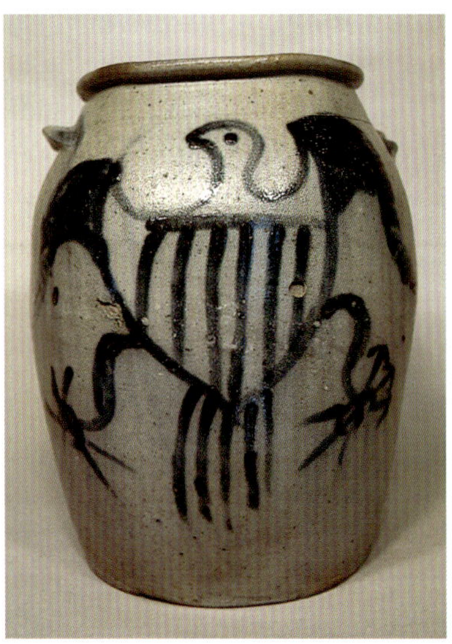

Figure 8 Jar, attributed to James Miller, Alexandria, Virginia, or Georgetown, District of Columbia, ca. 1820–1826. Salt-glazed stoneware with brushed and slip-trailed cobalt. H. 12". (Private collection.)

for normal household use. The jar in figure 5 shows that Miller could be a competent and artistic decorator of his pots. Cobalt floral decorations spring from the jar's handle terminals on the front and back. Applied through the use of a slip cup (a funnel-like tool that pours glazes in thin, exacting strokes), the decoration consists of a central stem girded by two outwardly curving leaves, each ending in a multipetal flower head. The style of the flower head, which is accomplished by a few looping strokes, has been seen on a few extant, pre-1825 Wilkes Street products, including a one-and-one-half-gallon stoneware pitcher stamped "HUGH SMITH & CO." This similarity in design supports the notion that Miller was once employed on Wilkes Street.

Miller's use of both the brush and slip cup to decorate his stoneware is a technique also found in the work of John Swann and his apprentice, B. C. Milburn. Milburn and his sons, who owned and operated the Wilkes Street Pottery from 1841 until 1876, used brushes and slip cups to decorate their ware to a level of ornamentation nearly unparalleled in American stoneware.

A stoneware pitcher stamped "J. MILLER" below the collar (fig. 7), with an underlying two-gallon capacity mark, is consistent in form with pitchers produced at the Wilkes Street Pottery before 1825. It is generally narrow and only slightly ovoid below the collar, lacking the extreme bulge at the waist most often found on Wilkes Street pitchers made for Smith and his son, Hugh Charles, later in the 1820s into the 1840s. The pitcher's brush-applied cobalt decoration, a horizontal garland of leaves ending in a large flower head, is unlike any seen on Alexandria stoneware of the period, resembling only slightly horizontal floral motifs found on some of the latest ware produced for Hugh Charles Smith circa 1845, long after Miller and his contemporaries were potting. The decoration may reflect an attempted copy of designs used at that time by the Parr family in Baltimore. The three-gallon stoneware jar with eagle-and-shield decoration illustrated in figure 8 may have been made by Miller at his Alexandria or Georgetown pottery. This attribution is based on the jar's body form and extraordinarily thin rim construction (see figure 4 for a similar example), as well as on the three-gallon capacity mark stamped on the jar's reverse; this mark, a reversed numeral 3 within a rectangular border, bears no resemblance to stamps known to have been used in Alexandria, Baltimore, or, later, in Washington.

The eagle, which covers nearly the entire front of the jar, holds stylized arrows and olive branches in its talons. A curved shield, emblazoned with the stripes of the American flag, forms its chest. The bird's eye and possibly other areas of the decoration are applied by slip cup, whereas the rest of the decoration is accomplished with the simple use of a brush, including heavily painted sections for the ends of the wings. Figural decorations of this size and quality were rarely produced below the Mason-Dixon line. In terms of District of Columbia stoneware, this jar is one of only a few vessels known to be decorated with a nonfloral motif—the others include a pitcher with face decoration, attributed to Swann, and a jar with a brush-

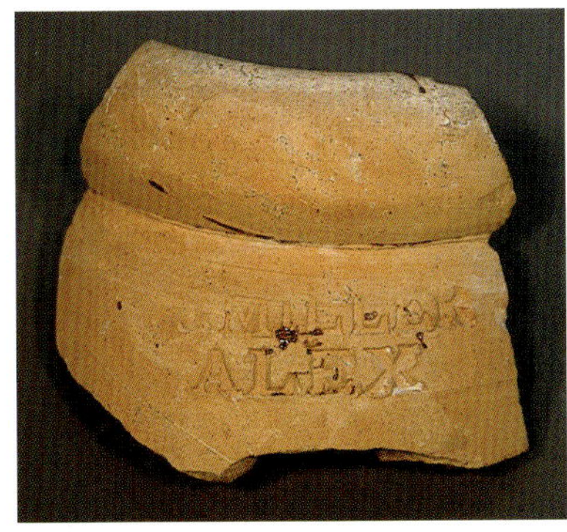

Figure 9 Sherd from sugar jar. Earthenware. W. 3⅛". (Courtesy, Alexandria Archaeology.) This sherd, which was excavated from the Alfred Street Sugar House Site, Alexandria, shows the impressed maker's mark, "J. MILLER / ALEX."

worked sailing ship on one side and a tree on the other, attributed to B. C. Milburn.[18]

In 1987 Alexandria Archaeology began excavation of a sugar refinery that had operated on the 100 block of Alfred Street from 1804 until 1828.[19] Among the countless fragments of earthenware sugar molds and syrup jars recovered during the dig were fifteen jar sherds clearly impressed "J. MILLER / ALEX." These pieces represent the entirety of extant earthenware attributable to Miller (fig. 9). No specific mention of earthenware as one of Miller's products appears in the 1820 Census of Manufactures or in any of the court records associated with his financial difficulties; if earthenware had been part of his regular production repertory, it was most probably a small one. In a marketplace dominated by other potters, he found at least limited success producing this highly specialized, industrial pottery.[20]

From the above material evidence, it is clear that Miller diverged but did not stray greatly from the style of stoneware potting and decorating conceived by John Swann circa 1810 to 1825. Miller pottery and that produced on Wilkes Street can be differentiated only by rim construction, handle placement, and certain subtleties in overall form. There is even very little difference in color and texture, suggesting that Miller used products and firing methods similar to those of his primary competitor (and likely former employer).

Some of Miller's jar forms may seem generally denser and less sophisticated than those produced by Swann; as a decorator, however, Miller may have been more creative than his contemporary, and it is important to note that all of his known products are decorated with cobalt. In contrast, several stoneware pieces impressed with Swann's mark, "J. SWANN / ALEXA," are merely salt-glazed and undecorated. Miller appeared to be aware of how stoneware manufacture in the country was evolving and as such embraced cobalt decoration, perhaps even more so than Swann. Nevertheless, Miller's attempt at state-of-the-art stoneware production—documented in written records and corroborated by his few surviving pots—met with great adversity. The small number of known pieces signed by or attributed to him suggest that his operations in Alexandria and Georgetown were small-scale and relatively short-lived. He was never a successful businessman.

Miller is a common name in nineteenth-century American pottery. It is also a prominent name among the merchants of Alexandria beginning in the eighteenth century. To further confuse things, a few of these businessmen associated themselves with local potteries. Alexandria merchant Robert Hartshorne Miller mentions the sale of locally produced stoneware in an advertisement in the *Alexandria Gazette* circa 1830. His son, Elisha Janney Miller, purchased stoneware bearing the mark "E. J. MILLER / ALEXA" from the Milburns a few decades later. Based on these bits of information, James Miller pieces may be labeled incorrectly as, for instance, the work of potters named Miller who were active in Virginia, Pennsylvania, or Kentucky, or, more logically, labeled as the work of Alexandria potters who made jars for one of the merchant Millers. With the information provided herein, it is the hope of the authors that more examples bearing the impression "J. MILLER" will come to light so that more can be understood about this somewhat mysterious but significant contributor to Alexandria's potting tradition.

1. A stoneware jar signed "J. MILLER / ALEX" in the Smithsonian collection is noted in Suzita Cecil Myers, "Alexandria Salt-Glazed Stoneware: A Study in Material Culture, 1813–1876" (master's thesis, University of Maryland, College Park, 1982), p. 98. Excavated earthenware jar sherds signed "J. MILLER / ALEX" were also found in the 1987 excavation of the Alfred Street Sugar House in Alexandria. However, the first stoneware jar signed by and correctly attributed to James Miller to have surfaced within the stoneware collecting community was found in February 2001. For an illustration of this jar, see figure 5.

2. The 1820 Federal Census Schedule for the District of Columbia lists James Miller as a free white male resident of Georgetown between the ages of 26 and 45. His household included five other young males and three young females (probably his sons and daughters), a woman aged between 26 and 45 (probably his wife), and a free male over the age of 45. One person in the household (most certainly Miller) was listed as engaged in manufacturing. Given the age range enumerated in the census, Miller was born sometime between 1775 and 1794; the age of his eldest child and his emergence as a potter in the late 1790s suggest a birth year circa 1780. U.S. Bureau of the Census, *Fourth Census of the United States, 1820: Population Schedules, District of Columbia,* Georgetown, Washington County, p. 27. (Microfilm copy available at the National Archives, Washington, D.C.)

3. The history of the early Alexandria potters was extensively researched by John K. Pickens in the 1970s. His notes and observations are available in the Pickens Papers (box 57), Local History / Special Collections, Alexandria Library, Alexandria, Virginia. For a detailed discussion of these early potters, see Barbara H. Magid, "An Archaeological Perspective on Alexandria's Pottery Tradition," *Journal of Early Southern Decorative Arts* (Winston-Salem, N.C.: Museum of Early Southern Decorative Arts) 21, no. 2 (winter 1995): 41–82.

4. *Alexandria City Records: Land Book and Personal Property Tax Assessments, 1797–1798, 1800,* microfilm reel 00027, Alexandria Library. These records were noted in the Pickens Papers.

5. Some researchers have given Miller a larger place in the history of early Alexandria than was warranted. Miller's role circa 1800 has been misconstrued based on the reference in city records to the partnership of "Miller & Hewes." This firm was not operated by James Miller and Thomas Hewes, however, but rather by the prominent Alexandria merchants-auctioneers Mordecai Miller and Abraham (Abram) Hewes. Numerous period land/tax records and newspaper advertisements confirm this.

6. Lewis Plum's decorations were limited to a reddish brown rust solution in which his stoneware vessels were partially dipped before firing. Reynolds apparently produced only plain, undecorated ware. For an extensive discussion of early stoneware manufacture in Alexandria, see Magid, "Archaeological Perspective on Alexandria's Pottery Tradition."

7. Myers, "Alexandria Salt-Glazed Stoneware," p. 19.

8. Swann's claim was that he "has been enabled lately to make a great improvement in his ware, although it has been at considerable expense and labor" (*Alexandria Gazette and Daily Advertiser,* August 5, 1819, quoted in Magid, "Archaeological Perspective on Alexandria's Pottery Tradition," p. 56). For a discussion of Swann's stoneware innovations in the late 1810s, see Suzita Cecil Myers, *The Potter's Art: Salt-Glazed Stoneware of 19th-Century Alexandria* (Alexandria, Va.: Alexandria Urban Archaeology Program, 1983), p. 9, and Magid, "Archaeological Perspective on Alexandria's Pottery Tradition."

9. Bureau of the Census, *Fourth Census of the United States, 1820: Census of Manufactures:* Georgetown, Washington County, District of Columbia, p. 322. James Miller was listed as the only potter operating within the limits of Georgetown. This entry is briefly mentioned in Myers, "Alexandria Salt-Glazed Stoneware," pp. 98–99.

10. The original record appears in the Bureau of the Census, *Fourth Census of the United States, 1820: Census of Manufactures,* and is mentioned in Myers, "Alexandria Salt-Glazed Stoneware," pp. 22–23, and Myers, *Potter's Art,* pp. 10–11.

11. Alexandria was part of the District of Columbia between 1791 and 1846. Thorough research by the authors has produced no references to potters within Washington or Georgetown pre-1820. Later potters/pottery owners operating within the limits of what is today considered the District of Columbia include M. Swan (ca. 1827), Richard Butt (ca. 1834–1843), John Walker (ca. 1835), Enoch Burnett (ca. 1845–1880), and many others late into the century.

12. All of this is discussed thoroughly in both Myers, "Alexandria Salt-Glazed Stoneware," pp. 18–31, and Myers, *Potter's Art,* pp. 8–11.

13. Alexandria City Deed Books, O-2 through P-2, 1824–26, pp. 79–81. (Available on microfilm through the Alexandria Library Special Collections.) Miller's trustee was George Catlett.

14. Ibid., p. 80. The Francis Peyton listed as the owner of the property was a prominent landlord in Alexandria. Although the document inexplicably fails to list the exact location of the James Miller pottery, a careful examination of tax records has enabled us to say, with near certainty, that it was located near the intersection of King and West streets.

As far as is known, every kiln site in the city of Alexandria has been located, either through land and tax records or through archaeological excavations, with the exception of James Miller's. Although this document makes clear the fact that Miller operated a "Pottery establishment" in the "County of Alexandria D.C.," it fails to list its precise location. No newspaper ads, directory entries, court documents, or other sources could definitively produce this address. An extensive search of land and tax records was conducted, but no rental agreement between Francis Peyton and James Miller was found. When Isaac Robbins and George Catlett (Miller's trustee) were also searched, these names also yielded no relevant results. However, a listing in the 1825 city tax assessment (Alexandria City Personal Property Tax Assessment roll, Ward 3, p. 5) shows James Miller renting a house and lot located near the intersection of King and West streets from the Franklin Bank with one shopkeeper, two stories, and an assessed value of $1,000. Since an exhaustive search of the 1824 city property tax assessment showed that virtually all of Francis Peyton's properties for that year were located in that immediate vicinity, this likely was the Miller shop. Whether this is the same property later operated by Tildon Easton as a stoneware pottery ca. 1841–1843 (also near the corner of King and West streets) is unconfirmed, although no signed James Miller sherds were found during the partial excavation of that site undertaken in the 1980s.

15. Alexandria City Deed Books, p. 80.

16. Arlington County Insolvent Debtors, 1826–1833, pp. 66–69 (available on microfilm through the Alexandria Library Special Collections). The federal law that enabled Miller to seek his release from debtor's prison was "An Act for the Relief of Insolvent Debtors within the District of Columbia." Mention of an *Alexandria Gazette* advertisement related to this case was found in T. Michael Miller, *Portrait of a Town: Alexandria, District of Columbia (Virginia), 1820–1830* (Bowie, Md.: Heritage Books, 1995), p. 256.

17. *Alexandria Gazette,* June 4, 1827, found in Miller, *Portrait of a Town,* p. 256.

18. Both of these pieces are in the Alexandria Archaeology Collection.

19. All told, over 11,000 fragments of syrup jars were recovered and determined through spectrographic analysis to be of local manufacture. How many of these were produced at Miller's pottery is uncertain, but it was likely a large portion. For a detailed description of these pots and the sugar house excavation, see Keith L. Barr, Pamela J. Cressey, and Barbara H. Magid, "How Sweet It Was: Alexandria's Sugar Trade and Refining Business," in *Historical Archaeology of the Chesapeake,* edited by Paul A. Shackel and Barbara J. Little (Washington, D.C.: Smithsonian Institution Press, 1994), pp. 251–65, and Barbara H. Magid, *The Sugar House Site, 44AX96, Interim Report: 1987 Field Session* (Alexandria, Va.: Alexandria Archaeology Publications, 1987).

20. Magid, "Archaeological Perspective on Alexandria's Pottery Tradition," p. 54.

Christopher T. Espenshade

Relatedness and Fluidity among Stoneware Potters of Washington County, Virginia

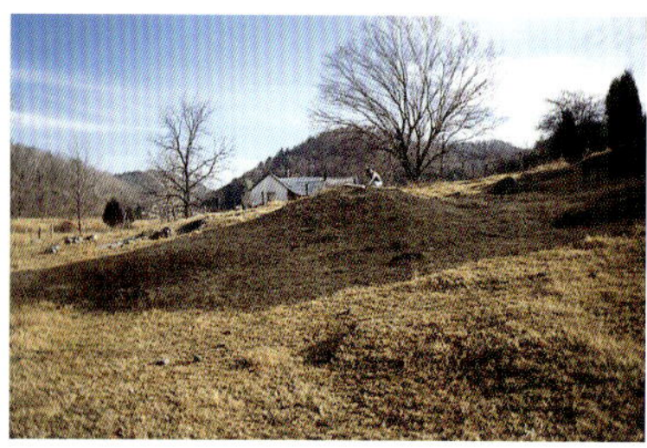

Figure 1 Kiln and waster mound at the Magee stoneware shop of the Osceola cluster. (Photos, Christopher T. Espenshade.)

Figure 2 Storage jar, attributed to J. M. Barlow, Alum Wells or Oceola, Washington County, Virginia, 1880–1896. Salt-glazed stoneware. H. 13". This vessel has been attributed based on its handle and rim forms and its decorative motif.

In 2001–2002, Skelly and Loy completed the survey of historic pottery-making in Washington County in southwestern Virginia.[1] The survey built on previous work by Klell Napps and Roderick Moore. Archival research was undertaken to identify potters and place them in the landscape, and an archaeological survey was conducted at thirty locations suspected of being former pottery shops (fig. 1).

The archival research indicated that earthenware was produced locally by 1780; stoneware appeared by 1850. Major clusters of earthenware shops developed in Osceola and stoneware ones on Mendota Road. The stoneware was typical of the pan-Northeast tradition of salt glaze over freehand, with cobalt underglaze decoration (fig. 2). The fieldwork included revisits to two previously excavated stoneware kilns, the discovery and sampling of seven stoneware shops, and the recording of the source of clay for several of the Osceola shops (fig. 3).

An interesting aspect of the Washington County study was the high degree of relatedness among the stoneware potters. Burrison and Zug have noted the clannish nature of pottery making in the South, and Washington County fits the pattern.[2] Thirty-eight of the forty-three known stoneware potters in the county are linked by descent, marriage, or shared workplace (fig. 4). Potting followed bloodlines: the Wootons, Vestals, Millers, Magees, and Gardners, for example, featured multiple generations of potters, which

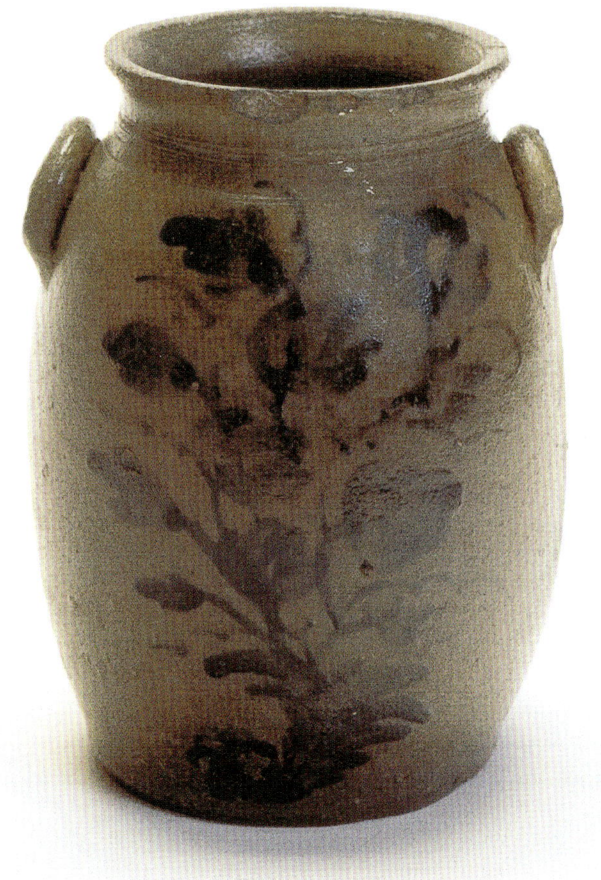

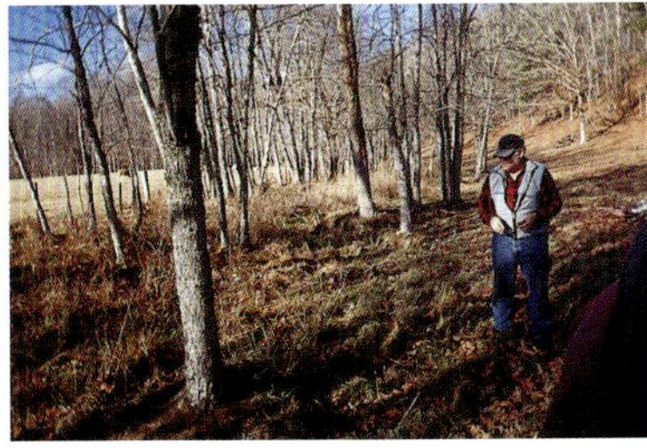

Figure 3 Clay Bottoms, an old back channel of the Middle Fork of the Holston River, at which potters from the Osceola shops quarried clay.

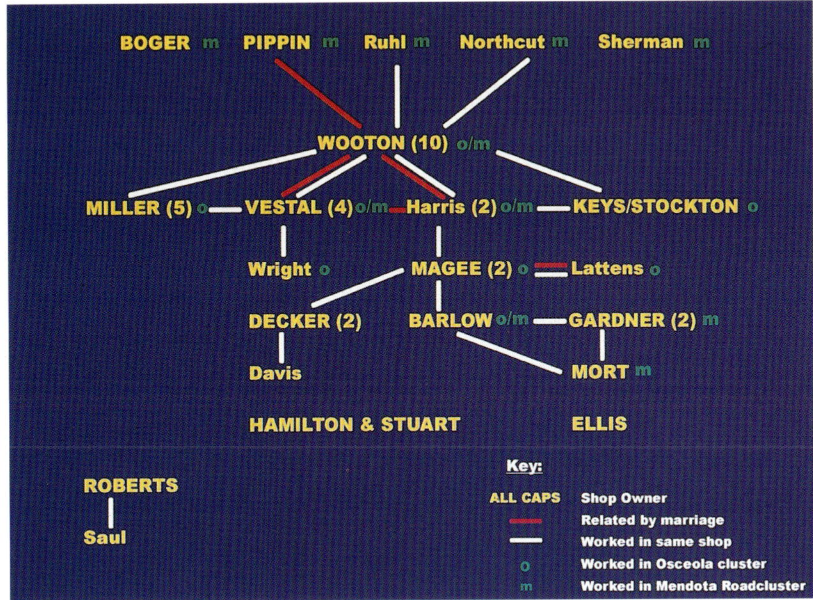

Figure 4 Relatedness diagram of the stoneware potters of Washington County, Virginia.

is consistent with the lack of formal potter apprenticeships found in the county records.

The major potting families strengthened their network through marriage. In most cases these links were in all likelihood simply the result of marrying within one's social circle. In other cases, however, the individual marrying into a clay family appears to have had no prior potting experience.

The potters were also linked as coworkers. It was common for many of the county potters to work in multiple shops with different coworkers as shops opened, evolved, moved, or closed. By 1870, it appears that there were few strangers in the pottery business in Washington County.

Fluidity, a second trait of the potters, refers to the ease with which a potter could move from one shop to another. In Washington County, the high relatedness allowed much fluidity. For example, although the Wootons were an established potting family, some remained in the Osceola shops even after John T. Wooton opened his shop on Mendota Road. Likewise, excavations at the Gardner kiln yielded more stamps of "E. W. MORT ALUM WELLS, VA" and "J. M. BARLOW" than of "J. W. GARDNER & SON / CRAIGS MILL, VA.," and there is no question that Gardner owned this shop and that Mort and Barlow had their own shops elsewhere on Mendota Road at that time. Clearly, Mort and Barlow were making pottery at the Gardner shop and the Gardners were allowing them to continue using their own stamps.[3]

The high degree of relatedness among the potters made it easy for a potter to follow work; by the same token, that very fluidity would have acted as a buffer against shortfalls of clay, fuel, orders, and/or capital. Washington County stoneware potters reaped the full benefits of fluidity without having to move beyond their local network of shops. The use of foreign stamps at the Gardner kiln might reflect some sort of etiquette associated with the movement of potters between shops. As research continues in the county, additional ties should be recognized.[4]

Christopher T. Espenshade
Cultural Resource Specialist
Skelly and Loy, Inc.
<cespenshade@monroeville.skellyloy.com>

1. The work was conducted under a Virginia Department of Historic Resources Cost-Share Grant; funding partners included Washington County, the Washington County Preservation Foundation, and the William King Regional Arts Center (WKRAC). The project built on the extensive previous work by the Cultural Heritage Program at the WKRAC. The Wolf Hills Chapter of the Archeological Society of Virginia and Marcus King of the WKRAC assisted in the fieldwork. See C. T. Espenshade, Skelly and Loy, Inc., Monroeville, Pennsylvania, "Potters on the Holston: Historic Pottery Production in Washington County, Virginia" (report on file, Virginia Department of Historic Resources, Richmond, 2002).

2. John A. Burrison, *Brothers in Clay: The Story of Georgia Folk Pottery* (Athens: University of Georgia Press, 1983), and Charles G. Zug III, *Turners and Burners: The Folk Potters of North Carolina* (Chapel Hill: The University of North Carolina Press, 1986).

3. It has been suggested by some researchers that the presence of foreign stamps at a shop site simply reflects that the potter in residence was copying his competitor's wares. However, the relative frequency of the Mort and Barlow stamps at the Gardner kiln suggests that Mort and Barlow were producing pottery at the Gardner shop. Moreover, the variability in rim and base forms at the Gardner shop suggests the work of multiple potters.

4. A proposal is pending for test excavations at the Mort kiln under the Virginia Department of Historic Resources, Threatened Sites Program. Due to landowner issues, the Mort kiln was not examined in detail during the 2001–2002 survey. The site features an extensive waster pile and intact kiln elements. A very brief examination of sherds suggests a wide variety of rim forms, possibly indicating the presence of multiple potters there as well.

William B. Liebeknecht

Jar or Jug? A Handled Stoneware Storage Vessel from the Delaware Valley

The two gray-bodied, salt-glazed stoneware vessels shown here (fig. 1) were purchased as a lot in an auction in southern New Jersey. The vessel on the left is stamped "RCR" (Richard Clinton Remmey) above "PHILA" (Philadelphia) within a clipped rectangle. This company produced stoneware from 1859 through the 1880s.[1] Although the second vessel is unmarked, it is believed to have been made by the same factory, possibly at the same time. Both vessels exhibit very similar handle attachments, body color, form, and glaze.

The vessel on the left is a standard, wheel-thrown, undecorated two-gallon jug. The one on the right is, for lack of a better term, a handled jar, undecorated and unmarked, with a semi-wide mouth. Unglazed patches along the shoulder represent points of contact with a jug saggar or stacker. Unglazed patches on the body below the shoulder represent points of contact from informal wads. The glaze around these points of contact exhibit a distinctive greenish yellow hue.

So what is this vessel? Is it a jar, a jug, or a crock? This vessel is unlikely to be a preserve jar since the diameter of the mouth is slightly smaller than contemporary glass canning jars, making removal of solid food stores difficult. In her book on American stoneware, Georgeanna Greer pictures a similar vessel, a handled, small-mouthed preserve jar with a wider mouth, more typical of contemporary glass canning jars.[2] Its plain, undecorated appearance suggests a utilitarian, storage-type function, possibly industrial (chemical storage).

Figure 1 Jug and handled jar, Richard Clinton Remmey, Philadelphia, 1859–1880s. Salt-glazed stoneware. H. 11" and 9". (Private collection; photo, Michael Murphy.) The jar holds 80 liquid ounces, or 5 quarts. Its mouth, formed by a collar with a flat lip, has an interior diameter of two inches. An internal lid or ledge seat suggests a formal lid, either ceramic or cork, was sealed to it with wax or tied to the collar.

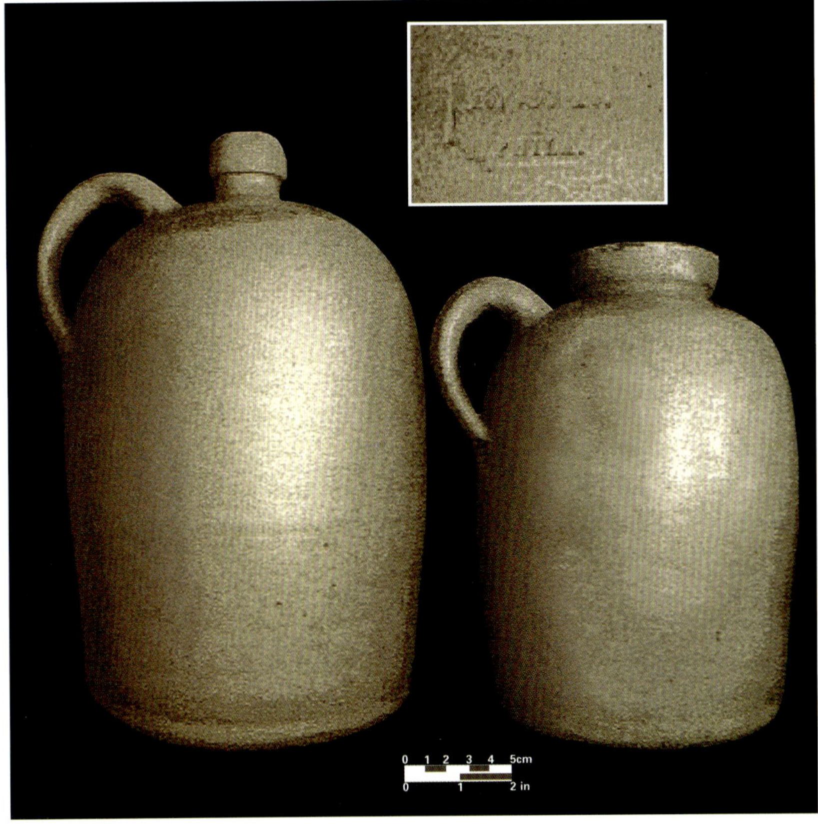

William B. Liebeknecht
Principal Archaeologist
Hunter Research, Inc.
wbl@hunterresearch.com
http://hunterresearch.com

1. William C. Ketchum Jr., *American Stoneware* (New York: Henry Holt and Company, 1991), p. 87.
2. Georgeanna Greer, *American Stonewares: The Art and Craft of Utilitarian Potters*, 3rd ed., rev. (Atglen, Pa.: Schiffer Publishing, 1999), p. 87.

John Kille

William Pecker Jar

The ovoid shape of the dusty stoneware pot on the table seemed at odds with the eclectic assemblage of mostly twentieth-century "antiques" offered at a recent Kentucky flea market. A quick turn of the jar confirmed the incongruities of time and place, revealing the presence of two very unusual stamped designs, as well as a rarely seen maker's mark belonging to one of New England's earliest and most talented potters, William Pecker (figs. 1–4).

The discovery of this decorated piece of stoneware is all the more surprising given that Pecker is best known for the redware vessels he produced as early as 1784 in Amesbury and West Amesbury, Massachusetts. In fact, in *Early New England Potters and Their Wares,* Lura Woodside Watkins focuses solely on Pecker's redware production without a mention of stone-

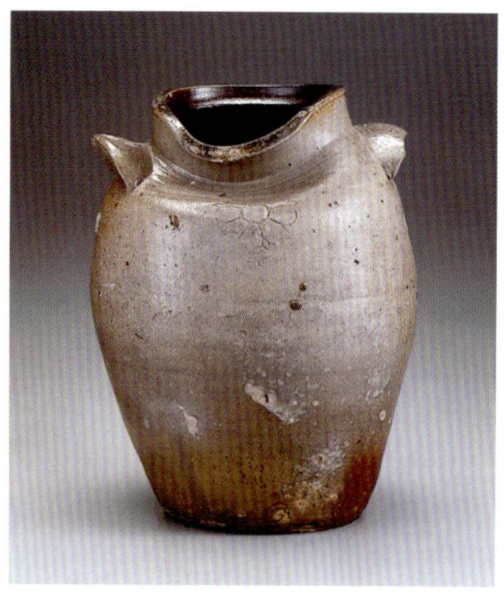

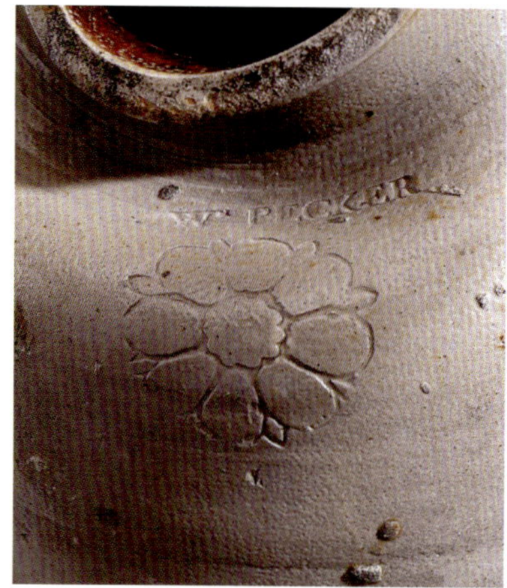

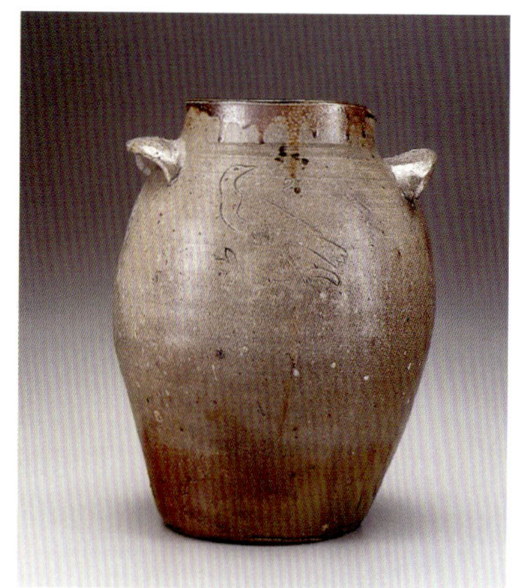

Figure 1 Jar, William Pecker, West Amesbury, Massachusetts, 1790–1810. Salt-glazed stoneware. H. 12¼". (All photographs, Gavin Ashworth.)

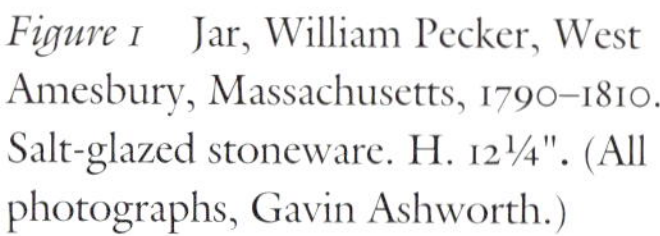

Figure 2 Detailed of the stamped flower and "WM PECKER" on the jar illustrated in fig. 1.

Figure 3 Reverse side of the jar illustrated in fig. 1.

ware manufacture. Watkins described his redware as being "beautiful" with "delightful rosy tones accented by brushings of dark glaze."[1]

The stamped motifs on the Pecker stoneware jar are reminiscent of stamped designs seen on stoneware vessels attributed to Boston and Charlestown potters Jonathan Fenton and Frederick Carpenter. Notably, the distinctive floral pattern on the Pecker jar is comparable to a five-petaled flower design used by Fenton (fig. 5). Further, all three potters—

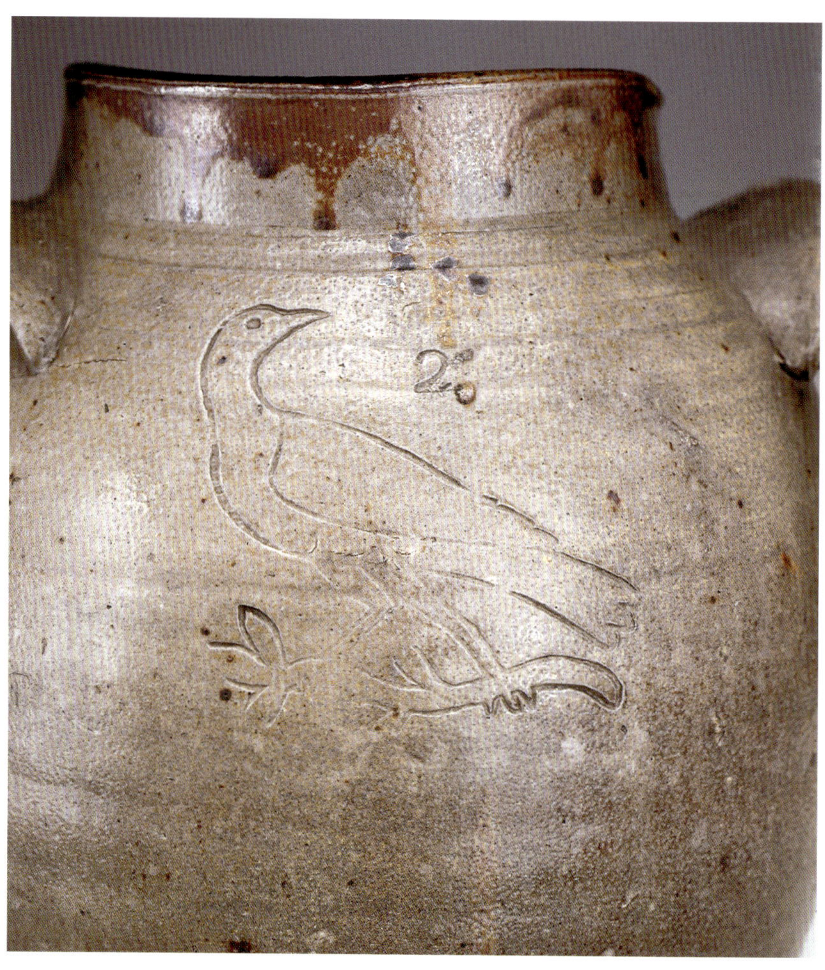

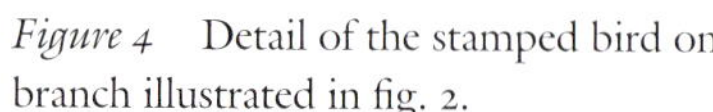

Figure 4 Detail of the stamped bird on branch illustrated in fig. 2.

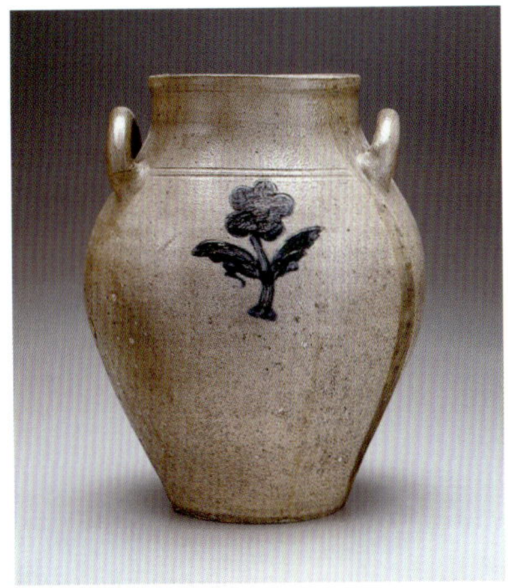

Figure 5 Jar, attributed to Jonathan Fenton, Boston, Massachusetts, ca. 1794–1797. H. 13". Salt-glazed stoneware.

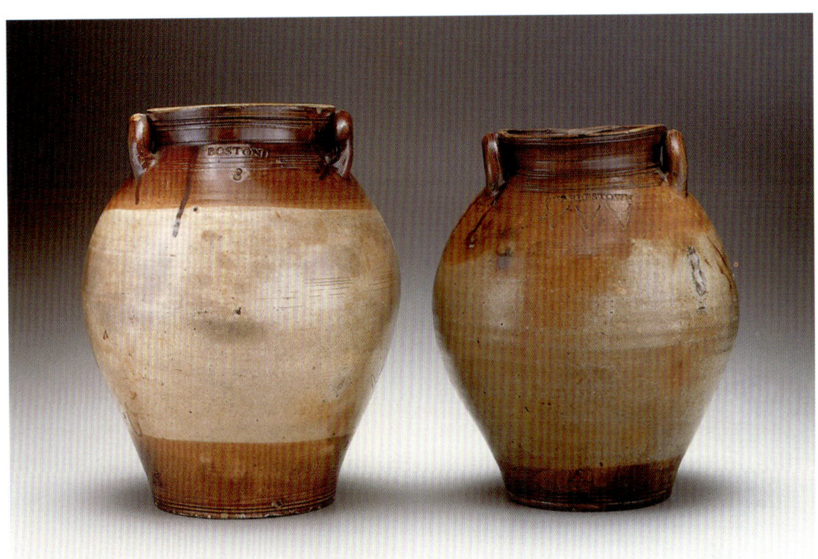

Figure 6 Jars, attributed to Frederick Carpenter, Boston/Charlestown, Massachusetts, ca. 1810. Salt-glazed stoneware with iron or ochre wash. H. 14¼" and 13".

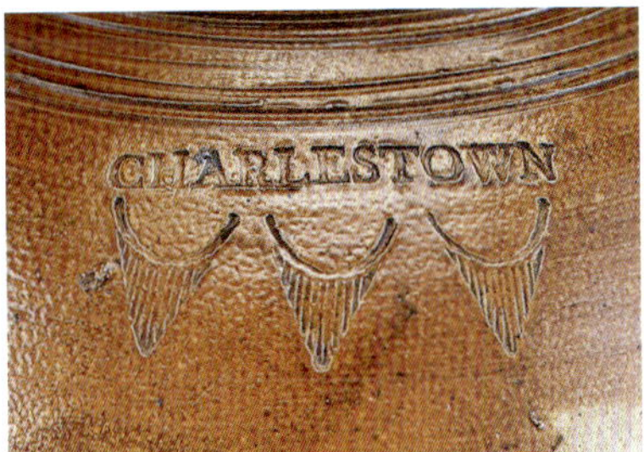

Figure 7 Impressed Charleston stamp from the jar shown on the right in fig. 6.

Pecker, Fenton, and Carpenter—stamped their stoneware vessels with highly detailed designs (figs. 6, 7).

Like their European predecessors, American potters relied on stamped designs to provide aesthetically pleasing decorations that could be applied with efficiency and economy.[2] However, as with molded, slipped, and incised decorations, the appearance of elaborate stamped designs on early American stoneware vessels is a relatively rare occurrence. Since Pecker chose to decorate this jar with two different designs and also applied a maker's mark, he may have intended this piece to be somewhat special.

Another notable feature of the Pecker pot is a decidedly slumped rim that probably occurred when stacked wares shifted during a kiln firing. Tragically, William Pecker himself was crushed to death when one of his kilns collapsed on him in 1820.[3] The misshapen appearance of the jar he made and decorated is a tangible reminder of the challenges, as well as the grave physical dangers, involved in operating a stoneware kiln during this period.

John Kille
Assistant Director
The Lost Towns Archaeology Project
Anne Arundel County, Maryland
<jkille@wam.umd.edu>
<http://www.geocities.com/londontown.geo/>

1. Lura Woodside Watkins, *Early New England Potters and Their Wares* (1950; [Hamden, Conn.]: Archon Books, 1968), p. 70.
2. Donald Blake Webster, *Decorated Stoneware Pottery of North America* (Rutland, Vt.: Charles E. Tuttle Co., 1971), p. 157.
3. Watkins, *Early New England Potters and Their Wares,* p. 70.

Jonathan Goodwin

Excavations at the Minton Factory: Shedding New Light on Nineteenth-Century Pottery Kilns

Recent excavations by Stoke-on-Trent Archaeology Service on the site of the Minton pottery factory have offered new insights into the methods employed in the construction of nineteenth-century pottery kilns. The project unearthed the remains of four "bottle"-shaped updraft kilns ranging in date from the mid-nineteenth to the early twentieth centuries, almost doubling in a stroke the total number of nineteenth-century kilns excavated to date at Stoke-on-Trent.

The site has been home to the present works since the 1950s, but throughout much of the nineteenth and early twentieth centuries the area was occupied by two potworks. The first of these, located in the southwestern corner, was a chinaworks established by Thomas Minton in the late eighteenth or early nineteenth century. In the eastern half of the site, separated from Minton's works by the Newcastle canal, was the Trent Potteries, erected by George Jones in 1864–1865.

The earliest and most complete of the four kilns found during the service's excavations formed part of Minton's chinaworks and was thought to date to the mid-nineteenth century. The base of the oven, discovered at the level of the ash pits, was located within a rectangular room (fig. 1). This indicates that the kiln did not have a separate hovel, but that the hovel was built on the shoulders of the oven chamber and projected through the roof of the building. It is not known whether this was a biscuit or glost kiln.

The three remaining excavated kilns related to George Jones's Trent Potteries and dated from the late nineteenth to the early twentieth century. Again, each kiln survived as an oven base situated within a rectangular or square room. All were of identical construction: the foundation of the oven was built rather like a brick donut with a core of bricks and waste sherds in the central void (figs. 2–4). The brick surface that formed the

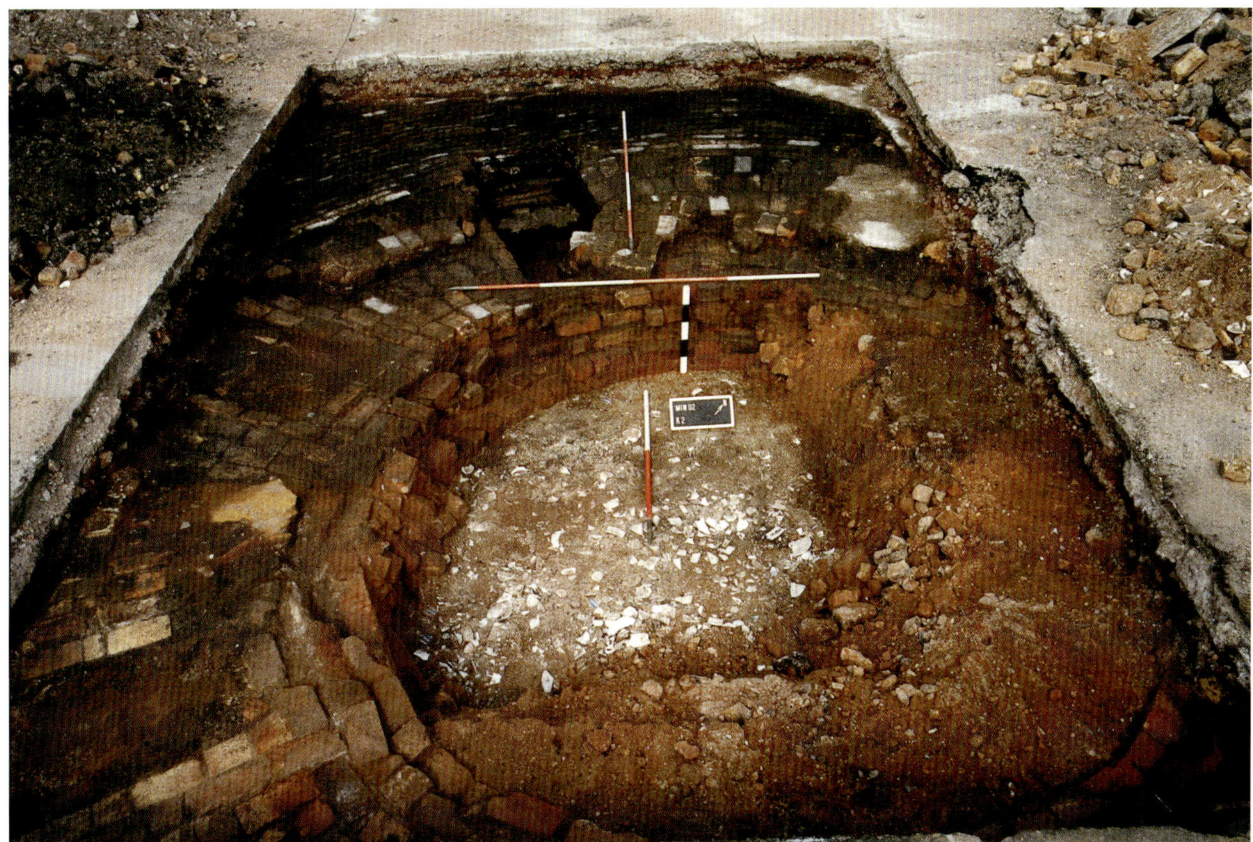

Figure 1 Excavated nineteenth-century oven base from Thomas Minton's chinaworks. Scales are 0.5, 1.0, and/or 2.3 m. (All photos, The Potteries Museum and Art Gallery, Stoke-on-Trent.)

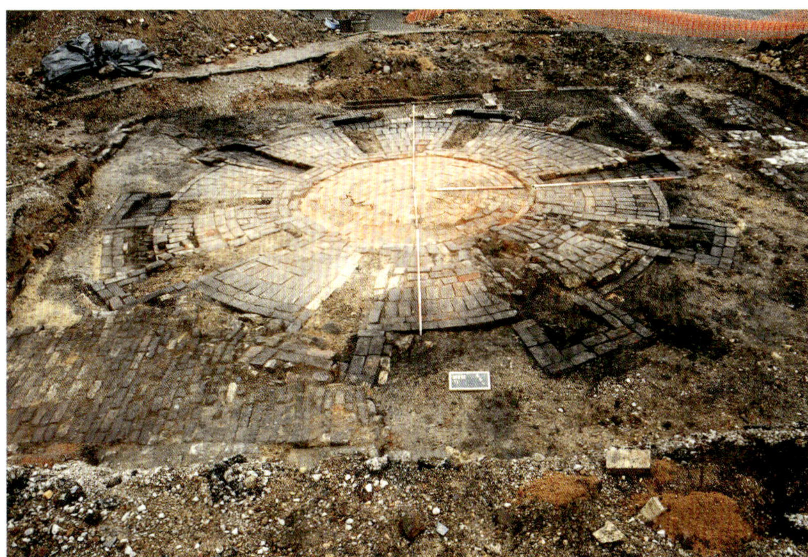

Figure 2 Mid- to late-nineteenth-century oven base from George Jones's Trent Potteries. Note the central void.

bottom of the flues and provided the base for the oven chamber itself was laid over the rubble core. This was something of a revelation, as it had been previously thought that kiln foundations were entirely of brick. Initially it seemed odd that a manufacturer would risk building such an essential part of the factory's operation on seemingly flimsy foundations. However, subsequent research has shown this to be a recognized practice and one that was entirely sensible.

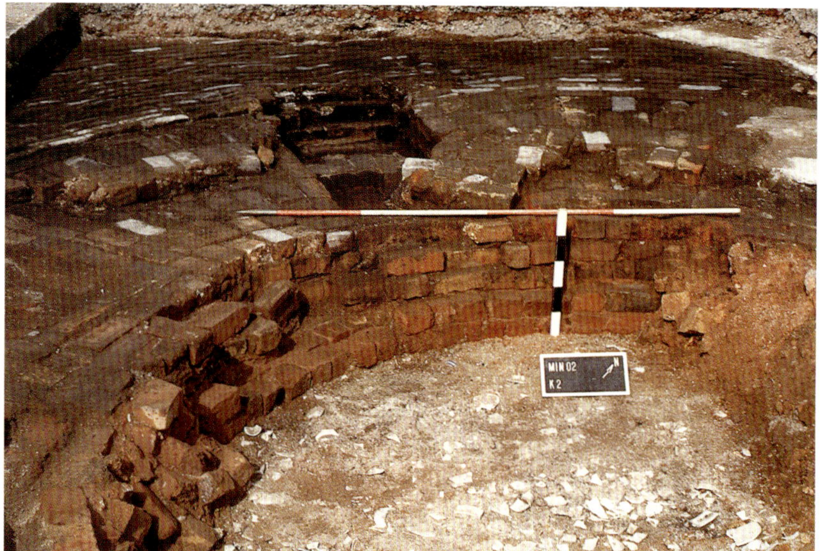

Figure 3 Detail of central void, showing fill of brick, sandy material, and pottery waste: Sandeman's "cork."

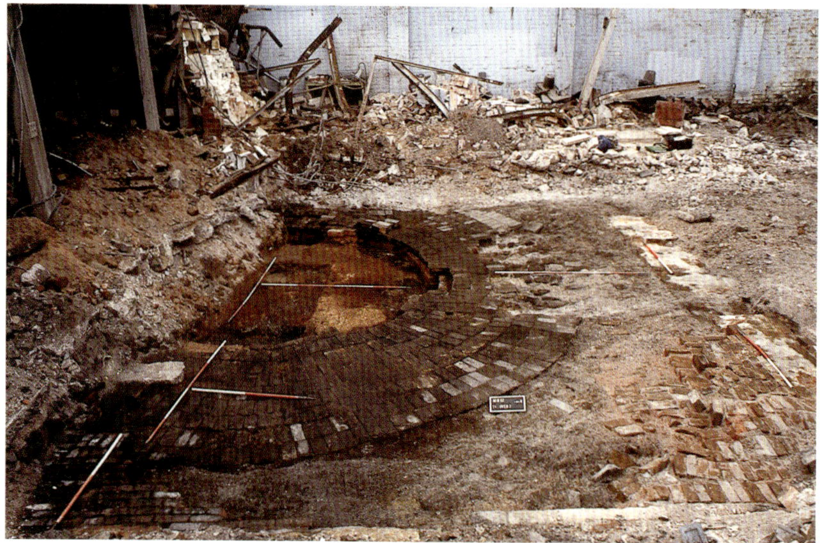

Figure 4 Another oven from the Trent Potteries, once again showing the central void.

In his 1901 *Notes on the Manufacture of Earthenware,* Ernest Albert Sandeman describes a similar construction method in which a foundation—known as the "cork" and composed of broken bricks, "grog" or ground-up saggars, and sherds—was used to form the base of the oven.[1] According to his account, three or four feet of soil were removed and filled with the cork material, which was then raised to the required height and the top graduated from side to center to match the required pitch of the flues. When complete, the cork was smoothed over with a layer of fine, fired sand that acted as a bed for the brick floor subsequently laid on top. It is not clear from Sandeman's account whether the cork was enclosed by a built outer brick ring, but he does state that the outer circles of the cork should comprise whole bricks to prevent subsidence caused by the oven sucking moisture from the soil beneath it during firing. All of the material used to form the cork was prefired and contained no moisture, thereby negating the costly problem of subsidence, which causes the kiln to list and crack its flues.

This is the first time that we have encountered this construction method archaeologically and recognized it for what it is, and future kiln excavations will no doubt show how widespread this practice actually was. Clearly, however, there is much to learn about these once commonplace structures.

Jonathan Goodwin
Assistant Field Archaeologist
Stoke-on-Trent Archaeology Service
The Potteries Museum & Art Gallery
<jon.goodwin@stoke.gov.uk.>

1. Ernest Albert Sandeman, *Notes on the Manufacture of Earthenware* (London: H. Virtue & Co., 1901), pp. 193–95.

Al Luckenbach

If This Pot Could Sing

Archaeologists and other students of historical ceramics are accustomed to extracting a narrative of the past from simple sherds and vessels. Ivor Noël Hume, in his recent work, referenced such activity with the beseeching title *If These Pots Could Talk*. Although Noël Hume proves himself an admirable interrogator of ceramics, the subject of this short paper goes one better: describing a pot that can sing of its past—in nursery rhyme!

The vessel in question seems unremarkable at first glance. It is a small English brown salt-glazed jug from the second quarter of the nineteenth century, dipped in iron oxide to produce the two-tone style of stoneware that had been popular in homes and taverns for well over a century (figs. 1, 2). It is the inscription that makes the vessel remarkable. Stamped in individual letters across the front are the words:

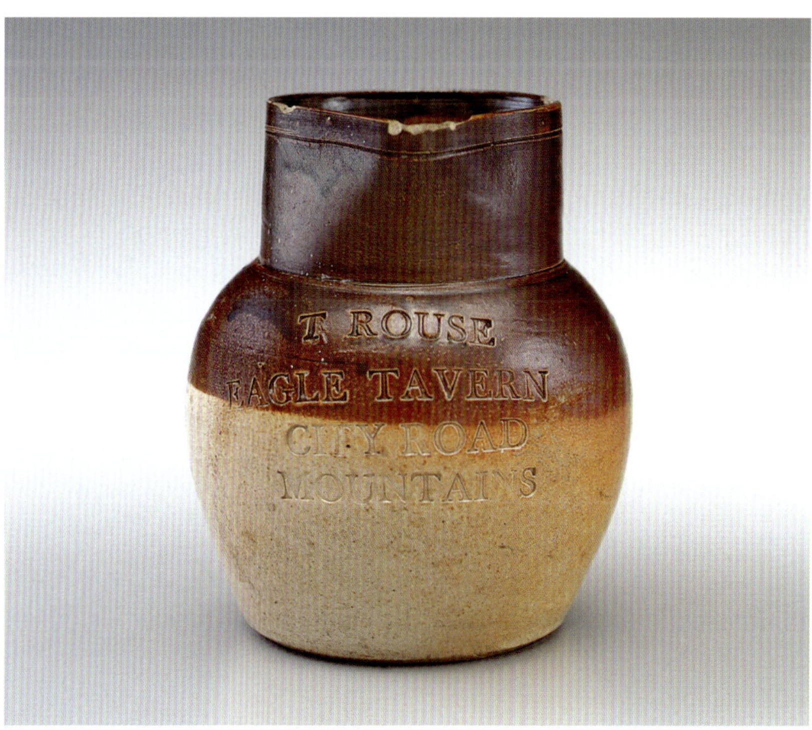

Figure 1 Jug, London, 1825–1850. Salt-glazed stoneware. H. 5½". (Private collection; photo, Gavin Ashworth.)

Figure 2 Detail of the inscription on the jug illustrated in fig. 1.

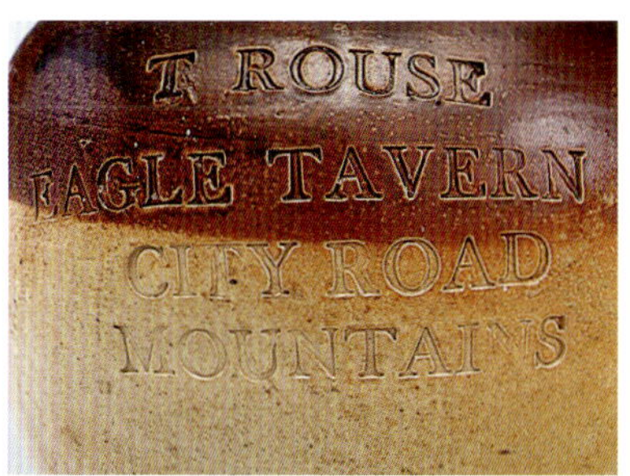

T. ROUSE
EAGLE TAVERN
CITY ROAD
MOUNTAINS

The nursery rhyme connection derives from the fact that throughout the nineteenth century pawnshops were located just up the City Road from the Eagle Tavern, close to Angel Islington. Add to this the information that to pawn one's watch (or coat) was once known in London slang as "popping" your "weasel," and one can decipher the song:

Up and Down the City Road
In and Out of the Eagle
That's the Place the Money goes
Pop goes the Weasel

The poem, of course, has many verses, and variations abound. It was first published as a dance song in Baltimore, Maryland, in 1850, but is actually much older, and obviously English in derivation.

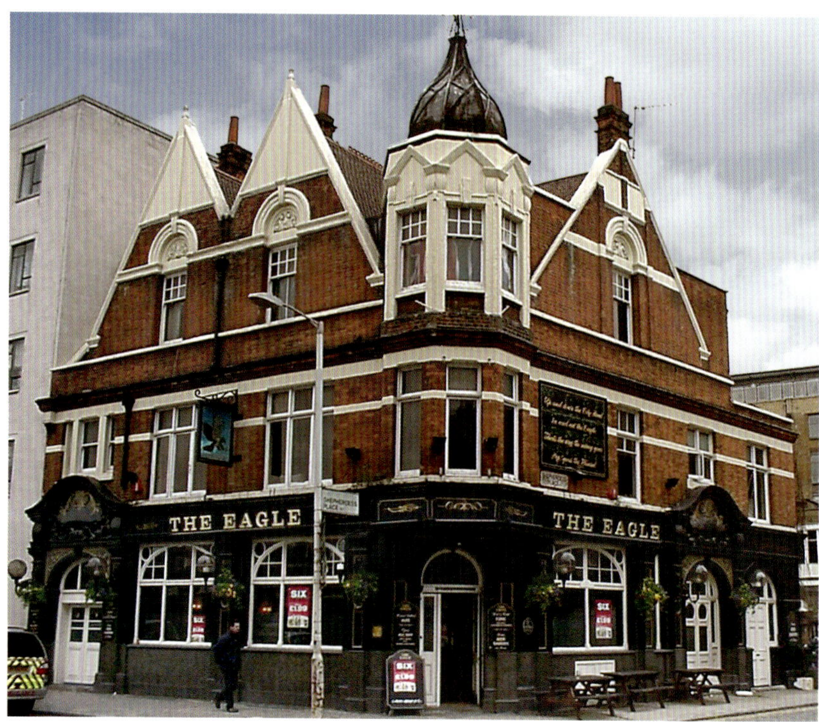

Figure 3 View of the Eagle Tavern, London, 2002. (Photo, Donna Ware.)

There is still an Eagle Tavern on City Road in London (fig. 3), although the current structure was built in 1901 after a fire consumed its predecessor and is, in fact, the third of its name to stand on the spot. The date of the original structure remains unknown, but the second to bear the name—built between 1825 and 1828—is the one referred to on the jug shown here (fig. 4). This can be established readily by the fact that a Thomas Rouse was the first (and longest) proprietor of the second Eagle Tavern, running the operation from 1828 until about 1850. His name can be clearly seen in a detail of an 1841 lithograph showing the street side of the tavern (fig. 5). The word "mountains" refers to a left-leaning political party of the late eighteenth to mid-nineteenth century.[1]

Figure 4 *Eagle Tavern,* steel line engraving on paper, John Shury (fl. 1813–1846), 1841, for *Finsbury Square, City Road,* publisher T. Bowyer. (Private collection.)

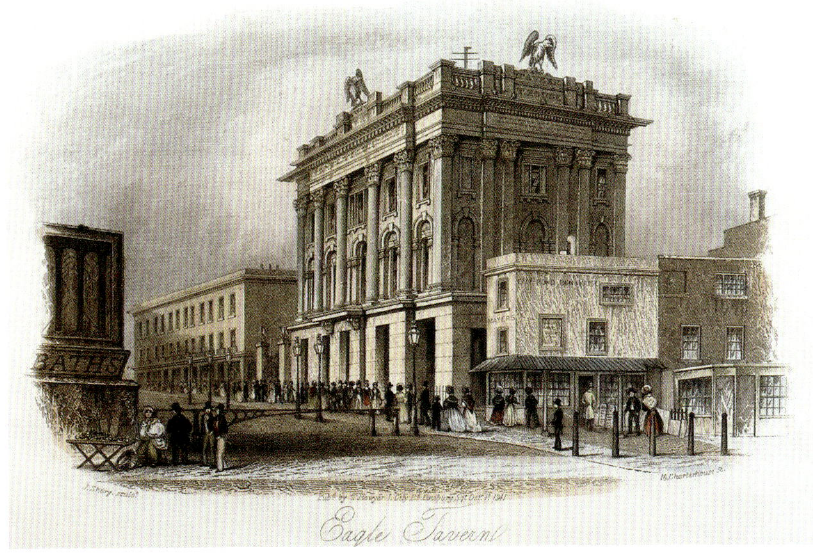

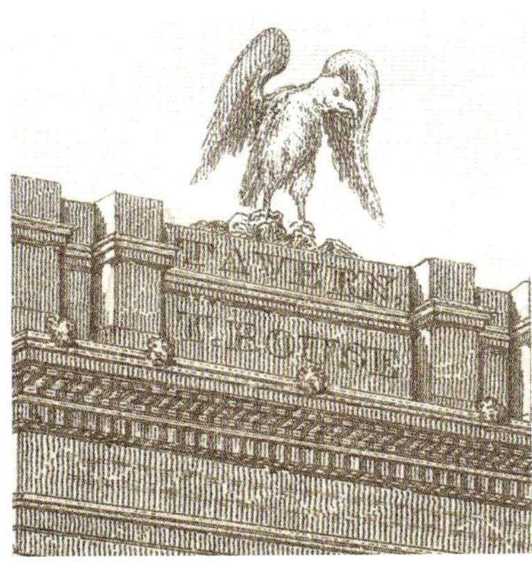

Figure 5 Detail of the engraving illustrated in fig. 4, showing the proprietor's name, T. ROUSE, in stone on the pediment.

Figure 6 *Pleasure Grounds, Eagle Tavern, City Road,* steel line engraving on paper, by John Shury (fl. 1813–1846), 1841, for *Finsbury Square, City Road,* publisher T. Bowyer. (Private collection.)

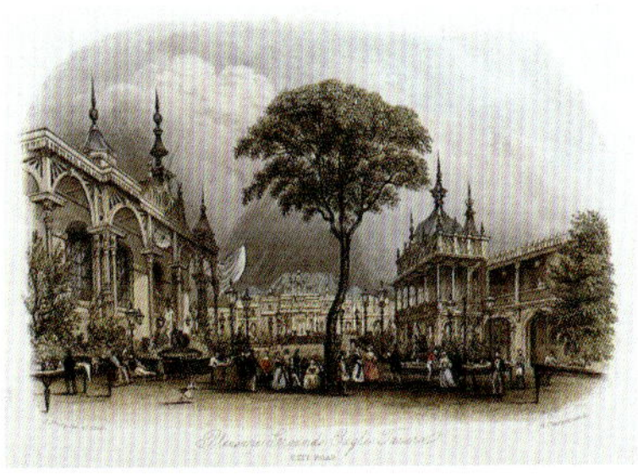

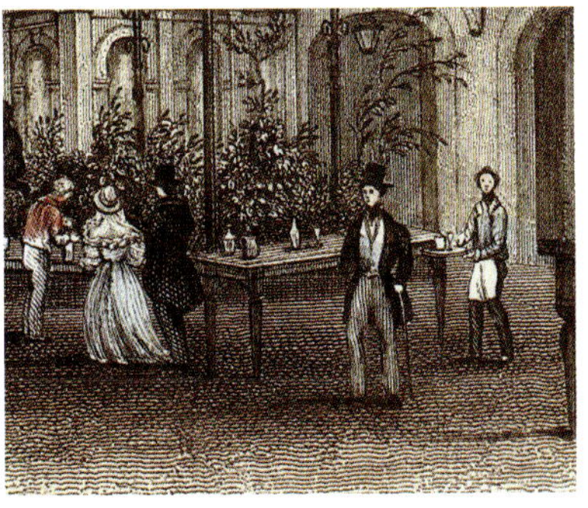

Figure 7 Detail of the engraving illustrated in fig. 6 showing alcoholic beverages being served in bottles, glasses, and a small, perhaps stoneware, jug.

Over its long history the Eagle Tavern seems to have undergone not only structural changes but also changes in social emphasis. The first building had repute both as a tea garden and as a venue for wrestling. In its 1828 incarnation it seems to have been best known for its large and popular outdoor theater (figs. 6, 7). Charles Dickens refers to this theater as the "Rotunda" in his *Sketches by Boz* (characters, "Miss Evans and the Eagle") written about 1835. After 1854 it was acquired by another owner and until the 1870s was known as the Eagle's "Grecian Theatre."

By the late nineteenth century the area around the Eagle Tavern had fallen into a state of disrepute, perhaps due in part to its proximity to the East India Docks. In order to combat widespread public drunkenness, the Salvation Army acquired the Eagle in 1883 and operated it as a "citadel," or rehabilitation center, until the structure burned down at the turn of the century. The Eagle Tavern apparently retained its name under the Salvation Army, however, for it is mentioned as such in articles in the *London Times* in 1888 concerning the murders of prostitutes by "Jack the Ripper."

So once again a long and storied history is revealed in a simple ceramic vessel. This stoneware jug sings of its past like a haunting childhood memory. Now, if I could just get that tune out of my head. . . .

Al Luckenbach, Ph.D.
Director
The Lost Towns Archaeology Project
Anne Arundel County, Maryland
<Alluck@aol.com>
<http://www.geocities.com/londontown.geo/>

1. Personal communication with Ivor Noël Hume, 2003.

Robert Werowinski

"THIS I MAD FOR YOV AND MOOM"

Earthenware decorated with white or colored slip was popular in England throughout the seventeenth and eighteenth centuries. All sorts of vessel shapes were made in slipware: plates, chargers, condiment dishes, porringers, honey pots, mugs, tygs, posset pots, and jugs.

One of the rarer slipware forms is the diminutive cradle, which was made in a variety of sizes from about the 1670s to the early eighteenth century.[1] Through the years, collectors and curators have speculated about their use. They may have served as christening gifts or perhaps as fertility symbols for newlyweds (today we throw rice). Some collectors believe they functioned as convenient containers on chests as "hold alls" for coins, rings, and all the small things otherwise easily lost in a drawer. Larger cradles may have been used to hold children's dolls.

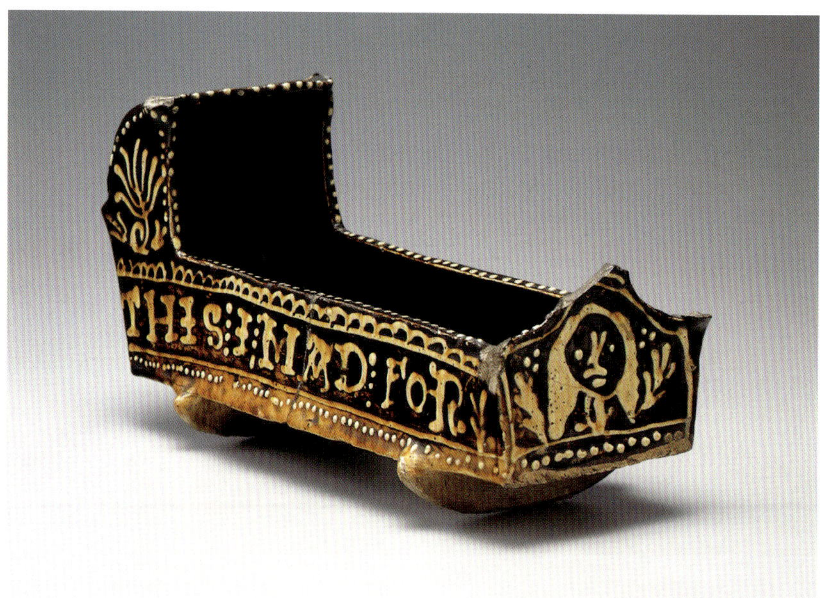

Figure 1 Cradle, Staffordshire, ca. 1710. Slipware. L. 14". The side shown is inscribed with trailed slip "THIS I MAD FOR." Note how the bonnet curves from front to back. (Photos, Gavin Ashworth.)

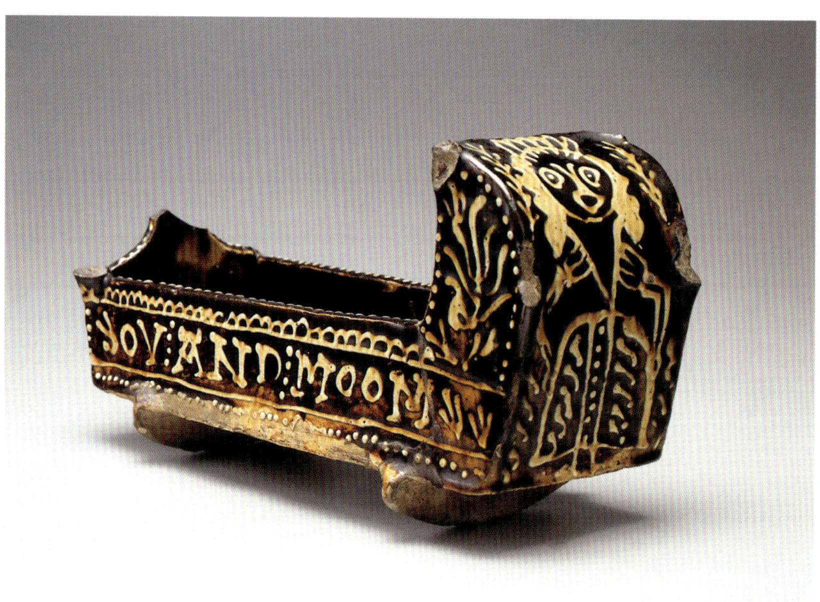

Figure 2 Opposite side of the cradle illustrated in fig. 1, inscribed "YOV AND MOOM."

Figure 3 Detail of the cradle bonnet decorated with the portrait of "MOOM."

Figure 4 Detail of the foot of the cradle with the portrait of "YOV."

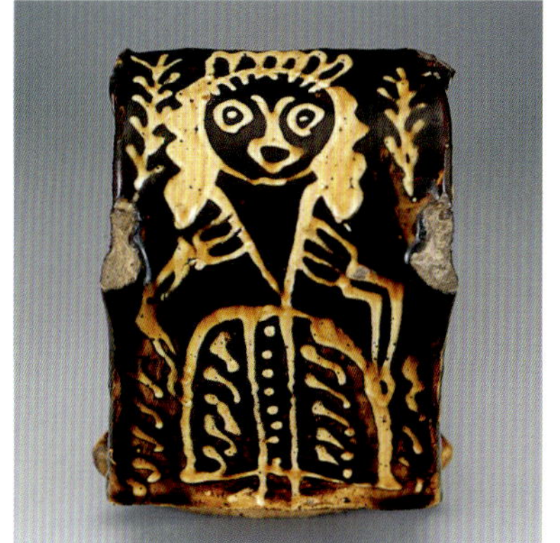

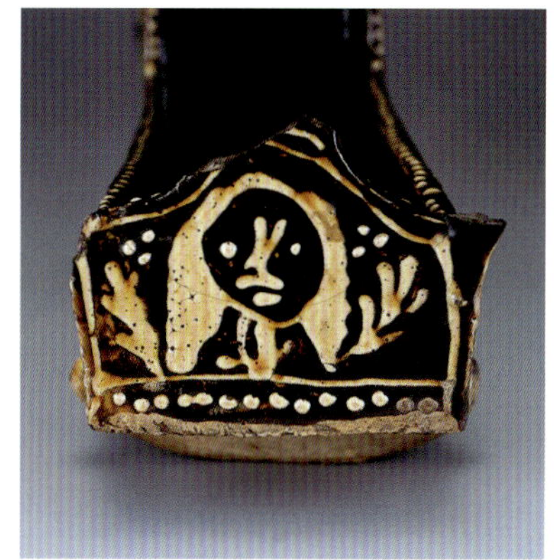

One such slip-decorated cradle, made in Staffordshire around 1710, displays some unique attributes (figs. 1, 2), the most unusual of which is the shape of its bonnet. The hoods of most slip-decorated cradles curve over the bed from side to side. The bonnet on this example, however, arches from front to back.

The buff-colored body is covered with a brown slip except for the exterior base and runners. A thick white slip was used to draw the portraits of a mother on one end and her child on the other (figs. 3, 4) as well as to inscribe on the sides: "THIS I MAD FOR YOV AND MOOM." White dots produce the jeweling that decorates the exterior and top edges of the cradle. A colorless lead glaze covers the decorated surfaces.

The inscription reveals that this cradle was probably made by the potter for his family.[2] It may have been a toy; possible evidence of this is its hard life: all six finials are missing, and at some point it was broken in half. Despite its rough condition, it is a favorite in my slip-decorated pottery collection.

Robert Werowinski
James Island Antiques
<JamesIslandAntiq@aol.com>

1. Leslie B. Grigsby, *The Longridge Collection of English Slipware and Delftware*, 2 vols. (London: Jonathan Horne Publications, 2000).
2. Many cradles are decorated with portraits of people wearing crowns. If the woman in this portrait is crowned—and she appears to be—then she would be a royal figure, not the potter's wife.

Robert Hunter

New Acquisitions at Chipstone

Three ceramic objects recently acquired by the Chipstone Foundation are connected to ongoing research related to articles published in *Ceramics in America*. Two of these objects are eighteenth-century earthenware punch bowls decorated with underglaze dragons (figs. 1, 2). Originating on late-seventeenth-century Chinese porcelain, this motif was used extensively on English delft and, subsequently, on Worcester and Bow porcelain. Examples of delft and soft-paste porcelain punch bowls abound. Famed painter and social commentator William Hogarth owned a large, circa-1730s one

Figure 1 Punch bowls. *Left:* Staffordshire or Yorkshire, ca. 1780. Pearlware. D. 7 15/16". *Right:* attributed to Enoch Booth, Tunstall, Staffordshire, ca. 1745. Creamware. D. 7 1/8". (Chipstone Foundation; photo, Gavin Ashworth.) The body of the dragon starts on the exterior of the bowl and continues over the rim into the well.

of English delft.[1] Both delft and English porcelain punch bowls of this type have been found in Williamsburg excavations.[2] There appears to be no record, however, of this decorative motif on creamware and pearlware bowls, such as those illustrated here.

The creamware dragon bowl is attributed to a small group of early earthenware items made by Enoch Booth in Staffordshire around 1745.[3] The underglaze decoration was created using manganese with yellow and green

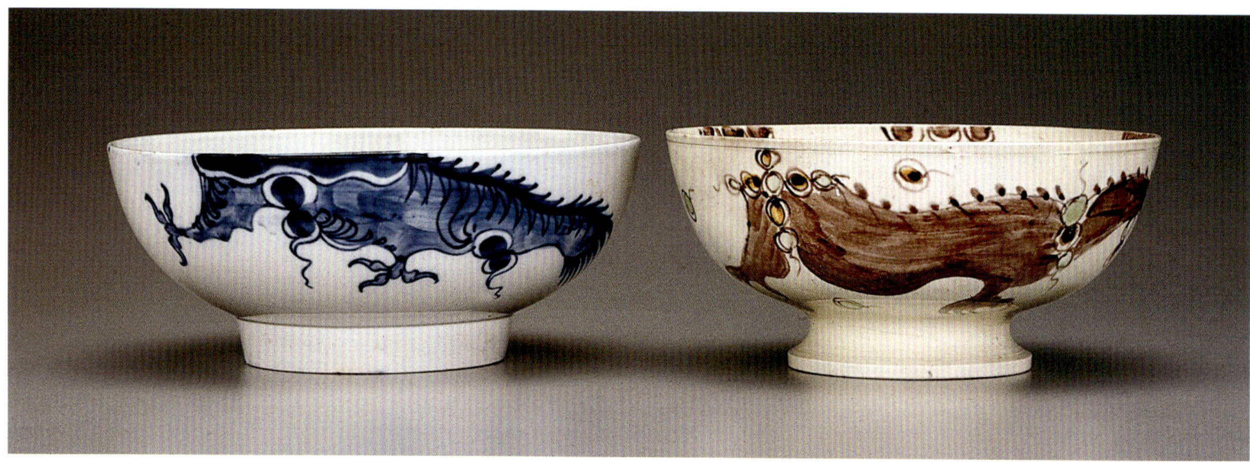

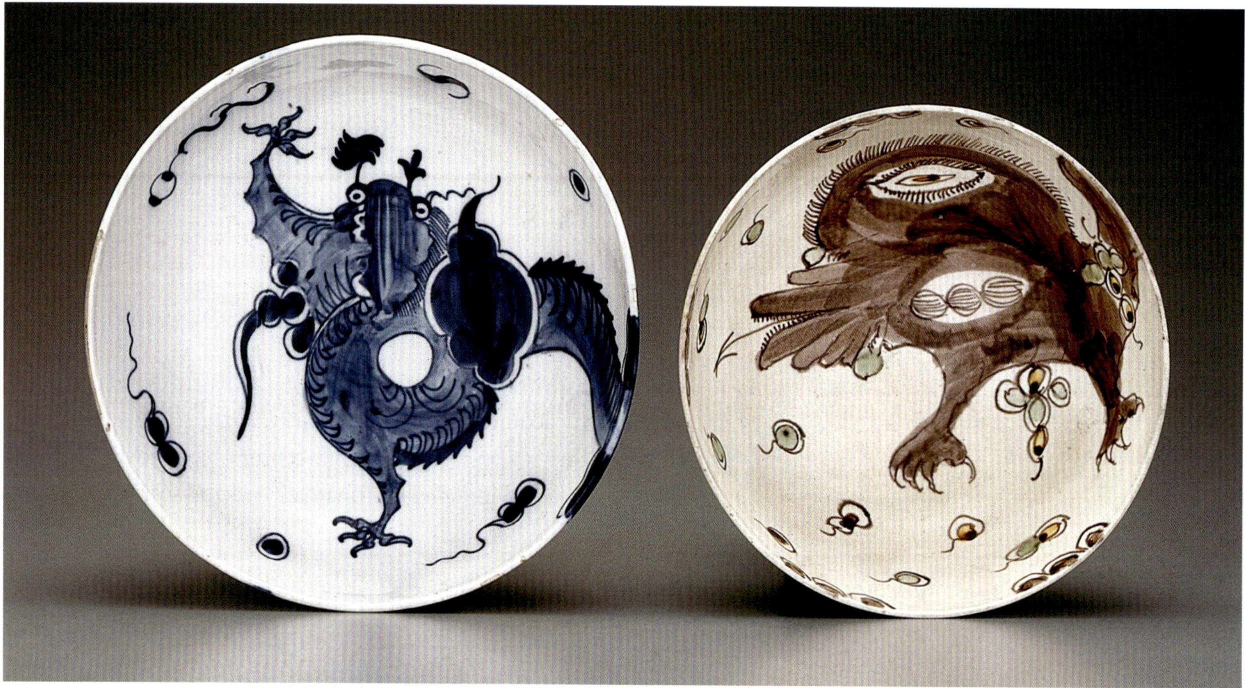

Figure 2 Details of the interiors of the punch bowls illustrated in fig. 1, showing the head and upper body of the dragons.

highlights. The circa 1780 Staffordshire pearlware punch bowl with underglaze cobalt decoration exemplifies what has been called "china glaze," a refined earthenware body imitative of blue-and-white porcelain.[4] These two examples demonstrate the enduring popularity of this motif, as documented on Chinese porcelain, English delft, Worcester and Bow porcelain, and, now, creamware and pearlware.

Figure 3 Teapot, Staffordshire, England, ca. 1770. Stoneware. H. 5½". (Chipstone Foundation; photo, Gavin Ashworth.)

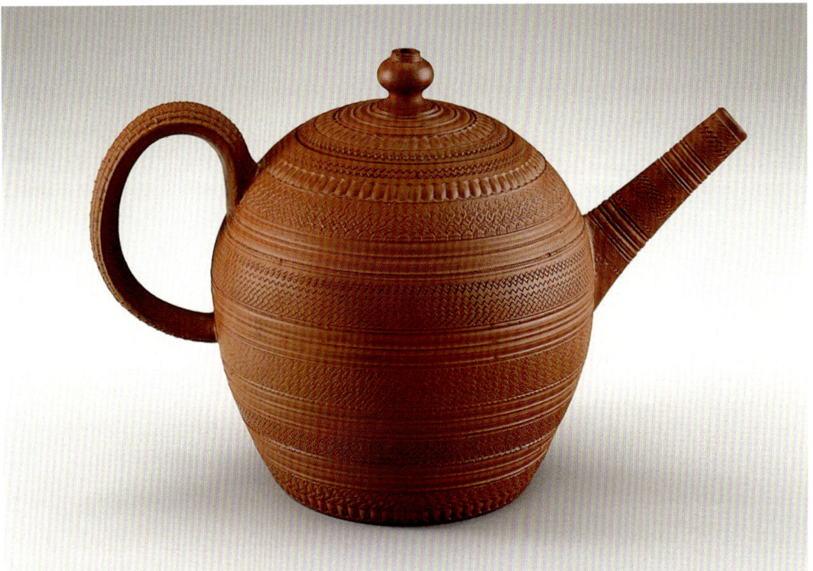

Figure 4 Detail of roulette decoration on the body of the teapot illustrated in fig. 3.

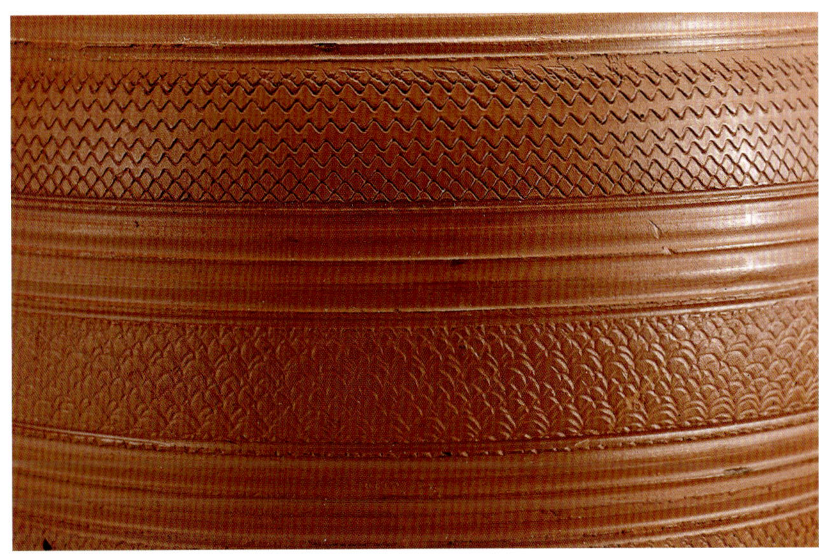

Figure 5 Detail of roulette decoration on the spout of the teapot illustrated in fig. 3.

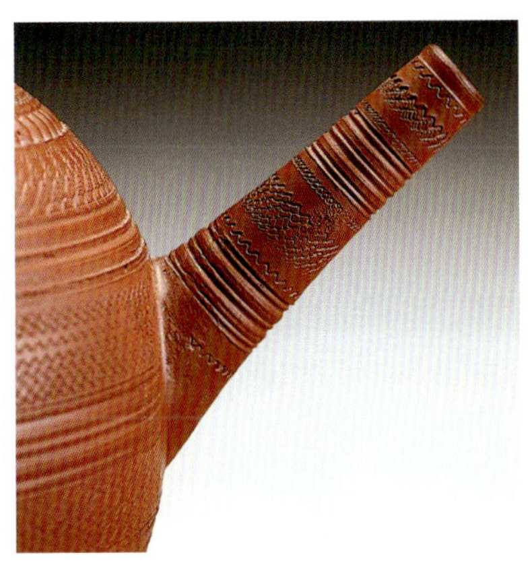

The third recently acquired object helps illustrate the economic constraints of surface embellishment on late-eighteenth-century Staffordshire red stoneware (fig. 3). As discussed in detail by Jonathan Rickard and Don Carpentier in this volume ("The Little Engine That Could," pp. 78–99), the creation of surface decoration by engine turning was a major development in Staffordshire after 1770. At first glance this redware stoneware teapot seems to bear the characteristics typical of engine turning, but close inspection shows that the surface treatment was applied using a series of decorative rouletting wheels (fig. 4). Even the spout and lid bear roulette decoration (fig. 5). This piece is further evidence of the use of roulettes to simulate engine-turning decoration without the expense of owning the more complicated engine-turning lathe.

Robert Hunter
Editor, *Ceramics in America*
<CeramicJournal@aol.com>

1. Lars Tharp, *Hogarth's China* (London: Merrell Holberton, 1997), p. 49.

2. John Austin, *British Delft at Williamsburg* (Williamsburg, Va.: The Colonial Williamsburg Foundation, 1994), p. 94.

3. Jonathan Horne, *English Pottery and Related Works of Art 2002* (London: Jonathan Horne Antiques, Ltd., 2002), p. 22.

4. George L. Miller and Robert Hunter, "How Creamware Got the Blues: The Origins of China Glaze and Pearlware," in *Ceramics in America*, edited by Robert Hunter (Hanover, N.H.: University Press of New England for the Chipstone Foundation, 2001): 135–61.

Mary C. Beaudry

A Pernicious Influence? Japanese Water Drop Ware

Over the years I have puzzled over an odd-looking type of ceramic ware found at archaeological sites in New England, usually represented by a single potsherd. It is a high-fired earthenware so dense it resembles dry-bodied stoneware, with a thick brown glaze that seems to curdle atop the surface of the pot (fig. 1).

An example of this ware found at the Narbonne House in Salem, Massachusetts, during excavations there in the 1970s was identified as German stoneware, but, as is usual in archaeology, the analysts were more interested in the preponderance of the ceramics than in this single, seemingly anomalous, find and did not undertake research into its history.[1] A similar single sherd among the ceramics recovered from excavations at a nineteenth-century boardinghouse in Lowell, Massachusetts, also generated little interest—our analysis did not even mention the ware because the single sherd was not statistically significant in the collection.[2] In the late 1980s, we found another single potsherd of the ware, this time beneath the kitchen floor of the Spencer-Peirce-Little House (SPL) in Newbury, Massachusetts; this was a rim sherd—a lid seating for a vessel like a tea canister.[3] Again it was a single sherd, found in a nineteenth-century context but not considered worthy of much attention. But in 1996 excavations at SPL began to turn up numerous examples of what my students referred to as "wormy ware," "dog-hair ware," or "ugly ware."

Soon we had enough fragments to make up at least one teapot and one tea canister, and I realized I needed to know what this ware was and what significance it might have, if any, to my interpretation of the site. A colleague in art history suggested the pottery was Japanese, so I began to look into the literature on Japanese pottery. None of the art books carried anything that resembled my "wormy ware,"[4] but I soon learned that after the United States opened trade with Japan in the Meiji period (1868–1912), Americans were seized with a passion for goods, particularly decorative art objects, from Japan.[5] *Japonisme,* as the craze was known, was fed by the ramped-up production of Japanese kilns and factories, which churned out goods for export that American consumers adored but that lovers of fine art declared gaudy and grotesque—one writer declared that "even in an industrial museum their influence would be pernicious."[6]

The definitive attribution for my mysterious "wormy ware" I found in trade catalogs for A. A. Vantine & Co. of New York, importers of fine Oriental art and furnishings.[7] My teapot and tea canister fragments were indeed

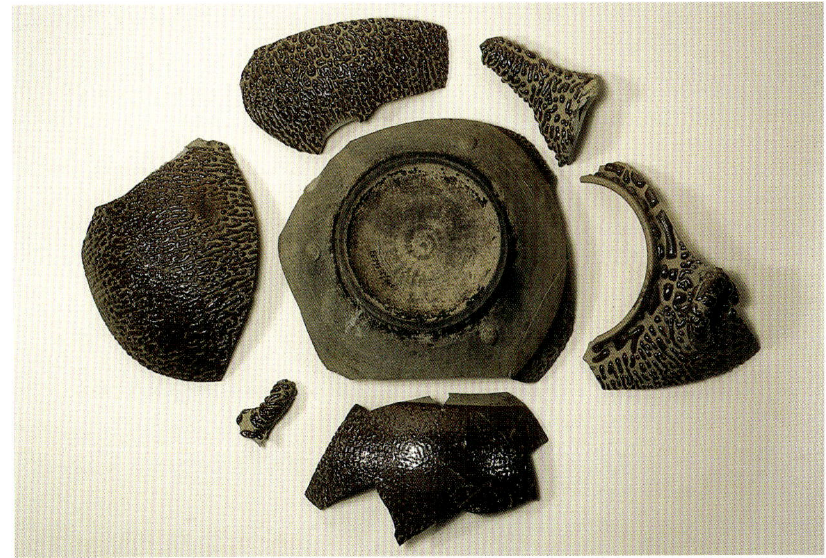

Figure 1 Sherds of a Japanese Water Drop ware teapot found in an 1870s context at the Spencer-Peirce-Little Farm, Newbury, Massachusetts. Note the charring on the base of the teapot. (Photo, Michael Hamilton.)

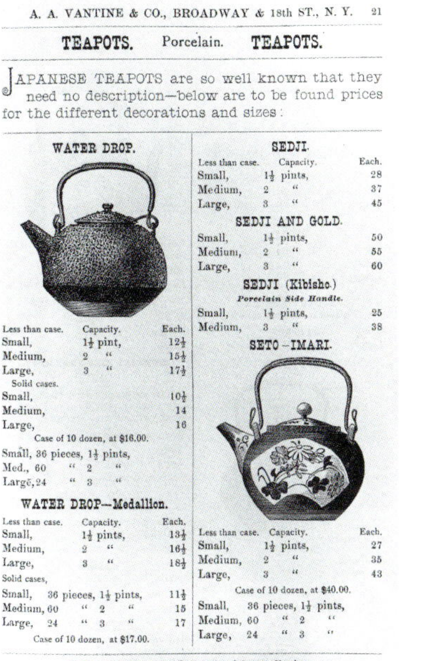

A. A. VANTINE & CO., BROADWAY & 18th ST., N. Y. 21

TEAPOTS. Porcelain. **TEAPOTS.**

JAPANESE TEAPOTS are so well known that they need no description—below are to be found prices for the different decorations and sizes:

WATER DROP.

Less than case.	Capacity.	Each.
Small,	1½ pint,	12½
Medium,	2 "	15½
Large,	3 "	17½
Solid cases.		
Small,		10½
Medium,		14
Large,		16

Case of 10 dozen, at $16.00.

Small, 36 pieces, 1½ pints,
Med., 60 " 2 "
Large, 24 " 3 "

WATER DROP—Medallion.

Less than case.	Capacity.	Each.
Small,	1½ pints,	13½
Medium,	2 "	16½
Large,	3 "	18½
Solid cases,		
Small, 36 pieces,	1½ pints,	11½
Medium, 60 "	2 "	15
Large, 24 "	3 "	17

Case of 10 dozen, at $17.00.

SEDJI.

Less than case.	Capacity.	Each.
Small,	1½ pints,	28
Medium,	2 "	37
Large,	3 "	45

SEDJI AND GOLD.

Small,	1½ pints,	50
Medium,	2 "	55
Large,	3 "	60

SEDJI (Kibisho.)

Porcelain Side Handle.

Small,	1½ pints,	25
Medium,	3 "	38

SETO-IMARI.

Less than case.	Capacity.	Each.
Small,	1½ pints,	27
Medium,	2 "	35
Large,	3 "	43

Case of 10 dozen, at $40.00.

Small, 36 pieces, 1½ pints,
Medium, 60 " 2 "
Large, 24 " 3 "

Prices Subject to Change without Notice.

Figure 2 Advertisement for Japanese teapots from an 1890s catalog produced by A. A. Vantine & Co. of New York. Water Drop teapots are here offered wholesale in a variety of sizes. (Courtesy, The Winterthur Library, Printed Book and Periodical Collection.)

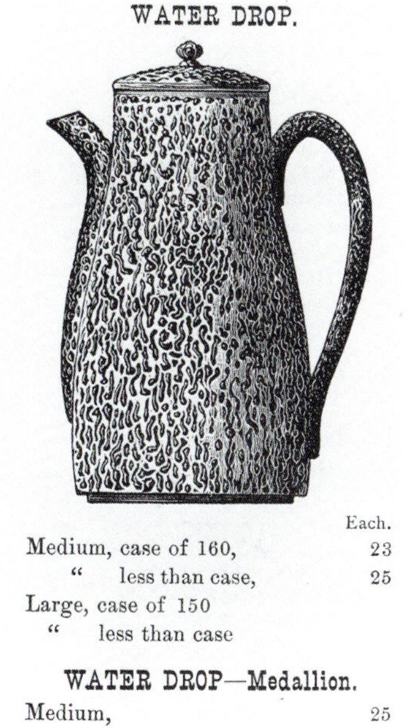

WATER DROP.

	Each.
Medium, case of 160,	23
" less than case,	25
Large, case of 150	
" less than case	

WATER DROP—Medallion.

Medium,	25

Figure 3 A Water Drop chocolate pot offered for sale by Vantine's in its 1890s catalog. (Courtesy, The Winterthur Library, Printed Book and Periodical Collection.)

among the vessel forms produced in Japan for export during the Meiji period (fig. 2). The Vantine catalogs refer to the ware as "Water Drop" and claim that it was so popular and well known it needed little description. A catalog from the 1890s explained that the ware was a porous earthenware, called "Water Drop" from the resemblance of the glaze to drops of water; made in teapots and water bottles, the latter used in hot countries to keep water cool by placing them in a draft, evaporation taking the place of ice. The teapots are known all over the country and need no special mention. Some have a medallion with paintings of flowers and shrubs in glazed paint on the side; those are known as Water Drop Medallion.[8]

The catalogs showed teapots and chocolate pots (fig. 3) and mentioned, but did not illustrate, Water Drop Medallion, nor have I seen any examples from archaeological or other contexts. Soon after my discovery in the

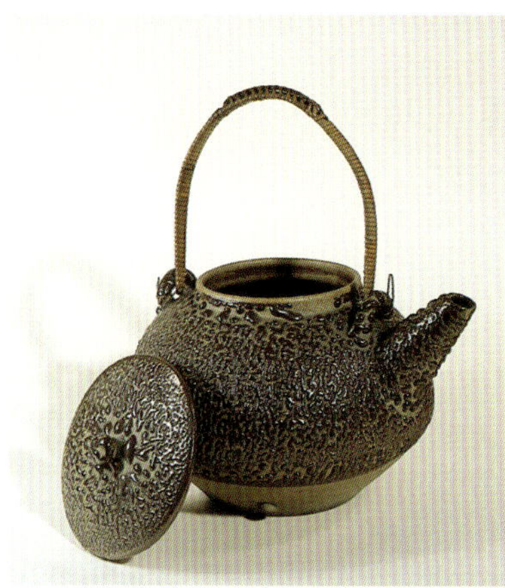

Figure 4 Teapot, Japan, 1870–1890. Earthenware. H. 4¾". An intact example of a Water Drop pattern. (Author's collection; photo, Michael Hamilton.)

archives, I came across an intact example of a Japanese Water Drop teapot at a local flea market (fig. 4). Like the example found at SPL, it is small in capacity and shows evidence (i.e., slight charring) of having been placed atop a burner of some sort; the base of each teapot has three small bumps that may have facilitated placing the vessel upon a burner.

Beyond the craze for things Japanese, the Victorians also found anything considered rustic to be very appealing as an element of household decor. Water Drop ware exhibits a certain rustic character, and this, along with its links to *japonisme,* may have been at the root of its appeal to Victorian Americans.[9] Archaeologists would do well to consider the cultural context in which this seemingly innocuous and, to many a modern eye, unattractive ware was used. It enabled its owners to express metaphorically an aesthetic of rusticity and to exhibit a knowledge of things Oriental. The number of sherds we find may be statistically insignificant but even a single Water Drop teapot carried complex meanings for its owners and for those invited to partake of tea poured from it.

ACKNOWLEDGMENTS My research on Water Drop ware was conducted in 2001 under the auspices of a National Endowment for the Humanities Fellowship for Advanced Study at The Winterthur Museum and Library. I am especially grateful to Neville Thompson, former librarian at Winterthur, for guiding me toward the A. A. Vantine & Co. trade catalogs in the Winterthur collection. I also thank Grace Ziesing for sharing with me her notes on the family history project she is conducting.

Mary C. Beaudry, Ph.D.
Associate Professor of Archaeology and Anthropology
Department of Archaeology
Boston University
<beaudry@bu.edu>

1. Geoffrey P. Moran, Anne E. Yentsch, and Edward F. Zimmer, *Archeological Investigations at the Narbonne House, Salem Maritime National Historic Site, Massachusetts,* Cultural Resources Management Study, no. 6 (Boston: National Park Service, North Atlantic Regional Office, 1982).

2. David H. Dutton, "'Thrasher's China' or Colored Porcelain: Ceramics from a Boott Mills Boardinghouse and Tenement," in *Interdisciplinary Investigations of the Boott Mills, Lowell, Massachusetts. Volume III: The Boardinghouse System as a Way of Life,* edited by Mary C. Beaudry and Stephen A. Mrozowski, Cultural Resources Management Study, no. 21 (Boston: National Park Service, North Atlantic Regional Office, 1989), pp. 83–120.

3. See, e.g., Mary C. Beaudry, "Scratching the Surface: Seven Seasons at the Spencer-Peirce-Little Farm, Newbury, Massachusetts," *Northeast Historical Archaeology* 24 (1995): 19–50, and Mary C. Beaudry, "Farm Journal: First Person, Four Voices," *Historical Archaeology* 32, no. 1 (1998): 20–33.

4. Kikusaburo Fukui, *Japanese Ceramic Art and National Characteristics* (Tokyo: N.p., 1926); Barry Till and Paula Swart, *The Flowering of Japanese Ceramic Art: Late 16th Century to the Present/L'épanouissement de l'art céramique japonais de la fin du seizième siècle à nos jours,* exh. cat. (Victoria, B.C.: Art Gallery of Greater Victoria, 1983); Tadanari Mitsuoka, *Ceramic Art of Japan,* 5th ed. (Tokyo: Japan Travel Bureau, 1960).

5. William Hosley, *The Japan Idea: Art and Life in Victorian America,* exh. cat. (Hartford, Conn.: Wadsworth Atheneum, 1990); Siegfried Wichmann, *Japonisme: The Japanese Influence on Western Art since 1858* (New York: Thames and Hudson, 1999).

6. A Professor Morse, as quoted by James Lord Bowes in *A Vindication of the Decorated Pottery of Japan* (Liverpool: Printed for private circulation by D. Marples and Company, 1891); in this book Bowes defended himself against criticism by Morse and others of his earlier work, *Japanese Pottery* (Liverpool: E. Howell, 1890), in which he had gone so far as to suggest that some examples of "Modern" Japanese pottery possessed artistic merit.

7. A. A. Vantine & Co., *Illustrated Catalogue of A. A. Vantine & Co., Importers from the Empires of Japan China India Turkey Persia and the East, Broadway and 18th Street, New York* (New York: A. A. Vantine & Co., 1880). Although there are several Vantine catalogs in the Winterthur Collection of Printed Books and Periodicals and one in the Trade Catalogue Collection of the Library at the University of Delaware, none produced after circa 1900 includes Water Drop ware among its offerings, so one might deduce that the ware went out of production and/or popularity before, or by the end of, the Meiji period.

Grace H. Ziesing, in her notes on her family history that she generously shared with me, records that A. A. Vantine & Co. was owned and operated by one of her ancestors, James Irving Raymond, who passed it on to his son Irving. The business originally operated at 827/829 Broadway, New York, but in 1913 it moved to 5th Avenue and 39th Street. Irving sold the business in 1922; Vantine's no longer exists.

8. Vantine & Co., *Illustrated Catalogue*, p. 5.

9. Katherine C. Grier, "Material Culture as Rhetoric: 'Animal Artifacts' as a Case Study," in *American Material Culture: The Shape of the Field*, edited by Ann Smart Martin and J. Ritchie Garrison (Winterthur, Del.: Henry Francis Du Pont Winterthur Museum, 1997; distributed by University of Tennessee Press, Knoxville), pp. 65–104, quote on p. 96.

Lisa Ellis

An Investigation into "Ghosts" and Gilding on a Kangxi Porcelain Pot in the J. Paul Getty Museum

In 2001 the J. Paul Getty Museum acquired a Chinese gilded porcelain teapot made between 1662 and 1690, in the Kangxi period (1662–1722). Finely worked European silver mounts encase this porcelain vessel, which is marked on its base with an artemisia leaf (fig. 1). The teapot exhibits two

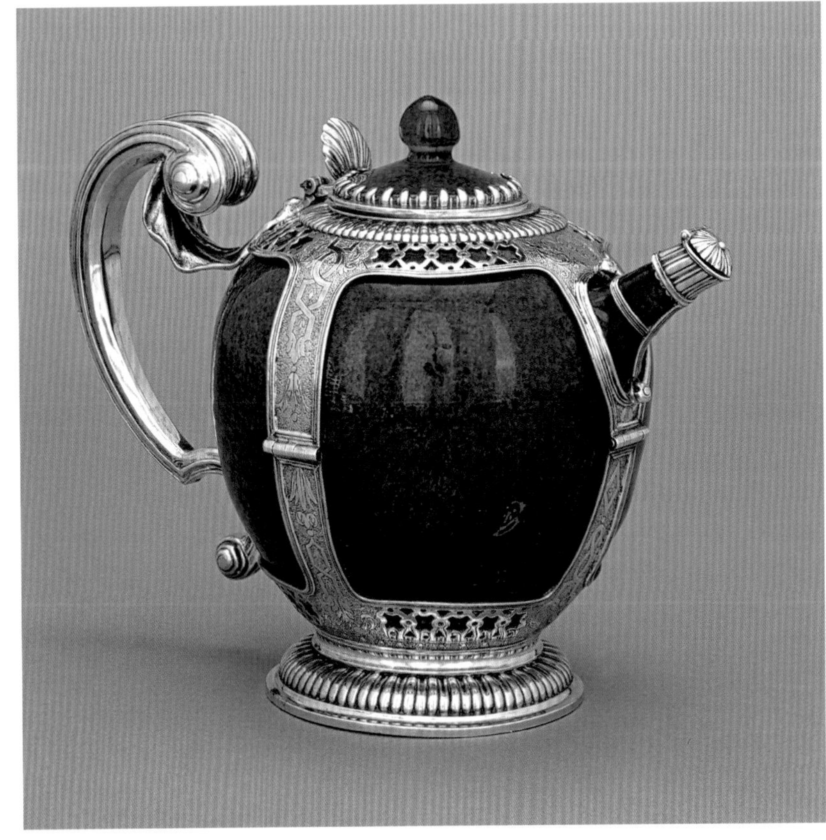

Figure 1 Gilded teapot, China, 1662–1690. Porcelain. H. 6". The vessel is fitted with European silver mounts. (Courtesy, J. Paul Getty Museum; acc. no. 2001.76.)

small but significant areas of damage, partially hidden by trellis work in the silver mounts. These suggest that the pot's handle originally spanned the top of the vessel. Most likely deliberate, the removal of the handle has damaged the glaze: the surface has been ground away, revealing a white body. The silver replacement handle is now located at the side, opposite the spout.[1]

The teapot's rich blue speckled glaze has many names that describe either the way it was applied, its color, or both: "blown blue," *blue soufflé, fouette,* the "Mazarin technique," and *ch'ui ch'ing*. This method of glaze application, by no means restricted to the color blue, was described by T'ang Ying, a director of the imperial porcelain manufacture at Jingdezhen in the mid-eighteenth century—or about fifty years after the creation of the Getty teapot:

> A bamboo tube one inch in diameter and some seven inches long has one of its ends bound round with a fine gauze, which is dipped repeatedly into the glaze and blown through from the other end. The number of times that this process has to be repeated depends partly on the size of the piece, partly on the nature of the glaze, varying from three or four times up to seventeen or eighteen.[2]

In the case of the Getty teapot, the "blown blue" glaze was further decorated with gilding. Not surprisingly, it is in very poor condition, and worn away where it was not protected by the silver mounts (fig. 2). While this is

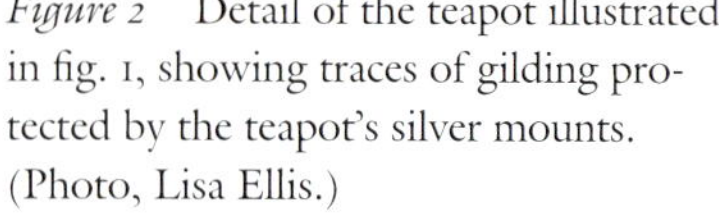

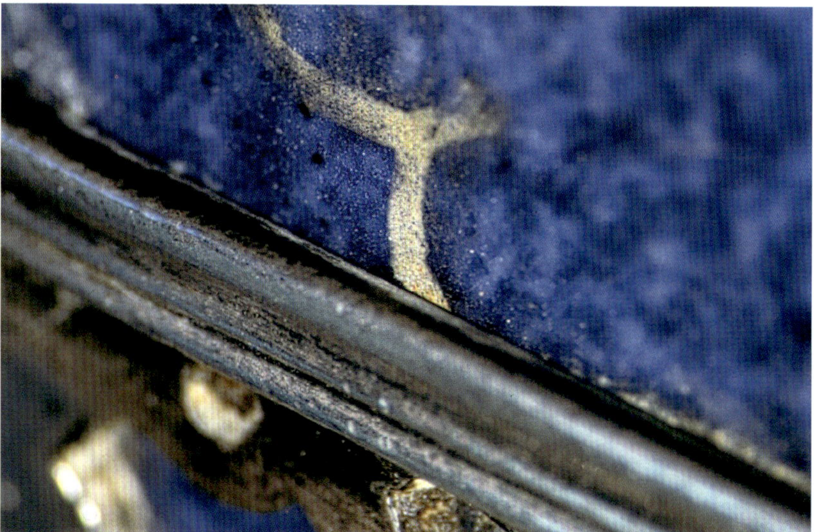

Figure 2 Detail of the teapot illustrated in fig. 1, showing traces of gilding protected by the teapot's silver mounts. (Photo, Lisa Ellis.)

typical of many surviving Kangxi gilded vessels, a well-preserved, gilded porcelain brush holder of the same date, from the collection of Augustus the Strong, is a fortunate anomaly.[3]

Although only traces of the gilding survive, the teapot's original appearance can be reconstructed. Areas that were once gilded can be distinguished, with some difficulty, from areas that were never gilded. The former appear matte, which evidently is linked to the method of gilding as described below. Unfortunately, photography of these areas is made nearly impossible by the vessel's shape and highly reflective glaze. A quarter of the gilded design was re-created by manipulating a digital image (fig. 3).

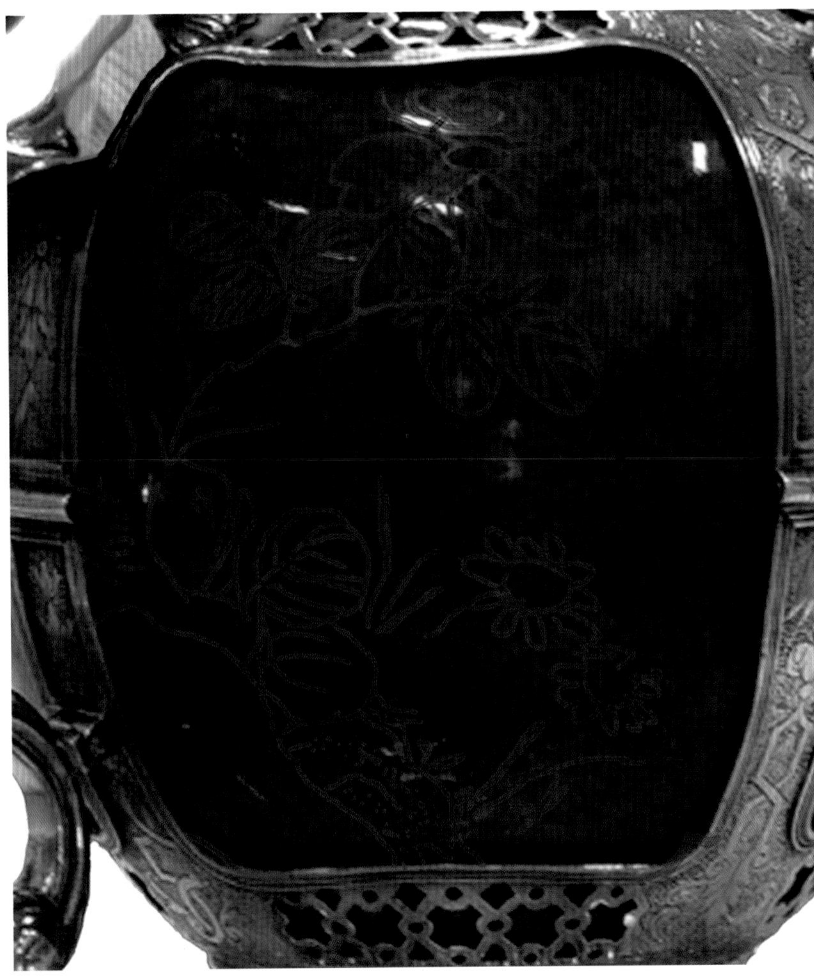

Figure 3 Digital reconstruction of a gilded area on the teapot illustrated in fig. 1.

Analysis of the Gilding

The teapot's gilding was analyzed using Quantitative X-Ray Fluorescence (XRF) analysis.[4] Two areas were tested: a gilded area and a matte area, or an area from which the gilding has disappeared. The results of the XRF analysis showed that, as expected, most of the gilding is composed of gold (table 1). Unexpected, however, were the lead counts: the results indicate that there is about twice as much lead in the gilded area as in the matte area.

TABLE 1

	Co	Ni	Cu	Zn	Ag	*Au*	Sn	Fe	Pb	As	Mn
Gilded Area	80.121	10.431	2.533	0.000	4.657	*146.675*	2.654	80.121	84.758	3.54	170.835
Matte Area	39.828	12.244	0.311	2.925	0.181	*1.927*	1.653	85.149	41.239	0.00	160.860

Results of XRF analysis: figures are given in counts/sec

Père d'Entrecolles, a Jesuit priest who was stationed in China in the late seventeenth and early eighteenth centuries, described in detail a gilding process he witnessed in the ceramic factories of Jingdezhen. It should be noted here that while some of the minutiae of the priest's accounts are clearly wrong, much of the information he relayed appears trustworthy.

In a letter sent on September 1, 1712, from Jao-chou, Kangxi province, the Jesuit priest describes the sequence of decoration, firing, and applying overglaze gilding in the manufacture of porcelain. After an initial firing, gilding was put on the surface of the porcelain, which was then refired in a special furnace.[5] Père d'Entrecolles then outlines how the gold and white lead mixture was prepared and applied:

> When one wishes to apply gold, one grinds it and one mixes it in the bottom of a porcelain vessel until one sees a little cloud of gold in the bottom of the water. One allows it to dry and then uses it by mixing it in a sufficient amount of gummed water. With thirty parts of gold one incorporates three parts of white lead, and then one applies it to porcelain just like a colored glaze.[6]

Evidently, the lead white or *ceruse* was employed as a flux to lower the much higher melting point of the gold. As indicated in d'Entrecolles's letter, this use of lead white is undoubtedly related to its use, together with gum water, in the preparation of overglaze, fired-on enamel colors in Jingdezhen, described elsewhere and in greater detail by d'Entrecolles.[7]

While the results of the XRF analysis of the matte areas on the Getty teapot indicate that lead, the metal with the lower melting point, is still on the surface, or shallowly embedded therein, its presence may not be exclusively responsible for the matte appearance of the glaze. Recently published is an account of fired-on gilding from a probably much earlier date, discovered on a Northern Song stoneware, a conical bowl with russet glaze.[8] As in the case of the Getty teapot, examination revealed patterns of "ghosts" in areas believed to have been gilded on the interior of the eleventh-century vessel. The "ghosts" seem to be permanently fixed in the glaze.[9] Subtle clues in the appearance of the matte areas led the investigators to believe that delicate patterns cut out of gold leaf, backed with a textile, were bonded to the ceramic before firing with an unidentified adhesive. While the authors admit there is no way to know whether garlic juice, as described in the writings of the late Song literatus Zhou Mi (1232–1298), was used in the preparation of the gold, they do believe that the gilding was fired in place, as Zhou Mi's accounts also suggest.

Identified with XRF analysis, the presence of lead in the gilding of the Getty teapot is corroborated by Père d'Entrecolles's accounts of porcelain manufacture in Jingdezhen in the early eighteenth century. While the presence of lead may be at least partially responsible for the appearance of the matte areas on the surface of the glaze, it must be stressed that similar matte patterns also appear to have been caused by a very different, lead-free gilding process. Further research might determine whether matte patterns or "ghosts" on Chinese glazes can be reliably linked to fired-on gilding processes, regardless of gilding composition or method of application.

ACKNOWLEDGMENTS This research was carried out while I was a graduate intern in the department of Decorative Art and Sculpture Conservation at the J. Paul Getty Museum. For their support I would like to thank Brian Considine and Jane Bassett of the department of Decorative

Arts and Sculpture Conservation; curator Gillian Wilson and associate curator Jeffrey Weaver at the J. Paul Getty Museum; as well as senior scientist Dr. David Scott and graduate intern Satoko Tanimoto, both formerly of the Getty Conservation Institute's Museum Research Lab. I would also like to extend gratitude to the Curator of Chinese Art, Robert D. Mowry, and assistant Adam Osgood for allowing me to examine the bowl in the collection of the Arthur M. Sackler Museum.

Lisa Ellis
Sherman Fairchild Fellow in Objects Conservation
Museum of Fine Arts, Boston
<LEllis@mfa.org>

1. For a well-documented and illustrated example of a similar case, please see the description of a mounted Kangxi porcelain vessel, also in the collection of the J. Paul Getty Museum, from which the spout, handle, and finial were removed in the eighteenth century to accommodate French gilt bronze mounts. F. J.B. Watson and G. Wilson, *Mounted Oriental Porcelain in the J. Paul Getty Museum* (Santa Monica, Calif.: J. Paul Getty Museum, 1982), pp. 74–76, no. 16.

2. See "Dipping into the Glaze and Blowing on the Glaze," in Robert Tichane, *Ching-te-chen: Views of a Porcelain City* (Painted Post, N.Y.: New York State Institute for Glaze Research, 1983), p. 156, no. 13, ill.

3. See Eva Ströber, *"La Maladie de Porcelaine": East Asian Porcelain from the Collection of Augustus the Strong,* exh. cat., Albertinum Dresden (Berlin: Edition Leipzig, 2001), no. 44.

4. X-ray fluorescence is a nondestructive analytical technique in which the elements present on an object's surface are detected using X rays. The analysis was carried out in the J. Paul Getty Museum Research Laboratory using a Kevex 0750A instrument, set at 50 kV, 3.3 mA, with a Ba/Sr secondary target and collimators of 3 mm on the X-ray tube and 4 mm on the detector of 200 seconds acquisition time. As there was no standard with which to compare, the readings of the gilded and ungilded ceramic were not normalized. The spectra were acquired by Satoko Tanimoto under the direction of Dr. David Scott, Senior Scientist, Museum Research Laboratory, Getty Conservation Institute. For a description of the analysis of silver embellishment on Chinese export wares, see Shirley Maloney Mueller, "Surface Silver Decoration on Chinese Export Porcelain: An Analytic Approach," *Oriental Art* 48, no. 4 (2002): 43–46.

5. In d'Entrecolles's own words, "on cuit la porcelaine; apres quoy on y applique l'or, & on la recuit de nouveau dans un forneau particulier"; Stephen W. Bushell, *Description of Chinese Pottery and Porcelain* (Oxford, Eng.: Clarendon Press, 1910), p. 195.

6. Ibid. The French text reads: "Quand on veut appliquer l'or, on le broye, & on le dissoud au fond d'une porcelaine, jusqu'à ce qu'on voye au dessous de l'eau un petit ciel d'or. On le laisse secher, & lorsqu'on doit l'employer, on le dissoud par partie dans une quantité suffisante d'eau gommée: avec trente parties d'or on incorpore trois parties de ceruse, & on applique sur la porcelaine de mesme que les couleurs"; Tichane, *Ching-te-chen,* pp. 83–84.

7. Tichane, *Ching-te-chen,* p. 81.

8. The bowl is in the Arthur M. Sackler Museum, Harvard University Art Museums (acc. no. 1919.207). See Robert D. Mowry, *Hare's Fur, Tortoiseshell, and Partridge Feathers: Chinese Brown- and Black-Glazed Ceramics, 400–1400,* exh. cat. (Cambridge, Mass.: Harvard University Art Museums, 1996), pp. 108–10, no. 15.

9. After examination, conservators washed these areas with purified water and conservation grade detergent, and applied an impermanent coating in acetone for research purposes without damaging the "ghosts." Earl S. Tai, "Analysis of a Sung Ceramic Bowl" (unpublished research paper for Fine Arts 202, Harvard University, fall 1990), unpaginated.

Linda R. Shulsky

Sherds of Chinese Porcelain Found at Old Mobile

Sherds of Chinese porcelain have been found at the site of Old Mobile, Alabama, which was occupied by the French from 1702 to 1711. The settlers at Old Mobile traded with the nearby Spanish settlements of Pensacola, and also with Havana and Veracruz, so it is likely that the porcelain came to Old Mobile via the Manila galleon trade. Most are decorated with cobalt blue but some were painted with overglaze red and gold enamels. Although some have been discussed in previous articles (the excavation under the direction of Dr. Gregory Waselkov began in 1989), continuing excavations have turned up additional sherds painted with red and gold enamels that are worthy of further comment.[1]

The sherds of thin, fine-bodied porcelain were most likely produced at Jingdezhen, the porcelain-making city in southern China. They are of a type called Chinese Imari, because they copied Japanese wares shipped from the port of Imari. The pieces were made during the latter part of the Kangxi period (1662–1722) of the Qing dynasty (1644–1911), by which time Chinese potters had the skill to manufacture pieces of any size and with almost any kind of decoration.

The Chinese had been making porcelain since the Sui dynasty (581–618), but Europeans could not manufacture true porcelain until 1710, when the Meissen factory in Germany was started. Chinese porcelain was coveted in Europe and in European colonies because of its white, dense body, which was resonant when struck, impervious to liquid, and translucent. Stoneware and earthenware did not possess these traits, making them less desirable alternatives.

Chinese and Japanese Imari wares were produced strictly for export, and European customers eagerly collected them. The usual palette for both Chinese and Japanese Imari included underglaze blue; the Old Mobile sherds, however, contain only red and gold enamels. This palette is called "blood and milk" in the Netherlands, and although rare in the United States, Dutch museums contain many examples. One of the largest porcelain collections in Europe in the early eighteenth century—formed by Augustus the Strong, elector of Saxony and king of Poland (1670–1733), and much of which is still intact at Dresden—contains many examples.

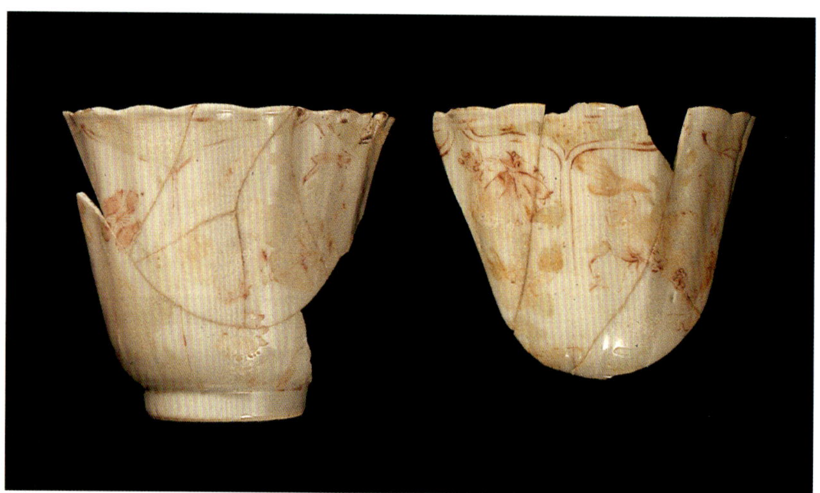

Figure 1 Fluted cups, China, early eighteenth century. Porcelain. *Left:* H. 3". (Photos, courtesy of the author.) The exterior is decorated with delicate flowers over the glaze.

The two fluted cups are similar but not identical; both are decorated with delicate flowers both on the exterior (fig. 1) and the interior (fig. 2). The six-sided cup (fig. 3) exhibits floral decoration on the exterior and an unidentifiable red decoration on the interior. The exterior base (fig. 4) is

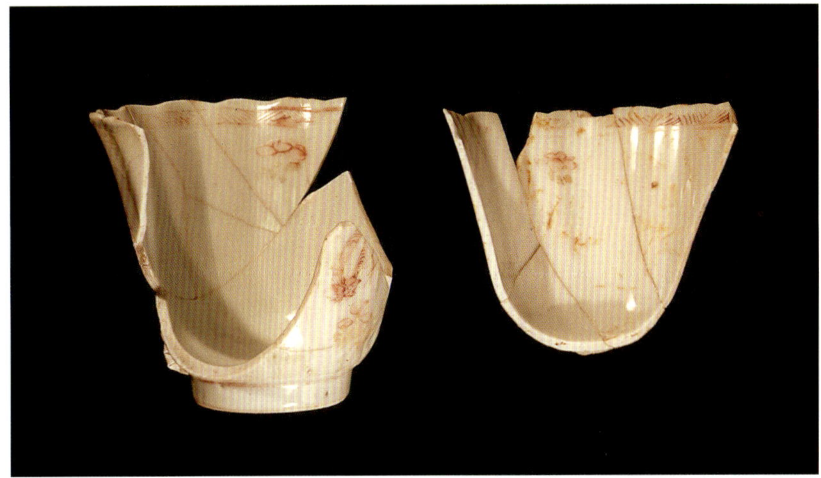

Figure 2 Interior of the cups illustrated in fig. 1. Overglaze flowers ornament the interior surfaces, as well.

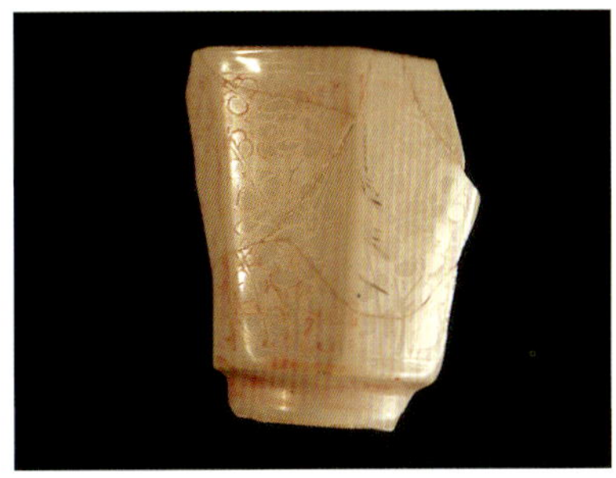

Figure 3 Cup, China, early eighteenth century. Porcelain. H. 2¾". This hexagonal cup is adorned on the exterior with a floral decoration.

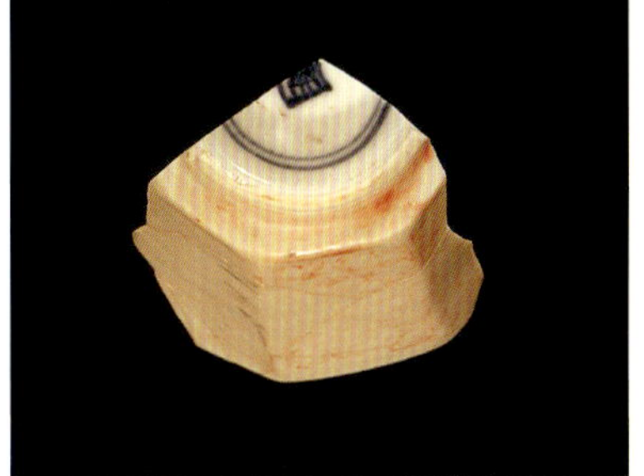

Figure 4 Base of the cup illustrated in fig. 4 displaying unidentified underglaze mark.

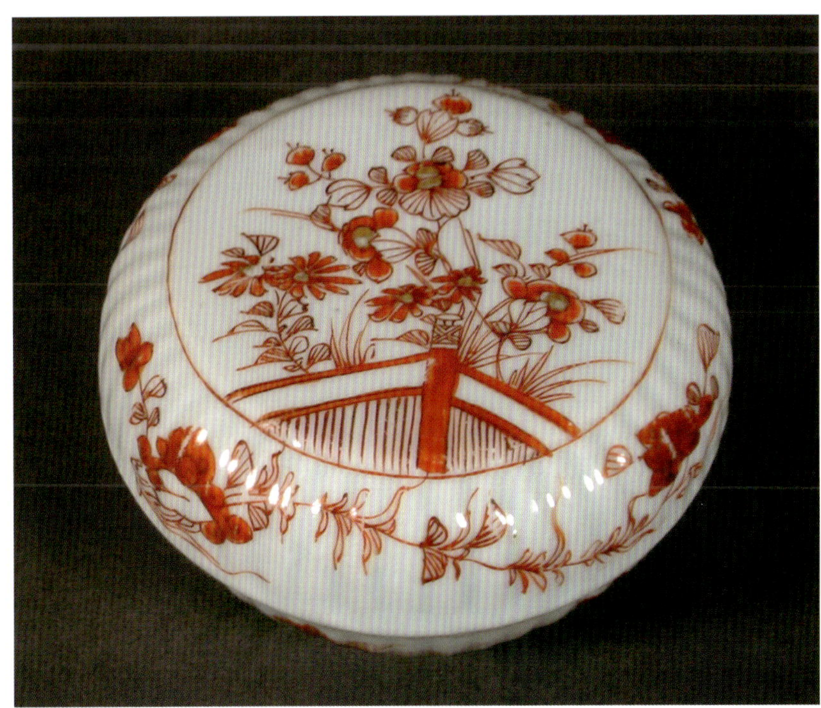

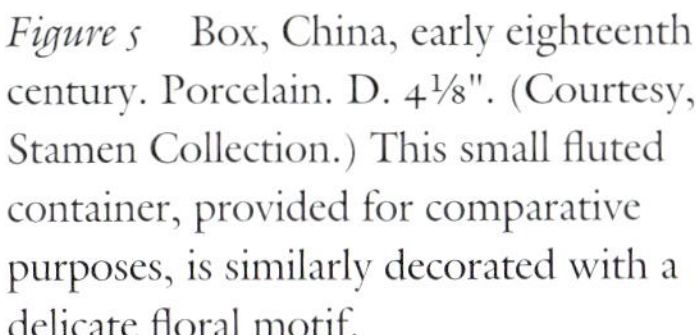

Figure 5 Box, China, early eighteenth century. Porcelain. D. 4⅛". (Courtesy, Stamen Collection.) This small fluted container, provided for comparative purposes, is similarly decorated with a delicate floral motif.

painted in underglaze blue with a mark inside the double ring typically found on pieces made during the Kangxi period. Unfortunately, the mark cannot be identified.[2]

The overglaze decoration on the cups is difficult to see because much of it has worn away from burial. I have provided a comparative piece (fig. 5) that is similarly decorated. The box has delicate floral decoration and fluted sides.

Linda R. Shulsky
Art historian and author
<Lshulsky@aol.com>

1. Linda R. Shulsky, "Chinese Porcelain in Old Mobile," *Antiques* 150, no. 1 (1996): 80–89.
2. Linda R. Shulsky, "Chinese Porcelain at Old Mobile," *Historical Archaeology* 36, no. 1 (2002): 97–104. Ceramic experts at the National Palace Museum in Beijing also were unable to identify this mark.

Sara A. Hahn

The John Dortch Site: Anglo Elegance on the Spanish Louisiana Frontier

The John Dortch archaeological site is located near St. Francisville, West Feliciana Parish, Louisiana. Occupied between 1794 and 1799, the site, then part of Spanish West Florida, is one of only a few Spanish-colonial period settlements in the area. Dortch, a Revolutionary War veteran from South Carolina, settled his family here while Spain was still in control of the region. While most contemporary sites in South Louisiana yield French ceramics despite being under Spanish rule, excavation of the Dortch site produced numerous English wares and very few French ceramics.

Approximately 5 percent of the artifacts recovered from the site are historic ceramics. These consist mostly of creamware and pearlware in a variety of decorations. Other English wares within the assemblage include black-glazed redware, delft, basalt, and unglazed red stoneware.

A mere seventy sherds of creamware are decorated, yet the variety of decoration is remarkable. The decorations employed include overglaze transfer-printed sherds in red as well as black; overglaze hand-painted sherds in red;

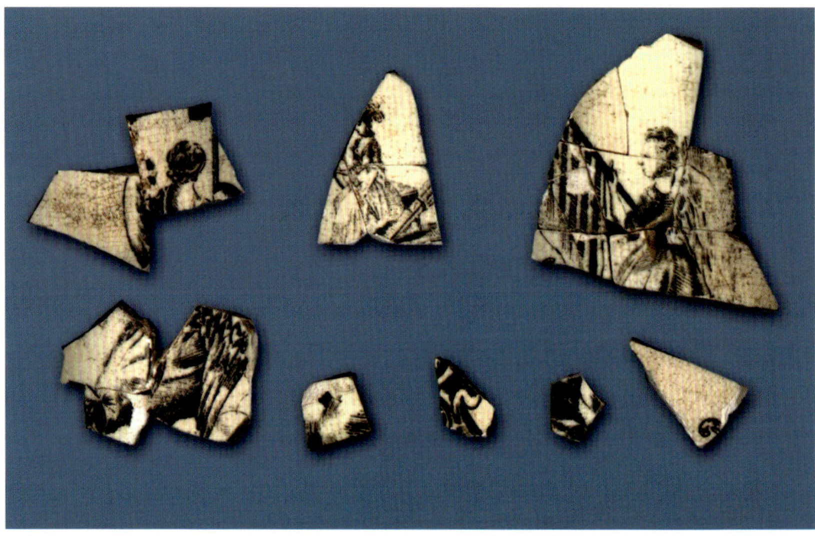

Figure 1 Jug sherds, Liverpool, ca. 1785–1790. Creamware. (Photos, courtesy Coastal Environments, Inc.) The transfer print commemorates the Revolutionary War with the "Success to the United States of America" pattern.

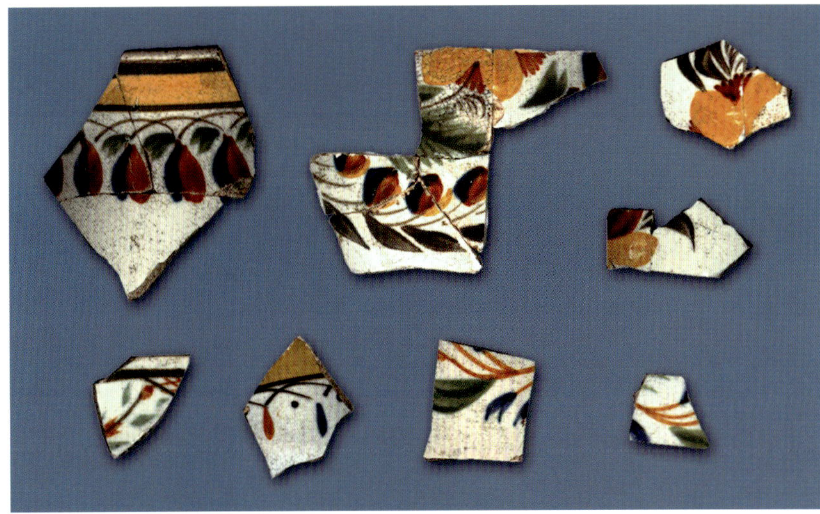

Figure 2 Fragments of hand-painted polychrome vessels found at the Dortch site, Staffordshire, ca. 1795–1799. Pearlware.

and molded sherds. Several of the black transfer-printed sherds were reconstructed into a portion of a Liverpool jug commemorating the Revolutionary War (fig. 1). The pattern, "Success to the United States of America," is considered rare in antique collections.[1] The molded sherds represent portions of a breadbasket and a candlestick.

Over half of the pearlwares are decorated and mostly represent teawares. The majority of these are polychrome hand-painted wares (fig. 2), whereas others exhibit molding, fluting, or annular banding. The remaining hand-painted pearlware vessels have blue Chinese motifs, in imitation of Chinese porcelain. One such motif occurs on a cup, a plate, and a saucer (fig. 3).

Blue and green edgewares represent the second most popular pearlware decoration recovered. A few pearlware sherds are also transfer-printed in blue, with Chinese motifs. One has even been fashioned into a gaming piece (fig. 4).

A small percentage of the ceramics recovered are tin-enameled wares, primarily identified as delft. Most of the delft sherds represent a large

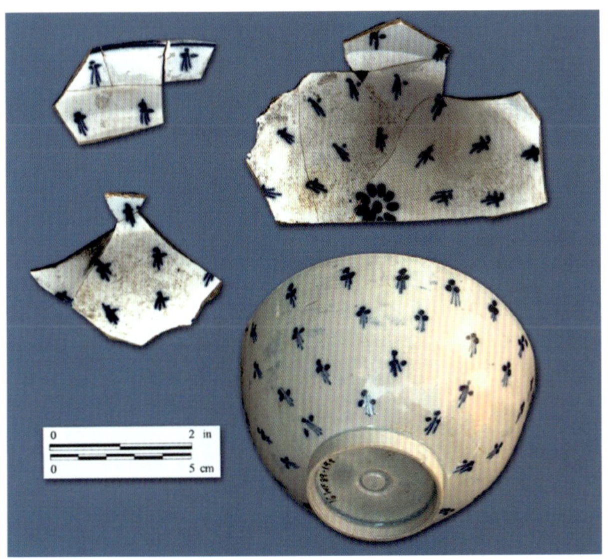

Figure 3 Hand-painted blue teawares, Staffordshire, ca. 1780–1799. Pearlware. Scale is in inches and centimeters.

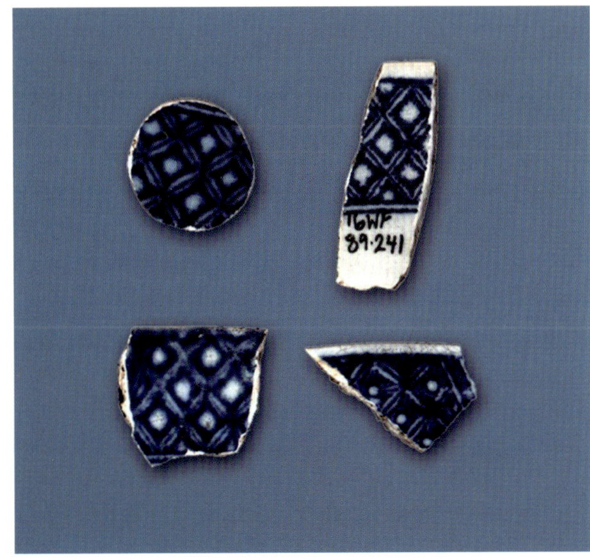

Figure 4 Transfer-printed blue wares from the Dortch site, Staffordshire, ca. 1790–1799. Pearlware. The sherd at the upper left was fashioned into a gaming piece.

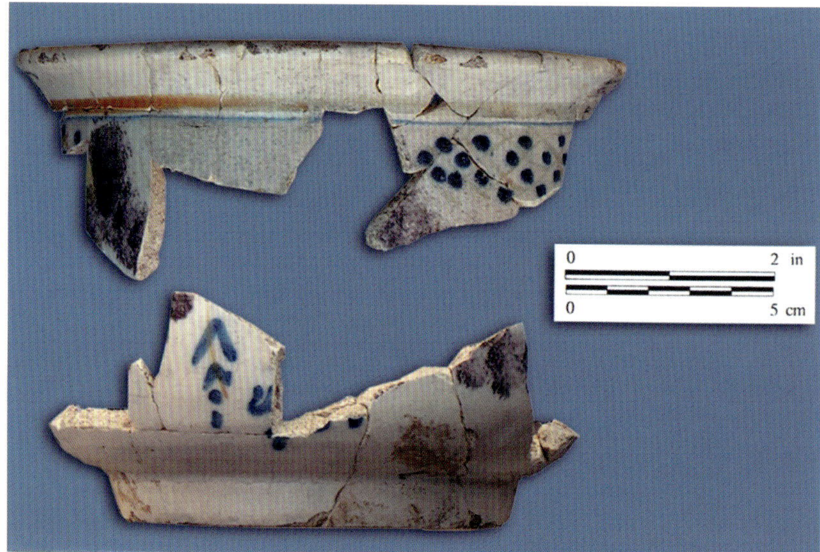

Figure 5 Flower bowl, England, eighteenth century. Tin-glazed earthenware. Examples of English delft are rarely found on Louisiana sites. Scale is in inches and centimeters.

portion of a flower bowl form (fig. 5)—one of the most remarkable finds from the Dortch site, with its powder purple and polychrome hand-painted decoration. Although delft is common at English-colonial archaeological sites, very few sherds of delft have ever been recovered from Louisiana archaeological sites, and even fewer have been decorated.[2]

Dortch apparently brought a number of English ceramics from South Carolina when he moved to Spanish West Florida circa 1793. The variety, quantity, and quality of English ceramics indicate that he was a man of means. The assemblage's well worn and highly fragmented condition suggests that the Dortch home served as an inn or meeting hall along a remote frontier road for wealthy businessmen, politicians, traders, and possibly even local revolutionaries.

Sara A. Hahn
Archaeologist
Coastal Environments, Inc.
<shahn@coastalenv.com>

1. David Arman and Linda Arman, *Anglo-American Ceramics Part 1, Transfer Printed Creamware and Pearlware for the American Market 1760–1860* (Portsmouth, R.I.: Oakland Press, 1998), p. 181.

2. Jill-Karen Yakubik, "Ceramic Use in Late-Eighteenth-Century and Early-Nineteenth-Century Southeastern Louisiana" (Ph.D. diss., Tulane University, New Orleans, 1990), pp. 289–91; Jeffrey P. Brain, *Tunica Treasure* (Cambridge, Mass.: Peabody Museum of Archaeology and Ethnology, Harvard University; Salem, Mass.: Peabody Museum of Salem, 1979), p. 44.

Book Reviews

Ivor Noël Hume. *If These Pots Could Talk: Collecting 2,000 Years of British Household Pottery.* Photographs by Gavin Ashworth. Milwaukee: Chipstone Foundation, 2001. 472 pp., 655 illus., 590 in color. $75 (clothbound).

My review copy of this large and weighty book never made it—modern transportation obviously defeated by the Atlantic. The copy I had the good fortune to purchase arrived with a batch of other, more handy works, and so this American giant was put aside to glance at when time permitted. It looked like a so-called coffee-table book—full of good illustrations but with little real meat—and the three ceramic faces that leered out from the dust jacket did not dispel this initial impression. Perhaps, too, the book's main title suggested that it was not a serious study.

How wrong I was, how very wrong! Once prompted to pick up this work, I could hardly put it down; garden, wife, and family took second place. In the week or so that I took to read this magnificent work I learned more about pots and how and why they were made and used—and not only pots, but about British (indeed world) history—than I had learned in all my seventy years.

This is very much a happy Anglo-American book. The author was born in London, and after the war he joined the staff of London's Guildhall Museum as an archaeologist, progressing to Colonial Williamsburg in 1957. American readers will not need reminding of his standing and experience, or of his fourteen previous books and many learned articles. His international honors are well known and richly deserved—few, if any, other American-based researchers have received the Order of the British Empire. Gavin Ashworth, another English-born master craftsman, who photographed so tellingly the hundreds of illustrations, deserves like praise and recognition. With the help of the Chipstone Foundation, this splendid partnership has produced a monumental work.

I have referred to the production partnership, but the partnership between Noël and his wife Audrey (1927–1993) was truly outstanding. The book tells of their great enjoyment as they hunted (pots) together, dug together, shared ideas as they traced the life of each pot, and generally worked as a mutually encouraging team.

Noël and Audrey indeed made their pots talk, made them tell of their times and their history, ancient and modern. The talk is certainly not one-sided, but rather a pleasing, often humorous, conversation. We are privileged to eavesdrop, to gain an impression of times gone by, of the delights of collecting and researching, of the joy of discovery.

The time scale is vast, commencing with B.C. pots and progressing (in time, not necessarily in quality or charm) to a trinket box commemorating the Queen Mother's hundredth birthday in August 2002. Obviously the coverage is biased, for this is a very personal book, not only in the selection of pots but in the story and the pleasing manner of the telling. I am a "porcelain man," Noël is a "pottery man" (very little porcelain is included in this work). He has very nearly won me over to the more ancient craft. It is a good read and a very well-produced, modestly priced book. It gives the reader pleasure as well as insight into pots and collecting, and it obviously gave the author much pleasure in the writing.

There are very few niggles, and none that detract from the importance and value of this fine work. I regret that the sizes of the objects are not included in the captions; one has to turn to page 375 to find such basic information.

On more material points, the F. & R. Pratt 1857 pot lid (fig. I.10) should not be described as lithographed because it was printed from a set of copperplates engraved by Jesse Austin. The bat-printed porcelain saucer (fig. XIII.28) is described both as bone china and as the collection's only example of New Hall hard-paste porcelain. It is almost certainly not New Hall, and at the stated period of circa 1815–1825 would not be of the hard-paste body. A pleasing and quite early Toby jug shown in figure XIV.13 is described incorrectly as classic polychrome decorated circa 1825–1835. It appears to have semitranslucent inglaze colors and to predate 1800 by several years.

The statement on page 294 that William Duesbury of Derby took over the Bow porcelain factory in 1763 surely needs more thought or research; I am not aware of any evidence to support this statement. At the head of the next page, the partner Weatherby in the Bow concern did have a recorded Christian name, John. On pages 322–23, the Doulton & Watt's Lambeth partnership of circa 1815–1858 is associated with the 1870s.

The lengthy glossary is helpful, but most British works would define *clobbering* as later decoration over an originally complete pattern, not as "often . . . part of the original design intent" (p. 363). To describe creamware as yellow (p. 364) is, to my mind, a bit strong. My dislike of the terms *tea poy* (p. 372) and *tea caddy* (pieces of furniture) rather than *ceramic tea cannister* is personal—but correct! There are several references to Llewellynn Jewitt's nineteenth-century work, but the main title should not include the word history.*

These are but small points, outside the author's main interest and period of study, and in no way diminish this truly amazing book that should be in every ceramic library, even if one has to invest in larger and stronger bookcases. Well done and thank you, Ivor Noël Hume, and your team.

Geoffrey Godden
Findon, West Sussex

* EDITOR'S NOTE: The title of the American edition, *The History of Ceramic Art in Great Britain from Pre-historic Times down through Each Successive Period to the Present Day* (New York: Scribner, Welford, and Armstrong, 1878), undoubtedly is less well known in the reviewer's Great Britain than in the United States.

Louana M. Lackey. *Rudy Autio.* Foreword by Peter Voulkos. Westerville, Ohio: American Ceramic Society, 2002. 278 pp., approx. 150 color illus. $65 (hardbound).

I have never actually met Rudy Autio, so I felt like something of a party crasher when reading Louana M. Lackey's new book on the well-known contemporary ceramist. On the dust jacket Lackey is described as a Research Scholar in Ceramics at the Maryland Institute College of Art, with previous experience in archaeology, anthropology, and art education. She seems to have had a colorful life, leaving college to be an art student at the Art Students League of New York, but her principal qualification to write this biography is that she is a friend of Autio.

Her volume is not a piece of scholarship nor is it meant to be. Rather, it is an affectionate account of Autio's life, written in a style approximating that of a local newspaper ("Rudy also has had fun making woodblock prints" [p. 136]). It strikes me as written mainly for people who, like Louana Lackey, already know and like Rudy Autio and enjoy being reminded of him for a few fond moments. While the book provides a useful overview of his career, it offers little more information than a decent oral history interview would do. Photographs of Autio, his work, and his studio environment are numerous, but, apart from some old black-and-white images, are of uneven and often amateurish quality. It is certainly not a book that will persuade anyone of Autio's significance as a potter or artist.

This would not be a cause for concern or even comment were it not for the fact that the jury is very much still out with regard to the importance of Autio's work. Autio has both benefited and suffered from his inextricable link with Peter Voulkos, who until his recent death had loomed over American ceramics like that other well-known, larger-than-life Greek, the Colossus of Rhodes. Autio and Voulkos became friends before either one knew a thing about pottery, when both were enrolled in an art class at Montana State College, Bozeman, on the G.I. Bill. The two men had more or less fallen into studying painting, and with an equal degree of casualness took up ceramics under the guidance of a woman named Frances Senska, who had studied with the Finnish immigrant potter Maija Grotell at Cranbrook. Autio and Voulkos were among a group of students who became interested in the medium and went on to help build a pottery in Helena, Montana, on the grounds of a brickyard. (The owner of the facility, Archie Bray, hoped to build a multifaceted artistic community at his factory. Although he passed away in 1953, his vision has been more or less fulfilled, and the Archie Bray Foundation remains a vital force in American ceramics.)

It seems that Voulkos committed to clay more readily and more fully than his friend. Autio, who for years dabbled in various artistic media, arguably did not hit his stride as a potter until two decades later. For the ceramic historian, what really captures the imagination about Autio in these early years is the company he kept: Voulkos, first and foremost, but also the triumvirate of Bernard Leach, Shoji Hamada, and Soetsu Yanagi, who visited Bray's manufactory in 1952 as part of their mission to expose Americans to the Japanese pottery tradition.

In a perfect universe, Autio would have become the Henri Matisse to Voulkos's Pablo Picasso—two giants with opposing aesthetic sensibilities who challenged one another to scale ever-greater heights of artistic achievement. Stylistically, the analogy holds true. Autio is a colorist who creates large, emphatically decorative pots festooned with cartoons of naked women and horses. His debt to late-period Matisse is almost total. Voulkos (who used to pin images of Picasso's own willfully clumsy ceramics to his studio wall) was deeply moved by the experience of meeting Leach and his colleagues and almost immediately entered a phase of wildly inventive construction—a freeform combination of Cubism, Abstract Expressionism, and Japanese aesthetics. He soon moved to California to teach at the Otis Art Institute. There he was able to play the Picasso role to the hilt, spawning a generation of followers, scandalizing his detractors, and abruptly adopting new styles when it suited his purposes.

Autio, by contrast, seems to have dithered. In 1957 he began teaching at the University of Montana, Missoula, and founded a ceramics program there; but his own work in the medium during the 1950s and 1960s took the form of architectural reliefs in a conservative W.P.A. style. He frittered away time and energy on outside projects such as a pair of bronze grizzly bears that serve as the mascots for the university. His tentative stabs at Voulkos's pioneering style ("bentware," as Autio amusingly calls it) were interesting but hardly the equal of work by other Voulkos acolytes such as Jim Leedy, John Mason, and Paul Soldner. Even when Autio finally found his signature style he remained a frankly derivative artist. Whereas Voulkos channeled Picasso, Autio merely imitated Matisse. His pots of the 1980s, with their whirling figural compositions, are impressive for their novel handbuilt construction and their freedom of drawing and color, but they are hardly revolutionary. They are also unbelievably repetitive. Autio's mature style calcified almost as soon as it appeared—a fact that Lackey clearly recognizes at some level, given that the last sentence in her book is a defensive one: "[J]ust as he would not 'always make the same picture' if he were a painter, Rudy does not always make the same pot" (p. 150). Actually he does, and though it is a nice pot, it would have seemed more artistically relevant in 1950, or even 1920, than it does today.

A photo in Lackey's book of Autio and Voulkos playing the guitar in 1953 tells the story with almost heartbreaking concision: the handsome Voulkos, a blur of energy and movement and clearly transported by the music, is turned away from Autio, who looks on with the appreciative, slightly befuddled expression of a faithful hound (p. 25). The photo is the most telling image in the book, because it shows Autio as a shy outsider even in a group of two. As an artist, he simply was not interested in rising to the historical circumstances that were thrust upon him. In Lackey's biography he perhaps gets what he deserves: not a good book, but a loving, nonjudgmental treatment in which he is celebrated simply for being himself. From a sentimental point of view this is unobjectionable; everyone should be so lucky. From a historical point of view, the book only confirms the impression that Autio is like most people—a good guy, doing his best—while Voulkos was a larger-than-life figure bent on transforming the course of ceramic history. The comparison is not fair, but, unfortunately, it is inevitable.

Glenn Adamson
The Chipstone Foundation and Milwaukee Art Museum

Richard D. Mohr. *Pottery, Politics, Art: George Ohr and the Brothers Kirkpatrick.* Urbana and Chicago: University of Illinois Press, 2003. 225 pp.; 22 color pls., 113 bw illus.; index (no bibliography). $60 (hardbound).

Richard Mohr, a philosophy professor at the University of Illinois, pretends to love the pots of George Ohr and the Kirkpatrick brothers in order to write about his favorite subjects—amateur Freudian psychoanalysis and anal sex. He wants to find big, universal issues in their work. He claims that his book will resurrect the Kirkpatricks "from obscurity wrought of curatorial storage, regional collecting, scholarly neglect, and well-intended prudery" (p. 6). One wonders what he means by obscurity. A Kirkpatrick snake jug recently sold for more than $38,000 at Christie's, and another is currently on permanent view in the Luce Center at the New-York Historical Society, interpreted in the public audio tour by nationally syndicated cartoonist Garry Trudeau ("Doonesbury"). But further reading in this slim volume will finally bring you to the crux of the matter. Mohr wants these potters to be shown in *art* museums, but, he complains, their pots have not been interpreted in a way that is sufficiently sexy to intrigue art museums. "It may not be the case," he argues, "that only in recent critical times could the brothers' work be given its interpretive due, but in light of the fusion of meaning and use in their work, it is particularly helpful to have available the critical tools of the present which emphasize strategy over structure, rhetoric over grammar, function over form, and which are sensitive to the political dimensions of art, to irony, fun, and to turns of meaning as well as of phrase" (p. 6). He refers to his method as "the interpretive techniques of contemporary literary and art criticism" and then names "deconstructive, historicist, rhetorical, and psychoanalytical strategies" (p. 6). Deconstruction, rhetoric, and psychoanalysis are easy to find in this book; historical fact is not.

I wrote on the Kirkpatricks many years ago, so I was especially excited about the possibility of new interpretations of their work.[1] I, too, wonder why Charles Demuth's quiet formalist paintings of Lancaster, Pennsylvania, for example, are hanging in the Whitney Museum of American Art, while the Kirkpatrick brothers' best snake jug is displayed across Central Park at the historical society. New arguments that cut through the old rhetoric of art versus craft or decorative versus fine art surely would be welcomed in the field of decorative arts scholarship. Indeed, Mohr promises to show us the light of cutting-edge interpretation: "If, along the way, the book helps academics take the decorative arts in general more seriously than they have been in even the recent past, that would be nice" (p. 7). Nice, however, is hardly the word one would use to describe a largely scatological text by a scholar who relishes the opportunity to write about excrement, anal sex, taut foreskins, vulvae, large breasts, and miscegenation. This is not a nice book, despite the author's best wishes for our enlightened future. I kept wondering as I slogged through Mohr's secretions whether taking the decorative arts "more seriously" meant that once we scholars began to uncover the scatological significance of Belter sofas, ball-and-claw feet, and over-upholstered seat rails, the decorative arts would become more accessible to art museum curators and aficionados.

For those readers unfamiliar with the work of Cornwall and Wallace Kirkpatrick, from 1859 to 1896, in their Anna, Illinois, pottery the brothers made standard utilitarian salt-glazed stoneware products, as well as some remarkable sculptural objects, including but certainly not limited to jugs covered with writhing three-dimensional snakes and whisky flasks in the shape of pigs. When I put together an interpretation of their pots nearly thirty years ago, I saw the work largely as radical temperance propaganda wrought by a pair of widely read, politically savvy Midwestern craftsmen with a keen observation of gesture and remarkable skill in modeling. But Mohr thinks the temperance angle is "too simplistic and probably flat out wrong, even though Wallace Kirkpatrick was himself involved briefly with the temperance movement" (p. 28). Ignoring that temperance advocates were socially radical in their belief that society could legislate morality, Mohr prefers to see the brothers as "appleknockers" (p. 2) with a scatological sense of humor. Temperance as a theme is too stodgy for the new scholarship. However, Mohr is so intent on dishonoring the temperance interpretation that he neglects the Kirkpatricks' contribution to the object dialogue that unites past and present. Dismissing temperance as a theme because the brothers did not use standard temperance imagery, Mohr fails to see that they invented their own iconography, which included references to classical sculpture. He writes instead:

> In general I will be arguing that the Kirkpatricks' body of work, far from being conformist and conservative, is critical and progressive, even as it advances a fairly dark view of the world. For the Kirkpatricks, the underbelly of existence is clammy, dank, and uneasy. Their work is streaked with misanthropy, a gentle, pitying mournful misanthropy, one which does not abandon humanity as hopeless. It at least goes to the bother of subverting social conventions such as it can—sometimes subtly, sometimes by scaring the horses outright. (p. 28)

Okay, that is a different train of thought, and one that might be worth following if the author had some command of the past that he conjures so glibly. The writer's facile command of the English language makes for easy reading, but he is disconcertingly loose with facts. We learn at the outset (p. 2), for example, that the Philadelphia Centennial Exhibition of 1876 was "America's first world's fair" (no, that would be New York City's famed Crystal Palace Exhibition of 1853); that Anna, Illinois, the site of the pottery, is a "delta town" (actually, it is landlocked, with nary a river in sight), and that Ott & Brewer's now famous Baseball Vases—the first American claywork to be officially classified as art and frequently shown in art museums since that time—were nothing more than "kitsch." I could be accused of favoring grammar over rhetoric here, but if we are going to have a new scholarship in the decorative arts, should we not start with the facts, as boring as some of them may be? I was sorry to see all these missteps from the start. I was hoping for a new paradigm, but found an old poseur.

The interpretive strain with the most promise is Mohr's exploration of the "grotesque" with regard to the Kirkpatricks' work using the analytical tools of Mikhail Bakhtin, a Russian literary theorist:

> Exaggeration, hyperbolism, excessiveness, obsessiveness, fantastic dimensions, and the resulting impossible nature of an image represented in these ways are all typical attributes of the grotesque style. . . . The essential characteristic of the grotesque . . . is that it is a mechanism by which the rational, the ideal, the prescriptive yearnings and highest aspirations of the human are transferred or projected downward onto the lower registers of life, especially on humans' nagging animal traits, the abdomen, the genitals, the rectum. In the grotesque, "the bowels and the phallus" become a second body with a life of its own. (p. 36)

Mohr loves this stuff, but he never takes it anywhere. His thesis is that the Kirkpatricks' work fits the definition of grotesque and that it is "a dethroning, a debunking, but it is not the narrow debunking that is satire. . . . Through the grotesque the Kirkpatricks took laughing aim not just at the Victorian value of soberness but at conscientiousness, discipline, hard work, prescriptivity, rational orderliness, competitive excellence, regulated self-improvement, better-than-thou-ism, optimism sustained by good deeds, thrift, prudence, and prudery, in short, the whole Victorian worldview" (p. 38).[2] He is so fond of the grotesque that he happily mistakes an airhole (a puncture in an applied figure to keep it from exploding in the kiln) for the results of a giant fart. And he is pleased to find the Kirkpatricks' repeated use of dung beetles rolling dung (which he delights in calling "shit") but fails to consider that this is low-caste imagery of industry. The usual symbol for industry in the 1800s would have been the busy beehive. Instead, the Kirkpatricks celebrated the dung beetle's ability to make something from nothing, just as potters craft their wares from dust.

Some of the interpretive directions Mohr takes are provocative—like comparing a short series of similar jugs to a rondel, a form of poetry—but others become morasses. One discussion about a small inkwell that seems to support protectionist tariffs is so convoluted that even the author loses track of his argument and finally flails it by calling the piece a "complex work of irony" (p. 42). Suffice it to say, there are enough problems with Mohr's analysis of the Kirkpatricks' work to draw this text into question. In any case, none of this will matter to the collector contemplating the $40,000 price tag on the next snake jug to come up for sale.

Mohr is more effusive about George Ohr, the self-styled "mad potter of Biloxi," and in many ways the book is really about him. There has been much written about Ohr, but none of it is sufficiently scatological to suit Richard Mohr, who waxes rhapsodic over Ohr's sexual penny banks of penises, vulvae, and breasts but fails to mention Ohr's reproductions of historic ceramic forms.

The best part of the Ohr section is where the author demonstrates Ohr's debt to the Kirkpatricks. The connection between the Kirkpatricks and Ohr was first noted in 1986, in an entry on Ohr that Bert Denker and I wrote for *"The art that is life": The Arts and Crafts Movement in America, 1875–1920*.[3] Robert Ellison Jr. expanded this connection greatly in the book he wrote with Eugene Hecht and Garth Clark that accompanied the landmark exhibition at the American Craft Museum in 1989,[4] but not to Mohr's satisfaction:

> Every critic admits that Ohr's wares with snakes derive significantly from the Kirkpatricks' and count as art pottery by any standard. . . . The snake wares of the Kirkpatricks and Ohr reveal a second, more important influence flowing from the former to the latter. The Kirkpatricks' jugs hold, I believe, the key to understanding the different levels of complexity in Ohr's forms—his overall aesthetic. Nearly every critic of Ohr points out that Ohr was trying to "transcend" the potentials offered by the traditional vessel form and that he indeed succeeded in taking the vessel where no vessel had gone before. That Ohr was able to do this, I suggest, is largely due to aesthetic innovations already worked out in the Kirkpatricks' snake jugs. (p. 121)

Mohr supports this assertion with a bold and convincing argument. Unfortunately, he follows this breakthrough with more of his usual nattering about excrement, anality, and obsessiveness, ultimately comparing Ohr with Howard Hughes. Mohr's conclusion is that:

> . . . in the fulfillment of his excremental vision, Ohr may have achieved even more than producing pottery as pottery *simpliciter*. If twentieth-century psychoanalytical theory is true, then Ohr in his very wooziness and compulsions may have given us a glimpse of art as art itself, or more modestly put, of artistic process as artistic process pure and simple. In regressing from the sexual and phallic stages of psychological development, Ohr in his work rejects the vision of the "adult genital personality type, the successful psychosexual development in psychoanalytic theory, characterized by capacity for mature heterosexual love, responsible concerns beyond the self, and productive living in society." (p. 163)[5]

Mohr is right that his book offers new ways of looking at objects. Whether this idiosyncratic form of psychosexual analysis can be applied to the Kirkpatrick and Ohr pots—or to any other objects, for that matter—is another issue.

Ellen Paul Denker
Museum consultant and writer

1. Ellen Paul Denker, "Forever Getting up Something New" (master's thesis, University of Delaware, Newark, 1978).

2. A catalog of Victorian virtues taken from Daniel Howe, ed., *Victorian America* (Philadelphia: University of Pennsylvania Press, 1976), pp. 17–24.

3. Ellen Paul Denker and Bert Denker, in Wendy Kaplan, *"The art that is life": The Arts and Crafts Movement in America, 1875–1920*, exh. cat. (Boston: Museum of Fine Arts, 1987), pp. 252–53, no. 110.

4. Garth Clark, Robert Ellison Jr., and Eugene Hecht, *The Mad Potter of Biloxi: The Art and Life of George E. Ohr* (New York: Abbeville Press, 1989), pp. 68–69.

5. Quoting Raymond Corsini and Alan Auerbach, eds., *Concise Encyclopedia of Psychology*, 2nd ed. (New York: Wiley, 1996), p. 721.

Richard L. Spivey. *The Legacy of Maria Poveka Martinez*. Photographs by Herbert Lotz. Santa Fe: Museum of New Mexico Press, 2003. xvi + 208 pp.; color and bw illus., bibliography, index. $60.00 (clothbound).

In the late 1800s the populations of the Pueblo tribes in the American Southwest declined precipitously. Museums in the eastern United States dispatched anthropologists to document what they feared were dying cultures and to collect and document their crafts. The production of pottery vessels to store water and grain and other necessities of life was also declining due to the availability of imported metal pans, dishes, and other vessels. The emergence of a huge, new, voracious market—tourists—led to further craft deterioration.

Anthropologists, archaeologists, and interested collectors in the Southwest endeavored to reverse the trend in the early 1900s. They helped Pueblo potters and other artisans sell their products at higher prices in urban centers such as Santa Fe and Albuquerque. In 1922, they organized an Indian fair in Santa Fe, which eventually became the enormous Indian Market that annually attracts about 1,200 artists and artisans and 100,000 buyers from around the world. The original organizers focused on traditional Indian crafts and rejected anything that was considered to be nontraditional. They purchased many of the objects in advance, to ensure the high quality of the displays, and (as they are today) prizes were awarded for significant examples.

One of the potters recognized at the first Indian fair was Maria Martinez (ca. 1887–1980) of San Ildefonso Pueblo, located northwest of Santa Fe. Initially she and her husband, Julian, made polychrome-decorated pottery. In 1907 Edgar L. Hewett—founder of the School of American Archaeology (now the School of American Research) and the Museum of New Mexico, as well as one of the major proponents of the Santa Fe Indian fairs—encouraged her to make copies of pottery he had excavated on the nearby Pajarito Plateau. Maria and her husband later developed a new style of decorating pottery, known simply as black-on-black, which became world famous. Maria Martinez eventually became the best-known Pueblo potter of all, widely recognized by just her first name. (In the following comments I shall mostly use the name Maria, but I recognize that the production of pottery associated with her and her family entailed the work of several gifted people. Indeed, this is true for almost all Pueblo pottery, which was usually made by family groups.)

Although Indian fair organizers focused on preserving traditional potting and decorating techniques, the objects that Maria and others made had a new and nontraditional function: they were, in the view of buyers, "art." In keeping with the production of art, organizers urged potters and other craftspeople to sign their wares. Some resisted, for it is anathema among Pueblo people to seek individual recognition, but Maria was one of the first to do so. Her pottery commanded significantly higher prices than did the work of other potters. Now, prices can be stratospheric: a large black-on-black storage jar by Maria and Julian sold in 1999 for a record auction price of $255,500.[1]

Maria's superior abilities as a potter were recognized almost immediately. She and her husband participated in the California-Pacific Exposition in San Diego in 1915. The first major biography on the potter was published in 1948, another was published in 1977, and several more have followed.[2] Richard Spivey's book is the latest contribution to our understanding of Maria, her family, and their pottery.

Spivey was personally acquainted with Maria and her descendants, and he writes knowledgeably about them and their work. He published his first book on Maria in 1979, followed by a revised edition in 1989. This book is technically a revised edition of the latter, but in many respects it is an entirely new work.[3] Notably, all of the pottery photographs were taken specifically for this edition, and there have been significant additions to the text, which has also been reorganized.

The text is now arranged chronologically, and Maria's work and contributions are put in the context of the history of potting at the Pueblo of San Ildefonso. Spivey discusses the pottery that Maria made for Hewett and details Julian's role in its decoration. (Maria almost never decorated her work.) Spivey also explains the accidental discovery, in about 1919, of the process used to make the quintessential Maria black-on-black pottery, and includes quotations from lengthy interviews he conducted with her in 1977, to help readers understand what she did, how, and why. There are several photos of her and her family; more important, however, is the inclusion of several early examples of her and Julian's work, including all seven of the known large storage jars.

Detailed histories of the work of Maria's sister (Clara), her daughter-in-law (Santana), her sons (Adam and Popovi Da), and grandson (Tony Da) follow. All of these discussions are major additions to earlier editions of the book. There are also chapters devoted to signatures on Maria's pottery and a listing of the numerous awards and honors she received. The book concludes with two interesting essays by Popovi Da (relating to Indian values and Indian pottery); a memorial to Popovi Da by the photographer Laura Gilpin; a letter from the famed English potter Bernard Leach; and a detailed genealogical chart of Maria's Pueblo family.

What are the significant contributions in this new edition? The text has been reorganized significantly from earlier editions, and it is much clearer as a result. (In the earlier editions, however, Maria's comments were coordinated with a series of photographs showing her and Julian making and decorating pottery, which helped make the process more understandable.) The discussion of signatures and their dating is clear and concise. The photographs of pottery are significantly better than in previous editions, with the objects placed against neutral backgrounds and well lighted. Gone are the artsy, disturbing, outdoor settings of pottery placed against backdrops of sandstone and yucca. (I suppose the photos in the earlier editions make for a sort of period piece in photographic style, but they certainly detract from the objects.) Likewise, the accuracy of the color in the new edition is vastly improved over the reproductions in earlier editions. The biographies and work of Santana and other family members are new or much expanded, and there are significant and lengthy quotations from several of the potters. For anyone interested in the work of Maria's descendants, this is the essential book.

What are the criticisms? Surprisingly, the pottery itself is largely ignored in the text. There is little discussion of any of the objects, and the author does not discuss the chronology of Maria's black-on-black pottery designs. While it may be impossible now to discern a progression of styles, if there were any hope of distinguishing a chronology in Maria's work, it would have been helpful to organize the illustrations chronologically. The present organization of the illustrations seems at times haphazard. Forgeries of Maria's pottery are mentioned (p. 161), but no examples are shown or discussed. Given the high prices that Maria's pottery and that of her family now command, it would be useful to know how to detect problem pieces. The photographs are the best published to date of Maria's work, and highlights emphasize the incredible mirror finish that Maria achieved on her pottery, but the matte decoration is not always clear. Photographing Maria's pottery using techniques perfected for silver objects might be advantageous. The index is incomplete. It is a technical issue, but to show such care and sensitivity in the reorganization and editing of text from earlier editions, and to invest the time and funds necessary to produce so many new photographs, it seems inconceivable that the index should receive less attention. Often personal names are not indexed, even when those names appear in the text as being significant. For example, the noted Pueblo artist Awa Tsireh (and brother of Santana, Maria's daughter-in-law) is discussed and his important influence on Julian Martinez is explained, but he is listed only as "Alfonso Roybal (Awa Tsireh)" once, without a corresponding cross-reference, and at least one reference to him as Awa Tsireh is missing altogether. Likewise, Sallie Wagner is quoted repeatedly and extensively, but her name is missing from the index. It is hoped that this technical fault will be corrected in future editions.

Despite these relatively minor complaints, this new edition of Spivey's book *The Legacy of Maria Poveka Martinez* is a major addition to our understanding of the work of this gifted potter and her family. In my view, it is mainly the ensemble of discussions of Maria's descendants that make Spivey's new book a major contribution to our knowledge. The title indicates clearly the author's intent: Maria's legacy is the focus, and the book is of value to anyone interested in a comprehensive overview of this pottery. In addition, for serious students and collectors of Maria's pottery, and for those who wish to understand her even better, I would recommend Susan Peterson's *The Living Tradition of María Martínez* for its additional quotes from Maria and photographs.

Dwight P. Lanmon
Santa Fe, New Mexico

1. *Important American Indian Art*, sale cat. (New York: Sotheby's, November 30, 1999), lot 4.

2. Alice Marriott, *María: The Potter of San Ildefonso* (Norman: University of Oklahoma Press, 1948); Susan Peterson, *The Living Tradition of María Martínez* (Tokyo and New York: Kodansha International, 1977).

3. Richard L. Spivey, *Maria* (Flagstaff, Ariz.: Northland Press, 1979 and 1989).

Bai Ming. *The Traditional Crafts of Porcelain Making in Jingdezhen / Jingdezhen chuantong zhi ci gongyi.* Translated by Mao Zengyin. Jingdezhen: Jiangxi Fine Arts Publishing House, 2002. 275 pp.; bilingual (Chinese and English), 600 color photographs, 16 line drawings; bibliography. $47 (clothbound).

The 600 photographs reproduced in this book document the stages of ceramic production in the "porcelain capital of the world," Jingdezhen, in Jiangxi Province, China. The images were culled from more than 2,000 slides taken over the course of seven years by the author, a well-known ceramic artist and painter in China, as well as a lecturer at the art college of Tsinghua University. While he is most likely not familiar to Western potters, he has been making porcelain in Jingdezhen for eleven years, and his list of accomplishments and memberships is impressive.

The front flyleaf states that Bai Ming has "not only documented the details of the magic skills of porcelain in the ancient town with a history over one thousand years for a vivid presentation to the world, but also given them a historic and documentary meaning as significance as the field survey." Two issues immediately become evident: the difficult and admirable but often quaintly awkward translation by Mao Zengyin, and the nearly impossible task of summarizing in one book the more than one thousand years of history and technology of porcelain production in Jingdezhen.

I was fortunate to attend the China Ceramic Cultural Exchange program in Jingdezhen in 2000, managed by Li Jiangsheng, the international program director. We visited the San Bao pottery, both the reconstructed Ancient Kiln and the new study center, which are featured prominently in the book. I spent time wandering the back alleys of the potters' district, where I nodded, smiled, and photographed the always generous and friendly potters and decorators, although I would not go so far as to say that I could "wholeheartedly listen to the merry songs arising from the hearts of honest potters" (p. 9).

Along with master potters from around the globe, I tried my hand at throwing, tooling, decorating, glazing, and firing. Any potter or ceramic historian who has visited the potteries in China, or has tried his or her hand at mastering Chinese methods of porcelain making, will appreciate this book. Jingdezhen is rightly considered the holy land for ceramic artists around the world, and "the delicacy of her products is [indeed] lost in wonder" (p. 34) to many of us.

This is not a technical volume, but rather a photo essay of the "magic skills" of the potter. A novice potter will not find much that thoroughly instructs, as there are no details of clay or glaze composition, or of kiln construction and firing. Unfortunately, as I discovered from my own slides taken there, still photographs, no matter how many you have or how well taken they may be, cannot fully capture the awesome technical ability of these potters and decorators. In this sense, then, the author's goal to provide Chinese and foreign ceramic artists with "a full knowledge of the skills and techniques of porcelain in Jingdezhen" (p. 6) is perhaps not realized.

The book discusses quarrying, processing, workshop structure, shaping, joint forming, trimming, glazing, decorating, firing, and rice-straw packing. Although it is stated that the photos are more convincing than pages of written materials, only the skilled potter will fully comprehend what is going on, and there are a few photographs that leave even the initiated a bit confused, despite the brief descriptions.

Nevertheless, the skill of the potters is evident in these photographs. Although most of the Western potters on my tour failed miserably to create wares using the same methods as the Chinese potters, it was evident that the Chinese potters themselves believe, as the author says, that "nothing can never be done" (p. 74). The author also states, "The skills look quite easy, but it is very difficult to master it" (p. 80). Too true. The Chinese ceramic artists are fearless, and the millennia-old knowledge runs directly through their bodies to their fingertips, as they throw bowl after bowl after bowl with speed, accuracy, and great panache.

Decorating gets short attention here. A photo of a "long biscuit board" of greenware bowls decorated in underglaze blue with the "rice-straw motif" (p. 87) does not begin to hint at the speed and grace of the decorators. The results are a somewhat standardized, age-old calligraphic design in upper and lower registers that takes seconds for the decorators to apply. (This is one aspect of the artistry that is lost when a single photograph is used as an illustration.) Also, there is quite an industry of reproducing designs and forms from the last five hundred years going on in the city, but it is not discussed. The decorations illustrated are, for the most part, "modern"—in a handsome but slightly dated way. The one technique that is truly modern, called "overglaze new colors" (p. 234), is a technique that uses camphor oil or kerosene in its production. Again, however, there is probably not enough technical information for most potters to be able to imitate this method.

As a ceramic historian I was a bit disappointed by the superficial nod to the historic record. Only one illustration from Tang Ying's eighteenth-century book and four small details from a book of the Ming dynasty are utilized to cover the story of ceramic production prior to 2002. The bibliography contains Chinese-language references only and so does not list such historic references as Walter A. Staehelin's *The Book of Porcelain*,[1] which reproduces an eighteenth-century set of gouache paintings of ceramic production, or the letters of Père d'Entrecolles,[2] written in 1712 and 1722, which detail the technical aspects of ceramic manufacturing in the early eighteenth century, nor does it reference a 1920 *National Geographic Magazine* article on the town of Jingdezhen[3] that illustrates ancient forms still being made in that year.

Technically, I found the illustrations of throwing the most engaging. These are of small pieces and—the most amazing—a large bowl, plate, and vase. By "large" he means, for example, approximately 42 inches for the plate (p. 106). I watched as two potters threw a plate larger than that, one working from the inside, one from the outside. It took 500 pounds of clay and five men to lift it off the wheel when it was completed. Although all the Chinese potters I observed created their wares with what seemed to us the utmost ease—even the large dish—I agree with the author that, "It is really no easy work" (p. 165, referring to glazing).

The section on the kiln is perhaps the most disappointing. The photographs are of the quite beautiful Ancient Kiln, outside Jingdezhen, which was reconstructed as a tourist site but is now idle. The group I traveled with visited several active kilns and we had the opportunity to participate in the firing of the Ancient Nanfeng Kiln in Foshan. It would have been nice if pictures of a kiln being loaded, fired, and unloaded had been included, especially since the author photographed over a seven-year period. While the old kilns are fascinating, most potters today fire in gas or electric kilns, and sometimes in coal-fired kilns, a fact that is not discussed; not to mention this is slightly misleading.

The text is minimal, so reading this small volume does not take much time. The reader is unfortunately left to decipher too much from the fine photography. The author says, "We have only one aspiration: We hope that all the readers would treasure the book" (p. 8). For those who have been there, the book is a treasured reminder of the ease and beauty of the work of the potters, even though it does not share much new information. For those who have not been there, perhaps this will inspire you to go. Meanwhile we await a film of the same subject, which may be the only way to fully capture the "magic skills" of the potters of Jingdezhen.

William R. Sargent
Peabody Essex Museum

1. Walter A. Staehelin, *The Book of Porcelain: The Manufacture, Transport, and Sale of Export Porcelain in China during the Eighteenth Century*, trans. from the German by Michael Bullock (London: Lund Humphries, 1966).

2. Published in English in 1725, in Jean-Baptiste Du Halde's *General History of China*, according to Ann Finer and George Savage, eds., *The Selected Letters of Josiah Wedgwood* (London: Cory, Adams and McKay, 1965), p. 162.

3. Frank B. Lenz, "The World's Ancient Porcelain Center," *National Geographic Magazine* 38 (November 1920): 391–406.

R. K. Henrywood. *Staffordshire Potters, 1781–1900: A Comprehensive List Assembled from Contemporary Directories with Selected Marks.* Woodbridge, Suffolk, Eng.: Antique Collectors' Club, 2002. 416 pp., numerous bw illus.; bibliography, index. $89.50/£45.00 (clothbound).

The information about manufacturers and their marks assembled by Dick Henrywood for his earlier books underpins the present volume, which has been eagerly anticipated for a number of years.[1] While much printed and molded pottery from the eighteenth and nineteenth centuries bears a maker's mark, the great majority does not. Even where a piece is clearly marked, it is usually necessary to consult other sources for confirmation of the date range in which a piece might have been produced or where it might have been made. Obvious sources to consult are the contemporary local, regional, and trade directories for the period, but these publications are by their very nature ephemeral, tending to be discarded when the latest edition comes out, and surviving copies are often rare and fragile.

Henrywood is to be congratulated on drawing together information on pottery manufacturers operating in the north Staffordshire Potteries between 1781 and 1900 by systematically examining the directories that covered this region. The former date is that of the earliest directory to include Staffordshire, while the latter is, as the author admits, an arbitrary, but logical, cutoff point. The present volume is not a wholesale reproduction of the Staffordshire directories in their entirety. He has kept strictly to pottery manufacturers, omitting references to engravers, color manufacturers, flint millers, and the scores of subsidiary trades that formed the infrastructure of the dominant industry. While these omissions might be regretted by some, it does make the information manageable and coherent.

Henrywood's aim is to provide a companion volume to the existing standard works on British ceramics, notably, Geoffrey Godden's *Encyclopaedia of British Pottery and Porcelain Marks* and his subsequent *Encyclopaedia of British Porcelain Manufacturers,* John Cushion's *Handbook of Pottery and Porcelain Marks,* and, from the nineteenth century, Simeon Shaw's *History of the Staffordshire Potteries,* John Ward's *The Borough of Stoke-upon-Trent,* and Llewellynn Jewitt's *The Ceramic Art of Great Britain.*[2]

As the author states in the introduction, the drawback with marks books is that not all pottery firms marked their wares. Contemporary books by Shaw, Ward, and Jewitt did not claim to be comprehensive in their coverage of Staffordshire companies. Many firms were short-lived, changing their names or company partners frequently; others were operating on a small scale; scores saw no commercial reason to mark their wares with their names. Regardless, most were listed in the directories and it is on these lesser-known companies that Henrywood's book sheds light.

The purpose of the directories was to list the businesses, tradesmen, and shopkeepers in a town or region, indicate the private addresses of the principal citizens, and give an outline of other commercial intelligence (railway stations, post offices, etc.), often including a history of the town. Over the 119-year period that Henrywood's book covers, such directories were produced by a variety of publishers, from the national coverage of the London-based Kelly directories of 1850 onward, to the single directory of the Staffordshire pottery towns published in 1796 by the Hanley-based printers, Chester and Mort.

The book is aimed at serious collectors but is not afraid to address some basic issues. Chapter 2, "The Staffordshire Potteries," for example, offers a useful overview of the six pottery towns that make up the modern city of Stoke-on-Trent, as well as the numerous villages, hamlets, suburbs, and districts in this heavily industrialized area. It draws extensively on contemporary descriptions from the various directories themselves. Combined with the simple map on page 10 illustrating the relative position of the places mentioned in the directories, the chapter provides a clear guide to the geography of this small but crowded part of the county.

Chapter 3, "The Directories, Compilers, and Publishers," gives short histories of the various companies that produced the directories and highlights some of the problems associated with individual directories. Tunnicliffe's 1787 list of potters, for example, was lifted verbatim from Bailey's 1784 directory, and Pigot's directories of 1842 and 1844 were simply reprints of the company's 1841 directory.

Chapter 4, "Potters' Marks," is a brief listing of the types of marks to be found on wares. It covers how marks were applied (printed, impressed, etc.), what the marks represent (makers' names, pattern or series names, types of body, etc.), and when and how different mark types were introduced and how they can assist in dating a piece. A notable feature of this chapter is the range of illustrations showing the different types of mark.

The majority of the book (more than 200 pages) is taken up by Chapter 5, "Alphabetical List of Manufacturers." This is the real meat of the book and will doubtless be the chapter that readers will turn to most often.

The alphabetical list extracts all the pottery companies and partnerships listed in the directories and gives a brief address, the date and name of the directory or directories in which they are listed, and an abbreviated classification of the types of wares made as described in the directory. While each directory had its idiosyncrasies and no one directory was fully inclusive, together they provide a broadly comprehensive list of the pottery firms operating at the time of the industry's greatest expansion. Henrywood has taken from sixty directories the details of all the pottery manufacturers listed. Every partnership and spelling variation is listed, and the author has wisely resisted any attempt to correct obvious inconsistencies or mistakes in the original directory entries, listing instead all spelling and partnership variations and cross-referencing them.

Organizing the entries from all the different directories and compiling this alphabetical list was a truly mammoth task. The text is augmented by a selection of black-and-white photographs of marks and by reproductions of advertisements that appeared in the directories. In many cases these expand considerably on the brief official directory entry.

The usefulness of this chapter is augmented by Appendix I, "Original Directory Listings," in which all relevant transcribed entries from each directory are listed as they appear in the original. Indeed, calling this section an appendix—it is more than 130 pages long—diminishes its significance. Many of the directories cited are rare, some extremely so, and almost impossible to access. In reprinting the entries Henrywood has placed the raw data into the hands of his readers, enabling them to extrapolate whatever additional information they may want. A minor criticism is that it would have been interesting to have had a checklist of directory titles and dates at the beginning of the appendix. It also would have been useful if, in addition to putting the directory name in the running header, the date had been given as well. These are, however, minor quibbles from one who uses the book frequently as an important reference tool. It is a great pleasure to see the extremely rare map from Allbut's 1802 directory, which includes the location of the various potteries, reproduced in redrawn form following its directory entries.

Appendix II, "Index of Partnership Surnames," is also extremely useful in that it lists all the partners' names mentioned in company titles. While it is usually straightforward to follow the dominant partner in a company, the second- and third-named partners are frequently lost in alphabetical listings of company names. Henrywood has rescued these other partners and in so doing reveals how, as partnerships changed, different individuals moved to the fore, either as dominant partners or as independent manufacturers.

This is a useful, authoritative, and important book and will be a valuable addition to the library of anyone interested in the north Staffordshire potteries. As the author himself acknowledges, it is not—and was not intended to be—a list of every Staffordshire pottery company, as some firms known to exist from marked specimens are not listed in the directories (for example, figure makers John Dale and Charles Tittensor and the company of Lakin & Poole).[3] Some may have been overlooked when the directories were compiled, and others may have come and gone in the period (sometimes five years or more) between published directories.

The number of pottery companies operating in north Staffordshire during the late eighteenth and nineteenth centuries was truly staggering. Although it is rarely stated in the directories themselves, it is known that hundreds of these companies were exporting either to North America, to the expanding British Empire, or to Britain's allies. Indeed, some companies' products were almost entirely destined for export, and wares bearing the marks of many of these companies can be found all over the world. No single source could possibly provide information on all the companies that made pottery in north Staffordshire, but Henrywood has significantly increased the information available in a magisterial and accessible form, and thereby enabled researchers to gain a better idea of the scale and complexity of the Staffordshire potteries.

Miranda Goodby
Collections Officer, Ceramics
Potteries Museum and Art Gallery, Stoke-on-Trent

1. R. K. Henrywood, *Relief-Moulded Jugs* (Woodbridge, Suffolk, Eng.: Antique Collectors' Club, 1984); R. K. Henrywood, *An Illustrated Guide to British Jugs from Medieval Times to the Twentieth Century* (Shrewsbury, Eng.: Swan Hill Press, 1997); A. W. Coysh and R. K. Henrywood, *The Dictionary of Blue and White Printed Pottery, 1780–1880,* 2 vols. (Woodbridge, Suffolk, Eng.: Antique Collectors' Club, 1982 and 1989).

2. Geoffrey A. Godden, *Encyclopaedia of British Pottery and Porcelain Marks* (1964; London: Barrie and Jenkins, 1991); Geoffrey A. Godden, *Encyclopaedia of British Porcelain Manufacturers* (London: Barrie and Jenkins, 1988); John P. Cushion and W. B. Honey, *Handbook of Pottery and Porcelain Marks,* 4th ed., rev. and exp. (London: Faber, 1980); Simeon Shaw, *History of the Staffordshire Potteries* (1829; Newton Abbot, Devon, Eng.: David and Charles; Wakefield, Eng.: S. R. Publishers, 1970); John Ward, *The Borough of Stoke-upon-Trent* (1843; Wakefield,

Eng.: S. R. Publishers, 1969; Stoke-on-Trent, Eng.: Webberley, 1984); Llewellynn Jewitt, *The Ceramic Art of Great Britain,* 2nd rev. ed. in a single vol. (1883; reprint, Chicheley, Eng.: Paul P. B. Minet, 1971).

3. Additional information on some of these principals can be found in Rodney Hampson's index and abstracts of pottery references from *The Staffordshire Advertiser:* Rodney Hampson, *Pottery References in The Staffordshire Advertiser, 1795–1865,* Occasional Publication, no. 4 (Hanley, Eng.: Northern Ceramic Society, 2000). While news items and advertisements are only a partial guide to pottery history, focusing primarily on crisis events such as fires and bankruptcies, this source supplements Henrywood's book and the other references mentioned.

Compiled by Amy C. Earls

Checklist of Articles, Books, and Electronic Resources on Ceramics in America Published 1998–2004

The checklist that follows, which contains approximately 350 entries, was compiled from online searches and from publications received as a member of organizations for ceramics collectors and researchers. Also provided is my list of the top twenty-five of these associations, specifically those that sponsor workshops, meetings, or publications relevant to ceramics made or used in America.[1] For the contact information of these groups, search at <http://www.Google.com>.

In the last year or so several organizations (the Northern Ceramic Society and the English Ceramic Circle, among others) have begun to include at least partial color photographs in their publications, without substantially raising membership rates. Collector organizations are following this trend in collector books and exhibit/auction catalogs, where the standard is full-color. This is a welcome change from fifteen to twenty years ago, when only black-and-white illustrations were available for ceramic identifications. Disciplines such as my own, historical archaeology, limit potential contributions to ceramic knowledge by offering only black-and-white photographs, often of substandard quality. The commitment to quality color photographs, such as those that illustrate *Ceramics in America,* may require underwriting of costs in order to keep publications affordable and therefore accessible to a wide audience. The $750 price of David Sanctuary Howard's new book on Chinese porcelain armorial services, for example, reflects the cost of including high-quality color plates in self-published books with small print runs, but surely it limits the audience.

I still have hopes that digital publishing will counter high prices for books with color illustrations. In a recent exhibit catalog of early Chinese ceramics, the printed version contains seventy-eight color and numerous black-and-white photographs.[2] The accompanying CD-ROM, on the other hand, contains color images of all 374 catalog entries plus a detailed description of all exhibits, including a brief description in Chinese.

Please send publication notices for books, articles, and web publications to the Book and Exhibit Review Editor, *Ceramics in America,* P.O. Box 121, Florence, New Jersey, 08518, U.S.A. <trentonpots@yahoo.com>.

1. Eastfield Village, Northern Ceramic Society, Winterthur's Ceramics in America conference, National Council on Education for the Ceramic Arts, American Ceramic Society, Potteries of Trenton Society, English Ceramic Circle, Society for Post-Medieval Archaeology, American Ceramic Circle, White Ironstone China Association, Friends of Blue, Transferware Collectors Club, Council for Northeast Historical Archaeology, Society for Historical Archaeology, San Francisco Ceramic Circle, Tea Leaf Ironstone Club, Flow Blue International Collector's Club, Wedgwood International Seminar, Wedgwood Society of New York, English Ceramic Study Group of Philadelphia, Friends of Terra Cotta, Oriental Ceramic Society, Stangl/Fulper Collectors Club, Medieval Pottery Research Group, and Washington Ceramic Seminar. I would be interested in hearing about other organizations. Ceramic organization news is posted on my weblog <http://www.greatestjournal.com/~trentonpots> and in my weblog community <http://www.greatestjournal.com/~potterynews>

2. Stephan von der Schulenberg and Rainald Simon, *The Birth of Form: Early Chinese Ceramics at the Museum of Applied Arts, Frankfurt* (Heidelberg, Germany: Wunderhorn, 2002). The ceramics in this catalog predate American colonization so are not in this bibliography.

Acton, Lesley, and Natasha Smith. *Practical Ceramic Conservation.* Marlborough, Eng.: Crowood; dist. in the U.S. by Trafalgar Square, 2003.

Adams, William H. "Dating Historical Sites: The Importance of Understanding Time Lag in the Acquisition, Curation, Use, and Disposal of Artifacts." *Historical Archaeology* 37, no. 2 (2003): 38–64.

Agnew, Antonia, David Doxey, and Felicity Marno. *Tea, Trade, and Tea Canisters.* Exhibit catalog, Stockspring Antiques. London: Stockspring Antiques, 2002.

Agnew, Antonia, and Felicity Marno. *The Dragon and the Quail: English Kakiemon Porcelain.* Exhibit catalog, Stockspring Antiques, February 23–March 11, 2000. London: Stockspring Antiques, 2000.

Anderson, Duane. *All That Glitters: The Emergence of Native American Micaceous Art Pottery in Northern New Mexico.* Santa Fe, N.M.: School of American Research Press, 1999.

———, ed. *Legacy: Southwest Indian Art at the School of American Research.* Santa Fe, N.M.: School of American Research Press, 1998.

Anderson, Scott L. "Robertson Art Tile Company, Morrisville, Pennsylvania, 1890–1982." *Trenton Potteries* [Newsletter of the Potteries of Trenton Society] 3, no. 3 (September 2002): 4–7.

Andres, Mark. "Wally Schwab: A Marriage of Austerity and Ostentation." *Ceramics Monthly* 51 (February 2003): 50–55.

Andrews, Susan C., and James P. Fenton. "Archaeology and the Invisible Man: The Role of Slavery in the Production of Wealth and Social Class in the Bluegrass Region of Kentucky, 1820 to 1870." *World Archaeology* 33, no. 1 (2001): 115–36.

"Animal Motifs on White Ironstone." *White Ironstone Notes* [White Ironstone China Association Newsletter] 7, no. 4 (spring 2001): 1, 4–13.

Armbrust, Margaret M. "The Phoenix Lives: Curtis Benzle on Porcelain and Repairs." *Ceramics Monthly* 52 (February 2004): 65–69.

Arnold, J. Barto, III, Thomas J. Oertling, and Andrew W. Hall. "The *Denbigh* Project: Test Excavations at the Wreck of an American Civil War Blockade-Runner." *World Archaeology* 32, no. 3 (2001): 400–412.

Ashworth, Frank. *Aynsley China.* Princes Risborough, Buckinghamshire, Eng.: Shire Publications, 2002.

Atterbury, Paul. "Architects and Ceramics in Victorian Britain." In *British Ceramic Design, 1600–2002,* edited by Tom Walford and Hilary Young, pp. 138–44. Paper presented at a colloquium celebrating the 75th anniversary of the English Ceramic Circle, September 21, 2002, Victoria and Albert Museum, London. Beckenham, Kent, Eng.: English Ceramic Circle, 2003.

Bai Ming. *The Traditional Crafts of Porcelain Making in Jingdezhen / Jingdezhen chuantong zhi ci gongyi.* Translated by Mao Zengyin. Jingdezhen: Jiangxi Fine Arts Publishing House, 2002.

Baker, Sara. "Sustaining a Standard of Living." *Ceramics Monthly* 51 (March 2003): 61–63.

Banks, Catherine. "The Archaeology of Enoch Wood" [lecture notes]. *Northern Ceramic Society Newsletter,* no. 129 (2003): 4–6.

Barclay, Katherine. *Scientific Analysis of Archaeological Ceramics: A Handbook of Resources.* Oxford, Eng.: Oxbow Books, 2001.

Bawden, Charles R. "A Proposal for an Archive of Metal Repairs." *Northern Ceramic Society Newsletter,* no. 132 (2003): 20–23.

———. "Words and Meanings: Work in Progress." *Northern Ceramic Society Newsletter,* no. 131 (2003): 33–37.

Benedick, Alain, and Ulrike Radunz. *Sarreguemines, la porcelaine.* Sarreguemines, Fr.: Pierron, 2002.

Bentley, R. Alexander, and Herbert D. G. Maschner. "Stylistic Change as a Self-Organized Critical Phenomenon: An Archaeological Study in Complexity." *Journal of Archaeological Method and Theory* 8, no. 1 (2001): 35–66.

Berg, Torsten, and Peter Berg, trans. *R. R. Angerstein's Illustrated Travel Diary, 1753–1755: Industry in England and Wales from a Swedish Perspective.* London: Science Museum, 2001.

"Berlin Swirl." *White Ironstone Notes* [White Ironstone China Association Newsletter] 5, no. 3 (winter 1998): 1, 4–7.

Black, John. "Tin-Glazed Earthenware: One Design, Two Painters?" In *British Ceramic Design, 1600–2002,* edited by Tom Walford and Hilary Young, pp. 28–32. Paper presented at a colloquium celebrating the 75th anniversary of the English Ceramic Circle, September 21, 2002, Victoria and Albert Museum, London. Beckenham, Kent, Eng.: English Ceramic Circle, 2003.

Blackwood, Robin, and Cherryl Head. *Old Crown Derby China Works: The King Street Factory, 1849–1935.* Ashbourne, Derbyshire, Eng.: Landmark, 2003.

Blakeman, Alan. *Bottles and Pot Lids: A Collector's Guide.* London: Miller's, 2002.

Blandino, Betty. *The Figure in Fired Clay.* London: A. and C. Black, 2001.

Blinkhorn, Paul. "Pottery." In "The Excavation and Analysis of an 18th-Century Deposit of Anatomical Remains and Chemical Apparatus from the Rear of the First Ashmolean Museum (Now The Museum of the History of Science), Broad Street, Oxford," by Graham Hull. *Post-Medieval Archaeology* 37, no. 1 (2003): 5–11.

Booth, Pauline. "The Staffordshire Pottery Industry in the Nineteenth Century and Its Markets." *Staffordshire Studies* 13 (2001): 109–26.

Borrell, Hector Rivero, Gustavo Curiel, Antonio Rubial Garcia, Juana Gutierrez Haces, and David

B. Warren. *The Grandeur of Viceregal Mexico: Treasures from the Museo Franz Mayer.* Exhibit catalog, Museum of Fine Arts, Houston, March 24–August 4; Henry Francis du Pont Winterthur Museum, Delaware, October 19, 2002–January 12, 2003; San Diego Museum of Art, March 9–May 25, 2003. Houston: Museum of Fine Arts; dist. University of Texas Press, 2002.

Bowers, Bruce. "Converting an Electric Kiln for Wood and Gas Firing." *Ceramics Monthly* 52 (February 2004): 72–75.

Branson, Helen K. "Yukio Ozaki's Marbled Ceramics." *Ceramics Monthly* 51 (June/July/August 2003): 26–28.

Brawer, Catherine C. *Chinese Export Porcelain from the Liebman Collection.* Madison, Wis.: University of Wisconsin Press, 2002.

"Bread Plates and Cheese Dishes." *White Ironstone Notes* [White Ironstone China Association Newsletter] 6, no. 4 (spring 2000): 1, 4–12.

Bresnan, Debra. "Blazing a Trail: New York's Hudson Valley Potters." *Ceramics Monthly* 51 (June/July/August 2003): 64–71.

Brown, Glen R. "Matt Long's Moments of Victory." *Ceramics Monthly* 52 (January 2004): 32–36.

———. "Xiaoping Luo's 'Time Square.'" *Ceramics Monthly* 52 (February 2004): 39–42.

Brown, Michael K. *The Wilson Potters: An African-American Enterprise in 19th-Century Texas.* Exhibit catalog, Museum of Fine Arts, Houston, November 3, 2002–March 3, 2003. Houston: Bayou Bend Collection and Gardens, Museum of Fine Arts, 2002.

Brown, Peter. "Derby Porcelain: The Work of Floral and Botanical Artists, 1790–1805." *Antiques* (June 2003): 102–11.

Bruce, Susan. *The Art of Handbuilt Ceramics.* Marlborough, Eng.: Crowood; dist. in the U.S. by Trafalgar Square, 2000.

Bruggeman, Rhue, and Beverly Curtis. "Building a Minigama at Mount Hood Community College." *Ceramics Monthly* 51 (June/July/August 2003): 72–75.

Busby, Eileen R. *Cottage Ware: Ceramic Tableware Shaped as Buildings, 1920s–1990s.* A Schiffer Book for Collectors. Atglen, Pa.: Schiffer, 2003.

Busch, Richard. "A Wood-Fired Look from an Electric Kiln." *Ceramics Monthly* 51 (February 2003): 45–47.

Butera, Anthony W., Jr. "'Informed Conjecture': Collecting Long Island Redware." *Ceramics in America* 3 (2003): 214–37.

Butler, Michael, Julia B. Curtis, and Stephen Little. *Shunzhi Porcelain, 1644–1661: Treasures from an Unknown Reign.* Exhibit catalog, Honolulu Academy of Arts; Trammell and Margaret Crow Collection of Asian Art, Dallas; University of Virginia Art Museum, Charlottesville. Alexandria, Va.: Art Services International, 2002.

California Heritage Museum. *California Tile: The Golden Era, 1910–1940, Acme to Handcraft.* Edited by Joseph A. Taylor. A Schiffer Book. Atglen, Pa.: Schiffer, 2003.

———. *California Tile: The Golden Era, 1910–1940, Hispano-Moresque to Woolenius.* Edited by Joseph A. Taylor. Updated ed. A Schiffer Book. Atglen, Pa.: Schiffer, 2003.

"Cambridge Shape aka Scalloped Decagon." *White Ironstone Notes* [White Ironstone China Association Newsletter] 5, no. 2 (fall 1998): 1, 4–8.

"Cameos and Faces." *White Ironstone Notes* [White Ironstone China Association Newsletter] 8, no. 3 (winter 2001): 1, 4–11.

Carruthers, Clive. "Spanish *Botijas* or Olive Jars from the Santo Domingo Monastery, La Antigua, Guatemala." *Historical Archaeology* 37, no. 4 (2003): 40–55.

Cartier, Jean. *Faïences du Beauvaisis au XIXe siècle: Manufactures de Saint-Paul et de l'Italienne.* Paris: Somogy/Beauvais, 2002.

———. *Grès, terres cuites et faïences: Chefs-d'oeuvre du Beauvaisis au XIXe siècle.* Paris: Somogy, 2002.

Cartier, Jean, and Audrey Magnan. *Céramiques de l'Oise: La Collection du Musée départemental de l'Oise.* Paris: Somogy, 2001.

Cassidy-Geiger, Maureen. "Fabled Beasts: Augustus the Strong's Meissen Menagerie." *Antiques* 164 (October 2003): 152–61.

"Ceramiche e corredi in epoca moderna" [Monastic Ceramics in Italy during the Modern Age]. 1998 conference, Finale Emilia. *Archeologia Postmedievale,* no. 5 (2001).

Chervenka, Mark. *Antique Trader Guide to Fakes and Reproductions.* Iola, Wis.: Krause, 2002.

Christie's. *Benjamin F. Edwards III Collection of Chinese Export Porcelain, Part III.* Auction catalog, Christie's New York, January 20, 2004. New York: Christie's, 2004.

Christie's. *Captains and Kilns: European Ceramics, Chinese Export, and Maritime Art, including Palissyware and French Majolica, the Property of Animal Art Antiques.* Auction catalog, Christie's New York, January 20–21, 2004. New York: Christie's, 2004.

Christie's. *European Ceramics including the Pompey Collection.* Auction catalog, Christie's New York, May 23, 2002. New York: Christie's, 2002.

Cincinnati Art Galleries. *Holiday Sale 2003: Including Fine Fulper and Grueby from the John Hunter and Allen Weisberger Collection, Rookwood from the Family of Indiana Artist William Forsyth, and Pieces from the Family of One of Rookwood's Last Owners; Also Items from Several Important Midwestern Collections.* Auction catalog, Cincinnati Art Galleries, November 1–2, 2003. Cincinnati, Ohio: Cincinnati Art Galleries, 2003.

Clark, Kenneth. *The Tile: Making, Designing, and Using.* Marlborough, Eng.: Crowood; dist. by Trafalgar Square, 2002.

Clark, Phyllis B. "Walter Ostrum." *Ceramics Monthly* 51 (April 2003): 50–55.

Clennell, Tony. "Up in Canada: An Appreciation of the Work of Bruce Cochrane." *Ceramics Monthly* 51 (June/July/August 2003): 55–59.

Clifford, Timothy. "Some English Ceramic Vases and Their Sources, Part 2." In *British Ceramic Design, 1600–2002,* edited by Tom Walford and Hilary Young, pp. 73–105. Paper presented at a colloquium celebrating the 75th anniversary of the English Ceramic Circle, September 21, 2002, Victoria and Albert Museum, London. Beckenham, Kent, Eng.: English Ceramic Circle, 2003.

Cloonan, Mary K. "Bernadette Curran." *Ceramics Monthly* 51 (November 2003): 82–83.

Coates, Carole. *Catalina Island Pottery and Tile, 1927–1937: Island Treasures.* A Schiffer Book for Collectors. Atglen, Pa.: Schiffer, 2001.

Cockerill, John, and Joyce Cockerill. "Naked Children on North East Pots." *Northern Ceramic Society Newsletter,* no. 131 (2003): 23–27.

———. "Pattersons—Potters of Gateshead." *Northern Ceramic Society Newsletter,* no. 129 (2003): 13–15.

———. "Produced by Hogarth, Copied and Engraved by Robson, and Printed at Middlesbrough Pottery." *Northern Ceramic Society Newsletter,* no. 130 (2003): 31–32.

Coleman-Smith, Richard, with P. E. Pickering, O. Rackham, A. Peterson, I. Peterson, W. Moore, A. Coleman-Smith, B. Gittos, and M. Gittos. "Excavations in the Donyatt Potteries: Site 13." *Post-Medieval Archaeology* 36 (2002): 118–72.

"Columbia Shape." *White Ironstone Notes* [White Ironstone China Association Newsletter] 9, no. 4 (spring 2003): 1, 4–13.

Conroy, Michel L., ed. *Mingei Legacy: Continuity and Innovation through Three Generations of Modern Potters.* Exhibit catalog, Mingei International Museum, San Diego, February 14–April 3, 2003. Erie, Colo.: NCECA (National Council on Education in the Ceramic Arts), 2003.

Constable, Peter. "The Manufacture of British Holy Water Stoups." *English Ceramic Circle Transactions* 18, pt. 2 (2003): 339–48.

Cooper, Emmanuel. *David Leach: 20th Century Ceramics.* Shepton Beauchamp, Eng.: Richard Dennis, 2003.

"Corn and Oats." *White Ironstone Notes* [White Ironstone China Association Newsletter] 6, no. 2 (fall 1999): 1, 4–10.

Cox, Alwyn, and Angela Cox. "Joseph Newton, Swinton Pot Painter." *Northern Ceramic Society Newsletter,* no. 131 (2003): 41–46.

Cruickshank, Graeme. *A Visit to Dunmore Pottery: A Contemporary Account, with Additional Commentary.* Stirling Smith Art Gallery and Museum, Scottish Pottery Studies, No. 4. Stirling, Scot.: Stirling Smith Art Gallery and Museum, 2002.

Cumberpatch, Christopher G. "The Transformation of Tradition: The Origins of the Post-Medieval Ceramic Tradition in Yorkshire." *Assemblage* [Sheffield graduate journal of archaeology], no. 7 (April 2003). <www.shef.ac.uk/assem/>

Currie, Christopher K., with Peter Foster and Kathy White. "Archaeological Excavations at Upper Lodge, Bushy Park, London Borough of Richmond, 1997–99." *Post-Medieval Archaeology* 37, no. 1 (2003): 90–125.

Darling, Trevor. "A Coffee Cup Conundrum." *Northern Ceramic Society Newsletter,* no. 129 (2003): 36–38.

———. "English 18th Century Porcelain Potting Pots and Pans." *Northern Ceramic Society Journal* 19 (2002): 93–104.

Davis, Steve. "Kazegama." *Ceramics Monthly* 51 (March 2003): 54–56.

Denker, Ellen. "Lenox China Easy Guide to Dating Dinnerware Patterns." *Trenton Potteries* [Newsletter of the Potteries of Trenton Society] 3, no. 3 (September 2002): 1–3.

De Waal, Edmund. *Twentieth Century Ceramics.* London: Thames and Hudson, 2003.

Dewar, Richard. *Stoneware.* Philadelphia: University of Pennsylvania Press, 2002.

Dieringer, Ernie, and Bev Dieringer. *White Ironstone Pitchers: An Identification Guide.* Redding, Conn.: White Ironstone China Association, Inc., 2003.

Dietz, Ulysses G. *Great Pots: Contemporary Ceramics from Function to Fantasy.* Exhibit catalog, Newark Museum, February 14–June 1, 2003. Madison, Wis.: Guild; dist. by North Light Books, 2003.

Docker, Keith. "A Cockpit Hill Teapot." *Northern Ceramic Society Newsletter,* no. 131 (2003): 47–48.

Dodd, Leigh J. "Excavations on the Site of the Lewis Pottery Complex, Buckley, North Wales, United Kingdom." *Ceramics in America* 3 (2003): 245–48.

Doherty, Jack. *Porcelain.* Philadelphia: University of Pennsylvania Press, 2002.

Draper, Jo, and Penny Copland-Griffiths. *Dorset Country Pottery: The Kilns of the Verwood District.* Marlborough, Eng.: Crowood; dist. in the U.S. by Trafalgar Square, 2003.

Eden, Victoria. "Bryan Trueman." *Ceramics Monthly* 51 (June/July/August 2003): 90–91.

Edmundson, Roger S. "Benthall Pottery, Shropshire and Its Salopian Art Pottery." *Northern Ceramic Society Journal* 19 (2002): 29–76.

Edwards, Diana. "English White Salt-Glazed Stoneware for the American Market." *English Ceramic Circle Transactions* 18, pt. 2 (2003): 315–34.

Eiland, Murray. "Ceramic Culture Innovation, 1851–2000." *Ceramics Monthly* 52 (February 2004): 61–64.

Ellis, Anita J. *The Ceramic Career of M. Louise McLaughlin.* Cincinnati: Cincinnati Art Museum; Athens, Ohio: Ohio University Press, 2003.

Emmerson, Robin. "Design for Dessert." In *British Ceramic Design, 1600–2002,* edited by Tom Walford and Hilary Young, pp. 58–72. Paper presented at a colloquium celebrating the 75th anniversary of the English Ceramic Circle, September 21, 2002, Victoria and Albert Museum, London. Beckenham, Kent, Eng.: English Ceramic Circle, 2003.

Erickson, Michelle, and Robert Hunter. "Swirls and Whirls: English Agateware Technology." *Ceramics in America* 3 (2003): 87–110.

Espenshade, Christopher T. "The Two Faces of Anthony Baecher." *Ceramics in America* 3 (2003): 256–58.

Eyles, Desmond, rev. by Louise Irving. *The Doulton Lambeth Wares.* Rev. ed. Shepton Beauchamp, Eng.: Richard Dennis, 2002.

Falk, Cynthia. "Sarah Bixler's Plates and Flowerpots." *Antiques* 164 (July 2003): 70–77.

Fennell, Christopher C. "Molded Malevolence: Instrumental Symbolism Rendered in Clay." *Ceramics in America* 3 (2003): 270–73.

Ferguson, Patricia F. *Cobalt Treasures: The Robert Murray Bell and Ann Walker Bell Collection of Chinese Blue and White Porcelain.* Toronto: George R. Gardiner Museum, 2003.

Finkelnburg, Dave. "Mark Issenburg." *Ceramics Monthly* 51 (March 2003): 72–75.

Fisher, Charles L., ed. *People, Places, and Material Things: Historical Archaeology of Albany, New York.* New York State Museum Bulletin 499. Albany, N.Y.: New York State Museum, 2003.

"Fluted Shapes, The." *White Ironstone Notes* [White Ironstone China Association Newsletter] 10, no. 3 (winter 2004): 1, 4–15.

Forbes, Sheila, and George Haggarty. "William Reid's Newbigging Pottery, Musselburgh, 1800–1932." *Northern Ceramic Society Journal* 19 (2002): 15–27.

Freestone, Ian C., Louise Joyner, and Ray Howard. "The Composition of Porcelain from the Isleworth Manufactory." *English Ceramic Circle Transactions* 18, pt. 2 (2003): 284–94.

Gabszewicz, Anton. "Bow Porcelain: A Suggested Chronology" [lecture notes]. *Northern Ceramic Society Newsletter,* no. 130 (2003): 9–11.

Garriott-Stejskal, Richard. "Maxine Chelini." *Ceramics Monthly* 51 (February 2003): 32–35.

Gavin, Robin Farwell, Donna Pierce, and Alfonso Pleguezuelo, eds. *Cerámica y cultura: The Story of Spanish and Mexican Mayólica.* Exhibit catalog, Museum of International Folk Art, Santa Fe. Albuquerque, N.M.: University of New Mexico Press, 2003.

Gibson, Ann. "Ceramics in National Trust Houses." *Northern Ceramic Society Newsletter,* no. 129 (2003): 41–44.

Gleason, Ann. "Leah Leitson's Altered Porcelain Pots." *Ceramics Monthly* 51 (June/July/August 2003): 84–88.

Godden, Geoffrey A. "C. 19th Porcelain in the Godden Collection" [lecture notes]. *Northern Ceramic Society Newsletter,* no. 129 (2003): 9–12.

———. *Godden's Guide to English Blue and White Porcelain.* Woodbridge, Suffolk, Eng.: Antique Collectors' Club, 2003.

———. "'A Set of Three Handsome Ornaments' (Daniels, 1846)." *Northern Ceramic Society Newsletter,* no. 130 (2003): 23–29.

Goldberg, Arthur F. "Highlights in the Development of the Rockingham and Yellow Ware Industry in the United States—A Brief Review with Representative Examples." *Ceramics in America* 3 (2003): 26–46.

Goodby, Miranda. "'Our Home in the West': Staffordshire Potters and Their Emigration to America in the 1840s." *Ceramics in America* 3 (2003): 1–25.

Goodwin, Jonathan. "The Excavations at the New Bridge Pottery, Longport: The Phillips, Davenport, Clarke, and Bodley Periods" [lecture notes]. *Northern Ceramic Society Newsletter,* no. 129 (2003): 6–8.

Graham, Roger. "The Kiln Exhaust Sniffer: A Do-It-Yourself Oxygen Probe." *Ceramics Monthly* 51 (March 2003): 84–85.

"Grape Shapes, The." *White Ironstone Notes* [White Ironstone China Association Newsletter] 8, no. 2 (fall 2001): 1, 4–16.

Graves, Alun. *Tiles and Tilework.* London: Victoria and Albert Museum, 2002.

Gray, Jonathan, ed. *Welsh Ceramics in Context.* Part 1. Swansea, Wales: Royal Institution of South Wales and City and County of Swansea, 2003.

Gray, Pamela L. *Ohio Valley Pottery Towns.* Mount Pleasant, S.C.: Arcadia, 2002.

Gristina, Margaret Kaelin, and James Cummings. *Chinese Export Porcelain Including Figures from the Collection of Mr. and Mrs. Robert Gill.* Exhibit catalog, Chinese Porcelain Company, October 10–26, 2002. New York: Chinese Porcelain Company, 2002.

Groninger Museum. *Umi o watatta tōjikiten: Keitokuchin imari derufuto Oranda furōningen hakubutsukan shozō Nichiran kōryū yonhyakunen kinen tokubetsuten / Ceramics Crossed Overseas: Jingdezhen, Imari, and Delft from the Collection of the Groninger Museum.* Exhibit catalog, Sogo Museum of Art, September 30–November 15, 1999; Nagasaki Prefectural Art Museum, February 4–27, 2000; Kaimaru Museum of Art, Tokyo, March 2–14, 2000; Nara Sogo Museum of Art, March 16–April 2, 2000; Kobe Daimaru Museum of Art, April 6–25, 2000. [Tokyo]: Mainichi Shinbunsha, 1999.

Gründig, Rita, and Hans-Dieter Roethe. *Lettiner Porzellan: Zur Geschichte einer mitteldeutschen Porzellanfabrik.* Exhibit catalog, Staatliche Galerie Moritzburg, Landeskunstmuseum Sachsen-Anhalt, December 1, 2000–March 4, 2001. Halle an der Saale, Ger.: Staatliche Galerie Moritzburg, Landeskunstmuseum Sachsen-Anhalt, 2000.

Hamer, Frank, and Janet Hamer. *The Potter's Dictionary of Materials and Techniques.* 5th ed. Philadelphia: University of Pennsylvania Press, 2004.

Hardy, Michael. *Handbuilding.* Philadelphia: University of Pennsylvania Press, 2000.

Harlow, Francis H., and Dwight P. Lanmon. *The Pottery of Zia Pueblo.* Santa Fe, N.M.: School of American Research Press, 2003.

Hauser, Mark W., and Christopher R. DeCorse. "Low-Fired Earthenwares in the African Diaspora: Problems and Prospects." *International Journal of Historical Archaeology* 7, no. 1 (2003): 67–98.

Heeney, Gwen. *Brickworks.* Philadelphia: University of Pennsylvania Press, 2003.

Henrywood, R. K. *Staffordshire Potters, 1781–1900: A Comprehensive List Assembled from Contemporary Directories with Selected Marks.* Woodbridge, Suffolk, Eng.: Antique Collectors' Club, 2002.

Herbert, Tony. "Clay as Canvas: Pictorial Tile Panels" [lecture notes]. *Northern Ceramic Society Newsletter,* no. 130 (2003): 6–8.

Hess, Catherine. *Italian Ceramics: Catalogue of the J. Paul Getty Museum Collections.* Los Angeles: Getty Publications, 2002.

Hewat, Margaret, and June M. Owen. *Hilditch Porcelain.* Clwyd, Wales: Avondale, 2003.

———. "Topographical Wares Produced by Hilditch and Hopwood during the Period 1845 to 1855." *Northern Ceramic Society Newsletter,* no. 130 (2003): 17–22.

Hillis, Maurice. "The Analysis of Shards from the Brownlow Hill Site in Liverpool." *English Ceramic Circle Transactions* 18, pt. 2 (2003): 335–38.

Holdway, Ruth. "Batman Returns" [Paul Holdway demonstrating bat printing]. *Northern Ceramic Society Newsletter,* no. 132 (2003): 3–4.

Hood, Graham. "Meditations on a Chinese Musician." *Ceramics in America* 3 (2003): 196–213.

Hopper, Robin. "Chosin Pottery Inc.: Stinking Fish in Paradise." *Ceramics Monthly* 51 (November 2003): 43–49.

Hoskisson, Don. "The Pattern and the Passion." *Ceramics Monthly* 52 (February 2004): 34–38.

Howard, David Sanctuary. *Chinese Armorial Porcelain.* Vol. 2. Chippenham, Wiltshire, Eng.: Heirloom and Howard, 2003.

Howarth, Jack, and Robin Hildyard. *Joseph Kishere and the Mortlake Potteries.* Woodbridge, Suffolk, Eng.: Antique Collectors' Club, 2004.

Hugoniot, Jean-Yves. *Terres de Saintonge: L'art de la poterie, XIIe–XIXe siècle.* Paris: Somogy, 2002.

Hunt, Bill. *21st Century Ceramics in the United States and Canada.* Westerville, Ohio: American Ceramic Society, 2003.

Hunter, Richard W. "The Pottery Decorating Shop of the Mayer Arsenal Pottery Company." *Trenton Potteries* [Newsletter of the Potteries of Trenton Society] 4, no. 2 (June 2003): 1–7.

———. "William Richards' Stoneware Pottery Discovered!" *Trenton Potteries* [Newsletter of the Potteries of Trenton Society] 1, no. 3 (August/September 2000): 1–3.

———, transcr. "Minutes of the [Trenton] Potters Union." *Trenton Potteries* [Newsletter of the Potteries of Trenton Society] 3, no. 4 (December 2002): 1–5.

———, transcr. "Minutes of the [Trenton] Potters Union." *Trenton Potteries* [Newsletter of the Potteries of Trenton Society] 4, no. 1 (January 2003): 1–5.

Jackson, Reg. "Late 17th-Century Stoneware Waste from the Tower Harratz Pottery, Bristol." *Post-Medieval Archaeology* 37, pt. 2 (2003): 217–20.

Jarrett, Chris. "The Pottery." In "The Post-Medieval Waterfront Development at Adlards Wharf, Bermondsey, London," by David Divers. *Post-Medieval Archaeology* 36 (2002): 102–8.

Johnson, Donald-Brian, Timothy Holthaus, and James Petzold. *Ceramic Arts Studio: The Legacy of Betty Harrington.* A Schiffer Book for Collectors. Atglen, Pa.: Schiffer, 2003.

Jones, David. *Raku: Investigations into Fire.* Marlborough, Eng.: Crowood; dist. in the U.S. by Trafalgar Square, 1999.

Jordan, Derek H. *Victorian China Fairings: The Collectors' Guide.* Woodbridge, Suffolk, Eng.: Antique Collectors' Club, 2003.

Jörg, Christiaan J. A. *Fine and Curious: Japanese Export Porcelain in Dutch Collections.* Amsterdam: Hotei, 2003.

Joseph, J. W., and Martha Zierden, eds. *Another's Country: Archaeological and Historical Perspectives on Cultural Interactions in the Southern Colonies.* Tuscaloosa, Ala.: University Press of Alabama, 2002.

Karskens, Grace. "Revisiting the Worldview: The Archaeology of Convict Households in Sydney's Rocks Neighborhood." *Historical Archaeology* 37, no. 1 (2003): 34–55.

Kelly, Sophia E. "The Potter's Mark: Redwares and Stonewares Recovered in Excavation of the Duncan-Bower House in the Hamlet of Enfield Falls, New York." B.A. thesis, Department of Archaeology, Cornell University, Ithaca, N.Y., 2003.

Kennedy, Rachel. *Between Bath and China: Trade and Culture in the West Country, 1680 to 1840.* Bath, Eng.: Museum of East Asian Art, [1999].

Killock, Douglas, John Brown, and Christopher Jarrett. "The Industrialization of an Ecclesiastical Hamlet: Stoneware Production in Lambeth and the Sanitary Revolution." *Post-Medieval Archaeology* 37, no. 1 (2003): 29–78.

Kyūshū Ceramic Museum. *Koimari no michi / The Voyage of Old Imari Porcelains.* Exhibit catalog, Kyūshū Ceramic Museum, October 3–December 3, 2000. Saga, Japan: Saga Art and Culture Foundation, 2000.

Lackey, Louana M. *Rudy Autio.* Westerville, Ohio: American Ceramics Society, 2002.
———. "Some Assembly Required: The Work of Richard Milette." *Ceramics Monthly* 51 (March 2003): 64–68.
Lawrence, Susan. "Exporting Culture: Archaeology and the Nineteenth-Century British Empire." *Historical Archaeology* 37, no. 1 (2003): 20–33.
Layton, Thomas N. *Gifts from the Celestial Kingdom: A Shipwrecked Cargo for Gold Rush California.* Palo Alto, Calif.: Stanford University Press, 2002.
Le Corbeiller, Clare, and Alice C. Frelinghuysen. "Chinese Export Porcelain." *The Metropolitan Museum of Art Bulletin* 60, no. 3 (winter 2003).
Ledger, A. P., comp. *The Bedford Street Warehouse and the London China Trade, 1773–1796: References from Original Documents.* Derby Porcelain Archive Research Reports, vol. 2. Derby, Eng.: Derby Museums and Art Gallery, 2003.
Lee, Angela. "Flushed with Pride: The Story of the Toilet" [lecture notes]. *Northern Ceramic Society Newsletter,* no. 130 (2003): 5–6.
Lehman, Dick. "Carrying the Empty Cup: Three Generations within the Japanese Master/Apprentice Tradition." *Ceramics Monthly* 51 (December 2003): 70–77.
Levin, Elaine M., ed. *Movers and Shakers in American Ceramics: Defining Twentieth Century Ceramics.* Westerville, Ohio: American Ceramic Society, 2003.
Lewington, John. "St. Anthony's Pottery, Tyneside, circa 1780–1878." *Northern Ceramic Society Journal* 19 (2002): 5–13.
Lewis, Ann-Eliza H., ed. *Highway to the Past: The Archaeology of Boston's Big Dig.* Boston: Massachusetts Historical Commission, 2001.
Lewis, Sue. "Rock Creek Climbing Kiln." *Ceramics Monthly* 52 (January 2004): 40–44.
Liebeknecht, William B. "Joseph Mayer's Arsenal Pottery Dump, Part 1: Yellow Ware." *Trenton Potteries* [Newsletter of the Potteries of Trenton Society] 1, no. 2 (April/May 2000): 1–2, 4.
———. "Joseph Mayer's Arsenal Pottery Dump, Part 2: Majolica." *Trenton Potteries* [Newsletter of the Potteries of Trenton Society] 1, no. 3 (August/September 2000): 4–5.
———. "Joseph Mayer's Arsenal Pottery Dump, Part 3: Cut Sponge Decorated Ironstone China." *Trenton Potteries* [Newsletter of the Potteries of Trenton Society] 2, no. 3/4 (December 2001): 1–4.
———. "William Richards' Sugar Processing Pottery, 1760–1786." *Trenton Potteries* [Newsletter of the Potteries of Trenton Society] 1, no. 4 (December 2000): 1–4.
Liebeknecht, William B., and Richard W. Hunter. "The Richards Face—Shades of an Eighteenth-Century American Bellarmine." *Ceramics in America* 3 (2003): 259–61.
Liebeknecht, William B., Rebecca White, and Richard W. Hunter. "A Coxon Waster Deposit of the Mid-1860s, Sampled in Trenton, New Jersey." *Ceramics in America* 3 (2003): 241–44.
Litzenburg, Thomas V., Jr., and Ann T. Bailey. *Chinese Export Porcelain in the Reeves Center Collection at Washington and Lee University.* London: Third Millennium Publishing; dist. by Antique Collectors' Club, 2003.
Lucas, Gavin. "Reading Pottery: Literature and Transfer-Printed Pottery in the Early Nineteenth Century." *International Journal of Historical Archaeology* 7, no. 2 (2003): 127–43.
Lucas, Gavin, Roderick Regan, Lucy Whittingham, Duncan Mackay, and Lorrain Higbee. "The Changing Vernacular: Archaeological Excavations at Temple End, High Wycombe, Buckinghamshire." *Post-Medieval Archaeology* 37, pt. 2 (2003): 165–206.
Lukacs, George H. *Poughkeepsie Potters and the Plague.* Mount Pleasant, S.C.: Arcadia, 2001.
Madrigal, Patricia. "Profiles in Pottery: The W. H. Tatler Decorating Company." *Trenton Potteries* [Newsletter of the Potteries of Trenton Society] 1, no. 2 (April/May 2000): 3.
Magid, Barbara H., and Bernard K. Means. "In the Philadelphia Style: The Pottery of Henry Piercy." *Ceramics in America* 3 (2003): 47–86.
Mallet, J.V.G. "Agostino Carlini, Modeller of 'Dry-Edge' Derby Figures?" In *British Ceramic Design, 1600–2002,* edited by Tom Walford and Hilary Young, pp. 42–57. Paper presented at a colloquium celebrating the 75th anniversary of the English Ceramic Circle, September 21, 2002, Victoria and Albert Museum, London. Beckenham, Kent, Eng.: English Ceramic Circle, 2003.
———. "The First Seventy Five Years of the English Ceramic Circle." In *British Ceramic Design, 1600–2002,* edited by Tom Walford and Hilary Young, pp. 1–14. Paper presented at a colloquium celebrating the 75th anniversary of the English Ceramic Circle, September 21, 2002, Victoria and Albert Museum, London. Beckenham, Kent, Eng.: English Ceramic Circle, 2003.
———. "The 'Gentleman Potters,' Part 1: Bernard and Janet Leach." *English Ceramic Circle Transactions* 18, pt. 2 (2003): 253–63.
Malone, Kate. *Kate Malone: A Book of Pots.* Woodstock, N.Y.: Overlook, 2003.
Manger, George, and Connie Manger. *Pottery from the Shenandoah and Cumberland Valleys: Selections from the Manger Collection.* Exhibit catalog, Washington County Museum of Fine Arts, May 16–September 14, 2003. Hagerstown, Md.: Washington County Museum of Fine Arts, 2003.
Markin, Trevor. "Anthony Keeling and Company, Part 2: The Partners John Shorthose, Thomas Shelley, and Thomas Heath."

Northern Ceramic Society Journal 19 (2002): 105–27.
———. "Thomas Baddeley, Engraver and Enameller." *Northern Ceramic Society Journal* 19 (2002): 1–4.
Martin, Colin. "De-particularizing the Particular: Approaches to the Investigation of Well-Documented Post-Medieval Shipwrecks." *World Archaeology* 32, no. 3 (2001): 383–99.
Massey, Roger. "The Isleworth Pottery Accounts, 1794–1805." *English Ceramic Circle Transactions* 18, pt. 2 (2003): 300–14.
———. "The Isleworth Pottery Insurance Policies, 1765–1800." *English Ceramic Circle Transactions* 18, pt. 2 (2003): 295–99.
Massey, Roger, Jacqueline Pearce, and Ray Howard. *Isleworth Pottery and Porcelain: Recent Discoveries.* Exhibit catalog, Stockspring Antiques, London, June 5–14, 2003. London: English Ceramic Circle and Museum of London Specialist Services, 2003.
Mathieu, Paul. *Sex Pots: Eroticism in Ceramics.* Piscataway, N.J.: Rutgers University Press, 2003.
McKeown, Julie. *Burgess, Dorling and Leigh.* Shepton Beauchamp, Eng.: Richard Dennis, 2004.
McLaurin, Arthur P., and Harvey S. Teal. *Just Mud: Kershaw County, South Carolina, Pottery to 1980.* Camden, S.C.: Kershaw County Historical Society, 2002.
Medieval Pottery Research Group. *Minimum Standards for the Processing, Recording, Analysis, and Publication of Post-Roman Ceramics.* Occasional Paper, no. 2. London: Medieval Pottery Research Group, 2001.
Meldrum, Rose. "Mr Campbell and Mr Drinkwater: Two Liverpool Delftware Potters." *Northern Ceramic Society Newsletter,* no. 131 (2003): 28–30.
Melosi, Martin V. *The Sanitary City: Urban Infrastructure in America from Colonial Times to the Present.* Creating the North American Landscape series. Baltimore: Johns Hopkins University Press, 2000.
Meslin-Perrier, Chantal, and Marie Segonds-Perrier. *Limoges: Deux siècles de porcelaine.* Paris: Amateur; Réunion des musées nationaux, 2002.
Meyers, Allan D. "West African Tradition in the Decoration of Colonial Jamaican Folk Pottery." *International Journal of Historical Archaeology* 3, no. 4 (1999): 201–23.
Mézin, Louis. *Cargaisons de Chine: Porcelaines de la Compagnie des Indes du Musée de Lorient.* Exhibit catalog, Musée de la Compagnie des Indes, Lorient, June 26–November 30, 2002. [Lorient, Fr.:] Musée de la Compagnie des Indes, 2002.
Michaud, Joyce. "Gary and Daphne Hatcher Creating a Cohesive Whole." *Ceramics Monthly* 52 (February 2004): 50–57.
Miller, Matthew R. *Decorated Stoneware of Cowden and the Stoneware Potteries of Harrisburg, Pennsylvania, 1852–1924.* Shermans Dale, Pa.: Harrisburg Stoneware Book, 2001.
Milne, Graeme J. *Trade and Traders in Mid-Victorian Liverpool: Mercantile Business and the Making of a World Port.* Liverpool: Liverpool University Press, 2000.
Minogue, Coll, and Robert Sanderson. *Wood-fired Ceramics: Contemporary Practices.* Philadelphia: University of Pennsylvania Press, 2000.
Miro, Marsha, and Tony Hepburn. *Robert Turner: Shaping Silence, a Life in Clay.* New York: Kodansha International, 2003.
Moes, Robert. *Quiet Beauty: Fifty Centuries of Japanese Folk Ceramics from the Montgomery Collection.* Exhibit catalog. Alexandria, Va.: Art Services International, 2003.
Mohr, Richard D. *Pottery, Politics, Art: George Ohr and the Brothers Kirkpatrick.* Champaign, Ill.: University of Illinois Press, 2003.
Molina-Morales, F. Xavier. "Industrial Districts and Innovation: The Case of the Spanish Ceramic Tiles Industry." *Entrepreneurship and Regional Development* 14, no. 4 (2002): 317–35.
Mommsen, H. "Provenance Determination of Pottery by Trace Element Analysis: Problems, Solutions, and Applications." *Journal of Radioanalytical and Nuclear Chemistry* 247, no. 3 (2001): 657–62.
Monsoon Guides. *Shopping for Antiques and Collectibles: Singapore and Malaysia, 2003/4.* Chicago: Art Media Resources, 2003.
Morgenthal, Deborah, and Suzanne J. E. Tourtillott, eds. *The Penland Book of Ceramics: Master Classes in Ceramic Techniques.* New York: Lark Books, 2003.
Mortimer, K. V. *Pot-Lids and Other Coloured Printed Staffordshire Ware: Reference and Price Guide.* Woodbridge, Suffolk, Eng.: Antique Collectors' Club, 2003.
Moulder, Enid, and Bruce Moulder. "NSC [*sic*] Members, Pray Raise Your . . . Tea Pot Lids!" *Northern Ceramic Society Newsletter,* no. 131 (2003): 31–33.
Murfitt, Stephen. *The Glaze Book: A Visual Catalogue of Decorative Ceramic Glazes.* London: Thames and Hudson, 2002.
Murphy, Pat. *Noritake for Europe.* A Schiffer Book for Collectors. Atglen, Pa.: Schiffer, 2001.
Musée des beaux-arts de Dijon. *Un cabinet des porcelaines: Porcelaines de Saxe dans les collections publiques parisiennes.* Exhibit catalog, Musée des beaux-arts de Dijon, June 16–October 1, 2001. Dijon, Fr.: Musée des beaux-arts de Dijon, 2001.
Nagatake, Takeshi. *Classic Japanese Porcelain: Imari and Kakiemon.* Combined ed. Tokyo: Kodansha International, 2003.
National Academy of Design, Caskey-Lees, and Sha-Dor. *The New York Ceramics Fair.* Exhibit catalog, New York Ceramics Fair, January 14–18, 2004. New York: National Academy of Design, 2004.
Nefedova, Olga. "Early Zsolnay Porcelain-Faience in the Tareq

Rajab Museum." *Ceramics Monthly* 52 (January 2004): 58–60.

Newell, Mark M. "Making His MARK." *Ceramics in America* 3 (2003): 273–75.

"New York Shape, Asia Shape, and Leaf Focus." *White Ironstone Notes* [White Ironstone China Association Newsletter] 9, no. 2 (fall 2002): 1, 4–11.

Nissen, Craig. *McCoy Pottery Wall Pockets and Decorations: Identification and Values.* Paducah, Ky.: Collector Books, 2003.

Noël Hume, Ivor. "Through the Lookinge Glasse; or, The Chamber Pot as a Mirror of Its Time." *Ceramics in America* 3 (2003): 138–71.

Norris, Scott. "Mark Shapiro." *Ceramics Monthly* 51 (September 2003): 51–58.

O'Donovan, Maria, and LouAnn Wurst. "Living on the Edge: Consumption and Class at the Keith Site." *Northeast Historical Archaeology* 30–31 (2001–2002): 73–84.

O'Malley, Nancy. "The Pursuit of Freedom." *Winterthur Portfolio* 37, no. 4 (2002): 187–217.

Oriental Ceramic Society. *The World in Blue and White: An Exhibition of Blue and White Ceramics, Dating Between 1320–1820, from Members of the Oriental Ceramic Society.* Exhibit catalog. London: Oriental Ceramic Society, 2003.

Orr, David G. "Samuel Malkin in Philadelphia: A Remarkable Slipware Assemblage." *Ceramics in America* 3 (2003): 252–56.

Orser, Charles E., Jr., ed. *Encyclopedia of Historical Archaeology.* London: Routledge, 2002.

Orser, Charles E., Jr., and Pedro P. A. Funari. "Archaeology and Slave Resistance and Rebellion." *World Archaeology* 33, no. 1 (2001): 61–72.

Ostermann, Matthias. *The Ceramic Surface.* Philadelphia: University of Pennsylvania Press, 2002.

Outlaw, Alain C. "Backcountry Sophistication: Anthropomorphic Elements from a Piedmont North Carolina Kiln." *Ceramics in America* 3 (2003): 265–68.

Owen, J. Victor. "The Geochemistry of Worcester Porcelain from Dr. Wall to Royal Worcester: 150 Years of Innovation." *Historical Archaeology* 37, no. 4 (2003): 84–96.

Owen, J. Victor, and John Sandon. "A Rose by Any Other Name: A Geochemical Comparison of Caughley (c. 1772–99), Coalport (John Rose & Co.; c. 1799–1837), and Rival Porcelains Based on Sherds from the Factory Sites." *Post-Medieval Archaeology* 37, no. 1 (2003): 79–89.

Owen, Nancy E. *Rookwood Pottery at the Philadelphia Museum of Art: The Gerald and Virginia Gordon Collection.* Exhibit catalog, for "Elegant Innovations: American Rookwood Pottery, 1880–1960," Philadelphia Museum of Art, November 15, 2003–March 21, 2004. Philadelphia: Philadelphia Museum of Art; dist. by Antique Collectors' Club, 2003.

Padwee, Michael. "The Manufacture of Ceramic Tiles in Trenton, Part 2: The Trent Tile Company (1882–1939)." *Trenton Potteries* [Newsletter of the Potteries of Trenton Society] 4, no. 4 (December 2003): 1–6.

Padwee, Michael, and Susan I. Padwee. "The Manufacture of Ceramic Tiles in Trenton, Part 1." *Trenton Potteries* [Newsletter of the Potteries of Trenton Society] 4, no. 3 (September 2003): 1–4.

Paradis, Joe. *Abingdon Pottery Artware, 1934–1950: Stepchild of the Great Depression.* A Schiffer Book for Collectors. Atglen, Pa.: Schiffer, 2000.

Paradis, Joe, and Joyce Paradis. *The House of Haeger, 1914–1944: The Revitalization of American Art Pottery.* A Schiffer Book for Collectors. Atglen, Pa.: Schiffer, 1999.

———. *The House of Haeger, 1944–1969: The Post-War Era.* A Schiffer Book for Collectors. Atglen, Pa.: Schiffer, 2004.

Partington, Matthew. "Studio Potters and Design: A Case Study of the Whieldon-Inspired Earthenwares of Walter Keeler." In *British Ceramic Design, 1600–2002,* edited by Tom Walford and Hilary Young, pp. 145–52. Paper presented at a colloquium celebrating the 75th anniversary of the English Ceramic Circle, September 21, 2002, Victoria and Albert Museum, London. Beckenham, Kent, Eng.: English Ceramic Circle, 2003.

Patrick, Stephen E. "A Maryland Grouping of Bow and Derby Figures of the 1760s." *Ceramics in America* 3 (2003): 249–51.

Peacey, Allan, and Alan Vince. "Chemical Characterization of Clay Pipes and Wig Curlers from Roy's Orchard, Pipe Aston, Herefordshire." *Post-Medieval Archaeology* 37, pt. 2 (2003): 207–16.

Peck, Pauline C., and Glenn Erardi. *Mustache Cups: Timeless Victorian Treasures.* A Schiffer Book for Collectors. Atglen, Pa.: Schiffer, 2001.

Pierson, Stacey. *Designs as Signs: Decoration and Chinese Ceramics.* Exhibit catalog. London: Percival David Foundation of Chinese Art/School of Oriental and African Studies, University of London, 2001.

Pipes, Marie-Lorraine. *The Polychrome Pearlware Pattern Book.* Newton, N.J.: Artifact Research Center, 2003.

"Plain White Ironstone: A Shaker Aesthetic." *White Ironstone Notes* [White Ironstone China Association Newsletter] 5, no. 4 (spring 1999): 1, 4–8.

Pomfret, Roger. "The Bleak Hill Site, Cobridge." *Northern Ceramic Society Journal* 19 (2002): 129–62.

Pos, Tania M. Buckrell. *Tea and Taste: The Visual Language of Tea.* A Schiffer Book. Atglen, Pa.: Schiffer, 2004.

Preller, Patricia. *A Partial Reconstruction of the New Hall Pattern Book.* Bude, Eng.: Pat Preller, 2003.

Priddy, Sumpter, III. *American Fancy: Exuberance in the Arts, 1790–1840.* Exhibit catalog, Milwaukee Art Museum, April 3–June 20, 2004;

Peabody Essex Museum, Salem, Mass., July 14–October 31, 2004; Maryland Historical Society, Baltimore, December 3, 2004–March 20, 2005. Milwaukee: Chipstone Foundation and Milwaukee Art Museum; dist. in the U.S. by Distributed Art Publishers, 2004.

Queensberry, David. "The British Pottery Industry in the Post-War Period: A Personal Perspective." In *British Ceramic Design, 1600–2002*, edited by Tom Walford and Hilary Young, pp. 153–62. Paper presented at a colloquium celebrating the 75th anniversary of the English Ceramic Circle, September 21, 2002, Victoria and Albert Museum, London. Beckenham, Kent, Eng.: English Ceramic Circle, 2003.

Ramsay, Ross, and Anton Gabszewicz. "The Chemistry of 'A'-Marked Porcelain and Its Relation to the Heylyn and Frye Patent of 1744." *English Ceramic Circle Transactions* 18, pt. 2 (2003): 264–83.

Ratherham, Terry. "Sprig Mouldings—Can They Identify Manufacturers?" *Northern Ceramic Society Newsletter*, no. 129 (2003): 29–35.

Raynor, Barrie. "The John Hawley Potteries in Longton and Fenton." *Northern Ceramic Society Newsletter*, no. 129 (2003): 20–28.

"Relish Dish Update." *White Ironstone Notes* [White Ironstone China Association Newsletter] 10, no. 2 (fall 2003): 1, 5–19.

Rendall, Richard, and Elise Abrams. *Hand-Painted Porcelain Plates: Nineteenth Century to the Present*. A Schiffer Book for Collectors. Atglen, Pa.: Schiffer, 2003.

Resta, Monica. *Starting in Polymer Clay: Techniques, Tools, and Projects*. New York: Sterling Publishing, 2003.

Rice, Paul. *British Studio Ceramics*. Marlborough, Eng.: Crowood; dist. in the U.S. by Trafalgar Square, 2002.

Roberts, Gaye Blake. "Ware for a Good Man." *Northern Ceramic Society Journal* 19 (2002): 77–91.

———. "'Wax and Wooden Wonders': Design Sources Used by Josiah Wedgwood." In *British Ceramic Design, 1600–2002*, edited by Tom Walford and Hilary Young, pp. 106–23. Paper presented at a colloquium celebrating the 75th anniversary of the English Ceramic Circle, September 21, 2002, Victoria and Albert Museum, London. Beckenham, Kent, Eng.: English Ceramic Circle, 2003.

Rogers, Connie. *Illustrated Encyclopedia of British Willow Ware*. A Schiffer Book for Collectors. Atglen, Pa.: Schiffer, 2003.

———. "The Origin of the Willow Pattern." *Northern Ceramic Society Newsletter*, no. 130 (2003): 41–46.

Rogers, Phil. *Ash Glazes*. 2nd ed. Philadelphia: University of Pennsylvania Press, 2003.

———. *Salt Glazing*. Philadelphia: University of Pennsylvania Press, 2002.

Rosen, Kenna, and Bob Rosen. *Bluebird China*. A Schiffer Book for Collectors. Atglen, Pa.: Schiffer, 2003.

Sandon, John. *Starting to Collect Antique Porcelain*. Antique Collectors' Club, 2003.

Santos, Maria Carmen. "18th-Century Buen Retiro Porcelain." *Ceramics Monthly* 51 (December 2003): 57–59.

Scarlett, Timothy J. "Narcissus's Mirror: Manufacture and Modernism in the American Great Basin—The Case of Pottery." *International Journal of Historical Archaeology* 3, no. 3 (1999): 167–75.

Schaltenbrand, Phil. *Big Ware Turners: The History and Manufacture of Pennsylvania Stoneware, 1720–1920*. Bentleyville, Pa.: Westerwald Press, 2002.

Scharfenberger, Gerard P., and Richard F. Veit. "Rethinking the *Mengkom*-Mixing Bowl: Salvage Archaeology at the Johannes Luyster House, A Dutch-American Farm." *Northeast Historical Archaeology* 30–31 (2001–2002): 53–72.

Schneider, Ulrich, and Belinda Petri. *Kobaltblau: Meissener Porzellan des 18. Jahrhunderts aus einer rheinischen Privatsammlung*. Exhibit catalog, Couven Museum, Aachen, June 30–September 30, 2001. Aachen, Ger.: Museen der Stadt Aachen, [2001].

Schopp, Paul W., and David L. Weinberg. "National Ceramic Company, Trenton, New Jersey." *Trenton Potteries* [Newsletter of the Potteries of Trenton Society] 2, no. 1 (March 2001): 1–5.

Schroedl, Gerald F., and Todd M. Ahlman. "The Maintenance of Cultural and Personal Identities of Enslaved Africans and British Soldiers at the Brimstone Hill Fortress, St. Kitts, West Indies." *Historical Archaeology* 36, no. 4 (2002): 38–49.

Schulenberg, Stephan, Graf von der, and Rainald Simon. *Feuergeburten: Fruhe chinesische Keramik im mak.frankfurt/ The Birth of Form: Early Chinese Ceramics at mak.frankfurt*. Exhibit catalog, Museum für Angewandte Kunst (mak.frankfurt), June 20–September 15, 2002. Frankfurt: mak.frankfurt; Heidelberg: Wunderhorn, 2002.

Scotchie, Virginia. *Setting up Your Ceramic Studio: Ideas and Plans from Working Artists*. New York: Lark Books, 2003.

Scott, David. *Clays and Glazes in Studio Ceramics*. Marlborough, Eng.: Crowood; dist. in the U.S. by Trafalgar Square, 1998.

Scott, Paul. *Ceramics and Print*. 2nd ed. Philadelphia: University of Pennsylvania Press; London: A. and C. Black, 2002.

Signy, Michael. "A Sample Plate." *Northern Ceramic Society Newsletter*, no. 131 (2003): 38–40.

Singleton, Theresa A. "Slavery and Spatial Dialectics on Cuban Coffee Plantations." *World Archaeology* 33, no. 1 (2001): 98–114.

Skinner, Deborah. "The Story of Decorative Tiles at the Gladstone Museum" [lecture notes]. *Northern Ceramic Society Newsletter*, no. 130 (2003): 3–4.

Slitine, Florence. *Samson: Génie de l'imitation.* Paris: Editions Massin, 2002.

Smith, Roger. "'It Is Not in the Power of Porcelain To Be Commanded': Some Problems in the Design and Manufacture of Vulliamy's Sculptural Clocks." In *British Ceramic Design, 1600–2002,* edited by Tom Walford and Hilary Young, pp. 124–37. Paper presented at a colloquium celebrating the 75th anniversary of the English Ceramic Circle, September 21, 2002, Victoria and Albert Museum, London. Beckenham, Kent, Eng.: English Ceramic Circle, 2003.

Spasskii, Yu. I., S. V. Kurlakov, A. A. Kobelev, and I. S. Kurlakova. "Decoration of Ceramic Articles by Polymer-Powder Pigments." *Glass and Ceramics* 59 (2002): 386–88.

Spencer, Cynthia. "When Bad Glazes Happen to Good Potters: An Unsolved Mystery." *Ceramics Monthly* 51 (March 2003): 86–88.

Spero, Simon. *Annual Exhibition of 18th Century English Porcelain, 1745–1792.* Exhibit catalog, Simon Spero, London, October 7–18, 2003. London: Simon Spero, 2003.

———. "Vauxhall Porcelain: A Tentative Chronology." *English Ceramic Circle Transactions* 18, pt. 2 (2003): 349–72.

Spivey, Richard L. *The Legacy of Maria Poveka Martinez.* Santa Fe: Museum of New Mexico Press, 2003.

Staniforth, Mark. "Annales-Informed Approaches to the Archaeology of Colonial Australia." *Historical Archaeology* 37, no. 1 (2003): 102–13.

Stapleton, Annamarie. *John Moyr Smith, 1839–1912: A Victorian Designer.* Shepton Beauchamp, Eng.: Richard Dennis, 2002.

Stott, Annette. "The Dutch Dining Room in Turn-of-the-Century America." *Winterthur Portfolio* 37, no. 4 (2002): 219–38.

Straube, Beverly A. "The Prodigal Son Returns to Jamestown." *Ceramics in America* 3 (2003): 262–65.

"Syllabub, Posset, Punch, and Toddy Bowls and Cups." *White Ironstone Notes* [White Ironstone China Association Newsletter] 6, no. 3 (winter 2000): 1, 4–11.

Taylor, Alan. *Stoke-on-Trent Past.* Chichester, West Sussex, Eng.: Phillimore, 2003.

Taylor, Sue. *Bullers of Milton.* Leek, Eng.: Churnet Valley Books, 2003.

———. "Studio Ceramics in the Potteries Museum and Art Gallery." *Northern Ceramic Society Newsletter,* no. 129 (2003): 54–55.

Terpstra, Karen. "Australia's Bendigo Pottery." *Ceramics Monthly* 51 (January 2003): 66–68.

———. "Traditional Values from Down Under: La Trobe University's David Stuchbery." *Ceramics Monthly* 51 (March 2003): 57–60.

Tourtillott, Suzanne J. E. *500 Bowls: Contemporary Explorations of a Timeless Design.* New York: Lark Books, 2003.

Treadway Gallery. *American Art Pottery: Ohio Pottery, Roseville, Weller, Owens, Clewell, and Cowan, Auction Results from 1990–2000.* Cincinnati: Treadway Gallery, 2000.

———. *Glaze, Form, and Execution: American and European Art Pottery.* Sale catalog, John Toomey Gallery, Oak Park, Ill., May 7, 2000. Cincinnati: Treadway Gallery, 2000.

———. *Rookwood Pottery: Over Ten Years of Auction Results, 1990–2002.* Cincinnati: Treadway Gallery, 2003.

Turner, Anderson, ed. *Glazes: Materials, Recipes, and Techniques.* A *Ceramics Monthly* Handbook. Westerville, Ohio: American Ceramic Society, 2004.

———. *Pottery Making Techniques.* A *Pottery Making Illustrated* Handbook. Westerville, Ohio: American Ceramic Society, 2003.

———. *Studio Practices, Techniques, and Tips.* Westerville, Ohio: American Ceramic Society, 2003.

Uglow, Jenny. *The Lunar Men: Five Friends Whose Curiosity Changed the World.* New York: Farrar, Straus, and Giroux, 2002.

van Dam, Jan Daniël. "European Redwares: Dutch, English, and German Connections, 1680–1780." In *British Ceramic Design, 1600–2002,* edited by Tom Walford and Hilary Young, pp. 33–41. Paper presented at a colloquium celebrating the 75th anniversary of the English Ceramic Circle, September 21, 2002, Victoria and Albert Museum, London. Beckenham, Kent, Eng.: English Ceramic Circle, 2003.

van Lemmen, Hans, and Bart Verbrugge. *Art Nouveau Tiles.* New York: Rizzoli, 1999.

Van Patten, Joan F. *Collector's Encyclopedia of Nippon Porcelain: Identification and Values.* 6th series. Paducah, Ky.: Collector Books, 2001.

Veit, Richard. "Following the Yellow Brick Road: Dutch Bricks in New Jersey, Fact and Folklore." *Bulletin of the Archaeological Society of New Jersey,* no. 55 (2000): 70–76.

———. "Moving Beyond the Factory Gates: The Industrial Archaeology of New Jersey's Terra Cotta Industry." *Industrial Archaeology* 25, no. 2 (1999): 5–28.

Veit, Richard, and Mark Nonestied. "Taken for Granite: Terracotta Gravemarkers from New Jersey and New York." *Ceramics in America* 3 (2003): 172–95.

Ventura, Carol. "Ceramics in Guanajuato, Mexico: A Look at Five Contemporary Studios." *Ceramics Monthly* 51 (March 2003): 78–81.

———. "A Maya Ceramics Tradition Survives in the Yucatan." *Ceramics Monthly* 51 (December 2003): 64–65.

Vodrey, Catherine S. *A Centennial History of the Hall China Company.* East Liverpool, Ohio: Hall China, 2002.

Von Dassow, Sumi, ed. *Exploring Electric Kiln Techniques: A Collection of Articles from Ceramics*

Monthly. Westerville, Ohio: American Ceramic Society, 2003.
Walford, Tom, and Hilary Young, eds. *British Ceramic Design, 1600–2002*. Papers presented at a colloquium celebrating the 75th anniversary of the English Ceramic Circle, September 21, 2002, Victoria and Albert Museum, London. Beckenham, Kent, Eng.: English Ceramic Circle, 2003.
Walls, Wuanda. "Heeseung Lee." *Ceramics Monthly* 52 (January 2004): 61–63.
Wang Qingzheng. *A Dictionary of Chinese Ceramics / Zhongguo taoci ci dian*. Translated by Lillian Chin and Jay Xu. Singapore: Suntree; dist. in the U.S. by Chinese Clayart, 2002.
Ward, Cheryl. "The Sadana Island Shipwreck: An Eighteenth-Century AD Merchantman off the Red Sea Coast of Egypt." *World Archaeology* 32, no. 3 (2001): 368–82.
Warren, David B., Michael K. Brown, Elizabeth Ann Coleman, and Emily Ballew Neff. *American Decorative Arts and Paintings in the Bayou Bend Collection*. Houston: Museum of Fine Arts; Princeton, N.J.: Princeton University Press, 1998.
Washburn, L. Madison. "Toy Story." *Ceramics in America* 3 (2003): 268–70.
Watts, Andrew. "Developments in Glaze Composition and Application in Staffordshire during the 18th Century." *English Ceramic Circle Transactions* 18, pt. 2 (2003): 248–52.
Weaver, Jim. "Melissa Greene." *Ceramics Monthly* 51 (March 2003): 69–71.
Wegars, Priscilla. *Uncovering a Chinese Legacy: Historical Archaeology at Centerville, Idaho, once the "handsomest town in the basin."* Idaho Cultural Resources Series, no. 5. Boise: University of Idaho, Bureau of Land Management, 2001.
"Well and Tree Platters." *White Ironstone Notes* [White Ironstone China Association Newsletter] 8, no. 4 (spring 2002): 1, 4–13.
Wensley, Doug. *Pottery: The Essential Manual*. Marlborough, Eng.: Crowood; dist. in the U.S. by Trafalgar Square, 2002.
Wertkin, Gerard C., ed. *Encyclopedia of American Folk Art*. London: Routledge, 2003.
Wettstaed, James R. "Perspectives on the Early-Nineteenth-Century Frontier Occupations of the Missouri Ozarks." *Historical Archaeology* 37, no. 4 (2003): 97–114.
White, Leslie. "Knife Rests Old and New—A Potted History." *Northern Ceramic Society Newsletter*, no. 129 (2003): 16–19.
White, Mary. *Lettering on Ceramics*. Westerville, Ohio: American Ceramic Society; London: A. and C. Black, 2003.
White, Rebecca, and William B. Liebeknecht. "Rebekah at the Marriott: Marriott Site Yellow Ware Waster Dump, circa 1863–1868, Trenton, New Jersey [Part 1]." *Trenton Potteries* [Newsletter of the Potteries of Trenton Society] 3, no. 1 (March 2002): 1–4.
———. "Rebekah at the Marriott: Marriott Site Yellow Ware Waster Dump, circa 1863–1868, Trenton, New Jersey [Part 2]." *Trenton Potteries* [Newsletter of the Potteries of Trenton Society] 3, no. 2 (June 2002): 1–4.
"White Ironstone Molds and Moulds." *White Ironstone Notes* [White Ironstone China Association Newsletter] 9, no. 1 (summer 2002): 1, 4–15.
Whiting, David. "Jennifer Lee: The Circumnavigation of Form." *Ceramics Monthly* 51 (October 2003): 38–41.
Wilders, David. *Hartley's: Brick by Brick, Pot by Pot*. Wellinborough, Eng.: Castleford Press, 2003.
Wilkie, Laurie A., and George W. Shorter, Jr. *Lucrecia's Well: An Archaeological Glimpse of an African-American Midwife's Household*. Mobile, Ala.: Center for Archaeological Studies, University of South Alabama, 2001.
Williams, Peter. "The Talbot Hotel Pit Group." *Ceramics in America* 3 (2003): 111–37.
Wood, Karen A. *Tableware in Clay from Studio and Workshop*. Marlborough, Eng.: Crowood; dist. in the U.S. by Trafalgar Square, 1999.
Wood, Nigel. *Chinese Glazes: Their Origins, Chemistry, and Recreation*. Philadelphia: University of Pennsylvania Press, 1999.
Woolliscroft, Pam. "A Conservation Project for The Spode Museum Trust's Pattern Books." *Northern Ceramic Society Newsletter*, no. 130 (2003): 33–40.
Wyman, Colin. "The Stoneware of Chetham and Woolley, c. 1795–c. 1820." *English Ceramic Circle Transactions* 18, pt. 2 (2003): 208–47.
Young, Hilary. "The Birth of the Ceramic Designer in England." In *British Ceramic Design, 1600–2002*, edited by Tom Walford and Hilary Young, pp. 15–27. Paper presented at a colloquium celebrating the 75th anniversary of the English Ceramic Circle, September 21, 2002, Victoria and Albert Museum, London. Beckenham, Kent, Eng.: English Ceramic Circle, 2003.
Young, Lucie. *Eva Zeisel*. San Francisco: Chronicle Books, 2003.

Index

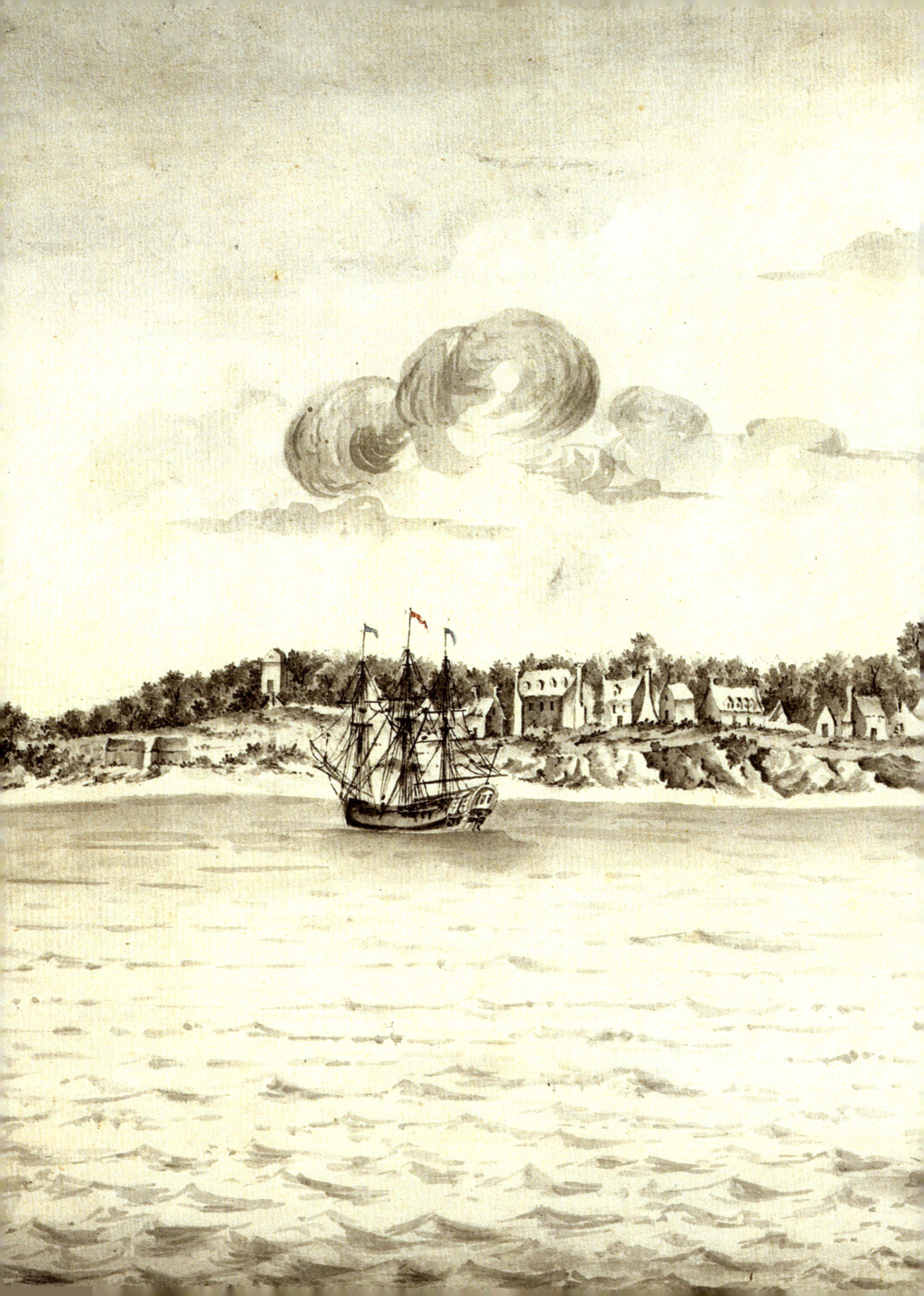